THE WORLD OF THE CRUSADES

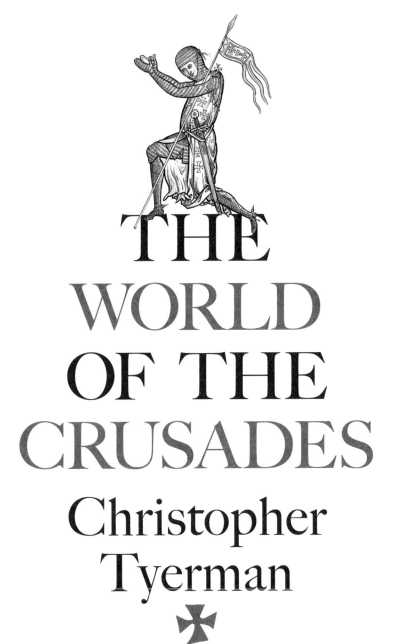

THE
WORLD
OF THE
CRUSADES

Christopher Tyerman

✠

An Illustrated History

YALE UNIVERSITY PRESS
NEW HAVEN AND LONDON

For information about this and other Yale University Press publications, please contact:
U.S. Office: sales.press@yale.edu   yalebooks.com
Europe Office: sales@yaleup.co.uk   yalebooks.co.uk

Set in Fournier MT Regular by IDSUK (DataConnection) Ltd
Printed in Great Britain by Gomer Press Ltd, Llandysul, Ceridigion, Wales

Library of Congress Control Number: 2019931656

ISBN 978-0-300-21739-1

A catalogue record for this book is available from the British Library.

10 9 8 7 6 5 4 3 2 1

In Memoriam
J.H.W.M.

CONTENTS

THE CRUSADES IN DETAIL

ILLUSTRATIONS, FIGURES AND MAPS

ILLUSTRATIONS

ILLUSTRATIONS, FIGURES AND MAPS

ILLUSTRATIONS, FIGURES AND MAPS

FIGURES

MAPS

ACKNOWLEDGEMENTS

I t is a pleasure as well as duty to thank those who have smoothed the path of this book. The idea for it emerged in conversation with Heather McCallum who has thereafter deftly shepherded the project to completion. The team at Yale, Marika Lysandrou, Rachael Lonsdale and Clarissa Sutherland, have guided production with conscientious accommodating efficiency. As ever, my agent, Simon Lloyd, has proved an effective ally and advocate. Sara Ayad undertook with tenacity and enthusiasm the initial labour of realising the images I had chosen, and Percie Edgeler kindly completed the task. Richard Mason, in copyediting, and Martin Brown, in drawing the maps, supplied vital structural support. The press's three anonymous readers generously took pains to note deficiencies and suggest improvements, saving me from blunders and greatly improving the whole. The remaining errors and misconceptions are mine alone. Any general study exposes its author's limitations perched atop a pyramid of others' scholarship. To the alert and interested my own debts will be apparent throughout the text and the notes. The Principal and Fellows of Hertford College, Oxford allowed me important sabbatical research leave at an early stage of preparation. The Ludwig Fund for the Humanities at New College, Oxford generously offered a grant towards the sourcing of pictures. These two colleges have provided enriching academic havens over many years. During the writing of the book, unlucky coincidence saw the deaths of a number of close personal and academic friends and mentors. To the memory of one, for half a century the most generous, effervescent co-conspirator in the human comedy, it is dedicated.

C.J.T., October 2018

PREFACE

The medieval crusades are both well known and much misunderstood. For almost a thousand years, the startling narratives of disruptive ideological commitment, military conflict and international conquest have excited, disturbed, intrigued and repelled. In mobilising, over many generations, hundreds of thousands of recruits to fight for causes physically distant and emotionally transcendent, the crusades appear extraordinary while simultaneously exposing in sharp relief the psychological and material resources of the distant societies from which they sprang and on which they preyed. With violence in the name of religion no longer appearing as outdated, eccentric or alien as it did only half a generation ago, the crusades persist in giving pause for thought. Yet they were of their time not ours. Modern fascination with the motivating force of religion has tended to simplify the crusades as 'wars of faith'. This misleads most obviously in two ways. It imposes a false binary cohesion on the identities and incentives of the warring parties, as in 'Christians versus Muslims', when the reality was more confused, cooperative as well as coercive, a matter of contact as well as competition. It also discounts the realities of warfare. Like religion, public violence is social and cultural. Crusaders' involvement varied from the devout to the forced, from free choice to the demands of employment, from enthusiasm to indifference to resentment. The crusades were wars fought under the banner of religious belief and are inexplicable without recognising that. However, they were also both more and less than that: more, in that they fitted wider general patterns of cultural and territorial aggression; less, in that, as wars, they were fought like any other, a matter of money and men, tactics and technology, castles and carpentry.

A third misconception is to see the crusades only in the context of a unique concern with the Holy Land. A useful and often effective means to recruit, fund and justify military enterprises across half a millennium of Eurasian history, the crusades operated as part of a material, political and cultural expansion of medieval western Europe, a path of connection and contact as well as alienation and conflict. The crusades did not initiate contacts with the Islamic world, for these had been growing in the decades before the First Crusade through pilgrimages; shared frontiers and conquests in Iberia and Sicily; and, especially, increased commerce, particularly with north Africa. While the original incentive to control Jerusalem and the Holy Land remained the defining inspiration, crusades, as proclaimed by church authorities, were not confined to wars and conquests in the Near East. They contributed to the political re-ordering of Iberia and the radical cultural transformation of the Baltic. Just one aspect of the penetration by western Europeans into the eastern Mediterranean, they played a part in the creation of an idea of distinctive European identity. The ideological legacy extended into the Atlantic and to the Americas while, at home, helping to sharpen intolerance towards social and religious minorities and dissidents. Despite an intrinsic supranational dimension, the crusading mentality of providential exceptionalism and divine favour bled into emerging national identities, sometimes, as with the Danish national flag, visibly so. The crusaders' reach straddled continents. Victims included Turks, Arabs, Greeks, Balts, Livs, Spanish Moors, Syrians, Palestinians, Egyptians, Moroccans, Tunisians, Russians, Finns, Bosnians, west German peasants, English rebels, Bohemian nationalists, political enemies of popes in Germany, Italy and Aragon, French and Savoyard dissenters, and Jews. However, the special influence of crusading can be exaggerated. In almost all cases, the crusades formed part of wider processes of engagement, competition and conflict, a makeweight not the pivot. Even the iconic First Crusade to Jerusalem owed its inception to existing western involvement in the Mediterranean and developments in the politics of Asia Minor and the Levant.

Crusades were wars; not all were fought by earnest idealists or for altruistic ideals, or, for that matter, by cynical opportunists. For most involved, their intentions, ambitions and choices were mixed and inevitably constrained by social and economic circumstances, not dictated by unfettered enthusiasm. The world of the crusades was the world of non-crusaders. The gloss of clerical idealism covers much of the surviving evidence with a distractingly coherent sheen. One aim of this book is to peer behind the constructed contemporary images to explore how the ideas and practice of the wars of the cross reflected and influenced the society that produced them. Much continued interest in the crusades has been sustained by the inclination to project current concerns – from the allure of religious or ideological warfare to the political fate of Palestine – onto the crusading past, paradoxically viewed as simultaneously alien and instructive, a habit that has been around since the Renaissance. The crusades even find themselves corralled into the self-serving unhistorical polemical myth of an immutable clash of civilisations. Yet the crusades do not hold up a mirror to the modern world so much as a window into remote past experience. What follows, therefore, seeks to examine crusading in its own muddied and muddling political, social, economic and cultural setting, not as a dimension of some inevitable cosmic struggle.

In recent decades, particularly in anglophone scholarship, there has been a renewed emphasis on the ideological dimension of crusading and the piety of participants. This came in reaction to previous economic and social interpretations that tended to relegate faith claims as cover for more temporal incentives and causes. Concentration on religious motives attempts to understand medieval crusaders – or, perhaps more accurately, those who wrote about them – on their own terms, through empathy not judgement. Material and visual evidence help ground the exploration of the subject. Tangible objects can be as eloquent of beliefs as written texts. The crusades were neither aberrations nor universal obsessions. They depended on material and physical resources as much as on popular and elite mentalities. People create objects – clothing, armour, weapons, utensils, buildings, ships – which then condition their creators. Crusaders may have been motivated by idealism or compulsion; but their actions rested on things not slogans. These are what will be illustrated.

The physicality of crusading did not deny its religiosity. It has been said that religion in medieval Christianity represented the physical body of believers rather than, since the Reformation, an abstract body of doctrine. While, as in all periods, individual conviction varied in degree from devotion to indifference to scepticism, faith, in medieval Christian communities, was openly enacted and performed, a matter of demonstrative acts, deeds not words. Faith acts included modes of living: celibacy, chastity, or entering enclosed communities; ritual behaviour such as participation in the Christian liturgy, observing church festivals, attending sermons, joining church processions, attending confession, fasting, performing public penance or going on pilgrimages; and charitable gestures such as alms giving and ecclesiastical donations. Performance, ritual and charity: crusading drew on all three. In theory, crusaders offered their lives to help fellow Christians in a penitential exercise during which they were expected to lead exemplary lives. The reality may have been less ideal. Crusading existed in public, from taking the cross to the conventions of leave-taking to the celebrations of return. Crusading was defined by physical trappings. Ideological in justification and publicised incentive, its objectives were concrete: conquest and defence of territory or people, accompanied by the customary detritus of war – armour, weapons, banners, tents, horses, mules, carts, wagons, ships, rations, siege machines, castles. Crusaders relied on provisions and pay. Their defining symbol was a physical cross worn on their clothes. Conquests required economic exploitation and governing through written bureaucracy; laws; commercial regulations; coinage; secular, ecclesiastical and military buildings. Individual crusaders travelled with possessions, which, for noble crusaders, could be lavish and luxurious. Campaigns necessarily generated plunder, booty, tribute, trade and gifts – between allies, patrons and comrades or in diplomatic exchange. Remembrance was constructed in glass, stone, paint and manuscript. In material terms, crusading created little original or exclusive to it, endowing familiar objects and activities with especial relevance or resonance. This book is partly about how the ordinary became extraordinary.

1. *The crusader knight, from a thirteenth-century English manuscript.*

THE HOLY SEPULCHRE

With the help of local tradition, the alleged site of the burial and resurrection of Jesus in Jerusalem was identified by Christian Roman authorities in 325/6, encouraged by the Christian emperor Constantine (306–37), who had just united the eastern as well as western Roman Empire under his rule. Around an excavated rock-cut tomb, a pilgrim church was constructed, the Martyrion, consecrated in 335. The site of the Crucifixion and the supposed burial place of Adam were also conveniently included in its complex. The tomb itself was incorporated into a small building known as the Edicule. The creation of the Church of the Holy Sepulchre coincided with the gradual emergence of Christian reverence for holy places and relics in general, a devotional development that made Jerusalem a major goal for wealthy pilgrims from across the Christian world, some of whose accounts of their visits became widely circulated. The physical image of the site was disseminated through such pilgrim descriptions and by visual representations in mosaics, manuscripts and commemorative religious artefacts. With the seventh-century Arab conquest, pilgrimage from western Europe became more difficult, expensive and rare, adding to the sense already implicit in the status of its holy sites that the Jerusalem pilgrimage possessed uniquely great penitential value. Understanding of the mystical importance of Jerusalem and the Holy Sepulchre was sustained through the prominence of the Holy Places in familiar scripture and repeated liturgy as the scenes of man's Redemption and of the coming Apocalypse, at once terrestrial and celestial, the empty tomb divine territory and a metaphor for a Christian life and God's promise of salvation.

From the late ninth and tenth centuries pilgrimages from western Europe increased as Mediterranean trade picked up and land routes became more accessible through Hungary's conversion to Christianity *c.* 1000 and Byzantine territorial advances in the Balkans, Asia Minor and northern Syria. By the early eleventh century, pilgrimages to the Holy Sepulchre were more frequent and increasingly fashionable, the bellicose Count Fulk Nerra of Anjou (987–1040) even going three times 'for fear of hell', while the Holy Sepulchre itself attracted donations, such as 100 gold pounds from Duke Richard II of Normandy (996–1026).[1] This was needed. In 1009 the church and edicule of the Holy Sepulchre were wrecked on the

2. *Eichstätt model of the Edicule, twelfth century.*

orders of the fundamentalist Fatimid Caliph Hakim. Both were rebuilt with impressive magnificence largely with Byzantine money and completed in the reign of Emperor Michael IV Paphlagon (1034–41). This was the church the crusaders found on 15 July 1099 and which they proved cautious in altering. The edicule was embellished but remained more or less the same, while the rest of the church was gradually remodelled and expanded in European romanesque style to accommodate the increased numbers and liturgical expectations of western pilgrims. The rebuilding was finished by the late 1160s. Despite conquest by Saladin in 1187 and sacking by the Khwarazmians in 1244, the crusaders' main church structure still stands, while the edicule has been rebuilt twice, in 1555 and 1809–10.

Pilgrimage to Jerusalem in the Middle Ages, for all its popularity, was never a mass activity. To satisfy and stimulate popular desire to be associated with the Holy Sepulchre, replicas of the church or edicule were erected widely across western Christendom, a tradition that long pre-dated the crusades but which gained momentum after 1099, while churches and chapels were dedicated to the Holy Sepulchre. Some may have provided settings for liturgical dramas such as Easter plays. Others may have operated more generally as visual contexts for sacramental liturgy focused on the Passion and Resurrection. In such tangible ways, that 'remotest place' as it was described at the time of the First Crusade, became embedded in the daily devotions of distant western Christendom, visible reminders of what the crusades were originally all about.[2]

3. *Aerial view of the Church of the Holy Sepulchre today.*

WHAT WERE THE CRUSADES?

The crusades were holy wars fought, adherents insisted, in response to the will of God on behalf of the Christian faith in defence of lands, people or religion. The inception of this distinctive form of Christian warfare can be traced to Pope Urban II's launch of a campaign in 1095 to help eastern Christians in the Byzantine Empire resist attacks by Turkish invaders and to recapture Jerusalem from its Muslim rulers. The subsequent successful war of 1096–9, known now as the First Crusade, established an indelible precedent. Wars fought for religion or with the approval of the Church were hardly novel. However, this war possessed two special properties. It was to be regarded as a unique penitential exercise, removing from participants all penalties for existing confessed sin. In the words of the original papal decree in 1095: 'whoever for devotion alone not to obtain honour [i.e. office/estates/titles etc.] or money, goes to Jerusalem to liberate the Church of God can substitute the journey for all penance'.[1] Popular perceptions soon translated this into a straight offer of salvation, with those who fell in this holy conflict regarded as earning immediate entry to heaven and the aura of martyrs. The second distinctive aspect, the liberation of Jerusalem and the Holy Sepulchre, the supposed site of Christ's Passion and Resurrection, defined an especially numinous territorial objective that remained a dominant, although not exclusive, reference even for wars of the cross fought far from Palestine.

The emphasis on the Holy Sepulchre, Holy City and Holy Land of Palestine tapped into the cultural familiarity of western European Christians with the scenes of Christ's life, death and believed resurrection derived from scripture, legend and liturgical repetition in church services. Jerusalem provided a focus for physical pilgrimage and spiritual imagination, the temporal setting for the cosmic drama of human redemption and the promise of the Last Judgement, a location set between earth and heaven. Although Urban II did not necessarily use the language of pilgrimage, the easy equation with this increasingly popular devotional practice lent crusade warfare a familiar touchstone for its validity as a holy enterprise. The lasting magnetism of Jerusalem, as both physical goal and redemptive metaphor, found physical witness in the popularity of replicas of the Holy Sepulchre that dotted the devotional landscape no less than the obstinate ambition of ten generations of crusaders to capture the city despite increasingly prohibitive strategic obstacles. Unlike other Christian-led wars in defence of faith or territory, campaigns to Jerusalem addressed no urgent security necessity. Judea lay far from the frontiers of western Christendom. Nor was the crusade designed as a missionary war until its ideology became entangled with later European colonial conquests in the Baltic and the Atlantic.

Crusade armies were distinguished by troops who had taken very particular vows of service. Unlike monastic vows, which were permanent, crusade vows, like those of pilgrims, were temporary, operative until the specific commitment had been satisfied (when exactly satisfaction occurred – just setting out? journey's end? death en route or before? – becoming a subject of later scholarly argument). Vows were signalled by the adoption of a physical cross, usually made of cloth or other textile, occasionally metal, and worn on the shoulder or other part of the recipient's garments. The cross symbolised a transcendent obligation to adhere to Jesus Christ's injunction to 'take up your cross and follow me' (Matthew 16:24; Mark 8:34; Luke 9:23). On departure, crosses were blessed in special liturgical ceremonies. During the fulfilment of the vow, the cross-bearer, the male *crucesignatus* or, in fewer but not rare cases, female *crucesignata*, assumed a privileged social and religious status under church protection. Authority for such privileges and the wars themselves came from the pope, acting in the name of Christ. Individuals' crusade vows were validated locally by priests. The crusades formed part of wider papal efforts to assert jurisdiction over penitential, pastoral and ecclesiastical legal systems in western Christendom. In the first decades after 1099, spiritual privileges similar or equivalent to those offered by Urban II were promulgated by local clergy without papal authority, for example in Iberia, Germany and the Baltic, each with traditions of wars with non-Christians. However, by the end of the twelfth century, the papal prerogative to initiate crusades, with the attendant spiritual and temporal benefits for crusaders, had generally asserted itself (see 'Taking the Cross', p. 4).

There were a few exceptions. In the Baltic from the mid-thirteenth century, popes permanently delegated the power to summon a crusade against non-Christians or Christian schismatics in the region to the military religious order of the Teutonic Knights, who had conquered and were ruling wide tracts of territory in the region. During efforts to resist the Mongol invasion of central Europe in 1241, the archbishops of Mainz and Magdeburg in Germany proclaimed a formal crusade – taking the cross, protection of property, remission of sins – without prior papal authorisation. Occasionally, for example in the Netherlands around 1230, local clergy applied crusade privileges – chiefly indulgences – to campaigns attempting to impose regional ecclesiastical discipline or political order. More eccentrically, trappings of the crusade were appropriated by those opposing papally authorised crusades against political enemies, for instance in Germany in 1240 and England in 1263–5. Crusades against crusaders signal how deeply crusading motifs and institutions had by then penetrated habits and mentalities.[2]

Papal authority provided the crusade with the apparatus of an accessible and apparently coherent legal, political and ideological structure. Using the crusade as a tool in claiming to represent God's purpose on earth, popes exercised a controlling share in the theology and formal mechanics of the enterprise. Lavish spiritual incentives were justified by the extreme penitential hardship, effort, danger and risk: full remission of penalties of confessed sins and the prospect of equal forgiveness in the afterlife. By the mid-thirteenth century this had elided into a plenary indulgence, remission of the sins themselves, absolving guilt as well as remitting punishment. Until the Jubilee indulgences of 1300 offered to pilgrims to Rome, the crusade indulgence offered the most generous relief available to the faithful. From the early thirteenth century the spiritual privileges became available to those beyond military recruits: partial indulgences (ideologically awkward: how can you divide sin?) proportionate to the giver's means and the material assistance provided (men, money, materiel, etc.); full indulgences earned by taking the cross and then redeeming the vow for a cash payment; indulgences available to relatives and the deceased. Wide sections of the community beyond the combatants themselves were thus given access to the salvific benefits – the old, the young, the weak, the infirm, the sick, the indolent, the cowardly, the preoccupied – while simultaneously providing the crusade with finance.[3] From the beginning, the Church had offered protection of family and property. During the twelfth century further legal and financial

TAKING THE CROSS

During his tour of France in 1095–6, Urban II instituted a new ceremony for those who had vowed to undertake the military journey to Jerusalem. Recruits were to receive and wear a cross, usually of cloth or silk, which they sewed onto their cloaks or tunics, commonly on the right shoulder, distinguishing their status both from other laymen and from Holy Land pilgrims who carried the scrip and staff (although many crusaders also adopted these in addition). Customarily, crosses were coloured red, although during the Third Crusade (1187–92) regional styles were adopted: red for followers of the king of France; white for those of the king of England; green for those of the count of Flanders; crusaders against papal enemies in Italy in the thirteenth and fourteenth centuries wore red and white two-toned crosses. Usually given by the clergy, crosses could be handed out by lay commanders,

4. Metal cross, similar to those adopted by some crusaders.

such as Bohemund at Amalfi in 1096. Women as well as men took the cross. Despite the initial assumption that crusaders needed to be of practical use to the enterprise, the only formal restrictions rested with status – technically only the legally free could undertake such a dislocating commitment – and conjugal rights, these requiring the acquiescence of wives for young married husbands (a condition dropped by Innocent III). By 1123, when taking the cross appeared in Canon 10 of the First Lateran Council, the ritual was well established. By the later twelfth century, liturgies of blessing the cross of departing Jerusalem-bound crusaders were being devised, displaying considerable local diversity.[4] Such ceremonies confirmed the cross as symbolising this form of penitential warfare, recognised by victims as different as Rhineland Jews and Languedoc heretics and, by the 1180s, in various regional vernaculars (*criosier, croiser, croisé, croisié* or, in England, *crusiatus*, a Latin word derived from a vernacular; a generation later forms included *croçada, croçea, croçeia*). From the Third Crusade, *crucesignatus* – signed with the cross – became a near-ubiquitous description, although one not unique to crusaders: the Crutched Friars and reformed heretics were also termed *crucesignati* and members of the Military Orders, although not in a strict legal sense crusaders, wore distinctive crosses on surcoats and clothing.

The symbol of the cross drew explicitly on the New Testament texts of Matthew 10:38 and 16:24, where Christ enjoined his followers to take up their crosses and follow him. It provided a pledge of penance and mortification, a sign of God's leadership and favour, a pledge of redemption through suffering, an ensign of sacrifice and salvation, a banner for Christ's *militia*, affirming the crusades' Christocentric focus, the penitential journey both a duty and an imitation. After the loss of the Jerusalem relic of the True Cross at the battle of Hattin in 1187, the recruiting propaganda for the Third Crusade from pope to jongleurs became saturated with cross-centred rhetoric, evoking the Passion and Resurrection, suffering and reward, penance and redemption. The cross increasingly dominated the descriptive language of the crusade, by the mid-thirteenth century becoming canonists' shorthand for the crusades as a whole, whether to the Holy Land (*crux transmarina*) or in Europe (*crux cismarina*). The metaphorical malleability even allowed one crusade preacher and veteran to declare '*crux enim gladius est*; the Cross is the sword'.[5] Crusaders marked their physical passage by carving crosses on walls, whether in Holy Trinity Church, Bosham, Hampshire, or the Chapel of St Helena in the Church of the Holy Sepulchre in Jerusalem.

Taking the cross played more than an emblematic role in the crusading process. It conferred precise obligations and privileges. By acknowledging a sworn commitment, the *crucesignatus* became subject to ecclesiastical protection but also discipline. Unfulfilled vows risked penalties including excommunication. Exemptions were deliberately hard to obtain as well as expensive until the system of payment for vow redemptions was introduced after 1213. The efficacy and exact nature of the spiritual privileges – remission of penance and/or sin, on earth and/or in heaven – and exactly when they became merited – on taking the cross, on departure, on death or fulfilment of the vow – remained subjects of academic debate. Yet the operation of the temporal privileges – protection of rights and property, immunity from credit interest and repayment of debts, delay in answering civil lawsuits – rested on public acceptance of status, which depended on knowledge of by whom and when the cross was taken. The status of *crucesignatus* could also afford tax exemption, as with the Saladin Tithe of 1188, which made backsliding appear as tax avoidance. For these reasons as well as for military preparations, by the end of the twelfth century and probably earlier, written lists of *crucesignati* were compiled by recruiters and civil authorities. As a thirteenth-century canon lawyer put it, 'no cross, no obligation'. Taking the cross was seen as a formal contract with God.[6] The ceremonies themselves provided neutral spiritualised spaces that became favoured occasions for otherwise delicate diplomacy or political posturing: Vézelay and Speyer 1146; Gisors and Mainz 1188; Rome 1220; Paris 1313.

The cross was both physical and personal. Preachers habitually used crosses as dramatic props, sometimes claiming they contained relics of the True Cross. Some *crucesignati* tattooed or even branded crosses on their skin. A famous manuscript illumination in a presentation copy of Robert of Rheims' popular chronicle of the First Crusade produced in 1188–9 depicted the dedicatee, Frederick Barbarossa, surrounded by crosses, on his robe, his shield and a globe he is holding. The cross operated to the theoretical advantage of the *crucesignatus* on a number of levels, one English liturgy proclaiming it 'an especial means of assistance, a support of the faith, the consummation of his works, the redemption of his soul and a protection and safeguard against the fierce darts of all his enemies'.[7] More prosaically, a Somerset *crucesignatus*, arguing crusader privilege in court in 1220, insisted that 'the crusade (*crussignatio*) ought to improve my condition not damage it'.[8] The actual crosses handed out could act as talismans of protection in this life and the next. In 1250 the German emperor Frederick II, a crusader in 1228–9, was buried wearing his cross.[9] *Crucesignati* unable to fulfil their vows bequeathed their personal crosses to the Holy Land or sent proxies carrying them; in 1183 the cross of the recently deceased Henry, eldest son of Henry II, sewn onto his cloak, was taken to Palestine by his companion William Marshal. The physical cross provided an intimate mystical union with Christ, a bond repeatedly emphasised by crusade preachers.[10] Some suggested extensive benefits, from exorcising demons, curing deformities or easing childbirth to remitting time in purgatory for deceased loved ones (*caros suos*) and relatives.[11] At least from the time of the Third Crusade, taking the cross became a metaphor for the Christian life incorporating devotion, obedience, penance, suffering, redemption and salvation. Combined with crusaders' uniquely generous privileges, this evangelic force could hardly be restricted to the fit, healthy, well-funded or military. From 1213, confirmed in 1234, the cross could be redeemed by payments without hindrance to the exercise of the spiritual advantages: crosses for cash. Although later evolving into the straightforward sale of indulgences, such vow redemptions helped transform crusade financing in the thirteenth century and embedded crusading widely into Christian society. Taking the cross became a habitual, if sporadic, demotic aspect of pastoral management, church liturgy and ecclesiastical fund-raising, far removed from yet umbilically linked to its invention by Urban II in 1095.

5. *Giving the cross.*

inducements were devised: immunity from civil lawsuits and repayment of debts; the ability to mortgage property, even if held as a tenancy or fief, and to receive interest-free loans; and escape from certain tax obligations. Involvement of direct Jewish credit was prohibited. Such measures, designed to encourage recruitment, exerted significant impact on the jurisdiction of law courts; the operation of land markets, commercial credit and public finance; and the scope of secular authority.

The social reach of the crusade caught all sections of free society. The legally un-free were excluded by virtue of their lack of independent legal agency or ownership of assets, which prevented them from entering into voluntary contracts such as the crusade vow and meant they also lacked the property to support their commitment or enjoy the temporal privileges. Becoming a *crucesignatus* implied freedom; for a serf, it implied manumission. Of course, some, perhaps many, un-free went on crusade, but in service to the great: not all who followed the cross had necessarily taken the cross. Otherwise, *crucesignati* came from all walks of life and most regions of western Europe: lords, knights, merchants, artisans, servants, soldiers, minstrels, other support staff, clergy of all ranks, clerks, to write and keep accounts as well as to pray, and even converts from Judaism.[12] Although highly gendered around the rhetoric of masculine martial valour, the crusade attracted women as active *crucesignatae*, as well as accompanying wives, civilian auxiliaries (e.g. laundresses) and army camp-followers. The crusade also directly affected them as relicts of departed crusaders, as financial contributors or as ideological devotees, expressed in many ways including through association with convents attached to military and preaching orders (see 'Women and the Crusades', p. 10).[13] The crusade paraded across society in recruitment, funding and social rituals of support: blessing departing crusaders, their crosses, weapons and even their ships; processions; alms-giving; special religious services; preaching; and the public imagery of sculpture, frescoes, mosaics and stained glass.

Crusading formulae also appeared outside canonically full-blown crusades. Different remissions of sins, associated with the Jerusalem war or not, could be offered, the terms varied by the scope or length of remission or the terms of qualification. Not all non-Holy Land campaigns that attracted indulgences also saw preaching and cross-taking or grants of temporal privileges. This 'pick and mix' flexibility eased the use of crusading forms across an expanding variety of conflicts from the twelfth to the seventeenth centuries. By the later fifteenth century, the crusade was commonly used as a mechanism to extract secular funding and clerical taxation. Few corners of Europe, the Mediterranean or western Asia entirely escaped the presence of crusaders, although not all minorities or fringe communities became formal crusade targets. There were no crusades against Celtic Christians of Ireland or Jews, although the latter suffered civil persecution and physical violence as victims of the extreme emotions inherent in crusading mentalities.

The crusade did not conform to modern norms of inter-ethnic conflict. Although crusading propaganda, literature and popular responses (as recorded in Latin and vernacular verses and songs) were tinged with cultural supremacism, the crusades were not racist in origin or intent. Ideologically, the enemy was defined and demonised by faith not blood. Hostility was tempered by circumstance. In theory binary – 'Pagans are wrong and Christians are right' ('*Paien unt tort e crestiens unt dreit*') in the words of the contemporary French *Song of Roland*[14] – in practice, when convenient or necessary, crusaders not only welcomed converts but negotiated with opponents, accepting tribute, protection money, surrenders and alliances, adapting to and taking advantage of local political and diplomatic realities. Thus in post-First Crusade Syria and Palestine cross-border treaties, alliances with Muslim rivals, even condominiums became regular. Within a few years of 1099, northern Syria witnessed battles between armies each composed of both Christian westerners, including First Crusade veterans, and local Muslim Turks.[15]

The sequence of mass Holy Land crusades ended in the mid-thirteenth century. The western European outposts on the mainland of the Levant established after 1099 were finally extinguished in 1291. However, the final large-scale medieval attack on Egypt came in 1365, with piratical raids on the Levantine coast continuing into the early fifteenth century. Crusades against Muslim rulers in Spain lasted until the conquest of Granada in 1492. Crusades were proclaimed and regularly fought against the Ottoman Turks from the mid-fourteenth until the late seventeenth century, with people still taking the cross to fight them. The last formal crusade may have been the anti-Ottoman Holy League of 1684–99. Crusades against heretics, begun in 1208 to suppress dissenters in Languedoc, were still fought in Bohemia and Savoy in the fifteenth century and against Protestants in the sixteenth century. As papal weapons against political enemies, crusades continued sporadically from the twelfth to the sixteenth centuries. Other legacies lasted

WOMEN AND THE CRUSADES

Despite the male-gendered military imperatives of crusading and entrenched clerical cultural misogyny, from the start women were closely involved: as fellow travellers, servants and companions; as spouses giving permission for a husband's departure or for the mortgaging of dower lands; as wives and daughters either on campaign or as relicts attempting to keep the home fires burning and family property intact; as transmitters of dynastic memories and traditions of service; and as *crucesignatae* in their own right. Western chroniclers, who noted their presence on campaigns from the First Crusade onwards, stereotyped women on crusade into familiar gendered categories, as wives, servants, market traders, laundresses who doubled as de-lousers, or prostitutes; while Greek and Arabic sources noted the exceptional number of women in crusader forces, Arabic writers mixing prurient fascination at western prostitutes' erotic skills, complete with breasts tattooed with crosses, with cultural disdain that many of the women fought and died in action. Women from all sections of free society took the cross. Crusade ordinances, in 1147 or 1190, assumed the presence of women, whose behaviour they sought to regulate. It has been estimated that 3 per cent of known participants on the Fifth Crusade were women, which may exclude servants and other menials. Women and children were afforded a separate tariff in the distribution of booty after the fall of Damietta in 1219.[16] Some of these would have taken the cross, not all of them necessarily in partnership with husbands, indicating possibly independent agency and individual vocation.

Crucesignatae appear in lists of non-noble Cornish crusaders after the Third Crusade and references to others are scattered across legal and administrative documents over the following century. In 1250, 9 per cent of a shipload of 453 crusaders were women, some travelling alone and unchaperoned or with other women. Aristocratic women could play significant roles. Ida of Austria led a military contingent on the 1101 crusade. Eleanor of Aquitaine conducted her own diplomatic if not domestic policies in Syria in 1147, and suffered gendered condemnation as a result. Queen Margaret of France presided over the ransom negotiations for the captive Louis IX at Damietta in 1250 – intriguingly opposite Shajar al-Durr, ruling sultana of Egypt, a unique example of women leading in the male preserve of crusade diplomacy. In 1200, Innocent III, in accordance with papal curial legal opinion at the time, suggested rich women *crucesignatae* could take paid troops on crusade.[17]

Women clearly also fought, certainly during crises and *in extremis* when all members of the army, including non-combatants, were necessarily pressed into action. They also appear regularly in support roles, such as ferrying water and supplies to front-line troops. The story of Margaret of Beverley, an educated Cistercian nun, detailed her early career as a *crucesignata*, saw her in arms defending the walls of Jerusalem in 1187 and later involved in fighting around Antioch, as well as various hair-raising escapades with Turkish captors. As a *virago* (literally manlike female warrior), Margaret was assuming a masculine identity, almost as an honorary man; in other passages she reverts to cliché feminine roles: carrying drink to soldiers; performing forced labour in captivity; and later earning money as a laundress. Although, like almost all accounts of *crucesignatae*, the narrative of Margaret's life was written by a man, her brother, so hardly reflects unfiltered feminine perspectives, the variety of experiences recounted would not have been unfamiliar, not least Margaret's devotion to the Virgin Mary, whose association with crusading as a patron and protector may have encouraged the participation of women.[18]

6. *Women at a siege, from* Histoire ancienne jusqu'à César, *late thirteenth century.*

Male clerical disapproval of women on crusade expressed itself in moral judgmentalism and legal restrictions. Chronicle tales of illicit intercourse and lascivious women, such as the nun of Trier at Nicaea in 1097 who preferred sex with her Muslim captor to returning to her life of chastity, were fuelled by a belief that crusaders should be without sin or the stain of carnality (killing excepted), pointing to Christ's injunction to those who would take up their crosses to follow him that they should abandon their domestic ties. Jerome of Prague blamed the failure of the Second Crusade on the presence of women.[19] Wives could not go without permission of their husbands; unmarried daughters without that of their fathers; ideally, unattached younger women were not to go at all. Wives' conjugal rights, which initially had allowed them formal control over their spouses, were swept away by Innocent III, permitting husbands to vow to go on crusade without their wives' permission.[20] Crusade preachers increasingly typecast women as obstacles to recruitment, symbols of carnal pleasure and domestic entanglements. The reality contradicted this: women in Genoa in 1217 and Marseilles in 1224, for example, materially assisted crusade promotion. Women attended crusade sermons alongside men. Countess Alice of Blois led her own regiment to Acre in 1287. Away from military campaigns, women were associated, through donations, legacies and, after 1213, vow redemptions, the offer of which potentially greatly increased women's institutional engagement. Similarly, during the first half of the thirteenth century, church authorities determined that wives and children fully shared in a crusader's plenary indulgence, although whether as recognition of family ties or an incentive to women not to take the cross themselves is hard to measure. What is clear, from active *crucesignatae* who travelled and died on crusade, to twelfth-century nuns who wanted institutional association with the Templars, to women who paid to redeem a vow or put money into a parish collecting chest, beneath the clouds of misogyny, the variegated appeal of the crusade reached across gender. Equally, women found themselves as victims, of legal and occasional physical perils of abandonment by husbands; of sexual exploitation or disparagement on campaign; and, among the crusaders' enemies, subject to violence, slavery, rape and death.

even longer. Cyprus, conquered from Greek rule by crusaders in 1191, remained under westerners' rule until 1571. The Hospitaller Knights of St John, founded in Jerusalem in the wake of the first great crusade of 1096–9, ruled the island of Rhodes between 1309 and 1522 and, from 1530, Malta, before being expelled by Napoleon Bonaparte in 1798. The Teutonic Knights, founded *c.* 1190 during the Third Crusade, created German Prussia which, with Livonia, they ruled from the thirteenth to the sixteenth centuries.

The Development of Christian War

The ideological roots of the crusades lay deep in Eurasian faith traditions. All three Abrahamic faiths – Judaism, Christianity, Islam – developed ideologies of justified warfare when faith became synonymous with political communities: the Old Testament Israelites; the Christian Roman Empire and its successors from the fourth century AD; the Islamic Caliphate and its heirs from the seventh century. These polities fused the religious and the secular, in ways paralleled by some modern nationalisms. Classical arguments for

7. *The iconic legendary Christian warrior Roland as a crusader.*

just war were philosophical and legal. Aristotle argued that 'war must be for the sake of peace' (*Politics* VII:14), a just end that could encompass aggression as well as defence. The requirements of a supposedly virtuous state justified even genocide of opponents. Where classical public religion resembled a civic cult, the specific category of religious war hardly arose. Roman Law added just cause, a *causa belli*, to Aristotle's just ends. Justification rested on upholding of contractual relations (*pax*, the Latin noun for peace, derived from the verb *pangere*, to enter into a contract). For jurists such as Cicero, this included right conduct in defence of the state, recovery of lost goods and punishment. As a form of legal redress, a just war required formal declaration by properly constituted authorities. Behind the legalisms lay the practical implications that all war against Rome's public enemies, *hostes*, was just. Theories of just war tend to support established political power.

Theories of Christian war only developed in response to Christianity becoming tolerated and then the official religion of the Roman Empire in the fourth century. When Christianity became an attribute of citizenship, it acquired necessary attendant obligations, including military service. Only the clergy, with their tenacious claims to immunity, were exempt. Laymen were encouraged to regard Christian Rome's wars as Christianity's wars, the empire and Church now providentially united to fulfil God's purpose, a symbiosis promoted by the influential theologian and former imperial official Ambrose, bishop of Milan (d. 397). Enemies of the state were enemies of the Church and vice versa. With the erosion of the Western Roman Empire in the fifth century, a more general theory justifying war by Christians based on first principles emerged, associated in particular with Augustine (d. 430), bishop of Hippo in north Africa, whose chief interest lay in the problem of sin and the more immediate threat of Christian dissidents. Although insistent on the separation of the secular from the divine, and never producing a codified theory of Christian just war (that had to wait for medieval canon lawyers and theologians, notably Thomas Aquinas in the thirteenth century), scattered throughout his writings Augustine suggested it might be legitimate to use a sinful act, violent war, to fight sin provided the act was performed with right intent, in a good cause – defence, protection or restitution of property or rights – and under legitimate authority. A key text was Romans 13:4: 'for he beareth not the sword in vain: for he is the minister of God, a revenger to execute wrath upon him that doeth evil'. This could hardly be construed as wholly metaphorical, unlike St Paul's martial metaphors ('armour of God . . . the breastplate of righteousness . . . the shield of faith . . . the helmet of salvation': Ephesians 6:11 and 11–17). For Augustine: 'it is the injustice of the opposing side that lays on the wise man the duty of waging war', and 'the commandment forbidding killing was not broken by those who have waged war on the authority of God'.[21] Later interpreters used Augustine to turn classical just war into something much closer to all-out religious war.

Ambrose, Augustine and their contemporaries did not invent Christian violence. Christian scripture and theology demonstrated a complicated relationship with violence, at no time solely focused on pacifism. The Old Testament is shot through with accounts of violence explicitly condoned or commanded by God, which Christian writers such as Origen (d. *c.* 254) interpreted as temporal prefigurations of the spiritual struggles against sin embodied in the truths of the New Testament and the New Dispensation of the Incarnation.[22] Christ in the New Testament preaches peace and forgiveness of enemies and a kingdom of heaven not of earth. The message of the Gospels, Acts and Epistles concentrated on moral and social not political hostility and violence, condemning envy, hatred and force against individuals, not communal aggression or defence. In the Latin translation of the New Testament most influential in the medieval Christian west, the Vulgate of Jerome (d. 420), the invariable word for 'enemy', as in the apparently unequivocal insistence to love one's enemy (Matthew 5:43–4), was *inimicus*, a personal foe, not *hostis*, a public enemy. New Testament pacifism skirted the public sphere. St Paul urged prayers for secular rulers (I Timothy 2:2); the tribute Christ advised the Pharisees to pay to the Romans ('Render unto Caesar', Matthew 22:21) subsidised the army; John the Baptist accepted the occupation of soldiers (Luke 3:14) and Christ admired the faith of the centurion (Matthew 8:8–13). The Book of Revelation, a late addition to the canonical texts, provides an apocalyptic vision of Christ, at the head of a heavenly army, bearing a sword to smite the nations (Revelation 19:14–15), a favourite subject for medieval religious artists. With the emergence of Christianity as the official state religion of the Roman Empire, religious precept was forced to accommodate a public role. In Christian accounts of Constantine's conversion, Christ is shown as giving temporal military victory to believers. The new Christian empire required the faithful to combat *hostes* not just *inimici*. The solutions of Ambrose, Augustine and others established a legitimate form of Christian public war conditioned by temporal necessity, a legal

8. Christ leading holy warriors dressed as crusaders, from an early fourteenth-century manuscript.

category that did not contradict traditional Christian moral teaching on private violence and personal forgiveness. Physical warfare could combine a metaphor or imitation of the spiritual struggle against internal or external sin with necessary temporal protection of Christian lands and people.[23]

This fusion, or confusion, of the physical and spiritual struggle, provided an emotional as well as ideological prop to the legal category of Christian just war. It also chimed with the beliefs of the newly Christianised warrior elites that dominated western Europe from the fifth century for whom war provided a central social institution and defining cultural activity, with its own aesthetics and moral code, the central proving ground for aristocratic personal virtue and public status as well as the prime mechanism for political power and economic reward. Christian missionaries thrived by promoting scriptural models sanctifying temporal authority and its associated violence, bestowing saintliness on martial Christian kings and kingship.[24] The relationship was mutually beneficial. Secular warrior elites endowed and protected the Church. In return, clergy, mainly drawn from the same aristocratic milieu, sanctioned political violence through ritual: prayers; liturgies; blessings for warriors, banners and weapons. Clerically written eulogies, propaganda and chronicles justified the wars and conquests of favoured rulers. Soldier-saints made their appearance in devotions and on battlefields. Icons and relics of Christ, such as fragments of the cross, or the Virgin Mary, or dead saints habitually accompanied armies across Christendom.[25] Violence became as embedded in western Christian culture as its antithesis, the monastic vocation.

The wars of Christian rulers against non-Christians attracted special approval. This could be grounded in the need for defence, as Christendom in the early Middle Ages (*c.* 700–1000) faced attacks from Muslim rulers in Iberia and pirates in the Mediterranean, pagan Hungarian Magyars in central Europe and pagan Scandinavians from the north, while expansionist conquest could imply conversion. Although forced conversion remained theoretically invalid, in practice Christianity was regularly imposed on subjected peoples, apologists being able to employ Christ's parable in Luke 14:23: 'And the lord said unto the servant, Go out into the highways and hedges and compel them to come in, that my house may be filled', a favourite text with later popes faced with the missionary opportunities of an expanding Latin Christendom. The archetype of the new minted Christian warlord was the Frankish king and emperor Charlemagne (r. 768–814), ruler over most of western Europe, whose conquests, notably the brutal annexation of Saxony from the 770s, were robustly proclaimed as religious wars, attended by prayers, masses, fasts, litanies, processions and the bearing of relics into battle. For the conquered, religion became the test of loyalty and citizenship, a means of social control and colonial oppression.

Charlemagne's legend as a holy warrior grew to include campaigns to Muslim Spain (where he had campaigned briefly) and even to the Holy Land (where he had not). As invasions by non-Christians persisted, so his reputation continued to exert powerful influence among military elites. The earliest written vernacular verse epics (formalised from earlier oral stories in the twelfth century), such as the *Song of Roland* or the stories of William of Orange, featured Carolingian wars against Muslims of Spain. The involvement of faith and churchmen in war was taken for granted. The legendary figure of Archbishop Turpin of Rheims, companion of Roland in the final battle at Roncevalles in the *Song of Roland*, continued to split Saracen skulls in romance and epic into the thirteenth century.[26] While the contrary tradition of pacifist escape from the world, realised in monasticism, remained prominent in ideal and practice, rhetorically it complemented the martial culture of lay society. The orders of monks were seen as battling the spiritual devil in parallel to the order of earthly warriors, the *ordo pugnatorum*, combating the devil's material agents. The association of faith and justified violence became entrenched. Popes Leo IV (847–55) and John VIII (872–82) offered spiritual rewards to those who fought and died for the *patria Christianorum*, Christendom, against 'pagans and infidels' in Italy.[27] Wars against invading Danes in France and Britain were cast by clerical observers in terms of faith. King Alfred of Wessex (r. 872–99) was eulogised as a religious warrior against the Danes, in some sources invariably described as pagans. Otto I of Germany (r. 936–73) bore a relic of the Holy Lance (the spear reputed to have pierced Christ's side on the cross) when he defeated the invading pagan Magyars at the river Lech in 955. Saints continued to support the faithful in battle while St Michael, armed and fighting the dragon of disbelief and sin, looked down on the faithful from church sculptures and frescoes. The warrior was sanctified and the saint militarised.

The eleventh century saw two political developments that defined a more distinctive form of religious war: the conquest by Christian lords of Muslim-ruled territories on the peripheries of western Christendom in Iberia, the western Mediterranean and Sicily; and the harnessing of Christian just war theory and practice in the cause of ecclesiastical reformist ideas centred on the Roman papacy. Both reflected and exploited the growing class of military entrepreneurs, specialists and trained thugs, later elevated to elite social status as knights: heavily armed horsemen, mobile in action and career opportunism, encouraged and sustained by the fractured competitive politics and expanding economic wealth of western Europe – princes, counts, lords and even bishops with armed retinues to put to use. The Church sponsored wars against infidels in Sardinia, Sicily, Tunisia and Spain. Some campaigns attracted papal remission of penances for sin, for example the Normans fighting in Sicily in 1076. When he conquered Toledo in 1085, King Alfonso VI of León-Castile declared it had been achieved 'under the leadership of Christ'.[28] Such religious militancy chimed with the assertion of clerical independence from lay control, led by a succession of popes from the late 1040s content to annex both the language and the use of force to secure what they described as freedom of the Church, *libertas ecclesiae*, in particular, the jurisdictional primacy of the papacy. In Italy and Germany, warriors for papal interests received blessings, banners and remissions of penance. The Norman invasions of Sicily and England in the 1060s were conducted under papal banners, as well as the Sicilian invasion attracting papal offers of spiritual rewards. Pope Gregory VII (1073–85) liked to quote Jeremiah 48:10: 'Cursed be he who keepeth back his sword from blood.' He attempted to recruit a network of armed supporters, the *militia sancti Petri*, during his struggle to unseat the German emperor Henry IV (1056–1106). In 1074, Gregory tried to raise an army to defend the eastern Empire of Byzantium and 'to rise up in armed force against the enemies of God and go as far as the sepulchre of the Lord under his leader-ship'.[29] The reference to the Holy Sepulchre in Jerusalem added an aura of holiness to the military enterprise, as of a pilgrimage, but also more visceral implications of providential apocalyptic contest.

Pope Gregory framed service in papal just wars as an imitation of Christ's sufferings, a holy act directed against 'the enemies of the cross of Christ' (in this case other Italians).[30] This was a short step to regarding wars fought for the Church as in themselves penitential acts, a view Gregory promoted towards the beleaguered end of his pontificate. This represented a marked shift. In church theory, just war was sinful but mitigated by circumstances, just cause, right intent, due authority. The victors at Hastings in 1066, despite fighting under a papal banner, were expected to perform penance for the slaughter of battle, even though a lighter one than for ordinary homicide. Now Gregory argued that certain sorts of fighting themselves constituted penance earning absolution and remission. This formed the ideological bedrock of the spiritual benefit of the war launched by Gregory's protégé Urban II in 1095. The official accommodation of war and religion was almost complete, as the Jerusalem war rhetorically translated traditional Christian acceptance of war as a necessary evil into a holy obligation, a penitential observance in its own right. Contemporary intellectuals noticed the change. One commented that while previous wars in defence of the Church had been deemed legitimate (*legitima bella*), now God had instituted an expressly holy war (*praelia sancta*).[31] Not a legal category, as just war was, the crusade was a devotional duty commanded through the pope by God Himself.

Crusading in Practice

The crusade was a category of war but also a lived experience, a pattern of behaviour and a cultural mentality. As such, it defies neat delineation. Much modern scholarship has attempted to discover a unitary definition of the crusade through its theology, law and propaganda. In the twelfth and thirteenth centuries, crusade promoters in papal circles, certain orders of monks, mendicant friars and the emerging universities, presented crusading as a coherent Christian exercise. However, in practice, uniformity was impossible in medieval Christendom. Central church authorities lacked the bureaucratic apparatus or executive power to impose it. As an example, the central moment of individual commitment, the *votum crucis*, showed wide variation. The votary received the cross as a sign of the vow in many different circumstances: after public sermons; as part of a pre-arranged ceremonial, perhaps associated with the Mass; or in private conclave with local priest or confessor. The wording of vows and specific rites on these occasions – if any – were ad hoc. Chroniclers and preachers seem to have taken the details of initial assumptions of the cross for granted, describing the settings and the act in general terms. Rituals were then developed for a subsequent ceremony, chiefly associated with departure, when the cross worn by the votary was blessed, by a bishop, abbot or other priest. In some rites the cross is given as well as blessed. Local variation dominated, in common with blessings for crusaders' weaponry apparent from the 1090s. Despite the existence in the thirteenth century of a papal formula for the blessing of crusaders' crosses, distinctive local rituals persisted, for instance in northern France, southern Italy, or the English west Midlands. The surviving written texts of these rituals may conceal even more divergence in practice. As they are, they illustrate the crusade as a lived not just preached phenomenon, with little fixed consistency of form or language.[32] Other more personal or demotic rituals may have attached themselves to the performance of commitment, such as the Irish crusader who cut off his hair (see 'Splitting Hairs', p. 22).

Descriptive language showed similar fluidity and regional difference. Until the fifteenth century, there was no agreed or consistent word for the crusade in Latin or the European vernaculars. Unlike modern historians, contemporary savants appear reluctant to provide the wars of the cross with a distinctive name. Despite ever more elaborate canonical refinement of the attached rewards and institutions, the crusade occupied no independent sacramental or juristic category. Sermons on the crusade were collected with other non-crusading ones under the general heading of 'penance'. The theology and operation of the crusade indulgence continued to perplex academics well into the thirteenth century before the formulation of the non-crusade specific idea of a universal Treasury of Merit, a celestial deposit account banked by Christ's sacrifice, accessible to all repentant sinners. Into the thirteenth century, papal descriptions of crusade spiritual privileges lacked clarity, consistency or precision. The text of Urban II's 1095 decree offering the Jerusalem war as substitute for penance only survives in a single late manuscript of possibly doubtful authority. From the beginning it was unclear whether remission applied to penances on earth or to penances due in the afterlife. However, the language of penance quickly evolved into the language of sin, perhaps reflecting popular understanding of the crusade simply as a bargain with salvation as the reward. The phrase *remissio peccatorum* – literally 'remission of sins' – appears to have been used freely by twelfth-century popes, but implying the narrower remission of penalties consequent on sin, not the guilt or the sins themselves.[33] Neither compendia of canon law, such as Gratian of Bologna's seminal *Decretum* (first redaction *c.* 1139), nor theological treatises offered a definition of the crusade; not even Thomas Aquinas (d. 1274), who consolidated categories of just war, did so. For an intellectual culture characterised by attempts to define categories in law, theology, natural philosophy and social status, the omission of the crusade is notable. Academic diffidence contrasted with the popular understanding of the incentive of remission of sins and reassurance of instant salvation for those who died in a crusade battle. Even here hesitancy persisted. Observers frequently afforded the glorious dead martyrs' palm, yet there were no crusader martyr saints. Louis IX of France (r. 1226–70), who died on his second crusade, was canonised in 1297 as a confessor not a martyr, to the disgust of his friends.

Language remained imprecise. Non-specific metaphorical euphemisms of travel were popular: *iter, profectio, passagium, via, voyage, passage* etcetera, combined with epithets of holiness or destination. Directly military vocabulary circulated in blessings, descriptions of the cross (as a *vexillum* or martial banner) and recruiting metaphors of military service, but was less common in general descriptions of the activity, although Urban II used the term *expeditio*, meaning a military campaign. The extension of crusade objectives away from Jerusalem and the Holy Land from the late twelfth century, and the integration of crusading into wider systems of religious observance, prompted the use of even less specific official language. The crusade became the *negotium sanctum*, holy business, or, in the case of the brutal early

SPLITTING HAIRS

In common with other religious activities, going on crusade was attended by ritual, performance and gesture. Histrionic public ceremonials of accepting blessed crosses and pilgrims' scrips and staffs or wearing penitents' garb underlined the holiness of the undertaking. More private rituals of leave-taking and departure, at least in the eyes of clerical commentators, also assumed set patterns: the crusader painfully but steadfastly tearing himself regretfully from the comforts and lures of home, focused on his higher calling; his dependants, relatives and neighbours left behind suitably lachrymose and destitute. If less staged, the reality may not have been far removed. The departure of a local lord and his retinue would inevitably have been a public affair, as would that of any householder, while supportive even festive crowds have been the perennial accompaniment to troops marching off to war. Private attitudes may have been less celebratory or stoical. Recalling leaving for the 1248 crusade some decades later, John of Joinville, perhaps channelling a literary trope familiar in vernacular poems about departing crusaders, provided an emotional vignette: 'I did

9. *Departing crusaders.*

not want to cast my eyes back towards Joinville at all, fearful that my heart would melt for the fine castle and two children I was leaving behind.'[34] The solemnity of the undertaking could invite extravagant symbolic gestures. The Gaelic poet Muireadhach Albanach Ó Dálaigh, who went on the Fifth Crusade (1217–21), recorded in verse how he had grown his hair so that he could then offer it to God as a votive offering before leaving on crusade, a sort of crusader's tonsure: 'Great till tonight my share of sins/this hair I give you in their place . . . Four years has the whole head of hair/been on me until tonight;/I will shear from me its curled crop: my hair will requite my false poems.'[35] Before the Second Crusade (1147–9) the Anglo-Norman Earl William of Warenne and his brother Ralph signalled the transfer of some property and rights to Lewes Priory 'by hair from their heads' cut with a knife by the bishop of Winchester. Whether the hair cut from Warenne's head was linked, as in all likelihood the property deal was, to the earl's impending departure for the east is tantalisingly unknowable.[36] However, such idiosyncratic rituals of commitment may well have been common. The personal importance of going on crusade invited such significant gestures.

thirteenth-century campaigns against heretics in southern France, the *nego-tium fidei et pacis*, the business of faith and peace. As an obvious analogy, the language of pilgrimage was common: *peregrinatio, pèlerinage*. The liturgies for blessing the cross witnessed at once the umbilical association of crusade and pilgrimage and their distinctive characteristics; the pilgrim's scrip and staff alone did not make a crusader even though the cross could, at least in the twelfth century, be borne by a non-fighting pilgrim. Taking the cross and receiving the scrip and staff remained separate acts even when under-taken during the same ceremony. As expressed in language, the under-standing of the crusade as a pilgrimage persisted, not least in the Baltic crusades and their German recruiting grounds.

From the Third Crusade (1187–92), the cross appeared more centrally in promoters' rhetoric and wider responses, as a banner and totem, symbol of Christ's suffering, his offer of redemption and the command to defend his heritage. The term *crucesignatus*, although not new, became commonplace. From the early thirteenth century, related words emerged in northern and southern French and Catalan vernaculars (*croisier, croiser, croisé, croʒeia, croʒea, cruʒea, croʒats, croʒada*, and so on). From 1190, Latinised vernacular *crusiati/cruisiati* appear in English government records. By 1300, the noun *croiserie* had gained currency in England and northern France, not least in advertising the chests for crusade alms in parish churches. Elsewhere *croʒada/cruʒada* (southern France and northern Spain) and *crociata/cruciata* (Italy and, later, the papal bureaucracy) became familiar. Some academics preferred the simplicity and suggestive universality of *crux*. From the four-teenth century, the Latinised vernacular word *cruciata* (later Spanish *cruʒada*, French *croisade*) took on a technical meaning to describe the process and the proceeds of the sale of crusade indulgences, a term for a financial expedient, effectively a form of taxation, that deliberately harked back to the dignified origins of crusading. By the sixteenth century, this association of the crusade and fund-raising seriously compromised popular and political reaction to continued appeals to crusade. Throughout, linguistic variety and inconsis-tency remained, reflecting the diversity of local engagement and tradition in defiance of any imagined homogeneous conformity. At the same time, the distinct development of vernacular terms and the adoption of some of them by the Latin-writing elites reveal a non-hierarchical, non-deferential mutual exchange of ideas far from the one-way, top-down monolithic institution suggested by official pronouncements and some modern historiography.[37]

The crusades were characterised by such processes of exchange, between church leadership and provincial custom, between ecclesiastical precept and lay response. Any definition must embrace the differences in reception as much as the consistencies in the core official message. Essential features of crusading included perceptions of external or existential threat; opportunities for spiritual and material gain; feelings of communal solidarity or collective and individual obligation, often fuelled by uplifting and exciting stories of crusading history and heroics or of atrocities and humiliations. Different regional or local experiences conditioned responses. Some local clergy adapted crusade appeals to suit their audiences, from overtly anti-Jewish hate campaigns in the commercialised Rhineland to using images of pole-vaulting over canals as a metaphor for attaining salvation in the waterlogged Netherlands. One of the greatest twelfth-century crusade polemicists, Bernard of Clairvaux, explicitly modulated his sales pitch according to his target audience (knights or merchants), a technique that later became standard in preaching instruction manuals. Clergy repeatedly resisted papal attempts to impose fiscal and administrative control. Local rulers modified or rejected provisions of papal offers of secular privileges for crusaders. The merchants of Lübeck, Cologne, London, Marseilles, or Genoa, while far from immune to notions of spiritual duty and reward, may have viewed the balance sheet of crusading in terms different both from one another and from recruits from rural, less commercial environments. While crusades may not have been inspired by material gain, they were sustained by material acquisition. Crusaders from regions that had frontiers with non-Christians – in Spain, Germany or the Baltic, for instance – held their own autonomous traditions of intercommunal war and material profit coloured by religious differences of identity to which the crusade merely added conceptual gloss. Beneath the equivalence of official formulae and the tropes and clichés of clerical commentators, the experience of the wars granted crusade status in Iberia and the Baltic differed from each other and from those fought in the eastern Mediterranean or within the rest of Latin Christendom.

Similarly, while the ecclesiastical authorities and canon and secular law treated all *crucesignati* the same, social and economic reality determined otherwise. Most of those who served on crusade, even those who had taken the cross, fought for pay, often concealed as gifts.[38] Armies were recruited and held together by networks of lordship, patronage, clientage, loyalty, kinship, employment or, occasionally, fraternities, formal associations of mutual assistance. From the later twelfth century, recruitment patterns adapted to increased royal government involvement and the availability and greater prevalence of central lay and church funds. Each campaign operated an internal market of paid service. For those whose livelihood depended on service to a lord, the voluntary nature of the crusade commitment may have remained notional. While some of the crusades to the east appear to have been unusually reliant on the private commitment and enterprise of individual lords, those lords' entourages included many who had little or no effective choice. Similarly, recruitment among the growing commercial communities and artisans ensured a diversity of motives, attitudes and experience. Peasants, artisans and clergy crusaders did not necessarily share the increasingly exclusive chivalric mores of the military leadership. Not all laymen would necessarily agree with or even understand the spiritualised vision of the enterprise promoted by the clergy. However, most of the surviving written evidence, inscribed and composed by clerics, emanates from the context of the knightly classes, the leaders, not the led. Most modern historical definitions of the crusade and crusading do the same. The appeal to women further exposes the hazard of generalisation. Crusading might appear strongly gendered, a masculine activity involving women only to the extent of consent, domestic and occasional financial support or, later, the proceeds from their redeemed vows. Did the crusade mean the same to the nuns who attached themselves to the Military Order of the Templars, or to those who abandoned their convents to join up, as to their knightly comrades? Like many male crusaders, women who followed the cross pursued occupations: servants, laundresses, prostitutes, but also, in one case at least, as a medical physician. Male anxieties about the differences in female responses surface in chronicle accounts that tacitly recognise contrasting gender experiences. Women are rendered as honorary men, supporting the war effort in labour or sacrifice, or confined to woman's work, such as de-lousing the troops and their clothes, or as dangerous libidinous threats to masculine clerical constructs of sobriety and chastity. Within the domestic setting at home, women played significant roles – in protecting family property and in the process of memorialising crusading family members. On crusade they did not abandon agency.

The sociology of crusaders suggests contrasting experience and perhaps understanding of the enterprise between volunteers and conscripts, leaders and led, the rich and the un-rich, men and women. Inevitably, in the cacophony of publicity, recruitment and response, the nuances of official messages could get lost, reducing them to ones of anxiety, excitement, reward, violence and salvation. Active crusading faced the perennial paradoxes of war: idealism and squalor; nobility and degradation; excitement and tedium; service and ambition. No definition can ignore the risk and sacrifices, the sheer awfulness of so many of the campaigns, disease and death. The immediate experience of camp life and combat may well have superseded ideological awareness. Nor can the suffering of victims be shunted to the margins. The crusade was a cruel act of religious devotion aimed at the violent suppression (i.e. killing and enslavement) or expulsion of opponents who, in many cases, only constituted a threat within the aggressors' own invented belief system. Ironically, crusades against those who did pose a direct danger to western Europe, the Mongols in the mid-thirteenth century or Ottoman Turks from the fourteenth century, attracted only disjointed and relatively modest support.

The crusade was originally constructed as an act of charity towards fellow eastern Christians while it explicitly denied the equality of shared humanity with non-Christians. Of course, this did not make the crusade unusual or uniquely vicious in medieval Eurasia. Nonetheless, the strenuous idealism of much eastern Mediterranean crusading must be set beside the use of the crusade as cover for German conquest and lucrative colonisation in the Baltic; the crusade as sanctifying Spanish annexation of Moorish al-Andalus; or the crusade as offering entrepreneurial nobles novel opportunities to enhance status, prestige and dynastic profit both at home and abroad. By casting profane actions in a sacred setting, the crusade was defined as special, in war, penance and politics.

That did not make crusading immune from criticism, entertainment, humour or satire. Rather the reverse. It is testament to how quickly the Jerusalem wars became embedded in western European culture that they quickly generated diffuse popular as well as elite commentary, from erudite scrutiny to ribald lampoon. It is hard to imagine, without the new focus on the history of Jerusalem, that a mid-twelfth-century lord of Montboissier in northern France would have called his son Heraclius, the name of the Byzantine emperor who restored the Holy Cross to Jerusalem in 630.[39] Similarly, the appearance of St George and scenes from the siege of Antioch in 1097–8 on friezes and frescoes across the west demonstrates the free embrace of First Crusade legends and motifs and a general acceptance, at least by artistic patrons, of a fusion between the religious and the martial.[40]

Yet beside acknowledgement and enthusiasm came criticism, a constant companion from the start. Critics fastened on the ideology and conduct of crusades and their associated institutions, from the Military Orders to the cash redemption of vows and sale of indulgences. The tension between religion and war continued to attract notice, the awkward alliance of self-indulgent warrior values with the puritanical selflessness of religious idealism, honour and glory embracing penitent self-abnegation. Repeated failures cast nagging doubt on God's approval as well as on crusaders' motives and behaviour. The triumph of the First Crusade in 1099 proved a toxic inheritance, insistent yet impossible to repeat. The material cost, human price and scale of violence provoked unease. By the later thirteenth century some argued that the crusade was actually impeding efforts to overcome Islam, a criticism later applied to crusades against Baltic pagans. The extension of penitential war to targets within Christendom stimulated concerted opposition, and not just from those targeted. Whereas crusading as a form of Christian expression remained widely popular, individual crusades were not docilely accepted. They had repeatedly to be sold, a process not without difficulty if surviving sermons are any indication. The apologist tone in public pronouncements and narrative accounts tells its own story. Charges of folly, hubris, hypocrisy, deceit, avarice and peculation swirled around all crusading ventures. Not all regions provided equally fertile recruitment grounds. Indifference marked much contemporary witness. The crusade never became a compulsory religious observance; active crusading remained a minority pursuit. Among the engaged, the tone of Latin chroniclers or vernacular versifiers spanned reverence, enthusiasm, admiration, objectivity, scepticism, irony, lament, cynicism and hostility, sometimes in the same work, as in the thirteenth-century English monk Matthew Paris's massive *Chronica Majora* (to 1259).[41]

Social engagement expressed itself in diverse vernacular settings: poetry, songs, plays, sculpture, painting, stained glass, sacred relics and commemorative *objets d'art*. Popular stereotypes of the crusader appeared. Romances of crusade heroics and images of great warriors gained wide currency. Frescoes of Richard I in fictional combat with Saladin adorned English royal palaces. Less exalted but perhaps no less familiar appeared the thirteenth-century French poet Rutebeuf's *descroisié*, the self-justifying armchair crusader enjoying in comfort the benefits of his redeemed crusade

10. *Richard I jousts with Saladin: tiles from Chertsey, made for King Henry III c. 1250.*

vow, afraid of the sea and of risking his material possessions by actually going on crusade.[42] The abuse of the crusade was a ripe topic in fiction. In versions of the twelfth- and thirteenth-century *Roman de Renart* the conventions of crusade narrative are subverted, for grimly comic effect. The crusader's cross is described as a cheap cloth or valueless rag (a charge repeated less humorously half a century later by a Languedoc heretic).[43] The anti-hero, Renart the Fox, unabashed, takes the cross to avoid punishment, having no intention of fulfilling his vow, or uses the crusade as an excuse to rob and murder his supposed companions. The satire exposes the naivety of clerics and lords in trusting superficial crusade gestures. The insincerity of *crucesignati* represents a running theme of contemporary commentary, here deployed for comic effect. Renart pokes fun at the whole idea that Muslim rulers might be frightened of a crusade. However, as notable as the ridiculing of crusade piety, the *Renart* cycle closely mimics the themes presented by crusade promoters.[44] The humour depends on the audience recognising what is being satirised, as it did in Jean Bodel's play *Jeu de St Nicholas* (*c.* 1200), in which satire becomes farce, as a crusade is fought, crusaders are massacred, and Saracens improbably converted by a statue of St Nicholas that also proves handy at protecting their treasure.[45]

In a different register, acquaintance with core elements of crusade ideas and propaganda is reflected in popular sacred songs and in vernacular verses of troubadours, *trouvères* and minnesingers where the competing loyalties of the lovelorn crusader, torn by loyalty to his beloved and obligation to the cause of the cross, provided a rich seam for poetic invention, the tropes of crusade, courtly love and chivalric duty playing against each other in lively tension. Vernacular poems and songs across western Europe reference motifs of the crusade message – cross, obligation, outrage, infidel insult, revenge, honour, collective shame, the hope of salvation, the celebration of violence, the conflict between secular desire and religious obligation – as staples of lay mentalities, adding varied context to the images of holy warriors in stone and glass.[46] Liturgies for blessing the cross and sacred songs commemorating the triumph of 1099 shared emphasis on temporal battle, physical struggle. Stories associated with the sacred booty of relics or secular campaign trophies were of human adventure. The vernacular and Latin verse and prose epics and romances are drenched in blood, as are the equivalent accounts by participants. Associated manuscript illuminations dwell on images of the warriors of Christ. Stories of carnage and death pepper the uplifting anecdotes used by preachers. The qualities of the crusade heroes and anti-heroes were those of the warrior. The Church's offer of penitential release and salvation supplied necessary reassurance for a duty cast in terms of death and glory.

Not all were impressed. Henry II of England was reported as commenting acidly on attempts by the patriarch of Jerusalem to persuade him to go on crusade in 1185: 'these clerks can incite us boldly to arms and danger (*arma et pericula*) since they themselves will receive no blows in the struggle'.[47] This was slightly unfair. Many clergy, including Henry's own archbishop of Canterbury, campaigned and died alongside the warriors they recruited. However, the king's assessment was correct: 'arms and danger'. Cast as a spiritual ideal, crusading became a pattern of social behaviour, but one derived from armed combat both as metaphor and fact. Despite the elevated promise of salvation, war defined the crusade.

CHAPTER ONE

THE MEDITERRANEAN CRISIS AND THE BACKGROUND TO THE FIRST CRUSADE

He attacked and broke into the city by force and sacked it. Large numbers were killed, even those who had taken refuge in the Aqsa mosque and Haram. He spared only those who were in the Dome of the Rock.

... our men entered the city, chasing the Saracens and killing them up to Solomon's Temple ... They killed whom they chose, and whom they chose saved alive ... After this our men rushed round the whole city seizing gold and silver, horses and mules, and houses full of all sorts of goods.[1]

Both passages describe the capture of Jerusalem in the late eleventh century by foreign invaders. The first, by a thirteenth-century Arabic historian from Mosul using earlier sources, recounts the sack of Jerusalem in 1078 by Atsiz, a freelance mercenary commander of nomadic Turcomans originally from the steppes beyond the Caspian Sea. The second, from one of the earliest surviving Latin chronicle narratives of the First Crusade, celebrates the victory of the western European army at Jerusalem on 15 July 1099. The similarity between the two should give pause before assuming the uniqueness of the First Crusade. Jerusalem changed hands four times in the thirty years before the western armies' arrival. The crusaders were relative latecomers to the violent piecemeal annexation of the cities and resources of Syria and Palestine by warlords from outside the region. The image sometimes presented of the First Crusade as a barbaric irruption into the irenic peace of a stable, sophisticated and tolerant Arab Muslim world misleads. The crusaders were just one among many bands of intruders on the make. It was precisely because the Near East was already

11. The Dome of the Rock, Jerusalem.

a scene of violence, competition, disruption and dislocation that they prevailed at all.

The great Jerusalem expeditionary force of 1096–9 was made possible by simultaneous crises of political authority across western Eurasia. Over a couple of generations in the mid-eleventh century, the already ragged political map from the Atlantic to the Iranian plateau was further shredded as old and new empires were undermined, collapsed or replaced. Regional fragmentation of political authority increased competition for power. Foreign intruders proliferated: nomadic steppe Turks in western Asia; northern Christian warlords in Muslim Spain, al-Andalus; Normans in southern Italy and Sicily. Driving forces ranged from tribal searches for improved economic prospects to elite mercenary opportunism. The disruption to established political systems offered rewards to mobile groups around the Mediterranean basin: north African Berbers, Ethiopians, Nubians, Kurds, Armenians, Scandinavians, Normans and other 'Franks', or the tribes of the Eurasian steppes attacking or serving the armies of Greek emperors and Egyptian or Iraqi caliphs and sultans. Such dislocation prompted changes in commercial networks, demographic patterns, systems of economic exploitation and relations between established religions and civil society, from new legal

12. Cultural exchange across geographic, political and religious frontiers: an eleventh–twelfth-century central Mediterranean ivory casket.

emphases in Sunni Islam in the east to the assertion of ecclesiastical independence in the west. These transformations revealed strands of exchange between the three continents surrounding the Mediterranean in goods, objects, ideas, information, texts, fashions, mercenaries or slaves. Although such contacts could operate over long distances and across confessional and religious frontiers, societies in medieval Eurasia were inevitably constrained by geography and technology. For most, horizons were local; even on the vast Eurasian steppes locality was tribal. Yet the political eruptions of the eleventh century that produced the First Crusade exposed a connected world.

The Fraying of Empires

In 1000 the Mediterranean was circumscribed by four empires: the Abbasids of Iraq; the Fatimids in Egypt; the Greeks of Byzantium; the Umayyads in Spain; and a fifth of more evanescent aspiration, the Germans in Italy. By 1300, the Abbasids, Fatimids and Umayyads had gone; the German role in Italy had been reduced to transience; and Byzantium only survived in severely reduced circumstances. Even at the height of their strength, each empire

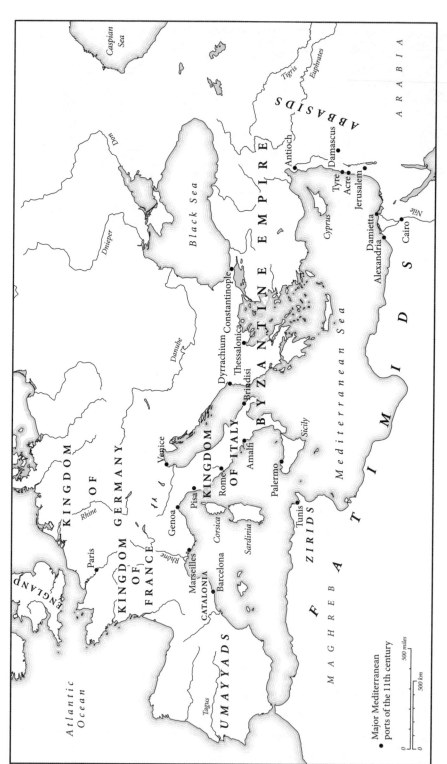

1. *The Mediterranean powers in the eleventh century.*

concealed faltering or unrealised cohesion. In largely mono-faith European Christendom power and legitimacy rested on the exploitation of mainly agrarian societies, geographically rooted in local regions and confected tribal identities (Franks, English, Saxons, Flemish, Burgundians, Danes, and so on), making ideals of pan-European political unity inherited from the Christian late Roman Empire and revived by the Frankish empire of Charlemagne (768–814) victims of material localism. Islamic polities were different. Fusing belief, law and political authority within the conceptual universalism of a frontierless Muslim community (the *umma*) of shared language and culture, the original Arab empire created in the seventh and eight centuries inherited and maintained a more urbanised, commercially prosperous economic system from its Romano-Byzantine and Persian predecessors. Its assertion of supra-tribal and supra-regional political legitimacy was matched by international exchange of commerce and learning. Merchants and scholars passed relatively freely across an Arabised society that stretched from the Atlantic to India. Below this internationalism, diversity of ethnicity and religious affiliation were recognised, as conversion to Islam was slow and regionally patchy. Significant Christian and Jewish communities remained. The heterogeneous culture of the Arab empire thus stood in contrast to more monochrome identities fashioned in the fragmented polities of western Europe.

However, Islamic absence of formal separation of religious, legal and political authority invited problems of legitimacy. While the caliphate embodied the inherited authority of the Prophet within the *umma*, providing a focus of political legitimacy, this did not necessarily imply an active caliphal role. Beneath the caliph's theoretical authority, local political power could emerge in a succession of regional dynasties without disrupting the perceived theoretical unity of the Islamic system even when central caliphal authority was ignored or, by 1000, rejected, as in Spain and north Africa. Given a monetised economic system reliant on a taxpaying populace, ruling elites could be mobile, dependent less on long-standing local roots than on control of cities and access to urban and rural rents in order to recruit mercenary or enslaved troops. This structure of power reflected the Arab empire's construction in the seventh and eighth centuries. It imposed a foreign ruling elite on existing Roman and Persian fiscal structures, buttressed by Arab migration and the military harnessing of nomads, such as the Bedouin and those from the steppes on the new empire's peripheries. The system that emerged sustained diversity of regional power within a cohesive Islamic cultural polity that stretched across two continents.[2] In contrast with the divisions in Christian Europe, in the Arab sphere political rivalry and dynastic ambition played out beneath a unifying cloak of a caliphal authority that bestowed legitimacy while wielding little direct power. The common western European insistence that title to power depended on its substance, seen in the anathematising of do-nothing kings, *rois fainéants*, belonged to a different political universe. However, medieval Islamdom was to change during the two centuries of the Near Eastern crusader interlude with the end of the traditional caliphates and the emergence of more recognisably unitary autonomous states.

The Abbasids

In Iraq, from the 940s, the once-dominant Abbasid caliphate, established in the mid-eighth century, had been controlled by a succession of emirs from a north Iranian Shi'ite dynasty, the Buyids, who, behind formal deference to the politically emasculated Abbasid caliphs, exercised power through a family coalition of rulers across Iraq and western Iran. They relied on accommodation between their Shi'ite beliefs and those of their Sunni subjects and taxpayers, and on polyglot armies, including Turkish slave troops in a system that lacked cohesive unity. From the 1020s, nomadic tribes from the central Asiatic steppes beyond the Arab world began to migrate south and west, towards Anatolia, attracted by political instability and access to new pasture. In contrast with the Turkish troops recruited by the caliphate from the ninth century onwards, the concerted Turkish invasion from the 1040s and 1050s, led by the Seljuks, transformed the Abbasid polity.

The Fatimids

The gradual implosion of Baghdad's central control over the northern arc of the Fertile Crescent (the region from the Persian Gulf through Mesopotamia, the Jazira and Syria to the Nile valley) was mirrored by the fates of the Abbasid's two rival caliphates: the Fatimid Shi'ites in Egypt and the Umayyad rulers of Cordoba in al-Andalus. In 969, from their base in north Africa, the Fatimids had conquered Egypt, the economic powerhouse and commercial hub of the Levant, establishing a new administrative capital at Cairo and ruling over a population of predominantly Sunni Muslims, Coptic and Melkite (i.e. Greek) Christians. Armed with the wealth of the Nile valley, they competed with the Sunni Abbasids for dominance over the wider Islamic world. The political contest was pursued largely in Palestine and Syria, making them a frontier zone to be fought over by outside powers. However, by the early eleventh century, direct Fatimid rule over their original north African centre of power had itself broken down as nomadic Arab and Berber tribes ranged freely and local dynasties asserted themselves, such as the Zirids in Tunis, while control of Sicily veered between Zirid overlordship and warring island dynasties.

In Egypt itself, as in Baghdad, the executive authority of the caliphs, after the robust fundamentalism of Caliph al-Hakim (996–1021), devolved onto competing court factions, a process intensified after the accession as caliph in 1036 of a six-year-old child, al-Mutansir (1036–94). Beside the court and administration, Fatimid armies comprised distinct, at times competing polyglot elements – Arab, Berber, Turkish, sub-Saharan African, Armenian – providing further scope for factionalism and dissension. As political control within the caliphate swung towards military not bureaucratic leadership, competition between Turkish and African regiments intensified, the consequent instability exacerbated by the influx into Egypt of nomads and Bedouin. In the 1050s plague and disappointing levels of the Nile flood reduced tax and rent returns, sharpening competition for control of diminished resources. In the 1060s violence between factions undermined Fatimid rule in Syria and threatened the regime in Egypt before some order was restored under the military rule of the vizier Badr al-Jamali (1074–94), an ethnic Armenian who had carved out a successful career in Fatimid Syria. Power in Egypt remained fragmented. The Fatimid caliphs claimed to be heirs to messianic imams, wielding supreme authority over both faith and law, their rule legitimised directly by God, not, as in Sunni political thought, by the collective authority of the *umma*. This transcendent status bestowed legitimacy on whoever held actual power under them. However, except with forceful caliphs such as al-Hakim, these theoretical claims made little difference to the realities of a heterogeneous political and social system with inherent centrifugal dynamics of communities and geography.

The Iranian poet, scholar and court official Naser-e Khosraw (1004–88), in his account of his extended travels across the Near East between 1045 and 1052, provides insight into the concurrent diversity and cohesion of the Arab world. A polymath, his leaning embraced Greek as well as Arabic philosophy and his career took him from India to Egypt to Afghanistan. Remembered chiefly for his Persian poetry, Naser had once worked for the Seljuks, visited

Mecca and studied Shi'ite teaching in Egypt. His observations of the territories he crossed and the people he encountered ranged from a young pupil of the great Persian philosopher Avicenna (*c.* 980–1037) in a town near the Caspian Sea conducting a seminar on Euclid, to a sixty-year-old Bedouin at Harran in the Jazira who insisted he neither knew nor understood the Koran. Along the way Naser observed the military defences in Levantine and Egyptian ports prompted by fears of Byzantine naval attack, but also recorded the diplomacy that allowed the Byzantine rebuilding of the Church of the Holy Sepulchre in Jerusalem. Everywhere he noted the international trade with Byzantium, north Africa, Spain, Sicily and Italy, especially in textiles and slaves. Naser's picture of the Arab world of the 1040s revealed mobile civilian a well as military elites, an international community of scholarship, doctrinal diversity, urban living and lively commerce – all within a context of political upheaval and the presence of war.[3]

The Umayyads

Further west, similar forces of decentralisation overwhelmed the Umayyad caliphate of Cordoba. Like its eastern Mediterranean equivalents, this Sunni caliphate, formally established in 929 after 150 years of Umayyad rule in Spain, relied on a professional literate bureaucracy, the approval of local Muslim aristocracies, and a mercenary and slave army, made up chiefly of Slavs and Berbers. In 1000 the caliphate appeared at the height of its power – rich, internally peaceful, externally effective – its de facto ruler, al-Mansur (d. 1002), launching a successful raid in 997 on the great Christian shrine of Compostela in Galicia. Yet, by the 1030s, the caliphate had disintegrated. One factor was the attempt by al-Mansur's heirs to move towards a Christian European model of uniting legitimacy and executive power by usurping the caliphate from the Umayyads. This loosened the bonds of loyalty with the local rulers, already strained by their exclusion from administrative and military patronage. Factional struggles, Umayyad pretenders and uncontrolled Berber freebooters destroyed central authority. Al-Andalus became a cockpit for competition between its Muslim princes, exploitation by Christian rulers to the north, and invasion by Moroccan religious fundamentalists from the south.[4]

Western Christendom

The north-western shores of the Mediterranean presented even less unity. Power resided with regional territorial princelings and rulers of small cities and emerging maritime entrepôts in Catalonia, Provence, Liguria, Lombardy, Tuscany, Campania, Apulia and the Veneto. Around 1000, the Ottonian kings of Germany, who had revived Charlemagne's western empire in 962, seemed to be laying foundations for a new lasting *imperium* based on a trans-alpine alliance between Germany and northern and central Italy under the young charismatic Otto III (r. 983–1002). This proved evanescent, the political future of Italy resting with local lordships, such as those in Apulia and Calabria annexed by Norman adventurers from the 1040s onwards, and cities such as Genoa, Milan, Florence, Pisa, Venice and Rome. Whatever power German emperors wielded in Italy was achieved by negotiation laced with occasional invasion. They were further challenged after 1060 by polit-ical and ecclesiastical alliances constructed by belligerent Roman popes, who supported challenges to imperial rights and authority from the Elbe to the Tiber. Further east, in newly Christianised Hungary, Bohemia and Poland, the German emperor's power to influence local rulers became atten-uated. The two generations of conflicts between German emperors and popes, known as the Investiture Contest (to 1122), limited German imperial intervention into wider Mediterranean affairs. At the same time, those seeking alternative sources of legitimacy for military adventurism in the region could look to popes eager for useful political alliances.

Byzantium

By the 1020s, the largest, wealthiest and oldest Christian power, the Eastern Roman Empire of Byzantium, had experienced a half century of extensive if expensive territorial expansion. The empire's borders stretched from northern Syria to Apulia, the Danube to Cyprus and Crete. Its diplomatic reach touched Eurasia from Russia, the steppes north of the Caspian, Scandinavia and the British Isles, to Iran and sub-Saharan Africa. In mid-century, Greek recruiting agents left coins and seals in Winchester while their emperors had paid for the rebuilding of the Church of the Holy Sepulchre in Jerusalem (1036–40; see 'The Holy Sepulchre', p. xxiii). Like its neighbours to the east, Byzantium relied on a professional bureaucracy, a pliant aristoc-racy, a peaceful capital, an increasing role for polyglot mercenaries in its armies, the legitimising glue of religion, and taxpayers. Also in common with their eastern neighbours, this aggregation of support splintered as the elev-enth century progressed, the tension between defence and taxation matching that between noble, military and bureaucratic factions competing for the imperial throne. Political unrest undermined administrative efficiency. From the 1040s, the once inviolate gold currency began to be debased, losing two-thirds of its value by the 1080s. In the middle of the century, plagues exacerbated economic and fiscal problems, undermining the tax base and intensifying the contest for power. Unlike in Islamdom, where inert legitimacy clung to ancient lineage while power was exercised by others, in Byzantium – as in its classical Roman predecessor – with sufficient support from the Church, army, civil service and the capital, Constantinople, might became right. Despite periods of dual monarchy between empresses and more or less pliant spouses or juvenile relatives, there could be no lasting system of *empereurs fainéants*. The throne passed by military coup at least three times in the eleventh century, while the empire's territorial integrity was compromised.

Eastern Anatolia, the core province of the empire, was penetrated by Turkish nomads from the 1020s, as was northern Syria from the 1060s. Other nomadic groups, the Cumans and Pechenegs, threatened the Danube frontier. In 1071, Bari, the last Byzantine outpost in Italy, was taken by Norman forces, who then launched a series of attacks across the Adriatic on the western Balkans. In the decades after 1070, northern Syria and Armenian Cilicia were lost and most of central Anatolia overrun by more organised Turkish invaders. Although the merry-go-round of new emperors stopped in 1081 with the seizure of power by the general Alexius Comnenus, the empire was reduced to reliance on the coastal plains and ports of Asia Minor, on Greece and the Balkans. The massive loss of taxpaying subjects and lands with which to barter internal support was not matched by any commensurate lessening of the financial and military needs of defence: far from it.[5]

By 1100, the existing Mediterranean polities had been overtaken by internal dislocation and foreign invasion from the Eurasian steppes, northern Europe and the deserts of Arabia and north Africa. Power became more decentralised, focused on competing city states and dominated by warrior rulers with origins outside the region, who found their own attempts to rule as challenging as it had been for those they replaced. Nomadic Turks from steppes beyond the Caspian Sea now lorded it over ancient cities of Iran, Iraq, Syria and Palestine, and occupied the ancient Anatolian heartlands of the Eastern Roman Empire. Adventurers from northern France ruled in Palermo and Messina and, from 1098–9, Syrian Antioch and Jerusalem. The cities of the north African seaboard were regular victims of Arab nomads. Moroccan Berbers determined the politics of al-Andalus. Political power in

Cairo was swapped between Iraqi, Armenian, Syrian and Kurdish viziers, their armies recruited from the steppes north of the Black Sea to the Sudan. Kurds found preferment from the Caspian to the Nile. Byzantine armies welcomed Slavs, Armenians, Turks, Scandinavians, Anglo-Saxons and Frenchmen. Italian merchants appeared as increasingly familiar presences in the trading posts and markets of north Africa and the Levant. In this context, the invasion of Syria and Palestine by armies from western Europe in the 1090s and their subsequent establishment of new warrior governments based on the region's cities, while extreme, were hardly eccentric. Local Syrian observers, by the 1090s only too familiar with alien foreign conquerors and overlords, could be forgiven for initially regarding the crusaders' invasion as yet another, if peculiarly violent and determined, foray by foreign mercenaries, hardly breaking a long and familiar line.[6]

A New Dispensation: Nomads, Mercenaries and Conquerors

Seljuks

Of all the eleventh-century invaders of the Mediterranean region, the most significant were the Seljuk Turks. They reordered the Muslim world. Unlike previous usurpers of power in the caliphate, the Seljuks came from outside the old Arab empire. While steppe mercenaries and slaves had been employed throughout the caliphate for generations, the Seljuks added not just different rulers but fresh social and economic direction. Driven by pressure on resources in the steppes and attracted by long-standing economic links with surrounding sedentary societies, Turkish tribes had been infiltrating the Near East, Iran, Khoresan, Iraq and eastern Anatolia for some time before the Seljuk chieftains, leaders of the Oghuz Turks originally from the region between the Aral Sea and the Volga, moved south into Khoresan in the 1030s and to Iran in the 1040s.[7] The mobile armies of mounted steppe nomads rapidly outmanoeuvred and defeated the forces of indigenous rulers, establishing Seljuk rulers in Khoresan and Iran in the 1040s, in the process forcing other Turkish nomads, often called Turcomen, to seek their fortunes further west in Armenia, northern Iraq, northern Syria and eastern Anatolia. By 1051, the western Seljuk commander, Tughril Beg, had annexed Isfahan as his capital. With north-eastern Iran in their hands, the Seljuks' attention turned to Iraq and the fading Buyid regime in Baghdad. Unlike other nomad groups eager for a place in the sun, Tughril harboured political ambition to rule as well as to exploit.

13. A Turkish archer.

At some point in the tenth century the Seljuks were converted to Islam. They emphasised their orthodox Sunni Islamic credentials to secure their status, in nominal loyalty to the Abbasid caliphate and in obvious contrast to the Shi'ite Buyids in Iraq and the Fatimids in Syria. In 1055, Tughril led his forces into Baghdad, sweeping aside the last Buyids and receiving from Caliph al-Qa'im the title of sultan (literally in Arabic, 'rule' or 'power'), a new title for a new regime with imperial pretensions. Tughril married one of his nieces to the caliph while more significantly securing one of the caliph's daughters for himself, an event, it was later noted, 'as had never happened to the caliphs before'.[8] These assertions of legitimacy were aided by opposition to the Shi'ite Fatimids. An Iraqi rebellion against the Seljuks attracted Fatimid patronage and support in briefly capturing Baghdad in 1058–9 before being crushed as Tughril reasserted control. The mantle of protector of orthodox Islam was to provide a convenient cloak for more than one parvenu insurgent seeking power in the Arab empire. However, despite their orthodox posturing, it is hard to cast the Seljuk invasions in religious terms. For some generations they retained aspects of steppe culture, such as burials with grave goods and the consumption of alcohol, their beliefs and rituals exhibiting an eclectic mix of steppe shamanism and adopted local Arab custom.[9] Their ascendancy was achieved not by religious or cultural accommodation but by extreme violence that did not end with the creation of the sultanate in Baghdad.

Seljuk conquests, whether of Shi'ites or Sunnis, were accompanied by massacres, plunder, rapine, the payment of lavish protection money and the saturation of slave markets: after one raid in Armenia, 'the cost of a beautiful girl came down to five dinars and there was no demand for boys at all'.[10] This was not simply a matter of barbarian nomads running amok through the ancient treasure houses of Arab wealth. Soon after occupying Baghdad, the Iraqi Seljuks were employing the same polyglot mercenary and slave armies as their predecessors. However, the disruptive injection of a nomadic element into the sedentary economy and society of the Near East held lasting significance. Other nomadic Turkish tribes roamed with increasing freedom across the whole of the Fertile Crescent and Anatolia. The Seljuk Empire was run by coercion and collaboration, targeted brutality not mindless mayhem, the exploitation of urban and rural resources calibrated to secure elaborate networks of patronage and alliance.

The Seljuk system contrasted with its predecessors in ways that accidentally facilitated the later success of the crusade enterprise. Power rested with Seljuk princes who ruled the various cities and provinces of the empire as a family business, not necessarily harmoniously. Any Seljuk prince could aspire to the sultanate in Baghdad, a feature that guaranteed simultaneous cohesion and competition. The princes' power depended on their own permanent personal military households – *askars* – and their paid or enslaved armies, commanded by emirs, who also recruited their own *askars*. Emirs and prominent *askar* leaders were rewarded with allocation of tax revenues from specified areas of land (*iqta*), or governorships of cities or regions, sometimes as *atabegs*, in theory guardians, mentors and military advisors to young Seljuk princes. In practice atabegs assumed independent authority, subservient in name only, a model familiar to Islamic politics. The new ruling elite was not initially territorial, princes, emirs and atabegs swapping or accumulating cities and regions according to politics and preferment not geography, a fluidity and mobility reflected in the continuing nomadic elements in the Seljuk armies.

The Seljuks and the Turks they promoted were aliens in a world of local Arab rulers and the civilian class of Arabic administrators and lawyers, notably the religious scholars, the *ulema,* who interpreted the law. Language presented a stubborn barrier. In the late twelfth century one Arab Syrian nobleman recalled his days fighting in the armies of Zengi, the Turkish atabeg of Mosul and Aleppo in 1135. He remembered Zengi discussing tactics with one of his commanders: 'they were both speaking Turkish, so I did not understand what they were saying'.[11] Seljuk public espousal of Sunni Islam proved important in reassuring indigenous elites and providing necessary levers of patronage and control. The great Baghdad vizier Nasim al-Mulk (d. 1092) initiated a policy of founding religious schools for the study of law and theology, *madrasa.* These schools provided a physical focus of Seljuk influence in buildings that became prominent features in cities from Iran to Syria; they supplied grateful members of the *ulema* with lucrative employment; and, in their officially directed syllabus, they helped engineer a practical accommodation between often disruptively competing Islamic legal traditions. Nevertheless, for all the techniques of soft power, the Seljuk Empire was a military system, sustained of necessity by violence. Few areas witnessed the consequences more destructively than Syria.

Syria

Greater Syria (*al-Sham*), including Syria and Palestine, presented a paradox in the Arab empire, at once a region of special sanctified religious signifi-cance and a frontier between the *dar al-Islam* (Abode of Islam) and the *dar al-hab* (Abode of War), the front line against the infidel.[12] Since the eighth century, the centre of Arab power had rested further east, in Iraq and Iran. The northern frontier with Byzantium from the Upper Euphrates to Cilicia remained porous and contested while in the 970s the Fatimids annexed much of southern Syria and Palestine. In the later tenth century, the Byzantines reconquered parts of northern Syria, including Antioch, establishing a fron-tier with Fatimid-controlled territory north of Levantine Tripoli. Despite occasional recourse to standard religious rhetoric, these wars hardly gener-ated the aura of holy wars on either side. Syria remained unstable, open to attack from Iraq, Egypt and the nomadic tribes of the Syrian and Arabian deserts, divided by competition between Greeks, Armenian, and rival Arab emirs loyal to Abbasids or Fatimids and disturbed by squabbling factions within the great cities of the region – Damascus, Aleppo, Antioch, Tripoli, Edessa, Mosul. From 1064, warring Aleppans sought the help of Turkish mercenaries, who added to the embattled political scene by challenging those who had invited them in the first place.

In 1071 the Seljuk sultan, Tughril's nephew and successor, Alp Arslan, intervened, forcing the submission of Aleppo before being called away to combat the Byzantines in Anatolia, marking the start of Syria's integration into the Seljuk Empire. Seljuk dominance was challenged by the Fatimids in the south, by indigenous Arab elites, and by freelance Turkish and Turcoman chiefs across the whole region. In 1078 a second Seljuk invasion, led by Alp Arslan's son Tutush, began a wholesale conquest in the name of his brother, the sultan Malik Shah (whose name symbolically combined the Arabic and Persian words for king). By 1086, Tutush had imposed Seljuk overlordship on Antioch (taken from the Byzantines), Damascus, Aleppo and Jerusalem. However, the coastal ports (Tripoli, Tyre, Acre, Jaffa, Ascalon) remained independent or nominally under Fatimid rule while the governors appointed by the Seljuks to administer the cities of the interior tended to act in their own autonomous interests, continuing regional rivalries and divisions that existed long before the arrival of the Turks. In comparison with the main centres of Seljuk power in Iran and Iraq, inland Syria lacked material and human resources, making it peripheral to Seljuk dynastic power games while forcing local rulers into fiercer competition for those limited opportunities for wealth that did exist. This combination of relative poverty and stubborn localism ensured that Seljuk power in Syria proved ephemeral. By 1115, Seljuk princes had disappeared from Syria, although the empire continued further east until the end of the century.

Division appeared early. A civil war for the sultanate after the death of Malik Shah in 1092 led to the defeat and death of Tutush in 1095. Tutush's sons were children – Ridwan of Aleppo (d. 1113) was thirteen and Duqaq of Damascus (d. 1104) even younger. While Ridwan ruled as well as reigned, Duqaq was overshadowed by his mamluk atabeg, Tughtakin, who ultimately succeeded him in Damascus. By the winter of 1097, when the crusaders arrived before Antioch, northern Syria had fragmented into feuds between Ridwan and Duqaq and the governor of Antioch, Yaghi-Siyan, against the atabeg of Mosul, Kerboga, while further south Jerusalem was held in the name of the Seljuks by a Turkish governor until the city was captured by the Fatimids in 1098. The failure of Seljuk control in Syria proved almost unimaginably propitious for the crusaders.

Byzantine Crisis

The Seljuks were not alone in finding imperial power precarious. When he abandoned his invasion of Syria in 1071, Alp Arslan had marched to confront a Byzantine army under Emperor Romanus IV Diogenes (1068–71) advancing from Anatolia into Armenia. The subsequent Seljuk victory at the battle of Manzikert near Lake Van confirmed that there would be no effective halt to continuing Turkish penetration of the Greek Empire's eastern provinces. However, the Turks presented only one threat to Greek imperial power. One of Romanus IV's unreliable allies at Manzikert, the Norman mercenary captain Roussel of Balleul, set himself up as an independent lord in Anatolia. Balleul and other western-hired swords proved a mixed blessing for Byzantium, adding to the complexity of private enterprise opportunism that characterised both sides of the struggle with the Seljuks. After 1071, Turkish infiltration of Armenia and Anatolia gathered pace. In 1077 a Seljuk cousin of Alp Arslan, Suleiman ibn Kutulmush, established a sultanate based on Konya, called the sultanate of Rum. In 1078, Nicaea, less than a hundred miles from Constantinople, fell to him. Soon most of the hinterland of Asia Minor and parts of the Aegean coast were in the hands of various Turkish warlords and pirates, threatening supply lines to the Byzantine capital. Across the former eastern provinces, Turcic tribes, including a nomadic group known as Danishmends, preyed on towns and settled agriculture more or less at will. In the west, the loss of Bari in 1071 to Norman freebooters led by Robert Guiscard was followed by Norman campaigns along the eastern Adriatic coast around Dyrrachium in 1081 and 1085. In the northern Balkans the Pechenegs, a coalition of steppe tribes from beyond the Danube, had penetrated the empire's frontiers. After their defeat in 1091, another group of nomads, the Cumans, menaced the region. Closer to the throne, the loyalty of army high command proved unreliable.

Although Alexius I (1081–1118) managed to stabilise the Balkans in the 1080s and 1090s, this hardly inhibited the threat from Nicaea or in the Aegean. The losses of Bari and, later, Antioch (1084/5) were not reversed. Diminishing territory, especially in Anatolia, created manpower and fiscal problems: fewer taxpayers and recruits without any diminution of military needs or expense.

Increasingly, Byzantium recruited troops from neighbours and former enemies, including Normans and Turks, but also western and northern Europeans, such as the Varangian Guard of Scandinavians and Anglo-Saxons. Self-interest dictated the establishment of Italian trading posts in Constantinople. In 1082, Alexius granted Venice tax exemption and free access to trade and ports within the empire in return for their assistance against the Normans in the Adriatic. Constantinople had long been a truly cosmopolitan city, attracting residents from across Eurasia from the Atlantic to the steppes. In the strategic crisis facing Alexius I in the 1090s, of particular interest were mercenaries from western Europe. It was his good fortune that a ready supply became available, although not exactly in the guise he may have expected. Like the rulers in the Arab empires who summoned steppe nomads to serve in their armies, Alexius found the westerners who answered his call had ambitions of their own.

The Rise of Western Europe

Superficially, western Europe had little to offer its eastern neighbours. Its rural economy precluded monetised systems of regular taxation. In the eleventh century, rents and renders from land were still received largely in kind not cash. In Byzantium and the lands of the former Arab empire, a commercial system was supported by gold as well as silver-based currencies and large towns and cities. In western Europe, the availability of coin, minted from various silver alloys, was limited; labour was cheaper than to the south and east, so labourers had less disposable income; cities were of negligible size. In the early eleventh century, the populations of Baghdad and Cairo may have numbered around half a million; Constantinople perhaps 600,000; Cordoba at least 100,000. By contrast, the largest western European cities, Cologne, Florence, Milan, Rome, Venice, may have harboured 30,000–40,000. By the end of the century, London and Paris may have contained about 20,000 each, hardly even third-rate by Near Eastern terms. While the quickening of economic activity, an increase in long-distance trade, a growth in markets and political centralisation greatly expanded urban populations across western Europe over the next two centuries, even cities such as Paris, which by 1300 approached a size of 100,000, were still dwarfed by the great emporia of the Near East.

However, unlike the Near East, where climate change caused droughts, western Europe benefited from the climatic warming of the period.

BYZANTIUM AND THE CRUSADES

The Byzantine perspective on the crusades was wholly different from that of western Christendom. In the historical context and world view of the surviving Eastern Roman Empire, the crusades formed one episode in a centuries-long sequence of disruptive incursions, distinctive as much in retrospect as in reality. Although periodically significant and finally transformative in Byzantine imperial politics, the crusades simply did not matter as much to the Greeks as they did in western Europe. The crusaders and their settlements competed for Byzantine attention with Bulgars, Pechenegs, Cumans, Serbs, Armenians, Italians, Arabs and Turks as disparate clients, subjects, rivals or neighbours within the wide Byzantine sphere of influence that stretched from the Adriatic and Danube to Cilicia and northern Syria, from the Russian steppes to the Levant. The crusades deepened and expanded ties between Byzantium and western Europe but did not initiate them. Assumptions of inevitable entrenched wariness and hostility between Byzantium and crusaders or the Franks of Outremer ignore constant economic, commercial, diplomatic, cultural and political exchange, a diversity of relationships variously marked by competition, cooperation, exploitation and co-existence. Byzantium itself covered widely disparate societies, demographics and geography. Trade between Byzantium and western and northern Europe in silks, soldiers, pilgrims, saints, slaves, metals, furs, spices or icons operated on their own separate lines, many of them long-standing by the late eleventh century. Foreign paid troops had long been a feature of Byzantine armies, for example the Scandinavian and Anglo-Saxon Varangian Guard, while the mid- and later eleventh century saw an increase in western European recruits and settlers – the so-called *frangopouloi* – whose style of cavalry warfare was admired. The Greek call for western aid in 1095 rested on an established tradition. However, western troops were not alone; foreign recruits included Slavs, Armenians and Turks. The Byzantine polity was cosmopolitan in nature and international in reach, not least in what might be called soft power: culture, language, religion. Greek ecclesiastical and political presence in Italy and Sicily was not extinguished by the loss of the last territorial holding of Bari to the Normans in 1071. Bohemund of Taranto may have proved belligerently hostile, but he held a Greek birth name (Mark) and may well have spoken Greek.[13]

14. The walls of Constantinople.

Byzantine rulers assessed the crusades in customary terms of geopolitical advantage. The absence of overt ideological support grated on western observers, but Greek Orthodoxy, while traditionally embracing the idea of war in defence of religion, never embraced the western idea of penitential warfare. The failure of Greek rulers to provide crusaders with more substantial material and military aid in 1147 or 1189 fuelled suspicion and resentment. This provoked Henry VI of Germany's bullying in 1195–6, when he demanded money with menace from Byzantium for his crusade, and encouraged the leaders of the Fourth Crusade to accept the future Alexius IV's fanciful offer of lavish assistance in 1203. The overriding primacy of Byzantine strategic interests, which embraced alliance with Turks when expedient, and diplomatic habits including necessary deceit, offended some western observers. Consequently relations could be constructive when interests coincided, as when the Byzantines tried brokering an anti-Seljuk alliance between the crusaders and the Egyptian Fatimids in 1097–9, but they could also be fraught when they did not, as over the status of Antioch after its capture by the First Crusade in 1098. Even there, ultimately long-term Byzantine objectives were peacefully achieved with acceptance of Byzantine overlordship in 1137, 1145 and 1159. Despite tensions over Antioch, Byzantine aid assisted Frankish leaders such as Raymond of Toulouse and the 1101 crusade. Relations with Outremer Franks were pragmatically friendly, producing in the mid-twelfth century a series of marriage alliances with Antioch, Tripoli and Jerusalem, close diplomatic agreement with Jerusalem in the 1170s and joint campaigns against Ayyubid Egypt executed (1169) or planned (1177). In 1176, Manuel I and Pope Alexander III even floated a scheme for a joint crusade.

The context of the crusades was of ever closer connections with Byzantium. Despite theological and institutional divisions between the eastern and western Churches that had prompted a public schism in 1054, Greek emperors maintained regular diplomatic correspondence with popes: between 1198 and 1202, during preparations for the Fourth Crusade, Innocent III and Alexius III exchanged at least eight embassies and twelve extensive letters. Manuel I was famously sympathetic to western influences at court, marrying an Outremer Frank in 1161, one of numerous dynastic alliances linking Byzantium to the nobility of the west. Westerners became entangled in Byzantine politics: members of the north Italian

15. *Alexius I, Empress Irene and the future John II.*

Montferrat family were closely involved in bloody coups in 1182 and 1187 as well as, more famously, 1203–4. Byzantium appeared to some a land of opportunity long before 1204. Less dramatically, Greek clergy worked in tandem with Roman Catholics in Outremer, Sicily and Calabria, as they were to do after 1191 in Cyprus. Trade provided the staple contact, fostered by the mutually profitable commercial privileges agreed with western shippers, notably the Venetians. Venetian raids in 1122–3 and anti-western riots in Constantinople in 1171 and 1182 did not inflict lasting damage; in 1198 a treaty restored all Venice's trading rights, commerce with Byzantium comprising up to half the city's commercial activity. Crusading quickened cultural exchange, like the western dissemination of Greek texts and translations from centres like Antioch or from shared artistic projects elsewhere in Outremer, as in the decoration of the Church of the Nativity in Bethlehem (c. 1170), jointly sponsored by Baldwin III and Manuel I. The flow of Greek art, relics, icons and texts increased hugely after 1204, but it had begun earlier.

The chief source of conflict came from immediate political crises not existential cultural alienation. For two centuries from the late eleventh century the rulers of Sicily – Normans (1060s–1194), Hohenstaufen (1194–1266) and Angevins (1266–82) – had contested Byzantine power in the central Mediterranean, usually

16. *Byzantine-Frankish cooperation: the mosaic of Jesus on Palm Sunday in the Church of the Nativity, Bethlehem.*

without association with the crusades (Bohemund's 1107–8 Balkan campaign and the threats during the Second Crusade and by Henry VI in the 1190s being exceptions). Whatever the subsequent political or literary gloss, on each twelfth-century large-scale land crusade issues of supply, not culture or religion, provoked armed confrontation, as they did again in 1204. One of the ironies of the Fourth Crusade rests in the evidence of desired cooperation not confrontation displayed in the treaties with Alexius IV. After the debacle of 1204, except for lacklustre attempts from the 1230s to shore up the Latin empire of Constantinople (1204–61) and, later, other westerner-held enclaves in Greece, crusading more often sought to include an alliance with Byzantium against mutual opponents, notably from the fourteenth century the Ottomans. However, the westerners' price of such an alliance, union of the Greek Orthodox with the Roman Catholic Church, was impossible for successive Greek emperors, wielding much reduced religious and political authority, to deliver. In 1204 a cultural legacy of mistrust and hostility was created among Byzantines that had not existed so virulently before. The unions agreed in 1274 and 1439, as well as a plan in 1355, came to nothing. Nonetheless, a few western anti-Turkish naval leagues in the fourteenth century included Byzantium, now little more than a city state, hardly a major regional still less world power. In the last sixty years before the fall of Constantinople to the Ottomans in 1453, crusades were planned and deployed to save not defeat Byzantium. As in the 1090s, Byzantium in the fourteenth and fifteenth centuries was regarded as a potential, if awkward, crusading ally not enemy.[14]

Agricultural yields improved; populations grew; commerce expanded; the need and use of markets and money grew. With it came social changes: modest urbanisation; enhanced levels of numeracy and literacy; and greater wealth for the aristocratic military elites who exploited these increasingly lucrative agricultural and commercial resources. The growth of towns stimulated inter-regional and international transmission of goods, people and ideas as well as the creation of newly prosperous, mobile groups of merchants and artisans. However, power remained largely concentrated in the hands of those who controlled land and the people who worked it. Political fragmentation from the late ninth and tenth centuries encouraged local lords to assert largely autonomous power, improving agricultural and commercial revenues and the consequent ability to employ military entourages to impose their authority, allowing them to sustain their independence. Castles provided visible signs of how increased wealth consolidated lordship power. Capricious rule and unbridled violence were tempered by traditional law, custom, accepted communal processes of arbitration and conflict resolution necessary within intimate social and economic communities. Competition for control of economic exploitation was fierce, pursued by technologically more sophisticated elites of armed mounted warriors. These arms-bearers, of whatever social origins, gradually developed into a distinct community of shared function, behaviour, social importance and cultural values: the knights so vividly illustrated in the Bayeux Tapestry. By 1100, a knight was synonymous with power and, as even kings depicted themselves as armed mounted warriors on their seals, symbolised authority: all nobles were knights; by 1200, all knights were noble.[15]

17. William of Normandy giving arms to Harold of Wessex as a sign of honour.

The competitive dynamics of lords, landed knights and paid armed retainers stimulated aristocratic social and geographic mobility. The landed warrior classes were not farmers; like their Near Eastern counterparts, they were rentiers although, unlike Turkish emirs, western lords' legitimacy remained tied, rooted in specific localities, by ancestry, adoption, appointment or acquisition. However, a lord could exercise lordship wherever he possessed retinues and income. While this usually imposed geographic limits, in a social context where enhanced profit, status and power could be gained by force or patronage, territorial constraints could give way to more distant career opportunities, whether in a neighbouring valley, province, kingdom or beyond: for German Saxon nobles, across the Elbe into the lands of Slavs and Balts; for French lords, into Spain to fight the Moors of al-Andalus or across the English Channel; for Norman knights, over the Alps into southern Italy, Sicily and Byzantium. The availability and capabilities of western knights joined with opportunity in the Near East and crisis in Byzantium to make the First Crusade possible. It also explains why Alexius I asked for their help in 1095.

Continental Exchange

This conjunction was not random. The image of the First Crusade devised by contemporary Latin sources emphasised its unexpected uniqueness, a divinely inspired irruption of the west into the east. Much of this involved deliberate mythologising. The leaders of the western armies that set off in 1096 knew where they were going and how to get there. The caustic monastic observer Guibert of Nogent's sneering commentary on the peasant children who set out with their parents only to ask at each town they came to whether it was Jerusalem only works as the comic insult it was intended to be if it was assumed Guibert's preferred elite knew better.[16] The speed with which a sequence of large armies reached the agreed rendezvous of Constantinople in 1096–7 alone indicates cooperation with the Greeks and prior understanding of the eastward routes, knowledge available from pilgrims, diplomats, adventurers, mercenaries, merchants and exiles. At least one leader, Peter the Hermit, had been to Jerusalem, as had the father of another, Count Robert II of Flanders. The south Italian Norman commander Bohemund had intimate experience of fighting the Byzantines in the west Balkans in the 1080s. Other crusaders, such as Guibert of Nogent's childhood friend

Matthew, from the Beauvaisis, had seen service with Alexius I in the years before the First Crusade.[17] The Latin narrative sources' almost total avoidance of Alexius's request for military aid in 1095 tells its own story. Even if not deliberate suppression, ignoring the Greek invitation elevated the role of the pope and gilded the autonomous agency of the faithful of western Christendom. Yet paradoxically these same sources reveal how the grand interpretation of a campaign into *terra incognita* misleads.

On 7 June 1099 the armies of the First Crusade finally reached Jerusalem after, for most of them, almost three years on the road. That evening Duke Robert of Normandy, camped outside the Damascus Gate, received an unexpected visitor, Hugh Bunel, a fellow Norman and notorious celebrity murderer. Twenty-two years earlier, Hugh had decapitated Mabel of Bellême at her castle of Bures, 'where she was relaxing in bed after a bath'. Fleeing Mabel's sons, William the Conqueror's agents, and bounty-hunters, Hugh had lived among Muslims for twenty years.[18] Hugh was far from the only expatriate westerner the crusaders encountered. In Constantinople in the winter of 1096–7 they found settled western communities, the *frangopouloi* – 'the Frankish people'. By the 1090s, these included Hungarians, Germans, Danes, Anglo-Saxons, Swedes, Venetians and Amalfitans as well as Frenchmen and south Italian Normans who had thrown in their lot with the Greeks after being defeated in the Balkans in 1085. Some joined the crusaders for the march across Asia Minor in 1097. *Frangopouloi* were not the only familiar faces in the east. When Bohemund's nephew Tancred arrived at Adana in Cilicia in late September 1097 he may have been met by a Burgundian adventurer called Welf. More certainly, in the same month, another crusade leader Baldwin of Boulogne was joined at Tarsus by a privateer fleet of Flemings, Antwerpers and Frisians who, it was alleged, had been plying their piratical trade for eight years under the command of a certain Winemar, a former member of the Boulogne comital household. Winemar's flotilla later seized the port of Latakia during the crusaders' siege of Antioch.[19] Whether these pirates had followed the crusade east, as other western fleets did, or had been preying on Mediterranean shipping before the crusade set out, is unknown. However, their presence and that of other convoys from the North Sea and Italy suggests that the Levant was far from inaccessible to western shipping by the 1090s.

Another feature of the crusaders' progress towards Palestine was revealed by their adaptability to Near Eastern politics and diplomacy. The Byzantine alliance provided the catalyst for negotiations with the Fatimids, spread over nearly two years before finally breaking down a few weeks before the assault on Jerusalem.[20] Surviving crusaders' letters and early narratives suggest they quickly grasped the divided circumstances of the Seljuk princes and how they had terrorised the indigenous peoples of the region. The crusaders could call upon Byzantine diplomats and their own interpreters who knew Arabic, probably from southern Italy (see 'Interpreters', p. 58).[21] Bohemund himself probably spoke Greek, useful as it was also spoken by many Antiochenes and others in northern Syria. Close contacts with Armenians were forged by Tancred of Lecce and Baldwin of Boulogne during campaigns into Cilicia in the autumn of 1097. Baldwin soon after found himself ruling the Armenian city of Edessa beyond the Euphrates. Armenian sources reflect an initial welcome for co-religionists. A Provençal clerk appeared alert to relative eastern and western currency exchange rates in Syria in 1099.[22] None of this is surprising, as it continues the tradition of contact and exchange between western Europe, Byzantium and, more remotely, the Arab world. The story of Peter the Hermit, the outraged Jerusalem pilgrim who in some accounts sparked the whole enterprise, epitomised the threads of contact, the movement of people and goods.

The most apparent human links were elite exchanges. The chief agent was Byzantium, the commodity military service. Scandinavians and Russians had been in imperial service for generations, joined by the 1080s by Germans and Anglo-Saxons. From the 1040s and 1050s, recruits were actively sought from England and Normandy. From the 1030s and 1040s, companies of Normans from southern Italy, valued as heavy cavalry, were regularly hired to supplement Byzantine troops defending frontiers in the Balkans and eastern Asia Minor. Their commanders often secured imperial titles, grants of lands and political influence. From the 1070s, Norman regiments appeared in imperial service under Byzantine rather than their own command. Turks were also recruited, like the polo-playing Tatikios, son of a prisoner of war, who later accompanied the First Crusade to Antioch, having previously commanded a regiment against the Pechenegs in the Balkans in the 1080s.[23] Good relations with the German emperor in the 1080s had produced German contingents. After 1089 a rapprochement with the papacy under Pope Urban II opened other opportunities. In 1090, Count Robert I of Flanders, a Jerusalem pilgrim a few years earlier, sent 500 troops to defend strategic areas of Asia Minor against the Turks. By the 1090s, western clergy, including Englishmen, were permanently settled in Constantinople.[24] Until the early

1070s, Byzantium had been a territorial Italian power. In the 1040s it was sending expeditions to contest rule over Sicily (and recruiting Normans to help), while Italy was still viewed from Constantinople as within its sphere of interest and influence. Southern Italy and Sicily retained significant communities of Greek speakers and Orthodox Christians. Greek emperors continued close, if sporadically fraught, correspondence with the papacy and other Italian leaders, such as the abbot of Monte Cassino. Italian commercial cities established trading posts and workshops in Constantinople, and beyond. Silk, manufactured or shipped through Byzantium, was widely sought after in western Europe. The regular commerce of people produced an eleventh-century northern French Latin–Greek phrase list for such useful things as asking for food, drink, clothes, beds and transport.[25]

Byzantium stood at one corner in a much larger trading area that was transformed during the eleventh century, with the First Crusade as much a symptom as a cause. In 1000 the carriers of long-distance trade in the Mediterranean had chiefly been Muslim and Jewish shippers, working out of ports in Egypt, north Africa and Muslim Sicily: 'not a single Christian boat floated on it'.[26] By the 1090s, Italian merchants and Italian shipping had intruded and begun to dominate, especially Genoese, Pisans and Amalfitans, with Venice assuming a controlling interest in Greek waters. In part the reasons for this were political. The great fourteenth-century Tunisian historian and historiographer Ibn Khaldun (1332–1406) argued that Christian conquests around the Mediterranean, combined with the decline of the Umayyads in al-Andalus and of the Fatimid Empire, had undermined Muslim investment and interest in sea power. This can be traced to the Genoese and Pisan naval competition with Muslim pirates over Sardinia in 1015/16 or the Pisan raid on Palermo in 1063, as well as the Norman conquest of Sicily (1060–91). Trans-Mediterranean commerce developed in parallel with the political disruption.[27] The weakening of Byzantium, the disintegration of the Fatimid Empire in north Africa and the Norman conquest of Sicily damaged traditional trading networks, presenting fresh opportunities for western, particularly Italian merchants already embedded in international trade in slaves, gold and textiles, carried in the early part of the eleventh century mainly on Muslim and Jewish ships. Amalfitan merchants founded a pilgrims' hospital in Jerusalem in the 1070s. Muslim commercial communities were settled in west Italian ports such as Naples, whose linen was probably exported in quantity to north Africa. Cheaper labour costs

INTERPRETERS

The inevitable obstacles of language that confronted crusaders as they moved east, south and north out of western Europe were novel only in degree. Many regions in medieval Europe and the Mediterranean were linguistically heterogeneous. The unifying languages of religion, learning, law and government such as Latin, Greek or Arabic concealed extremes of divergent local dialects and different tongues, such as northern and southern French or High and Low German. French-speaking elites ruled English speakers in England, Flemish speakers in Flanders, Italian, Greek and Arabic speakers in Italy and Sicily, just as Germans increasingly ruled over Slavs and Balts. Turkish lords in the Near East ruled subjects speaking or worshipping in Arabic, Greek, Armenian, Syriac and Hebrew. Byzantine Greeks employed speakers of French, English, Latin, Turkish, Norse and Slavic. Politics, diplomacy, government, administration, commerce, even law relied widely on translation, multi-lingualism and, thus, interpreters.

For crusaders, interpreters were important in promotion, during campaigns, in diplomacy, and in ruling conquests. While crusade sermons were often preached, and almost always recorded, if at all, in Latin, although at times with macaronic elements, audiences demanded the vernacular. Where, as often, the preacher was foreign, interpreters became essential, as in Wales and Germany in 1188 or England in 1267.[28] Communication presented similar problems on campaign. When persuading the cosmopolitan crusaders of the North Sea fleet in 1147 to attack Lisbon, the Portuguese bishop of Oporto used Latin as a lingua franca so that interpreters could translate his words to each separate linguistic group.[29] This cannot have been confined to formal occasions; few large eastern cities until the mid-thirteenth century were internally linguistically homogeneous and most at some stage had to deal with the different languages of locals, in central and eastern Europe, Byzantium, Sicily or Cyprus. Familiarity through previous trade or pilgrimage eased some of these contacts, as witnessed by an eleventh-century Latin–Greek phrase book.[30] Dealing with the different languages of the Near East during the First Crusade's march to Antioch would have been facilitated by Greek and Armenian interpreters; Tatikios, the

18. *Woodcut from the* Credo *of the crusader John of Joinville showing crusaders and Arabs or Turks with an interpreter on crutches.*

Byzantine general attached to the crusade, was a Christianised Turk. The necessary further translations from and into Frankish languages may have depended on the bilingual skills of western settlers in Byzantium or French settlers in southern Italy and Sicily. At Antioch, negotiations with Kerboga of Mosul were conducted by Herluin, possibly a southern Italian Norman, who 'knew both languages', implying Arabic but probably not Turkish (an ignorance shared by Arab emirs), his naming a rare event for interpreters who in the sources usually remained anonymous or unmentioned.[31]

Once established in the Levant, western conquerors and settlers constantly required translators, to conduct fiscal, commercial and legal business and diplomacy: treaties, surrenders of castles and cities, and ransoms. Accounts of detailed discussions across linguistic divides are either formal inventions or suggest the availability of sophisticated language skills. Until the dragomen (from the Arabic *tarjuman*, interpreter) who shepherded later medieval Levantine pilgrim-tourists, it is hard to find servants of Arabic- and Turkish-speaking rulers with mastery of western tongues, so it appears much of the translation work – oral and scribal – rested with Syrian and Palestinian subjects of the Franks or increasingly with bilingual Franks themselves, such as Reynald of Sidon and Humphrey IV of Toron who appear as translator-negotiators with Saladin in 1191–2. The precision of diplomacy required deeper knowledge than demotic Arabic, French, or the lingua franca of port and marketplace. Parallel difficulties were encountered in the Baltic. When the German conquerors staged a Christian morality play for new Lettish converts at Riga in the winter of 1205/6, interpreters were needed to explain what was going on to no doubt bemused locals.[32] Despite sharp cultural and religious divisions, prolonged settlement and rule extended the network of bilingual and multi-lingual officials, although identifying formal interpreting roles has proved elusive, in Outremer and elsewhere. Two remarkable features remain: the apparent ease of contact across linguistic divides and the absence in sources of a ubiquitous presence without which no crusade beyond western Christendom could have functioned.

19. Byzantine silk in the west: the cope of St Alboinus, Brixen, Italy.

encouraged these exports to high wage economies of the Maghreb: Amalfi even shared a currency with Muslim Sicily and north Africa.

The main driver of increasing western involvement in cross-sea trade lay in huge economic inequalities. Monthly shop rentals in Egypt may have matched entire annual royal revenues in some northern European kingdoms. Payment in gold for goods and slaves from the north made southern markets attractive for northern exporters, encouraging aristocratic investment, especially in cities that lacked an extensive rural *contado* or hinterland, such as Genoa, Venice or Amalfi. Subsequent economic and political problems in north Africa, Egypt and Byzantium then encouraged Italian shippers to cut out the Muslim and Jewish middlemen by building their own fleets and increasing the capacity of their ships. After the Norman conquest of Sicily, ports such as Palermo resumed their position as commercial hubs for the whole Mediterranean and facilitated plundering the north African coast, such as the Pisan raid on Tunisia in 1087. While perishable food remained restricted to local traffic, grain, olive oil, wine, sugar, timber, pottery, ceramics, as well as slaves, gold, ivory, silk and other textiles, began to circulate. As northern wealth increased, so did the import to Europe of higher-value goods from Egypt: ivory, rock crystal and spices. Trade knew few denominational boundaries. Eleventh-century Pisans decorated their churches with north African ceramic pottery. By the mid-twelfth century, Genoa's combined trade with Egypt and north Africa made up about 45 per cent of the whole, while its largest market (30 per cent), Latin Syria, acted as the entrepôt for the Muslim interior.[33]

Growing commercial links opened new channels of transmission, some unexpected. In 1076, Pope Gregory VII (1073–85) was engaged in diplomatic exchanges with an-Nasir, emir of eastern Mauretania (in modern Algeria). Commending two papal associates to the emir, Gregory indulged in an uncharacteristic burst of ecumenism: 'we believe in and confess, albeit in a different way, the one God, and each day we praise and honour him as the creator of the ages and ruler of this world'.[34] Such knowledge of Islam in the west was extremely rare – at least in public – but ever more available. Both the Norman conquest of Sicily and the northern Spanish advances into al-Andalus (Toledo fell in 1085) placed significant Muslim populations under Christian rule. The lords of the Maghreb in north Africa, controlling one of the supply lines of gold and ivory from sub-Saharan Africa to the north, were clearly worth cultivating. By the twelfth century, permanent Italian trading posts dotted the north African littoral, in one of which, Bugie in Algeria, the Pisan merchant and mathematician Leonardo Bonacci, better known as Fibonacci (*c.* 1170–*c.* 1240/50), encountered Hindu-Arabic numerals, which he later popularised across western Europe. Similar protected and privileged status was afforded to Italians around the Mediterranean, from Algeria to

20. Eleventh-century Amalfitan coin with cufic epigraphy: 'There is no God but God. Muhammed is the Prophet of God.'

Alexandria to Constantinople, a process in places accelerated but not initiated by the First Crusade. Cultural exchange flowed in the wake of commerce and conquest, such as Norman Sicily entertaining Fatimid art, architectural design and administrative practices, or the language skills of south Italian Normans. Generations before the First Crusade, the links between western Christendom, Byzantium and the Muslim world had been tightening, a process the great expedition to Jerusalem reflected, disturbed, but ultimately strengthened.

CHAPTER TWO

THE FIRST CRUSADE

The impact of the Jerusalem war of 1095–9 on Latin Christendom can be exaggerated but was profound. It enhanced papal authority, invested western European culture in the politics of the eastern Mediterranean, and bequeathed an acrid legacy of unrealistic geopolitical ambition. The First Crusade disrupted those who took part; those it left behind; and those it encountered across Europe and the Near East. The religious dynamism of the Jerusalem war was shaped by a bleak world view of urgent conflict between good and evil, sin and virtue, eternal life or eternal damnation. However, while the conception of holy war rested on scripture, legend and law, its realisation was grounded in economic and social systems in which power and authority lay with arms-bearing ruling classes, the targets of Pope Urban II's summons to fight: 'the knights who are making for Jerusalem with the good intention of liberating Christianity . . . since they may be able to restrain the savagery of the Saracens by their arms and restore the Christians to their former freedom'.[1] Beyond religious rhetoric, the campaign was framed by agricultural incomes; patterns of trade; the nature of lordship, kinship and service; and the ways men, materiel and money were assembled for war. Not everyone was convinced. Traditional beliefs in Christian pacifism or the primacy of the monastic ideal were not universally abandoned. Support for the First Crusade was political, following the contours of current controversies. Involvement was tempered by circumstance and self-interest. Large numbers of those who took the cross soon abandoned it. Others, such as the papally backed Norman rulers of the recently conquered Sicily, in contrast to their cousins in southern Italy, showed little appetite for the new adventure, preferring to consolidate their new possessions on the island and their trading relations with their Arab neighbours in north Africa and Egypt. Over a century later a northern Iraqi historian, Ibn al-Athir, described how Count Roger of Sicily (*c.* 1072–1101) reacted to suggestions of shipping a Frankish army to north Africa with a loud fart, adding the less percussive arguments that any such campaign would leave him out of pocket and destroy his existing agreements with the emir of Tunisia. Instead, Roger proposed: 'if you are determined to wage holy war on the Muslims, then the best way is to conquer Jerusalem'.[2] Although evidently *ben trovato*, the anecdote recognised the reality of Mediterranean politics, and by extension the politics of the crusade, driven by material concerns as much as religious compulsion.

The Plan

The plan to relieve Byzantium in Asia Minor followed by an invasion of Syria and Palestine was devised by Pope Urban II after a council held at Piacenza in Lombardy in early March 1095, at which Greek ambassadors asked for military aid against the Seljuk Turks. This was not the first such Byzantine appeal. As with earlier Greek invitations, it may have been accompanied with a substantial financial inducement, which might have contributed both to Urban's enthusiasm and his ability to fund an extensive preaching and recruitment exercise and attract support.[3] The decision to include the liberation of the Holy Sepulchre carried wide significance, not least by tapping into current eschatological excitement, a perception, encouraged by some popular preachers, a series of poor harvests and some unusual celestial phenomena, that the world was facing the Apocalypse, as prophesied in the Book of Revelation when Christ would return with a New Jerusalem. More pragmatically, Urban may already have been aware of requests for help from clergy in Jerusalem and returning pilgrims.[4] The Council of Piacenza represented the first international church assembly of Urban's troubled pontificate. Taking leadership of a movement to inspire the laity to aid fellow Christians in the east powerfully furthered papal assertion of primacy within Christendom, a natural corollary to Urban's fostering of better relations with Byzantium and the eastern Church in a neat upstaging of his opponents, the German emperor Henry IV and his client pope Clement III. One later commentator, born during the preaching of the First Crusade, repeated gossip that Urban had plotted with the Normans of

URBAN II

When he began promoting the First Crusade in 1095–6, Pope Urban II had been at the centre of international ecclesiastical politics for over fifteen years. Born Eudes (Odo) of Châtillon-sur-Marne around 1035 into a second-rung seigneurial family in Champagne, he received his early education and training at Rheims, where one of his teachers was the future founder of the austere Carthusian order of monks, Bruno of Cologne, who remained a lifelong mentor and confidant. After preferment as a canon and archdeacon at Rheims, in about 1068 Eudes entered the great Burgundian monastery of Cluny where he rose to be grand prior. Called to Rome to assist Gregory VII, in 1080 Eudes was installed as cardinal bishop of Ostia, quickly assuming a leading role in promoting and defending the pope's ambitious moral and ecclesiastical policies, earning the disparaging epithet of Gregory's *pedisequus* or lackey. He cut his teeth as an effective polemicist, networker, political operator and combative diplomat, especially while papal legate in Germany, 1084–5. Regarded as *papabile* on Gregory's death in 1085, he was elected pope in succession to Victor III (1086–7) in 1088. Although committed to the full ideological quasi-monastic rigour of Gregorian reform, Pope Urban pursued his objectives with greater flexibility and collegiality, slowly managing to rebuild support against Emperor Henry IV and his protégé the anti-pope Clement III, as well as establishing a more cohesive identity for papal administration, known from 1089 as the curia. Preaching the First Crusade formed part of this process, providing Urban with a popular international cause, a unique diplomatic opportunity to consolidate reconciliation with Byzantium and a chance to ally moral reform with political action that involved the laity as well as clergy: most of the canons of the Councils of Piacenza and Clermont in 1095 addressed issues of church discipline. The alliance of secular and religious commitment found its definitive symbol in the granting to crusaders of the cross, a ceremony which Urban instituted at Clermont. The crusade sat easily in Urban's wider policies of offering spiritual rewards for religious loyalty, as in his encouragement of Spanish Christian advances against the Moors, as well as exploiting his political alliances – notably with the Normans of southern Italy, whose crusade commander, Bohemund, was a personal

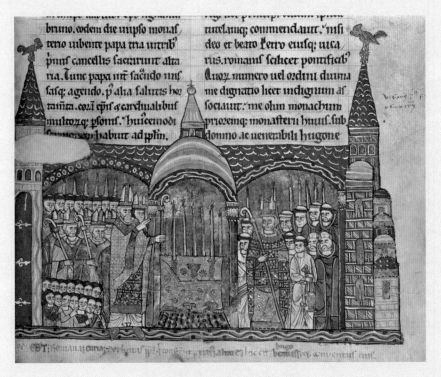

21. Urban II at Cluny, October 1095.

acquaintance – and his ecclesiastical contacts: on the way to Clermont, Urban consecrated the high altar of the new church at Cluny. Theoretical papal authority over the crusade was maintained through legates, Adhemar of le Puy and then Daimbert of Pisa, and accepted by the expedition's leadership, who wrote to Urban from Antioch in 1098 asking for his assistance after Adhemar's death. Although Urban died a fortnight after the fall of Jerusalem in July 1099, before he could learn of the triumph, his mark on the memory of the campaign and on subsequent crusade history remained indelible.[5]

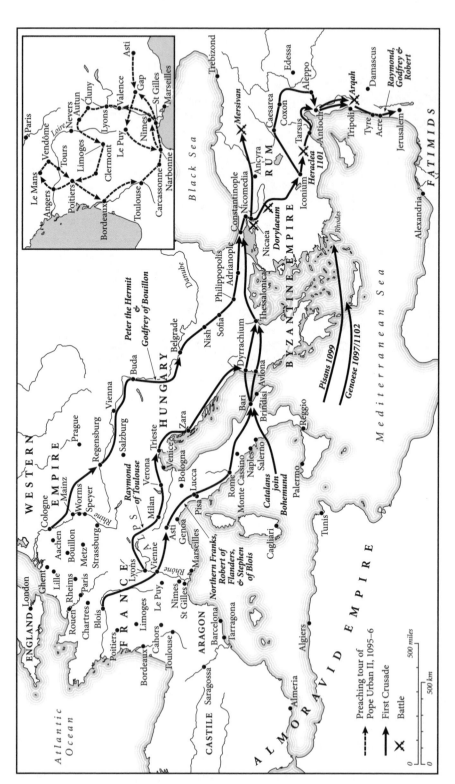

2. *The routes of the First Crusade and that of 1101, with Urban II's preaching tour of 1095–6.*

Preaching tour of
Pope Urban II, 1095–6

First Crusade

Battle

ENGLAND
London
Ghent
Lille
Rouen
Rheims
Paris
Chartres
Blois
FRANCE
Poitiers
Limoges
Cahors
Bordeaux
Toulouse
St Gilles
Nîmes
Le Puy
Lyons
Vienne
**Northern Franks,
Robert of
Flanders &
Stephen of Blois**
Marseilles
Genoa
Asti
**Raymond
of Toulouse**
**Catalans
join
Bohemund**
Monte Cassino
Rome
Salerno
Naples
Lucca
Pisa
Bologna
Venice
Verona
Milan
A L P S
Vienne
Lyons
Rhône
ARAGON
Barcelona
Tarragona
Saragossa
CASTILE
Almería
Algiers
Tunis
Cagliari
Palermo
A L M O R A V I D   E M P I R E

WESTERN
E M P I R E
Cologne
Aachen
Bouillon
Metz
Strasbourg
Worms
Speyer
Mainz
Rhine
Regensburg
Prague
Salzburg
Vienna
Buda
HUNGARY
Trieste
Zara
Danube
**Peter the Hermit
&
Godfrey of Bouillon**
Belgrade
Nish
Sofia
Philippopolis
Adrianople
Dyrrachium
Avlona
Brindisi
Bari
Réggio
Thessalonica
BYZANTINE EMPIRE
Black Sea
Constantinople
Nicomedia
Nicaea
Dorylaeum
Mersivan
Ancyra
R Û M
Iconium
*Heraclea
1101*
Caesarea
Coxon
Tarsus
Trebizond
Edessa
Aleppo
Antioch
Tripoli
Arqah
Damascus
**Raymond,
Godfrey &
Robert**
Tyre
Acre
Jerusalem
FATIMIDS
Alexandria
Rhodes
Mediterranean Sea
Pisans 1099
Genoese 1097/1102

Le Mans
Angers
Vendôme
Paris
Tours
Poitiers
Limoges
Bordeaux
Toulouse
Narbonne
Carcassonne
Clermont
Le Puy
Nîmes
St Gilles
Marseilles
Gap
Valence
Lyons
Cluny
Autun
Nevers
Loire
Atlantic
Ocean

500 miles
500 km
0
0

southern Italy to use the commotion created by the crusade to regain control of Rome, then in imperialist hands.[6] Whatever the truth of this, Urban energetically exploited the Jerusalem war to his political advantage. He also recognised the recent precedents of Christian rulers' conquests of Muslim territories. As he put it in 1098: 'in our days with the force of Christians, God has attacked Turks in Asia and Moors in Europe'.[7] Urban's predecessors had regularly branded recoveries of lost Christian realms meritorious, religious wars, acts of liberation and restoration: in 1089, Urban himself had associated reconquest in Spain with penance and remission of sins.[8]

Recruiting in northern Italy may have begun soon after Piacenza; a Lombard army reached Constantinople by the summer of 1096. Urban's close diplomatic links with the leaders of the Normans in southern Italy probably alerted them to the papal initiative at an early stage. Between July 1095 and September 1096, Urban toured much of southern, central, western and south-eastern France. The novel presence of a pope north of the Alps caused a sensation, heightened as the ageing pontiff maintained a gruelling schedule of public appearances, often in the open, even in winter. Urban combined preaching with presiding over important local religious ceremonies, such as the translation of relics or the dedication of altars. Wherever he went he negotiated with local ecclesiastics and lords for their support for the Jerusalem scheme. Letters and legates were sent to those regions that, because of distance or political impediment, such as the excommunications of the king of France and the emperor of Germany, he could not visit. By the time he held a council at Clermont in the Auvergne in late November 1095, Urban had already secured the commitment of a string of notables. The council itself was intended to attract secular as well as ecclesiastical leaders from across France. In a carefully staged and choreographed performance, at the end of the assembly, on 27 November, Urban preached on the Jerusalem war.

It is not known what Urban said. No verbatim record exists, and attendance was patchy. The decrees of the Clermont council chiefly reiterated papal policies on church authority, independence, organisation and discipline. The decree on the Jerusalem war, which only survives in seventeenth-century copies of a dossier of council documents kept by one of the attendees, the bishop of Arras, offered a special form of penitential exercise that forged together Gregory VII's idea of penitential violence, the papal concept of inviolate church freedom, and a campaign to Jerusalem.[9] Church protection was extended to those who undertook this task and to their property. Tendentiously, the pope's God-given authority over human spiritual affairs was assumed. The uniquely generous spiritual benefit of full remission of penance was open to all who confessed their sins. This full remission coupled with the explicit goal of Jerusalem transformed a mundane scheme to provide mercenary troops to Byzantium into a cause of ostensibly transcendent significance. Unlike his mentor Gregory VII's similar proposal in 1074 to assist Byzantium and march on to Jerusalem, Urban's provided a clear structure of message, response and reward: the positive incentive of remission of penance instead of Gregory's bleaker, more amorphous emphasis on martyrdom; the replacement of Gregory's vague promise of 'eternal reward' with precise spiritual and temporal rewards signalled by swearing a vow and taking the cross.[10] Oaths provided a familiar, serious bond of commitment. Simple, memorable slogans were deployed: 'Take up your cross and follow me', 'Liberate Jerusalem', 'expel the infidels', 'earn salvation', 'God Wills it'. The subsequent campaign of public ceremonies, private conversations, sermons, letters, legates, and the recruitment of local opinion formers, notably monastic networks, displayed propaganda management of a high order.

The idea that Urban had originally intended only limited aid for Byzantium is contradicted by his proposals' inclusion of Jerusalem, the unique spiritual rewards on offer, and his own extensive recruitment tour and efforts to communicate with regions beyond his itinerary. Letters, eyewitness accounts and land deeds of departing crusaders paint a fairly consistent outline of the pope's plan: a penitential military campaign to Jerusalem to recover the Holy Sepulchre, free eastern Christians and thus, in Urban's own words, 'liberate Christianity'.[11] Relief of the burden of sin struck a chord with arms-bearing aristocrats whose warrior values sat awkwardly with increasingly well-articulated clerical insistence on the unavoidable penalties of temporal sin. Many likened the expedition to a pilgrimage. Urban's few surviving letters used more general words with penitential associations of journeying and labour (*iter, via, labor*), while at the same time employing the precise language of divinely ordained sacralised holy warfare (*procinctus, expeditio*). Witnesses remembered the pope emphasising the armed nature of the struggle at Limoges in December 1095 and a war 'to hunt the pagan people' in Anjou in March 1096. The message got through: 'to fight and to kill' the defilers of the Holy Sepulchre, as one Gascon charter put it. The sense of a Christian *militia* suffuses crusaders' campaign letters.[12]

At Clermont, Urban announced the appointment of Bishop Adhemar of Le Puy as his surrogate to lead the expedition and the date of his departure, 15 August 1096. Land routes and a general rendezvous and muster at Constantinople must have been agreed in advance of the contingents setting off. Despite increasing naval capacity, the shippers of Italy hardly possessed the resources or technology to carry very large armies, with adequate rations and horses, across the Mediterranean. Equally, crusade commanders probably lacked sufficient ready cash to pay shipping costs or the appetite to test the ubiquitous landlubbers' suspicion of the sea that many would never have seen before. Strategically, the question as to why the crusade took three years to reach Jerusalem rather than the few months of a sea voyage, can be explained by the bifurcation of Urban's plan: help for eastern Christendom and the recovery of Jerusalem. Acceptance of the Greek invitation, and perhaps money, made Constantinople the necessary and obvious first destination. The main land armies mustered across western Europe in the autumn of 1096; reached Constantinople between November 1096 and May 1097; and gathered as one host at the siege of Nicaea by early June 1097, a process speaking loudly of coordination with the Byzantines.

The military effort stretched from the Mediterranean to the North Sea. Some recruitment appeared distinct from the papal campaign. The excommunicate French king, Philip I, held a conference in Paris in February 1096 to discuss the crusade. Meanwhile, a separate preaching initiative, begun perhaps before the Council of Clermont, was conducted by the charismatic diminutive Picard preacher Peter the Hermit. Later a figure of legend, in practice he apparently combined revivalist oratory with the ability to raise and organise troops, including a number of lords from the Ile de France and surrounding regions, and to provide active leadership for a substantial army of cavalry and infantry from northern France and western Germany.[13] Peter retained some standing in the crusader armies even after his own forces had been cut to pieces in Asia Minor in September 1096. How Peter acquired sufficient authority to command such forces is hard to fathom. Remarkably, his contingents – possibly tens of thousands strong – were ready to depart by early March 1096, reaching Constantinople in July and August. His relationship with Urban's mobilisation is unknown, although early accounts after 1099 linked the two. Peter's apparent pitch of serving Christ and restoring Jerusalem certainly echoed Urban's.[14]

PETER THE HERMIT

Peter, known as the Hermit (d. *c.* 1115), was a popular travelling evangelist from Picardy who preached moral and social reconciliation in northern France, establishing a strong reputation as a charismatic ascetic holy man in the years before the First Crusade. All chronicle accounts note his leading the first wave of crusaders eastwards that came to grief in Asia Minor in the autumn of 1096 and later his role at Antioch in heading the crusaders' embassy to Kerboga of Mosul. Some suggest his continuing prominence once the expedition had taken Jerusalem. After the crusade, he is said to have returned home, founding a religious house at Neufmoutier near Huy (in modern Belgium). One western German tradition ascribed the initiative for the crusade to Peter, calling him the '*primus auctor*'.[15] This tradition gained historiographic traction by being included, alongside prominence given to Urban II, in William of Tyre's *Historia*, the great late twelfth-century historical compendium of crusade history that dominated perceptions of the First Crusade until the nineteenth century when Peter's initiating role was dismissed as fiction.

Recent scholarship has reassessed Peter's contribution, noting that, while also a figure of legend, the historical Peter combined his revivalist oratory with raising and organising a coherent thousands-strong armed force, largely of infantry but led by lords and knights.[16] This force set out for the east in March 1096, only a few months after the Council of Clermont following Peter's preaching in areas Urban avoided, from Berry, the Orleannais, Champagne to Lorraine and the Rhineland, with additional recruitment from the Ile de France. The speed of his army's departure suggests he began to promote the Jerusalem journey before the Clermont speech, possibly in collusion with the pope, indicated by the only detailed account of Peter's preparations. This describes how Peter, prompted by his own ill-treatment on pilgrimage to the Holy Sepulchre, and armed with a written appeal for western aid from the Patriarch of Jerusalem (neither of which is impossible or even improbable), persuaded Urban to launch the crusade. Peter's own preaching lacked offers of the cross and in retrospect was seen as more populist than the pope's, aimed beyond the knightly classes. Yet the two campaigns shared essential elements: a call from the east; the

22. Peter giving out crosses.

plight of Jerusalem; the direct order of Christ (in Peter's case via a dream); and the offer of spiritual reward. It is easily conceivable that Urban, in exploiting the Greek invitation for aid into his scheme of a papally led Christian renewal, incorporated appeals from the Christian community in Jerusalem and the evangelical activism of Peter the Hermit.[17] The legend may not be groundless.

Preparation

Receiving the cross formed part of a process of engagement driven by material as well as emotional and religious forces. No recruit could hope to participate without material assets, his or her own or someone else's. The offer of church protection probably agreed at Clermont assumed crusaders possessed property.[18] Lords subsidised their entourages and relatives. Poorer crusaders without such material support had to abandon their journey. The staggered times of departure in 1096 depended on the harvest, raising money from property deals or recruits finding a paymaster. Accounts of the crusade note the large-scale involvement of what were frequently, at times derisively, termed 'the poor' (*pauperes*). Leaving aside the moral heft of the 'poor in spirit' (Matthew 5:3), the 'poor' on crusade were defined in comparative terms, not necessarily indigent but non-rich, subsidised by others. Such numbers grew proportionately as the campaign drained recruits' assets, necessitating the creation of common funds to bail them out.[19] Economic and financial constraints provided the frame for the expression of religious enthusiasm through emotional triggers of anxiety (fear of sin, hell, or bogeymen infidel), hope (salvation, virtuous conduct, self-improvement, enhanced status), revenge (for Christian and by analogy Christ's suffering) and reward (remission of penalties of sin, privileged legal protection, employment) that sought physical resolution through the military campaign. The crusade was always about more than a supposed existential Turkish threat. In records of their fund-raising transactions, departing crusaders were depicted as desiring escape from the burden of sin through the penance of the crusade. However, the Clermont decree implied that, given righteous intent, spiritual and material ambitions did not contradict one another. One eyewitness later described Urban offering knightly recruits self-respect, fame and a land 'flowing with milk and honey' (Exodus 3:8). Another had the pope promising crusaders the possessions of their defeated enemies, the usual accompaniments of successful warfare.[20] A famous crusader battle cry held out the prospect of 'all riches' (*divites*) as a reward for steadfastness in faith and victory in battle.[21] The ambiguity of spiritual and material gain was inherent.

Recruitment spread unevenly but extensively: in France, the Limousin, Poitou, the Loire valley, Maine, Chartrain, Ile de France, Normandy, Burgundy, Languedoc and Provence; in Italy, Lombardy, the Norman south and the ports of Liguria and Tuscany; in Germany, the Rhineland and western provinces. Enthusiasm is recorded from Catalonia. There is limited evidence of participants from Denmark and England. However, the English paid a land tax levied by King William II (1087–1100) to raise 10,000 marks for mortgaging the duchy of Normandy to subsidise his brother Duke Robert's expedition. Everywhere, the lead was given by what a Genoese observer called the 'better sort' (*meliores*): lords, abbots, members of mercantile urban elites.[22] Participation relied on existing networks of lordship, kinship, clientage, shared locality, commerce and employment, and therefore centred on aristocratic, ecclesiastical or commercial communities, families and courts with their immediate dependants – relatives, tenants, military households, client clergy, servants. The Church furthered international contacts through its increasingly cosmopolitan episcopates and monastic orders. Towns and cities provided focal points for recruitment and muster, news and recruitment passing along trading networks. Crusading traditions quickly became established in market centres such as Limoges, Poitiers, Tours, Chartres, Paris, Troyes, Lille, Cologne, Milan and Genoa. The high nobility operated internationally through extensive dynastic connections across regional frontiers.[23]

The total number of those who left for the east is unknowable. Some estimates put the figure as high as 70,000–80,000 recruited during the year after Clermont.[24] A regular stream of reinforcements in smaller groups joined them during the three-year campaign, by land but also by sea, chiefly on Italian fleets from Genoa, Lucca and Pisa. Many who took the cross thought better of it, could not find a patron or failed to raise adequate funds, without which, it was later observed, participation was impossible.[25] The impression given by crusaders' surviving property grants – sales or various forms of mortgage chiefly to monasteries, in return for cash, materiel or pack animals – is of free-standing, independent, knightly or noble recruits incurring considerable capital loss, many times annual landed income. However, these records are those of the leaders not the led, the paymasters not the paid. Most of those who went with the First Crusade at some stage, some at every stage, received payment in kind or cash, sometimes disguised as gifts, much of it in addition to basic survival rations. Lords paid their retinues and got their clerks to keep written accounts. On the march, payment could attract new followers and create fresh allegiances, a process fully exploited by ambitious junior commanders such as Bohemund's nephew Tancred of Lecce. Crusaders took considerable quantities of silver bullion with them in coin and ingots; a Burgundian knight received 2,000 shillings on just one land deal with the abbey of Cluny; Godfrey of Bouillon extorted 1,000 silver pieces from the Jews of Cologne and Mainz as well as raising 1,300 silver marks from selling his estate at Bouillon.[26] Affluent crusaders took negotiable wealth with them: jewels, plate or luxury textiles. Although very little gold was available until the crusaders reached the eastern Mediterranean, most leaders took some if they could. On campaign, the crusaders' resources were regularly replenished: by gifts, bribes and payment from the Greeks; tribute and protection money from cowed opponents; and booty from victories and conquests. The scramble for supplies, subsidies for poorer crusaders, arguments over exchange rates, and the creation of central communal funds witnessed the material imperatives.

Not all fund-raising was loss. Mortgages and ecclesiastical protection de facto recognised a crusader's title to property. The pious motives attributed to crusaders in some of the charters recording such financial transactions may have been genuine, or the gloss of the clerical scribe, or simply technical formulae indicating gifts rather than sales or mortgages.[27] Nevertheless, the availability of the necessary moveable wealth is striking, especially given the series of very poor harvests before the bumper crop of 1096, and the late eleventh-century western European dearth of silver. Even with the unlocked bullion assets of monasteries, the apparent surplus of liquid capital indicates developing monetisation in commerce and artisan trades. Wealth was no longer confined to ecclesiastical corporations, successful merchants and landed aristocrats. The head chef of Count Stephen of Blois, Hardouin Desredatus, possessed vineyards, land and houses that he assigned to the abbey of Marmoutier before setting off east. The abbey, near Tours in the Loire valley, played an active role in seeking such deals, monks and abbot openly touting for trade in what they clearly saw as a profitable business as well as spiritual opportunity.[28]

As the armies lumbered east from the early spring to late autumn of 1096, led by expanded retinues of great nobles, lesser lords and wealthy knights, the pattern of mutually sought-after lordship, secured by wages, gifts, subsistence, service and shared booty, provided the glue that held together the crusade. New subsidised units formed following a lord's death, impoverishment or another's success. Groups from the same area and across the social spectrum could travel together, mess together and pool resources. All recruits would have been used to acting and making decisions as a community. Alongside hierarchical lordship, much of society operated communally, from crop planting to law courts. On the crusade itself, the non-noble elements, characterised as the *populus*, periodically acted in concert to influence the decisions of the leaders who regularly consulted them. Besides the non-combatant support staff necessary to any armed force – cooks, farriers, carpenters, blacksmiths, writing clerks, valets, priests, prostitutes, laundresses and others – the First Crusade armies attracted non-fighting pilgrims seeking military protection. Some apparently set out with their belongings, intent on settling near the Holy Places. If so, hope proved a mirage or a nightmare. Non-combatants and the less well-off tended to be the first and heaviest casualties from disease, hunger and exhaustion: accounts of their privations and losses make harrowing reading. The genuinely poor could not go on crusade with much prospect of progress let alone survival.

The Campaign to Syria, 1096–7

The campaign of the First Crusade fell into four stages. The first saw the western forces converge on Constantinople in the autumn, winter and spring of 1096–7. In the second stage, over the six months from June 1097, the crusaders, acting in collaboration with the Byzantines, captured Nicaea in western Asia Minor, forced a passage across Anatolia, annexed Cilicia and besieged Antioch in northern Syria. During the third stage, in 1098, the crusaders emancipated themselves from the Greek alliance as they took Edessa, Antioch and its surrounding regions for themselves. The final act, beginning in January 1099, saw most of a much reduced crusade army march south into Palestine where, on 15 July 1099, Jerusalem fell after a month's siege, a triumph secured by victory over a Fatimid relief army at Ascalon in August. The majority of survivors then returned home leaving meagre garrisons in Jerusalem, Antioch and Edessa.

Two main routes to Constantinople were used. One went south-east from the Rhineland to follow the Danube to Belgrade before striking south-east across the Balkan peninsula to the Byzantine capital. This was used by forces that passed through or originated in western Germany, such as the armies of Peter the Hermit, some German counts, and two substantial contingents raised by two German priests, Gottschalk and Volkmar, which were destroyed in Hungary during June and July 1096 after provoking disturbances over supplies and markets. The surviving armies, including Peter the Hermit's, passed down the Danube from the early spring of 1096 onwards. Some months later, they were followed more peacefully by Godfrey of Bouillon, duke of Lower Lorraine, and his Lorrainers. The second route east led to the ports of Apulia in southern Italy and the short sea crossing to the Albanian coast and the old Via Egnatia across the Balkan peninsula to the Byzantine capital. This was used by the armies from northern France led by Hugh of Vermandois, brother of Philip I of France, Robert of Normandy, and the counts Eustace III of Boulogne, Robert II of Flanders and Stephen of Blois, as well as by southern Italian Norman troops under Bohemund of Taranto. The Lombards who reached Constantinople by August 1096 plausibly also travelled the Apulia–Albania–Via Egnatia route. These routes were familiar from trade and pilgrim traffic. Exceptionally, Raymond of Toulouse's large force, accompanied by the legate Adhemar of Le Puy, marched from Provence through Lombardy, around the head of the Adriatic and down the Dalmatian coast of the Adriatic before picking up the Via Egnatia, a longer journey that crossed difficult terrain where the Provençal troops encountered local hostility. It has been suggested that Raymond's Dalmatian itinerary had been planned with Alexius I to discipline a rebellious Serb leader, Constantine Bodin.[29] While evidence for this is circumstantial, general Byzantine-papal-

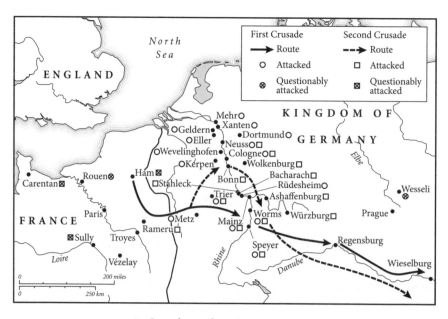

3. *Crusade attacks on Jews, 1096–1146.*

crusader cooperation may be assumed, not least in the provision of supplies and markets in Greek territory and the well-framed diplomatic preparations that greeted the crusaders when they reached Constantinople.

One unplanned consequence of the mass recruitment saw lethal attacks on Jewish communities of the Rhineland in May, June and July 1096, initially orchestrated in Speyer, Worms, Mainz and Cologne by troops under Count Emich of Flonheim. Feeding off local economic and social tensions, the violence was fuelled by the aggressive Christ-centred crusade rhetoric of victimhood, resentment and revenge. Although no part of official policy, these anti-Jewish atrocities exposed a fissile intolerance inherent in the crusade's ideology (see 'Jews and the Crusade', p. 80).[30]

The second stage of the crusade saw the western forces operating as Emperor Alexius's mercenaries, hired confederates of the Byzantine state. On reaching Constantinople, crusade commanders swore personal oaths to the emperor, receiving lavish gifts of gold, silver, jewels, cloaks, textiles, food, horses and military equipment in return. In the crusaders' own testimony, desire and expectation of material reward are palpable. Certain objects conveyed more than aesthetic or financial value. Tancred of Lecce, Bohemund's ambitious nephew, asked – unavailingly – for Alexius I's enormous imperial tent 'marvellous both by art and by nature . . . it looked like a city with turreted atrium [and] required 20 heavily burdened camels to carry'. Despite its highly inconvenient bulk, Tancred intended the tent as a meeting place for his growing band of clients and followers. Just as money allowed the great to attract support, so Tancred's hoped-for tent would have elevated his status. Display formed a crucial aspect of lordship, on crusade as at home. The luxury that attended rich crusaders on campaign played a social and political role beyond private gratification.[31] Alexius, who similarly used conspicuous wealth to politically dazzle and impress, understood this. He was paying on a number of levels for specific military aid.

The initial object was the recapture of Nicaea, within striking distance of Constantinople, held by the Seljuks since 1081. Earlier western recruits had been stationed nearby, as had been the forces led by Peter the Hermit until their near annihilation by the Turks in September 1096. Alexius's wider strategy included challenging Turkish power in Anatolia, Cilicia, Armenia and northern Syria, with Antioch fixed as a target. Using the crusaders on his eastern flank left Alexius freer to combat Turkish threats in the Aegean. In addition to money and supplies, he provided strategic advice, regional

JEWS AND THE CRUSADE

Although no crusade was launched against the Jews of western Europe, their communities were profoundly affected: directly from crusaders' physical attacks and financial extortion; and indirectly by increasingly overt anti-Semitic prejudice and discrimination arising from the development of a culture of aggressive Christian piety and religious xenophobia that crusading reflected and stimulated. Both lay and ecclesiastical Christian authorities were conflicted. Secular rulers generally welcomed Jewish commercial and financial activity as sources of revenue, which encouraged them simultaneously to protect and exploit Jews within their jurisdictions. Jews' urban trades, businesses and access to liquid capital made them attractive as both protégés and milch cows. As rich corporations, churches and monasteries similarly took advantage of Jewish finance. At the same time, official church teaching created a contradictory tension. On the one hand, Jews were depicted in the liturgy and elsewhere as responsible for the Crucifixion and obstinately blind to the Christian revelation: in short, enemies of Christ. On the other, the Book of Revelation describes how the final conversion of the Jews will mark a stage in the Apocalypse and the fulfilment of God's providential scheme and therefore implictly demands protected status for Jews. The crusades initially sharpened these contradictions before contributing to the spread of a climate of cultural uniformity and religious intolerance in which Jews found themselves increasingly exploited, marginalised, ghettoised and excluded.

Jewish communities spread from the Mediterranean into northern Europe from the tenth century, becoming established in some numbers in market towns and cities across parts of France and western Germany, increasingly prosperous regions later, not coincidentally, significant as centres of crusade recruitment. Attacks on these communities did not start with the crusades, reports of the Egyptian caliph al-Hakim's destruction of the Holy Sepulchre in 1009 provoking anti-Jewish violence in France. However, the concerted atrocities inflicted on Jewish communities in the Rhineland and northern France in 1096 during the early stages of the First Crusade appeared of a different order and set a new pattern for persecution that revolved around money, faith and civil protection. From May until July various Franco-German contingents of crusaders wrought

23. *Tombstone of a Jewish victim of crusader violence, Mainz, 1146.*

havoc in Jewish communities the length of the Rhineland and elsewhere in
northern France. From both Christian and Jewish sources, their motives
appeared both material and religious. The desire to seize Jewish cash to pay for
crusade expenses was widely shared; Godfrey of Bouillon extracted 1,000
marks from the Jews of Cologne and Mainz, later victims of the depredations of
the followers of Count Emich of Flonheim, who committed a series of the
worst outrages. The desire for money was nonetheless closely allied to a declared
collective sense of vengeance on enemies of the cross. While religious claims
may have acted as a cover for violent mercenary grand larceny, it appeared to
some victims as a potent ideological inspiration, supported by the many instances

of enforced conversion. Such excesses may have aided corporate bonding among the crusaders, a source of identity and the first action of the campaign. It also signalled a failure and collapse of political control by church and secular authorities: in attacking the Jews, Count Emich was clearly defying the authority of Emperor Henry IV as well as the local prince-bishops.

This combination of material greed, sincere or feigned enthusiastic religious hostility, and the limits of establishment protection was displayed again during the Second Crusade, when, among other outbreaks of persecution, a charismatic Cistercian preacher Radulph whipped up anti-Jewish violence again in the Rhineland in 1146; and in England during the early stages of the Third Crusade in 1189–90, attacks that culminated in the massacre and mass suicide of Jews at York in March 1190. The authorities' loss of control on these occasions contrasts sharply with the effective public protection afforded the Jews of Mainz by Frederick Barbarossa in 1188. However, the dangers for Jewish communities were not confined to sporadic explosions of violent hostility but embraced a gradual erosion of social tolerance, while whatever wealth they possessed was never immune from peaceful sequestration. Although successive popes from Eugenius III's 1145–6 crusade bull onwards had outlawed direct involvement of Jewish credit in funding crusades, as this risked siphoning crusaders' money to Jews, secular rulers felt free to extort money directly for their crusades, a move advocated by influential clerical anti-Semites such as Abbot Peter the Venerable of Cluny (d. 1156). In England, Jews were tallaged (a form of arbitrary royal expropriation) for crusades in 1188, 1190, 1237, 1251 and 1269–70. In 1245 the First Council of Lyons directed that all Jewish profits from interest be confiscated for the crusade. In 1248–9, to help pay for his crusade, Louis IX of France, a notoriously devout anti-Semite, expelled Jewish money-lenders and seized their assets.

It is incontestable that the culture of the crusade encouraged the range of disparagement of the Jews. During the later twelfth and thirteenth centuries, increased official alarm, academic contempt and political violence aimed at religious unorthodoxy and dissent, coupled with, in promoting the crusade, greater emphasis on the figure of Christ Crucified, placed those branded as enemies and killers of Christ in an ever more precarious position. Material exploitation was matched by deliberate social alienation in the name of faith, witnessed equally by formal discrimination, such as the legislation passed by the Fourth Lateran Council in 1215, and the emergence of blood libels from the mid-twelfth century (the first, invented in the 1150s by monks at Norwich cathedral priory, concerned an unsolved murder in 1144 of William an apprentice tanner). While the crusades did not create anti-Semitism, crusading's ideology and practice high-lighted some if its core sources, from financial resentment in a cash-strapped but increasingly monetised society to the promotion of an exclusive religion as marker of social identity. For those encouraged to think that their intent to fight the infidel represented an ultimate laudable ambition, Jews made awkward neighbours.[32]

contacts, for example with Armenian émigrés, and diplomatic intelligence, including putting the crusaders in touch with the Fatimids of Egypt. Direct Byzantine military cooperation was provided at the siege of Nicaea and a Byzantine regiment accompanied the march across Anatolia to Antioch to protect Alexius's interests and receive the surrender of captured cities. As one veteran noted, the crusaders needed Alexius as much as he needed them: 'without his aid and counsel we could not easily make the journey'.[33]

The muster of the armies at Nicaea encouraged field cooperation and unity in a host numbering many tens of thousands speaking many different languages. During the siege (May–June 1097) the leaders had to coordinate their actions consensually and pool resources: a common assistance fund was created, paying, among other things, for siege engines and engineers. The need for unity became even clearer after the fall of Nicaea (19 June). On 1 July, only a few days after setting out towards Syria, the expedition narrowly escaped disaster when its vanguard under Bohemund and the Byzantine general Tatikios became separated from the rest of the army and was attacked by a substantial Turkish force. Only the timely arrival of the main army saved the day and led to a sweeping victory, known subsequently as the battle of Dorylaeum. There followed a painfully slow march (perhaps between 5 and 11 miles a day for up to 800 miles) in harsh summer conditions. A number of Turkish-controlled towns and cities capitulated. Casualties from heat, hunger and disease were high. In September, at Heraclea, facing the barrier of the Taurus Mountains, the army divided. The main force followed a northern route through potentially friendly Armenian territory, approaching Syria from the north-west. Smaller contingents under Tancred of Lecce and Baldwin of Boulogne turned south, competing against each other as they swept up coastal towns in Cilicia before reuniting with the main army to besiege Antioch in October. This pincer strategy had probably been devised on Greek advice to maximise Armenian Christian support in the Taurus region and Cilicia while cutting off Antioch from the resources of its hinterland.

Antioch 1097–8

The crusade's third stage, the siege of Antioch, followed by a six-month hiatus in the expedition's progress, established the crusaders' independence from Byzantium, at the same time forging within the army a distinctive

24. *Antioch in the 1830s showing the fortifications on Mount Silpius behind the city.*

identity. Battered by disease, hunger, fear, anxiety, uncertainty, heavy casualties and battle trauma, the crusaders apparently developed a fierce sense
of providential community in adversity, encouraged by stories of heavenly
assistance, visions and miracles. Genuine demotic impulses were exploited
by the high command to keep the beleaguered army intact, fostering the
crusaders' image as the new Israelites, specially chosen, tested and protected
by God, in death as in life. This provided a defining template for subsequent
crusades. With the departure of the Greek regiment and the subsequent
much publicised and highly controversial failure of Alexius to help the
crusaders, Antioch transformed the crusade from a subordinate mercenary
army into the fiercely independent, self-conscious army of God.

The first siege lasted from 21 October 1097 until the city fell on 3 June
1098. The crusaders then immediately found themselves besieged by a large
relief army from Mosul. This second siege lasted until the breakout of the
crusader forces on 28 June, which achieved a surprising but decisive victory.
Antioch in 1097, a city of Greeks, Armenians, Arabs and Turks, was ruled
as a semi-autonomous dependency of Aleppo by its governor Yaghi-Siyan.
Throughout the first siege, the crusaders had been unable to surround

Antioch completely or prevent the city being supplied and reinforced. Despite defeating relief armies from Damascus (late December 1097) and Aleppo (February 1098), and constructing a number of siege forts around the city, Antioch only fell to them through the treachery of a disaffected local commander who helped spirit a small force under Bohemund over the walls at night (2/3 June). Even then the citadel remained untaken, only surrendering after the victory of 28 June. The concentration of tens of thousands of besiegers created severe problems of supplies, provisions being sought from as far away as Crete, Cyprus and Rhodes as well as the northern Syrian hinterland. As the winter of 1097–8 progressed, famine and disease became endemic. Desertions mounted, ironically assisted by the arrival in Syrian waters of fleets from Italy, Byzantium and possibly northern Europe. Morale sagged. Privations deepened. With the threat of Turkish relief forces undimmed, to stiffen resolve the leadership began to circulate stories of heavenly soldiers and saints fighting for the crusaders, and of visions and dreams that confirmed the providential nature of their cause and the certainty of paradise for fallen comrades.

The departure of Tatikios in February 1098, possibly to secure more supplies and troops, allowed some, notably Bohemund, to suggest treachery and dereliction from the agreements sworn between the crusaders and Alexius in Constantinople. These oaths, which can only be reconstructed from subsequent special pleading from all parties, seemingly implied that, in return for his active assistance, Alexius would receive the allegiance of crusader conquests, at least as far as Syria. What was envisaged for acquisitions further south is wholly unclear, except that some form of imperial overlordship would probably have been expected by the Byzantines. By the time they reached Antioch, the crusaders may well not have worked out how to organise a political settlement for Jerusalem. Their early contact with the exiled Greek Patriarch Simeon of Jerusalem may have alerted them to the complexity of implementing their slogan of liberation for Palestinian Christians.[34] The destiny of Antioch, by contrast, presented a more clear-cut objective. It is possible that Alexius had offered Bohemund a role as client ruler of a buffer province in Cilicia or northern Syria. However, buoyed up by his success in leading the defeat of the Aleppan army in February 1098, Bohemund developed an independent strategy to establish his own principality, a move eased by Tatikios's departure. As the crusaders stayed outside Antioch, foraging across the region, political options opened up. Fatimid negotiators appeared in the crusaders' camp in February and March 1098. A splinter group under Baldwin of Boulogne, who had again left the main army in October 1097, had offered service to Armenian lords in the upper Euphrates region, a move culminating in Baldwin's assuming control of the city of Edessa in March 1098. As commander of an alien elite military corps in control of a Near Eastern city, Baldwin was adopting a role similar to a Turkish emir or atabeg. In doing so, he showed his former comrades what was possible.

The outcome at Antioch assumed regional significance. With the crusaders still receiving supplies from Byzantine territory, naval reinforcements from the west presented a threat to the ports of northern Syria. In the wake of the failures of the rulers of Damascus and Aleppo, the atabeg of Mosul, Kerboga, assembled a large coalition, drawing allies from southern Syria, northern Iraq and Anatolia. His spring offensive in 1098 sought to impose his rule from the Jazira region of Syria to the Mediterranean. Antioch formed only one part of this strategy, as was apparent from Kerboga's unsuccessful three-week attempt to capture Baldwin of Boulogne's Edessa in May. This delay saved the crusade itself as Kerboga's army reached Antioch only hours after the westerners had entered the city and gained the protection of its walls. Bohemund's own parallel ambitions had also become clear. By the end of May, he had persuaded his fellow leaders to agree to his keeping Antioch if he could capture it and if no help came from Alexius. Four days later, on 2 June, a possible rival, Stephen of Blois, who only two months earlier had been boasting of his appointment as the expedition's 'lord, guardian and governor', conveniently fled the siege.[35] Once he had gone, Bohemund revealed to his remaining colleagues his plan to enter the city with the assistance of an Armenian commander of one section of the walls.

Timing was crucial for Bohemund. Not only was Kerboga's army fast approaching from the east, but he may have got wind that Alexius, accompanied by thousands of new crusaders, was slowly advancing across Anatolia to consolidate the rapid gains the Byzantine-crusader army had secured the previous year. While it is unlikely that Alexius, a cautious commander and more concerned with western Asia Minor than northern Syria, had firmly decided to advance as far as Antioch, his caution was compounded by learning of the crusaders' plight directly from Stephen of Blois in late June at Philomelium (Asksehir). The emperor withdrew westwards as a precaution against being cut off by renewed Turkish incursions. While it would stretch the evidence to suggest that Bohemund had planned Stephen's departure and loaded him with forecasts of doom in order to persuade Alexius to withdraw, Stephen's absence and the emperor's failure to proceed to Syria suited Bohemund's purpose. It left him free to demand Antioch and provided a very effective weapon of propaganda to excuse the crusaders' breaking their obligations to the emperor on the grounds of Alexius's own supposed breach of contract.

The sensitivity of the issue was reflected in the attention it received from later commentators, both Latin and Greek, who identified it as a pivotal moment in subsequent Byzantine relations with the western principalities in the Near East and later crusade expeditions. However, despite the mutual polemics, the breach was not total. Negotiations over Greek military help only finally ended in April 1099. Food still came from Byzantine territories; diplomatic contacts with Armenians and Fatimids, brokered by the Byzantines, were maintained; some crusade commanders, such as Raymond of Toulouse, still acknowledged Byzantine primacy and accepted Greek assistance. However, the removal of Byzantine direction in 1098 transformed the First Crusade into an independent player in Near Eastern politics whose uncomfortable ideological ambitions challenged regional expectations. The crusaders' increased autonomy was further supported by western fleets that allowed them independent access to supplies from across the eastern Mediterranean, naval protection for the land operations, and direct material aid, their presence arguably tipping the military balance towards the crusaders.

None of this would have mattered without victory at Antioch. After the occupation of the city on 2–3 June 1098, now themselves besieged by Kerboga, with Antioch's citadel still in Turkish hands, and the impossibility of defending the whole circuit of the walls, the crusaders plumbed new depths of desperation. Lack of food, high prices and illness sapped the army's physical strength. The vital supply of horses fell dangerously low. Morale was corroded by fear and helplessness at the only too visible prospect of imminent brutal death. Collective nerve snapped in a night of mass panic and flight (10–11 June). The expedition was saved by deft deployment of the carefully fostered sense of providential and eschatological purpose developed over the previous six months. In the days after the night of panic, supportive visions of Christ and the Apostles were reported to have been received by members of the Provençal army. One vision usefully indicated that the Holy Lance that had pierced Christ's side on the cross was buried in

Antioch's cathedral. Despite general scepticism, the claim was tested and on 14 June an object appropriate for the Lance (or rather its spear-head) was unearthed. The leadership reinforced the consequent positive change in mood with mass rituals of solidarity and penance and by imposing puritanical rules of behaviour. However, visionary politics failed to alter grim military reality. An embassy to negotiate with Kerboga in late June, led by the neutral figure of Peter the Hermit, may have sought a negotiated surrender to permit the crusaders to withdraw.[36] If so, it failed, leaving the crusaders little option but to chance survival on battle.

The crusader victory against the odds at the battle of Antioch (28 June 1098) saved the expedition and created a new political context. Effectively recreating under new management the former Byzantine province of Antioch lost to the Turks in 1084–5, perhaps a Byzantine strategic aim all along, the crusaders were now firmly established in northern Syria, with control over the lower Orontes valley and access to Mediterranean ports, a position consolidated over the following six months as more towns were captured. The beginnings of western administrative rule emerged in Antioch and elsewhere; a Latin bishopric was created at al-Bara. Urgency dissipated, as the army enjoyed novel peaceful prosperity while their commanders jockeyed for power in Antioch and exploited regional resources. The death of Adhemar of Le Puy (1 August 1098) removed a unifying and purposeful influence. With Bohemund successfully defending his hold over Antioch, Raymond of Toulouse, no less eager to secure a Near Eastern principality for himself, led raids that secured a swathe of territory to the south of the city, including Ma'arrat al-Numan, taken in December 1098 amidst stories of desperate crusaders' cannibalism. In early January 1099, Raymond attempted to assert supreme command by offering to take Godfrey of Bouillon, Robert of Normandy, Robert of Flanders and Tancred into his paid service. Only Tancred, the youngest and poorest of them, seems to have accepted, separating his fortunes from those of his uncle Bohemund, who was intent on staying in Antioch.[37] Revival of the crusade's momentum only came from the mass of crusaders gathered at Ma'arrat al-Numan whose purpose remained fixed on Jerusalem and not on their commanders' lucrative land grabs in northern Syria. Raymond's own Provençal followers dismantled the walls of Ma'arrat, leaving the town indefensible and forcing Raymond to accede to their demands to set out to Jerusalem. The rank and file's suspicions of the leadership, sometimes collectively discussed in formal consultative assemblies, had simmered ever since victory at Antioch; now they determined the course of the campaign.[38]

Jerusalem 1099

Raymond's departure from Ma'arrat al-Numan on 13 January 1099 opened the last act of the crusade. Rapid progress south, between mid-February and mid-May, was halted as Raymond, still determined to gain territory of his own, besieged Arqah, fifteen miles inland from the port of Tripoli on the route from the interior of southern Syria to the coast. Once joined by all the other leaders, except Bohemund, Raymond's strategy collapsed. Godfrey of Bouillon emerged as the spokesman for the mass of disgruntled crusaders, exploiting a new set of visions calling for an immediate assault on Jerusalem. The credibility of the Holy Lance, and by association Raymond who was using it as a talisman, was questioned after its advocate and finder, the Provençal visionary Peter Bartholomew, underwent an ordeal by fire (8 April) from which he died (20 April). Godfrey of Bouillon broke up the siege of Arqah on 13 May. Simultaneously, a Fatimid offer of free access to Jerusalem by unarmed Christians was refused. From Arqah progress was swift, the collapse of negotiations with the Fatimids making speed essential. Following

25. Jerusalem from the Mount of Olives, *a watercolour by Edward Lear, 1859.*

the coast road from Tripoli, shadowed by western fleets, the crusaders encountered minor opposition from Sidon; Tripoli, Beirut and Acre agreed treaties; Tyre, Haifa and Caesarea put up no resistance; Jaffa was abandoned by the Fatimids, who, under the active vizier al-Afdal, had recently reasserted control in Palestine, in 1098 regaining control of Jerusalem from the Ortoqid Turks. At Ramla in early June the crusaders briefly toyed with a direct attack on Egypt. This was rejected. Soon crusade detachments fanned out across the Judean hills. On 6 June, Tancred entered the largely Christian town of Bethlehem where locals overcame initial suspicion in welcoming the crusaders.

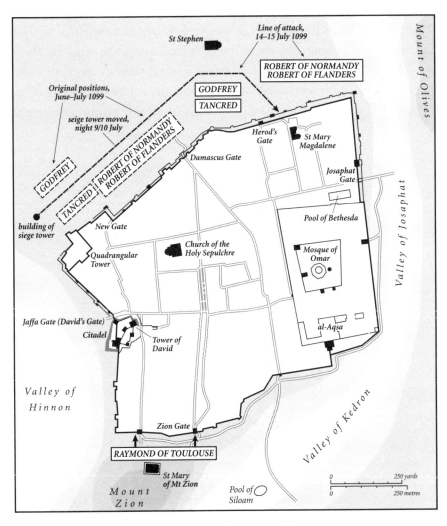

4. *The siege of Jerusalem, June–July 1099.*

The siege of Jerusalem began on 7 June and lasted until a final assault breached the walls on 15 July, leading to a sustained massacre in the hysteria of success, followed three days' later by a more cold-blooded mass killing, a move prompted by shortage of food and fear of the approaching Fatimid army.[39] The Fatimid garrison had clearly counted on relief from Egypt, adopting oddly passive tactics before, seeing the city was lost, quietly surrendering and being allowed to depart. Both sides appeared mindful of events at Antioch, the garrison hoping to sit it out behind Jerusalem's double walls until rescue appeared, the invaders determined not to be caught in a vice between the city and a relief army.

The month-long siege of Jerusalem prompted far less epic coverage than the drama of Antioch. Militarily it was very different. Conducted against the threat of the imminent arrival of a Fatimid army, the siege revolved around assault not blockade. The battle-hardened veteran army of a few thousand achieved a remarkable victory accompanied by the now familiar orchestrated religious enthusiasm – visions of divine favour, penitential

26. Sicilian twelfth-century reliquary of the True Cross, possibly similar to that of the kingdom of Jerusalem.

processions, etcetera – and technical ingenuity – elaborate siege machines built with the help of professional engineers and material cannibalised from Genoese ships. The brutal exultation of success gave way to a final episode of political infighting as the leaders chose Godfrey of Bouillon not Raymond of Toulouse to rule the conquered city. There was no suggestion of handing authority to local Christians, not least because they lacked a suitable political elite. The conquerors quickly imposed their own secular and ecclesiastical hierarchy. A new fragment of the True Cross was usefully discovered that was to serve as the iconic totem of the new regime for the next eight decades. Divine support was immediately called upon, as the still fractious crusade leadership united for one last time to defeat the Fatimid relief army under al-Afdal himself at Ascalon on 12 August. As with the victory over Kerboga at Antioch in 1098, triumph at Ascalon was crowned in the eyes of those reporting it by the seizure of material booty: 'the treasures of the king of Babylon' (the crusaders' name for Egypt): 'pavilions, with gold and silver and many furnishings, as well as sheep, oxen, horses, mules, camels and asses, corn, wine, flour'.[40] This victory marked the end of the First Crusade (see 'Plunder and Booty', p. 94).

The improbable success of the First Crusade was a triumph of organisation, determination, morale, improvisation, military leadership and luck. Given its disjointed command structure, the crusade's achievements appear even more remarkable. Yet the crusaders were quick learners. Following the near-disaster of a split army at Dorylaeum, the feuding, rancorous and competitive leaders thereafter united when confronting sieges, battle or political crisis. Funds were pooled at Nicaea, Antioch and Jerusalem. Bohemund assumed agreed tactical command during the siege of Antioch. The assault on Jerusalem was coordinated. This collective leadership challenged assumptions about optimum command structures while allowing for tensions between leaders and between the leadership and the mass of troops to be aired and defused without the army falling apart. Cut off for long periods from outside help, in constant fear of annihilation, the crusade's unity came from circumstance: divided they were sure of failure. The leadership's effective use of targeted spiritual interventions exploited the ideological imperative. The politics of conviction did not exclude the politics of acquisition; one led to the other.

Nonetheless, the crusaders' success owed as much to the incompetence, ill-fortune and divisions of the polyglot city states of the region as to their

PLUNDER AND BOOTY

Writing a decade after the Council of Clermont, Abbot Baldric of Bourgueil imagined Urban II offering crusaders 'the goods of your enemies . . . because you will plunder their treasures'.[41] This was hardly a surprising promise. Crusades, like all medieval armies, relied on plunder and booty to incentivise troops and sustain campaigns. Violent foraging, seizure of food when access to markets failed, signalled the transit of notionally friendly regions in central and eastern Europe of the land expeditions during the First, Second and Third Crusades, while shaping the progress and prospects for armies in hostile territory. Every major crusade to the eastern Mediterranean sought re-endowment, by agreement (with Alexius I in 1097 or Tancred of Sicily's 40,000 gold ounces in 1191), conquest (Thrace by Frederick I in 1190, Cyprus by Richard I in 1191 or Constantinople in

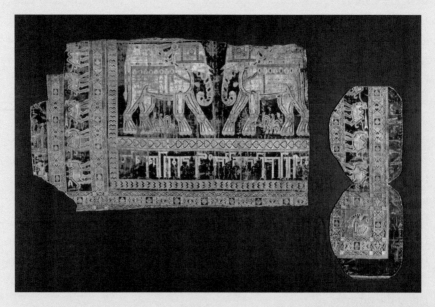

27. *First Crusade booty: the Shroud of St Josse, from the abbey of St Josse, Normandy; Persian embroidered silk allegedly brought back by Count Stephen of Blois.*

28. *The most famous crusader booty: the Four Horses of St Mark's, taken from the Hippodrome, Constantinople, after the Fourth Crusade, 1204.*

1203–4), coercion (the payment of substantial – 20,000 gold pieces – protection money by Tripoli and Jabala in 1099), or victory in battles or sieges (on the First Crusade alone, at Dorylaeum, Antioch and Ascalon, or at Iconium in 1190). Booty could feed directly to the troops who collected it or indirectly through endowing lords with fresh resources to pay their followers. Division of spoils formed a settled expectation among recruits both before and during campaigns. Formal sharing arrangements featured in agreements between crusaders at Dartmouth in 1147, Richard I and Philip II in 1190, and the crusaders and Venice in 1201. Anxiety, suspicion, competition and resentment over distribution of plunder marked the aftermath of successful operations, for example at Nicaea (1097), Ma'arrat-al-Numan (1099), Lisbon (1147), Acre (1191), Constantinople (1204) or Alcazar (1217). Despite the image and reality of reckless mayhem, and frequent appeals for restraint by commanders, plundering could also be chillingly ordered. Following the Genoese capture of Caesarea in 1101, booty was carefully allocated: the bulk of goods went to the commanders, ships' captains and 'men of quality', with a fifteenth going to the galley crews; the remaining 8,000 troops received 48s of Poitou and two peppercorns each.[42] At Constantinople in 1204, after an initial licensed free for all, collection and distribution were centralised.

After the capture of Damietta in 1219, allocation was calculated according to status: knights; priests and local recruits; non-noble troops; wives and children.[43]

The importance of booty went beyond necessity, constituting in the minds of contemporaries and participants justified reward. The earliest narrative of the First Crusade combined the spiritual and temporal dividends of steadfast faith and success in recording the crusaders' supposed morale-boosting battle cry at the battle of Dorylaeum: 'today if it pleases God you will all be given riches – *divites*'. These could be massive: Tancred allegedly stripped 7,000 marks worth of silver from Jerusalem's Dome of the Rock alone.[44] The diversion of the Fourth Crusade to Constantinople in 1203 was driven, one observer suggested, 'partly by prayers and partly by reward – *precio*'.[45] This could be taken for almost all crusades, from Palestine to Spain, from German merchants' profits in Livonia to northern Frenchmen's freebooting and land-grabbing in Languedoc. Provided the intent was suitably devout, material gain was not seen as a deplorable ambition, even in the original Clermont decree. Doing God's will, crusaders were free to indulge in legitimate grand larceny, the fruits of force and victory, although their plundering was no more extravagant than that by any other contemporary armies. In inspiration and action, piety and pillage operated in tandem, as on the piratical Venetian crusade of 1122–5 that gained territory for the cross along with brutal plunder and stolen relics for Venice. Crusading treasure seized as booty from the Levant was enthusiastically welcomed home by Genoa between 1099 and 1101, as was Spanish crusade plunder by the citizens of Cologne in 1189. The most obvious and possibly most widely disseminated booty were relics (see 'Sacred Booty', p. 252). Temporal swag could include silks, gold, gems, precious rings, arms, military fittings, statuary and other exotic items from the Orient, sometimes – as in Genoa after 1099 or Venice in 1125 and after 1204 – in very large quantities: the plunder from Constantinople has been estimated as more than enough to fund a European state at the time for a decade.[46] A Limousin lord, Gouffier of Lastours, was alleged to have befriended a lion during the First Crusade and more reliably to have displayed looted cloth hangings as mementos of his adventure. Fatimid linen, silk and cloth of gold embroideries obtained during the First Crusade, possibly loot from the Egyptian camp at Ascalon, came to be deposited in Cadouin Abbey in Perigord and Apt Cathedral in Provence, transfigured into objects of Christian reverence.[47] Alfonso VIII of Castile claimed an Almohad banner after his victory at Las Navas de Tolosa (1212). John of Alluye, a French crusader in the 1240s, returned with a sword made in China, although this, like other souvenirs, may have been a purchase not a battle prize.[48] Such trophies enhanced the prestige of the returning hero (John of Alluye's sword is carved on his funerary *gisant*, p. 104) as well as offering the chance of being converted into cash or property. The most famous crusade booty were the four horses from the hippodrome at Constantinople displayed from the 1260s on the west front of St Mark's in Venice. Most plunder possessed more mundane nature and use, providing immediate subsidy for crusaders on campaign, pay for return passages or means to recoup initial capital outlay.[49] Crusading could not have functioned without the reality of plunder and booty in a balance of military pragmatism, material attraction and spiritual inspiration that belies easy construction of conflicting motives or an unhistorical dichotomy of the secular versus profane.

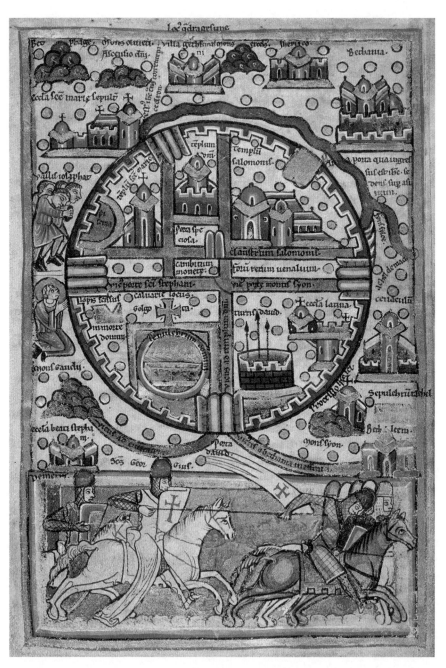

29. *The defence of Jerusalem.*

own resilience. The campaigns of 1097–9 were played out against the regional aftershocks of the Seljuk invasions. Long a politically fractured region, the civil wars in Syria and Iraq following the deaths of Malik Shah and his dominant vizier Nasim al-Mulk in 1092 opened political space for foreign intrusion, an opportunity encouraged by the Fatimids, who initially saw the crusaders as useful allies. A notable feature of the First Crusade was how easily it surfed the shifting currents of regional politics and how quickly its leaders became politically acclimatised. Yet the crusaders' capture of Jerusalem in 1099 bequeathed a costly legacy. The defence of the Holy City and the Holy Land became a totem of western Christian identity, a culturally defining obsession and an impossible political ambition.

Trophies and Memory

The immediate impact on western Europe came with returning veterans laden with trophies, mementos, plunder, stories and scars: pet lions, luxury linens, loose chippings, lost hands and tall stories.[50] Critics were silenced or won over. Survivors rapidly dictated or penned descriptions of the Jerusalem war, which were quickly refashioned by professional monastic writers into more crowd-pleasing literary accounts. Writing a generation later, a monk who had attended the Council of Clermont passed over the events of the crusade because he assumed his audience was already familiar with them through books, secular songs and sacred hymns.[51] The memorialising literary genre reached from liturgical songs to monkish chronicles to more overtly secular Latin and vernacular poems, some of epic content and length. Reputations were made (and a few destroyed) by stories of the Jerusalem journey. Old soldiers' tales were legion, as each area claimed their own particular heroes, such as who was the first man across the walls at Jerusalem: Raimbold Creton from Chartres, who lost a hand, or the brothers Ludolf and Engelbert of Tournai.[52] Bohemund helped fashion his own heroic legend during a promotional tour of the west in 1106–7 and earlier when he shipped Kerboga's tent to his home port of Bari.[53] The exotic drew attention to the special status of returned crusaders, such as palm leaves from Jericho or the sensational legend of Gouffier of Lastours' tame lion, which, after being rescued by Gouffier from a snake, followed him everywhere before drowning in pursuit of his saviour's departing ship. Gouffier brought back more tangible treasures such as Muslim banners, textiles and

30. *Commemorating the First Crusade in stained glass at St Denis in the mid-twelfth century.*

rings.[54] Families – like Gouffier's – later played on their links to crusaders by curating and displaying war trophies. Other veterans sought to enshrine their crusade credentials by donating relics acquired on campaign to religious houses. Fame operated reciprocally. Robert of Flanders milked his status as a Jerusalemite in his donations of Holy Land relics and in his charters. Conversely, he and Robert of Normandy were luminously commemorated as crusaders in mid-twelfth-century stained-glass windows at the French royal abbey of St Denis.

The rapid memorialisation crossed art forms. Carvings and frescoes in parish churches across western Europe alluded to crusading ideology, its Biblical context or directly to incidents on the campaign, the heavenly intervention of saints at Antioch proving especially popular. The twinned emphases on militant violence and religious conviction, on the agency of devout warriors and the immanence of Christ, were common across visual, aural and literary representations, the victories at Antioch and Jerusalem praised as acts of faith and feats of arms. Such transference could endow secular material objects with numinous quality, as in the case of two famous luxury Egyptian silks woven in the 1090s that survive at Cadouin in the

31. Shroud of Cadouin.

Dordogne and Apt in Provence. The Cadouin silk has been associated from the thirteenth century with Adhemar of Le Puy. Both were perhaps acquired by crusaders either as part of gift exchanges with Fatimid ambassadors or as booty after the battle of Ascalon. While other bits of eastern loot preserved their crusading provenance, these silks were reinvented as sacred icons by the religious communities where they were housed: the Cadouin silk became the shroud of Christ; that of Apt the veil of his grandmother St Anne.[55] In some ways such a transformation was appropriate as the crusade powerfully witnessed the physicality of Christian history, a process of literally getting near to Christ and to the events of the Bible, to tread in holy footsteps. Thus were crusaders lastingly transfigured into the new Maccabees and the new Israelites.

CRUSADE MEMORIALS

Memory played a prominent role in medieval European culture. This took many forms: commemorative endowments of monasteries, churches and chapels; special liturgies and religious services; written ecclesiastical calendars memorialising events or the deaths of patrons; the collection of letters or creation of literary memory in chronicles, verse or family histories; the conservation of relics of past deeds or their portrayal in statuary, frescoes, mosaics or stained glass; the oral record in family legend, domestic story-telling and public performance, such as sermons. Such memorials promoted crusading and the reputation of crusaders. Past events framed present action and inspired future behaviour. The repeated appeals to the luminous example of the First Crusade, 'the worthy deeds of our famous ancestors', resonated for centuries.[56] Liturgies and hymns celebrating the conquest of Jerusalem proliferated.[57] The circulation of chronicle accounts of past crusades featured prominently in preparations for new enterprises, as did evocations of past triumphs (and disasters) in crusade preaching and propaganda.

Crusade memorialisation assumed concrete forms. Some were ostentatious, such as crusaders' ceremonial presentation to churches or religious houses of plundered eastern sacred relics, often in lustrous reliquaries, a habit especially noticeable after the First and Fourth Crusades; the secular loot displayed as symbols of dynastic or corporate achievements; the First Crusade Levant textile hangings in the Lastours family museum at Pompadour in the Limousin or the public display of Venetian trophies from Constantinople; or the programme of First Crusade stained-glass windows at the abbey of St Denis in the 1140s.[58] More private, if also designed to be seen, were statues, such as that of the returning Lorraine Second Crusade veteran Hugh of Vaudemont at Belval; or the Joinville family epitaph at Clairvaux, composed by the crusader John of Joinville in 1311, which expressly honoured his many crusading ancestors.[59] The crusader John of Alluye was buried at the abbey of La Charité-Dieu, near Tours in northern France, around 1248. The monks remembered him in their prayers. His stone effigy conveyed a subtle message commemorating his crusade (1241–4) as it shows him, in full armour, wearing a sword whose elaborate

32. *Crosses carved on the walls of the Church of the Holy Sepulchre.*

33. *Statue commemorating the return of Hugh of Vaudemont from the Second Crusade.*

34. *The tomb effigy of crusader John of Alluye, c. 1248, showing his Chinese sword.*

pommel indicates a Chinese origin. At the very least visitors to the abbey might have been impressed by the exoticism of the carving.[60]

Generically, the path of the crusader was the path of Christ, the path of the cross, an act self-consciously following the commands to 'take up the cross' (Matthew 16:24; Mark 8:34; Luke 9:23) and to 'do this in remembrance of me' (Luke 22:19). It was not only the rich for whom these injunctions held power. The less wealthy could participate in memorial ceremonies and liturgies or brag of their exploits with equal vigour and imagination. For concrete memorial, they had fewer options. However, one habit may reflect a common desire to leave a mark: the crosses carved on church walls from the chapel of St Helena beneath the Church of the Holy Sepulchre to parish churches like that in the English village of Bosham on Chichester Harbour, each testimony to an instinct for recognition and record.

CHAPTER THREE

'THE LAND BEYOND THE SEA': LATIN CHRISTIAN LORDSHIP IN THE LEVANT, 1099–1187

Looking back a century later, the Mosul historian Ibn al-Athir described the appearance of western reinforcements in the Levant in 1104: 'There arrived ... from the lands of the Franks ships carrying merchants, troops and pilgrims and others.' He used the same formula in an account of the westerners' attack on Damascus in 1129: 'They all gathered, the king of Jerusalem, lord of Antioch, lord of Tripoli and other Frankish [rulers] and their counts and also those who had come by sea for trade or for pilgrimage.'[1] Military strength, commercial opportunity, religious magnetism, sea power and links with the west established the Franks (as the settlers were universally if ethnically misleadingly known; *ifranj* in Arabic), in their settlements in Syria and Palestine that came to be called *Outremer*, the land beyond the sea.

Settlement

The lands occupied by the western invaders were never very extensive. At their greatest extent, they stretched from Cilician Armenia and the Upper Euphrates valley in the north to the Negev and Gulf of Aqaba in the south, a distance of some 600 miles. Except for the isolated enclave of Edessa beyond the Euphrates to the east, the conquests were physically limited by chains of mountain ranges running north/south, with only a few rivers (such as the Orontes and Litani) and natural gaps (as at Homs, the Biqa valley and the road from Acre through Galilee to Damascus) allowing access from the coast to the interior. Beyond the mountains to the east, agrarian plateaux gave way to the fertile valleys of the Jazira in the north and arid scrub leading to desert in the south. Cutting north/south through this region, the great rift valley of the Jordan led to the Dead Sea. The narrow fertile coastal plain, interrupted by hills in the Lebanon and around Haifa, and flanked in Palestine by the dry Judean hill country, opened out in the south towards the intractable Negev desert between Palestine and Egypt. Failure to annex the great cities of the Syrian interior, Aleppo and Damascus, or extend control to the Nile valley, let alone challenge the Seljuks in Iraq, left the invaders without the major economic and political centres of the region. They were restricted to an area of immense cultural significance for all three Abrahamic faiths, but of patchy economic productivity, embracing fertile valleys and constricted plains, arid hillsides, semi-desert and parched wilderness, an inconveniently configured territory not much larger than modern England or a medium-sized state of the USA, such as Alabama.

Control even of this modest expanse proved strenuous to conquer and maintain. It took the Franks half a century to establish complete command over the coast. In the north, the city state of Antioch failed to secure stable frontiers either in Cilicia or towards Aleppo, which remained conspicuously beyond its grasp. While an important strategic buffer for the rest of northern Outremer, the county of Edessa proved ephemeral, lacking wealth, administration and settlement, reliant on constant military activity to manipulate local rivalries between Muslim and Armenian lordships. Its demolition between 1144 and 1151 proved impossible to resist. In the south, the expansion of the kingdom of Jerusalem to cover, at its height, not only the Biblical Holy Land but large tracts of land beyond the Jordan and Dead Sea and in the desert towards the Red Sea, never secured it from invasion from Syria or Egypt. The absence of permanent regional allies rendered Outremer vulnerable if its neighbours united against it, as happened in the 1180s, a fragility seemingly confirmed when it was all but annihilated in 1187–8 by the sultan of Egypt and Syria, Salah al-Din Yusuf ibn-Ayyub (i.e. 'the Righteousness of the Faith Joseph son of Job'), known to westerners then and now as Saladin (1137/8–93).

Hindsight imposes a teleological pattern of transience and decay. The obstacles to permanent settlement were formidable: the alien, hostile physical, cultural and political environment; the failure to reach the natural frontiers of mountains to the north and desert to the south or to annex major cities of the interior; the untamed and untapped economic, demographic and strategic power of Egypt. Limited settlement by westerners disguised the inadequacy of material resources within the Frankish territories necessary to support the numbers of immigrants that might have secured a more lasting presence. As it was, the Franks were too few to dominate and too many to integrate. Except in politics and superficial domestic manners, unlike other foreign invaders of the region, the Franks could not conform to indigenous linguistic and religious culture: the Frankish kings of Jerusalem revealingly called themselves 'king of the Latins', namely the Franks, those who followed the Latin rites of the western Catholic Church. Arabic presented a barrier to accommodation even where, as with Syrian and Palestinian Christians, religion did not. The Franks lacked the resources to compete numerically with the continuing influx of Islamicised steppe nomads into the Near East or prevent the rise of Turkish and Kurdish warlords to regional political domination. Demography denied Outremer's survival. However, the impression of a doomed venture obscures the social reality of the Frankish experience. By the 1180s, Outremer had become home to three or four generations of Franks, tens of thousands of people who, however conscious of their special status in ethnicity, language, law and religion, no longer could see themselves or, except in Muslim polemic, be regarded as intruders. For them, Outremer, as its greatest twelfth-century spokesman, the Jerusalem-born scholar, prelate, royal servant and chronicler William, archbishop of Tyre (c. 1130–86), insisted, was their *patria*, for the love of which 'if the needs of the time demand, a man of loyal instincts is bound to lay down his life'.[2]

35. *Farming in the Nile valley, the economic dynamo of the eastern Mediterranean.*

WILLIAM OF TYRE

William, archbishop of Tyre, intellectual, tutor, administrator, diplomat and pre-eminent historian of the Latin settlements in twelfth-century Syria and Palestine, was born *c.* 1130, probably in Jerusalem, into a local Frankish non-noble burgess family. After his early education most likely at the school run by the canons of the Church of the Holy Sepulchre, *c.* 1146–65 William received first-class academic training in the liberal arts, theology and civil law at Paris, Orléans and Bologna. On his return to the kingdom of Jerusalem in 1165, he soon garnered elite church preferment, first at Acre then as archdeacon of Tyre. Entering royal service as a diplomat to Byzantium (1168) and Rome (1169–70), in 1170 he was appointed tutor to King Amalric's son and heir the future Baldwin IV. In his own account, it was William who first discovered Baldwin's leprosy; tutor and pupil seemed to have continued on good terms into the 1180s. Through the good offices of the regent Raymond III of Tripoli, with whom William forged a lasting political affinity, he became the new King Baldwin's chancellor in 1174 and in 1175 archbishop of Tyre, the second-ranking cleric in the kingdom. Although his active political and secular administrative roles are unclear, his duties as chancellor (1174–84/5) frequently if not permanently delegated and his patron Raymond regularly out of favour, William's civil law skills were used in diplomacy. He led a delegation to the Third Lateran Council (1178–9) and negotiated at home and abroad with Byzantium (1168, 1177, 1179–80). As archbishop of Tyre (1175–84/6), he proved himself a vigilant diocesan.

However, his most distinctive activities were literary. He built up the library at Tyre and wrote an account of the decrees of the Third Lateran Council as well as two major historical works: the *Gesta orientalium principum*, a history of the Muslim world from the Prophet to the 1180s; and the *Historia Ierosolymitana* (or *Chronicon*), a detailed account of the First Crusade and the Latin east, beginning with the Byzantine Emperor Heraclius's return of the True Cross to Jerusalem (629/30) and ending with events recorded contemporaneously in 1184. Only the *Historia* survives, although the *Gesta* had a limited circulation in western Europe in the thirteenth century. William had begun collecting historical material soon after returning to Palestine in the 1160s, attracting early

36. William of Tyre.

support from King Amalric. The *Historia*, composed between 1170 and 1184, was explicitly conceived as an account of the foundation and fortunes of William's *patria*, although after his attendance at the Lateran Council in 1178–9 he began to revise and recast the work more as an apologia for the Latins of Outremer and, increasingly, a description of their growing travails in the face of resurgent Muslim neighbours, his analysis of the material rise of Saladin remaining a classic. While too cumbersome (almost 1,000 pages in the modern edition)[3] for simple propaganda for a new crusade, the *Historia* invites understanding and sympathy for the plight of the heirs of the First Crusaders, while not concealing William's partisan reflections on the immediate, and to him all too depressing, politics of his own time. It was later alleged that William had been disappointed not to have been elevated to the Patriarchate of Jerusalem in

1180 and had later fallen victim to the malice of the successful candidate, Patriarch Heraclius. Alternatively, William's vivid depictions of Jerusalemite factional rivalries may have been those of a close observer not political player, even if the gloom that pervades the later passages of the book at times conveys an almost existential despair. William's *Historia* stands as a monument to its author's erudition, human sympathy and literary mastery in its coherent expression of themes, clarity of style, breadth of learning, control of detail and range of material. Deploying extensive scriptural, classical and Christian allusions, motifs and models, William, who died before October 1186, combines sustained analytical synthesis, and vivid delineations of people, character and events, with an engaging individual voice. Extensively copied, continued and translated over the following centuries, it stands as one of the greatest historical works of the Middle Ages.

While it is impossible to calculate the raw numbers of Frankish inhabitants or their proportion in the total population, their presence in cities and certain rural areas was significant. By the 1180s, the Frankish community in the kingdom of Jerusalem possibly generated an armed force of around 20,000 including lightly armed auxiliaries known as Turcopoles, comprising local Syrians and some Franks.[4] Unlike the nomadic Turks, the Franks were accustomed to sedentary agricultural society, as lords, farmers and peasants, and to cities, as merchants, shopkeepers and artisans. Many immigrants were already familiar with a Mediterranean economy of cereals, olives and wine. The chief agricultural novelty most settlers would have encountered was sugar cane, only grown in the west by 1100 in parts of Sicily and Spain, yet integral to Outremer's prosperity, with centres of production at Acre, Sidon and Tyre, Galilee and the Jordan valley.[5] Rural settlement was patchy, clustered in areas of existing Syrian Christian occupation in southern Samaria, north of Jerusalem; western Galilee in the hinterland of Acre; and on the royal demesne around Nablus. Rulers, landlords and estate-owning religious corporations actively encouraged rural settlers in a deliberate policy of rural colonisation. As Franks, they were ipso facto free from the sort of restrictive or servile tenancy burdens familiar in the west. While in Antioch and Tripoli, Frankish settlement was largely restricted to towns and cities, and in parts of the kingdom of Jerusalem local peasant occupation could be significant. By the 1160s, the new Frankish village of al-Bira (Magna Mahomeria) near Jerusalem may have housed between 500 and 600, with a new settlement, Qubeida (Parva Mahomeria), being established nearby in mid-century, dedicated to producing olive oil. In 1170, al-Bira sent at least sixty-five troops to the defence of Gaza. As the villages' names suggest, the Franks probably replaced Muslim inhabitants, indicating some process of ethnic cleansing to match that in the city of Jerusalem.[6]

Al-Bira and Qubeida were two of a number of planned villages. Lists of settlers suggest that the bulk of rural immigrants came from other Mediterranean regions, especially southern France, but also northern Italy and Spain. Others came from Burgundy and the Ile de France. Although it may reflect more plentiful surviving evidence, settlers in cities appeared to come from a slightly wider international background, including most parts of France as well as Italy and Spain. Mention too is made of Scots, English, Germans, Bohemians, Bulgars and Hungarians.[7] Some towns and cities had been evacuated during the First Crusade and those conquered before 1110 had their inhabitants massacred or expelled. Thereafter, most contained mixed populations of Syrians and Franks. In cities many of the immigrants were clerics or associated with ecclesiastical institutions. The cities also harboured transient populations of visiting pilgrims, warriors, clergy and traders. The new Orientals (*nunc orientales*), as they were optimistically described by one of their number,[8] if non-noble, pursued a wide range of skilled and unskilled occupations: catering to elites as servants, coiners, goldsmiths and furriers; skilled artisans; carpenters, masons, cobblers, blacksmiths, butchers, bakers, grain and wine growers, and traders; humbler shopkeepers, gardeners, drovers and herdsmen. In ports such as Acre, Tripoli and Tyre, Italians from maritime communes enjoyed privileged quarters as did members of religious orders, monks and canons, and of the Military Orders drawn from across Europe. Rural landscapes were marked with castles, estate towers, manor houses, new villages, mills, oil-presses, vineyards and pigs. Urban centres were reconfigured to suit Frankish social, commercial and religious requirements, what the German pilgrim John of Würzburg called in the late 1160s 'new Holy Places, newly built'.[9] The motives of emigrants from Europe are hidden, but, like the Mormons trekking westwards in nineteenth-century North America, incentives of piety

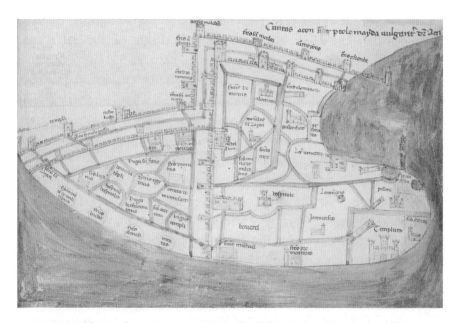

37. *Map of thirteenth-century Acre, showing the different Pisan, Venetian and Genoese quarters.*

38. *Frankish-built entrance to the Cenacle, the supposed Upper Room of the Last Supper story, Mount Sion, Jerusalem.*

and material opportunity plausibly combined. Some arrived with succeeding waves of crusade armies, but others, perhaps a majority, such as Constantine, a cobbler from Châlons, or John, a Vendôme mason, did not.[10]

Creating Outremer

The early years saw precarious garrisons become distinct principalities. In Antioch, Bohemund's military entourage proved sufficiently large and robust to maintain control even after their leader was captured by Danishmend Turks in August 1100. In Jerusalem, Godfrey of Bouillon's small garrison force of perhaps 300 knights and 2,000 infantry, having secured the Holy City, a handful of Judean towns and villages, and a narrow strip of land leading down to the coast and the port of Jaffa, began to assert Frankish power in the coastal plain, Judea and Galilee. A generation of Turkish-Egyptian contest had left no united local opposition to Frankish expansion. At Antioch and Edessa, the unstable political mosaic of the region offered the Franks greater opportunities for local alliances, as did the larger proportion of non-Muslims in the population. Taking advantage of a society where small committed companies of well-trained, heavily armed

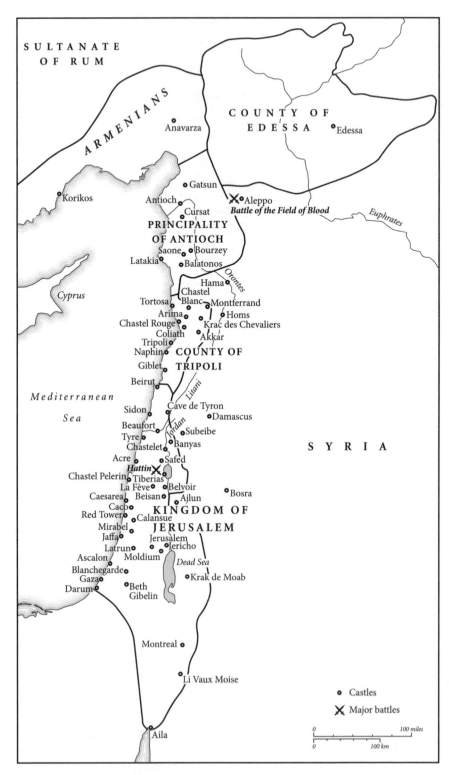

SULTANATE
OF RUM

ARMENIANS

COUNTY OF
EDESSA

Anavarza

Edessa

Korikos

Gatsun

Antioch

Aleppo
Battle of the Field of Blood

Cursat

PRINCIPALITY
OF ANTIOCH

Euphrates

Saone   Bourzey

Latakia   Balatonos

Orontes

Cyprus

Hama

Chastel
Blanc   Montferrand

Tortosa

Arima   Homs

Chastel Rouge   Krac des Chevaliers

Coliath   Akkar

Tripoli

Naphin   COUNTY OF

Giblet   TRIPOLI

Beirut

Litani

Mediterranean

Sea

Sidon   Cave de Tyron

Damascus

Beaufort   Jordan

Tyre   Subeibe

Chastelet   Banyas

Acre   Safed

SYRIA

Chastel Pelerin   Hattin
Tiberias

La Fève   Belvoir

Caesarea   Beisan   Bosra

Caco   Ajlun

Red Tower   Calansue

Mirabel   KINGDOM OF

Jaffa   JERUSALEM

Latrun   Jerusalem

Ascalon   Moldium   Jericho

Blanchegarde   Dead Sea

Gaza   Beth
Darum   Gibelin   Krak de Moab

Montreal

Li Vaux Moise

∘ Castles

✕ Major battles

| 0 | | | | | 100 miles |

| 0 | | | 100 km | |

Aila

5. *Political map of Outremer in the twelfth century.*

troops could impose themselves on people and resources across wide swathes of territory, Frankish rule in Palestine began more as a form of banditry and coercion than administration. Local resistance was feeble, as Muslim elites fled as refugees or were killed in the massacres that attended early Frankish conquests of the coastal cities. The major threats to Frankish success came from outside: Iraq, the Jazira and Egypt.

Systems of governing the conquests emerged from events not prior planning. In Jerusalem, in 1100 the new papal legate Archbishop Daimbert of Pisa unsuccessfully sought to install a theocracy, perhaps in line with Urban's liberation policy.[11] Material constraints imposed extemporised solutions. Each of the Latin principalities established after the First Crusade, while never entirely obliterating existing or traditional regional political structures, was perforce self-created. Antioch sought, not always successfully, an independent path between repeated reliance on the Franks of Jerusalem and the occasionally enforced claims of the Byzantine emperor. The county of Edessa existed alternately as a coalition with local Armenian interests and an adjunct to Antioch. The status of the county of Tripoli emerged only slowly as a semi-autonomous lordship in the orbit first of Jerusalem and then, from the 1180s, of Antioch. Jerusalem, a self-proclaimed kingdom after 1100, exerted some de facto responsibility over the other Frankish areas but its own status remained equivocal, from grudging acceptance by the papal legate in 1100 to prudentially recognising some general Byzantine overlordship in the 1150s and 1170s. Collapse of the male line of the Jerusalem royal dynasty in the 1180s even prompted the idea of asking the rulers of western Europe to arbitrate in choosing a ruler. However, Outremer's claims to legitimacy lay elsewhere. While each principality was the result of military and political expediency, ideologically, their legitimacy sprang from the pious heroism of the First Crusaders and the explicit favour of God, the autonomous justification presented by William of Tyre in his great narrative account of Outremer written in the 1180s.[12]

In Jerusalem, the immediate strategy secured access to the coast and pacified the interior. In the first decade and a half after 1099, Fatimid attacks from the south and those from the north-east sponsored by the Seljuks in Baghdad were undermined by Seljuk and Fatimid rivalry. This did not remove a lasting asymmetry in the Franks' predicament. Outnumbered and culturally alien, the Jerusalem Franks were always only one major military defeat away from a potentially fatal crisis while their opponents could always regroup, sustained respectively by the resources of the Syrian interior, the Jazira, Iraq, Egypt and the steppes. Nonetheless, Baldwin of Edessa's reign in Jerusalem after the death of his brother Godfrey in 1100 as King Baldwin I (1100–18), during which he extended Frankish control east across the Jordan, southwards towards Egypt, and along the Palestinian coast, demonstrated how much could be achieved through energetic use of limited military resources, aided by regular modest reinforcements from the west.

The coastal ports became the most urgent targets. Between 1099 and 1124 the Franks captured all the ports of the Syrian and Palestinian coast except Ascalon, which held out until 1153. Each success was achieved with the assistance of western fleets: Jaffa in 1099 (Pisans); Haifa 1100 (Venetians); Arsuf and Caesarea 1101 (Genoese); Tortosa and Jubail 1102 (Genoese); Latakia 1103 (Genoese); Acre 1104 (Genoese); Tripoli 1109 (Genoese and Provençal); Beirut 1110 (Genoese and Pisan); Sidon 1110 (Norwegian); Tyre 1124 (Venetian). Without a fleet, as at Tyre in 1111, or where a fleet failed to impose a complete blockade, as at Sidon in 1108, sieges failed. At Ascalon in 1153, reinforcements from the bi-annual passage of fleets from the west helped the Frankish fleet tip the balance after months of failed naval blockade. The dual role of Italian maritime cities as military allies and commercial entrepreneurs was recognised by grants of extensive lucrative trading immunities and privileges to the Genoese at Antioch, Jubail, Acre and Jerusalem, and the Venetians' reward of a third of the city of Tyre after its capture in 1124. Such commercial encouragement directly benefited rulers through tolls on trade and the thousands of pilgrims the Italian shippers transported each year.

Beyond pious tourism, imports to Outremer included leather, fur, timber, warm textiles such as wool and some culturally specific foodstuffs, including bacon. The Franks' taste for pork remained undimmed, as excavated rubbish dumps and middens testify, some of it probably supplied by local Christian communities. Apart from a booming trade in relics, the most high-value exports were cane sugar, luxury textiles and spices. The rulers of Outremer took advantage of shifting trade routes across western Asia which, with the growing dominance of western shippers in the Levant, increased the volume of trade through the ports controlled by the Franks. Acre emerged as a major entrepôt, with links to the west, to the Asian interior via Damascus and to Egypt. The importance of cosmopolitan commerce was recognised by Baldwin III (king of Jerusalem 1143–63), who granted a safe conduct to a

Muslim merchant from Tyre, a copy of which found its way into a storeroom at the great mosque in Damascus. Commercial success depended on a contradiction noticed by a Spanish Muslim visitor in 1183, the Franks giving free access to their ports from the Turkish-held interior, even during times of war.[13] Other sources of income for the new rulers came chiefly from minting coinage; exploitation of inland caravan routes in the desert and semi-desert beyond the Dead Sea and Judean hills; and control of the agrarian economy as rent-collecting landlords. The distribution of castles and stone towers across the interior of the kingdom of Jerusalem shows that oversight of rural estates was as important as frontier protection and defence.[14]

The Franks' investment of Outremer followed strategic necessity. Antioch sought to annex the Upper Orontes valley and Cilicia and threaten Aleppo; Edessa to establish strongholds across the Upper Euphrates valley; and Tripoli to conquer the Biqa valley and the Homs gap that led from the sea through the Lebanese mountains to the Syrian interior. Each pursued immediate political advantage, willing, if convenient, to ally with Armenians, Arabs or Turks. This did not obscure a religious dimension. Antiochene coins showed the head of St Peter. The priorities for the Jerusalem Franks were more constrained by their role as defenders of the Holy Places, emphasised on coins that depicted key sites in the Holy City (e.g. the Tower of David or the Holy Sepulchre).[15] The chief religious sites were quickly secured: Jerusalem itself, where non-Christian residence was symbolically outlawed, Bethlehem, Nazareth, Hebron (supposed site of the tombs of the Old Testament patriarchs), and the rest of the Biblical Holy Land from the Jordan to the sea, Banyas and the Dog River in the north to Ascalon and Beersheba in the south. However, the settlement remained vulnerable. Egyptian attacks in 1101, 1102 and 1105 on occasion penetrated to within twenty-five miles of Jerusalem. Invasions by Mawdud of Mosul between 1110 and his assassination in 1113, and a further attack from Mosul in 1115, devastated parts of the county of Edessa and, in 1113, threatened Galilee. The Franks were helped by the fragmented politics of their Syrian neighbours, who were equally dismayed by the prospect of dominance from Iraq as by the presence of the Franks. The febrile relations between Aleppo, Damascus, Mosul and Baghdad offered the Franks opportunities for alliances regardless of religious scruples. The Franks of Antioch occasionally allied with the Turkish ruler of Damascus against Aleppo and even, some sources suggested, against fellow Franks at Edessa.[16] Diplomatic alliances, such as between Damascus and Jerusalem, were commonplace during the first half-century of Frankish occupation and temporary truces were frequent throughout. The Outremer lordships took their places among the competing city states and regional principalities jostling for survival and ascendency. Their existence demanded a high degree of non-confessional political flexibility and ingenuity (see 'Coins in Outremer', p. 120).

Politics

The kingdom of Jerusalem became the leading polity of the Frankish settlement in charisma and resources. The early kings managed to subordinate the territorial ambitions of their acquisitive nobles to fashion a coherent political system in which precedence was afforded the royal High Court; land and money fiefs were held from the monarch; and military obligations to the king's summons were accepted and performed. This was achieved by mutual recognition of rights. Territorial lords were autonomous in their own lands, such as the great fiefs of Jaffa, Ascalon, Transjordan or Galilee, but in cases of rebellion or other conflict, royal jurisdiction was accepted by them and their Frankish subjects. By the reign of King Amalric (1163–74), under a legal procedure known as the *assise sur la ligece*, subtenants were to swear allegiance directly to the king and thus, in theory, were given the right to sue in the High Court, even against their own lords (although none is known to have actually done so). The king exercised the right to summon to arms his tenants and popular militias; to call assemblies to discuss matters of common interest, such as an emergency tax in 1183; and to make church appointments. This last flew in the face of the very principles of church autonomy that underpinned the policies of the papal reformers who had conceived of the idea of the Jerusalem war. Despite the impression retrospectively given by thirteenth- and fourteenth-century law books, the kingdom was governed by pragmatism not legalism. Survival depended on cooperation and mutual self-interest between king and nobles, with the crown holding the most lucrative parts of the kingdom based on Jerusalem, Acre, Tyre and the region north of the capital around Nablus, and, although lacking an extensive or sophisticated bureaucracy, dispensing lucrative preferment and protection.

This accommodation became especially important as the kingdom's stability was threatened by a sequence of dynastic and political crises.

Succession to the crown was openly disputed in 1100, 1118, 1163 and 1186. Civil war threatened in 1133–4, 1152 and 1186. The chief minister was assassinated in 1174. Baldwin II (1118–31) spent a year in Turkish captivity (1123–4), a fate similarly suffered by significant numbers of Frankish nobles throughout the period. The marriages of two kings, Baldwin I and Amalric, were successfully challenged as bigamous or uncanonical. Only twice in eighty-eight years did a son succeed father (in 1143, a child; and 1174, a leprous child). Minors inherited in 1143, 1184 and 1186. Baldwin I may have been homosexual; Baldwin IV (1174–85) was a leper. Of the eight kings between 1100 and 1188, Fulk (1131–43) died as a result of a hunting accident, his sons Baldwin III (1143–63) and Amalric died in their thirties, Baldwin IV in his twenties and Baldwin V (1185–6) succumbed as a child of nine. However, dynastic misfortune and complexity were not the unique preserves of Jerusalem. With the exception of France, orderly royal succession was rare throughout twelfth-century Christendom. Muslim Syria and Egypt also shared confused successions, rule of minors and political assassination. Similarly disrupted inheritance among the Frankish nobility allowed kings to exploit the lack of adult male heirs that also attracted ambitious nobles from the west eager to enhance status, most famously Raynald of Châtillon, younger son of a minor lord from central France who rose, through two successive marriages, to become Prince of Antioch (1153–61) and lord of Transjordan (1177–87). Such figures relied on royal patronage or approval, as did church appointments where a colonial dimension was most marked. Almost all episcopal appointments went to western immigrants, often second- or third-raters who stood little chance of similar preferment in the increasingly competitive home ecclesiastical job market.

The political history of Frankish Jerusalem is commonly divided into three broad periods: expansion with a focus on northern Syria to the 1140s; competition with Nur al-Din of Aleppo in Syria and then Egypt from the mid-1140s to late 1160s, encompassing the failure of the Second Crusade and Amalric's abortive attempt to control the Nile; and subsequent decay and defence in the face of Saladin's ascendancy in uniting Egypt and Syria in the 1170s and early 1180s, culminating in the disastrous defeat of the Jerusalem army at Hattin in 1187 and the subsequent loss of most of the kingdom. This conceals continuities, such as the unstable intimacy of the domestic political scene, dominated by a handful of nobles jostling for access to or control over the wealth at the king's disposal. There was no clear trajectory of stability or

COINS IN OUTREMER

The coinage of the Frankish Levantine conquests revealed the extent of the conquerors' reliance on the region's economic and commercial system. Unlike in western Europe, where currency was silver-based, gold provided the high-value coins in the eastern Mediterranean. In general the Levantine economy was far more monetised than in the west, despite a marked increase in the amount of bullion and coin in circulation and use in Europe during the twelfth and thirteenth centuries. Initially, the Outremer Franks operated a hybrid system that included silver coins from western Europe, mainly northern Italian and southern French; copper coins based on local Arabic or Byzantine designs with modest Frankish iconographic modifications; and local silver and gold coins, dirhams and dinars. Under Count Bertrand (1109–12), Tripoli issued silver pennies of Toulousain design. In the early years, Antioch used Seljuk coins. The gold coins minted in Tripoli and, after 1124, in the kingdom of Jerusalem (bezants), were simply copies of Fatimid dinars, complete with Arabic Koranic inscriptions, a habit that lasted until banned in the 1250s by an outraged visiting papal legate. Even then the new Christianised designs were in Arabic. Only in the 1130s and 1140s did Antioch, Tripoli and Jerusalem begin to mint their own silver coins, billon (i.e. debased silver) pennies. In Jerusalem the initial reform under Baldwin III by the 1140s was superseded by a lasting new issue under Amalric in the 1160s. The chief mints were located in Antioch, Tripoli, Tyre, Acre and Jerusalem. Re-coinages appear to have been irregular. Some local lords minted their own silver and copper coins, as at Jaffa, Beirut and Sidon, while others produced, presumably for immediately local consumption, lead tokens, perhaps as small change, or

39. A Tripoli imitation of a Fatimid bezant.

to pay labourers and tradesmen, or even for use in gambling. In addition, Turkish coppers seem to have been in common use across Outremer, as small change.

This heterogeneous eclectic coinage reflected Outremer society and its commercial needs. Inevitable economic exchange between the different communities required a degree of currency synergy between Frankish and neighbouring currencies as well as coins that would be familiar across social, religious and linguistic divides within Outremer. The Franks were never in an imperial position to impose a wholly exclusive financial system on the indigenous population. Equally, the high-value bezants' aping of Egyptian currency acknowledged the mutual dependence between Frankish rulers and Syrian and Egyptian traders and merchants. Although lighter, and of less fine gold, than the dinar, the Frankish bezant could act almost as a proxy common currency. It formed part of the Franks' rapid assimilation into the regional gold-based monetary system; the great Jerusalem tax of 1183 was calculated and paid in bezants as were land values and wages.[17] On the other hand, the introduction of a distinctive Frankish silver penny across Outremer at roughly the same time in the 1130s and 1140s suggests an advance of government administration and political reach, as well as possibly an increased Frankish demographic footprint.

The collapse and limited reconstruction of Outremer after 1187 left its mark on minting and coins in circulation. The Third Crusade, and probably the Fifth as well, saw an immense influx of western coins, mainly silver pennies, a trend that continued into the thirteenth century. There appears to have been no systematic attempt to re-mint these coins into local currency, suggesting they circulated within ports where multiple currencies operated, while pointing to the new limits to the power of the local Frankish rulers. These continued to mint coins as before, still on an ad hoc and perhaps restricted basis. The needs for bezants remained in the prosperous commercial centres such as Acre. Local lords in Tyre, Beirut and Sidon continued to issue their own silver pennies and coppers. This is hardly surprising

40. A denier of King Amalric of Jerusalem showing the rotunda of the Holy Sepulchre.

as, proportionately, incomes increasingly came from trade not land. However, the production of copies of Ayyubid drachmas after 1251 mirrors shrinking Frankish dominion and underlined the constant reality of Outremer's integration within the wider economy and commerce of the eastern Mediterranean and the Fertile Crescent.[18]

decadence. The early conquests of 1099–1124 were punctuated by serious defeats, in 1102 or 1123 when Baldwin II was captured. Despite setbacks in 1129 and 1148 at Damascus; the near civil wars, in 1134 between the Angevin King Fulk and the local baronage, and in 1152 between Baldwin III and his mother Queen Melisende; and the rise of Nur al-Din to dominate Syria in the 1150s, Baldwin III was still able to broker power in Antioch and Tripoli and extract tribute from Egypt. Comparably, Antioch suffered repeated defeats and the death or capture of its leaders, in 1100, 1104, 1119, 1130, 1149 and 1161, and disruptive power struggles within the ruling family in the 1130s, yet survived as a Frankish city state until 1268. Tripoli managed to assert and maintain its separate identity from the 1120s despite limited territory, a series of succession disputes down to the 1140s, the assassination of one count (Raymond II in 1152) and the long captivity of another (Raymond III 1164–74; his first cousin Amalric of Jerusalem acting as regent). The kings of Jerusalem regularly intervened to rescue the other principalities during such crises, an involvement that assumed a dynastic dimension after two of Baldwin II's younger daughters married into the ruling houses of Antioch and Tripoli.

The paradox of vulnerable strength persisted. In the 1160s, despite the loss of Banyas in northern Galilee, Amalric of Jerusalem was able to compete vigorously for control of Egypt. In 1176–7 an assault on Saladin in Egypt, with help from a large Byzantine fleet and western arrivals, remained possible. From mid-century, the increasing use of the new Military Orders of Templars and Hospitallers to garrison strategic castles showed both an awareness of the mounting threat from Muslim Syria and a policy to deal with it, while simultaneously signalling a lack of royal resources forcing kings into dependence on the Military Orders (see Chapter 4). At the same time, increased fortification of strong-points deep within the kingdom, even near Jerusalem itself, spoke of resources and resilience as well as the heightened reality of danger. Land for sale around the Holy City remained at a premium in the 1160s.[19] Between the 1120s and 1170s most of the kingdom of Jerusalem was free from attack. The power vacuum of a leper king between 1174 and 1185 exacerbated internal divisions but did not prevent military victory over Saladin at Montgisard in 1177 or raids to the Red Sea and Arabian coast under the auspices of Raynald of Châtillon in 1183. In the same year, the levy of a general tax following a fiscal survey of the realm and the consultation of a representative assembly spoke of financial strain

1. Rulers of Jerusalem
1099–1192

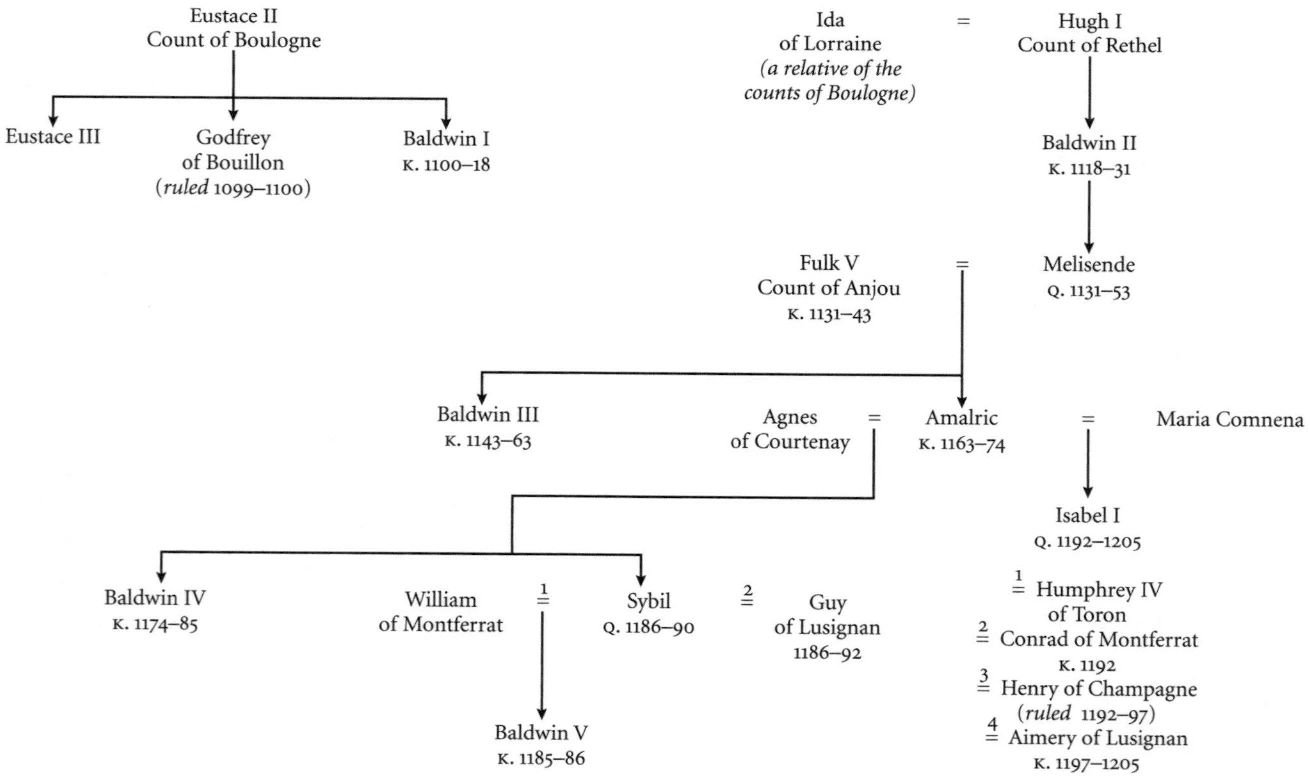

Eustace II
Count of Boulogne
=
Ida
of Lorraine
(a relative of the
counts of Boulogne)

Hugh I
Count of Rethel

Eustace III

Godfrey
of Bouillon
(ruled 1099–1100)

Baldwin I
K. 1100–18

Baldwin II
K. 1118–31

Melisende
Q. 1131–53
=
Fulk V
Count of Anjou
K. 1131–43

Maria Comnena
=

Baldwin III
K. 1143–63

Amalric
K. 1163–74
=
Agnes
of Courtenay
2 =
Guy
of Lusignan
1186–92

Isabel I
Q. 1192–1205

1
= Humphrey IV
of Toron
2
= Conrad of Montferrat
K. 1192
3
= Henry of Champagne
(ruled 1192–97)
4
= Aimery of Lusignan
K. 1197–1205

Baldwin IV
K. 1174–85

William
of Montferrat
1 =
Sybil
Q. 1186–90

Baldwin V
K. 1185–86

yet robust political institutions.[20] Saladin's own serious illness in 1185–6 threatened the unity of his empire. His death would have destabilised it, letting the Franks off the hook, if only temporarily.

On such a narrow stage damaging factionalism could not be avoided. In 1100 a group of Boulogne loyalists ensured the succession of Godfrey of Bouillon's brother Baldwin in the face of opposition from the legate Daimbert and the ambition of Tancred of Lecce. A coup in 1118 led to the accession of Baldwin II to the exclusion of the legitimist heir Eustace of Boulogne, Baldwin I's elder brother. The deal brokered by Baldwin II for Count Fulk V of Anjou to marry his eldest daughter Melisende and for them, after his death, to rule jointly, in association with their son, the future Baldwin III, almost came unstuck twice. In 1133–4 local nobles, under Count Hugh of Jaffa (himself an incomer who spent his youth in the west), a cousin of Baldwin II, rebelled against what they may have seen as an Angevin takeover of power and the marginalisation of the rights of Queen Melisende. The rebels even called in help from the Fatimid garrison at Ascalon. Fulk survived but Angevin influence was reined in. In 1152 the now adult Baldwin III had to use force to prise power from his mother and her protégés. In 1163, before allowing his coronation, baronial opposition forced Amalric to repudiate his first wife, Agnes of Courtney, possibly on the grounds of bigamy, certainly to prevent Agnes wielding patronage. In 1174 the chief minister, Miles of Plancy, another westerner, was murdered during a baronial struggle to control the new leper king. From 1174 to 1186 the political vacuum caused by Baldwin IV's illness and his nephew Baldwin V's infancy removed the safety net of royal arbitration as different factions near the throne scrapped for control of patronage and policy. On Baldwin V's death in 1186 these rivalries almost spilled into open civil war in a move orchestrated by the disruptively ambitious Raymond III of Tripoli, by marriage lord of Galilee. The dead child king's first cousin twice removed, Raymond, tried to deny the crown to Baldwin's mother Sybil, elder daughter of King Amalric, and her second husband, Guy of Lusignan. When his counter-putsch failed, Raymond seceded from obedience and allied with Saladin, treason only repudiated when the whole kingdom was threatened with invasion the following year.[21]

The hindsight of the catastrophic defeats of 1187–8, when Outremer was almost completely overrun by Saladin after his devastating victory over the Franks at the battle of Hattin, frames a seemingly dismal picture. Yet such teleology misleads, masking a more uneven narrative of opportunity and accident. Factional feuding, succession crises, rebellion and civil war were as rife in twelfth-century England as in Jerusalem. The rise and the ultimate fall of the kingdom were far from determined or inevitable. Attacks on Damascus in 1129 and 1148, Aleppo in 1124–5 or Shayzar in 1111, 1138 and 1157 could have expanded Frankish rule into the Syrian interior and annexed major centres of power. The losses of the strategically important northern Galilean strongpoints of Banyas in 1164 or Jacob's Ford in 1179 were exceptional; they were neither preordained nor were their consequences inevitable (see 'A Day at Jacob's Ford', p. 128).

Baldwin III had imposed tribute on the rulers of the decayed Fatimid caliphate of Egypt and the full conquest, planned by him and pursued by his brother Amalric in the 1160s, came close at least to military success. The effectiveness and adaptability of Frankish arms should not be underestimated. Diplomatic alliances with Byzantium in the 1150s and 1170s, with the marriages of Baldwin III and Amalric to Greek princesses, potentially offered much. Famous defeats such as the Antiochene disasters at the Field of Blood (1119) or Inab (1149) were avoidable, as was the disaster at Hattin in 1187, a battle as notable for how nearly the Franks won it as for the annihilating scale of Saladin's victory.[22]

Society and Shared Space

The internal development of Outremer society cannot be assessed solely in terms of a failed or doomed community. Despite impediments of religion, culture, geography and resources, the Franks secured their occupation and even thrived for generations. The elites governed themselves according to agreed structures of law, judicial procedure and convention. As in the west, rulers consulted their officials, great lords, clerics and others in deliberative councils, as at Nablus in 1120, which promulgated canons mainly concerning moral behaviour and relations with the Church, or in 1183 to agree a general tax in the kingdom of Jerusalem. Military contingency required constant informal as well as formal consultation. Politics and patronage sought validation in legal process, the ruler's High Court providing a cockpit for factional contest as much as judicial settlement. This could be writ large, as at Tripoli in 1109, where Baldwin I presided over a council of all Outremer to settle outstanding territorial claims.

While Frankish institutions were imported, elements of continuity survived in the configuration of lordships, partly a product of geography, as in the boundaries of the county of Tripoli. In Antioch and Edessa the presence of large indigenous Greek and Armenian Christian communities enforced a degree of institutional accommodation. In Antioch it seems the mainly Norman ruling elite adopted the local Greek title of *dux* (duke) for the leading civilian official.[23] In general, Franks imposed their own officials to administer their military, judicial and administrative responsibilities while Frankish land-lords relied on their own or local mediators with their indigenous subjects and tenants, Syrian *dragomanni* (literally interpreters) or a *ra'is* (headman).[24] As elsewhere around the Mediterranean, internal self-determination allowed for separate communities to co-exist as neighbours. The Franks' relations with the indigenous Syrian population within Outremer were primarily economic not social, as taxpayers, workers or slaves, not citizens.

This produced a layered political and legal society, in which each commu-nity regulated itself, with relations between them – fiscal, commercial or criminal – ordered and scrutinised by ruling Franks, through law courts and lordships. Syrian Christians, Muslims and Jews held their own courts for civil disputes and petty crimes, as did the Franks, but serious offences and any involving Franks came before the Frankish *cour des bourgeois*, often presided over by Frankish officials called viscounts, operated by local Frankish lords according to western legal norms, such as trial by combat. Freedom was assumed for all Latin Christian settlers of whatever social or economic standing, in marked contrast to social systems in the west. Local Syrian Christians, Muslims and Jews were largely excluded from this ruling legal and political community. In ports, such as Acre or Tyre, inevitable inter-communal exchange was regulated by commercial courts dealing with judicial and fiscal responsibilities. Syrian Christians acted as port officials. In the market court (*cour de la fronde*), both Latins and Syrians could act as jurors while witnesses across the faith communities swore oaths on their respective holy books, 'because be they Syrians or Greeks or Jews or Samaritans or Nestorians or Saracens, they are also men like Franks' – necessary pragmatism not ecumenical tolerance.[25]

Community parallelism determined interfaith contacts and infra-Christian denominational relations. Limited religious syncretism did exist, in shared shrines, religious space, rituals (for example, Muslims receiving baptism as a curative superstition, not a sign of conversion) and objects of devotion, such as the Greek Orthodox shrine of the Virgin Mary at Saidnaya near Damascus, the icon of the Virgin at Tortosa, or the Tombs of the

A DAY AT JACOB'S FORD,
29 AUGUST 1179

At dawn on 29 August 1179, following a siege of five days, troops led by Saladin launched a final assault on the Frankish castle of Le Chastellet overlooking a strategic crossing of the River Jordan on the main road from Acre to Damascus in Upper Galilee know as Vadum Iacob, or Jacob's Ford, a site associated with the Patriarch Jacob and of scriptural and spiritual significance for both Muslims and Christians. The castle, commanded by Templar knights, was unfinished, having only been begun the previous October, which meant that its defenders, a substantial force perhaps numbering 1,500 men, included many civilian masons, carpenters and other building workers and Muslim captives as slave labour. The importance of the castle, only a day's walk from Damascus, on the Ayyubid side of the porous frontier with the kingdom of Jerusalem, was recognised by the attendance of Baldwin IV of Jerusalem and his army from October 1178 to April 1179 to protect the early stages of construction and to prevent Saladin's repeated attempts to stop the building by diplomacy or force, even by offering 100,000 dinars in compensation if the Franks withdrew. In late August, knowing a Frankish relief force would take time to assemble, Saladin, aware that time was of the essence, attacked in strength. Although his siege machine failed to effect a decisive breach, after five days, early on 29 August, sappers finally managed to bring down sections of the walls, the fire used in the process setting alight the Franks' final makeshift wooden lines of defence. It was reported that the commander of the garrison deliberately leapt to his death in the flames. Saladin refused a negotiated surrender. Perhaps as many as 800 defenders were killed, with 700 captured, along with armour, weapons and animals. Some of the captured were converts from Islam who were summarily executed. The loss of Le Chastellet at Jacob's Ford was both a tactical success for Saladin after his defeat in 1177 at Montgisard and a strategic one, as it left Galilee open to future attack. Some have seen this day as the beginning of the military process that ended at the battle of Hattin in 1187.

The site of the castle was left relatively undisturbed until excavations in the 1990s uncovered what was in effect a time capsule of both the siege and the

41. Aerial view of Ateret Fortress showing the north-west wall of the castle.

42. A horse killed during the siege.

elaborate building work at the castle. Construction was evidently interrupted by the Ayyubid attack, tools and materials being left where they lay. The unfinished nature of the project was clear, as was the nature of the fighting and of injuries suffered by the combatants. The defenders had been bombarded with intense volleys of arrows before the final assault, skeletons showing evidence of arrow wounds prior to death blows from close-quarter weapons, swords, spears or axes. As well as the remains of men and horses who fell that day, the site was littered with tools – axes, chisels, spades, hoes, spatulas for spreading plaster and mortar and picks – as well as sickles, knives, daggers, iron bowls, mace heads, arrow-heads, crossbow bolts, a wheelbarrow, a stone sundial and a board for *marelles*, or Nine Men's Morris, a strategy board game permitted by the Templars. The castle was equipped with a cistern and a communal oven and apparently used its own lead coins to supplement royal gold bezants and silver pennies. Le Chastellet was planned on a grand scale, to house a large Templar community of knights, sergeants, servants and, probably, Muslim slaves. Its construction and loss show the scale of the Franks' ambition, human and material resources, their technical skills and their vulnerability.[26]

Prophets at Hebron, each venerated by Muslim as well as Christian pilgrims. Inter-faith association relied on linked folk beliefs, as in the generalised efficacy of baptism, not theological exchange, tolerance or ecumenism. Jews and Muslims were formally banned from living in Frankish Christian Jerusalem. In the twelfth century, few Franks mastered the literary Arabic to engage fully either with Islamic culture and beliefs or with local Christians, although many probably necessarily acquired a smattering of demotic oral Arabic.[27] Muslims and non-Latin Christians lived beyond the pale of Frankish citizenship, like serfs in the west, although, like Frankish non-fief holders, they could be arraigned in the Frankish *cour des bourgeois*. Unable to plead in Frankish civil courts, technically they could hold neither office nor land. There were some exceptions, such as Hamdan ibn Abd al-Rahmin (*c.* 1071–1147/8), a local Muslim intellectual, whose medical services to the Frankish lord of Atharib, a town near the Antioch/Aleppo border, was rewarded with the fief of a local village. A member of the Arab ruling family of Shayzar leased a village from a neighbouring Frankish knight. In Nablus, Muslims and Frankish Christians lived side by side, operating neighbouring businesses, even intermarrying.[28] Obviously, the Franks exploited Muslim labour, including slaves, while encouraging Muslim entrepreneurs to use their ports. They also drew distinctions between the largely quiescent Muslim fellahin living within Outremer, the often-accommodating Bedouin on the frontiers and the hostile Turks across the borders with whom, nonetheless, diplomatic treaties of convenience or even active alliances could be entertained. The Franks' mission to defend the Holy Land and Holy City did not preclude civil relations with Muslims of equal social standing on an individual basis, such as the Templars in Jerusalem providing space for Muslim visitors to pray towards Mecca.[29] The great hospital in Jerusalem, run by the Order of St John, the Hospitallers, was open to all in need regardless of faith.

Nonetheless, within Outremer, religion stood as an absolute barrier to integration, reinforced by civil and criminal laws that discriminated against Muslims. As slaves, labourers, taxpayers, skilled artisans, doctors and traders, Muslims were useful; otherwise, collectively, they existed socially as separate and invisible. Only conversion to Latin Christianity, for Muslims as well as Syrian Christians, secured full citizenship, and the Franks were notoriously negligent in proselytising. A similar picture emerges of Jews, who were left to arrange their own affairs, controlled by rabbinical courts, while

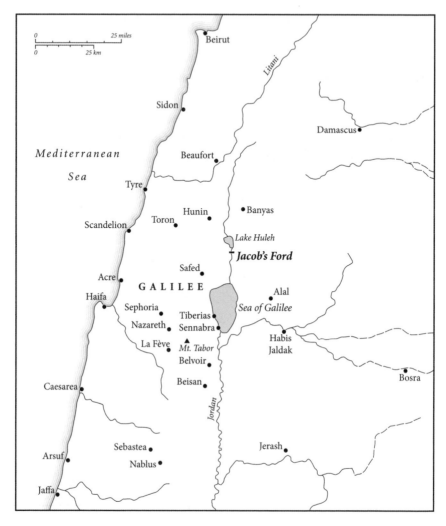

6. Jacob's Ford.

contributing to the economy through agriculture in areas of settlement such as Galilee, and in particular, it seems, the dyeing business. At Nablus, the local Samaritan sect was allowed to hold its annual Passover festival, attracting the faithful from across the Near East, a unique example of tolerance of such a non-Christian religious event.[30] Religious segregation operated in a two-way street. Although some Christian commentators, such as William of Tyre, noted the differences between Sunni and Shi'ite Islam, most Muslim observers largely ignored the complexity of Christian denominations, dismissing Christians as polytheists.[31] Religious bigotry was not the unique preserve of the Franks.

Language and culture also limited assimilation with local Christians. Two main Christian groups confronted the Franks in Outremer. The Orthodox Church shared belief in the Trinitarian doctrine agreed at the Council of Chalcedon (451). Strong in the kingdom of Jerusalem and Antioch, the Orthodox community divided between a Greek elite and the mass of Arabic speakers who used Arabic or Syriac in their services. On doctrinal grounds, the Franks regarded the Orthodox as members of the same Catholic Church. The other Christian group included ancient indigenous denominations with origins in doctrinal disagreements stretching back to Chalcedon and beyond: Jacobites, Armenians, Nestorians and Maronites. Relations with all these communities depended on politics, status, space, patronage and precedence as much as observance, doctrine or dogma. Ironically, official Latin Catholic relations with the Chalcedonian Orthodox Church proved more fraught than those with the non-Chalcedonians. All were tolerated but the latter, having no hierarchical association with the Latin Church, were afforded protected autonomy, even patronage, whereas the Orthodox Church presented direct competition, at least at the level of episcopal appointments and jurisdiction. Twelfth-century Antioch saw a bitter protracted battle between Latin and Orthodox hierarchies. In Jerusalem, the Latin patriarchs were shadowed by absentee Greek equivalents based in Constantinople. By contrast, ecclesiastical contacts with the Jacobites, strong in northern Syria, and the Armenian Church, prominent in Edessa, were broadly amicable, if largely characterised in the secular sphere by indifference and what has been described as 'rough tolerance'.[32] Political expediency played a role, such as the availability of Armenian noblewomen for Frankish marriages. The Maronites of Lebanon, valued for their military capability, were even persuaded to enter into communion with Rome in 1181 despite their historic doctrinal and continued linguistic and cultural differences.

Away from ecclesiastical politics, contacts were governed by expediency. Flushed with victory in 1099, the Franks initially banned all non-Latin clergy from the Church of the Holy Sepulchre. The failure of the Easter Holy Fire 'miracle' in 1101 prompted a relaxation of the ban, allowing access to Orthodox clerics (who presumably knew the secret of generating the miraculous flame, important for Easter tourism), an arrangement followed in other shared churches in Jerusalem. Local Orthodox bishops cooperated with the Latin hierarchy, such as Archbishop Melitus of Gaza who received property for the Hospitallers in the 1170s and was a *confrater* of the order.[33] Greek monasteries around Jerusalem and Antioch flourished during the twelfth century; St Sabas in the Judean desert attracted Frankish patronage. Orthodox monasteries such as St Sabas, those on the Black Mountain near Antioch or the famous monastery of St Catherine at Mount Sinai acted as cultural entrepôts for manuscripts, icons and artists. Funds from Byzantium flowed into the Orthodox community but also paid for redecoration in Latin churches, such as the Church of the Nativity in Bethlehem and the Holy Sepulchre. Syrian Orthodox Christians acted as scribes and customs officers. The small Jacobite community in Jerusalem, despite being regarded as heretical by the Latins, was allowed to build a chapel near the entrance to the rebuilt Church of the Holy Sepulchre and on at least one occasion received royal protection for property rights.[34] Circumstances could impose inter-denominational contacts and accommodation or the reverse. The Edessan Frankish lord Baldwin of Marasch (d. 1146) apparently spoke Armenian and employed an Armenian priest as his confessor.[35] However, Count Joscelin II of Edessa (1131–59) regarded the county's Jacobites as fifth columnists cooperating with the Turks and harassed them accordingly.

Outremer's heterogeneity inevitably eroded formal apartheid, although the loss of most of the material evidence of Frankish settlement makes uncovering informal assimilation difficult, as surviving written evidence points to sharp religious division and much archaeology is of culturally exclusive religious or military sites, although many castles reflected long periods of occupation both before and after Frankish tenure. New ecclesiastical architecture showed European inspiration most clearly, although in the twelfth century largely immune from fashionable contemporary French Gothic. In places, it also borrowed distinctive local Near Eastern features – flat roofs, domes, simple geometric lines. Domestic architecture and decoration have mainly vanished, although what does survive suggests Franks imported some styles and features familiar from the west, such as houses opening directly onto the street with plots of land behind. Other vernacular structures – water mills, bridges, store houses, etc. – displayed local pragmatism not cultural imperialism, as did the use of plentiful stone, not scarce timber, as the chief domestic construction material.[36] Prestige buildings could attract an eclectic mix of aesthetic and material influences. An early thirteenth-century pilgrim's literary description of palatial apartments in the Frankish castle at Beirut is suggestive: the interior was dominated by marble floors and fountains, trompe-l'oeil mosaics and frescoes produced by skilled local craftsmen (see 'Syrians, Muslims and Greeks', p. 230).[37] Cultural exchange from patron to designer to artisan to labourer is evident elsewhere. The cover and illuminations of the famous psalter prepared for Queen Melisende, now in the British Library, combine western, Byzantine, Armenian and Islamic influences (see 'The Melisende Psalter', p. 138). The decorative scheme at the Church of the Nativity in Bethlehem, financed by the Byzantine emperor Manuel I, displays a similar cultural mix (see p. 51). In a polyglot, multi-faith and, in cities, cosmopolitan society, accommodation was inescapable. The written record of the land deal between the Hospitallers and Archbishop Melitus of Gaza is in both Latin and Greek, as were inscriptions in the Church of the Nativity. Baldwin III issued safe conducts for Muslim merchants and Arab lords, such as the peripatetic Usama ibn Munqidh of Shayzar, whose large library of Arabic books he apparently seized.[38]

The Franks adapted to a monetised economy very different from that in western Europe. Local currency, such as gold bezants, continued under the Franks, who persisted in minting imitation Arabic coins. Although Tancred produced his own copper coinage at Antioch by 1110, in Jerusalem no distinctive Frankish currency was produced before the 1130s at the earliest, while imported foreign currencies from Lucca and Valence long remained standard tender. Baldwin III may have been the first king to engage in a substantial re-coinage programme, asserting a royal monopoly on minting in the kingdom, a policy followed by his successor Amalric.[39] The fiscal and social role of money was more immediately adopted. Patronage dealt in money fiefs drawn on the revenues of cities, some still calculated in Saracen *hypereroi*, as well as grants of land.[40] The 1183 tax on incomes and property was assessed in bezants. Absorption of indigenous culture had limits. The Arabic texts left by the Franks on the walls of the Dome of the Rock and the al-Aqsa mosque (under the Franks the headquarters of the Templars), or on the imitation bezants minted at Acre, did not suggest understanding of the Koran from which they came; rather they were seen as decorative and, in the case of the bezants, usefully familiar and convertible for indigenous merchants.[41]

43. *A twelfth-century bishop's crozier found at the Church of the Nativity, Bethlehem.*

Diversity

The courts of the Frankish rulers, like those of their Syrian and Egyptian neighbours, reflected diversity. Nur al-Din (d. 1174), the Turkish atabeg of Aleppo and conqueror of Muslim Syria, ruled over Jews, Muslims, Christians, Arabs, Turks and Armenians, and employed Kurdish mercenary chiefs. The Fatimid caliphs in Egypt employed Christian Copts and Armenians as secretaries, generals and administrators; the Vizier Bahram (1135–7), called the 'Sword of Islam' (*Saif al-Islam*), was originally an Armenian Christian

CHURCH OF ST. ANNE AT JERUSALEM, RECENTLY GIVEN BY THE SULTAN TO THE EMPEROR OF THE FRENCH.

44. The church of St Anne's, Jerusalem, an 1856 engraving.

whose brother was the Armenian patriarch of Egypt. Kurdish Saladin's entourage included Jewish physicians, Iranian and Iraqi civil servants as well as Turks, Arabs and fellow Kurds. Franks not only allied with Turks; some also fought for them, as was permitted under Jerusalem law. The court of King Amalric (1163–74) shared the cosmopolitan Near Eastern pattern. His mother, Queen Melisende, was half-Armenian; his father a Frenchman from Anjou. His first wife was a Palestinian Frank; his second a Byzantine Greek princess. Apparently, he unsuccessfully sought the medical aid of the great Jewish scholar and physician Maimonides (1135–1204), then living in Egypt. The academic tutor of Amalric's son Baldwin – William of Tyre – was a Jerusalem Frank educated for two decades at the grandest schools of the west – Paris, Orléans and Bologna – while young Baldwin's riding master was a Palestinian Christian whose father and brother served as the king's doctors before the family decamped after 1187 to serve Saladin. Jewish, Samaritan, Syrian Christian and Muslim physicians were popular with the Frankish nobility, much to William of Tyre's disgust. Raymond III of Tripoli's doctor, a local called Barac, treated the ailing Baldwin III in 1163.[42] Antioch, with its rich intellectual history and continued contacts with the

THE MELISENDE PSALTER

Despite the image of Frankish exceptionalism promoted by William of Tyre, the courts of twelfth-century kings of Jerusalem were as diverse and multicultural as any other in the Levant. Royal dynasticism promoted close association with Greeks and Armenians while royal patronage acted as a magnet for indigenous professionals and servants, from medical doctors to artists and craftsmen. The brothers Kings Baldwin III and Amalric had an Armenian grandmother, Morphia, wife of Baldwin II, and a French father, King Fulk; both married Greek princesses (Theodora Comnena and Maria Comnena respectively). The court of Amalric attracted Arab and Jewish doctors, Syrian instructors in horsemanship and, in William of Tyre, tutor to the future Baldwin IV, a Jerusalem Frank possessed of the grandest elite western European academic training. This was not a new development. Baldwin I had employed local Syrian converts, and kings regularly patronised local Syrian Christian religious houses. Frankish Outremer was not hermetically sealed from either its non-Frankish subjects or neighbours. Cross-border alliances of convenience, even against fellow Franks, were not unknown. Aristocratic Muslims visited the Haram al-Sharif and the al-Aqsa mosque. The rebellious Count Hugh of Jaffa attempted to make common cause with the Fatimid garrison at Ascalon in 1134. The refurbishment of the Church of the Nativity in Bethlehem *c.* 1170, whose bishop was born in England, was paid for by King Amalric and his father-in-law, the Byzantine emperor Manuel I, and included Greek mosaics with Latin inscriptions.

The so-called Melisende Psalter provides exquisite illustration of such cosmopolitan cross-cultural fertilisation. Produced between 1134 and 1143, probably as a special presentation volume from King Fulk to his wife Queen Melisende (the half-Armenian daughter of Baldwin II and heiress to the kingdom), the psalter, a diminutive book (22 cm x 14 cm) of over 200 folios, contains twenty-four illuminated scenes from the New Testament painted by an illustrator with the Greek name of Basilius; an English-style calendar of saints' and commemoration days, including for Melisende's parents King Baldwin and Queen Morphia, illustrated by a different artist with monthly signs of the Zodiac showing combined western European and Arabic influence; a copy of the Latin

45. *Front cover of the Melisande Psalter.*

psalms written in northern French script, with a third illuminator contributing initial letters showing a hybrid Italian-Arabic style, possibly Sicilian; and, in the same hand as the psalms, prayers to nine saints, illustrated by a fourth artist who tried to incorporate Byzantine motifs into a western European style. The delicate Islamic-style geometrically designed ivory and gem-studded covers depict, on the front, scenes from the life of King David, and, on the back, a king (perhaps Fulk) performing the Six Works of Mercy from Matthew's Gospel (feeding the hungry; giving water to the thirsty; clothing the naked; sheltering the homeless; visiting the sick; and visiting the imprisoned). Even the spine, decorated with Byzantine silk and the Greek crosses of the Jerusalem royal arms, breathes a mixture of eastern and western styles and the highest luxury. Probably created in workshops associated with the cosmopolitan Church of the Holy Sepulchre, the psalter bears striking witness to a fertile and eclectic congregation of international styles – northern French, English, Byzantine, Arabic, Islamic and Armenian – that cannot have been as unique as the psalter's own survival. (It is now in the British Library.)[43]

academic centres of inner Syria and Iraq, provided a forum for cultural exchange, although chiefly via local Greek- and Arabic-speaking Christians.[44] Such cross-community links only grew as the Franks entrenched their presence in Levantine society, settlers picking up demotic Arabic. Frankish rulers could receive similar deference as that afforded their Arab or Turkish predecessors. The process began early. An Arabic poet celebrated the deeds of his employer, Raymond IV of Toulouse, at the battle of Ascalon (1099). The funeral processions of Baldwin I (1118) and Baldwin III (1163) attracted locals from across the ethnic and religious divides, including Muslims, some of whom may have been professional mourners.[45]

Outremer did not become a cultural catalyst or melting pot. Intercommunal contacts remained circumstantial and superficial. Each community retained its sealed identity, regarding the others – if at all – as strange. The Arabisation of Syria and Palestine had taken centuries. The Franks never continuously occupied anywhere on the Levantine mainland for longer than 186 years (Qal'at Sanjil, the castle site of Mount Pilgrim outside Tripoli, 1103–1289). Some adopted habits of dress, eating, housing, even military tactics appropriate to the environment. Tancred of Lecce issued

46. *Qal'at Sanjil, Raymond of Tripoli's castle that remained in Frankish hands 1103–1289 and still stands today. A late nineteenth-century view.*

CASTLES IN OUTREMER

Castles such as Crac des Chevaliers in Syria or Marienburg in Poland represent the largest, most iconic surviving relics of the crusades, symbols of military conquest and rule that lay at the centre of active crusading. This is appropriate, as fortified sites for aggression, defence and authority were central to the imposition and consolidation of political and social control, from the start of campaigns to the enforcement of continued civil power. In every region of crusader conquest – the Levant, Iberia, the Baltic or Greece – castles served a dual function as military bases and as focal points for the protection, subjugation or exploitation of local populations and resources. This merely extended to areas of crusading the use of castles familiar across western Europe from the tenth century onwards. Crusaders brought their expectations and technologies with them, while borrowing from local traditions, adapting existing fortifications, and developing their own innovative sophisticated designs and styles. Each region of conquest imposed distinctive patterns and features.

In Outremer, the earliest castles were simple towers, scores of which, of one or two storeys, were erected in the first fifty years of Frankish occupation, chiefly as centres of lordships in which to dispense justice, receive taxes and store renders. They were very much on the model of the Norman castles that festooned England after 1066, except that in Outremer the castles were of stone and were not constructed on artificial earth mounds (mottes) as in the west. The great nobles of the new Frankish principalities built their own large keeps, which could extend to substantial palatial complexes, in the cities from which they derived their power and wealth, such as Beirut, Tyre, Jubail or Jerusalem, where the king's castle incorporated the existing Roman Tower of David. On arrival in the east, crusaders found local enclosure fortifications (*castra*), common across the eastern Mediterranean, which they adapted and copied as these provided relative ease of construction – walls surrounding a courtyard – and convenient shelter for local Franks, especially in remote areas such as Transjordan (Montreal from 1115 and Kerak from 1142), in frontier regions, such as southern Palestine where from the 1130s a string of *castra* ringed the Fatimid port of Ascalon (e.g. Ibelin, Darum and Gaza), or on suitable sites such as the small islet

47. *Crac des Chevaliers.*

off Sidon. The Military Orders, whose wealth meant they began to take over most of the rural castles of all types from the mid-twelfth century, also built *castra*, essentially as fortified cloisters. Some enclosure castles also contained keeps (as at Darum and Jubail) or were surrounded by often extensive protective outworks (as at Ibelin). In the later twelfth century, additions to initial designs charted increased investment and the growing Ayyubid military threat; some fortified manor house complexes were thus transformed into regular castles (for example, Belmont near Jerusalem).

From these basic enclosure castles came the famous concentric castle design, simply one *castra* surrounding another, a double defensive system that echoed Byzantine fortifications such as the Theodosian walls of Constantinople familiar to successive generations of crusaders. The concentric design was pioneered by the Hospitallers at Belvoir, a hilltop site overlooking the Jordan valley and the road from Damascus to Jerusalem bought by the Order in 1168. Completed probably a decade or so later, Belvoir's concentric design withstood Saladin's forces for eighteen months to two years (1187–9) before the garrison surrendered once the outer defences had been penetrated; the inner walls were never breached. Belvoir provided a model for later thirteenth-century castle building in Outremer (such as the extensions at Crac des Chevaliers and Margat, both

48. Belvoir.

belonging to the Hospitallers) and in the west, notably a number of Edward I of England's castles in Wales.

Location and topography exerted as much influence on castle design as purpose, the contrasting settings of cities, coastal plain, hill country or desert determining salient features. Accessible hilltops, as at Montreal or Saphet in Upper Galilee, offered attractive sites, although more favoured were those naturally protected on three sides by deep river valleys or, in the case of the great fortress of Athlit, Château Pèlerin, built with the help of pilgrims and crusaders during the Fifth Crusade (1217–18), protected by the sea. Some of the largest and most imposing castles were built on such spurs of land, often in contested hill country or near vital trade routes: Crac des Chevaliers protecting the Homs gap behind Tripoli; Saone on the Latakia to Aleppo road; Margat on the coast road between Tortosa and Antioch. The Teutonic Order's headquarters (1229–71) at Montfort in Upper Galilee was unusual in being an administrative capital not a strategic military post. Outremer's eclectic castle system reflected varying Frankish needs: internal oversight of material possessions and the local population; political control; settler protection; ostentatious display of power; control of trade routes; extending areas of influence; and defence along flexible and porous frontier zones. The usefulness and flexibility of castles in different contexts was eccentrically if ingeniously confirmed by Richard I's prefabricated wooden castle, *Mattegriffon*, which he brought with him from Sicily to the siege of Acre in 1191.[46]

As elsewhere, cost dominated the provision of castles in Outremer. Increasingly in the twelfth century and completely in the thirteenth, oversight, ownership and construction of castles became the preserve of the Military Orders who had access to resources beyond the means of the richest secular lords. The costs of construction and maintaining the Galilee Templar castle of Saphet, rebuilt from 1240, were huge: 1,100,000 gold bezants in the first two and a half years, and 40,000 bezants a year thereafter for a garrison of 50 Knights Templar, 30 sergeant brothers, 50 Turcopoles, 300 crossbowmen, 820 servants and labourers and 400 slaves, slave labour having played a necessary part.[47] The garrison at Vadum Iacob had been of similar strength, while the complement at Athlit was around 4,000.

Behind their massive walls and extensive outer defences, achieved by extraordinarily skilled and ingenious feats of engineering in moulding the unforgiving landscape to their purposes, these large castles operated as homes and communities not just barracks. Internally, they were furnished, equipped with cisterns, kitchens, stables, dining halls, chapels, domestic quarters, and, at Belvoir at least, a bathroom. Inside walls were plastered and decorated with frescoes. Inside and out, the stonework and vaulting were finished to a high quality, not least the fine ashlar of the outer walls of most of the grandest castles. Yet despite their architectural sophistication and effective defensive designs, these castles could not survive indefinitely on their own resources. Without relief they were doomed to fall to determined attack, as their capture by Saladin and later Baibars and his successors showed only too decisively.[48]

coins in Antioch portraying himself as an eastern potentate, bearded and perhaps wearing a headdress, possibly a turban. Loose-fitting clothes, veils, surcoats over armour, cool summer fabrics, furs for the cold winters were dictated by the climate. Some acclimatised Franks took to eastern cuisine, although others stuck firmly to a western diet, including pork. Archaeological evidence indicates that the constant stream of new arrivals from the west, as pilgrims or settlers, hardly helped raise the standards of health as they appear to have been generally poorly nourished and riddled with intestinal parasites. Some adaptation to local hygiene can be traced in Frankish maintenance of aqueducts, water cisterns and, in the Hospitaller castle at Belvoir overlooking the Jordan, a bathroom. Militarily, the Franks proved fast learners, coming to terms with Turkish field tactics by developing counter-measures in the delayed massed charge and the fighting march, where the cavalry was protected by flanking infantry. But the Franks did not copy their enemies' mounted heavy and light archers or the battle-field feints.[49] Despite their sustained military endeavours, by the 1180s, Outremer Franks could strike their western European contemporaries as exotic or dissolute, the Jerusalem embassy to Europe in 1184/5 being remembered by one hostile witness for its ostentation and attendant clouds of perfume, features that made it easier to blame the *poulains*, as the Franks were derisively known in the west, for the political and military setbacks and disasters that engulfed them.[50]

CHAPTER FOUR

CRUSADES AND THE DEFENCE OF OUTREMER, 1100–1187

Twelfth-century Outremer stood at the extreme physical frontier of Latin Christendom while at the same time occupying a central space in Latin Christian thought, emotion and cosmology. One veteran of the First Crusade and a Jerusalem resident asked, rhetorically, why, despite overwhelming numerical superiority, the Franks' enemies had failed to crush the newcomers: 'Why did they not, as innumerable locusts in a little field, so completely devour and destroy us?' Obviously because of the power and protection of God, but he added, alongside the Almighty, 'we were in need of nothing if only men and horses did not fail us'.[1] Faith and military reinforcements sustained Outremer as an intrinsic, familiar, if exotic, part of Christendom. The phrase 'shouted aloud at the crossroads of Ascalon' became a metaphor for common gossip, a twelfth-century version simultaneously of the Clapham omnibus and Timbuctoo, at once popular space and the ends of the earth.[2]

The Crusade of 1101

Even before the fall of Jerusalem in 1099, further armies were being prepared. In response to news of the success at Antioch and the crusaders' pleas for reinforcements, new preaching campaigns were launched in Italy and France attracting backsliders who had failed to fulfil their vows of 1095–6; those eager to hop onto the bandwagon of success; and shamefaced veterans who had abandoned the 1096 expedition. With songs, letters and early narratives all unblinkingly emphasising the raw, violent physicality of the bloody victory of 1099 and material success, there was little abstract about the new appeal.[3] There was talk of conquering Baghdad or Egypt.[4] The heroics of 1097–9 seemed to confirm God's favour and immanence and a turn in the tide of history. The subsequent dismal failures of the campaigns of 1101 served notice that such high ambitions were spiritually and practically unsound, setting a more restricted, realistic frame around future strategies for defending the new conquests.

While there had been no pause in contingents leaving for the Levant in the years after 1096, the promotional campaigns of 1099–1100 raised very substantial forces, in total perhaps as great as the armies of 1096. Among the leaders were Duke William IX of Aquitaine, Count William II of Nevers, Duke Odo I of Burgundy, Count Stephen I of Burgundy, Duke Welf IV of Bavaria, and even Conrad, constable to Urban II's arch-enemy Henry IV of Germany. The regions of recruitment mirrored those of 1096. A Lombard army set off from Milan on 3 September 1100, reaching Constantinople in late February or early March 1101, to be met by Raymond of Toulouse, who had been Emperor Alexius's guest since the previous year. By early June, northern French troops under Stephen of Blois, the Burgundians and Constable Conrad's small German force had joined Raymond and the Lombards at Nicomedia on the Asiatic side of the Bosporus. Accompanied by the Milanese relics of the city's patron Saint Ambrose and Raymond's Antioch Holy Lance, the army's religious identity did not prevent its Italian leadership deciding on the quixotic political priority of rescuing Bohemund, who had been in Turkish captivity in north-eastern Asia Minor since being defeated in 1100 by an army of Danishmend Turks while trying to relieve the Armenian city of Melitene in eastern Anatolia. Rejecting the advice of the First Crusade veterans to follow the glorified path of 1097, the army captured Ankara before breaking up under sustained Turkish assaults at Merzifon in early August, the leaders fleeing back to Constantinople, abandoning the infantry and non-combatants to massacre or slavery.

The pattern was repeated. The bulk of the other western armies arrived in Constantinople in June 1101. Leaving William of Aquitaine and Welf of Bavaria behind, William of Nevers immediately set out after the Lombard army. After reaching Ankara in mid-August, he changed course, turning towards Iconium (Konya) which he failed to capture. Pressing forward towards Cilicia, his army was destroyed by the Turks at Heraclea (Ereghli). Following an increasingly familiar scenario, the cavalry deserted the infantry, the leaders escaping to reach Antioch. A similar fate awaited William of Aquitaine. Setting out from Constantinople in mid-July along the 1097 route, in early September his army was also defeated at Heraclea, only some of its leaders, including Duke William, managing to flee to the coast or make it through to Syria. These disasters were not down to inadequate preparation or ignorance of local politics and conditions. Some accused the Greeks, most blamed the crusaders' own sins, cover for over-optimism and incompetence. Despite Emperor Alexius providing material and logistical support, the experience of 1101 showed how difficult it was to sustain large armies in hostile terrain facing an undefeated united enemy. This highlighted the good fortune enjoyed by the First Crusade, gilding even further the lustre of the first Jerusalem journey.

Western Aid for Outremer

The failure of 1101 reshaped western responses. With the exception of what is now known as the Second Crusade (1145–8), subsequent armed assistance for Outremer before 1187 rested with smaller expeditions, whose numbers made travelling by sea possible, in rhythm with the increasingly popular bi-annual Levant marine passages of pilgrims and merchants. The timing of cross-Mediterranean sea travel was regulated by the prevailing Mediterranean winds and currents, which effectively restricted access to spring and autumn. Such military tours, usually lasting months not years, were attuned to the incremental needs of the Franks of Outremer not cosmic strategy. Occasionally, direct Outremer appeals elicited wider efforts at western recruitment, as during the crisis after the defeat and death of Roger of Antioch at the battle of the Field of Blood in 1119, which led to the Venetian crusade of 1122–4 and the capture of Tyre (1124); or in 1127–9, with the recruitment of an army to attack Damascus coinciding with the arrival of Count Fulk V of Anjou to become the future king of Jerusalem. Other expeditions appeared more speculative, offering service to whatever project the rulers of Outremer had in hand. In 1110, as part of an extended Mediterranean progress that took in Byzantium as well as a pilgrimage to the Holy Sepulchre, King Sigurd of Norway was persuaded to join Baldwin I's siege of Sidon. Reputation came from physical presence in the Holy Land. Sending sums of money hypothecated on some future promised expedition instead, as Henry II of England (a grandson of Fulk V of Anjou through the count's first wife and so the nephew of Kings Baldwin III and Amalric) discovered, earned few plaudits.[5]

The roll call of visiting western luminaries testified to the status a Jerusalem veteran could hope for back home: Eric I of Denmark (1102–3, though he died in Cyprus before reaching Palestine); Sigurd of Norway (1107–10); Charles of Denmark (1111, nephew of the First Crusade commander Robert II of Flanders and a future count of Flanders himself); Conrad of Hohenstaufen (c. 1124, the future Conrad III of Germany and leader of the Second Crusade, the only European crowned head to campaign twice in the Holy Land itself). Some, like Conrad, made more than one trip: Fulk V twice (1120 and 1128); Count Hugh I of Troyes thrice (1104–8, 1114,

49. *Countess Sybil of Flanders's cross. She settled in Jerusalem 1157–65.*

1125); Count Thierry of Flanders four times (1138, 1147, 1157 and 1165); his son Philip twice (1177–8 and 1190–1). Crusading ran in families, such as the dukes of Burgundy; the counts of Flanders, Burgundy, Blois-Champagne; the Italian Montferrats or the English Beaumonts; or the minor French comital houses of Montléry, le Puiset, Lusignan, Brienne or Joinville and the upwardly mobile English Glanvills. The prestige of a Holy Land campaign reflected the glamour that clung to the heroes of 1096–9 whose reputations had quickly been transformed into legend. Those left out of the glory of the First Crusade appeared eager to gain some post hoc association, which may explain why Philip I of France, excluded by excommunication from a role in 1096, allowed his daughter Constance to marry Bohemund, the son of a parvenu Norman adventurer, during his 1106–7 tour recruiting for a new eastern enterprise. Such was Bohemund's fame, witnessed by his starring role in the earliest narratives of the First Crusade, that men apparently flocked to get him as godfather to their children and Henry I of England had to ban him from entering England lest he signed up too many Anglo-Norman lords for his new *via Sancti Sepulchri* (in fact an invasion of the western Balkans designed to topple Alexius I, an expedition that met with dismal failure in 1108).[6] Bohemund's reputation survived failure, giving his name (originally a nickname; his baptismal name was Mark) to six successors as princes of Antioch and earning him a distinctively eastern-style domed mausoleum over his tomb at Canossa in Apulia that may have been designed to evoke the Holy Places. These micro-crusades help shape a tradition. Despite persistent uncertainties over crusaders' privileged entitlements, by the 1120s taking the cross had become familiar.[7] In the early years of the settlement, there was always some necessary campaigning on offer, to defend or expand the frontiers. This in turn attracted more permanent recruits in the shape of the Military Orders.

The Military Orders

The Military Orders provided crusading's most original contribution to the institutions of medieval Christendom. Their combination of charitable purpose, religious discipline and armed violence tapped into aristocratic mentalities of aggressive piety and anxious self-justification. Their defining visual as well as institutional images of militancy, charity and the cross, as displayed for example on Templar seals, expressed the complexity of

50. Bohemund's tomb, Canossa, Puglia, Italy.

Christian teaching on the crusades. In retrospect appearing a logical extension to the militant religiosity that produced the First Crusade, originally
the Military Orders were products of the circumstances of the Frankish
enclave in Palestine and the plight of the increasing numbers of visiting
pilgrims. After 1099, the countryside around Jerusalem and roads from
the coast remained unsafe, especially for unarmed pilgrims now arriving
in large numbers. In 1119 a group of pious knights, already attached to

51. *Templar seal.*

the canons of the Holy Sepulchre, established a formal confraternity to provide military protection for pilgrims to Jerusalem and Jericho. Led by Hugh of Payns from Champagne and Godfrey of St Omer in Picardy, these knights followed the canons' rule, swearing vows of chastity, poverty and obedience, and depended for income on alms. Recognised by the Council of Nablus (1120) and licensed by the patriarch of Jerusalem to defend pilgrims in return for remission of their sins, the knights were given quarters at the royal palace in the former al-Aqsa mosque on the Temple Mount (Haram al-Sharif), known to the Franks as the Temple of Solomon. After the king moved across the city to the Tower of David a few years later, the knights took over the whole al-Aqsa site as their headquarters, providing them with their resonant name, the Order of the Temple of Solomon, Templars for short. After a successful European recruiting tour in 1127–9, Hugh of Payns received recognition of his Order

52. *The al-Aqsa mosque, headquarters c. 1119–87 of the Templars.*

at the Council of Troyes (1129), confirmed by subsequent papal privileges, and enshrined in a detailed rule. Lingering, and never wholly suppressed, disquiet at such a blatant confusion of the spiritual and the material, of the profession of a regular canon with that of a knight, elicited a famous polemical apologia from the leading preacher, pastoral theologian and ecclesiastical publicist of his day, Bernard of Clairvaux's *De laude novae militiae* (*In Praise of the New Knighthood*, c. 1130). This wove traditional motifs of Christian self-sacrifice, martyrdom and salvation together with a conveniently radical refashioning of St Paul's spiritual metaphors for fighting for Christ into literal exhortations to physical warfare for the faith, in Bernard's catchy phrase, the Templars transforming sinful warfare, *malitia*, into God's *militia*.[8]

The Templars proved immediately popular, attracting international recognition, recruits and patronage in Outremer and across western Europe. Visiting pilgrims and crusaders could become temporary *confratres* (as did Fulk of Anjou on his first trip in 1120). Others joined permanently, some after long secular careers, bringing with them lucrative donations and further networks of family contacts. Rapidly, from the 1120s, the Templars built up a large pool of patrons and estates across western Europe as well as the Levant, supplying Outremer with troops and external funding, as a proportion of profits from Military Order holdings in the west was sent to the east. This cross-Mediterranean presence led to the Order becoming used by crusaders and others as bankers. By the time of the Second Crusade, the Templars were providing loans, military advice, leadership and a de luxe hotel service for western crusaders. In places, the Templars created lasting physical symbols of their calling in building round churches on their property, evoking the Holy Sepulchre or the al-Aqsa in towns and countryside across western Europe. Within Outremer, the Order was soon manning forts and castles, especially to protect strategic roads, as well as providing a standing military regiment.

The Order of the Hospital of St John began with a pilgrim hospice in Jerusalem founded in the early 1080s to cater for pilgrims and funded by Amalfitan merchants. In common with hospital institutions across western Christendom, the laymen who ran the hospital assumed the character of a religious community, with nursing as their vocational duty. After 1099, under its administrative head Gerard, the hospital and its community attracted lavish donations from local rulers and western patrons

53. Templar round church, Tomar, Portugal.

and, in 1113, recognition and protection from the pope. By the 1120s, the hospital had acquired extensive estates in Italy, Catalonia and southern France as well as lands and rents across Outremer. The Jerusalem hospital grew into a huge business, with hundreds of beds for patients of all religions and both sexes, providing a social service for exhausted and sick pilgrims, the local community, pregnant women, abandoned children and the destitute. Nursing remained an obligatory vocation for all brothers of the Order. Early military association may have come from its provision of field hospitals on military campaigns. The Order's lay religious brotherhood may have acted as the model for the early Templars. The debt was soon reciprocated when the Hospitaller Order assumed direct military functions. As an increasingly well-funded private institution, a wider social and political role in cash-strapped Outremer was almost inevitable. In 1126 members of the Order were made responsible for units in the Jerusalemite army that attacked Damascus. In 1136 a castle built at Bayt Jibrin to resist raids from Ascalon was assigned to the Order, possibly the second to be so assigned. By the 1140s, the Order appears to have become militarised on the lines of the Templars, in the process becoming more aristocratic in recruitment, although not abandoning the formal obligation of nursing. With their military function came further responsibilities for manning (and funding) castles. The Jerusalem hospital continued providing an ecumenical service to the whole community, its local importance transcending politics as well as religion: apparently Saladin allowed ten Hospitaller brothers to continue to tend the sick in the hospital for a year after his capture of the city in October 1187.[9]

The two Jerusalem Military Orders became leading political players in Outremer (and, indeed, the west). Although frequently at odds with each other, the Orders featured prominently in deciding military strategy. Jurisdictionally independent of all except the distant papacy, they could act as supposedly neutral arbiters in politics and financial management. As the costs of defence rose, decreasingly matched by the resources of the crown and local secular nobility, the Orders' power and influence increased as they controlled more castles and frontier military sites.[10] By the 1180s, the combined Templar and Hospitaller contribution of around 700 knights to the full muster of the kingdom of Jerusalem was roughly equal to that from all other sources. The Orders grew into large international corporations, their fighting knights an elite minority, supported by military sergeants, clergy, lay officials, servants. Some professed knights were more estate managers than warriors. There were even groups of nuns who wished to be attached to the Orders. Effective in channelling funds, faith, recruitment and property management, the Orders prompted imitation. As efforts to conquer Muslim al-Andalus gathered pace, local Iberian Military Orders were founded: Calatrava (Castile, 1164); Santiago (León, 1170), Alcantara (Castile, 1176) and Avis (Portugal, c. 1176). Within Outremer, the Order of Lazarus (1130s) was modelled on the Templars, mainly attracting knights with leprosy; in 1198 the hospitaller Order of St Mary of the Germans, founded at Acre in 1190, was militarised under a Templar-style rule, later known as the Teutonic Knights; so, in 1228, was the English Order of St Thomas of Acre, originally founded for canons in 1190/1. The institutional alliance of mission, holy war, ecclesiastical exemption and religious discipline proved popular on Christendom's northern frontiers, with the Swordbrothers of Livonia (c. 1202) and the Prussian knights of Dobrin (Dobryzn, c. 1220).[11]

Members of the Military Orders were not technically crucesignati. As brothers they did not take the cross, and, except for the temporary confratres, their commitment, like a monk's, was for life. However, they shared the crusader's purpose, idealism and spiritual privileges. They also shared a

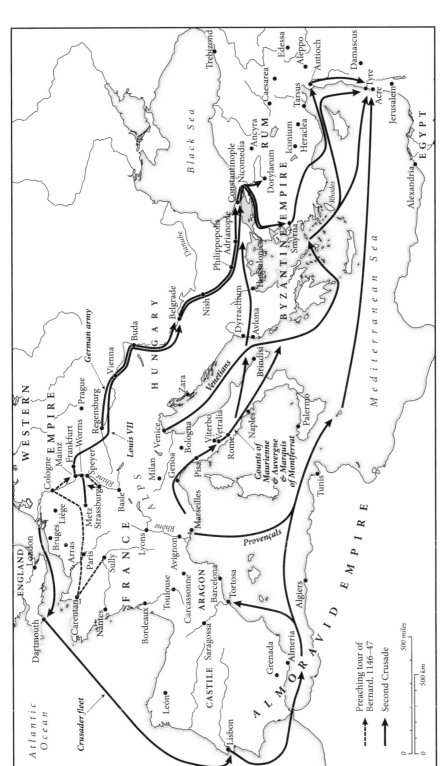

7. *The crusades of 1122–48 and the Second Crusade.*

social and cultural milieu. Involvement in crusading and the Military Orders often ran in tandem through families. As striking, the Orders left tangible and lasting memorials to crusading, in castles and fortified headquarters in the east, in Iberia and the Baltic and, across western Europe, in their round churches evoking Jerusalem, the remains of their religious houses and manorial properties, or the preserved names of the places and estates they owned: the Rue du Temple in Paris; the Temple Church, St John's Gate, Knightsbridge, and St John's Wood in London; Tempelhof in Berlin.

The Holy Land Crusades of the 1120s

The Venetian Crusade, 1122–5

A series of major crises in Outremer in the 1120s provoked the first concerted western military campaigns since 1101. Antioch was leaderless after the defeat and death of its prince, Roger of Salerno, at the Field of Blood in 1119. Baldwin II of Jerusalem, previously count of Edessa, acted as Antioch's regent, having only assumed the crown after a divisive succession struggle following Baldwin I's death in 1118. Baldwin II failed to impose as firm a grip on his factious nobles, some of whom still questioned his right to rule. Although attacks from Iraq had ceased after 1115, banditry and raids from the Fatimid garrison at Ascalon as well as the continuing threat from Egypt itself undermined security in the south, while in the north Aleppo and Damascus alternated between alliance and attack. Gloom was deepened by economic and environmental difficulties, such as earthquakes (1113, 1114, 1117) and plagues of locusts (1114 and 1117). The Jerusalem government appealed to the papacy and Venice for help. Pope Calixtus II responded by sending the doge of Venice, Domenico Michiel, a papal banner. The doge took the cross in 1122. The subsequent Venetian campaign (1122–5) demonstrated how enthusiasm for holy war operated in collaboration with a range of material and pious objectives while confirming the significance of sea transport's increasing ability to convey substantial forces.

One Jerusalem witness put the Venetian fleet at 120 ships, carrying 15,000 Venetians and pilgrims, the latter presumably paying customers, and, significantly, for the first time, 300 horses. The fleet also carried timbers for catapults, ladders and siege machines, a precedent for future sea-borne expeditions.[12] On their way eastwards, the Venetian crusaders plundered Corfu to put pressure on the new Byzantine emperor, John II Comnenus (1118–43), to confirm

54. *Relics of St Isidore taken by Doge Michiel during the Venetian crusade. Fourteenth-century mosaic, St Mark's, Venice.*

Venetian trading rights. The capture of Baldwin II by Balak, ruler of Aleppo, in April 1123 coincided with the fleet's arrival at Acre. In May 1123 the Venetians decisively destroyed an Egyptian naval squadron patrolling the southern Palestinian coast, and captured Egyptian supply vessels with their cargos of weapons, siege timbers, gold, silver and spices.[13] Except for the siege of Sidon in 1110, the Venetians had not previously played much of a distinctive role in Outremer, unlike Genoa and Pisa. Now they took the opportunity to gain a permanent stake in the increasingly lucrative Levantine trade. Over the winter of 1123–4 they negotiated a deal with the regency Jerusalem government for the capture of Tyre. In return for their assistance and a loan of 100,000 gold pieces to pay the Jerusalemite army, Venice would receive a third of the conquered city, free trade, legal autonomy, the use of their own weights and measures, and an annual tribute of 300 bezants. After a five-month siege, the Damascene garrison surrendered in July 1124. Returning to Venice in 1125, Michiel's fleet terrorised its way through the Aegean and Adriatic, sacking cities and looting islands of booty and relics. The Venetians staked men, money and ships on a grand scale, a substantial investment risk from which they derived substantial capital return, holy relics and remission of sins: good business all round.[14] The crusade's benefits were material, enhancing Venice's civic identity, not least in physical terms through the display of holy booty, such as the relics of St Isidore deposited in the treasury of the Cathedral of St Mark's.

The Damascus Crusade, 1129

The capture of Tyre, the release of Baldwin II a few weeks later and the arrival in Outremer in 1126 of the heir to Antioch, Bohemund II, son of the First Crusade hero, seemed to promise greater stability. After besieging Aleppo in 1124 and defeating a Mosul army in 1125, Baldwin II now planned a major assault on Damascus, to follow raids towards the city in 1125 and 1126. An embassy sent to Europe in 1127, including the Templar leader Hugh of Payns, sought soldiers for the Damascus campaign; the securing of Fulk V of Anjou's agreement to marry Baldwin's heir, his eldest daughter Melisende; and papal recognition for the Templars. Crusaders came mainly from France: Champagne, Flanders, Normandy, Provence as well as Anjou, although equivocal evidence exists of Hugh recruiting in England and Scotland.[15] Subsequent coordination betrayed inept strategic management. While Fulk arrived with the spring passage of 1129, Hugh, having to secure his Order's recognition at the Council of Troyes in January, only reached Palestine months later, which may explain why Baldwin launched the attack on Damascus as late as November. The Frankish army penetrated to within ten miles of Damascus before bad weather, inadequate supplies, indiscipline among its foragers, and effective Turkish harrying tactics forced a retreat. One local chronicler stated that the Damascenes paid 20,000 dinars for the Franks' withdrawal, with a promise of annual tribute to follow.[16] If true, this was not what the western crusaders had come 2,500 miles to achieve. For Baldwin, while welcome, it would hardly shift the terms of Syrian politics decisively in his favour. Unlike the siege of Tyre, the Damascus campaign lacked the advantages of being able to invest the city closely from territory already held. Supplies, communication and mobility all presented predictable problems. Baldwin II's political imperative to use the Damascus enterprise to assert his authority, newly upholstered by the presence of Count Fulk as an experienced heir, failed to mitigate the logistical shortcomings. Extending Frankish rule to the cities of the Syrian interior made political, strategic and economic sense. However, successful inland sieges usually came not by forced conquest but by military pressure producing political negotiation or diplomatic accommodation, as at Antioch in 1098, only taken through treachery. The Franks at Damascus faced an additional obstacle. A Damascene witness noted that the Turkish auxiliaries were eager to fight the Franks because they were infidels.[17] The politics of the *jihad* soon became a public touchstone for the politics of Syria.

The Unification of Turkish Syria

The political history of Syria and Palestine between 1099 and 1187 is dominated by the successive conquests between 1127 and 1174 of Imad al-Din Zengi and his son Nur al-Din, which united inland Syria and the Jazira, followed by the incorporation of these lands between 1174 and 1186 into the empire of Saladin, sultan of Egypt, prior to his annexation of most of Outremer in 1187–9. The reordering of the politics of the region was furthered by Saladin's suppression of the Fatimid caliphate in 1169–71. In 1187, for the first time in over two centuries, the great cities of Mosul, Aleppo, Damascus, Jerusalem, Alexandria and Cairo, as well as the Holy Places of the Hijaz, acknowledged the same overlord.

Zengi, atabeg of Mosul in 1127 and Aleppo in 1128, with a deserved reputation for ruthlessness and brutality, had extended his power on both sides of the Euphrates and southwards towards Damascus. In 1144 he captured Frankish Edessa, the dismemberment of the principality completed by his son Nur al-Din in 1151. After Zengi's assassination in 1146, Mosul and Aleppo had been divided between his two sons, only reunited under his second son, Nur al-Din of Aleppo (1146–74) in 1149. In 1154, Nur al-Din finally occupied Damascus. Both Zengi and Nur al-Din chipped away at neighbouring Frankish territory, especially in the north. After his victory over Prince Raymond of Antioch at Inab in 1149, Nur al-Din threatened Antioch itself and symbolically washed in the Mediterranean to signal the wider Muslim advance. The implosion of the Fatimid regime in Egypt in the 1160s drew Nur al-Din to send his Kurdish general Shirkuh to annex the country, in competition with the Franks of Jerusalem. Victory in 1169 left Shirkuh's nephew Saladin as sultan and, although nominally subject to Nur al-Din, de facto ruler, a position he consolidated by abolishing the Fatimid caliphate. On Nur al-Din's death in 1174, Saladin moved quickly to control Damascus, then dispossess or subjugate Zengid and other rulers in

55. Saladin, a contemporary image.

Syria, Aleppo submitting in 1183 and Mosul in 1186. Despite a few forays against Outremer, and a few successes, such as at Jacob's Ford in 1179 (see 'A Day at Jacob's Ford', p. 128), only after commanding the united resources of Egypt, Syria and the Jazira did Saladin move to conquer Outremer.

It has become common for the unification of Syria, Egypt and Palestine in the twelfth century to be ascribed to a Muslim religious revival. The First Crusade had attracted a call for *jihad* from a Damascene religious scholar

'Ali ibn Tahir al-Sulami (d. 1106), who regarded it as part of a general Christian assault on Islamic lands stretching from Iberia and Sicily to Syria, its success attributed equally to Muslim political divisions and the abandonment of the tradition of *jihad*. This embraced both the military struggle against infidels (*al-jihad al-asghar* or lesser *jihad*) and the more important inner contest against enemies of the soul (*al-jihad al-akbar* or greater *jihad*): 'Put the *jihad* against your souls ahead of the *jihad* against your enemies, for truly your souls are greater enemies to you than your human enemies.'[18] The association of politics with religion became standard among twelfth-century Arabic commentators on the wars in Syria and Outremer, although some preferred more temporal analyses of greed and danger. Whatever their private commitment, Zengi, Nur al-Din and Saladin each proclaimed their status as leaders of the *jihad*. However, the alleged Muslim revival might more accurately be described as a process whereby successful Turkish and Kurdish warlords harnessed suitable strands of Muslim law and theology to bind the administratively vital indigenous judicial, academic and bureaucratic elites, the *ulema*, to accept their usurping rule. In 1130, Zengi's announcement of a *jihad* against the Franks concealed his designs on Muslim Hama and Damascus.[19] Almost six decades later, Saladin was accused of similar dereliction of duty in his persistent campaigning against fellow Muslims, not the Franks.[20]

Following Seljuk precedent, conquest came hand in glove with lavish investment in religious institutions and promotion of the parvenu rulers' Islamic credentials, Koranic virtues and deferential lip-service to the Abbasid caliphate. However, as mujahidin, these rulers could also distinguish themselves from their increasingly ineffectual Seljuk or Arab predecessors. Fostering good relations with the members of the *ulema* such as Saladin's influential minister, the Palestinian writer, lawyer and poet al-Fadil (1135–1200), granted thuggish warlords respectability.[21] This process was supported by endowing religious schools, *madrasas*, that offered employment for educated civilians and military nobles alike. New Turkish and Kurdish rulers built their regimes on war, wealth, patronage and propaganda but also on indigenous administration, justice and accommodation of diversity. *Madrasas* were visible symbols of this alliance, prominently situated within major urban centres, such as Damascus. Unlike their Frankish conquerors, the unifiers of Muslim Syria respected local interests, where convenient, allowing a patina of continuity to cover new regimes. In 1136, after capturing

56. *Teaching in a mosque.*

Ma'arrat al-Numan from the Franks, Zengi restored property to owners who had been dispossessed by the Franks in 1098 or their heirs, their title checked against the Aleppan land tax archives.[22] The political use of religion rested on theological and scholarly trends in west Asian Islam stimulated by uncertain political legitimacy and lent focus by the Frankish occupation's creation of an influential body of vociferous refugees. The Seljuks' patronage of *madrasas* in Iran and Iraq had encouraged the identification of religion, politics and social community, emphasising conservative Sunni textual tradition in the study of the Koran and the *hadith* (sayings of the Prophet), rather than innovative philosophy or natural science. In a parallel investment in religious study, some schools were founded in early twelfth-century Shi'ite Fatimid Egypt, perhaps to combat the influence of the Christian Copts.[23] Scholarly promotion of uniformity through *madrasas* helped rulers counter political dissent and encourage identity between the nomadic warrior Turkish lords and their settled subject peoples, with, in Syria, the Franks providing a convenient rhetorical focus of threat.

Inscriptions even before his capture of Edessa in 1144 praised Zengi as 'tamer of the infidels and the polytheists, leader of those who fight the holy war, helper of the armies, protector of the territory of the Muslims', all rather far from the reality: the early Seljuks and other Turkish rulers adopted a rather relaxed adherence to Islam, retaining many aspects of steppe culture.[24] By contrast, Nur al-Din, seemingly a man of sincere private piety, went further, hugely increasing the number of *madrasas* in his lands, many with personal endowments.[25] In 1168 he commissioned a pulpit (*minbar*) in Aleppo decorated with exhortations to *jihad*, which was intended for the al-Aqsa mosque once Jerusalem was recovered. It was, by Saladin, in November 1187.[26] The recovery of Jerusalem became a symbol for spiritual as well as political renewal, a theme exploited by Saladin and his propagandists, particularly once that goal had been achieved. The courts of the Zengids and Ayyubids (namely Saladin, son of Ayyub, and his family) were staffed with members of the *ulema* steeped in the new orthodoxy; at Nur al-Din's court Ali ibn Asakir (1105–76), the leading scholar of his generation, also collected *hadith* on the *jihad*; another of Nur al-Din's civil servants, the Iranian Imad al-Din Isfahani (1125–1201), had taught in a Damascus *madrasa*, later becoming Saladin's secretary and biographer. The Iraqi Beha al-Din ibn Shaddad (1145–1234), a noted legist, taught in *madrasas* in Mosul and Baghdad and, among other works, composed a monograph on *jihad*; hired by Saladin in 1188 as judge of the army, he repaid the compliment by writing a flattering biography of the sultan showing him in the best light of a Koranic mujahid as befitted his honorific title Salah al-Din, 'Righteousness of the Faith'.[27]

Jihad provided a legitimising cause as part of the wider promotion of Koranic Islamic virtues, what has been described as a 'recentring' rather than a revival.[28] Enthusiasm for armed *jihad*, as distinct from the habitual round of regional warfare, was not a creation of the Zengids. They merely took advantage of a vocal minority within the educated elites, reinforced by articulate refugees at Iraqi and Syrian courts with carefully preserved memories of crusade atrocities such as the massacre at Ma 'arrat al-Numan in 1098. Territorial competition became rebranded as religious war. *Jihad* proved especially significant for Saladin. The Zengids were Turkish nobility, with experience of rule stretching back to the reign of Malik Shah, when Zengi's father was governor of Aleppo. The Kurdish Ayyubids were upstarts, mercenary generals who traded their military service under the Zengids for political power, beginning with Saladin's father Ayyub's appointment as governor

57. Nur al-Din's minbar *in the al-Aqsa before its destruction in 1969.*

of Baalbek by Zengi in 1139. Saladin himself owed his position to his role as his uncle Shirkuh's lieutenant in the conquest of Egypt in 1168–9 under the nominal suzerainty of Nur al-Din. Helped by a remarkable series of convenient (and not necessarily coincidental) deaths – Shirkuh in 1169; the twenty-two-year-old last Fatimid caliph al Azid, 1171; Amalric of Jerusalem, 1174; Nur al-Din, 1174, and his teenage son al-Salih of Aleppo, 1181 – Saladin imposed his family's rule in Egypt and abolished the Shi'ite caliphate in 1171, cloaking usurpation with the aura of a Sunni champion. Careful to pay formal obeisance to the Abbasid caliph, between 1174 and 1186 Saladin swept aside the Zengids in Syria and the Jazira through force, bullying, bribery, patronage and diplomacy, drawing to himself and his family the adherence both of the civilian *ulema* and the mercenary regiments, the *askari*, on whom political control depended. Across Egypt and Syria, Saladin methodically placed his relations in control of key economic, fiscal, military and administrative resources through grants of political office and tax revenues (*iqta*). A conquering parvenu with no legitimacy beyond his own agency, Saladin needed to demonstrate his religious credentials to rule through the overt performance of Koranic models: public ritual piety; puritan domestic simplicity; strict but merciful legal judgement; generosity in finance, charity and patronage; dedication to the culture of *jihad*. Regardless of Saladin's private beliefs, and it might be noted that Nur al-Din founded many more religious schools than he did, politics required such behaviour.

Saladin's empire also relied on fresh conquests to consolidate new alliances and reward new followers. The Franks presented unique adversaries. Totems of enmity for the revived Islamic seriousness, they were immune to Saladin's usual carrot-and-stick tactics of annexation. Legally, Saladin could only agree temporary truces with the infidel. Politically he had nothing to offer, as the Franks could not submit to his overlordship. Mortal confrontation was therefore inevitable, encouraging the presentation of power politics as *jihad*. Thus, the presence of the Franks ideologically as well as materially assisted Syrian unification and the development of the strong Muslim militarised polities of the Zengid and Ayyubid Empires.

The Second Crusade, 1145–8

The Franks' greatest opportunity to contest Syrian unification came in response to Zengi's serendipitous capture of Edessa in December 1144. Although leading to no immediate assault on the rest of Outremer, as Zengi turned his attention to policing his existing conquests, the loss of Edessa and the Franks' failure to retake the city in 1146 presented a strategic and moral blow, exposing the lack of providential certainty in the Franks' occupation. The political context was confused. The deaths of Fulk of Jerusalem and John II of Byzantium in hunting accidents in 1143 were balanced by a Mosul revolt against Zengi in 1145, his murder in 1146, and the division of his empire between his sons. In 1145 the new Byzantine emperor, Manuel I (1143–80), received the homage of Prince Raymond of Antioch (r. 1136–49), who otherwise stood to gain most by a new crusade in northern Syria. Jerusalem was adjusting to the uneven joint rule of the widowed Queen Melisende and her teenage son Baldwin III (1143–63). Any substantial crusader intervention in Syria threatened to undermine Byzantine interests there, as would the involvement of Sicily and Germany, rivals to the Greeks in Italy. Equally, Byzantium saw no advantage in disturbing relations with Muslim neighbours, while wariness of western motives had grown since the First Crusade, with Antioch remaining a source of potential conflict. The diplomatic bouillabaisse was thickened by the precarious position of Pope Eugenius III (1145–53). Elected in February 1145, after his predecessor had been killed in street fighting in Rome, overshadowed in Italy by rivalry between Sicily, Germany and Byzantium, Eugenius's decision to follow Urban II's precedent in calling for a mass redemptive military campaign to the Levant operated, as had the 1095 appeal, as part of a policy of consolidating papal influence and authority.

Eugenius's letter calling for a new crusade, *Quantum praedecessores* ('How much our predecessors'), was framed by the glorious memory of the First Crusade. While citing the loss of Edessa as the specific *casus belli*, Eugenius repeated Urban II's formula of the urgency of help for the 'eastern Churches', perhaps as a sop to Byzantium, but certainly in evocative imitation of the 1095 call with its implicit claim of papal responsibility for the universal Church. Urban's precedent was again cited for the grant of remission of sins, while papal authority was invoked in offering the crusaders' temporal privileges, fully described for the first time with reference to a Holy Land campaign.[29] Initial response was muted, and the bull, first sent in November 1145, was reissued in March the following year. The call was first taken up at Christmas 1145 by Louis VII of France, who may already have been toying with an eastern expedition of his own, but preaching and recruitment only gained momentum with the involvement of the pope's mentor Bernard of Clairvaux and the network of his Cistercian order of monks, of which Eugenius had been a member (see 'Bernard of Clairvaux', p. 170). Thereafter, in contrast to 1095–6, the pope played a secondary role, easing diplomatic contacts and issuing bulls in response to requests to extend crusaders' privileges to campaigns in northern Spain and the Baltic. Conrad III of Germany admitted to the pope that he had taken the cross (from Bernard at Christmas 1146) 'without your knowledge'.[30] Although he attended Louis' ceremonial departure from St Denis near Paris in June 1147, Eugenius left set-piece exhortations and the necessary grind of promotional touring to others, especially his old tutor, the charismatic Bernard.

Recruitment for the new venture probably outstripped that for the First Crusade, the consequence of careful orchestration between the papally authorised preaching campaign of Bernard and the Cistercians and the commitment of the kings of France and Germany and leading regional nobles, such as the counts of Flanders, Champagne, Savoy and Toulouse and the duke of Bavaria. A series of high-profile theatrical assemblies, at Bourges (December 1145), Vézelay (March 1146), Speyer (December 1146), Etampes

(February 1147), Regensburg (February 1147) and Frankfurt (March 1147) established domestic support for two monarchs whose authority was otherwise limited or contested. Crusade leadership paid political dividends; for Louis VII it provided the first instance of a French king commanding a large national army on an international campaign since the 870s. Recruitment stretched from Languedoc to the eastern marches of Germany, from the North Sea to Tuscany, pulling in urban elites as well as rural lords, knights, merchants, soldiers for hire, townspeople, artisans, men and, to the misogynist disgust of clerical critics seemingly after the event, women. Recruits included at least two who were dumb from birth.[31] Local habit, family connections, dynastic traditions and political convenience were again as instrumental as inspirational oratory. Bernard set a tone of general religious revivalism. Already a champion of the Templars and an enthusiast for redemptive holy war, he argued that the crisis in Outremer provided a unique opportunity: in serving the 'cause of Christ', to paraphrase St Paul, 'to conquer is glorious, to die is gain' (cf. Philippians 1:21): win win.[32]

Bernard's success cast him as the victim of aggressive stalking by audiences who identified in him Christ-like qualities.[33] Other preachers were less fastidious. One, a Cistercian called Radulph, thrilled crowds in the Rhineland during the summer and autumn of 1146 preaching against 'the foes of the Christian religion', including local Jews.[34] Popular anti-Judaism faced equivocal church policy. At almost the exact time Radulph was stirring up racial hatred, Abbot Peter the Venerable of Cluny was writing to Louis VII comparing the Jews of Europe unfavourably to Muslims, regarding their presence in Christendom as polluting and calling for them to be punished, short of actually killing them. Anti-Jewish riots and murder accompanied crusade recruitment in eastern France and central Europe as well as those encouraged by Radulph in the Rhineland. Ecclesiastical and secular protection appeared to be more effective than in 1096, with violence, though extreme, less widespread or concerted. Bernard's main concern was that Radulph had preached without licence. Crusading was popular in the Rhineland where some, perhaps many, resented what appeared to them the privileged status of the Jews, protected by the king, wealthy bishops and rich lords, enjoying financial benefits while poorer crusaders plunged into debt. Eugenius III had forbidden crusaders access to Jewish credit in *Quantum praedecessores* if they wished to enjoy immunity from interest. The theological refinement of protecting those proclaimed by the Church as the oldest enemies of Christ

BERNARD OF CLAIRVAUX
AND THE CISTERCIANS

The influence of Bernard of Clairvaux (1090–1153) on the development of the ideology and practice of crusading ranks in significance beside that of Urban II and Innocent III. An early recruit (1113) to the new austere Cistercian monastic order (founded in 1098 at Cîteaux in Burgundy), from his position as abbot of Clairvaux, which he founded in 1115, Bernard became the dominant pastoral voice in western Christendom, promoting a distinctive theological message of intense spirituality and direct personal religious commitment. A spare, ascetic, charismatic figure, he pursued his advocacy of monastic rigour and the need for the laity to abandon luxury and materialism to transform their lives and secure salvation through his writing, preaching, public debate, political lobbying and formidable administrative skill. Coming from minor Burgundian nobility, he saw the potential of crusading and the new Military Order of the Templars in his programme of devotional renewal. In the 1130s his treatise *De laude novae militiae* (*In Praise of the New Knighthood*), composed in support of the Templars, decisively transformed the metaphorical New Testament language of spiritual conflict, such as employed by St Paul, into unequivocal religious justification of literal physical warfare in defence of the Christian faith, a task that invited salvation, the *malitia* of secular war transmuted into the *militia* of Christ. Bernard's appeal combining spiritual and physical Christian militancy became central to the promotion campaign he led for the Second Crusade (1145–8). Recruited by his former pupil and fellow Cistercian Pope Eugenius III, his sermon at Vézelay at Easter 1146 to the French king and nobility, despite leaving no surviving record of what Bernard actually said, became iconic, as did stories of the power of his preaching and associated miracles. His orchestration of publicity, sustained by sending letters and well-briefed agents to those regions he could not visit personally and his use of the growing network of Cistercian monasteries, became a model for future organisers, as did the message he projected. His letters read like sermons, repeating central themes of vengeance, reward, duty, redemption and amendment of life. Despite the failure of the Second Crusade, acknowledged in Bernard's own pained apologia *De Consideratione* (1149/52), his

58. Bernard preaching.

underlying emphasis on the crusader's personal responsibility to and relationship with Christ and the cross became standard features of the preaching of subsequent crusades. Any squeamishness at the elevation of Christian violence was swept away as much by Bernard's intense conviction, clarity of argument, vitality of imagery and power of rhetoric as by his startling reworking of scripture. The concentration on personal spiritual commitment in the context of communal religious responsibility sharpened the evangelic force of recruitment while allowing for the easy accommodation of different terrestrial military objectives. In 1147 Bernard himself authorised the application of crusade privileges to that summer's campaigns against the Slavs in the southern Baltic, even suggesting that the pagans 'shall either be converted or wiped out', an extreme and canonically precarious view of Christian militancy.[35]

The subsequent prevalence of Bernard's language and his theology of Christian warfare rested on the rapid expansion of the Cistercian Order across western Christendom during and after his lifetime. Despite the Order's original emphasis on isolation and the simplicity of the monastic vocation, it became a wealthy corporate power in church affairs, its members becoming bishops and many of its abbots acting as willing public promoters of ecclesiastical causes. The Order's centralised federal structure, with regular general assemblies at

Cîteaux, provided a convenient and dynamic network for the transmission of ideas, information and promotional material. Its close association with crusading was reflected in prayers for *crucesignati* within its liturgies. Cistercians played a central role in every major eastern crusade from the 1140s to the early thirteenth century. Apart from the Second Crusade, in preparation and leadership especially a Cistercian enterprise, preaching the Third Crusade was spearheaded by Cistercians such as Cardinal Henry de Marcy of Albano and Archbishop Baldwin of Canterbury, who used local Cistercian abbots in his recruiting tour of Wales in 1188. The Order hosted promoters and leaders of the Fourth Crusade at Cîteaux in 1198 and 1201, provided preachers and a number of abbots joined the expedition (e.g. Abbot Gunther of Pairis, the abbots of Loos in Flanders, Les Vaux de Cernay and Luciedo). The militant Bernardine legacy found similarly vigorous expression in the assault on heretics in Languedoc, Henry of Marcy leading a military expedition there in 1181 and Arnaud Aimery, abbot of Cîteaux, with other members of the Order, playing a prominent active part in the opening stages of the Albigensian crusades. The alignment of institutional ambition and Christian imperialism found further outlet in the occupation of new Christian territories in the southern Baltic. After 1200, in Livonia, Cistercian entrepreneurs, such as Theodore of Treiden and Bernard of Lippe, himself a veteran former soldier, followed colonising German merchants and warriors under the banner of the cross. Unlike more traditional lavish Benedictine monasteries, Cistercian houses were cheap to found and relatively simple to operate, ideal as centres of missionary work and the expression of crusading ideology. They also, more widely, preserved collective corporate memory of Bernard and of their other crusade champions. The dominant role of the Order in crusading only diminished from the early thirteenth century when preaching and organisation increasingly fell to Paris-trained secular clerics and academics and then, from the 1220s, decisively to the mendicant Orders. However, the Bernardine vision remained an indelible element in crusade preaching and ideology.

may have been lost on those summoned to avenge the insult to Christ in the east. To the authorities the disturbances constituted acts of civil disobedience, unwelcome distractions to crusade planning. Radulph was silenced by being returned to his monastery; the agitation subsided.

Rulers involved in regional frontier conflicts with non-Christians quickly associated themselves with the greater enterprise. Alfonso VII of Castile rebranded his campaign against Almeria as a holy war, earning remission of sins before extracting a papal bull from Eugenius confirming its status in April 1147. A further papal grant of indulgences, harking back to Urban II's offer in1095, supported an ultimately successful Catalan siege of Tortosa in 1148. Both these campaigns involved the Genoese. In Germany, a deal brokered by Bernard of Clairvaux allowed the dissident Duke Henry the Lion of Saxony and Saxon nobles to assume crusader status for the 1147 summer campaign against the pagan Abotrites and Wends across the Elbe along the southern Baltic shore (see Chapter 8). While the agreement reflected the need for political stability in Germany and suggested the usefulness of the crusade in notionally binding hostile factions together in a common cause, Bernard trenchantly urged the need for the pagans to 'be converted or wiped out'.[36] Once again the pope obliged with retrospective approval. Such dressing scarcely concealed the material motives of the 1147 Baltic campaigns, which in the event spent as much time harassing Christian cities as pagan recalcitrants. Spanish and German frontier wars had increasingly been promoted in terms resonant with the ideology of the Jerusalem holy wars, in Spain explicitly so for the previous thirty years. In 1146–8 the extensions of crusade institutions to Iberia and the Baltic were clearly not coincidental; but neither were they planned as part of some grand strategy. The process remained reactive not premeditated.

Eugenius had set no date for muster or embarkation. Despite an apparent flirtation with a Sicilian offer to carry the French army by sea, Louis VII decided to follow Conrad III along the land route of Godfrey of Bouillon to Constantinople. Others reached the Byzantine capital via Italy and the Adriatic crossing. Alfonso-Jordan, count of Toulouse, son of the First Crusade leader Raymond IV, born outside Tripoli in 1104, sailed directly from Provence. Sea transport of armies with horses and materiel, pioneered by the Venetians in 1122–4, now offered a viable alternative. A fleet gathered from around the North Sea that mustered at Dartmouth in Devon in May 1147 may have comprised 150 to 200 ships capable of carrying up to

10,000 people. This international force, which bound itself into a sworn commune for purposes of command, discipline and sharing booty, came from the rural areas of eastern England and the Low Countries but also the commercial ports of the region: London, Dover, Southampton, Hastings, Bristol, Ipswich, Cologne, Boulogne. Sailing down the Atlantic coast, in June the armada was hired by Afonso of Portugal (1128–85) to help besiege Lisbon, then in Muslim hands (July–October 1147), the first of a number of opportunist attacks on ports in al-Andalus by passing crusaders over the next seventy years. Once the city was captured, many crusaders chose to stay. Others, mainly from Flanders and Germany, after winter refits to the ships, sailed into the Mediterranean, probably reaching the Holy Land the following spring where it is likely many were taken into service by Conrad III.

Although such disparate forces from so huge a geographical region cannot have been minutely coordinated, contingents assembled through forward planning. The North Sea fleet cannot have gathered at Dartmouth and then immediately agreed to form a restrictive commune by chance. Commerce, lordship and the Church provided regular conduits of communication to transmit crusade plans. Most forces departed between April and June 1147 and, despite contrasting fortunes, reached Outremer a year later, suggesting at least a general understanding of the timing of the mission, as well as of the determining factors of seasons, harvests and, at sea, winds, currents and, for those from northern Europe, the need for winter quarters. The precedent was known: it had taken the bulk of the first Jerusalem campaign between a year and a year and a quarter to reach Syria. The Second Crusade was slightly faster.

Not all lessons of the First Crusade were well learnt. Louis VII, despite raising money through special taxes, rapidly ran out of cash, having to seek substantial loans from the Military Orders. Militarily, the Germans suffered the same fate as the crusaders of 1101. Assembled perhaps in too great haste between the winter and spring of 1146–7, after reaching Constantinople in September 1147, the German army, possibly concerned about food supplies, refused to wait for the French army close behind, only to be severely mauled by the Turks near Dorylaeum. The army disintegrated as it retreated to Nicaea, where the battered survivors encountered the French forces. Unlike the Franks in Outremer, the Germans had not mastered the technique of a fighting march to counter the harrying tactics of the Turks. Conrad, who had been wounded in the withdrawal from Dorylaeum, retired to Constantinople for the winter before sailing to Palestine the following spring. The French fared slightly better in Asia Minor, battering their way to Adalia on the southern coast by early 1148 despite a bruising encounter with the Turks at Mount Cadmus (Honaz Daghi, January 1148). However, short of money and ships, in another echo of 1101, Louis sailed to Syria with his knights and cavalry, abandoning the bulk of the infantry to fight overland to Antioch: few made it. The Germans and the French had been undone by optimistic strategies, bad tactics, poor intelligence, indiscipline, failed logistics, canny opposition and bad weather. The Greeks, pilloried in the west as treacherous scapegoats, had not requested the crusade and were powerless to provide adequate surplus supplies even in Byzantine territory. By contrast, the Turks proved far more effective opponents than fifty years earlier.

Despite these setbacks and the Lisbon diversion, the crusaders who reached Outremer in the spring of 1148 constituted a very substantial fighting force, many thousands strong, although the French army now mainly comprised knights. On arrival in Palestine, Conrad III, flush with Greek money, hired a new army from freshly arrived crusaders. With retaking Edessa ruled out as the city's defences had been levelled in 1146 after a failed Frankish attempt to recapture it, a campaign in northern Syria, against Shayzar or Aleppo, was also rejected, ostensibly because of a diplomatic rift between Louis VII and Prince Raymond of Antioch (1136–49) attributed by gossip to an affair between Raymond and Louis's wife, Eleanor of Aquitaine, Raymond's niece. More certainly, assistance to Antioch invited complications with Byzantium whose overlordship Raymond had acknowledged in 1145. In any case, most crusaders had gathered in Palestine. Conrad III emerged as the dominant western voice. The crusaders and the Jerusalemite leaders, after debating whether to attack Damascus, as in 1129, or Ascalon, decided on Damascus, with Ascalon a second option.

In 1148, Damascus was no longer a Frankish ally as it had been for most of the time since 1129. Nor had it yet been absorbed into Nur al-Din's growing empire. While the presence of so many troops encouraged Frankish hopes of success, the campaign turned into a dismal failure. A rapid march to Damascus in July 1148 was followed in days by an equally precipitate withdrawal. Although the Latin and Arabic sources do not agree, poor and indecisive tactics, the absence of a plan for a proper investment of the city, tensions within the leadership over who should rule the conquered city, perhaps

COMMUNES ON CRUSADE

Crusade armies were held together through a combination of lordship, kinship, clientage, affinity, peer pressure, shared locality and language, enthusiasm, compulsion, necessity and pay. Frequently, these pressures and conditions encouraged the creation of agreed mutual associations, from ad hoc agreements to pool financial and material resources to formal communes and fraternities, bound by oaths, in which disparate or connected groups and individuals combined together outside or complementary to the other cohesive social forces on campaign. Some associations were agreed in advance; some freely entered into during operations; some enforced by leaders during periods of crisis or to impose discipline. Such mutual alliances were necessary in crusade armies that were gathered from multiple localities, different lordships and diverse rural and urban communities, and in which allegiances could shift through the death or impoverishment of leaders. The presence or absence of monarchs on crusade made little difference. Beneath the outward display of hierarchy, most large-scale crusades depended on communal cooperation and consent without which they could not have functioned.

The pattern of communal arrangements fell into four broad categories. First, exigencies of campaigning required leaders to cooperate in providing supplies or the military needs of troops across the army through common funds such as those established at the sieges of Nicaea, Antioch and Jerusalem during the First Crusade; at the siege of Acre in 1189 or at Damietta in 1219. Sometimes these arrangements, as during the siege of Antioch in 1097–8, were secured by oaths, the leaders entering into temporary formal confraternities. One of the more remarkable of these sworn fraternities was established by Louis VII of France with 'common consent' after his army's mauling by the Turks at Mount Cadmus early in 1148 when he put his troops under the discipline and command of the Templars.[37] The second general form of communal arrangements was similar in providing for discipline within armies at the instigation of commanders but secured by oaths. Beyond simply reinforcing martial order, such provisions were necessary as in any one large army crusaders came not just from different lordships but from regions with distinct legal systems and expectations. Such

59. Collective decision-making on crusade, Jerusalem 1099.

communal ordinances first emerged at the siege of Antioch in 1098. They were characterised by an agreed set of detailed rules for behaviour and dispute resolution backed by judicial processes armed with draconian penalties: Louis VII's at Metz in 1147 (although these proved abortive); successive ordinances regulating the polyglot Angevin forces in 1188–90; or the stern regulations agreed by Frederick Barbarossa, his commanders and 'sworn in every tent' as he set out east in 1189. These ordinances could cover everything from theft and violent crime to sexual conduct, gambling, cheating, fraud, hoarding of supplies, food prices, disposal of property, division of booty, suitable dress and the treatment of women. Not all were imposed by kings.[38]

In 1147 and 1217 similar regulations were agreed by fleets from the North Sea that organised themselves into the third category of public association, the communes and confraternities established by crusaders' mutual agreement at the very start of a campaign. The most famous of these was the commune established in May 1147 at Dartmouth, a port on the extreme south-west coast of England, by a coalition crusade fleet drawn from across the North Sea region including west Germany, northern France and southern and eastern England. Besides the agreed regulations of behaviour and punishment, all significant decisions were reached by occasionally rancorous debate in open assembly.[39] This model bore similarities to corporate civic institutions appearing in increasing numbers in towns and cities across western Europe. For urban crusaders pooling resources in such a communal arrangement made logistical and business sense. A shipload of Londoner crusaders in 1190 adopted Thomas

Becket (a Londoner himself) as their commune's patron. Sea travel encouraged such sworn associations as companies frequently possessed no previous formal social ties. In 1250 one such crusade company engaged a collective class action against their cheating shippers. However, such associations were more normal than may appear: English crusaders in 1190 were generically described as *coniurati*, joined together by oaths.

A final method of communal organisation can be found in crusade confraternities that existed on a more permanent basis to organise donations, recruitment, funding and material support for members on crusade. While some, like those of Florence and Pistoia during the Third Crusade, Châteaudun in northern France established in 1247 or the Parisian *confrarie* of the Holy Sepulchre of 1320, were based on specific urban centres, others, such as the North Italian confraternity of the Holy Spirit, operated with an extended geographical reach across a number of cities.[40] Founded during the Fifth Crusade, its statutes received papal confirmation in 1255 and members played a significant part in the defence of Acre in 1291. However, the communal aspect of crusade was not class distinctive. Nobles played prominent parts in the North Sea fleet communes of 1147 and 1217 and the Paris *confrarie* of 1320. Kings swore with their followers to communal ordinances. Setting out on the Second Crusade in 1147, Milo, lord of Evry-le-Châtel in Champagne, swore oaths of mutual loyalty with his knights ('*se federaverunt juramentis*').[41] The idea that the political and ideological dominance of lordship and hierarchy precluded other forms of social engagement and association is misleading. Outside lordship or kindred, communal bonds, of friendship, commerce, occupation or belief, were ubiquitous. For crusaders, technically equal as *crucesignati*, such associations could be both convenient and essential.

sterner resistance than anticipated that dashed hopes of a quick surrender or early successful assault on the walls, all undermined the attackers' resolve, as did rumours of an approaching Zengid relief army. No sustained operation, with catapults, sapping, battering rams and siege towers, was even attempted. As in 1129, the contrasting odds for successful sieges of inland cities and coastal ports were made clear. The retreat to Galilee was chaotic, with heavy casualties. Despite continued German support for an attack on Ascalon, divisions within Frankish and crusader ranks, exacerbated by the simmering rivalry between Queen Melisende and Baldwin III, prevented further action. Conrad left for home in September; Louis the following spring. In 1154, Damascus submitted to Nur al-Din.

The Waning of the Crusade, 1149–87?

The failure at Damascus represented a major humiliation, spawning an industry of blame, finger pointing and soul searching. Although papal bulls continued to call for new eastern expeditions, usually in response to appeals from Outremer, enthusiasm for using crusade formulae elsewhere became patchy. The tradition of associating campaigns against al-Andalus with the Jerusalem war continued, promoted chiefly by papal legates and church councils, holy war becoming embedded within the foundation of Iberian Military Orders. In the Baltic, while the language of religious war was bandied about, between 1147 and the 1190s only a bull of 1171 explicitly offered vows, cross and indulgence to war in the region. For Outremer, the Second Crusade signalled a wasted opportunity to construct a new frontier and stall the advancing unification of Syria. In the west, at least in the eyes of William of Tyre who saw the consequences first hand at both ends of the Mediterranean, enthusiasm to assist Outremer declined as the Damascus debacle was attributed to the allegedly duplicitous behaviour of the Outremer Frankish nobility.[42] Despite papal attempts to excite new expeditions (at least seven between 1157 and 1184) and repeated embassies from Outremer calling for aid, western rulers tended to maintain only lip service to the cause.[43] From the 1150s to 1180s, veterans of the Second Crusade, such as Louis VII and Frederick I Barbarossa (1152–90), Conrad III's nephew and successor, but also Henry II of England, (1154–89) talked of taking the cross but failed to do so. Instead, in 1166 and 1185 the French and English kings agreed to levies on income as well as property to help

Outremer, the first European income taxes. By the 1180s, Henry II, a close relative of the Jerusalem kings, had salted away a considerable treasure in Jerusalem supposedly to await his arrival. When in 1177–8, Count Philip of Flanders led a substantial army in the Holy Land chiefly drawn from northern France, he fell out with the Jerusalem government and his campaign in northern Syria proved ineffectual, fuelling western disenchantment. The increasingly dysfunctional internal politics of the kingdom of Jerusalem after the accession of the adolescent leper Baldwin IV (1174) presented particular challenges to visiting crusaders.[44] Either, like Philip of Flanders, they came with sufficient forces to dictate their own policy that might not fit local plans; or they brought with them contingents too small to alter the military balance in Outremer.

The Holy Land still offered career advancement for nobles and clerics with limited prospects in the west. The pious and those obligated by penance, punishment or oaths still sought Jerusalem. William Marshal, the future Regent of England (1216–19), went east in the mid-1180s to fulfil the crusade vow of his dead master, Henry, the eldest son of Henry II (d. 1183). The north Italian nobleman William of Montferrat was attracted by the promise of a royal marriage to Baldwin IV's sister Sybil and heir in 1176. The pilgrimage trade still flourished, adding to the growth in the commercial profits of Italian cities whose fleets still underpinned Outremer's survival. However, short of a defining crisis in Outremer, European politics precluded the necessary diplomatic consensus for a new grand expedition. The papacy was involved in a series of disputes with potential crusade leaders, most draining and damaging being those with Frederick Barbarossa from 1159 to the early 1180s over power in Italy, but also with Henry II of England over his struggle with Archbishop Thomas Becket of Canterbury over church jurisdiction in the 1160s. England only emerged from a long civil war in the mid-1150s. Louis VII and his successor Philip II (1180–1223) conducted a near-permanent feud with Henry II who, as duke of Normandy and Aquitaine and count of Anjou also ruled most of western France. Successive ineffectual treaties between the contestants included mutual agreements to depart on crusade, convenient diplomatic cover rather than binding commitment. In Italy, Frederick Barbarossa's attempts to assert imperial rule met decades of local opposition that drew in the rulers of Sicily as well as the papacy. The maritime cities remained willing partners but not initiators of an eastern crusade. The failure to take advantage of a papal and Outremer-backed Byzantine alliance in the 1170s represented an opportunity that, after Manuel I's defeat by the Turks at Myriokephalon in 1176 and death in 1180, followed by the overthrow of the pro-western Greek regime in 1182, did not recur.

Revulsion at the failed Second Crusade did not abolish interest in the Holy Land. Surviving vernacular literature, much of it critical of the antics of crusaders, kept both the images and stories of holy war in the east alive, reflecting continued interest and understanding. Outremer remained a focus of absentee religious devotion and occasional pious chivalric self-fulfilment. General understanding of holy war remained: reward for fighting for the faith. An assumption of Outremer's permanence naturally grew with the passage of time and the mundane reality of contact through pilgrimage, immigration and trade, consolidating a normalisation of attitudes. Outremer became just another in the community of states in Christendom, elevated by its status not its predicament, its demands assessed on politics not eschatological transcendence. The traditions and memories of past crusades did not disappear. Physical mementos did not lose their attraction. Outside academic refinement, ecclesiastical rules or political calculation, popular understanding, for example of the act of taking the cross, persisted, providing a receptive audience to the dramatic call to arms in 1187 when the sudden collapse of Outremer turned general sentiment into shocked action.

SECOND CRUSADE MANUSCRIPTS

Chronicle accounts of crusades can provide a barometer of contemporary responses. The explosion of texts concerning the First Crusade told its own story not just of the initial reception of those startling events but, in subsequent copying and circulation, of how the memorialised narratives continued to be used in promoting later expeditions and encouraging crusading commitment more generally.[45] The reverse is also evident. A dismal crusade left fewer immediate literary traces and even less succeeding interest. Contemporary written accounts of the Second Crusade (1145–8) exemplify this, while simultaneously demonstrating the often precarious and random bases of modern historical information. The most detailed accounts of any parts of the crusade cover the siege of Lisbon in 1147 and Louis VII's campaign to Antioch in 1147–8. They only survive in a single manuscript each without which our knowledge of events would be both very diminished and very different.

The *De expugnatione Lyxbonensi* (*The Siege of Lisbon*) survives in one messy copy written on poor parchment probably dating from the 1160s or 1170s, now bound into a volume of other texts collected in the sixteenth century by Archbishop Matthew Parker of Canterbury and in the library of Corpus Christi College, Cambridge.[46] Both its original authorship and subsequent provenance are obscure, although the dedicatee (Osbert, clerk of Bawdsey in Suffolk) and probably the author ('R' in the manuscript) came from the circle of a prominent East Anglian family, the Glanvills, one of whom, Hervey of Glanvill, led a contingent of crusaders at Lisbon.[47] The text is in a short book form, a *libellus*, familiar from texts that lay behind First Crusade chroniclers. It describes the course of a North Sea crusade fleet between May and October 1147, from assembly at Dartmouth to the successful completion of the Lisbon siege. Composed in a common narrative epistolary format, despite its apparent eyewitness immediacy, the text's content is artfully composed, shot through with tropes of canon law, classical and scriptural allusion, and contemporary arguments for holy war. When recording one of Hervey of Glanvill's speeches to the troops, in a marginal note the text warns the reader that these were not his actual words.[48] The general accuracy of the narrative finds some corroboration

60. De expugnatione Lyxbonensi.

from a much shorter German account, also in letter form.[49] Without the survival of the sole manuscript, we would know little about the Dartmouth commune or details of how the crusaders were hired to besiege Lisbon, and less about the organisation of such fleets and armies or the cultural penetration of central themes of crusade ideology and advocacy in the mid-twelfth century.

The sole manuscript of Odo of Deuil's account of the crusade of Louis VII of France from Christmas 1145 to his arrival in Antioch in March 1148, *De profectione Ludovici VII in orientem* (*The Journey of Louis VII to the East*), is also couched in the context of a letter, in this case to Odo's monastic superior Abbot Suger of St Denis. Odo claimed to be providing material for the abbot's putative biography of King Louis.[50] Twelfth-century St Denis had established itself as a centre for royalist historiography. Odo (d. 1162), who served as one of King Louis' household chaplains on crusade, wrote within this tradition, placing the king at the dramatic and didactic heart of the narrative as an exemplar of Christian kingship and personal virtue whose piety prevailed over personal

– 183 –

61. *Seal of King Louis VII of France.*

mistakes and extreme challenges. The work's lack of circulation and its critical appraisals of the crusaders' actions have led some modern critics to wonder, perhaps implausibly, whether the text is a contemporary literary fiction critiquing crusading ideology and practice. To a standard scriptural and classical education, Odo, who succeeded Suger as abbot of St Denis in 1151, added close awareness of chronicles of the First Crusade, a copy of one of which he took with him on the journey east. Yet Odo's work led nowhere. Suger died before using it; other writers either ignored or did not encounter it. It survives in a single later (*c.* 1200) high-class manuscript, probably copied at the Cistercian abbey of Clairvaux in whose library it was until the French Revolution.[51]

The survival of these two unique texts allows detailed insight into singular perspectives on just two limited parts of the campaigns of the Second Crusade. While numerous other sources exist, none is as full or seemingly immediate. If these two solitary manuscripts had not survived, our knowledge of the crusade would have been at once severely curtailed and more balanced. Thus they can stand for the study of much of the crusades: inverted triangles of imposing interpretive superstructures perched on narrow evidential support.

CHAPTER FIVE

THE THIRD CRUSADE
AND THE REINVENTION
OF CRUSADING, 1187–1198

O n 4 July 1187 a 20,000-strong Frankish army led by King Guy of Jerusalem (1186–92) was destroyed near Hattin in the hills above the Sea of Galilee by superior forces commanded by Sultan Saladin of Egypt and Damascus. The battle was long and hard fought; the Frankish defeat was total, leaving Outremer denuded of troops, money and morale. Within three months, all bar one of the major cities and ports of the kingdom of Jerusalem had been captured or surrendered, their Frankish populations becoming either refugees or slaves. In most places, resistance was absent, forlorn or minimal. Jerusalem itself, crowded with displaced Franks, capitulated on terms after a sharp siege on 2 October. The great castles of the interior succumbed one by one; the Hospitallers at Belvoir held out until January 1189, Montreal in the desert beyond the Dead Sea until May 1189; and, thanks to some clever if desperate diplomatic shadow boxing by its Arabic-speaking lord Reynald of Sidon, Beaufort on the River Litani above Tyre until April 1190, by which time the verdict of Hattin was being challenged in the sand dunes before Acre. Only Tyre remained of the Frankish cities of the kingdom of Jerusalem, saved in the summer of 1187 by the fortuitous arrival of a western adventurer with close connections with the east, Conrad of Montferrat. Saladin's 1188 campaign continued the rout, reducing northern Outremer to Tripoli, a tower in Tortosa, the castles of Margat and Crac des Chevaliers and the city of Antioch itself. Saladin's conquest of Outremer provoked the largest international western European military enterprise of the whole Middle Ages.

62. *The Horns of Hattin.*

The Fall of Outremer

The fall of Outremer in 1187–8 was neither predicted nor predictable. The shock in the west was seismic. Even in the Near East, Saladin's triumph appeared to some, including the Abbasid caliph, unexpected and not entirely welcome.[1] Within Outremer, despite acute political difficulties, many had retained confidence in the Franks' survival, famously witnessed by the building programme still underway in 1187 at the Church of the Annunciation at Nazareth. To escape the attention of Saladin's conquerors, newly carved but not yet installed capitals were buried, suggesting hopes for Frankish recovery even in the depths of disaster.[2] Two years of intense factional conflict over the succession and control of government in Jerusalem after the death of Baldwin IV in 1185 had threatened the unity of the kingdom, provoking near civil war. However, the army that King Guy led in Galilee in July 1187 drew on a full muster across the kingdom, with contingents from Tripoli and Antioch. While poisonous relationships among the high command complicated strategy and tactics, the link between political dysfunction and defeat at Hattin is not simple, clear or direct.

The failure of a Jerusalem embassy to western Europe led by Patriarch Heraclius of Jerusalem in 1184–5 to elicit either substantial military aid or a new candidate for the throne threw the kingdom back on its own resources. While commerce and religious tourism thrived, the nobility and government struggled to meet growing expenses of military readiness. To cover costs of defence, in 1183, a general census of all subjects had led to the levy of a general tax on income and property on the whole population, falling, in the way of such things, disproportionately on the poorer. Lordships and castles were increasingly transferred to wealthy religious corporations, especially the Military Orders, and the crown. At the same time as this increased the importance of royal patronage, consistent or effective royal leadership was eroded by the declining health of Baldwin IV and the succession of the child king Baldwin V (1185). Factional infighting revolved around the succession to the crown; the strategy to combat Saladin; assertion of independence by the great lordships of the kingdom; and personal political rivalries.

The future succession to the crown excited three factions: those of Baldwin IV's elder sister, Sybil, and her husband Guy of Lusignan; of Baldwin's younger half-sister Isabel and the family of her mother the dowager queen Maria's second husband, Balian of Ibelin; and of Raymond III of Tripoli, allied to the Isabel faction, but with royal designs of his own as Baldwin IV's first cousin once removed and, after the death of young Baldwin V in 1186, the closest male heir to the throne. Married to the heiress to the rich lordship of Galilee, as intermittent regent for Baldwin IV and V, Raymond, who had spent a decade in Muslim captivity (1164–74), relied on truces with Saladin, including one of four years in 1185 which meant that the Franks failed to take advantage of Saladin's near-mortal illness in the winter of 1185–6. The state of royal finances and the vulnerability of Raymond's agrarian estates in Galilee may have encouraged this approach: his enemies accused him of treachery. An alternative strategy called for aggression not diplomacy. Despite setbacks in northern Outremer, the kingdom of Jerusalem had retained most of its territorial integrity even after the unification of Muslim Syria with Egypt after 1174. The Jerusalemites maintained confidence in their military strength. Saladin's armies had been defeated at Montgisard in 1177 and Le Forbelet in 1182, the year he failed to take Beirut. Twice in 1183 the Jerusalem host had forced Saladin to withdraw, first from a siege of Kerak and then by outfacing his army in Galilee. The leading exponent of taking the attack to the enemy, Raynald of

Châtillon, lord of Transjordan and hero of the Montgisard victory, orchestrated dramatic raids on ports on the Red Sea in 1183 which, while militarily insignificant, threatened severe damage to Saladin's prestige. Like Raymond, Raynald's policy chimed with his particular self-interest, as revenues in his desert lordship came from predation on passing caravans.

As royal power was swopped between factions in the 1180s, nobles were increasingly free to feather their nests. Raymond of Tripoli and Raynald of Châtillon pursued wholly different policies in their frontier lordships. Guy of Lusignan, when count of Jaffa and Ascalon, defied the ailing Baldwin IV's attempts to dispossess him in 1183–4. In turn, after becoming king in a coup engineered by his wife Sybil and her allies in 1186, Guy was unable to prevent Raymond of Tripoli making a private treaty with Saladin. The gathering crisis of external threat, enfeebled monarchy and rotating regencies fed a culture of toxic mistrust. Yet, cutting across fratricidal divisions were broader loyalties to the monarchy and genuine disagreements over how best to secure the kingdom's survival. Raynald of Châtillon, a previous prince of Antioch by marriage (1153–61), after his release from fifteen years of Muslim captivity (1161–76), displayed consistent support for the king, often as the army's commander-in-chief. The majority of barons, when faced with the fait accompli of Sybil and Guy's coronation in 1186, despite strong hostility towards the pair, recognised the need for unity and submitted.

Nevertheless, the papal encyclical launching the Third Crusade saw the disaster of 1187 as God's judgement on 'the dissention which the malice of men at the suggestion of the devil has recently roused in the land of the Lord'.[3] Baldwin V's death left the kingdom divided into separate enclaves. In 1187, Raymond of Tripoli allowed Saladin's troops access to Galilee and even stationed some of them in Tiberias, while Raynald of Châtillon broke the 1185 truce with Saladin by attacking an Egyptian caravan bound for Damascus. Only the destruction of an outnumbered Templar-Hospitaller force by a Muslim foraging army at the Springs of Cresson near Nazareth in May 1187 compelled unity. Saladin's troops had been given permission by Raymond to pillage the countryside beyond his Galilee lordship. The disaster forced Raymond's reconciliation with Guy to face Saladin's expected invasion. A general muster of the Jerusalem forces met at Sephoria in Galilee in late June, perhaps 1,200 knights, around 18,000 infantry and additional Turcopole auxiliaries. Facing them, Saladin had mustered an army of 30,000 professional fighters augmented by significant detachments of volunteers.

Saladin's success in luring the Franks into battle on 4 July on unfavour-able terms and waterless terrain has been much debated. The sultan needed a victory to justify his grand mobilisation and retain his allies' support. Guy too appeared compelled to fight to secure his own credentials. Talk of Fabian tactics or withdrawal to the cities, especially when voiced by Raymond of Tripoli, smacked of passive defeatism and contradicted past Frankish success and Outremer's culture of providential confidence symbol-ised in the relic of the True Cross the army carried with it. Unusually in this period, battle suited both sides. Poor local intelligence and faulty tactical decisions loaded the dice against the Franks, who nevertheless withstood more than twenty-four hours of Turkish attacks on the march to Hattin on 3–4 July. During the battle itself, despite being surrounded and short of water for their horses, the Franks resisted for almost a whole day in mid-summer heat despite desertions and undisciplined infantry, a tenacity that spoke of high levels of physical and psychological strength. The customary massacre of the defeated did not engulf the leaders or many of the knights. Some, like Raymond, had escaped through the enemy cordon, while Guy, Raynald and most of the remaining commanders were taken prisoner. Two hundred Templars and Hospitallers were executed, as was Raynald, appar-ently by Saladin himself. The other leaders were led off to captivity. The Mosul chronicler Ibn al-Athir, who crossed the bone-strewn battlefield two years later, commented: 'Seeing the slain, you would not imagine that anyone had been taken alive, while seeing the captives, you would think that none could have been killed.'[4] A shattering loss was the relic of the True Cross, the ensign of God's favour, its capture providing important propa-ganda for Saladin but also for recruiters of the crusade that followed.

The captivity and subsequent release of the Frankish leaders revealed a feature of Outremer contemporaries took for granted. While commentators on all sides tended to emphasise the binary nature of conflict, exchanges across political and cultural divides were commonplace, from trade, employ-ment and diplomacy to spying. Constant warfare inevitably drew contending parties close. Three of the main Jerusalem politicians in 1187 – Raymond of Tripoli, Raynald of Châtillon and the Seneschal, Joscelin III of Courtenay, titular count of Edessa – had spent long periods in Muslim prisons, their release being matters of extended negotiation. Frankish knights served in Turkish armies for pay and, if stories circulating among western crusaders in the early 1190s can be believed, some even negotiated with Saladin in the

1180s to apostatise and attack Outremer.[5] The regiments of light-armed mounted archers, known as Turcopoles, who fought using Turkish battle-field tactics, comprised Franks, Syrian Christians and converted Muslims.[6] Diplomatic links with Muslim neighbours went back to 1098; alliances and treaties to the earliest years of Outremer. The intense diplomacy with Saladin that characterised Richard I's Palestine campaign during the Third Crusade in 1191–2, and the subsequent negotiated truces by the restored kingdom of Jerusalem after 1192, were unexceptional.

In 1187 each side was familiar to the other, their relations based more on politics than faith. Saladin's relative generosity in his treatment of Frankish captives and refugees earned him some retrospective Muslim disapproval. In addition to allowing ten Hospitallers to continue working in the Jerusalem hospital, Saladin also permitted Frankish refugees from Jerusalem wishing to reach Europe access to the port of Alexandria. There they received the protection of the city's governor, who put pressure on reluctant Italian ship-pers to take them on board. The refugees were well treated and the wealthier

63. *An Arab slave market.*

among them even indulged in some commercial enterprises of their own. Apart from his diplomatic relations with Raymond of Tripoli, it was claimed that Saladin was in correspondence with the wife of the lord of Burzey, a castle in the south of the principality of Antioch, who 'exchanged gifts with him and used to inform him of many significant matters'. She was the sister of the wife of Bohemund III of Antioch and allegedly it was on her account that the lord of Burzey and his family were freed after the castle's capture in 1188. Even if fabricated to extol the sultan's generosity and Frankish ladies' lack of scruple, the story suggests fluidity in cross-community relations. Ibn al-Athir mentioned meeting a Muslim who had served the Hospitallers of Crac des Chevaliers, fought with them against fellow Muslims, and even claimed to have accompanied a Hospitaller embassy to western Europe.[7]

Saladin understood the public requirement to emphasis religious conflict. A prime target during the battle of Hattin was the seizure of the True Cross. Symbolism was important. However, the conquest of Outremer in 1187–8 was not without compromise. Antioch was saved by a truce agreed with Bohemund III in 1188. After Saladin's victories, not every surviving Frank was enslaved or expelled. As late as 1217, a Frankish widow was living in the village beneath the castle of Montreal south of the Dead Sea.[8] The fall of Outremer led to a glut of slaves in the markets around the Near East, providing Arabic moralists with a host of touching, pointed, tragic or uplifting stories that fail to disguise the brutal horror of people trafficking. However, the victims of 1187–8 were not unique, even if their numbers were greater. The Franks enslaved those they defeated as readily as did their opponents. In 1187–8 wealth, payment of ransom or conqueror's caprice spared thousands, some providing the basis for a Christian counter-attack. The fall of Outremer in 1187–8 revealed the limits of Frankish assimilation into the Near Eastern world. Paradoxically, it also showed how far Franks had adapted and been accommodated within the Levant.

The Third Crusade: Preparation

News of Hattin and the loss of the True Cross reached the west by early autumn 1187. Before word of the capture of Jerusalem had arrived, Pope Gregory VIII issued a call to arms, *Audita Tremendi* (October/November

PREACHING

Preaching the cross provides some of the most iconic images of the crusades: Urban II at Clermont in 1095; Bernard of Clairvaux at Vézelay in 1146; Fulk of Neuilly before the Fourth Crusade; Oliver of Paderborn in Frisia before the Fifth Crusade. Both actual preparations and literary descriptions pivoted around the initiating rituals of the promotional sermon. Theoretically, these assumed regular form, open to modification according to an audience's social, professional, gender or regional complexion: opening exhortation (*exordium*); the point of the address (*narratio*); then detailed explications and arguments (*divisio, confirmatio* and *confutatio*) before a final peroration. Increasingly, to spice the message and keep the listeners' attention, sermons were invigorated with uplifting moralising anecdotes (*exempla*), perhaps often in the vernacular, featuring crusade heroes or addressing everyday anxieties of would-be recruits. By the early thirteenth century, crusade preaching, with its general Christ-centred appeal to Christian obligation, sacrifice, reward and redemption, had been assumed into a wider academic industry promoting broad pastoral evangelism to the laity. Model examples featured in formal sermon collections on penance in general. The potential for demagoguery, apparent in charismatic preachers such as Peter the Hermit in 1095–6 or the renegade Radulph in 1146, became tempered by closer coordination and licensing by the papacy and by the institutional dominance of the Cistercians, Paris-trained academics such as Gerald of Wales, Fulk of Neuilly, Robert Courson, Oliver of Paderborn or James of Vitry, and, from the 1220s, the friars. With the thirteenth-century extension of the crusade to the mass of the population with cash redemption of vows, preaching the cross became a more regular feature of communal religion; mere attendance at sermons earned increasing spiritual reward.

However, from the start, the literary and polemical image of sermons inspiring spontaneous commitment to the crusade misleads. Taking the cross came as part of a process of information, consultation, negotiation, decision and action involving the crusader's family, superiors, dependants, religious advisers and possible financiers. Although the climax of crusade sermons happened when members of the audience came forward to take the cross – often in

64. Preaching in grand style.

carefully staged and choreographed performances – the liturgy for blessing the cross only occurred much later when the crusader was about to embark. Sermons acted as much as rituals of encouragement and commitment as they did recruiting shows, preached to congregations already fully aware of what was going to happen, alerted by the preachers' outriders or by newsletters. Preaching formed part of a multi-media publicity scheme that included written texts in support of the crusade message or to broadcast the success of the current recruiting campaign. The spiritual significance of sermons was habitually sharpened by coinciding with local saints' days, the great penitential Christocentric festivals of the Church (Advent, Christmas, Lent and Easter) and the context of the Mass, the impact of these occasions frequently enhanced by the use of props – crosses, relics and visual aids, canvasses illustrating infidel atrocities; crucifixes identified in clouds – and moving guest appearances by veterans and victims: ritual as drama. While sermons were recorded and probably often delivered in the lingua franca of Latin, interpreters or preachers versed in the local vernaculars were on hand to convey the detail, even though the central message was, like the liturgy of the Mass, formal, familiar and understood whatever the language employed. Not all listeners were impressed; crowds could be rowdy, bored, distracted, disruptive, their interest held by organised community chanting and singing as well as thespian tricks and stagecraft. With their unique element of necessary audience participation, crusade sermons, even if not as central to the conversion of laymen into crusaders as official accounts required, nonetheless supplied a very distinctive devotional activity in western European religious culture as well as representing a core feature of the crusade in practice and imagination.

1187). Within six months the king of Sicily had sent a fleet to Syria; the kings of England and France and the Holy Roman Emperor had taken the cross with many of their leading nobles; special taxation had been instigated in France and England; official preaching under the general direction of papal legates had been in operation since November. Recruitment had started immediately, from Denmark to the Mediterranean, from Austria to the Atlantic. Plans, armies and fleets had been put in motion; international negotiations over routes, supplies and transport had been instigated; and one monarch, Frederick Barbarossa of Germany, a veteran of 1147–8, had even fixed a muster date (23 April 1189 at Regensburg) for departure.

Numbers taking the cross possibly outstripped those of the great recruiting drives of 1095–6 and 1146–7. All the traditional centres of enthusiasm were affected: Flanders, Champagne, Burgundy, Poitou, the Rhineland, the Low Countries, northern Italy; and great trading cities such as Cologne, London, Pisa and Genoa. Contemporaries recorded massive support across social, gender and geographic frontiers with the departure of local contingents throughout 1189–91. Armies numbered in the tens of thousands; Frederick Barbarossa's in 1189 perhaps as many as 15,000; Richard I's in 1190 about the same. Substantial fleets from Italy, France and the North Sea each carried hundreds if not thousands. Whole regions lost their lords, sometimes to the detriment of local law and order. Sicily contributed fleets, in 1188 and 1189. A whole generation of crusaders was formed and with it a lasting legacy of cultural involvement and recognition. One eyewitness summed up a common feeling: 'it was not a question of who had received the cross but of who had not yet done so'.[9] The commitment of monarchs made the crusade a function of government and royal power: people signed up 'for the love of God, remission of sins and respect of kings'.[10] Without rulers' leadership, support stuttered. Official Sicilian involvement ended on the death of King William II in 1189. The refusal of King Sverre of Norway or King Canute VI of Denmark to take the cross stunted participation among their nobilities, a pattern repeated across Europe from Toulouse to south Wales.

Mobilisation was backed by effective propaganda. A carefully worked crusade message provided arguments for service, consistent across papal and legatine letters; polemical and academic tracts; sermons; correspondence from veterans of the 1187 disasters; chroniclers' accounts, some by participants; poems; and descriptions of visual propaganda. The main features of *Audita Tremendi* were widely broadcast in an elaborate exercise

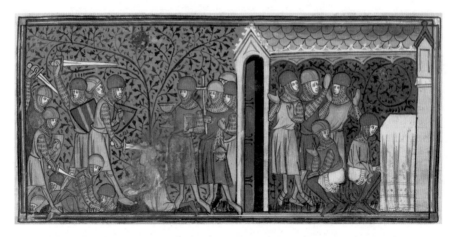

65. Muslims defecating on a Christian shrine, a theme of Third Crusade visual propaganda.

led by the chief crusade legate to Germany and France, Henry of Marcy, former Cistercian abbot of Clairvaux and cardinal bishop of Albano. The promotional networks included local archbishops and bishops, internationally well-connected intellectuals such as Alan of Lille or Peter of Blois, and, as in the 1140s, the Cistercians. Preachers doubled as recruiting agents, organisers and commanders: Bishop Godfrey of Würzburg and Archbishop Baldwin of Canterbury both led contingents and died in the crusader camp at Acre in 1190. Drama was added by the circulation of emotional letters, allegedly from the Holy Land front line, and the witness of Outremer refugees such as Archbishop Joscius of Tyre who had brought the news of Hattin to the west and given the cross to Henry II, Philip II and Philip of Flanders in January 1188. Stories reached the Near East of troupes of dispossessed Franks in penitents' garb parading large canvass cartoons of Saladin's obscene desecration of the Holy Places and of combat between Mohammed and Christ, images picked up in one of Henry of Albano's recruiting polemics.[11]

The tone of this multi-media campaign came from *Audita Tremendi*: the atrocities committed by Saladin; the loss of the True Cross and profanation of the Holy Places; the universal Christian responsibility for the catastrophe through the sins of all the faithful, not just the Franks; the consequent duty to accept the God-given opportunity for service and repentance with the associated remission of confessed sin and temporal privileges. The crusade offered a test of Christian devotion and the chance to earn eternal life.[12]

Subsequently, the pope's criticism of the Outremer Franks was tempered: they came to be seen as victims, focus shifting to the injury done to the cross and Christ. Exhortation invoked duty, shame, honour, vengeance, self-sacrifice, repentance, salvation and chivalry. The cross provided a comprehensive image and slogan, fusing the personal and universal, the material and the mystical. In Henry of Albano's phrases, copied by other promoters, the cross was 'the ark of the vassal of the Lord, the ark of the New Testament . . . the glory of the Christian people, the remedy of sin, the care of the wounded, the restorer of health', both physical battle standard for the faithful warrior and symbol of Christ's redeeming sacrifice, demanding service while guaranteeing *Audita Tremendi*'s reassurance of death 'in a brief moment' to 'gain eternal life', or, as one Third Crusade preacher wrote, 'the seal of our religion'.[13] The cross dominated preaching and recruitment. Followers of different commanders were distinguished by the colour of their crosses: red for the forces of Philip of France; white for Henry II's; green for those of Philip of Flanders. As the defining signal of commitment since the 1090s, words in Latin and the vernacular now decisively identified crusaders with the cross (*crucesignati*, *cruisiati*, etcetera). A famous manuscript illumination in a presentation copy of Robert of Rheims's chronicle of the First Crusade, produced in 1188–9, showed the dedicatee, Frederick Barbarossa, surrounded by crosses, on his robe, on his shield and on a globe he is holding.[14] Preachers employed crosses as props and spread stories of crosses in the sky to accompany descriptions of their sermons.

Symbols mattered, but *Audita Tremendi* also argued that material costs acted as an investment in salvation, sending earthly riches to 'the heavenly barn'. A blanket exemption on interest repayment was developed from the Second Crusade privilege by simplifying the protected category to all 'usurious interest' (*dandas usuras*). Although this acknowledged crusaders' need to borrow on the open market to fund their campaigns, the imprecision of *Audita Tremendi* soon led to local clarification and modification to reassure creditors and sustain crusaders' credit-worthiness. Taxation stimulated support. Justified by *Audita Tremendi*'s extension of responsibility for the fate of the Holy Land to all Christians, the Saladin Tithe of 1188–9 exempted *crucesignati* as they were committing their own resources to the struggle. A levy of a tenth on lay and ecclesiastical revenues and movables for one year, the tithe was agreed in early 1188 by Henry II and Philip II, although the latter found himself impotent to collect it and in 1189 cancelled it. In

66. *Frederick Barbarossa the* crucesignatus *receiving a copy of Robert of Rheims's history of the First Crusade.*

England, the tax was raised. Propertied *crucesignati* were supposed to be given the proceeds from the non-crusading taxpayers on their lands. The material incentive to gain exemption by taking the cross was obvious. As Roger of Howden, a royal official and crusader, archly observed, 'all the rich men of his [Henry II's] lands, both clergy and laity, rushed in crowds to take the cross'.[15]

How much of the Saladin Tithe was spent on the crusade is not easy to judge. More generally, money and materiel were sought from subjects and dependants. Hearth taxes were widespread (used for example by Frederick Barbarossa in Germany and the count of Nevers in France); land was sold, leased or mortgaged, with the Church still the chief lender and beneficiary. In 1189–90, Richard I of England (1189–99), who had succeeded his father Henry II in July 1189, indulged in an orgy of asset-stripping, selling offices, titles, property and rights. An experienced general, Richard recognised the huge expense of war and the especially great costs of crusading. Government receipts for 1190, at over £30,000, showed a 50 per cent increase on normal revenue in the 1180s, excluding income from the Saladin Tithe, which a contemporary optimistically believed may have reached upwards of £60,000; and other extraordinary levies, such as that on the Jews, which may have brought in a further £10,000.[16] Even so, equipping and manning Richard's crusade fleet of about one hundred vessels of various sizes alone may have cost almost £9,000 just for the first year's wages, a further £5,700 for hiring ships and thousands more on equipment (from horses to siege engines) and food (bacon, cheese as well as grain for biscuits). These expenses did not cover the costs of Richard's own military entourage or subsidies to allies, such as the king of France (over 13,000 gold ounces) or the count of Champagne (4,000 measures of wheat, 4,000 sides of bacon and 4,000 pounds of silver). Small wonder Richard sought every opportunity to re-endow his campaign, in Sicily where he wintered in 1190–1, and in Cyprus, which he conquered in May 1191. While English bureaucratic procedures allow uniquely precise insight into the nature of costs, the pattern was familiar. Frederick Barbarossa calculated a minimum of three marks per head for two years' service, costs he avowedly did not even attempt to meet from royal resources, leaving fund-raising for those outside his service to individual crusaders. Philip II of France's contract with Genoa in 1190 to ship a force of 650 knights and 1,300 squires plus their horses, at 5,580 marks, cost the equivalent perhaps of 60 per cent of ordinary annual royal income. The bailing out of some of his leading magnates in Sicily in 1190–1 may have cost Philip the equivalent of a quarter of ordinary annual income.[17]

Beyond the recruits themselves, taxpayers, shipping contractors, artisans supplying war materials, or farmers selling provisions, all felt the effect of the great mobilisation. Increased demand drove prices higher. Domestic sacrifices could be considerable. As one veteran recalled: 'And none to sell his heritage/Delayed the holy pilgrimage'.[18] While outright disposal of property was not universal, mortgages and loans could strain family resources. Creditors, mortgagers or buyers of property benefited, prompting resentment and violence. Despite official disapproval, anti-Jewish riots in London and other English market towns culminated in the massacre and mass suicide of Jews in York in March 1190. By contrast, in the Rhineland, the centre of crusader anti-Jewish violence in 1096 and 1146, Frederick Barbarossa personally guaranteed and enforced royal protection of the Jewish community, preventing crusaders from attacking the Jewish quarter in Mainz during March 1188, riding through the streets of the city with a leading rabbi, and issuing an edict imposing corporal and capital punishments for those who assaulted Jews.[19] However, like Richard I, asserting royal protection did not inhibit Frederick from taxing the Jews for his crusade.

The ability of western European economies to sustain such extensive investment in war, demanding huge quantities of cash and bullion, speaks of robust and diverse capacity. Yet the translation of these material fundamentals into concerted military action required a diplomatic and political transformation that only the disasters of 1187–8 could provoke. Frederick Barbarossa was able to come to accommodation with both Philip II of France and the papacy over contentious issues of territory and preferment. The association of Frederick and the papal legate, Henry of Albano, in the emperor's taking the cross in March 1188 symbolised new mutual acceptance of their reciprocal roles and interests, not least in Italy. Taking the cross together helped Philip and Henry II appear to resolve differences without either side losing face. Across society, the cause of the cross provided an opportunity to settle or suspend disputes. This could be evanescent. The coalition of German princes that followed Frederick Barbarossa presaged no new accumulation of imperial power. The great feudatories of France, the duke of Burgundy or the counts of Flanders and Champagne, operated as independent commanders, their association with Philip II's commitment based on convenience not subservience. Nevertheless, the recovery of Jerusalem challenged normal political constraints.

Preparations proceeded at different paces. In Germany, the imperial army was hurriedly – perhaps inadvisedly – ready by the spring of 1189. While smaller contingents, such as those of Louis of Thuringia (1189) or Leopold of Austria (1190–1), and forces from Bremen, Frisia and Cologne (1189–90), travelled by sea, Frederick's army planned to follow the Danube to Constantinople and the Asia Minor route of the First and Second Crusades. Although both Henry II (in 1188) and Philip II (when stuck in Sicily in the winter of 1189–90) toyed with travelling overland at least some of the way, outside Germany the bulk of crusaders faced the prospect of sea voyages. Contingents from the Baltic, North Sea, Low Countries, England, the French Atlantic and Mediterranean seaboards, and Italy, were able to requisition or hire merchant shipping and exploit local shipbuilding expertise. From around the European coastline, fleets of a few score to hundreds of vessels embarked eastwards in 1189–90. French nobles commissioned at least four substantial fleets in 1189 and 1190. Richard I of England built, bought or hired his own fleet in England and western France in 1190 and secured a flotilla of Mediterranean galleys. Besides resourcefulness in shipping, armies required war engines, fiscal ingenuity, budgets for wages, provision of health care and navigational mapping. Armies travelled with ambulance carts; fleets with prefabricated throwing engines and even, in the case of Richard I, a wooden field fortress. Expenses were estimated in advance, with cash and bullion transported accordingly. As well as galleys, of various sizes, large cargo-carrying round ships, known as cogs, were deployed, capable of carrying hundreds of men and horses. Frederick Barbarossa and Richard I sought to impose discipline on the behaviour of their inter-regional coalitions of troops through punitive ordinances covering anything from murder and theft to excessive gambling.

Planning was supported by past experience, trade, diplomacy, reconnaissance and espionage. Detailed itineraries had been a feature of chronicles describing crusades since the early twelfth century. By the second half of the century, maritime guides for the Mediterranean were being produced in ports such as Genoa and Pisa that seemed to borrow from Arab geographers, including the north African and Sicilian al-Idrisi (d. 1165). Roger of Howden, crusader and royal clerk, not only produced a very precise itinerary of his voyage from Spain to the Holy Land and back again to Marseilles in 1190–1, he also noted prevailing winds and provided a schematic account of sea lanes that reads like a description of a diagrammatic map. On return he may even have compiled his own guide to the coasts from eastern England to the Mediterranean, and beyond, citing the work of another Third Crusade veteran, the admiral Margarit, commander of the Sicilian fleet in 1188. Ship's companies were advised to employ a *conductor*, an expert in sea routes. Nautical information was shared widely, both across cultural frontiers and within Christendom: a Pisan maritime handbook on the Mediterranean was copied in Winchester, a centre for Third Crusade organisation.[20]

PAYING CRUSADERS

The idealised crusader, as extolled by generations of crusade promoters, took the cross out of faith alone and, as a sign of devotion, funded his service out of his own resources. Many crusaders did both, yet more relied on the patronage and assets of lords or other associates, the need to provide board and wages representing a major element in recruiting and fund-raising. Every crusade depended on paid troops. These fell into three broad categories: obligated vassals, clients and members of lords' entourages, often knights themselves, who expected to provide their own war materials but to serve on campaign for pay; employees, such as household servants, who had little choice but to follow their lords but also customarily received wages; and a much wider pool of troops who owed no tenurial obligations to a lord but fought for necessary reward without which they could not have served. Pay did not preclude devotion but supported it as a necessity for continued participation, especially as crusaders were supposedly driven by free individual commitment not dragged by the shackles of hierarchy. The reality was rather different, with the usual constraints of social and economic power, service and employment fully in operation. Within crusade armies, the death or destitution of commanders led to fluid employment markets where knights and other soldiers looked for new patrons and successful ambitious lords sought additional followers, using pay as a necessary lure, sometimes in competition with other eager would-be patrons. This pay could go beyond simple rations or providing funds for basic subsistence. Rates were not restricted to costs but to generous purchase of loyalty. In 1195, Henry VI of Germany explicitly offered to pay knights and sergeants on his crusade salaries in gold above specified rations.

From the First Crusade onwards, chronicles are littered with words for money contracts (*conventio solidorum*), wages (*vadia*, *stipendia*), paid troops (*stipendiarii*), retaining (*retinere*), hiring (*conducere*). Paid retainers and financial contracts appear in accounts of the First Crusade; Tancred of Lecce was both a paymaster and a recipient of a paid contract to serve Raymond of Toulouse. Engineers at the sieges of Nicaea and Jerusalem were paid to work on siege machinery, while Bohemund claimed at Antioch that he could not afford to

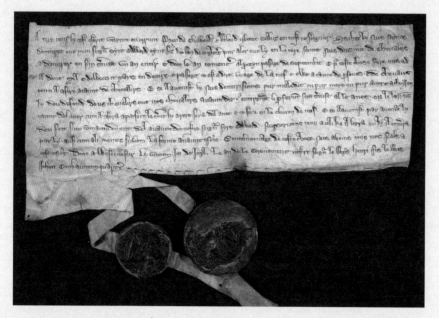

67. *Contract of Robert Tibetot and Payn de Chaworth to accompany the Lord Edward on crusade in 1270 with five knights each in return for shipping, water and 100 marks per knight.*

continue paying his followers, producing an account book to prove it. On the Second Crusade, in 1148, Conrad III used money he had been given by the Byzantine emperor Manuel I to hire a new army when he arrived in Palestine. In 1190, Richard I fixed payment for the soldiers and salaries in his crusade fleet (2d a day for soldiers; 4d for steersmen). At the siege of Acre, Archbishop Baldwin of Canterbury led a paid regiment of 200 knights and 300 sergeants. Other knights were paid for guard duty. On arrival at Acre, Richard I hired archers with '*bona stipendia*' and outbid Philip II in competing for the paid service of knights, bidding first 2 then 4 gold pieces. Thereafter, the evidence of pay becomes more prominent. In 1201, Theobald II of Champagne left 50,000 livres to pay for crusaders, while the treaty of Venice stipulated the inclusion of 20,000 paid sergeants in the crusade host. Crusaders in Languedoc were paid fixed daily rates, as were Louis IX's household troops on crusade in 1248. At the same time, John of Joinville was paying his knights slightly less than the king's rates. In the second half of the thirteenth century, crusaders were retained through written fixed contracts specifying the rates of pay and terms of employment. Schemes for fresh eastern expeditions in the fourteenth century were accompanied by detailed lists of salaries for knights as well as infantry.

The ubiquity and importance of pay on crusades exerted significant influence on their character and organisation. Pay helped secure a measure of order and discipline on campaign. The cost stimulated paymasters' financial expedients, from mortgages and sales of property to innovative schemes for attracting donations; estate, national and clerical taxation; and vow redemptions. The requirements of pay forced commanders to have access to large amounts of coin. One Champagne crusading lord raised as much as 200 *livres* in pennies (48,000 of them), a physically inconvenient but more adept currency to pay his followers. The ultimate recognition of the tension between the idea of a free *crucesignatus* and the reality of a paid warrior came with the advocacy around 1300 of paid professional preliminary assaults on Egypt prior to any traditional mass crusade. Pay did not contradict the ideals of crusading or exclude the presence of self-funded crusaders, but perhaps it gave both more chance of success.[21]

The Campaigns of the Third Crusade

The Siege of Acre

Saladin's victories in 1187–8 were incomplete. Crucially, the port of Tyre, still in Frankish hands, provided a relatively safe harbour for western fleets. Protected from landward attack by a narrow isthmus, Tyre had resisted Saladin in the summer 1187 thanks to the fortuitous arrival of Conrad of Montferrat, a paternal uncle of the late Baldwin V. Without Tyre, the sultan's navy would have made any future crusader landings almost impossible. Sea power determined the pattern of the western military response, with the regular arrival in Levantine waters of western fleets from the spring passage of 1188 onwards. With prevailing currents and winds more or less confining naval expeditions to spring and autumn, direct passages from western Mediterranean ports took from a few weeks to a couple of months. While Tyre supplied defensive cover, reconquest demanded aggression. This came from an unlikely source. On his release from Ayyubid captivity in the summer of 1189, Guy of Lusignan had been excluded from political authority over the rump of Outremer by Conrad of Montferrat exploiting his role as the saviour of Tyre. In August, Guy suddenly took advantage of the arrival of the first substantial group of crusaders with a Pisan fleet to march south and lay siege to Acre. A typically cautious reaction by Saladin allowed Guy to dig in across the sand dunes around the port. Despite a serious defeat in October 1189 and heavy losses through disease as well as combat, the Frankish crusade army clung on with attritional trench warfare. Although unable to impose a complete blockade of Acre, time favoured the crusaders provided they could keep open the sea lanes for new arrivals and food supplies while Saladin's difficulties in keeping his coalition in the field only increased. As the numbers in the western camp swelled to many thousands, the siege of Acre began to acquire epic dimensions for participants, many of whom wrote vividly of their experiences. Comparisons were even drawn with the siege of Troy.[22]

The siege fell into three phases. The bridgehead around the city was established and defended for a year from August 1189. Substantial western reinforcements then arrived in the summer and autumn of 1190, including a French force under Henry of Champagne, the remnants of the German crusade under Frederick of Swabia, and an English advance guard under Archbishop Baldwin of Canterbury and the former Chief Justiciar Rannulf Glanvill, followed by stalemate, hunger, disease and low morale. Finally, the

kings of France and England landed in May and June 1191 and the city fell
in July. The crusaders in their fetid and overcrowded camp were consistently harried by Saladin's forces. Epidemics cut through all ranks. Problems
of supplies and distribution were exacerbated by hoarding and too much
bullion chasing stretched resources of food. Until the arrival of the French
and English kings with their heavy siege weapons and throwing machines,
direct assaults on the city walls were ineffectual, while Egyptian ships
repeatedly broke the naval blockade. Discipline was undermined by tensions
over tactics, food, and between regional groups, mirroring acute rivalries
within the leadership, especially the competing claims of Guy of Lusignan
and Conrad of Montferrat to the kingship of Jerusalem. The deaths of
Queen Sybil and her and Guy's daughters in the camp in October 1190
provoked an unseemly wrangle over the succession. In November, Conrad
of Montferrat married Sybil's half-sister and heiress, Isabel, who had to be
summarily divorced from her existing husband, Humphrey of Toron. Guy
still insisted on his rights as the anointed monarch. Political deadlock
persisted. Yet, with Saladin unable to cut supply lines or dislodge the camp,
the crusaders' cohesion, reinforced by newcomers, held, in anticipation of
the arrival of the kings from the west.

68. Acre, from an engraving of 1839.

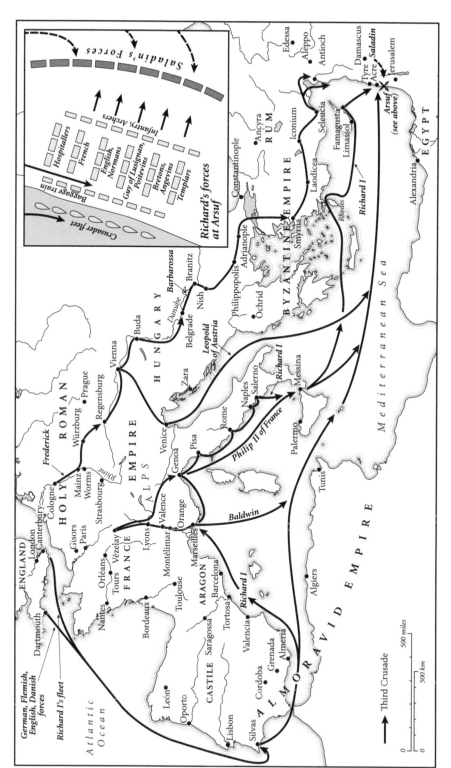

8. *The Third Crusade.*

Delay?

The First Crusade had taken two years from Urban II's Clermont speech to reach northern Syria; the Second Crusade two and a half years from the first papal encyclical to the arrival of the French and German kings in Outremer in the spring of 1148. One criticism of the Third Crusade, at the time and since, concerned its slow progress. This misleads. The strategy of the Third Crusade differed from that of its predecessors: travel by sea played a dominant role, allowing the main armies to set out serially from 1189 onwards: a Pisan flotilla, the German land army, a large French force and fleets from northern Europe in the spring of 1189; another northern European force later in 1189; a French army under Henry of Champagne in the spring of 1190; the first section of the Anglo-Norman–Angevin army in the summer of 1190; the main French and Angevin forces in the summer of 1190 but leaving Sicily only in the spring of 1191. The laborious pace of the expeditions of Richard I and Philip II, who only reached Palestine three and half years after the initial papal call to arms, was exceptional. Smaller forces were quicker. In 1190 the English advance guard that left central France in July managed to reach Acre that October. If the German army had not disintegrated after the unexpected death of Frederick Barbarossa in Cilicia in June 1190, the largest crusade force would have appeared in Outremer just over two and half years after recruitment began, and joined an already large army besieging Acre. Even the Anglo-French armies took less than a year from departure to arrival in Palestine, as Richard I's budget to pay his troops anticipated. The stepped pattern of departure eased supply difficulties and became a feature of later expeditions. Sea transport, despite organising shipping and embarkation ports, was quicker, if costlier, than travel by land. The requirements of provisioning determined regular landfalls; horses needed substantial quantities of fresh water to survive. Given the size and shape of most open-decked oared twelfth-century ships, long-distance travel by sea in winter was dangerous and rarely undertaken. If embarking from northern Europe after spring, this almost inevitably meant finding winter quarters to shelter and refit: Marseilles for the great North Sea fleet in 1189–90; Messina for Philip II and Richard I in 1190–1. The problem of winter campaigning was not confined to sea-borne armies. Frederick Barbarossa prudently wintered in Thrace in 1189–90 rather than follow the unfortunate precedent of Conrad III and Louis VII of attempting a winter crossing of Asia Minor.

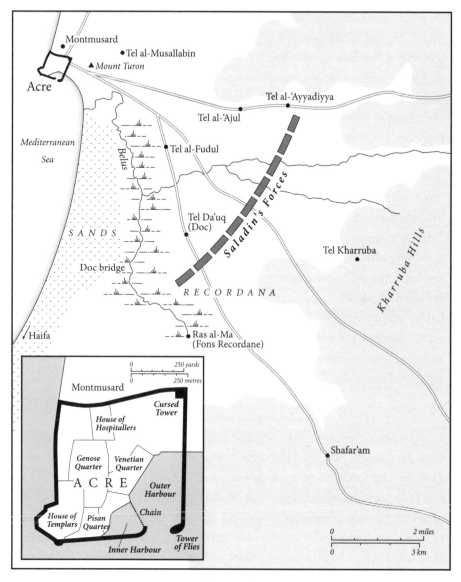

9. *The siege of Acre.*

The German Expedition, 1189–90

Frederick Barbarossa's accommodation with the papacy and the acceptance of his son Henry VI as his heir and regent in Germany made an early muster in May 1189 possible. Frederick's army made good progress through Hungary thanks to a negotiated agreement over access to markets. Once in

Byzantine territory, the Germans encountered opposition, in part due to the impotence and vacillation of Emperor Isaac II Angelus (1185–95). Frederick solved the diplomatic and supply problems by occupying the rich province of Thrace to the west of Constantinople from November 1189. A new treaty with the Greeks (February 1190) provided transport across the Hellespont and access to markets at moderate exchange rates, although the latter proved nugatory once the Germans crossed into Asia Minor in late March. The need to resupply the army and secure adequate provisions drove it forwards despite heavy Turkish assaults. Victory at Iconium in May restocked the army with money, supplies, food and morale. By June, Frederick had brought his battered but still impressive force to the borders of Christian Cilician Armenia, one of the more remarkable feats of western arms in crusading history. The achievement was immediately undone by Frederick's sudden death on 10 June during the crossing of the River Saleph. His army rapidly disintegrated, only a remnant reaching Acre the following November led by the emperor's son, Frederick of Swabia. The loss of the German army changed the course of the crusade, prolonging the siege of Acre, reducing the chances of recovering Jerusalem, and exposing the delay of the kings of France and England.

The Anglo-French Crusade

In the Anglo-French realms, the peace brokered when Henry II and Philip II took the cross in January 1188 soon collapsed. While Henry's death in July 1189 and the accession of Richard I allowed crusade plans to reach fruition, carefully sculpted agreements over sharing profits and the choreographed progress of the Anglo-Angevin and French royal armies highlighted tensions, exacerbated by an obvious disparity in wealth and organisation. Richard was able to hire his own fleet and subsidise many of his followers, who came to include Philip and other prominent French commanders whom he then outbid for siege engines and hired service once he had arrived at Acre. After leaving together from Vézelay on 4 July 1190, exactly three years after Hattin, and agreeing to muster at Messina in Sicily, each king made his separate way, Philip via Genoa and Richard to Marseilles where he hoped to meet his fleet. Gathered from England, Anjou and Poitou, the fleet comprised about one hundred ships carrying, according to a well-informed witness, over 10,000 sailors, knights and infantry, rations for a year (presumably chiefly flour and dried biscuits) and military equipment.[23] A year's pay was calculated in advance with the royal treasure evenly distributed across the fleet to reduce losses from shipwreck. From its full muster at Lisbon in July 1190, the fleet was scheduled to meet the king at Marseilles the following month. They missed each other by three weeks, the king hiring a flotilla of galleys to take his military household, perhaps numbering 3,000, from Marseilles to Messina where army and navy were finally united in late September.

The Sicilian interlude in the winter of 1190–1 was marked by worsening relations between Richard and Philip and open hostility between Richard and the island's inhabitants, especially King Tancred (1189–94). However, the stay provided supplies, ships, refits and funds, including 40,000 gold ounces extracted from Tancred by Richard in lieu of a legacy of Tancred's predecessor William II (1166–89) to Henry II for the crusade and the dower of William's widow, Richard's sister, Joan. A third of the gold went to Philip, along with 10,000 marks to release Richard from a promise to marry Philip's sister, and some ships, a windfall that allowed Philip to re-equip and continue by sea. Philip sailed for Acre on 20 March, arriving on 20 April. His forces and large siege machines, given suitably belligerent nicknames (for example, Bad Neighbour and God's Stonethrower) made an immediate impact on morale and tactics.[24] However, the French fleet paled beside the armada assembled by Richard I, possibly containing over 200 vessels, 17,000 soldiers and crew, as well as trebuchets and Richard's prefabricated wooden castle. Richard sailed from Sicily on 10 April. Dispersed by bad weather, the fleet reassembled at Cyprus which, after a lightning campaign during May against its independent Greek ruler, Isaac Comnenus, fell to Richard. Whether planned or opportunist, the conquest of Cyprus proved the most durable achievement of the Third Crusade, made at the expense of fellow Christians. The island may already have been a major supplier for the Christian army at Acre. Immediately, it became a milch-cow for Richard. He initially sold the island to the Templars for 100,000 bezants (of which 40,000 were forthcoming) and later in 1192 to Guy of Lusignan, no longer king of Jerusalem, for a further 60,000 bezants. Guy originally came from Poitou, his family Richard's vassals in France. The Lusignans were to rule Cyprus (from 1196 as kings) until the late fifteenth century, with the island remaining in western hands until conquered by the Ottoman Turks in 1571.

Richard reached Acre on 8 June 1191 to find the siege already in its final stages. The garrison surrendered on 12 July. Despite vicious squabbling

FOOD AND DRINK

While enthusiasm and ideology may have initiated crusades, their viability, conduct and course depended on the availability of adequate food and drink.[25] Harvests determined the departure time for land armies on the first three major eastern crusades, all of which subsequently experienced problems in accessing markets and securing fair prices or sufficient supplies. The need to refit and restock directed crusades to winter in Constantinople (1096–7; 1147–8; 1203–4); Thrace (1189–90); Sicily (1190–1); Cyprus (1248–9); and ports in Iberia (1147; 1217–18) and the western Mediterranean (the Flemish fleet in 1203–4; the Frisians in 1217–18). The search for supplies drove crusade itineraries, diplomacy and military action. The great long sieges conducted by the First, Third and Fifth Crusades required provisioning from across the Greek- and Turkish-held Levant. Louis IX of France's agents spent two years stockpiling grain and wine in Cyprus before his 1248 crusade. Failure to find adequate supplies compromised the Germans and French in 1147–8 and the crusaders at Venice in 1202 when they ate the food intended for the forthcoming campaign. Calculations of required amounts of food and drink were integral to crusaders' treaties with Genoa (1190); Venice (1201 and 1268); and Henry VI of Germany's contracts with his knights and sergeants in 1195. Almost all detailed descriptions of crusade campaigns emphasise the importance and difficulties of obtaining sufficient food supplies. The depredations in Hungary by the forces of Peter the Hermit in 1096 were caused by the loss of their baggage train of over 2,000 wagons carrying corn, barley and meat. Land armies were slowed by packhorses and food carts, as well as the need to forage for items such as grain, honey and vegetables, and to allow animals for slaughter and horses to graze. All crusade armies, whether transported by land or sea, faced the problem of the sheer bulk of provender needed to sustain men, pack animals and horses.

Modern estimates, based on contemporary calculations in treaties and advisory tracts, suggest that a crusader might have consumed 1.3 kilos of food a day, mainly grain or flour (which weighed less) to make bread or the ubiquitous unappetising hard ship's biscuit, supplemented by small amounts of cheese, salted meat (predominantly pork), and dried legumes, with between 3 and 8

69. *Eating and drinking on campaign: Normans in England 1066, with the meal blessed by a future 1096 crusader, Bishop Odo of Bayeux.*

litres of liquid, depending on activity, more if actually fighting. Horses, even on land if stall fed, required daily 5 kilos of grain, 5 of hay and 32 litres of water. The 1201 Venetian treaty specified provision of *c.* 400 kilos of bread, flour, grain and legumes per man and *c.* 340 litres of wine, enough for about ten months, with *c.* 800 kilos of grain for each horse. In his compendious early fourteenth-century guide to crusading, the Venetian Marino Sanudo produced precise estimates for consumption of biscuits, wine, meat, cheese and beans. Richard I's preparations for his fleet in 1190 showed that commanders were well aware of what was needed. Exchequer records itemised the collection of food for the fleet: 140 large cheeses and 300 bacon carcasses from Essex and Hertfordshire; 100 cheeses, 800 bacon carcasses and 20 measures of beans from Hampshire; 100 measures of beans from Cambridgeshire and Huntingdonshire and 276 measures of beans from Gloucestershire. These staple ingredients aside, crusaders might expect to supplement their diet where possible with local perishable produce – eggs, meat, fruit and vegetables (rarely enough if the apparent ubiquity of scurvy-related conditions is a guide), and local wine (although Norwegians in 1110 fatally underestimated the strength of Greek retsina).

On campaign, one of the most frequently noted civilian groups were cooks, some of whom were evidently master chefs, while others ran the equivalent of mess tents or soup kitchens. Apart from occasional mass shortages, access to food became a divisive mark of status as well as stimulating cooperation in messing together. At Antioch in 1098 and Acre in 1190, the rich were criticised for pushing up prices for the poor. Hoarding appeared a perennial problem. Stories of famine, of eating horses, pack-animals, vermin or roots, and even of cannibalism highlighted the contrasting degrees of access to supplies, an inequality that could strain army cohesion. The usually loyal John of Joinville may have voiced a general feeling when in retrospect he condemned the French barons after the fall of Damietta in 1249. They 'should have preserved their resources in order to make good use of them'; instead they 'took to serving splendid meals and lavish dishes'.[26] Some of these may not have been good for the diners. Although some Franks in Outremer adopted local Levantine cuisine, the evidence of excavated middens suggests that westerners stuck to familiar diets, notably in their enthusiasm for pork. The latrines at Acre also show they were infested with parasitic intestinal worms.[27]

over the distribution of booty, Acre gave the crusade a secure harbour and military base, crucial for prospects both for the crusade and the restoration of a viable Frankish Outremer for which the city came to act as both capital and major economic centre, one of the chief commercial entrepôts of western Asia. After Acre's capitulation, a pattern to the Palestine war quickly emerged. Even before the city fell, Richard opened diplomatic contact with Saladin, his purpose to seek an agreed restoration of the kingdom of Jerusalem, including the Holy City, by presenting the sultan with an implacable military threat. The departure of Philip II at the end of July to secure his interests back in France, leaving the bulk of French troops behind under the duke of Burgundy, gave Richard dominant command. Although Conrad of Montferrat and elements of the Outremer baronage pursued their own negotiations with Saladin, Richard's tactics and strategy determined the remaining fourteen months of the Holy Land conflict.

The confrontation between Saladin and Richard I caught the imaginations of the sultan's entourage and later observers. Diplomacy shadowed force. Richard signalled his determination by his massacre of 2,500–3,000 prisoners from Acre when Saladin delayed implementing the agreement over the city's surrender. Saladin responded by killing captured Franks and crusaders. The two-handed chess of diplomacy and war continued. Moving south from Acre in late August 1191, Richard, flanked by the crusader fleet providing protection and supplies, led a fighting march along the coast towards Jaffa, shadowed and harried by Saladin's troops. On 7 September, near Arsuf, the skirmishing developed into a set-piece encounter. Although the crusaders had the better of the exchange, Saladin's army remained intact. The practical problems for both sides became apparent. With neither able to achieve a decisive victory, the military and diplomatic goals of each remained out of reach.

Between September and December 1191, Richard methodically occupied the coastal plain of southern Palestine, positioning himself for either of his two strategic options, an assault on Jerusalem or an attack on Egypt. The latter was made more difficult when Saladin demolished the fortifications of Ascalon, although Richard toyed with a Genoese-backed assault on the Nile. Diplomacy ran on, apparently including an offer of Richard's sister Joan in marriage to al-Adil as a means to a Palestinian condominium, a suggestion that incited her incandescent fury. After painfully slow progress towards Jerusalem, the crusaders reached Bayt Nuba, twelve miles from the

Holy City at the turn of the year. Bad weather and the fears expressed by the local baronage and Military Orders over the risks of an assault on Jerusalem, and the difficulty of defending it once captured, encouraged Richard to order a withdrawal on 13 January 1192, turning the crusaders' attention to rebuilding the fortifications at Ascalon. In June, following six months consolidating his hold over southern Palestine and the northern Negev, a reluctant Richard was forced by his allies and followers again to march towards Jerusalem. This time he took a week not two months to arrive at Bayt Nuba, only to withdraw once more on 4 July.

In January and June 1192 tactical and strategic obstacles prevented hazarding a repeat of 1099. Saladin's field army remained intact. The likely departure of most crusaders once Jerusalem had been captured and the absence of control over Transjordan allegedly made the Holy City untenable. However, these problems had not changed since the first march to Bayt Nuba. Richard's withdrawal in January 1192 had already shown Saladin the weakness of his policy of trying to strong-arm diplomatic concessions. As Saladin could not afford to surrender Jerusalem he had no option but to call what turned out to be Richard's bluff. The January withdrawal undermined the crusade's unity, the prospect of Jerusalem being the only glue holding the Angevin-French coalition together. Richard's alternative strategy of reinforcing Frankish control over the coastal plain and threatening Saladin's supply routes to Egypt made military sense but denied the higher purpose of the whole enterprise. Why were the crusaders fighting in southern Palestine if not for Jerusalem, only a few miles away? By withdrawing without a fight for the Holy City, Richard undermined the providential assumptions behind the expedition, damaging morale while showing his hand to the enemy. Whether from over-subtle, conservative tactics or loss of nerve, by twice conceding Jerusalem was out of reach, Richard reduced pressure on Saladin, leaving a negotiated settlement for a condominium or two-state solution his best option. Details of such an agreement occupied discussions between Richard and al-Adil throughout 1192 alongside continued jockeying for military advantage.

Political events further north cast a shadow. An unsatisfactory compromise over the Jerusalem succession had left Guy of Lusignan as king but forced to divide the lands and revenues with Conrad of Montferrat who was recognised with his wife Isabel, King Amalric's younger daughter and since the death of Queen Sybil in 1190 heir to the kingdom, as Guy's heirs. This agreement collapsed as Conrad threatened a separate treaty with

Saladin. In April 1192, Richard was forced to accept Conrad as king of Jerusalem, with Guy's purchase of Cyprus as compensation. The new settlement immediately unravelled when Conrad was assassinated in Tyre on 28 April, some said at Richard's instigation, although other culprits, including Saladin, were equally plausible. Further dispute was prevented by the marriage of Conrad's pregnant widow, Isabel, to Henry of Champagne, a crusade veteran of two years and conveniently a nephew of both Richard and Philip II. With Richard distracted in Acre, in late July Saladin attempted to break the deadlock in southern Palestine with a surprise attack on Jaffa only to be thwarted by the sudden appearance of Richard himself at the head of a small scratch naval relief force. Saladin's failure at Jaffa gave Richard his most memorable and dramatic victory. It also proved to be the last shot at a military solution.

Both sides now sought a settlement. Saladin's political and financial capital was fast running out. Richard's health, poor since contracting a form of scurvy or trench-mouth at Acre, took a turn for the worse. He also learnt of serious threats to his power in England and France. The sticking point was Saladin's insistence on the demolition of the refortified walls at Ascalon, which Richard finally conceded in order to achieve an immediate deal. Under the Treaty of Jaffa (2 September 1192) a three-year truce was imposed across all remaining parts of Frankish Outremer. Palestine was to be partitioned, the Franks retaining Acre, Jaffa and the coast between. The walls of Ascalon were to be demolished; the plain around Ramla and Lydda was declared a condominium with open access to Christians and Muslims alike; Christian pilgrims were allowed to visit the Holy Sepulchre. To facilitate future pilgrim trade, Saladin separately conceded the presence of small numbers of Latin priests at the Holy Sepulchre, the Church of the Nativity in Bethlehem and the Church of the Annunciation in Nazareth. The crusaders' demand for the return of the relic of the True Cross lost at Hattin was dropped despite the relic being in Saladin's treasury. Richard left the Holy Land on 9 October. If he had delayed until the spring passage in 1193, as he had promised in June 1192, he would have been available when Saladin died in Damascus on 4 March 1193 and the Ayyubid Empire descended into intra-dynastic feuding.

Consequences

The timing of Saladin's death poses one of the many 'what ifs?' surrounding the Third Crusade: what if Saladin had pressed the siege of Tyre or the

WEAPONS

Except against pagans in the Baltic, crusade armies enjoyed no significant technological advantages over their opponents. Different social and economic conditions determined contrasting resources, training and battlefield tactics, as in the contrast between the mass male military habits of the horsemen of the Eurasian steppes and the selective mounted elites of the sedentary societies of Europe and the Near East. Emphasis consequently varied in the balance of infantry and cavalry, mounted or foot archers, close combat or mobile harrying. However, the fundamental tools of war were broadly similar, especially between crusaders and their Syrian Arab, Egyptian Fatimid or Iberian Moorish enemies: swords, bows, spears, lances, maces, axes, body armour and artillery.

Swords used by western European crusading knights could be around 75 cm long, sometimes longer, with two-edged blades, weighing around 1.5 kg, designed more for hacking and cutting than stabbing or thrusting (which may have been the function of daggers in close combat). Good swords were expensive, symbols as well as equipment for the socially elevated. Sword pommels could be decorated, part of a ubiquitous visual aesthetic of war that even extended to painted arrow shafts. Near Eastern straight swords, which tended to be narrower, were used alongside curved sabres. The best blades were western European, Chinese or Indian, and could be traded over thousands of miles: in one mid-thirteenth-century case (see p. 104) a Chinese sword appears to have reached Touraine in northern France via Syria, brought by a returning crusader. The intimacy of battle made the sword a central weapon for knights fighting on horseback or on foot. While lances and javelins were also used as offensive weapons, spears were employed by infantry in defence, to help shield cavalry or secure positions. Infantry also used weapons derived from agriculture – axes, flails, picks. Both infantry and cavalry on all sides used daggers and maces.

The most common civilian utensil used in war was the bow. Because of its importance in hunting, the simple bow, used by all fighting forces, was not socially exclusive to elites or commoners. Some regions – such as Wales or Armenia – seemed to specialise in producing archers. Given the limited range of

70. Weapons of war: bows, spears, axes, swords.

the simple bow dependent on basic muscle power, crossbows (or arbelasts) became popular as being more effective and over a much longer range; both aspects led to a wholly ineffectual ban by the Second Lateran Council in 1139 on use of the crossbow by Christians against any except the infidel, who also widely employed it. Only when the native Prussians acquired crossbow technology in the 1260s could they mount a real challenge to the Teutonic Knights. The longbow probably featured in Richard I's army on the Third Crusade. Archers played a central role in all forms of battles and sieges, to pin down the enemy, inflict casualties at long range, weaken opponents' resolve, and disrupt formations. They operated most effectively in open battle when coordinated with the cavalry or in sieges. The exception was the composite bow, made of wood, bone or horn and sinew, the weapon of the steppe horseman, essential to the Turkish tactic of harrying and feint.

Besides hand-held weaponry, artillery (throwing machines such as mangonels, petraries, trebuchets) was deployed extensively during the many sieges that dominated warfare in the Near East (see 'Sieges', p. 372). Eastern Mediterranean armies, but not crusaders or Outremer Franks it seems, also used Greek Fire, sometimes in grenade form.

Armour was conditioned by class and function. The western knight customarily wore a hauberk or body armour of chain mail (weight *c.* 11kg) with, by around 1200, added mail head cover (coif), leggings and mittens. Helmets were conical, rounded or pothelms, cylindrical with flat tops. Visors were introduced to help sight, breathing and ventilation. Chain mail and metal helmets were also used by Turkish and Arab mounted warriors. Shields were of wood and leather, kite-shaped with the Franks; small and round for the Turks. Plate armour began to be introduced in the west from the late twelfth century, but slowly. Surcoats were worn to reduce the heat of the metal armour that was worn over leather or textile padding. Horses could also be protected by various forms of armour. Turkish horses tended to be smaller than their Frankish counterparts, as the Turkish steppe environment precluded protected stud farms to selectively breed equine height and strength, a difference that literally supported the contrasting fighting traditions – the lighter-armed Turkish mounted archer against the heavily mailed Franks, who found the lack of suitable local horses a problem on long crusading campaigns.[28] Most fighters wore little protective clothing beyond perhaps a leather tunic; armour was sometimes improvised from kitchen pots and pans. The effectiveness of weaponry is attested by the archaeological evidence of wounds inflicted, direct testimony to the butchery of battle and the tenacity or courage of those involved.

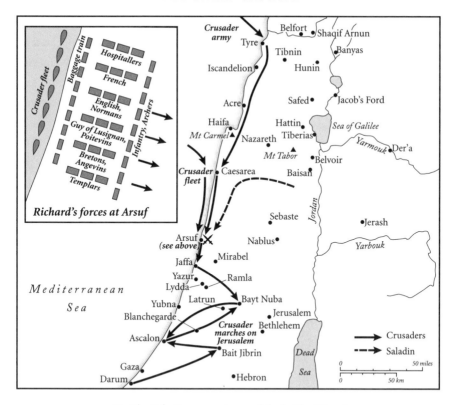

10. *The Palestine campaigns and the battle of Arsuf.*

annexation of Antioch in 1188 or had not released Guy of Lusignan in 1189; or Frederick Barbarossa's great army had reached Syria in 1190; or Richard had risked an assault on a nervous and panicked Jerusalem in January or June 1192; or he had been allowed to secure Ascalon before Saladin dismantled its fortifications in September 1191; or if he had arrived too late to relieve Jaffa in July 1192? The lasting impact of the Third Crusade rested on none of these, but on the striking conclusion of the transcendent redemptive mission and mass mobilisation of 1187–90 in the realpolitik treaty of Jaffa and the division of power over Palestine. The subsequent rhythm of Holy Land crusades was set by the expiry of the truces such as that of 1192 as much as by special political crises, and ended in negotiated agreements, usually to the crusaders' disadvantage. The failure to take Jerusalem in 1192 imposed military and logistical reality on future planners and recast the terms of propaganda. Richard's appreciation of the crucial importance of Egypt to the security of a restored Jerusalem became standard in theory and practice. The focus for recovery shifted, becoming the near-permanent business of the Holy Land, *negotium terrae sanctae*. In material terms, the Third Crusade bequeathed an example of tightly organised preaching, a carefully modulated coherent propaganda message, innovative financial expedients, and new strategies for sea transport, diplomacy and military objectives. However, the human cost was devastating. Out of ten leading companions of Duke Leopold V of Austria, nine died on the crusade. One veteran declared that of the 12,000 who arrived at Acre early in 1190, barely 100 were still alive by the summer of 1191. A sceptical observer from northern England reckoned a casualty rate of 75 per cent, while a confidant of Saladin quoted the Jerusalemite noble Balian of Ibelin as telling him that fewer than half of the westerners returned home.[29] Many of those who did had endured privations horrifying even by the standards of war. Not a few wondered at the price.

The experience of the Third Crusade also challenged the idea, popular with its promoters, that crusading represented a contest between irreconcilable opponents. It never did. Saladin's accommodating treatment of Outremer refugees and captives was just as typical of exchanges with the Franks as his massacre of members of the Military Orders after Hattin or the summary execution of prisoners after the killings at Acre. Third Crusade commanders' integration of war with diplomacy followed an Outremer tradition established during the First Crusade and pursued consistently thereafter. Frederick Barbarossa's pre-crusade treaty with Iconium operated as part of a pragmatic not confessional foreign policy. Arriving at Latakia in July 1188, Admiral Margarit of Sicily visited Saladin to warn him to his face of the impending onslaught from the west.[30] Both Richard and Philip began talks with Saladin as soon as they arrived at Acre; members of the local baronage never stopped dialogue with the sultan. Each side dealt with the other as fellow politicians not devils incarnate, a realism reflected in Richard's message to Saladin in July 1192: 'You and we together are ruined; our best course is to stop the bloodshed'.[31] After the Jaffa truce, Bishop Hubert Walter of Salisbury, unlike Richard, took advantage of the chance offered by the treaty to redeem his vows at the Holy Sepulchre. While in Jerusalem, he held convivial meetings with Saladin at which they gossiped about the qualities and failings of Richard I, and Walter persuaded the sultan to allow Latin clergy to officiate at the major Christian shrines in Jerusalem, Bethlehem and Nazareth. Such encounters stood far removed from the cartoonish demonisation of Saladin in the west four years earlier. Links

71. Hubert Walter's sandals, buskin and amice, buried with him and more than forty items of luxury textiles in 1205.

across the battle lines were not confined to diplomacy. On one occasion during his negotiations with al-Adil, Richard I asked to hear Arabic song, leading to a command performance by a local harp-playing chanteuse that the king apparently enjoyed. Among the booty from a great caravan captured by Richard's troops in June 1192 were notebooks belonging to a prominent Iraqi geographer and traveller, al-Harawi.[32] Once checked for military secrets (there were none), the notes were offered back to al-Harawi with an offer of compensation and an invitation to meet the king, which was declined. After the crusaders' departure, Henry of Champagne apparently sought and received robes and a turban from Saladin, which he wore as a sign of mutual respect.[33] For all the hostile rhetoric and pointedly crafted memories, while the Third Crusade perfected faith propaganda it also exposed how material accommodation was necessary to fulfil religious ambition. The following century was dominated by these two apparent opposites.

Socially and institutionally, the Third Crusade transformed the business of the cross. Rhetorically, the emotionally and politically inadequate result stood in lasting rebuke to the sins of Christendom. Increasingly crusading was cited as a metaphor for Christian struggle as the mass public involvement of 1188–92 extended its social reach. Privileges began to be offered beyond those who fought, with vow redemptions purchased by the wealthy. Pope Clement III (1187–91) offered shares in crusade indulgences to those who sent aid or proxies.[34] The extension of crusade privileges to noncombatants developed widely over the following century, broadening into a system of alms giving, partial rewards, vow redemptions and direct purchase of indulgences that extended the embrace of crusading far beyond those who took the cross, embedding it as a normative feature of western Christendom's devotional habits.

The German Crusade, 1195–8

The Third Crusade's immediate political legacy lay in the frequency of campaigns away from the Levant to which some or all of crusade elements – papal authority, vow, cross, preaching, spiritual and temporal privileges associated with the Jerusalem war – were applied. By the end of the 1190s, wars equated to Near East crusading, chiefly through remission of sins, had been proclaimed in Spain (including, in 1197, a crusade against a renegade Christian King Alfonso IX of León) and the north-east Baltic.[35] The nonagenarian Pope Celestine III (1191–8), a veteran of papal legations to Spain that encouraged wars against the Moors, proved an enthusiast. In the Holy Land the three-year truce of 1192 imposed its own timetable. The German crusade of 1195–8 marked the start of regular Holy Land crusades between 1192 and 1271. The new crusade was initiated early in 1195 by Emperor Henry VI of Germany out of personal commitment, dynastic tradition and political ambition.[36]

Having secured the throne of Sicily late in 1194 as husband to the legitimate heiress, Constance, Henry VI controlled suitable ports for a new eastern campaign. Successor, son and great-nephew of previous royal crusaders, Frederick Barbarossa and Conrad III respectively, Henry's interest in the eastern Mediterranean was more than sentimental. As part of his preparations, Henry consolidated imperial links with local rulers. In return for homage, he gave crowns to Aimery of Lusignan, ruler of Cyprus since the death of his brother Guy in 1194, and to Leo II of Cilician Armenia (Aimery was crowned by the bishop of Hildesheim in September 1197, Leo by the archbishop of Mainz in January 1198). Only after Henry's announcement of a crusade at Easter 1195 was Pope Celestine persuaded to back it (August 1195). Henry planned to provide a substantial military core, demanding tribute as well as military aid from the new Byzantine emperor, Alexius III (1195–1203), to pay for it. The threat of a revival of Sicilian aggression in the Balkans in the event of Greek refusal was clear. The resulting so-called Alamanikon (i.e. German) tax was thus a form of protection money. Extremely unpopular in Byzantium, signalling a more focused approach to forcing Greek assistance for crusading, born of the frustrations of 1147 and 1189, this aggressive policy to extract Greek aid found extreme expression during the Fourth Crusade (1201–4).

Preparations for the German crusade were at least as thorough as for the Third Crusade, the total number of Germans who embarked probably nearly matching those in 1189. Although preaching had been authorised across western Europe, the venture remained a national enterprise. Despite chronic ill-health, Henry emphasised his commitment in taking the cross and at a series of imperial diets in 1195–6. Recruitment revolved around Hohenstaufen loyalists, in particular from southern and western Germany, and those with existing or dynastic crusade associations. Contingents came from Lübeck, Bremen, Saxony, Thuringia, Franconia, Brabant, the Rhineland, Austria, Carinthia and Dalmatia. Departures were staggered across the spring and summer of 1197. A northern fleet of forty-four ships only arrived at the muster point of Messina in August; the main force reached Acre on 22 September, some months after the first arrivals. Cohesion was further compromised by the death of Henry in September 1197. Once in the Holy Land, the Germans managed to restore the Frankish position that had just been undermined by the accidental death of Henry of Champagne (he fell out of a window) and the loss of Jaffa to al-Adil, now sultan of Egypt, who had begun to unite the Ayyubid possessions under his leadership. In late October 1197 the Germans under Henry of Brabant recaptured Beirut and tried unsuccessfully to capture Toron in Galilee (November 1197–Februry 1198). Under German auspices the Jerusalem succession was settled in January 1198 by the marriage of Queen Isabel (her fourth at the age of twenty-five) to Aimery of Lusignan, who now added the crown of Jerusalem to that of Cyprus. News of the death of Henry VI and the desire of King Aimery to avoid further military provocation led to a truce with al-Adil that lasted from July 1198 to 1204. Beirut was retained by the Franks; Jaffa by al-Adil (it was returned by diplomacy in 1204).

The results of the German crusade failed to match its promise. Beirut provided an important link between Acre and the north and, during

THE SOCIOLOGY OF CRUSADING: WHO WENT?

The traditional image of crusaders depicts lords, knights and undifferentiated infantry, with the occasional addition of camp-followers and hangers-on. Emphasis is often afforded the contrast between the rich, and their followers, and the so-called poor, often characterised as undisciplined feckless zealots. In action and by promotion a gendered activity, the role of women was ignored, underestimated, denigrated or caricatured by largely misogynist clerical observers (see 'Women and the Crusade', p. 10). The reality was more complicated, mirroring increasingly diverse social structures in western Europe. No one embarked on crusade, or got very far, without assets, their own or those of a lord, employer, relative, neighbour, colleague, friend or fraternity. The term 'poor' represented a literary or theological construct more than a precise economic condition, at best a relative term embracing social and financial status, the unrich or the commoner, not just the impoverished or destitute. Campaign vicissitudes could alter status, a knight becoming, in one veteran's phrase, a 'pauper since yesterday'.[37] Non-combatant pilgrims, accompanying crusade armies for protection, a feature of forces travelling overland, could be pressed into military service. This economic and social fluidity within large crusade forces was reflected in the repeated need for additional common funds to bail out the impoverished outside the normal structures of subsidy by occupation, lords, associates or employers. It may also be noted that not all those on crusade, perhaps particularly among the domestic servants, were necessarily *crucesignati*.

The enterprise was inevitably dominated by the wealthy, powerful and militarily adept from the social elite, the knights Urban II appealed to, Bernard of Clairvaux's 'mighty men of valour'.[38] They provided the social, material, strategic and tactical leadership and warrior expertise. Surrounding them were men also trained in arms, either from lords' own military entourages and client networks or from the wide circle of smaller landholders or property-holders. The clergy, from bishops to writing clerks, served the spiritual and bureaucratic needs of crusade armies, as well as, in many cases, leading their own regiments and assisting in military operations. The network of actually, potentially or

72. A demotic image from a thirteenth-century engraved ceramic.

partially self-funded crusaders was joined by prosperous burgesses, many of whose occupations were solely civilian not military. In some crusading arenas, such as the Baltic and on certain Mediterranean crusades, urban mercantile involvement proved crucial.

Chronicles, government records, crusader wills and evidence from fund-raising property deals identify commoner crusaders with occupations that were integral to the military establishment: sergeants, squires, engineers, archers, crossbowmen, infantry troops, steersmen and sailors. These were joined by an array of household servants, officials and hangers-on: priests, clerks, pages, valets, cooks, dog-handlers, farriers, grooms, horse-boys, butlers, seneschals, stewards, marshals, constables, chamberlains, notaries, physicians, minstrels and laundresses (who doubled as de-lousers on the Third Crusade and probably on other campaigns). Wealthy crusaders travelled in often lavishly ostentatious style, display and consumption remaining part of the performance of lordship on crusade as elsewhere: some thirteenth-century crusaders' wills expose truly astonishing levels of luxury. A wider circle of crusading artisans could provide necessary supporting services, some employed by the knightly leaders, others perhaps freelance: judges, academics, schoolmasters, rectors, vicars, provosts, archdeacons, merchants, moneychangers, goldsmiths, blacksmiths, carpenters, carters, ditchers, masons, millers, bakers, barbers, surgeons, physicians, butchers, weavers, fishmongers, cobblers, tailors, dyers, potters, vintners, peasants and prostitutes who, on Louis IX's 1249–50 campaign in Egypt, appear to have been organised in brothels by members of the royal household.[39] Disapproving clerical commentators suggested that crusading held special attractions for criminals, perhaps lured by the legal protection afforded crusaders, the need to make themselves scarce, or the potential pickings in the chaotic conditions of often cash-rich crusader camps. Within artisan categories status varied enormously: some dyers were international entrepreneurs, while master chefs operated on a far elevated social and economic plane from the scullions who defended the crusader camp at Constantinople with pots and pestles in 1203. Not all artisans were likely to have signed up to ply their trades on campaign, their occupations being recorded more as a means of identification in domestic legal and fiscal records. Nonetheless crusading can be seen as much as a phenomenon of artisans as of knights, of carpentry as much as of castles. Like other wars, crusading attracted a preponderance of young men. Yet the bulk of crusaders came from rural and urban underclasses. At the bottom of the scale, men and women took the cross with the most modest of incomes, small farmers and villeins teetering on the edge of serfdom with property worth only a few shillings a year.[40]

Yet, in whatever reduced circumstances, when they took the cross these crusaders possessed some subsistence of their own and enjoyed sufficient freedoms to take the cross and enjoy the material privileges of protection of property, debt relief, delay in answering lawsuits and the right, even as tenants, to seek mortgages. However, most lacked freedom of choice or action outside the orbits of landed or urban elites. With few exceptions (see 'The Children's Crusade', p. 258), the image of crowds spontaneously leaving fields or workshops to follow the cross is largely mythical, the fictions of preachers, commentators and canon law designed to emphasise the supposed spontaneity of religious commitment – taking the cross an epiphany of faith or a spasm of spiritual fervour. In reality, crusade recruitment relied on property and planning, while crusade armies, microcosms of the society that produced them, were held together by cats' cradles of formal and informal mutual dependence, lordship, booty, handouts and, for many, pay, in cash and kind.

preparations in 1196, Henry VI had obtained papal privileges for the fledgling, still non-military Teutonic Hospitaller Order. The truce of 1198 supplied the context and timetable for the next campaign, initiated in August 1198 by the new pope, Innocent III. Although Henry VI's death prevented further exploration of imperial influence over Cyprus and Armenia, he bequeathed the policy to his son and ultimate heir Frederick II (b. 1194; king of Germany, 1212–50). Nonetheless, the German crusade demonstrated the effectiveness of the tested Third Crusade techniques of preaching, recruitment and funding; the need for central payment of troops; and the comparative ease and speed of sea passage to Palestine from friendly ports. The popularity of the crusade beyond the noble elites pointed to the creation of a broadening social engagement with the wars of the cross, a phenomenon exploited to the full in the remarkable pontificate of Innocent III (1198–1216).

A PALACE IN BEIRUT

Sometime in the late summer or early autumn of 1211 an aristocratic German traveller Wilbrand of Oldenburg (d. 1233) arrived in the Levant port of Beirut. Wilbrand, son of Count Henry II of Oldenburg, was a canon of Hildesheim, later rising to the bishopric of Paderborn and archbishopric of Utrecht. Besides his main purpose in the east as ambassador from the German King Otto IV to King Leo of Armenia, Wilbrand took the opportunity to make a tour of the region, taking in the Holy Places, later writing up an account of his journey.[41] Beirut had been recaptured from the Ayyubids by the German crusade of 1197 and by 1211 was in the hands of John of Ibelin (*c.* 1179–1236), known as the Old Lord of Beirut. The son of Balian of Ibelin and Maria Comnena, widow of King Amalric, John, half-brother to Isabel I (q. 1190–1205), acted as regent of the kingdom of Jerusalem from 1205 to 1210 on behalf of his niece, Isabel's daughter, Mary of Montferrat (b. 1192; q. 1205–12). John rebuilt Beirut's fortifications including the castle by the sea.

Within one of its towers, with wide views across the harbour on one side and fields and orchards on the other, John constructed domestic quarters, including what a clearly intrigued and awestruck Wilbrand described as a very ornate

73. Beirut, a nineteenth-century view.

palatium, or hall where the lord and his courtiers could relax. The marble floor mimicked a sandy seashore, with 'water agitated by a light breeze', giving anyone walking on it the impression of wading through water. The *trompe l'oeil* effect was maintained by ceiling frescoes of scudding clouds in a windy sunny sky, 'there the sun to define the year and months, the days and weeks, and the hours and seconds by its movement in the zodiac', and walls of marble inlay imitating curtains. In the centre of the hall stood a pool of marble flowers, at its centre animals and a dragon fountain whose spray, in hot weather, cooled the air wafting in from windows on every side of the hall.

Almost as striking as what Wilbrand describes is his own alertness to natural details – the wading through water on a sandy shore; the chasing clouds; the views of ships and orchards from the windows, etc. Wilbrand also reveals that the workmanship on John's palace came from Syrian Christian, Greek Orthodox and local Muslim craftsmen, a sign that beneath law and politics Outremer was positively as well as exploitatively multicultural, at least in major building works and prestige artistic projects.[42] Similar cross-cultural cooperation and influences can be seen elsewhere in religious art and architecture and manuscript production. The quality of marble appears comparable to the best examples in the great mosques of Damascus or Jerusalem. The decorative programme in Beirut opens vistas onto the secular domestic lifestyle of Outremer Franks, or at least the fabulously rich ones such as John of Ibelin. Although a grand, privileged noble ambassador, Wilbrand cannot have been the only western traveller impressed by such visible evidence of the riches of the east. The great hall at Beirut cannot have been unique in lavishness. While not a stone, flake of paint or marble chipping survives from John's palace, Wilbrand's testimony suggests that behind the austere facade of castle walls the lords of Outremer lived in a style of luxury and cultural eclecticism not far removed from that of their Arab, Turk and Mamluk neighbours.

74. *Mosaic of date palm, horses and water, Great Mosque, Damascus, a possible parallel to those in the palace of Beirut.*

2. Kings and Queens of Jerusalem
1192–1291

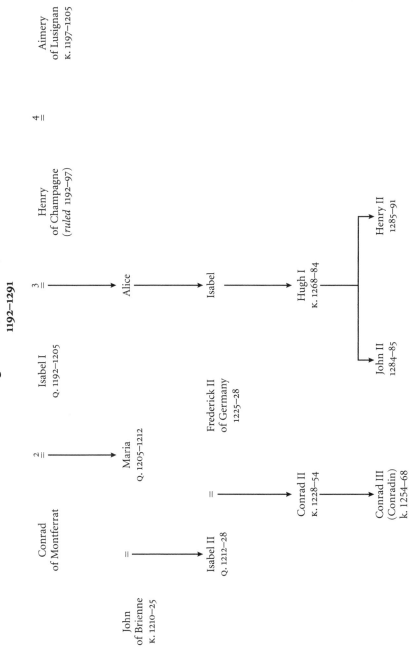

CHAPTER SIX

RESHAPING THE EASTERN MEDITERRANEAN: EGYPT AND THE CRUSADES, 1200–1250

Egypt and the Crusades

'This is a mighty affair. Great forces have passed thither long ago on various occasions. I will tell you what it is like; it is like a lap dog yapping at a mastiff, who takes little heed of him.'[1] The French nobleman and Levant veteran Erard of Valery was attempting to inject a note of realism into discussions in 1274 for a new planned attack on the Mamluk sultanate of Egypt while recognising the thirteenth-century consensus that the key to power in the Levant lay on the Nile.[2] Although proving a geopolitical cul-de-sac, appreciation of the importance of Egypt was as old as the crusades themselves. When the armies of the First Crusade arrived in Syria in the winter of 1097–8, they immediately confronted Egypt's importance and the threat it posed to western conquests in Palestine, negotiating with the Fatimids, each eager to seek common cause against the Seljuks. The thirteenth-century historian ibn al-Athir fancifully suggested the Fatimids had invited the crusaders into Syria for that purpose.[3] Crusader-Fatimid discussions only ceased a few weeks before the crusaders advanced into southern Palestine to besiege Fatimid-held Jerusalem in June and July 1099. One veteran recalled the leaders debating whether they should attack Egypt: 'if through God's grace we could conquer the kingdom of Egypt, we would not only acquire Jerusalem but also Alexandria, Cairo and many kingdoms'. Against this, it was successfully argued that the expedition lacked sufficient numbers to have any chance of lasting success.[4] The importance of Egypt was confirmed when the crusaders had to defend their capture of Jerusalem from a Fatimid relief army. Thereafter, no Latin ruler in Palestine ignored Egypt.

As the Fatimid caliphate crumbled, kings of Jerusalem took advantage with sporadic raids on the Nile Delta. By the 1160s they were extracting regular tributes from a succession of tottering regimes in Cairo. The stakes were of the highest. In 1200, during preparations for the Fourth Crusade, Innocent III admitted the insufficiency of land and population in the Holy Land alone to sustain many artisans and agriculturalists from the west.[5] One way out of this bind was to leech onto Egypt's monetised economy, already being tapped by Italian merchants. Short of conquest, protection money produced gold to pay for troops and defences. This was a game more than one could play. In the 1160s and 1170s the kings of Jerusalem competed directly with Nur al-Din and his Kurdish generals; the ultimate victory of Saladin secured for him precisely what the Latins had hoped for themselves, Egypt's gold allowing him to reward followers and recruit vast companies of soldiers he then employed to overawe rivals in Syria and encircle the Latin principalities.[6] The need to contain, accommodate, coerce or exploit Egypt remained a constant in all western Holy Land strategies.

To recruit for an Egyptian war required a plausible narrative of urgency and obligation: Egypt was not Jerusalem. Sensitivity to criticism of diversion promoted the concealment by the leaders of the Fourth Crusade of the agreement with Venice in 1201 to attack Egypt.[7] Crusade propagandists sought rhetorical devices from scripture: in Exodus, the path to the Holy Land had come from the Nile, a precedent Innocent III used in citing the overthrow of Pharaoh before the Fourth Crusade. The Exodus story invited spiritual analogies: Isaiah 31:3: 'Egypt is man and not God', the epitome of transient materialism.[8] A second rhetorical device placed Egypt in a cosmic setting. Throughout western European media, Cairo and by extension Egypt was known as Babylon, injecting the right note of eternal spiritual conflict into the otherwise severely material business of dealing with a serious political problem. The military challenge was recognised by Richard I during the Palestine war of 1191–2 when, as part of his diplomatic dance with Saladin, he floated a plan in October 1191 to hire (at 50 per cent of cost) a Genoese fleet to ferry his troops to attack the Nile in the summer of 1192.[9] The following century saw two major western invasions of Egypt (1218–21 and 1249–50); one aborted effort (1202–4); and earnest diplomacy backed by armed force, as in 1228–9 and 1239–41.

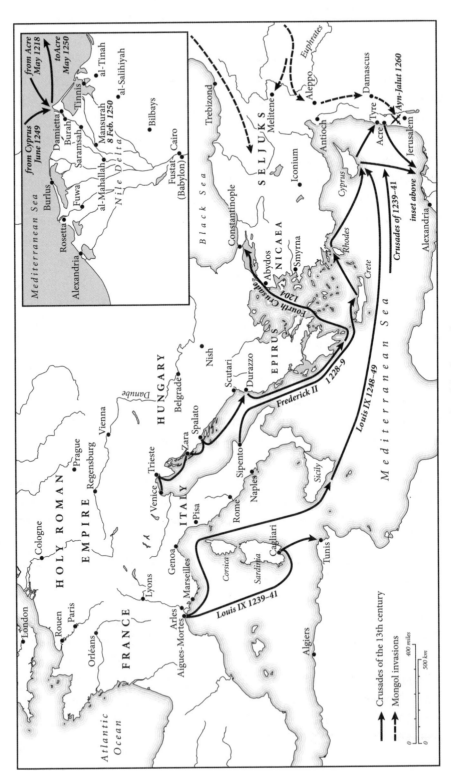

11. *Eastern crusades of the thirteenth century.*

The Fourth Crusade, 1198–1205

The first test of the policy came in 1198 when the new pope, Innocent III (1198–1216), summoned a crusade to shore up the gains and restore the losses of the German Crusade. The truce of 1198, set to last until 1204, only covered hostilities in Syria and Palestine, implicitly marking Egypt as a target. Innocent sought first-hand intelligence on the state of the Ayyubid Empire and Sultan al-Adil's power. Logistics of an invasion had been made easier by the Latin conquest of Cyprus, the western alliance with Cilician Armenia and the recapture of Acre and other Palestinian ports. Innocent attempted unsuccessfully to engage Alexius III of Byzantium in an eastern Mediterranean coalition. The subsequent Venetian involvement in the Fourth Crusade was driven by the prospect of trading privileges in Alexandria and other Egyptian ports where Venice had been overshadowed by competitors such as Genoa. In the event, although the bulk of the Fourth Crusade diverted to Constantinople, where Venice already held the commercial whip-hand, some contingents separately reached Acre and joined a raid on the Nile in 1204.[10]

Recruitment for Innocent III's new crusade began despite dynastic rivalries, civil wars and succession disputes in France, England and Germany that prohibited royal participation. Networks of preachers were appointed by the end of 1198, including a prominent charismatic publicist, Fulk of Neuilly. The death of Richard I in April 1199 opened the way for his allies in France, such as the counts of Flanders, Blois and St Pol, to reach accommodation with Philip II. Taking the cross operated as part of the process of reconciliation, binding former enemies to an honourable common enterprise approved by the king. In a coordinated sequence, the cousins, the counts of Blois and Champagne, took the cross at Ecry in November 1199; the pope appointed crusade legates and instituted a clerical income tax of a fortieth to help pay for the expedition in December 1199 (the failure of which cast a financial shadow over the whole enterprise); preaching was authorised from Ireland to Hungary; the count of Flanders, the count of Champagne's brother-in-law, took the cross in February 1200, followed shortly by the count of St Pol. At meetings in the summer of 1200 at Soissons and Compiègne the sea route east was agreed and ambassadors despatched to Italy to negotiate a shipping contract. With neither Genoa nor Pisa interested, the ambassadors concluded a treaty with Venice in April 1201.

INNOCENT III

Lothar (1160/1–1216; pope 1198–1216) was the son of the count of Segni, a town south-east of Rome, and nephew of Pope Clement III (1187–91). After studying theology in Paris and canon law at Bologna, Lothar was appointed a cardinal by his uncle in 1190. His early writings show an intense engagement with the image of the cross as a metaphor for the spiritual reality of a Christian life. Although sidelined during the pontificate of the nonagenarian Celestine III (1191–8), he was quickly elected pope on the same day as his predecessor's death. The election of a thirty-seven-year-old signalled a decisive move away from the line of cautious, usually elderly curial veterans who had tended to be preferred over the previous half-century. Innocent proved to be one of the most dynamic and effective popes of the Middle Ages. His policies revolved around the assertion of papal ecclesiastical and temporal rights and spiritual authority; the development of church reform through the evangelisation of the laity and the exercise of canon law; and the material protection of the faith against heretics and infidels. In the scope, detail and success of advocacy and development of the crusade, Innocent proved to be the most significant pope after Urban II. Innocent's marriage of theological clarity to institutional frameworks established the character of official crusading for following generations.

While in general terms more of a codifier than an absolute innovator, Innocent clarified the nature of the crusade indulgence to include remission of sins not just penance; instituted crusade taxation of the clergy (in 1215, after an aborted attempt in 1199); organised comprehensive papal licensing of regional crusade preaching across western Christendom (1198); proposed proportionate indulgences according to contributions below actual service (an idea canvassed as early as 1157 by Hadrian IV); and offered redemptions of crusade vows to any who wished to take the cross but were unable to fulfil their vows in action (1213, building on an idea of Clement III). Vow redemptions, clerical taxes and donations transformed crusade finance. From Innocent's reign regular special prayers and processions for the crusade became familiar across western Europe, as did the appearance of chests in local churches to receive alms and donations. More indirectly, his sponsorship of the early Dominican and Franciscan friars

75. Innocent III.

presaged their later rise to dominate crusade preaching. The great crusade decrees *Quia Maior* (1213) and *Ad Liberandam* (1215) provided lasting rhetorical and administrative templates. Innocent extended crusade privileges to political conflicts in southern Italy and Sicily (1199); to campaigns against Languedoc heretics (1208–9), Spanish Moors (1212) and, partially, to the Baltic. The Fourth Lateran Council (1215) provided the cornerstone of Innocent's policies. Summoned to confront reform, heresy and the crusade, the council approved the instruments as well as principles in support of Innocent's embracive concept of evangelising the laity through offering sacramental, penitential and physical protection in a Christendom directed by the Church and united under papal authority. The crusade combined Innocent's core message of penance, redemption and active obligations demanded by Christ of all the faithful. Beyond political, polemical and administrative skills, Innocent was no armchair organiser. After losing control of the Fourth Crusade, he ensured close papal involvement in the Fifth, engaging in active proselytising. A seasoned preacher in Latin and the Italian vernacular, not afraid to extemporise, his sudden death in July 1216 may well have been hastened by his exhausting public preaching tour for his new eastern crusade.

The Venetian treaty, for all its later infamy, displayed understanding of what an invasion of Egypt required. For 85,000 marks, payable in four instalments from August 1201 to April 1202, the Venetians contracted to supply ships, including specialist horse-carrying *huissiers*, for an army of 4,500 knights, with horses, 9,000 squires and 20,000 infantry, along with provisions for men and beasts for up to a year. The Venetians would additionally contribute a fleet of fifty galleys at their own expense, as well as the crews for the crusader ships, who could have numbered as many as 30,000. This great armada, after mustering at Venice on 29 June 1202, was to sail directly to Egypt, avoiding breaking the 1198 Syrian truce. The scale of the enterprise matched the ambition. To fulfil the Venetians' contractual obligation to build, equip and man the fleet, Doge Enrico Dandolo imposed a moratorium on all other commercial activity.[11] While the cost per head was in tune with previous shipping contracts, such as Philip II's with Genoa in 1190, the Venetian deal assumed not only the deep pockets of the crusade leaders but also that large numbers of those not directly attached to them would take advantage of the transport on offer. The former assumption may not have been too fanciful. Count Theobald of Champagne, the leading protagonist of the crusade in northern France before his early death in May 1201, budgeted for 50,000 marks to pay for his own and hired troops. It was the failure of sufficient numbers of independent crusaders to arrive in Venice in 1202 that scuppered the Venetian deal, threatening the whole enterprise. While the northern French core of the leadership remained robustly committed to the Venetian deal, and publicised the muster widely across France and Germany, thousands of recruits sought other more convenient ports. Even some followers of the counts of Flanders and Blois used southern Italian ports rather than Venice, while a Flemish fleet partly sponsored by Count Baldwin made its own way to the Holy Land.[12] The pope recognised this lack of unanimity by sending one legate to Venice and the other to Acre.

The preaching campaign followed previous patterns with local clerics and the Cistercians featuring prominently. Centred on Flanders, Champagne, the Ile de France and the Loire valley, recruitment extended from the British Isles to Italy, from Saxony to Provence. Fulk of Neuilly's preaching became notorious, both for its powerful effect and its ignominious end when he was accused of embezzlement of the alms he had collected.[13] The geographic breadth and moral force of the preaching campaign cut across political divi-

76. Venice.

sions. On the death of Theobald of Champagne in 1201, the French leaders chose as their nominal commander the well-connected northern Italian Boniface, marquis of Montferrat, from a family with extensive previous associations with Byzantium and the Holy Land as well as Germany, where Boniface's cousin, Duke Philip of Swabia, was a claimant to the throne.

Perhaps between 12,000 and 15,000 troops arrived at Venice during the summer of 1202. Although comparable with the largest crusader hosts, this fell far short of the numbers envisaged in the 1201 treaty, leaving the crusade leaders scrabbling to fulfil the financial terms. Despite a levy on every crusader at Venice, the leaders' personal funds and heavy borrowing, 34,000 marks remained outstanding, 40 per cent of the agreed price, presenting the crusaders and Venetians with the mutually unpalatable prospect of abandoning the expedition and the waste of an extremely powerful armed and mobile fighting force. To save a return on their great investment, the Venetians proposed a moratorium on the debt. This would now be repaid from profits on future conquests, beginning with the Dalmatian port of Zara (Zadar), despite it being a Christian city under the protection of the king of Hungary, who in 1202 happened to be a *crucesignatus*. The attack on Egypt was postponed to 1203. In return, the doge committed himself and the city more firmly to the crusade as active allies and participants, not just shippers. Although acknowledged as inappropriate, the Zara plan was accepted by the leadership, including the papal legate Peter of Capuano, as the only way of continuing the crusade. The high command showed their queasiness at the whole business by keeping most crusaders in the dark even after the fleet left Venice in early October 1202. The pope was less easily deflected; he sent letters prohibiting the attack and threatening all who took part with excommunication.

The goal of Egypt remained. The intensity with which the high command faced down papal objections and dissidents within their own ranks uneasy at fighting fellow Christians rested on the understanding that only such a large force had any chance of making an impact on Ayyubid power and so needed to be kept in being by agreeing to Venetian terms. This appreciation of the costs of the military requirements explains the attraction of the offer made by Alexius Angelus, nephew of Alexius III, son of the deposed Isaac II Angelus and claimant to the Greek throne. Backed by his brother-in-law, Philip of Swabia, and Boniface of Montferrat, Alexius attached himself to the crusade army at Zara in December 1202, promising, in return for being placed on the Byzantine throne, to assist the crusade with 10,000 Greek troops and 200,000 marks for the invasion of Egypt.[14] Despite offering a reunion of the Greek Church with Rome, Alexius had failed to secure the support of Innocent III, who still hoped for a rapprochement with Alexius III. Yet through the good offices of Boniface and later Doge Dandolo, Alexius presented the crusaders with an apparently alluring opportunity to gain Byzantine support and re-endow the crusade.

The seizure of Zara in November 1202 fitted a pattern of plundering familiar from both the First and Third Crusades, the latter's predation on Sicily and Cyprus showing that violence against Christians in pursuit of funds and provisions was not the novel prerogative of the Fourth Crusade. As Count Hugh of St Pol later explained, without more funds to pay for soldiers and materiel, the goal of Jerusalem was impossible.[15] Nonetheless,

3. Montferrat Family

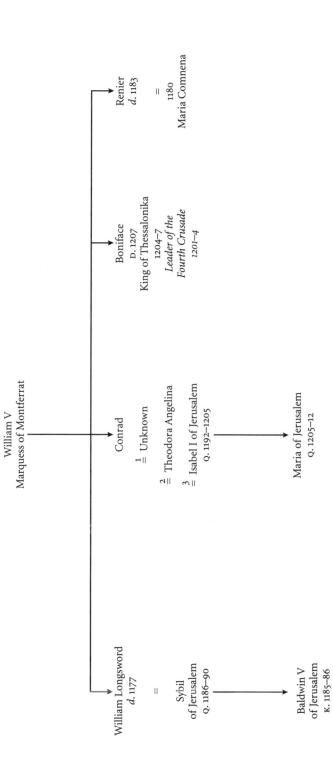

William V
Marquess of Montferrat

William Longsword
d. 1177

=

Sybil
of Jerusalem
Q. 1186–90

Baldwin V
of Jerusalem
K. 1185–86

Conrad

¹= Unknown

²= Theodora Angelina

³= Isabel I of Jerusalem
Q. 1192–1205

Maria of Jerusalem
Q. 1205–12

Boniface
D. 1207
King of Thessalonika
1204–7
*Leader of the
Fourth Crusade*
1201–4

Renier
d. 1183

=
1180
Maria Comnena

A SPRING DAY IN BASEL, 1201

During the spring of 1201 news of the fresh expedition to recover Jerusalem and rescue the Holy Land continued to circulate in the valley of the Upper Rhine in south-western Germany. In the city of Basel (now in north-west Switzerland) the year before, in May 1200, the city's bishop had taken the cross with a number of local abbots and monks, a gesture of ecclesiastical solidarity that appeared to lead to no immediate concerted general effort of promotion. By contrast, a year later, advance notice had prepared an expectant crowd of clergy and laity to gather in the cathedral, dedicated to the Virgin Mary but known locally as the Münster, then probably still a building site as the church was being restored after a devastating fire in 1185. The physical renewal and restoration provided an appropriate image and setting for what they had come to hear: the cross being preached by Abbot Martin of the Cistercian abbey of Pairis in Alsace, one of the local clerics authorised by Pope Innocent III to preach the cross in the diocese of Basel. The sermon had evidently been well publicised, the monk of Pairis who recorded the event a few years later noting that the large crowd, 'prepared in their hearts to enlist in Christ's camp, were hungrily anticipating an exhortation of this sort'. When Abbot Martin stood up in Basel cathedral that spring day he was preaching to the choir. As with modern evangelism, crusade promotion was carefully planned with advance publicity ensuring good attendance at its functions.

Martin's sermon operated as a focus in a series of ritualised responses. Rumours of the crusade and Martin's arrival created a fraught atmosphere of expectation and aspiration, tensions released during and after the sermon through emotional gestures: weeping, groaning, sighing and sobbing, emotionalism encouraged by the preacher who led the lachrymose histrionics. The sermon itself, recorded as a literary performance evoking the Cistercian tradition of crusade evangelism and clearly modelled on Bernard of Clairvaux's preaching, crystallised the papal appeal to Christians to acknowledge the transcendent redemptive importance of the Holy Land and their warriors' duty to 'hasten to help Christ', encouraged by the glorious crusading past, the prospect of future reconquest, and the bargain of spiritual and temporal gain, the latter quite explicit: 'in the matter if the kingdom of heaven, there is an unconditional pledge; in the matter of temporal prosperity, a better than average hope'. The whole show was completed by the abbot giving out crosses and promising to join the crusade. The account of Martin's sermon that spring day in Basel introduces a laudatory narrative of the abbot recruiting a regional contingent in which he takes a leading role on campaign, the story culminating in justifying his act of grand larceny during the sack of Constantinople when he and his chaplain filled their habits with over fifty looted relics from those of the Passion, Christ's life, body parts of John the Baptist and the Apostles, to pieces of lesser

77. *The Münster, Basel, site of Abbot Martin's sermon.*

saints such as the seventh-century Merovingian abbess Adelgonde or Agricius, the fourth-century first bishop of Trier. The relics were carried back by Martin to adorn his monastery of Pairis. His day in Basel formed just one act in this drama, but, in formal literary remembrance at least, it incorporated elements familiar across western Christendom at the opening of the thirteenth century: papal authority and influence over the promotional process; the central recruiting themes of Christian obligation, the urgent plight of the Holy Land, the importance of past glories, the unambiguous offer of spiritual and material profit. The crowds assembled in Basel Münster knew what they were there for and expected the performance Abbot Martin delivered, all concerned playing their choreographed parts in the cause of the cross. In fact, Martin may not have been at all remarkable; even fellow Cistercians who wrote of the Fourth Crusade never mention him.[16]

the capture of Zara threatened to end the campaign, exciting vocal opposition within the army – 'I have not come here to destroy Christians,' said one dissenter[17] – and a papal letter excommunicating any who took part. The letter was suppressed by the leadership in deft information management. Subsequently, faced with disbanding the crusade or tolerating its insubordination, Pope Innocent tacitly acceded to allowing the crusaders to avoid excommunication while travelling on the ships of the still-excommunicated Venetians. Even Innocent's prohibition on further attacks on Christians was qualified in cases of obstruction or necessity.[18] Disquiet over Alexius's plan persisted over the winter of 1202–3 at Zara and the following April when the fleet moved on to Corfu. While many deserted, the need for re-endowing carried the day. The Venetian-crusader fleet sailed on to Constantinople, which was reached, without any effective local resistance, on 24 June 1203.

The Greek failure to contest the crusaders' passage through the Hellespont provided a mixed augury. Weak Byzantine defences – apparently the Greek emperor had only twenty 'rotting and worm-eaten small skiffs' at his disposal[19] – suggested a decayed fiscal and administrative regime, hardly a solid basis for the promised lavish aid. However, Greek land forces, chiefly paid foreign troops, provided consistently stiff opposition in a series of encounters in and around Constantinople between June 1203 and April 1204. It is tempting to see the events of 1203–4 as a dual culmination: of long-standing hostility to devious, aloof and schismatic Byzantium; and of prolonged decline in Greek imperial power. Neither is fully justified. Each large crusade army that passed through Byzantium had encountered supply difficulties and diplomatic tensions, yet suggestions for conquest had repeatedly been rejected. By contrast, the 1203 crusaders' initial intervention was framed as a restoration of a legitimate heir who would then support the crusade and reunite the Greek Church with Rome. This differed from the sustained territorial ambitions of the Norman Sicilian rulers in the Balkans and Greece such as had led to the brief capture of Thessalonika in 1185. For many interested powers in the west, including the papacy, Byzantium was still seen as a potential, if awkwardly inscrutable, ally, enmity revolving around shifting political advantage not fundamental alienation. Religion and commerce bound as much as they divided. Even the often fraught Byzantine–Venetian relationship had been eased with Greek payment of reparations for attacks in 1182 on the Venetian community in Constantinople and the restoration of Venetian trading privileges. Byzantine imperial power had appeared impressive until dynastic feuding in the 1180s loosened central grip, so that by 1203 islands and provinces had begun to assume increased autonomy, a process the crusaders' conquest of the capital in 1204 did nothing to reverse.

The diversion to Constantinople was regarded by the crusaders as a means of keeping alive prospects of campaigning in the Levant. For the Venetians it offered an opportunity to further recoup their massive capital outlay; consolidate existing trading rights; and sustain the hope of breaking into the even more lucrative Egyptian market. However, immediately on

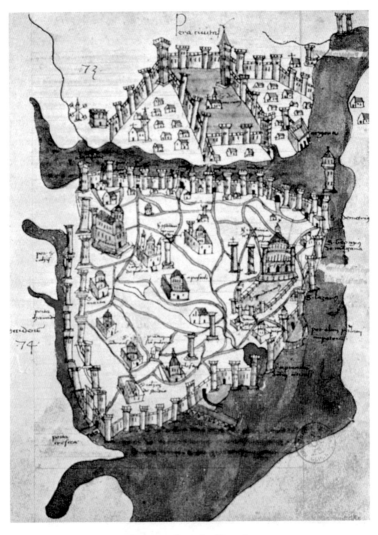

78. Constantinople in the fifteenth century.

arrival at Constantinople, westerners' expectations were confounded. Far from being welcomed as a liberator or returning hero, young Alexius was greeted with armed resistance. Even after his assumption of power following the crusaders' assault on the city in July 1203 and the flight of Alexius III, Alexius, now Alexius IV, attracted sullen Greek acceptance at best, a political situation further complicated by the unscheduled emergence from prison and restoration of the blinded Isaac II, who then ruled dysfunctionally with his son. To sustain his position, Alexius IV agreed new contracts with the crusaders securing their help for another year in return for more guarantees of assistance for a future Levant campaign. To pay for the deal, Alexius stripped Constantinople of treasure, consolidating Greek hostility to the foreigners and further isolating himself. The presence of the crusaders, camped at Galata across the Golden Horn from the city, with their demands on food supplies, added to the febrile atmosphere as winter closed in. With the Venetian fleet and crusaders' camp coming under attack from Greek dissidents, a confused series of palace coups ended in February 1204 with Alexius IV and his father dead and a new emperor, an anti-westerner, Alexius V, committed to destroy the crusaders.

Their deteriorating position left the crusaders few options. As one account recalled, 'they were neither able to enter the sea without danger of imminent death nor delay longer on land because of their impending exhaustion of food and supplies'.[20] Without supplies, money or seaworthy ships, their only escape lay through the city. Lingering doubts over attacking fellow Christians were allayed by clergy insisting that combating schismatics, regicides and oath-breakers who were impeding the cause of the Holy Land was both legitimate and meritorious, earning indulgences for those who died in the fighting.[21] The crusaders would take by force what the Byzantines had failed or refused to provide under treaty or alliance. In March 1204 the crusaders and Venetians agreed a new contract that settled the distribution of booty from the city, including the final settlement of the original crusader debt, and set the arrangements for carving up power within the Byzantine Empire once the city had fallen. The crusaders agreed to delay their departure east for yet another year, to March 1205, deferring the Egyptian campaign for the fourth time since 1202. The plan was a desperate throw; no foreign army had captured Constantinople since its foundation nine centuries before.

The final attack began on 9 April 1204. In the ensuing capture and sack of the city between 12 and 15 April the crusaders killed thousands of civilians, desecrated churches, destroyed buildings, and looted the city of the moveable wealth that had survived the fiscal predations of Alexius IV and a devastating fire the previous August. The sack of Constantinople was calculated and controlled after the first day of mayhem, the plundering systematic. It was not in the conquerors' interests to allow unbridled destruction of what was to become their new capital. It has been estimated that the total value of the plunder, in addition to 10,000 horses, may have been around 800,000 marks, enough to fund a substantial western European state for over a decade.[22] On top of this were boatloads of relics stolen not exclusively but chiefly by clerics – 'holy robbers'[23] – for whom such sacred loot constituted investment in their home churches' future prosperity (see 'Sacred Booty', p. 250). The gluttonous sack of Constantinople, while not outside the brutal military conventions of the time, struck contemporaries from ibn al-Athir in Mosul to Innocent III in Rome, no less than Byzantines and later observers, as an atrocity in its scale of rapine, slaughter and wanton destruction of centuries of classical and Christian civilisation.[24]

The capture of Constantinople did not end the Fourth Crusade. Baldwin of Flanders, chosen by the conquerors as the new emperor, insisted at his coronation that the relief of the Holy Land remained the objective for the following year. Only after defeats in 1205 at the hands of Bulgarians and Greeks did the papal legate unilaterally absolve the crusaders in Greece of their Holy Land vows, to the unrestrained but impotent fury of Innocent III. However, not all crusaders had joined the Constantinople excursion or travelled east via Venice. Substantial contingents, including the large Flemish fleet with Countess Marie of Flanders on board, sailed directly to Acre, perhaps up to a fifth of those nobles who took the cross in 1199–1200, with as many as 300 knights reaching the Holy Land, in comparison with the 500 to 700 knights at the Byzantine capital.[25] These Holy Land crusaders joined King Aimery of Jerusalem in raids into Galilee and to the Jordan, as well as a naval sortie in May 1204 to the Nile Delta port of Fuwa, which they briefly occupied and ransacked. This aggression encouraged al-Adil to reach a six-year truce favourable to the Franks.

While meagre in its impact on the Levant, the Fourth Crusade exerted a profound influence on future crusading. The schism with the Greek Church was rendered unbridgeable except as a paper diplomatic convenience. Consequent rule over parts of the Balkans, Greece and the Greek islands accelerated direct western investment and exploitation of the region that lasted into the early modern period. Yet western immigration remained a minority concern, initially largely confined to networks of northern French noble houses and the Venetians. The occupation of Latin Greece – or Romania as it was known in the west – hardly deflected support for the remaining outposts of Outremer. Attempts to harness crusades to defend Latin Greece met lukewarm responses from the 1230s and did not materially deprive the Holy Land of aid. More widely, the scale of planning and resources needed for any Egyptian enterprise had been clearly demonstrated.

Invasions: The Fifth Crusade, 1217–21

The Fourth Crusade prompted a refashioning of funding and administration when Innocent III launched a new mass eastern crusade in 1213. The bull *Quia Maior* offered the crusade *remissio peccatorum*, remission of sins, to anyone who contributed by personal service, proxy, subsidy or other material assistance. At the same time, overturning the official line adopted since Urban II, there was to be no restriction or test of suitability on who could take the cross, with the vow now able to be commuted, redeemed or deferred.[26] Formally systematised by Gregory IX in 1234, this policy gave non-combatants – including the old, young, infirm, aged, and weak, men and women – and those of modest means access to the crusade's uniquely comprehensive spiritual privilege, extending its social range while, through cash redemptions of vows, widening the source of funds. This spiritual largesse was supported by licensed regional teams of preachers, often led by University of Paris-trained theologians, keeping in direct contact with the papal curia. Congregations were encouraged to donate alms, bequeath legacies, and join in special prayers and processions. Chests for crusade funds were placed in parish churches across western Europe. Building on precedent, by further institutionalising crusade processions, prayers, vow redemptions, alms and legacies, Innocent III sought to embed crusading in the Catholic culture of the west. More directly, the pope raised taxes. The Fourth Crusade had demonstrated the consequences of the failure of his 1199 tax scheme. Now, Innocent deliberately secured the explicit assent of the assembled clerical representatives at the Fourth Lateran General Council of the Church in 1215 to an ecclesiastical income tax of a twentieth, a model for papal crusade taxes for another century and a quarter (the last such general tax was authorised in 1333) and a fiscal precedent for the rest of the Middle Ages.

SACRED BOOTY

Veneration of relics defined the spiritual mentality of medieval Christendom and nowhere more obviously than in the crusades. For believers, relics provided intimate tangible contact between the present and the eternal, proof of the living truth of the Gospel promise of salvation (the common medieval word for relic, *pignus*, also meant a pledge). Crusading's initial inspiration focused on the repossession of the most numinous relic of all, the Holy Sepulchre, Jerusalem regarded as a liminal space between earth and heaven, the terrestrial and the transcendent. The Holy Land provided the unique repository of physical remains of the Apostles and material witness to the life of Christ, the places He visited, the objects He touched, the Passion and especially the True Cross. As the setting of the early Church, the scene of miracles and martyrdoms, the whole of the eastern Mediterranean provided fertile ground for relic hunters. Just as pilgrims had done before, crusaders were avid collectors, by purchase, gift, theft, plunder or discovery. The excavation of the supposed Holy Lance briefly and vitally transformed the crusaders' morale at Antioch in 1098, while the convenient unearthing of a fragment of the True Cross at Jerusalem the following year provided the new Frankish settlement with its most iconic totem. The range of relics transported westwards is indicated by a fairly representative list of items brought back from Palestine and given to Gascon monasteries in the 1150s: splinters of the True Cross; Christ's blood mixed with earth; pieces of Christ's cradle, the Virgin Mary's tomb and the rock where Christ prayed at Gethsemane; hairs of the Virgin Mary and Mary Magdalen; and a miscellany of mementos of scriptural events and characters: the Apostles, John the Baptist, Abraham, Isaac, Jacob and Stephen Protomartyr.[27] Following their supposed role at Antioch in 1098, eastern martial saints were increasingly popular: Robert of Flanders brought back St George's arm and a portion of ribcage in 1099.[28] All had been authenticated by reputable Holy Land donors, who may have turned tidy profits on such transactions. Certainly the supply seemed limitless. The continuous flood of relics carried back to western Europe by crusaders and pilgrims served many purposes: securing mutually beneficial patronage links between monasteries and patrons; enhancing the attraction of abbeys that

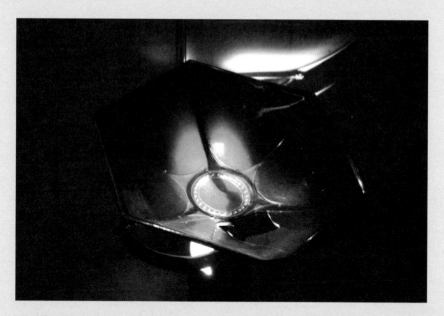

79. *The Sacro Catino, Cathedral of San Lorenzo, Genoa, acquired from Caesarea in 1101.*

80. *Byzantine loot: the Archangel Michael, St Mark's, Venice.*

housed the new holy objects as lucrative pilgrimage sites; promoting an internationalisation of scriptural and Holy Land saints' cults; gilding the reputation and securing the memory of those who had brought them. Through acquisition in the east on crusade, even obviously secular objects, such as luxury textiles, gems or military equipment, could acquire quasi-spiritual significance when presented as gifts to shrines and religious houses. Some, such as the Fatimid silks at Apt and Cadouin (see p. 101) or the Sacro Catino in Genoa (a Roman basin of Egyptian emerald glass looted from Caesarea in 1101), became rebranded as actual relics themselves.[29]

While relic-gathering was integral to the expectations and experience of all eastern crusading, nothing compared with the orgy of theft by 'holy robbers' at Constantinople, Christendom's greatest depository of holy detritus, after its capture by the Fourth Crusade in 1204.[30] In the mayhem following the city's fall, crusading clergy and laymen alike systematically scoured the churches and monasteries of the Byzantine capital in search of relics to transport home to glorify their own or a local church. Using trickery, bullying and force, some, like the bishops of Soissons and Halberstadt and the abbot of Pairis in Alsace, made off with cartloads of relics and reliquaries, as well as gold, silver, gems, silks and tapestries to decorate their new shrines, to be welcomed as miraculous benefactors when they returned home with their loot, 'triumphal spoils of holy plunder'.[31] Laymen were equally eager: the great Burgundian monastery of Cluny acquired the head of St Clement thanks to the burgling skills of a local noble crusader, Dalmas of Sercy.[32] The knightly chronicler Robert of Clari donated his probably purloined relics of the Passion to the monastery of St Pierre, Corbie. The trade did not stop in 1204. One calculation identified over 300 individual objects that reached western Europe taken between 1205 and 1215, with forty-six feasts instituted to commemorate the arrival of new relics in the west.[33] The benefits were clear, in new foci for miracles, a quickening of the pilgrim trade and the consequent rise in some ecclesiastical incomes, and hence increased investment in buildings and local infrastructure. The fortune of the previously struggling monastery at Bromholm in Norfolk was made thanks to the arrival in 1205 of a piece of the True Cross stolen from Constantinople. However, this sacred contraband created a glut on the market that highlighted the problem of duplicates and fakes. Relics were often subject to scrutiny of their authenticity, none more famously than the Holy Lance of Antioch during the First Crusade (a trial by fire proving inconclusive but seriously undermining its reputation). After 1204, the issue became so acute that the Fourth Lateran General Council of the Church in 1215 imposed a papal licensing system for all newly venerated relics to protect the faithful from 'lying stories or false documents as has commonly happened in many places on account of the desire for profit'.[34] The need for authentication led to a trade in provenances in Constantinople and a slew of simultaneously celebratory and exculpatory narratives of the Fourth Crusade designed to validate legitimacy of both relic and ownership, the latter often no less dubious than the former. However, despite the queasiness of some authorities, the centrality of relics persisted. Crusade preachers regularly used splinters of the True Cross as props, while Louis IX of France integrated his possession of Passion relics, especially the Crown of Thorns acquired from Constantinople via the Venetians, into his vision of sacral kingship and promotion of the crusade. After his canonisation in 1297, in a sort of sacred relay, his cult generated relics of its own.[35]

The promotional campaign emphasised the crusade as a metaphor and exemplar for the Christian life. Innocent's enthusiasm for the crusade's fusion of religious commitment and political action, while, as *Quia Maior* made clear, never losing sight of the primacy of the Holy Land as an objective, prompted the application of crusade formulae – cross, indulgence, privileges, prayers, processions, etc. – in various configurations to other arenas: against enemies of the papacy in Italy and Sicily; heretics in Languedoc; Muslim rulers in Spain and pagans in the Baltic. Such were the pope's predilections that petitioners actively sought the perceived benefits of crusade institutions for their own local battles, as did the bishop of Riga in the eastern Baltic in 1215. Victims, such as the Languedoc counts in 1215, facing a crusade against alleged heresy in their lands, argued equally vigorously for their cancellation.[36] Innocent III permanently influenced how future crusades were conducted and the ways in which crusading permeated western European society. His policies came close to establishing a near-permanent crusade by disseminating a sense of existential crisis, depicting Christendom beset by enemies: Turks in the east; Moors to the south; pagans in the north; and, no less toxic, within Christendom itself, heretics and dissenters. Popular mood was focused by the increased presence of preachers broadcasting messages of threat supported by the communal ritual of prayers and intercessory processions. The effectiveness of this programme received unexpected proof. In 1212 the failure of the Fourth Crusade, the dissemination of news of the dire threats to the faith and preachers' rhetorical revivalist emphasis on the sanctity of Apostolic poverty provoked demonstrations and marches in northern France and the Rhineland later configured as the Children's Crusade (see 'The Children's Crusade', p. 258).[37] Such awareness from those on the fringes of social power – the young, the rootless, the economically marginalised – revealed the reach of Innocent III's proselytising.

The new eastern crusade was intended as the most coherent yet. The well-attended Fourth Lateran Council in 1215 was framed by the call to the Holy Land crusade, part of an agenda including pastoral reform and the fight against heresy. At the council, the crusade led a programme of lay evangelisation including decrees establishing the doctrine of Real Presence of Christ's Body and Blood in the eucharist and the requirement for annual oral confession, both sacramental measures involving access to God's grace and salvation paralleled in the penitential commitment of crusading. The council confirmed the crusade preliminaries, with a few modifications, and fixed the time and place of the muster (Messina or Bari, 1 June 1217) and Egypt as the destination. Details, including bans on tournaments and trade with the enemy, were collected in the decree *Ad Liberandam*, which was to serve as a model for later crusades. The programme of preaching and recruitment initiated, in some regions, a decade-long engagement with the eastern crusade, only ending with the controversial expedition of the excommunicated Frederick II of Germany and Sicily in 1228–9. This commitment sustained through three pontificates (Innocent III, who died in 1216; Honorius III, 1216–27; and Gregory IX, 1227–41) confirmed crusading as a familiar and regular rather than exceptional feature of devotional life and politics, a process enhanced by parallel crusading ventures in the northeastern Baltic (against pagan natives) and Languedoc (against heretics).

Recruitment demonstrated the continued popularity of eastern crusading, although, unusually, this did not include the kingdom of France, due to war with the king of England, the distraction of the Languedoc crusade, and the unpopularity of the papal legate, Robert Courson. In Germany, England and the cities of northern Italy, all regions of civil war and festering political rivalries, the crusade, as a neutral higher calling, provided context for conflict resolution. Details of recruitment, surviving in greater quantity than for previous expeditions, show the mobilisation of all sections of free society, women as well as men.[38] As before, contingents revolved around traditional lordship and communal hierarchies. However, the scale of recruitment, combined with the absence of clearly established overall leadership, produced an uncoordinated muster. With sea travel now the only practicable means of transporting large armies, by the summer of 1217 two substantial coalitions gathered at opposite ends of Europe, one led by King Andrew of Hungary and Duke Leopold VI of Austria in the Adriatic, and the other, from Frisia, the Low Countries and the Rhineland, in the North Sea. Neither coalition stayed united. The Germans and Hungarians arrived separately at Acre in the late summer and autumn of 1217, to be followed the next spring by the northern Europeans, who had wintered severally in Iberia or Italy by which time Andrew of Hungary had already departed overland for home (January 1218). Staggered arrivals and departures became prominent features. The fluid rules for taking the cross and preachers' tone of easy spiritual reward seem to have encouraged vow fulfilment based on personal contribution rather than strategic completion.

THE CHILDREN'S CRUSADE

Popular engagement with the crusade found exceptional expression in the spring and summer of 1212 when crowds of enthusiasts in the Low Countries, the Rhineland and parts of northern France gathered in marches proclaiming devotion to the cause of the liberation of the Holy Land and return of the True Cross. Conditioned by a generation of blanket crusade evangelism, these demonstrations took the form of mendicant penitential processions, probably stimulated by Innocent III's institution of liturgical processions to solicit divine aid to counter Almohad advances in Spain in 1211 and the intense preaching campaign on behalf of the Albigensian Crusade in 1211–12. The deliberate promotion of an urgent sense of Christendom in crisis, coupled with preachers' persistent emphasis on the virtues of apostolic poverty, moral purity and the redemptive power of the cross, served to draw attention both to the failures of the elite-led expeditions to the east and the consequent frustrations of those prevented from participating in the crusade and its benefits by virtue of their marginal social and economic status.

The narrative of what happened in 1212 is impossible to determine with any certainty. Chronicle accounts cannot be reconciled, reflecting individual attempts to organise memories of events that appeared startling, eccentric and potentially unnervingly disruptive, from the start encouraging myths, morality tales and tall stories. What emerges is a picture of two centres of action. One in western Germany, focusing on traditional urban as well as rural centres of crusade recruitment, including Metz, Cologne and Speyer, appeared overtly directed towards the crusade to the Holy Land, with stories of massed processions from March to July, a leader called Nicholas carrying a tau cross, and of contingents carrying pilgrim insignia crossing the Alps into Italy and, largely vainly, seeking ships to the Levant. In the other area of agitation, in the Dunois, Chartrain and Ile de France south-west of Paris, the emphasis as recorded appeared more generally revivalist, although those marchers who converged on the abbey of St Denis near Paris for the annual Lendit Fair in June, apparently carried crosses and banners and chanted for the restoration of the True Cross. These were led, in some accounts, by a shepherd, Stephen of Cloyes, near Vendôme, a

81. *Modern myth images: the Children's Crusade in the Rhineland by Gustave Doré, 1877.*

symbolically significant profession in populist religious fundamentalism. Direct association between these two contemporary movements may have been real, accidental, coincidental, non-existent, imaginary or merely literary.

The intriguing element that has attracted subsequent attention came from descriptions of participants as *pueri*, literally 'children', but more likely indicating the powerless and rootless. Descriptions identify those involved as being on the fringes of the settled social hierarchy: youths, including girls; adolescents;

the unmarried; the old; shepherds; carters, ploughmen, farm labourers, artisans. Whether any reached Palestine is doubtful, although there were stories of some 'crusaders' finding employment in Languedoc and one writer placed Nicholas at Damietta on the Fifth Crusade. But such accounts fit moral not historical narratives. Nonetheless, the uprisings of 1212 reveal an extensive social engagement with crusading, providing strong testimony to the cultural penetration of crusading as a social and religious ambition; to the effectiveness of sustained preaching in stirring popular response; and to the existence of political awareness and agency among groups ostensibly far removed from traditional political elites. The issues raised by the 1212 demonstrators – moral reform, the threats to Christendom, the redemptive power of the cross – precisely fitted papal policy, even though there is no mention of these events in surviving papal records. The 1212 marchers exposed the dynamic popular appeal of crusading later illustrated in the so-called Shepherds' Crusades of 1251 and 1320 in France. They may also have exerted significant influence on the future direction of the crusade project. Faced by this potentially disruptive combination of popular enthusiasm with frustration at being excluded from the institutional apparatus and benefits of crusading, a year later, in his bull *Quia Maior* of 1213, Innocent III proposed a system of vow redemptions so that, regardless of military suitability, anyone could take the cross and enjoy crusade spiritual privileges while contributing whatever they could afford. This could thereby offer at least partial opportunity for direct general public involvement, a measure that at once recognised mass aspirations while simultaneously seeking to contain their expression.[39]

12. Places associated with the Children's Crusade.

82. A crusading bishop's mitre – that of James of Vitry.

Philip II in 1191 provided a precedent, while the short-term commitments of the Albigensian crusaders and the annual campaigners under the cross in Livonia offered immediate models.

The early arrivals helped secure the environs of Acre and its food supplies, culminating in the fortification of the Athlit promontory twenty-five miles to the south, necessary preliminaries to an attack on Egypt.[40] An alliance with the Seljuks of Iconium served to further protect the Outremer enclave. Once the northern European fleets had assembled at Acre, the only question for the crusaders and the king-regent of Jerusalem, John of Brienne (1210–25), widower of Queen regnant Mary (1205–12) and father of Queen Isabel II (1212–28), was which Egyptian port should be attacked. The choice fell on Damietta, at the head of the main eastern estuary of the Nile, already the target of a Byzantine-Frankish assault in 1169 and, unlike Alexandria, without a large western commercial presence. The combined crusader and Outremer fleet arrived off Damietta in late May 1217, the opening of a gruelling two-year siege that stretched the invaders' logistics, technological ingenuity and morale to their limits. Internal divisions within the Ayyubid regime surrounding the death of Sultan al-Adil in August 1218, and the rocky succession of his son al-Kamil, failed to weaken Egyptian resistance, while the regular bi-annual reinforcement and departure of crusaders undermined their strategic focus and campaign camaraderie.

This was matched by uncertainty over leadership. At the start of the siege, John of Brienne as king of Jerusalem was chosen as de facto commander, but with no explicit agreement over future control of any conquests. John lacked authority over the crusaders from the west. The arrival of German and southern Italian contingents from 1217–18 onwards, and the papal legate Cardinal Pelagius in the autumn of 1218, held out the prospect of the arrival and assumption of command by Frederick II of Germany, who had taken the cross in 1215. Pelagius's control of the substantial sums that reached the crusaders from the Lateran Council church tax, worth according to a 1220 papal account 35,000 silver marks and 25,000 gold pieces,[41] allowed him to create a central treasury for indigent crusaders and to hire those in search of regular payment, giving him a significant voice in any decisions. Competing interests made consensus in an inevitably collective leadership hard to achieve, especially as, in common with earlier expeditions, choices were regularly debated with the wider community of the army.

During the siege of Damietta, from May 1218 to November 1219, neither the crusaders, established on the west bank of the Nile opposite the city, nor the Egyptian field army, camped on the east bank to the south, risked a major confrontation. Operations revolved around blockading the city and starving it into submission. The waterlogged terrain, an Egyptian blockade of the Nile, and the lack of timber for barges and siege engines prevented direct assaults on the walls. Disease and supply problems periodically threatened the crusade with dissolution. Even after the main defensive system of a mid-stream tower and chains was captured in August 1218 and a new canal dug to outflank Ayyubid defences, it was only the abandonment of the forward Ayyubid camp early in 1219 that finally allowed Damietta to be surrounded. The new sultan, al-Kamil, had withdrawn to combat a possible

83. The Nile at Damietta.

coup and rebuild his control over his professional regiments. Thereafter, he conducted forays against the crusaders from a distance while trying to rally support from fellow Ayyubids in Syria and encourage them to launch attacks on Acre, a tactic that drew John of Brienne back to the Holy Land for a year, in 1220–1. Starvation and the absence of any prospective relief forced Damietta to surrender in November 1219. The nearby Delta port of Tinnis fell soon after, leaving the crusaders in control of the main eastern outlets of the Nile Delta. The next twenty-one months saw stalemate. Damietta was formally Christianised, its mosques converted into churches. One of those, dedicated to the English St Edmund the Martyr, the king of East Anglia, was immediately decorated with frescoes depicting the saint's martyrdom at the hands of the Danes in 869, a painting commissioned by an English knight, Richard of Argentan.[42] Such visual demonstration of new ownership formed a typical aspect of the aftermath of conquest by all sides during the eastern crusades where artistic and aesthetic assertions of power played essential public symbolic roles, as in Jerusalem in 1099 or 1187.

The turnover of crusaders continued alongside debates over the next course for the expedition; a negotiated settlement was mooted by the Egyptians. Diplomatic contacts were cast into unexpected relief by the appearance of the charismatic mendicant, Francis of Assisi, who attempted to convert al-Kamil in person during the summer of 1219, and by a shoal of prophecies that swept through the crusader army. Some foretold

84. Thirteenth-century wall painting of the martyrdom of St Edmund, Cliffe-at-Hoo, Kent, perhaps similar to the one painted by crusaders at Damietta.

victory; others offered garbled echoes of the Asiatic conquests of Genghis Khan. The sense of divine providence may have influenced the rejection of al-Kamil's offers to restore Jerusalem and Palestine west of the Jordan to the Latins in return for the crusaders' evacuation of Egypt: the first in 1219, shortly before the fall of Damietta; the second before the crusaders' advance towards Cairo in August 1221. Given the invaders' military advantage in 1219, refusal of al-Kamil's terms made sense, even though voices, probably including John of Brienne's, were raised in favour of acceptance. Two years later, the balance of advantage was less obvious. However, any negotiated settlement would have meant the end of the crusade, leaving thousands of vows unfulfilled. On both occasions, but especially in 1221, the influence of the absent leaders Pope Honorius III and Frederick II, who had again taken the cross in 1220, inhibited abandonment of the crusade. Frederick's arrival was regularly proclaimed as imminent, lending influence to the papal and German representatives, Pelagius and Duke Louis of Bavaria. By contrast, King John, who favoured acceptance, lacked a large army of his own and the death of his wife Queen Mary in 1212 had in any case effectively made him only regent for his daughter Isabel II.

More immediately, as in 1191–2, the defensibility of Jerusalem without the castles of Transjordan was questioned, while, with Palestine under the authority of al-Kamil's brother al-Mu'azzam, sultan of Syria, the Egyptian ruler's capacity to deliver on his promises was doubtful. By 1221 any negotiated peace would have challenged the carefully nurtured prophetic optimism among the crusaders and, under Muslim law and convention, would in any case be time limited. The 1219 and 1221 Egyptian offers spoke of tactical manoeuvres to cover al-Kamil's immediate political weakness rather than a lasting Near East settlement. The 1221 offer came as both sides were consolidating their forces for an impending crusader march on Cairo which, despite his doubts, King John had returned from Acre to Damietta to join. With al-Kamil reinforced by Ayyubid allies from Syria, his offer may have been designed to sow dissent. In the event, the crusaders' attempt on Cairo failed dismally, their army forced to surrender after being trapped by Nile floods and the Egyptian army. In return for the crusaders' freedom and safe conduct, Damietta was evacuated (September 1221), ending the central action of the crusade and casting a possibly distorting retrospective glow on earlier failed diplomacy.

The negotiations of 1219 and 1221 fully exposed the Egyptian strategy's contradictions. While the 1218 invasion stirred Ayyubid disunity, divisions that leaders of Outremer would exploit to their advantage over the following thirty years, the crusaders' repeated refusal to trade Jerusalem for a withdrawal from Egypt questioned their objectives. Rejection did not necessarily come from blinkered zealous optimism. Their reading of the geopolitics of the Middle East persuaded enough of them that Jerusalem without its hinterland or a subservient Egypt was not viable in the medium let alone long term; and they were right. The Fifth Crusade's intransigence implied that only conquest, a regime change or an inconceivable diplomatic volte face would allow for the safe return of Jerusalem, a city with a worrying tendency to succumb to hostile sieges (about six in 175 years to 1244). The Fifth Crusade seemed to be banking on a military knock-out or the implosion of the Ayyubid regime. Both were feasible. Latin armies from Palestine had campaigned throughout the Delta in the 1160s. Using methods of extreme brutality, Saladin had been able to subdue Egypt in a relatively few years. The Fifth Crusade and the later expedition of Louis IX both reached to within a hundred miles of Cairo. Yet no plan of how to manage Egypt in the aftermath of any victory existed. Perhaps some sort of Latin overlordship was envisaged, for which precedents were hardly encouraging. The diplomatic option held no better prospects. The demilitarised Jerusalem agreed in a deal struck between the Ayyubid Sultan al-Kamil and the western Emperor Frederick II in 1229 easily fell to Turkish freebooters in 1244.

The Crusade of 1228–9

The logic of the 1221 defeat was not lost on the rulers of the rump of Outremer or planners in the west. For the former, diplomacy was as important as conflict. Antioch and Tripoli, dynastically united since 1187, became increasingly absorbed in the politics of Christian Cilician Armenia and in cutting deals with local Syrian rulers. At Acre, territory was conserved and extended largely through a rhythm of diplomacy shaped by the expiry of the recurrent truces with Ayyubid neighbours in Damascus, Transjordan and Egypt, and by playing them off against each other. The politics of Outremer were complicated by the role of Frederick II, from 1225 absentee king of Jerusalem by virtue of his marriage to the heiress Isabel II (d. 1228). While preparing to honour his crusade vows of 1215 and 1220, he conducted direct negotiations with al-Kamil over returning Jerusalem. When Frederick finally arrived in Palestine in 1228, his role had been compromised by papal excommunication for dilatoriness, the death of his wife, and the hostility of sections of the Outremer political elite, including the Cypriot Franks, Templars and Hospitallers. After military manoeuvring by both parties, Frederick and al-Kamil reached a ten-year agreement (treaty of Jaffa, February 1229) that restored Jerusalem, Bethlehem, Nazareth and all of Sidon to the Franks, although the Haram al-Sharif (Temple Mount) was left in Muslim hands, with free access for Christian pilgrims. Despite attracting opprobrium from all sides, the 1229 treaty fitted a pattern established since 1192, signalling an asymmetrical concern over the status of Palestine: Transjordan and Syria were of far greater strategic and political significance to Egypt provided the religious sensibilities of the *ulema* were appeased by continued control of Jerusalem's Islamic holy places. A German poet in Frederick's army likened the deal to watching two misers trying to divide three gold pieces equally.[43]

The Politics of Thirteenth-Century Outremer

Frederick's difficulties with the local baronage mirrored the fractured politics of thirteenth-century Outremer more generally. Although by the 1240s having gradually reasserted control over the territory between the Jordan and the Mediterranean, the Franks depended on the coastal ports, especially Tyre and Acre, for their wealth and power, supported by castles such as Athlit south of Acre, Margat between Tripoli and Latakia, Crac des Chevaliers in the Homs gap or, from 1240, Saphet in Galilee, all funded and held by the Military Orders. Even during the Frankish reoccupation of the Holy City (1229–44), Acre remained the capital of the kingdom of Jerusalem, the titles and jurisdictions of the twelfth century continuing often only as legalistic antiquarian memories, shadows or imitations. From 1219, Tripoli and Antioch were dynastically united under Bohemund IV and his successors, although each had been reduced to coastal ports and scattered castles, effectively isolated city states. There was little if any renewed Frankish rural resettlement after 1191–2. Outremer's survival rested on income from commerce and its ability to defend itself, making it reliant on the trading Italian communes established in the ports – Venice, Genoa, Pisa – and the Military Orders – Templars, Hospitallers and Teutonic Knights, each with different, often competing, frequently hostile sets of interest. The potential for conflict was exacerbated by weak central political control. The royal dynasty failed to produce adult male resident rulers. From 1225, when Isabel II married Frederick II, until 1269, when Hugh III of Cyprus, a descendant of Isabel I, united the crowns of Cyprus and Jerusalem, the king was a distant absentee (Frederick and Isabel's son, Conrad, 1225–54, and grandson Conradin, 1254–68), nominal rule resting in a series of usually and often violently contested regencies. Even after 1269, until his death in 1285, Charles of Anjou, the new king of Sicily, vigorously claimed sovereignty (sold to him by Mary of Antioch, another descendant of Isabel I) through agents sent east, leading to the bizarre position in the 1270s of the fast-diminishing Frankish kingdom squabbling over Sicilian or Cypriot legitimacy.

In the absence of a resident monarch, the local baronage, notably the Ibelin family, assumed authority. However, neither the barons nor the Italian communes nor the Military Orders were united; nor were the dominant cities of Tyre and Acre. This created an extraordinary spectacle of near permanent factional contest both between local interest groups and between them and representatives of absent monarchs, conflicts that inevitably sucked in the rulers and nobility of Cyprus. Outremer politics most resembled the infighting familiar in and between contemporary Italian city states. Between 1228 and 1243 the so-called War of the Lombards pitted King Conrad's (in reality his father, Frederick II's) representative, Richard Filangieri, supported by Tyre, the Hospitallers, the Teutonic Knights and the Pisans, against the Ibelins backed by Acre, the Templars and the Genoese. In 1231, to resist Filangieri, his opponents in Acre formed a commune. In 1242 the Ibelin faction prevailed when Tyre was captured. Nominal rule then passed between a parade of Cypriot and Ibelin regents. From 1250 to 1254, Louis IX of France exercised a form of parallel authority, while in the 1260s his agent, Geoffrey of Sergines, commander of the French garrison at Acre, actually served as regent. Unity was not achieved. In 1256–8 the Venetians and the Genoese took up arms in the War of St Sabas, a dispute only finally resolved in 1288. Venice had the support of Pisa, the Templars, the Teutonic Knights and part of the Ibelin clan; the Genoese the backing of the Hospitallers and other Ibelins. In the 1270s further disruption was caused by Charles of Anjou's agent Roger of San Severino, who managed to secure the support of Acre, Sidon and the Templars, while Tyre and Beirut remained loyal to Hugh III (I of Jerusalem). All the while, from 1265, the Mamluks of Egypt were systematically dismantling what remained of the kingdom and Frankish Outremer.

This persistent internecine feuding was sustained by thirteenth-century Outremer's wealth. It funded political conflict as well as providing the prizes all factions wished to acquire. Henry III of England's brother, Earl Richard of Cornwall, reported after his crusade of 1240–1 that Acre alone was worth £50,000 sterling a year, significantly more than King Henry's entire annual royal income.[44] Until the advent of the Mongols in the Near East from the later 1250s gradually readjusted western Asian trade routes, Acre and the other Outremer ports provided major entrepôts for Mediterranean trade from across Eurasia: foodstuffs, spices, base metal, metalwork, porcelain, glass, sugar, perfumes, wine, jewels, slaves, pilgrims, relics, silk, linen, cotton, wood and specialities such as Tuscan saffron.[45] 'Antioch cloth', whether or not actually manufactured in Syria, was a label that commanded high prices and conveyed social kudos across western Europe.[46] A large suburb was added to Acre to accommodate its swelling population. The Templars were so wealthy that they were able to spend over a million bezants over two and half years after 1240, rebuilding their castle at Saphet. For families such as the Ibelins, in the east since the early twelfth century, Outremer was home and, just as elsewhere in Christendom, profits were there to be had. Visiting crusaders encountered a rich, polyglot and increasingly bilingual society (Arabic and Romance languages), where, as in Italy, the nobility lived in cities and where markets offered customers anything from exotic fruit to illuminated manuscripts. Viewed through an economic lens, Outremer was booming, its cities worth mercantile investment to the end. However, just as its wealth depended on international trade so its survival was predicated on international assistance.

The Crusades of 1239–41

By incremental diplomacy backed by threats of force, the thirteenth-century kingdom of Jerusalem had gradually recovered lands in Galilee and west of the Jordan, a process the crusades of 1239–41 reinforced. In the autumn of 1234, in good time to prepare for the end of the ten-year 1229 truce, Pope Gregory IX (1227–41), a veteran of preaching the Fifth Crusade, called for a new eastern campaign. In addition to the usual spiritual and temporal privileges to active *crucesignati*, he offered indulgences for vow redemptions to any who contributed materially, instituted a clerical income tax, and proposed a new ten-year garrison force for Outremer. Preaching was assigned to the

ACRE MANUSCRIPTS AND 'CRUSADER ART'

The aesthetics of the crusades lacked distinctive form. In painting, sculpture, architecture, manuscript illumination, songs, poems, plays, clothes, food, weaponry, heraldry, the art of crusaders drew technique, inspiration and styles eclectically from prevailing cultural ambience. For the Franks of Outremer this included local influences – Greek, Syrian Christian, Arab, Armenian – as well as European (see 'The Melisende Psalter', p. 138, and 'A Palace in Beirut', p. 230). Although almost all the artefacts created by or for the Outremer Franks have not survived, it is hard to identify special Outremer style, except perhaps in concentric castle fortifications and in deliberate religious imagery on coins (St Peter in Antioch or the Holy Places in Jerusalem). Frankish ecclesiastical architecture, while incorporating local features such as domes and flat roofs, also relied on borrowing from western Romanesque, then Gothic models, making a religious point.[47] Divorced from their devotional settings, Frankish architecture could be admired for itself: Mamluk conquerors seemed happy to incorporate looted Frankish Gothic doorways, columns and decorative sculpture as trophies into mosques and a *madrasa* in Cairo.[48] Secular and domestic architecture and decoration appropriated indigenous styles, although in places, such as planned villages and suburbs, they introduced western ground-plans, such as two-storied houses opening directly onto the street, with individual plots of land behind.[49]

Similarly for western crusaders, content not form distinguished works associated with the war of the cross. Images of warrior saints such as St George, and of militant episodes from the Old Testament, proliferated in sculpture and illumination, as did what has been described as a 'Christo-mimetic movement' in art and relic collecting.[50] Crusade-related themes became popular in devotional manuscripts, especially those associated with the court of Louis IX.[51] Decorative schemes directly or indirectly focused on the crusade, such as the stained glass at St Denis showing scenes of the First Crusade or Louis IX's Sainte Chapelle in Paris, a giant reliquary for the relics of the Passion. Inevitably, visual art needed to be framed in conventional styles to engage the conscious or subliminal understanding of the viewer. The luxurious textiles, clothes, jewellery or metalwork that wealthy

85. A volume commissioned in Outremer in 1250–4 on Louis IX's crusade.

crusaders took with them or acquired on campaign lacked specific crusader motifs, except perhaps in the manuscripts they purchased or commissioned.

In Outremer, the Franks embraced regional diversity while importing western styles and artisans, such as painters and illuminators from Italy, Germany, England and France. Louis IX's stay in the Holy Land between 1250 and 1254 appears to have stimulated local luxury manuscript production at Acre, probably supported by French artists in his entourage. One volume, the so-called Arsenal Bible, comprising lengthy vernacular extracts with 115 illuminated scenes showing Byzantine as well as French influence, has been attributed to Louis' stay and even to his personal patronage and use. Although only a handful of manuscripts have been tentatively identified as originating in Acre, it appears that production increased in the final years before the city's fall, a sign of Acre's international status and the continued presence of wealthy patrons, some possibly visiting crusaders, most probably laymen or members of the Military Orders, as the texts are in the vernacular: works of history, literature, law and military advice. The styles reflect continuing borrowing between Christian Levantine, western European and Greek models. This typified a cultural identity that, both in Outremer and western Europe, even when highlighting specific ideological messages, exploited but did not transform existing fashions, techniques and expectations.[52]

new mendicant orders of Dominican and Franciscan friars.[53] The funding system allocated proceeds from legacies, alms and vow redemptions to crusaders, chiefly the already well provided. With none of the crowned heads of western Europe committing themselves, recruitment revolved around great nobles, prominently Duke Hugh IV of Burgundy; Counts Theobald IV of Champagne (posthumous son of the lost leader of the Fourth Crusade) and Peter of Brittany; and Earls Richard of Cornwall and Simon of Montfort of Leicester (Henry III's brother-in-law). The muster of French nobles was the largest since the Fourth Crusade. On both sides of the Channel, aristo-cratic recruitment operated as part of complex arrangements of reconciliation after periods of rebellion and dissent. The resulting campaigns in Palestine in 1239–41 lacked coherent timing, direction or leadership. Modest diplomatic successes were achieved chiefly because of Ayyubid division. The main French contingents arrived in 1239, their stay of a year marked by indiscipline, confused strategy between Damascus and Egypt, and being mauled in battle with the Egyptians near Gaza (13 November 1239). Simultaneously, al-Nasr, ruler of Kerak, had briefly reoccupied Jerusalem. Nonetheless, the presence of western troops was unwelcome to the Ayyubids, so deals were secured with Damascus and Kerak covering Frankish control over Galilee and southern Palestine, including Jerusalem. Richard of Cornwall's even briefer stay (October 1240–May 1241) witnessed the rebuilding of a fort at Ascalon and a largely empty treaty with Egypt confirming the agreements of the previous year over lands outside the sultan's control. Prisoners taken at the battle of Gaza were released from Egyptian captivity and Earl Richard was allowed to bury the remains of some of those killed in the battle, gestures that earned the earl more praise than for any other action seen on these ramshackle crusades. Nevertheless, by the end of 1241, the kingdom of Jerusalem appeared secure, with most of its pre-1187 lands west of the Jordan restored except for Nablus; the port of Acre booming; the main Holy Places, barring Hebron, under Frankish jurisdiction; and calm diplomatic relations with the Ayyubid princes. Yet the insignificance of these arrangements in the wider scheme of Asiatic geopolitics was soon revealed.

The French Crusade, 1248–54

In August 1244, Khwarazmian Turkish mercenaries in the pay of Sultan al-Salih of Egypt, invading Syria and Palestine from Iraq on the sultan's

CRUSADERS' BAGGAGE

Whatever plunder and booty crusaders acquired on campaign, few initially set out empty handed. The symbols of pilgrimage, the scrip and staff, took their place alongside the necessities of travel: clothing, arms, armour, cash (in currency, plate or ingots), cooking utensils, containers for food and drink, pack animals, harnesses and wagons. The clergy carried travel altars, liturgical books, religious vessels and writing implements. According to one witness, in 1096 the less well off piled their children and modest possessions onto simple two-wheeled carts to which they tied their cattle.[54] The presence of extensive, slow-moving baggage trains provided a much commented on feature of land expeditions. The wealthy habitually travelled with the accoutrements of their class. Beyond direct military or obvious financial requirements, such as weaponry, silver ingots or, as in the case of the English noble William Longsword in 1249, saddle bags stuffed with cash, luxury items, such as gold or silver plate, jewels and precious textiles, could also be bartered for supplies or exchanged for local currency.[55] Some objects served social as well as military purposes. When he reached Constantinople in 1097, Tancred of Lecce wanted a tent large enough to act as a hall for his growing cohort of clients, while the Bolognese crusader Barzella Merxadrus used his tent at Damietta in 1219 to live in with his wife.[56] Barzella's tent was equipped with furniture. Commanders took signs of their cultural identities with them. Richard I travelled with what he claimed was King Arthur's sword Excalibur, while his great-nephew, the future Edward I, carried a manuscript of Arthurian stories with him to Acre in 1271. The sometimes lavish nature of the goods that accompanied crusaders is displayed in surviving wills and inventories. In his will drawn up at Acre on 24 October 1267, the English crusader Hugh Neville's bequests included, in addition to cash, horses and armour, a standing goblet decorated with the arms of the king of England, a gold buckle, other buckles studded with emeralds and a gold ring. A year earlier, an inventory of the goods at Acre of the recently deceased French crusader Count Eudes of Nevers provides elaborate insight into aristocratic travelling style, itemising rings, enamels, bejewelled belts and hats, gold and silver cups, goblets, jugs, ewers, bowls, basins and spoons, some garnished with

86. *Loading up, from the statutes of the fourteenth-century crusading Order of the Knot.*

gems and enamel; expensive cotton and linen fabrics including numerous bed hangings, tablecloths, napkins, quilts, even the count's cloth of gold shroud, as well as quantities of curtains and carpets; gloves, leggings and shoes, alongside a miscellany of whistles, armour, spurs, weapons, banners, trunks and chests, food, drink, culinary utensils, leather bottles; the contents of the count's wardrobe; the furnishings of his travelling chapel – chalice, vestments and breviary; and three books: two romances and a 'romanz de la terre d'outre mer', either a translation of William of Tyre or possibly a version of one of the texts in the popular *chanson de geste* Crusade Cycle. While some of this bounty may have been purchased in Outremer, where certainly the whole lot was put up for sale to pay the count's debts, the bulk would have come with him from France. Crusaders took their intimate possessions with them just as they did their servants, clerics and military entourages.[57]

behalf, captured Jerusalem, slaughtering Franks and desecrating Christian shrines, before joining an Egyptian Ayyubid army that routed a combined Syrian Ayyubid-Frankish army at Forbie near Gaza in October. Soon, most of the Frankish gains of 1241 in southern Palestine were wiped out; Ascalon was lost in 1247. The future of Frankish Outremer looked precarious, contingent on regional forces over which the Franks exerted no real influence. Al-Salih's consolidation of power over Syria as well as Egypt, supported by his increasingly powerful personal Mamluk *askar* (the Bahriyya or Salihiyya), seemed to recreate the encirclement of Saladin's day. The western European response, although more modest than that after 1187, produced the best organised eastern crusade. Its complete failure imposed a bleak, forbidding realism.

Louis IX of France took the cross in December 1244 while in the grip of a serious illness, when he was thought, and probably thought himself, to be dying. He may or may not have heard of the loss of Jerusalem. His crusading commitment expressed a very individual intensity of devotion, a profound religious conviction that embraced public acts of piety, political reform, aggressive anti-Semitism, elaborate personal penance, and the patronage of religious orders and relics. Louis' crusade became a French enterprise, an extension of the newly powerful Capetian monarchy's ability to exploit the human and financial resources of the kingdom, backed by access to international revenues: vow redemptions, donations and clerical taxes authorised by Innocent IV at the First Council of Lyons in 1245. Over five years, the clerical tax alone may have contributed as much as 950,000 *livres tournois*, perhaps equivalent to four years' royal revenue. Royal accounts later put the overall costs of the expedition at over 1,500,000 *livres tournois*. However, extraordinary income from the church levies, redemptions, donations, taxes on royal lands and extortions from the Jews largely covered the costs of the invasion of Egypt.[58] To facilitate transport, Louis constructed his own Mediterranean port at Aigues Mortes. Contracts for ships and men were carefully drawn up. While there was some international involvement, for example a contingent from England, the main recruitment revolved around Louis, his brothers, and French dukes and counts, many of whom were further bound by generous royal subsidies. Massive dumps of wine and grain – the staples of crusaders' diet – were collected in Cyprus to await the crusade's arrival in 1248.

Louis embarked from Aigues Mortes on 25 August 1248. He spent the winter and spring in Cyprus, gathering his forces. After receiving ambassadors from the Mongols who, only seven years earlier, had invaded central Europe to devastating effect, Louis despatched in return the Dominican friar Andrew of Longjumeau to explore possibilities for an anti-Muslim alliance, a fantasy that western rulers continued to pursue for another half century. In late May 1249 the crusade armada, carrying perhaps 15,000 troops and auxiliaries (clerks, cooks, servants, physicians and the like), left for Damietta. Despite having given Sultan al-Salih (son of Sultan al-Kamil) time to muster his army and prepare Egypt's defences, following a forced landing on 5 June, the crusaders captured Damietta in a day when its garrison abandoned the city, the sultan having decided to use Mansourah, forty miles upstream from Damietta, as his forward base. The speed of the city's fall caught the crusaders off guard. Unprepared to take immediate advantage of their victory, they preferred to await new arrivals, notably Louis' brother Alphonse of Poitiers in October; see out the annual summer Nile floods; and reconvert Damietta into a Christian seaport.

In November, Louis, having rejected a proposal to capture Alexandria, led his army southwards towards Mansourah where, later that month, al-Salih died, perhaps of tuberculosis. Although his heir, al-Mu'azzam Turan Shah, took three months to reach the Nile, Egyptian defences held firm under the control of al-Salih's widow, Shajar al-Durr, the army high command and al-Salih's increasingly dominant Bahriyya Mamluks. From early December to early February the two forces faced each other across a branch of the Nile, the Bahr al-Sagir, a stalemate only broken in early February when a ford was found across the river. The ensuing battle for Mansourah (8–11 February), its gruelling bloody combat preserved in the vivid eyewitness remembrance of one of Louis' closest associates, John of Joinville, ended in a pyrrhic victory for the crusaders.[59] Heavy casualties included Louis' brother, Robert, count of Artois. While the badly mauled Egyptian army withdrew into Mansourah itself, it remained intact, largely thanks to the discipline of the Bahriyya Mamluks who now moved to the centre of the political stage. Mansourah brought Louis no closer to Cairo, instead it confirmed his isolation. Further stalemate forced a withdrawal once more across the Bahr al-Sagir. Increasing food shortages, enemy harassment and devastating camp diseases were compounded when the Egyptians outflanked the crusaders by blockading the rivers between them and Damietta. Forced into a painful retreat, Louis' army disintegrated in early April between Sharamshah and Fariksur, only halfway to Damietta. Louis and his troops were taken into hazardous captivity.

In an unexpected irony, two of the dominant figures in the subsequent negotiations for the ransom and release of the crusader prisoners of war,

JOHN OF JOINVILLE

Perhaps the most vivid, personal description of the experience of crusading is contained in the *Life of St Louis* by John of Joinville (1224/5–1317), a Champenois nobleman and veteran of the 1248–54 French crusade to Egypt and the Holy Land. He could boast ancestors who had fought on every major eastern crusade since 1147. Written in northern French vernacular and completed in 1309, the account of the crusade in the *Life* may have first been compiled separately, perhaps in the 1270s, which may explain its autobiographical rather than strictly hagiographical focus. Joinville, hereditary seneschal of Champagne, became a close friend of Louis IX on crusade, during which the king had bailed him out with funds to help pay his retinue of knights. His proximity to the king did not prevent his voicing criticisms of the campaign's conduct or the behaviour of participants. However, Joinville's description of the crusade is distinguished by details of military preparations, observations on camp and court life, vivid anecdotes of opponents and local curiosities, and especially close-quarter accounts of the harrowing atmosphere of battle and captivity. Joinville captures the horror and terror of war and its consequences while being sustained by confidence in the holy cause, in the social code of chivalric behaviour and in the outstanding personal qualities of Louis IX, an admiration that does not, however, blind him to the king's faults or one that he extends to all members of the king's family. By the time Joinville composed the final text, which had originally been commissioned by Joan of Navarre (d. 1305), wife of Louis IX's grandson Philip IV, the crusader king had been canonised (1297), his example being used by Joinville in not so veiled criticism of the conduct of his successors. After Louis' death, Joinville was rarely at court, occupied with family and regional business in Champagne, and by the time he died, aged at least ninety-two, he had become disillusioned with the increasingly bullying Capetian regime, even putting his name to charters of protest against Louis X (1314–16), the dedicatee of the *Life*. The absence of royalist obsequiousness may help explain the apparent limited circulation of the work in the later Middle Ages. While in Syria with Louis between 1250 and 1254, Joinville also wrote a devotional commentary on the Creed, a *Credo*, and possibly a song arguing that the

87. *John of Joinville (recognisable from his horse's heraldic device) and Louis IX at the storming of Damietta, from a fourteenth-century manuscript of Joinville's* Life of St Louis.

king should remain in the east after his defeat in Egypt. In 1311, to underline his own and his family's crusading lineage, he composed an epitaph for the tomb at Clairvaux of his great-grandfather, Geoffrey III of Joinville (d. 1188), a veteran of the Second Crusade. Pious, literate, independent-minded, Joinville exemplified a certain type of thoughtful regional aristocrat in whom the cultures of crusading and chivalry seamlessly combined, and on whom continued support for the crusades depended.

and the ceding of Damietta back to the Egyptians, were women: al-Salih's widow, Shajar al-Durr, now the arbiter of power in Egypt, and Louis' heavily pregnant wife, Margaret, who took the lead in maintaining the morale of the remaining crusaders in Damietta. The agreement, which included a ransom the equivalent of *c.* 400,000 *livres tournois*, was further complicated by a coup, orchestrated by the Bahriyya Mamluks who, fearful of losing power under the new sultan, assassinated Turan Shah and installed Shajar al-Durr as sultana, ending Ayyubid rule in Egypt. On his release, Louis stayed in Palestine, effectively as its ruler, for the next four years, shoring up its defences. He only returned to France in 1254.

The scale of Louis' defeat in the Nile Delta in 1250 matched his ambition. His plan envisaged the conquest and occupation of Egypt. He apparently took with him agricultural equipment for western settlers – hoes, harrows, ploughs, ploughshares, etc. – and hoped to convert indigenous Egyptians to Christianity. The conquest of Damietta in 1249 was not envisaged as a bargaining chip for the return of Jerusalem. In rejecting an attack on Alexandria in favour of an assault on Cairo, Louis agreed with his brother Robert of Artois: 'if you wish to kill the serpent, you must first crush its head'.[60] However, even the ever-optimistic Louis saw the flaw in his scheme, regretting after the capture of Damietta that 'he had not enough people to guard and inhabit the territory in Egypt which he had already occupied and was about to seize'.[61] Once again the logistics of conquest proved defeating. The only alternative to occupation and settlement was regime change. Here Louis superficially had a better chance, as his invasion coincided with the death of the sultan and prompted a major Egyptian succession crisis. Unfortunately for the crusaders, this only resulted in the ascent to power of the militant Bahriyya Mamluks. Yet even with a sympathetic Muslim regime installed at Cairo, Louis' plan for domination possessed a fatal flaw. The ideology of the crusade precluded lasting accommodation with Muslim Egyptians. In restricted circumstances Muslim rulers or competitors for rule might tolerate Latins as allies, even co-rulers, but never as masters. Grandiose hopes of mass conversions were fanciful; seemingly there had been few in the Latin kingdom of Jerusalem in the twelfth century. The only stable contemporary Latin conquest in the Levant was Cyprus: its population was Greek Orthodox Christian; and, as an island, it was defensible. It remained in westerners' hands until 1571. Egypt, like Palestine, lacked any of these favourable qualities.

88. Aerial view of Caesarea, the perimeter walls built by Louis IX.

Louis' failure did little to suppress the Egyptian strategy. In 1270 his second crusade, a disastrous, ill-conceived and ill-executed expedition to Tunis, was declared to be preparatory to another assault on Egypt. From the second half of the thirteenth century, stimulated by defeat, the crusades to Egypt spawned an extensive genre of detailed descriptions and investigations of the Egyptian economy and society, many based on eyewitness testimony from merchants, travelling clerics or released prisoners of war. The sixty years from 1270 saw a wealth of treatises, pamphlets and policy documents examining, sometimes in minute detail, economic warfare, maritime blockade, Near Eastern diplomacy and ethnicity, campaign costs, shipping, and the requirements of professional amphibious attacks on the Nile.[62] Actions included trade bans on war materials – iron, timber, etc. – that Egypt lacked. Some strategists went further and insisted on a total cessation of all trade, while others argued that no sanctions should harm Christian merchants more than Muslim importers, recognition of the significance of the scarcely resistible attraction of Egyptian markets.[63] The Egyptian crusade strategy stimulated or forced European planners and commanders to engage with a wider Afro-Asian world beyond the politics of Syria and Palestine. By the beginning of the fourteenth century, western observers

MEDICINE

Healthcare was taken very seriously by crusade commanders and planners. Despite medieval Arabic condescension and modern commentators' disdainful superiority, medical provision for crusaders was extensive and neither wholly nugatory nor homicidal. Although wedded to classical notions of the four humours and privileging the academic learning of physicians over the artisan experience of surgeons, medieval western European medicine was not altogether ineffective in addressing the needs of crusaders and settlers in Outremer. If cures remained largely beyond medical knowledge or scientific skill, nursing was afforded respect and resources. The great twelfth-century hospital in Jerusalem run by the Order of St John catered for hundreds of patients regardless of class, race or religion, providing palliative care based on a regime of medicinal herbs, non-intervention, good diet, rest and a measure of cleanliness. The importance of medical care was recognised. Every crusade was accompanied by physicians and surgeons who complemented nursing the sick and wounded with necessary and not always ineffective campaign and battlefield surgery. Godfrey of Bouillon's life was saved by doctors (*medicos*) when he was badly injured while hunting a bear during the march across Asia Minor in 1097. They probably cauterised what appeared to be a serious arterial wound.[64] By the early thirteenth century, if not before, Italian cities were employing leading consultants to accompany their crusading contingents, while Louis IX took a cluster of physicians and surgeons with him to Egypt, including a laywoman doctor (*physica*). Formal provisions were made to cope with the high incidence of disease and sickness on campaign as well as battle injuries. In 1189, Frederick Barbarossa organised ambulance wagons for the sick to minimise both mortality and delay.[65] Hospitals or hospices were common features of campaigning on station. Besides the Hospitallers' customary provision, at the siege of Acre, field hospitals were established by the troops; one such hospital, manned by crusaders from Lübeck, Bremen and Hamburg was dedicated to St Mary, and another, by English crusaders from London, to Thomas Becket. The German hospital was the germ of what later became the Order of Teutonic Knights. During his campaign in Palestine in 1191–2, Richard I established a

89. Carts for the wounded.

hospice for his troops at Ramla, while in battle he equipped a medical station in a fortified cart.[66]

The effect of these expedients on morale may have been greater than their medical usefulness. Mortality rates on crusade are impossible to calculate accurately, but some have estimated levels among the knightly classes of between 25 and 35 per cent, possibly an underestimate and certainly lower than for the mass of crusaders: most probably succumbed to disease, bad diet, appalling sanitary conditions and malnutrition. Dysentery and scurvy seem the common ailments for which crusade physicians had awareness but no cure. Arguably, doctors achieved more, if limited success, with battlefield injuries. Wounds were cauterised or washed in wine or vinegar; broken bones were set; arrows removed; bone fragments extracted. Archaeology has revealed successful trepanning operations and recoveries from severe fractures and wounds. However, survival remained as much a lottery as a science, despite growing knowledge of superior Arabic medicine and empirical experience increasingly informing medical textbooks.[67]

were proposing alliances with the Il-Khans of Persia or with the Nubians of the Upper Nile. In the context of a new Egyptian crusade, a detailed gazetteer was produced by an Armenian prince describing Asiatic realms from Turkey to China while insisting that a necessary precursor to any crusade must be accurate knowledge of Egypt's policy and resources.[68]

The awareness of Europe being, in a phrase popular in the later Middle Ages, merely an 'angle of the world', produced among crusade theorists and later humanist scholars alike an almost existential anxiety, forcing them to assess Christendom in global and material terms, an encouragement to think geographically rather than confessionally. The portolan navigational maps included in manuscripts of crusade history and crusade advice by the Venetian merchant and crusade lobbyist Marino Sanudo (*c.* 1270–1343) in the 1320s bear witness to the early stages of this process.[69] More widely, western study of Egyptian society, particularly of the Mamluk system of recruiting foreign slaves as warriors, elicited interest in ethnology, just as the recognised manpower deficit facing western invaders of the Middle East stimulated serious analysis of international demography. One writer even suggested that the solution to combating the Muslim advantage was to infiltrate the harems of the east with trained regiments of bluestocking Mata Haris who would give birth to a Christian Fifth Column in the Muslim world.[70] Eccentricities apart, the understanding of the sheer scale of the task of overpowering Egypt inspired some genuinely global and innovative thinking.

The thirteenth-century attacks on Egypt produced paradoxical results. The Fifth Crusade assisted in sustaining the unity of the Ayyubid Empire after the death of al-Adil; the defeat of Louis IX set the Mamluks on the path to power and empire. For westerners, the Egyptian strategy opened new international horizons while exposing the impossible legacy of 1099: Erard of Valery's lap dog yapping at a mastiff indeed. However, another dimension lay not in geopolitical conflict, but in the experience of individuals, such as the veteran of the Fifth Crusade from Provins in the Ile de France who had stayed in Egypt after the crusade's withdrawal, probably as a prisoner of war, and had then converted to Islam and married an Egyptian. By the time he met an appalled King Louis after his defeat in 1250, he had risen to a position of some importance at the Ayyubid court. Or Magistra Hersende, a laywoman and physician from Paris attached to Louis' entourage on crusade, who was found cradling the sick, dysentery-ridden king when he was captured near Sharamsah in April 1250 (see 'Medicine', p. 282).[71]

CHAPTER SEVEN

CRUSADES IN SPAIN

The failure of western Christendom's armies in the eastern Mediterranean stood in contrast to Christian rulers' success in Spain. In 1248, the same year that Louis IX embarked for the Levant, Fernando III of Castile accepted the surrender of Seville, the last great metropolis of al-Andalus ('the land of the west'), leaving only Granada in Muslim hands on the Iberian Peninsula. For the previous two centuries Spain had presented both a parallel and a contrast to the crusades in the east. Observers as different as Urban II in the 1080s and 1090 and the Damascus scholar al-Sulami in 1105 regarded the wars in Spain as part of wider Christian assaults on Islamic lands. For al-Sulami, the Franks, encouraged by Muslim disunity, had conquered Sicily and made extensive conquests in Spain before descending on the Near East,[1] while during the First Crusade Urban encouraged Catalan counts to concentrate on the local struggle rather than the Jerusalem adventure: 'it is no virtue to rescue Christians from the Saracens in one place, only to expose them to the tyranny and oppression of the Saracens in another'.[2] However, except in rhetoric and possibly spiritual incentive, the circumstances of eleventh-century Christian advances in Spain were distinct from those surrounding the Jerusalem wars. Crusading did not inspire the conquest of al-Andalus, Muslim Spain. Instead, the formulae of cross, papal privileges and remissions of sins were applied to pre-existing secular rivalries, finding natural affinity within long-standing self-justifications of political contest.

90. Spanish Christian troops.

The Spanish 'Reconquest'

War between Christian lords in the far north of the Iberian Peninsula and Muslim rulers to their south was not new in the late eleventh century. Exchange and competition across Christendom's Spanish frontier pre-dated crusade indulgences, establishing patterns of conduct and traditions later coloured but not shaped by the *negotium crucis*. The political history of early medieval Spain hardly compared with that of Europe north of the Pyrenees. In the early eighth century, the former Roman province of Hispania, dominated by an entrenched Christian Visigothic kingdom based at Toledo, was overrun after 711 by north African Berber armies commanded by Arab generals. A Muslim emirate with a capital at Cordoba (756–1031), rebranded in 929 as an autonomous caliphate, emerged under descendants of the Near Eastern Umayyad caliphs of the seventh and eight centuries. Only in the north beyond the Duero valley, in the Cantabrian mountains and the Basque country, did Christian lordships survive. Elsewhere, the Arab conquest led to a slow process of Arabisation and even slower Islamicisation: by 900 only about 25 per cent while in 1000 perhaps about 75 per cent of the population of Spain may have been Muslims. Jews and Christians, as People of the Book, paid the *jiyza* or poll tax, and adopted the customs and language of their masters. Arabic-speaking Christians, known as Mozarabs, developed their own liturgies. Early medieval Spain, as elsewhere around the Mediterranean, witnessed a pragmatic *convivencia* (literally 'living together') characterised by separation and indifference not tolerance or harmony, cultural synthesis combined with economic competition and potential social hostility.

The earliest Christian enclave to cohere into a perceptible lordship developed around Orviedo in the Asturias which, by the early tenth century, had expanded south to incorporate a new capital, León, and the county of Castile in the upper Ebro valley. In the western Pyrenees, lordships later known as Navarre and Aragon emerged. In the early ninth century a Carolingian county was established in Catalonia after Charlemagne's attempts in 778 to create a Frankish march further south around Zaragoza had failed in a campaign later made famous by the *Song of Roland*'s embroidered stories of the defeat of its rearguard at Roncevalles. Apart from Catalonia's involvement in trans-Pyrenean Francia, the politics of the Christian principalities revolved around local rivalries and raiding across the frontier with the Cordoba caliphate. The *Song of Roland*'s depiction of the massacre of a Frankish regiment by Pyrenean Basques in 778 as an epic contest between heroic Christian knights and demonic armies of Islam reflected eleventh-century French fiction, not eighth-century Iberian realities. After the eighth century, the Spanish frontier wars only began to be incorporated into grander perceptions of cosmic religious confrontation once they attracted French recruits and serious papal interest in the eleventh century.

How far, if at all, these local struggles for material existence and advantage had previously been perceived by Christian Spaniards in religious terms remains unclear, as does the genesis of the idea that the conquest of Muslim Spain constituted a *re*conquest, the *Reconquista* of nationalist myth. Early versions of the Reconquest idea were crafted in the late ninth century in the Asturias to demonstrate a legitimising link between Asturian kingship, the old Visigoth rulers, and a providential mission to restore Christian rule to the peninsula. This justified raids and campaigns against the Moors (people from the north African coast, Mauretania, Berbers) in religious terms, an elevation of purpose and consolidation of political identity familiar across early medieval western Europe, and not restricted to Christian rulers. The great Cordoban vizier, al-Mansur (i.e. 'the Victorious', 976–1002), declared his attacks on Christian territory to be *jihads* and flaunted his Koranic credentials. However, religious frontiers competed with many others in early eleventh-century Iberia. While the power of the Cordoban caliphate made it a prime threat to its Christian neighbours, political competition saw Christians fighting Christians, Muslims fighting Muslims, and all engaging in alliances and economic and commercial exchange across religious divides.

Politics and cash, not religion, provided the impetus for the wars after the sudden collapse of the Cordoban caliphate in 1031, which was replaced by unstable but still wealthy so-called *taifa* or 'party' kingdoms.[3] These competing Muslim principalities actively sought external military aid regardless of religion. Christian rulers soon took advantage, entering into agreements under which they were hired by *taifa* rulers in return for *parias*, annual tributes, effectively protection money, paid in gold. The urban economy of al-Andalus had exploited the gold coming across the Sahara from west Africa. The *parias* gave Christian rulers of the north direct access to large quantities of gold, a very scarce commodity in the rest of western Europe, consolidating their power, creating new opportunities to expand their frontiers at their paymasters' expense and to attract attention from beyond the Pyrenees. This last included fashionable ideas of holy war. However, religion was not a factor in *paria* agreements. In one, with the emir of Zaragoza in 1069, for 1,000 gold pieces a month, Sancho IV of Navarre promised not to allow 'people from France or elsewhere' to cross his kingdom to attack Zaragoza or to ally with anyone, Christian or Muslim, against the emir.[4] Such arrangements encouraged a mercenary free trade. Anyone – Muslim or Christian – with sufficient military credentials and armed support could sell their services to the highest bidder. The most famous freelance was the Castilian nobleman Rodrigo Diaz, El Cid (c. 1045–99). As well as serving Fernando I of León-Castile (1035–65) and his son Alfonso VI (1065–1109), Rodrigo fought for the emir of Zaragoza (1081–6) against Catalans and Aragonese. From 1089, he operated his own army, fighting Christian as well as Muslim rulers in eastern Spain before creating for himself an independent *taifa* lordship at Valencia (1094–99) that survived until 1102.[5] Christian rulers still competed with each other, no more united than their Muslim neighbours.

Such opportunism sought the respectable cloak of ideology, conquest justified as reclaiming territories that 'originally belonged to the Christians' or as 'the recovery and extension of the Church of Christ', a claim made explicit by Alfonso VI after capturing Toledo in 1085 when he wrote of the city, after 376 years of Muslim rule, now restored 'under the leadership of Christ . . . to the devotees of His faith'. Urban II echoed the theme, writing that Toledo had been 'restored to the law of the Christians'.[6] The religious rhetoric of Reconquest hardly concealed the secular drivers of the campaigns against the *taifa* kingdoms once Christian rulers sought political control rather than financial exploitation. By the 1090s, the frontier of al-Andalus had been pushed south to a line roughly from Coimbra in the west to north of Tarragona in the east, with a Christian salient extending down to Toledo on the Tagus in the centre. The Christian gains were modest and hardly presaged any inevitable annexation of the whole peninsula; al-Andalus still dominated most of the richest regions. These late eleventh-century wars were of piecemeal conquest and, in places, expulsion. One abiding feature of the Reconquest remained the custom that cities were surrendered through negotiation, with garrisons and civilians allowed to depart, a pattern repeated right up to and including the final expulsion of the Moors from Granada in 1492. Unlike some Levant campaigns, and even where complicated by north African interventions, the Spanish wars were fought as between neighbours, not aliens.

Holy War

The indigenous political and religious justification of Reconquest provided fertile ground for holy war as developed by the eleventh-century papacy, just as the wars themselves attracted trans-Pyrenean recruits. A Catalan-Aragonese attack on Barbastro, north-east of Zaragoza, in 1064–5, drew recruits from Burgundy, Normandy, Aquitaine and possibly Norman Sicily perhaps lured by an offer of remission of penance and sins by Pope Alexander II, who around the same time provided a blanket just-war authorisation when fighting Muslims who oppressed Christians. In one respect, the warriors at Barbastro followed a new uncompromising militancy, their brief occupation of the town marked by violent atrocities later familiar from the First Crusade. Foreigners brought with them an ignorance of Muslims and a confident brutish martial spirituality that chimed with the policies of contemporary popes. Spain became a laboratory for hegemonic papal policies in replacing the Spanish Mozarab liturgy with a Roman one and in the spiritualisation of war, particularly against Islam. In 1073,

Gregory VII argued that Spain 'from ancient times belonged to the personal right of St. Peter' and, despite long Moorish occupation, still did, a claim combated by Alfonso VI in 1077 when he styled himself 'emperor of all Spain'.[7] Further trans-Pyrenean links were witnessed by the penetration of Cluniac monasticism into northern Spain, from mid-century under the lavish patronage of the kings of León. In 1064, Raymond Berenguer I of Catalonia promulgated a Peace and Truce of God, a mechanism popular in places north of the Pyrenees whereby local lords swore to keep the peace and protect ecclesiastical property. By the 1080s, marriages of Spanish princes and princesses to spouses from north of the Pyrenees had become familiar. All five of Alfonso VI's legitimate wives came from outside Spain, a sign his dynasty had entered the family of western European rulers, even if domestically Alfonso may have retained local tastes: one of his mistresses may have been the daughter-in-law of the emir of Seville.[8]

The fusion of border conflicts, Reconquest and holy war in Spain came from the coincidence of the invasion of al-Andalus by the Moroccan Almoravids in 1086 and the promotion of penitential war by the papacy in the generation before the First Crusade. Originally a radical group of Islamic fundamentalists from the margins of the Sahara, by the early 1080s the Almoravids – the *al-Murabitum* or 'people of the ribat' (Islamic frontier military monasteries) – had conquered Morocco, rigorously enforcing austere religious observance somewhat at odds with the relaxed sophistication of al-Andalus. By the mid-1080s they were ready to extend their authority across the Straits of Gibraltar into al-Andalus. With pressure growing from the north in the aftermath of Alfonso VI's capture of Toledo in 1085, the *taifa* emirs, led by Seville, had little option but to invite Almoravid aid. The invasion, under Yusuf ibn Tushufin, led to the defeat of Alfonso at Sagrajas in 1086. While providing apparent support for al-Andalus, over the next quarter of a century, by force, coercion and diplomacy, the Almoravids absorbed the *taifa* emirates into their own empire, the last, Zaragoza, falling in 1110. The Almoravids' destruction of the *paria* system and their military threat encouraged the reactive adoption of Christian holy war. The arrival of the north Africans added a new and, for both Christian opponents and indigenous Muslims, an unwelcome and complicating dimension to Iberian politics. This was recognised by the distinction drawn by twelfth-century Christian Spanish writers between the Muslims of al-Andalus, 'Moors' and 'Hagarenes', with whom business could be done, and alien invaders, 'Moabites'(Almoravids) and, later, 'Assyrians' or 'Muzmotos' (the Almohads, invaders from north Africa from the 1140s), with whom it could not.[9]

Into this new political situation arrived foreign soldiers with the ideology and institutions of penitential warfare. In 1089 and 1091, Urban II offered the same remission of sins given to Jerusalem pilgrims to those who helped rebuild the city and church of Tarragona, across the frontier fifty miles south of Barcelona, as the city was intended as a 'wall and bastion against the Saracens for the Christian people'.[10] The First Crusade did not deflect Urban from support of the Tarragona enterprise, urging local counts to fulfil their crusade vows not in the east but nearer home. In the event, Jerusalem seems to have proved a greater draw, in Christian Spain as elsewhere. However, Urban's elision of objectives stuck. Peter I of Aragon (1094–1104) took the cross for Jerusalem in 1100. A year later, besieging Zaragoza, he was described as wearing his cross and displaying banners of the cross. The siege castle he built was nicknamed 'Juslibol', 'God Wills it', the slogan of Clermont.[11]

The subsequent incorporation of crusading institutions – bulls, indulgences, temporal privileges and cross – only gradually refined older associations of conquest and religious war. The past was reinvented to accommodate holy war. From around 1115 the patronal saint, James the Apostle, became a 'knight of Christ', perhaps in part as a potent competitor to contest papal proprietary claims for St Peter.[12] Other saintly recruits included popular heavenly crusading patrons the Virgin Mary and St George, but also, in León, the less obvious seventh-century scholar Isidore of Seville. However, local traditions of non-violent association of Christians and al-Andalus Muslims continued to shade crusade stereotypes, as in the literary treatment of Rodrigo Diaz, El Cid. Both the twelfth-century *Historia Roderici* and the early thirteenth-century epic *Poema de Mio Cid* admit to Rodrigo's friendship with Muslims and the shortcomings of Christians as well as Moors. The tone of crusading is absent.[13] The insinuation of crusading into Spain through papal bulls and the example of the Jerusalem wars was not comprehensive. Crusading was not associated with every campaign nor did it determine politics or military strategy. The most concrete association of holiness with war found expression in the imported Military Orders, their indigenous imitators and crusade taxation. The Iberian reality of shared space with other religions tempered the demonising posturing and religious conflict familiar in the rest of Latin Christendom.

91. St James the moor killer by Tiepolo.

92. Convivencia? *A Christian and a black Moor playing chess.*

Only in the later Middle Ages did memorialised crusade models more obviously encourage aggressive cultural discrimination and the active social pursuit of an exclusive divine mission.[14]

The Spanish Crusades

The legacy of the First Crusade and its apparatus lent patchy definition to holy war in Spain. Special interest was shown by popes with experience as Spanish legates: Cardinals Rainier (Paschal II, 1099–1118), Guy of Burgundy (Calixtus II, 1119–24) and Hyacinth (Celestine III, 1191–8). However, the initiative for seeking crusade formulae came chiefly not from Rome but from Iberian commanders wishing to enhance existing military schemes. Paschal II offered remission of sins to encourage Spaniards to resist the lure of the Jerusalem war in favour of fighting the Moors and Almoravids at home.[15] At the request of the Pisans, the cross, a papal banner and remissions were granted to an ephemerally successful Pisan-Catalan-southern French campaign against the Balearic Islands in 1113–14, and possibly for a planned assault on Tortosa. Those who died helping Alfonso I 'the Battler' of Aragon capture Zaragoza in 1118 or contributed to restoring its church were rewarded with papal remissions. Spain's moral and strategic equivalence with the Holy Land was confirmed by Canon XI of Calixtus II's First Lateran Council of 1123. This equated those taking the cross for Jerusalem with those for Spain, a stance reiterated by regional church councils and Calixtus's granting to *crucesignati* in Catalonia the 'same remission of sins that we conceded to the defenders of the eastern church'.[16] The rhetorical incorporation of Spain with the Holy Land found an echo in Archbishop Diego Gelmirez of Santiago's 1125 fanciful project to attack Jerusalem via north Africa: 'let us become soldiers of Christ . . . taking up arms . . . for the remission of sins'.[17] By 1150, this redefinition of the Reconquest as cognate to the Jerusalem war was reflected in Leónese and Castilian chronicles, with their themes of revenge and militant scriptural references. Most strikingly, in 1131, Alfonso I of Aragon-Navarre (d. 1134) formally – if abortively – bequeathed his kingdom jointly to the Templars, Hospitallers and the canons of the Holy Sepulchre; in the 1120s he had toyed with the creation of a Templar-style *militia Christi* to combat Muslims and open a new way to Jerusalem.[18]

93. Archbishop Gelmirez blesses two knights.

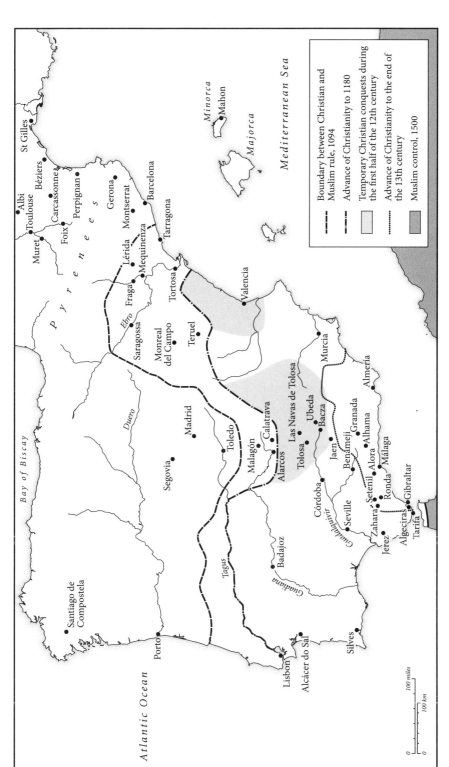

13. *The Spanish* Reconquista.

Legend:
- Boundary between Christian and Muslim rule, 1094
- Advance of Christianity to 1180
- Temporary Christian conquests during the first half of the 12th century
- Advance of Christianity to the end of the 13th century
- Muslim control, 1500

Atlantic Ocean

Bay of Biscay

Mediterranean Sea

Pyrenees

Minorca
Mahon

Majorca

St Gilles
Albi
Toulouse
Muret
Béziers
Carcassonne
Foix
Perpignan
Gerona
Montserrat
Barcelona
Tarragona
Lérida
Mequinenza
Fraga
Tortosa
Valencia

Saragossa
Ebro
Monreal del Campo
Teruel
Murcia
Almería

Duero
Madrid
Segovia
Toledo
Malagón
Calatrava
Alarcos
Las Navas de Tolosa
Tolosa
Ubeda
Baeza
Granada
Alhama
Benámeji
Jaén
Alora
Málaga
Ronda
Setenil
Zahara
Gibraltar
Algeciras
Tarifa

Córdoba
Guadalquivir
Seville
Jerez

Santiago de Compostela

Porto
Lisbon
Alcácer do Sal
Silves
Badajoz
Tagus
Guadiana

100 miles
100 km

The association of Reconquest with crusade remained contingent not automatic. In 1146 the Genoese attempt on the port of Almeria was described in secular terms whereas in 1147, with the Second Crusade to the east already launched, a renewed ultimately successful Genoese attack with Alfonso VII of Castile attracted both the rhetoric and institutions of holy war. 'Redemption of souls' had been offered even before Alfonso secured crusade status for the new attack from Eugenius III. While in practice the initiation and execution of the Almeria campaign owed nothing to the eastern expedition, it easily attracted the convenient aura of the Holy Land war, as did the Catalan-Genoese siege of Tortosa in 1148 that elicited a new papal grant of indulgences, 'which Pope Urban established for all those going for the liberation of the eastern church'.[19] The piggy-backing of the Reconquest onto the Jerusalem war was emphasised by Afonso of Portugal's employment of passing crusaders in the successful siege of Lisbon (July–October 1147). This represented part of a pattern whereby fleets bound for the Holy Land attacked Muslim seaports, for pay, plunder, glory and winter anchorages: King Sigurd of Norway in 1108 (Sintra, Alcácer do Sal); the North Sea fleets of the Second Crusade in 1147 (Lisbon), and their successors in 1189 (the Algarve and Silves) and 1217 (Alcácer do Sal). While lacking separate crusade bulls, these interventions reinforced a perceived unity of purpose and merit between Spain and the Holy Land. Yet the gloss of piety did not disguise the incentive of land and profit. The contemporary *Poem of Almeria*, celebrating the 1147 conquest, combined crusade motifs (St Mary, forgiveness of sins, 'the trumpet of salvation') with praise of chivalric values ('the glory of waging war is life itself'; the Castilian knights 'enjoy themselves more in war than one friend does with another') and the promise of 'reward of this life' as well as the next: 'prizes of silver, and with victory . . . all the gold which the Moors possess': a distillation of the distinctive flavour of the Reconquest crusades.[20]

In Spain, as elsewhere, the failure of the Second Crusade dampened the popularity of formal trappings of the crusade. Occasional deployments of papal grants, cross and indulgences persisted, as for a Catalan campaign in the Ebro valley in 1152–3. A council at Segovia in 1166 proposed Jerusalem indulgences for those fighting in defence of Castile while during Cardinal Hyacinth's two legatine missions of 1154–5 and 1172–3 the future pope, a tenacious crusade enthusiast, took the cross and offered remission of sins. In 1175, Hyacinth persuaded Alexander III to issue a fresh crusade bull in the face of a new danger posed by the Almohads, *al-Muwahhidun*, or 'Upholders of the Divine Unity'. Puritanically fundamentalist, and like the Almoravids from desert margins of south Morocco, the Almohads sought to impose their vision of the original purity of early Islam on the Maghreb and al-Andalus. Under their founder Muhammed ibn Tumart (d. 1130, declared a *mahdi* in 1121) and his successor Abd al-Mu'min (1130–63), the Almohads quickly overran the decaying power of the Almoravids in north Africa and, from 1146, began to subdue the emirs of al-Andalus. By 1173, Muslim Spain had been annexed under Yusuf I (1163–84), who now directly challenged the Christian rulers to the north. Over the next quarter of a century, many earlier Christian advances were reversed. In 1195, Alfonso VIII of Castile, supported by a crusade bull of 1193, was defeated at Alarcos and the Tagus valley raided. Yet, politics still trumped religion: disaffected Castilians fought for the Almohads at Alarcos; a Muslim regiment joined Alfonso IX of León's invasion of Castile in 1196. In response, in 1197 the nonagenarian Celestine III, former legate Hyacinth, promulgated full eastern crusading privileges against Alfonso IX.

The proposed crusade against Alfonso IX followed the Third Crusade's reignition of the Jerusalem war as the standard for church-approved violence. In 1188, Clement III extended Holy Land crusade privileges to Spain, including proportionate indulgences for non-combatant material contributors and a grant of church revenues. Thereafter, unlike crusades against Baltic pagans and apostates, heretics or other Christian religious or political dissidents in Europe, crusades in Spain were automatically assumed to be equivalent in merit to those to the Holy Land, even if not always as important.[21] In 1213, Innocent III cancelled the offer of crusade privileges in Spain except for Spaniards themselves in favour of his new Holy Land enterprise.[22] By the early thirteenth century, crusade privileges became customary accessories to the Reconquest especially after the strenuous international preaching campaign preceding the crusade of 1212 that led to the crushing victory of Alfonso VIII of Castile and Peter II of Aragon over the Almohads at Las Navas de Tolosa, the true beginning of the process of reconquest that ended in 1492. While this campaign included recruits from across the Pyrenees (most of whom left before the climactic battle), and later Christian conquests attracted foreign settlers, the thirteenth century saw the Spanish crusade become the preserve of Spaniards alone, its traditions and institutions developing in parallel but distinct from the rest of western Christendom.

94. The Almohad banner captured at Las Navas de Tolosa.

Military Orders

The Military Orders supplied one example of this Hispanisation of crusading. As providers of frontier garrisons, recipients of alms, estates, villages and castles, the Military Orders were integral to the Reconquest. While attracting patronage in the form of land grants by the 1130s, from the 1140s the Templars and Hospitallers exercised military roles. The Orders' combination of disciplined commitment, hierarchical control, directed endowment

95. A Templar tower on the Ebro near Tortosa.

and military efficiency proved a model for local rulers to establish their own national Orders. As in the Baltic, the proximity of a frontier with non-Christian territories gave the Spanish Military Orders a status, power and significance denied similar national Orders elsewhere in western Europe. By 1180 every Spanish kingdom except Navarre had their own Order alongside the Templars and Hospitallers (who remained prominent in Aragon and Catalonia): Calatrava in Castile (1158); Santiago (1170) and St Julian of Pereiro, later known as Alcantara (by 1176) in León; Evora, later Avis (by 1176) in Portugal. Local fraternities sprang up defending individual frontier castles, although lacking the resources or institutional permanence of the larger national Orders. Another Order, La Merced (*c.* 1230) in Barcelona, dealt with ransoming captives from the Moors.

Patrons included pious nobles or merchants, as well as kings and clerics. The larger Orders became sufficiently established to attract international investment: by 1200 the Order of Santiago held property from the British Isles to Carinthia in southern Austria. The Orders of Alcantara (1238) and Calatrava (1240) were granted papal indulgences to any who fought with them against the Moors, embedding the sort of 'eternal crusade' adopted later in the thirteenth century by the Teutonic Knights in the Baltic. That these privileges only came towards the completion of the conquest of al-Andalus signalled the Orders' wider political, social and cultural influence as they became firmly associated with royal power. Monarchs increasingly controlled them, helping configure Spanish politics as institutionally crusading long after any immediate Moorish threat had been extinguished.

The Thirteenth Century and Beyond

The patriation of the Spanish crusade allied the ideal of Christian holy war with wars that would have been fought anyway by armies gathered through normal secular processes of military obligation, dependence, clientage and alliance, with terms of service the same as for non-crusading warfare. The Spanish crusades could hardly be branded as pilgrimages. As the twelfth-century *Poem of Almeria* noted, beside religious inspiration, pay and booty provided necessary incentives. Increasingly, the Church, as a leading material beneficiary, provided fiscal subsidies. Initially, crusade privileges of the sort offered in 1123 may have been intended as a device to attract international support, southern France appearing especially fertile in recruits. However, cross-Pyrenean involvement declined. The battle of Las Navas de Tolosa on 16 July 1212 became iconic. Won by a coalition of Alfonso VIII of Castile, Peter II of Aragon and Sancho VII of Navarre, with most of their French allies having withdrawn a fortnight earlier, the victory over the Almohads under al-Nasir (1199–1214) was presented as providential and national, Spanish revenge for 711.

The victory's material as well as ideological legacy was profound. Politically, Castile reaped the main reward, with al-Andalus exposed by the rapid collapse of Almohad power. Castile lacked competitors with the long minority of James I of Aragon after the death of Peter II in 1213, and the succession to the throne of Navarre of the distant count of Champagne in 1234. Alfonso VIII's financial expedients that had paid for the 1212 coalition, including a 50 per cent levy on the Castilian Church's annual revenues, provided a lasting model. Wrapped in crusaders' mantles, subsequent Iberian rulers used the Church to subsidise their wars, including, from the mid-thirteenth century, a third of ecclesiastical tithe income (*tercias*) and regular appropriation of Holy Land clerical taxation, used alongside secular levies and forced loans. As with other European frontier regions in the later Middle Ages, the crusade allowed for the permanent extension of the fiscal and political power of the state.

By 1250, only the emirate of Granada survived in Muslim hands, effectively a client of Castile. After 1212, the traffic of attack and conquest was for the first time largely one way, the rapid collapse of the Almohad Empire leaving a newly enfeebled al-Andalus behind. Whereas after Las Navas, Innocent III concentrated his crusade policy on the Holy Land, his successors Honorius III, Gregory IX and Innocent IV were enthusiastic supporters of applying the crusade to Spanish annexations in Iberia and the Balearic Islands and to plans to invade Morocco. From the 1220s, Fernando III of Castile (1217–52, and of León from 1230) identified his expansion southwards towards the Guadalquivir valley as a religious mission. He appears to have used a crusade bull of 1231 as open-ended consecration for his conquests of Cordoba (1236), Murcia (1243) and Seville (1248). In the 1220s, James I 'the Conqueror' of Aragon (1213–76) received crusade bulls for his successful invasion of the Balearic Islands (1229–35) and, from the 1220s onwards, his campaigns against Peniscola, Valencia (annexed 1232–45) and Murcia. Crusades were employed in the 1230s and 1240s by the Portuguese kings Sancho II (1223–47) and Afonso III (1248–79) as they pushed south into the Algrave. The international context was recognised in regular suggestions of extending the holy war to north Africa and Palestine. Within the peninsula, limited foreign involvement persisted: English and French troops joined the siege of Valencia (1238) and foreigners were settled in Seville after 1248. Although schemes for the invasion of Morocco and forays across the Straits of Gibraltar punctuated the next three centuries, only James I, by then crusading's elder statesman, actively engaged with the eastern crusade, sending an Aragonese regiment to Acre in 1269 and attending the crusade discussions at the Second Council of Lyons (1274).

96. James the Conqueror besieging Palma, Mallorca, 1229–30.

As before, holy war was tempered by social and political reality. Annexations tended to be concluded by negotiation that secured some of the religious and legal rights of the conquered (for example, Mallorca in 1229, Valencia in 1238 and Murcia in 1243). Valencia retained its majority Muslim population. While some Muslims prudently apostatised, efforts at conversion were limited. Following conquest, in a reversal of roles, the *mudejars* (Muslims living under Christian rule) became protected second-class citizens with freedom to worship. Gradually, with increased Christian settlement, the Hispanisation and Christianisation of public spaces, religious sites, place names and secular landscapes, the accommodation with the *mudejars* frayed both locally and as part of public policy. Even by the end of the thirteenth century, there had been *mudejar* revolts. Thereafter, interfaith communal relations tended to be practical not principled. From the mid-fifteenth century, especially in Castile, a political and cultural revival of militant neo-crusading produced active state intolerance and the imposition of Christian uniformity under Ferdinand II of Aragon (1479–1516) and Isabella of Castile (1474–1504), and their heirs Charles V (1516–56) and Philip II (1556–98). Despite rhetorical echoes, the persecution and final expulsion (1609–14) of *mudejars* and *moriscos* (descendants of Muslim converts to Christianity) belonged to a different world to that of the Spanish crusades of the twelfth and thirteenth centuries.

The fall of Seville in 1248 concluded the rapid Christian territorial advances of the previous quarter of a century. However, wars continued with Granada; fresh threats came from the new Marinid rulers of Morocco, who invaded Spain in 1275, 1276 and 1282–3; occasional military excursions continued to north Africa (for example, the Castilian attack on Salé in 1260); and a prolonged struggle was waged for control of the Straits of Gibraltar, accompanied by a scattering of crusade privileges. Alfonso XI of Castile (1312–50) pursued a concerted Reconquest policy, regularly backed by crusade bulls. He defeated a major Marinid invasion at the River Salado in 1340 and, with international aid, captured Algeciras in 1344 as well as unsuccessfully besieging Gibraltar (which had been in Castilian hands since 1309) in 1333 and 1349–50, the second attempt ending when the king and many of his troops succumbed to the Black Death. The subsequent half-century of armed co-existence was broken around 1400 by a revival of Christian aggression. In 1410 the Castilians annexed Antequera. In 1415 the Portuguese capture of Ceuta on the north African coast was supported by crusade indulgences despite the complications of rival papacies during the Great Schism (1378–1417).

From popular literature to frontier plundering, the culture of crusading continued to suffuse Spanish aristocratic society, especially in Castile which from the thirteenth century possessed the only land border with Granada. Materially, in the fifteenth century, as elsewhere in Christendom, crusade bulls, preaching and indulgences were primarily fiscal devices, aimed at raising money through the sale of the crusade indulgences. From the pontificates of Martin V (1417–31) and Eugenius IV (1431–47), the Spanish *bula de crozada* became standardised, offering increasingly lowered fixed flat rates of purchase to attract more customers. In 1456 the Spanish Borgia pope Calixtus III (1455–8) extended the indulgence to the dead in purgatory. These bulls provided Iberian rulers with status and cash; and popes with international prestige and diplomatic influence. They became entrenched in Spanish public life, surviving the reforms of the penitential indulgence system at the Council of Trent (1545–63) and persisting in attenuated form until finally abolished by the Second Vatican Council (1962–5).

The ideology of crusade and Reconquest, sustained by the continued power of the Military Orders under royal command, lent an indelible providential tinge to the presentation of national identity. By the end of the fifteenth century, Castile itself was being promoted as a Holy Land in its own right, its Christian inhabitants the new Israelites, in clear appropriation of earlier crusade rhetoric.[23] Such claims suited royal domestic policy. Campaigning against Moors provided a convenient mechanism for controlling and directing energetic and restless nobles in an incontrovertibly respectable cause. An active crusading holy war tradition was revived in the mid-fifteenth century, with campaigns against Granada in the 1430s, a raft of papal bulls around 1450 and the capture of Gibraltar in 1462. The renewal of war against Granada by Isabella of Castile and Ferdinand II of Aragon, 1482–92, leading to the final expulsion of Moorish political rule from the peninsula in January 1492, regularly attracted full papal privileges. In a bull of 1482, Sixtus IV drew explicit parallels with the Holy Land crusades.[24] Crusade privileges were also extended to Portuguese campaigns in the Maghreb that had been a feature of their foreign policy since 1415. Indulgences were awarded for campaigns aimed at Tangiers, for example in 1471, and from 1486 these copied the full Castilian Granada grants, repeated in 1505, 1507 and 1515. Charles V's seizure of Tunis in 1535 was presented in crusading terms. As late as 1578, King Sebastian of Portugal (1557–78), supported by indulgences and papal legates, died fighting Moors in Morocco at the battle of Alcazar.

97. The surrender of Granada to the Catholic Monarchs by Muhammed XII in 1492, wood relief, c. 1495.

Wars in Morocco and Tunisia, driven by pursuit of fame, political advantage and commercial hegemony, could be fitted into traditional Reconquest justification of defence or recovery of Christian territory. However, Sixtus IV's 1482 Granada crusade bull also insisted on the crusade as a mechanism for spreading the Christian faith. This had become important as crusading formulae were applied to Spanish and Portuguese expeditions down the west African coast and to the islands of the eastern Atlantic from the reign of Eugenius IV (1431–47) onwards. Canon law going back to the thirteenth century allowed for the forcible subjugation of indigenous pagans if they resisted missionary work, hardly an objective or neutral test.[25] However, while the rhetoric and emotions of crusading were freely applicable to the conquests of the Canaries (1402–96) and later the Americas, formal crusade apparatus was less easily translated. Only by analogy could the Atlantic conquests be viewed as Reconquest or by stretching the reach of global crusade strategy, as in Christopher Columbus's insistence that his expeditions were conceived in the context of the recovery of Jerusalem.[26] In 1455, Nicholas V had granted the Portuguese the right to conquer and enslave African unbelievers. However, in the bull *Inter cetera* (1493) regarding conquests in the newly discovered Americas, Alexander VI (1492–1503), another Spanish Borgia pope, insisted that conversion was the sole justification for political dominion over indigenous peoples. In the event, the Spanish-Portuguese treaty of Tordesillas (1494), which carved up future global conquests, ignored papal authority, implicitly severing the new conquests from crusading. After the establishment of New Spain, America's formal connection with the crusade, as a province of the Spanish Empire, was confined to *bula de croẓada* fund-raising. The conquistadors do not seem to have sought crusade privileges. Despite sharing a historical, religious, emotional and psychological culture with *crucesignati*, the conquerors of America did not take the cross.

The revival of the crusade during the Granada war of the 1480s depended as much on a recasting of Catholic Spain's manifest destiny as it did on Aragonese and Castilian crusading traditions. Domestically, this conditioned the creation of an exclusive sectarian Christian society and, externally, informed the projection of Spanish imperialism. Images of past and future crusading combined to forge a dynamic sense of duty, supremacy and mission. Diplomatic rhetoric in early sixteenth-century Europe was larded with pious references to a new holy war against the Turks. In this, propagandists claimed a unique historic role for Spain, feeding a form of messianism that entered deep into national identity. The Spanish crusades played their part in the profound, occasionally dramatic, political, social and religious transformation of the Iberian Peninsula in the later Middle Ages. Their cultural legacy and tenacious myths coloured Spanish attitudes for centuries to come.

98. *The Fascist crusader: General Franco.*

CHAPTER EIGHT

BALTIC CRUSADES

The crusades in the Baltic were defined by materials: fish, fur, amber, timber, slaves; ships' carpentry and rigging; stone and brick for forts, castles and cathedrals; metal for weaponry. As in Spain, the use of crusading formulae overlaid existing contest for land and wealth. Like Spain too, the long-term political outcome was a triumph for Latin Christendom. However, unlike Spain, in two of the three areas where crusades were instituted in the Baltic – in Prussia (chiefly modern Poland) and Livonia (modern Latvia and Estonia) but not the Wendish lands east of the Elbe – new forms of government were established by a crusading Military Order, the Teutonic Knights, not secular rulers. The Baltic ideology of conquest was borrowed from other theatres of crusading: defence of Christians; retribution for apostasy; revenge for past wrongs; recovery of lost Christian territory supported by due authority and righteous religious intent. However, justifications for the northern crusades also fed off older German traditions and more recent Scandinavian experience of warfare against neighbouring pagans, all the time displaying the unmistakable reality of tangible profit.

The Baltic crusades were fought for territory, trade and the pursuit of secular and ecclesiastical glory and imperialism. Until the thirteenth century, the region's wars rarely attracted full Holy Land papal crusade grants of cross, preaching, remissions, privileges. The more frequent papal issues of limited remissions, of varying generosity and without other features of full crusade grants, built on pre-crusading attitudes to meritorious war. Two further aspects added to Baltic distinctiveness. For a century from the 1140s, German crusaders competed vigorously and occasionally violently with Danish kings.

Moreover, these crusade wars, unlike those in the Levant or Spain, were directly associated with forced conversion. Bernard of Clairvaux explained in 1147 when sanctioning the adoption of Holy Land crusading symbols and privileges by the Saxon summer campaign against the pagan Wends: 'They shall either be converted or wiped out'. This was, as Innocent III in 1209 declared to Valdemar II of Denmark, 'the war of the Lord . . . to drag the barbarians into the net of orthodoxy', a suspect principle in canon law, although elsewhere justified by Christ's parable in Luke 14:23: 'compel them to come in'.[1]

Origins

The Baltic crusades helped transform northern Europe. From the lower Elbe to Livonia, Estonia, Finland and the Gulfs of Finland and Bothnia, the subjugation, exploitation and ultimate Christianisation of its indigenous peoples imposed permanent political, cultural and environmental change. The campaigns revived German attacks on the western Slavs that had stalled after the tenth-century Ottonian kings of Germany had abandoned earlier advances following the great Slav rising of 983. The German tradition of sanctified wars against non-Christians in eastern and central Europe, stretching back through the tenth-century kings to Charlemagne in the eighth, provided precedents and an ideology of defending and expanding Christendom by force, an enterprise now joined by expansionist rulers of Denmark. The incentives for a new advance across the Elbe towards Pomerania were obvious, as a Flemish clerk put it in 1108: 'These gentiles are most wicked, but their land is the best, rich in meat, honey, corn and birds; and if it were well cultivated none could be compared to it for the wealth of its produce.'[2]

The region's politically fragmented lordships, tribes and extended families were divided by ethnic and linguistic differences. The Wends, western Slavs between the Elbe and the Vistula, were related to the Poles and Czechs. With territorial princes, market towns, ports and a polytheism ordered around a strong priesthood, well-stocked temples and numinous cultic sites, the structural similarities of Wendish society to its German and Danish neighbours eased frontier accommodation and post-conquest assimilation. The lands further east, from the Vistula to the Dvina and the Gulf of Riga, were inhabited by separate tribal groups of Balts: Prussians, Lithuanians,

Latvians and Curonians. Less centralised than the Wends, political power was exerted by local chieftans whose warrior aristocracies exploited the countryside from fortified earthworks, backed by control of fertility cults. North of the Balts, scattered Finno-Ugrian communities from the Gulf of Riga, Estonia and the Gulf of Finland comprised extended families, temporary local confederations and strong religious nature cults. Across the

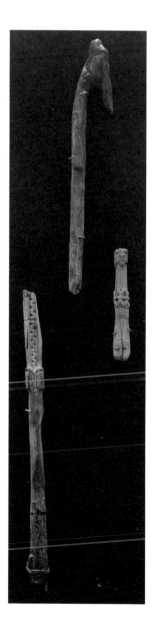

99. Baltic paganism: tree idols in Livonia.

region, religious practices supplied social cohesion and political identity. Whereas the Wends, after previous generations of regular contact, proved susceptible to German assimilation once conquered, the Balts and others proved more robustly hostile.

In Germany and Scandinavia, as elsewhere, the First Crusade left its mark on the rhetoric of war and the habits of the nobility. The emperor Henry IV appeared to contemplate a journey to Palestine in 1102; King Eric of Denmark (1102–3), King Sigurd of Norway (1107–10) and Conrad of Hohenstaufen, the future Conrad III (1124), all travelled there. In 1108 a scheme to attack the Wends explicitly drew a comparison with the defence of Jerusalem.[3] German literature cast epic heroes such as Roland as *milites Christi*.[4] This coincided with renewed German political and ecclesiastical expansion into pagan western Slavic lands such as Pomerania, with religion as the touchstone of political submission and allegiance on both sides. Obliterating pagan cultic centres symbolised the transfer of power, even if the new rulers were previously pagans who, like Henry of the Wendish Obotrites (d. 1127), had converted to retain their status in the new religious and political order. Resistance or conquest was expressed through religion. Wendish independence was reasserted following Henry's death by the reversion to paganism of the Obotrite prince Niklot (c. 1130–60). The Rugians' defeat by the Danes in 1134–6 was signalled by enforced baptisms, their subsequent resistance by apostasy, and their final subjugation in 1168 by Valdemar I of Denmark (1157–82) through the destruction of their pagan idols at Arkona. The religious complexion of political conflict was a Baltic commonplace long before Bernard of Clairvaux's offer of conversion or extermination of pagan races in 1147. However, conflicts were never binary. While in retrospect the missionary priest Helmold of Bosau justified the German campaign in 1147 as revenge for Wendish appropriation of previously Christian land and assaults on Christians, he also described the alliance shortly before between Count Adolf of Holstein, one of the 1147 campaign's leaders, and Niklot of the Obotrites, one of its targets.[5]

1147

The extension of Holy Land privileges to Saxon princes at the Diet of Frankfurt in March 1147 during the Second Crusade was an opportunist attempt to engage the disaffected and potentially rebellious Henry the Lion,

duke of Saxony (1142–80), in a general political reconciliation that King
Conrad III hoped to achieve before leaving for Palestine. Reluctant to join
the eastern crusade, Duke Henry posed a threat in the king's absence.
Having rejected his claim to the duchy of Bavaria, Conrad used giving the
cross to Henry and his followers for their summer campaign against the
Wends as a means of binding them into royal policy, the crusade acting as
both surety and reward for good behaviour. At Frankfurt, Bernard of
Clairvaux provided the necessary ecclesiastical blessing, subsequently
securing a papal bull authorising the initiative. The essentially political
context was reinforced by the involvement in the Wendish campaign of one
of the king's regents, Abbot Wibald of Stavelot; its peculiar character was
acknowledged by one Holy Land *crucesignatus* who later wrote that the
Saxon crusaders' crosses 'differed from ours in this respect, that they were
not simply sewed to their clothing, but were brandished aloft, surmounting
a wheel'.[6] While the religious panoply of the campaign was supported by
the presence of at least eight bishops, its priority remained secular. Church
approval attracted international support, with the Saxons joined by Danes,
including rival kings Canute V and Sweyn III, and Poles in a two-pronged
pincer attack on Dobin, a small recently fortified Wendish outpost, and
Demmin. The attack on Dobin under Duke Henry faltered, the Danes withdrawing before the fort surrendered. The Saxons followed soon after,
throughout appearing anxious to protect the future value of their conquests.[7]
The raid on Demmin failed to reach its objective, diverting to besiege the
richer prize of Stettin, a Christian city. Once the city's religion was recognised, the Germans retreated. The 1147 campaigns, despite their crusade
flag of convenience, proved entirely nugatory.

Conquest and Crusade

The official employment of precise crusade formulae did not recur in the
Baltic with any regularity until the 1190s. A crusade bull of 1171 looked
forward to an extension of holy war from Wendish Pomerania to distant
Estonia.[8] Otherwise the crusaders' vow, cross and Jerusalem remission were
absent. Depictions of the Danish and German conquest of Wendish Rugians
and Obotrites, while including the language of religious war, acknowledged
the motives of revenge, imperialism and greed. Of Henry the Lion's Slavic
wars, Helmold commented: 'no mention has been made of Christianity, but

only of money'.⁹ For pagans, too, material considerations balanced religious loyalty, one convert lord expressly demanding as a price of baptism the same rights of property and taxation as those enjoyed by Saxons.¹⁰ On both sides of a shifting frontier, priorities concerned political aggrandisement, German, Danish or Wendish; for the Danes and Germans, the creation of new trading posts and privileged immigrant settlements; for the Church, the endowment of new bishoprics and religious houses, in particular Cistercian monasteries. Despite occasional well-publicised brutality, conversion of the Wends consolidated conquest by offering integration: through baptism Slavs, Letts, Balts and Livs could become Germans. The convert son of the pagan Niklot ultimately inherited his father's lands as the Christian lord of Mecklenberg. He assisted the destruction of the pagan temples on Rugen by Valdemar I of Denmark (1168); supported Christian missionary work and the Cistercians; and went on pilgrimage to Jerusalem (1172). His descendants patronised the

100. Danish soldiers under Valdemar I.

101. Conversion: a Christian pendant in thirteenth-century Livonia.

Hospitallers and joined crusades to Livonia.[11] If sustained by material advantage, enforced conversion worked even in thirteenth-century Prussia and Livonia where resistance was stronger and integration harder.

By 1400, the Baltic was ostensibly a Latin Christian lake, even if older habits persisted below the surface. Through laws, language, bishoprics, taxes, immigrants and iron-fisted rule, Latin Christendom reshaped the physical, mental and human environment. Conversion operated as integral to the transformation of political control. Yet only with the thirteenth-century conquest of the heathen tribes of Livonia, Estonia, Prussia, and Finland did crusading specifically play a significant role, even if inconsistently as papal priorities and regional demands did not always coincide.[12] Papal enthusiasm to prosecute the Lord's War was exploited by ambitious commercial and ecclesiastical elites in cities trading with the eastern Baltic, such as Bremen and Lübeck, and sustained by a steady stream of available recruits: one contemporary account of the unfortunate Livonian crusade of 1198 mentioned bishops, clergy, knights, the rich, the poor and merchants (*negotiatores*).[13] Kings of Denmark and Sweden welcomed formal ecclesiastical sanction for their conquests. Ambitious clerics sought new ecclesiastical and monastic empires. Motives for conquest were grounded in material gain. Although technological limitations and political fragmentation made pagan communities of the eastern Baltic appear weak, their economic and commercial attractions were considerable as producers and traders in fur, fish, amber, wax and slaves. Recent archaeological study has suggested a thriving and growing economy that encouraged the heavy German investment to appropriate it.[14]

The crusade provided an ideology for exploitation and alliance with an imperialist church hierarchy. Conquests were justified as protecting missionary churches or punishing apostasy, their protagonists 'knights of Christ'.[15] In the Livonian mission capital of Riga, a religious order of knights, the Militia of Christ or Swordbrothers, was created by the missionary bishop c. 1202 that within a decade become co-ruler with him of Livonia and neighbouring Lettia (Latvia south of the Dvina). A few years later, a similar order, the Militia of Christ of Prussia, also known as the Knights of Dobrin (or Dobryzin), was founded at the Polish–Prussian border on the Vistula, receiving papal recognition in 1228. Unlike the Templars, whose rule they imitated, or the Teutonic Knights, these orders were parochial, tied to their local bishops, held no international property, and relied for endowment on what they could seize for themselves in the inhospitable Baltic terrain. As permanent Christian garrisons, they provided a precedent for the regional dominance established from the 1230s by the Teutonic Knights. The presence of holy warriors combined with the idea of holy space. The papacy claimed Livonia and Prussia for St Peter while the Livonian mission-aries at Riga took the Virgin Mary as patron. Albert of Buxtehude, the dynamic entrepreneurial bishop of Riga (1199–1229), apparently insisted Livonia was the land of the Virgin Mary as Jerusalem was that of Christ.[16] The identification with the Virgin was strengthened by the Teutonic Knights, whose patroness she was, when they ruled both Prussia and Livonia after the 1230s. The Baltic conquests were thus incorporated into a parallel transcendent narrative of defending Christian lands and proselytising the faith.

Reality challenged this narrative. Unity among the Christian conquerors was secondary to institutional and national rivalries. Danes fought the Swordbrothers and the Teutonic Knights in Livonia and Estonia. In 1234 the Swordbrothers in Riga massacred a hundred servants of the papal legate.[17] Later in the century, academics such as the Oxford scholar Roger Bacon and the Dominican preaching expert Humbert of Romans even questioned the justice and efficacy of violence as a tool of conversion. The image of eternal conflict ignored processes of conquest and colonisation. While Germans and Flemings settled in Prussia in some numbers, the few westerners in remote, harsher Livonia and Estonia largely confined themselves to defen-

sible riparian trading posts. In Prussia, faced with a repressive discrimina-
tory regime, indigenous Balts slowly acculturated to German religion, laws
and technology and over time, like the Slavs between the Elbe and Oder,
became German. In Livonia, foreign settlement was largely confined to
small military, clerical and commercial communities relying for survival on
force and the management of local trade through control of rivers and
coastal ports. This position inevitably encouraged a measure of accommodation with native rulers in pursuit of their own trading opportunities and
protection. The crusades overlaid such developments, but did not create the
circumstances for colonial exploitation.

Livonia, 1188–1300

The invasion of Livonia was launched through an alliance of commercial
and ecclesiastical interests in Bremen and Lübeck attracted by trade and
Christian mission in the increasingly prosperous eastern Baltic. The alliance
was initially the work of Archbishop Hartwig II of Bremen (1185–1207),
who had elevated a lone missionary station in the Dvina valley into a bishopric in the 1180s. Despite teaching the locals how to build forts in stone, the
missionary bishop, Meinhard, achieved few converts before his death in
1196. His successor, Berthold, followed a preliminary reconnaissance in
1196–7 with a military expedition in 1198 supported by a papal grant of
remission of sins from the crusade enthusiast Celestine III. Although
Berthold was killed during an otherwise successful German campaign, the
precedent was set. His successor, Archbishop Hartwig's nephew Albert of
Buxtehude, immediately began promoting German commercial interests as
holy war and turning trading posts into a missionary state. While the project
was largely a family business, Albert's core following and main beneficiaries of the conquest formed by his and Archbishop Hartwig's kindred, it
received international political support. In a papal bull of October 1199,
Innocent III offered non-Holy Land pilgrim remissions for those who took
up what was branded the defence of Livonian Christians.[18] Bishop Albert
ignored Innocent III's reluctance to equate the Livonian campaign with
a Holy Land crusade. Unilaterally appropriating the full panoply of a
crusade – cross, preaching, full remission of sins – for his enterprise, in
1199–1200 he recruited crusaders from Saxony and Westphalia and the strategically crucial mercantile community at Visby in Gotland, where five

HENRY OF LIVONIA

Crusading was a written phenomenon. The events of war, conquest and settlement are filtered through the interpretation contained in the texts describing them. There is no neutral witness. The *Chronicon Livoniae* by the German missionary priest known from his chronicle as Henry of Livonia is no exception. Despite its autobiographical tone, apparent narrative simplicity and unfussy Latin, this represented a skilfully fashioned political advocacy and religious polemic, artful in its superficial artlessness. Henry constructed a coherent creation myth that made the early thirteenth-century German conquest and settlement of Livonia (modern Latvia and Estonia) appear providential, proof of God's immanence, a triumph of truth, faith and justice against the eternal miscreant forces of darkness and evil.

Henry (*c.* 1188–after 1259) came from Saxony, near Magdeburg, before education at the Augustinian monastery of Segeberg in Holstein, where Meinhard, the first missionary bishop of Livonia (d. 1196), had been a canon. As well as sound training in Latin and the scriptures, at Segeberg Henry may have acquired Estonian and Latvian from Livonian hostages sent there by the brother of Abbot Rothmar, the redoubtable Albert of Buxtehude, bishop of Riga, a connection that determined Henry's future calling and career. In 1205, Henry joined Bishop Albert at Riga before being ordained in 1208 and assigned the missionary parish of Papendorf (near the modern Latvian/Estonian border). Henry's proximity to Bishop Albert provided him with first-hand experience of the German conquest and Christianisation of the region and the dynamic central character in the drama that Henry's chronicle, probably written between 1225 and 1227, unfolded.

Henry wrote an extended apologia for German invasion, conquest and military suppression of the native population. The language is heavily scriptural, much of it from the martial Books of the Maccabees, long associated with crusaders. The insistence was on the religious and canonical probity of the German occupiers confronted by the relentless perfidy and malice of the natives. Clearly aware of the canonical prohibition on forced conversion, Henry emphasised that the locals were punished for apostasising after initial free conversion or for attacking Christian communities. In Henry's vision, the German settlement

102. *A page of Henry of Livonia's* Chronicle.

was sustained with papal grants of remission of sins equivalent to those of Holy Land crusaders, a probably deliberate distortion by Henry or his source – Bishop Albert – exaggerating papal policy and practice. Henry aimed to secure the reputation and status of the see of Riga and to promote Livonia as the land of the Virgin Mary, a site of pilgrimage and grace. While not minimising violence or suffering, Henry provides insight into various methods of conversion, from coercion, bribery and entertainment to persuasion and genuine conviction. The force of Henry's polemic may have been stimulated by possible challenges to the Riga legend from papal legates, discontented locals or rival Danes. Henry's chronicle fits a medieval type as a colourful and coloured creation myth and a powerfully confident account of frontier conflict, Christian conquest and cultural annexation, in this instance blessed by the cross of the crusader.[19]

14. The Baltic crusades.

103. Baltic amber.

hundred apparently took the cross. He simultaneously negotiated with a potential rival, King Canute VI of Denmark (1182–1202), for safe passage to Livonia for his armada.[20]

Bishop Albert's expedition to Livonia in 1200, which he and his apologists insisted on portraying as a crusade equivalent to the concurrent eastern Mediterranean expedition, set the pattern for the next twenty-five years. Bishop Albert made annual recruiting tours of Germany and the western Baltic, providing soldiers, merchants, seamen, entrepreneurs, clerics and adventurers with absolution of sins in the pursuit of profit – even though, despite a bull of 1204 allowing Holy Land vows to be commuted to service in Livonia, Innocent III continued to avoid recognising Livonia's parity with the Holy Land. Albert's campaigns met with success. By 1210, the coast and lower Dvina had been subdued or overawed; a capital established at Riga whose harbour could be used by large cargo round ships, known as cogs; a cathedral had been started and the Swordbrothers founded. The new settlement rested on volatile foundations. The locals treated conversion as a temporary consequence of defeat to be reversed once the Germans moved on or away. Internationally, Bishop Albert faced challenges to his sovereignty from the papacy and the king of Denmark. Internally, clerical rule

104. People-and-cargo-carrying cogs on the seal of the Baltic trading Hanseatic League (left) and in the port of Riga (below).

depended on the support of the German merchants, whose interests were primarily economic not spiritual; for them conversion was useful as a means to bind locals to German trading practices. The Swordbrothers controlled a third of all territory and claimed rights to share future conquests. The interests of the ecclesiastical, commercial and military establishments regularly conflicted, united only by an entrepreneurial imperative to exploit the indigenous people and economy. The Christian mission imitated secular acquisitiveness in creating bishoprics and monasteries. The whole project relied on Bishop Albert's almost annual crusades providing physical force and ideological respectability.

The conquest of the lower Dvina valley, the Semigallians to the south and west and the Letts to the north and east, secured the Livonian coast.

105. Conquest: Turaida Castle, begun by Bishop Albert of Riga in 1214.

This allowed the Germans to protect local allies and control trade from the interior, both incentives for indigenous rulers to come to terms. Further advances between 1209 to 1218 northwards into Estonia were checked by the competing ambitions of Valdemar II of Denmark (1202–41), who built a fort on the north coast at Reval (now Tallinn) in 1219, leading to the partitioning of Estonia in 1222. The Danes dominated the sea-lanes from Lübeck, the vital entrepôt for manpower and trade without which the German Livonian enclave could not survive. Bishop Albert died in 1229. Contending interests remained: the Danes; the papacy; settlers; merchants; the Swordbrothers; local converts, allies and pagans; disturbed or hostile neighbours: the Curonians, Lithuanians and Russians of Novgorod. Internal divisions were matched by threats of rebellion and invasion. Territorial advances were balanced by fierce rivalry for land, desperate revolts by the hard-pressed peasantry (1222 and 1236), and the Swordbrothers' increasing violence and gangsterism. Pursuing an aggressively independent military policy under Master Folkwin (1209–36), from 1225 the Swordbrothers annexed Danish northern Estonia, allied with Livonia's enemies to acquire more territory, plundered church property, impeded baptisms and massacred converts. The Swordbrothers appeared more interested in locals as slaves not Christians, an intriguing, but not unique, attitude for a religious Order. The papacy had been scrutinising the Order for years before the massacre of the legate's men in 1234. The death of Folkwin with fifty brothers, almost half the Order's knights, at the battle of Saule against the Lithuanians in 1236, provided the opportunity the following year for the transfer of the remnant of the Order, its prerogatives and property, to the equally violent but more orderly Teutonic Knights.

The Teutonic Knights reshaped Livonia. They ended the awkward duopoly with the Rigan Church; mended relations with the papacy and the Danes (restoring Estonia to them in 1238); and used diplomacy as well as force to pacify neighbours. Hardly eirenic in dealing with internal opposition, their wider resources helped the Order overcome revolts and resistance from satellite provinces. From the late thirteenth century, the Teutonic Knights imposed security for the German settlement by creating a depopulated scorched earth *cordon sanitaire* in Semigallia that protected Livonia from Samogitia and Lithuania. The consequent struggle with Lithuania dragged into the fifteenth century. Ruling an autonomous province within the Order, with its own Master answerable only to the Grand Master based after 1309 in Prussia, the Livonian Teutonic Knights survived until 1562, when the last Livonian Master made himself duke of Courland and Semigallia.[21]

Danish and Swedish Crusades

Territorial ambitions of Scandinavian kings were linked to efforts to elevate their internal as well as foreign status through alliance with the international Church. While the crusade provided a suitable context, motives for conquest were material: to police piracy, exploit maritime trade and manipulate access to valuable raw materials. So were the means: raiding, a sort of counter-piratical piracy, and planting combined religious and trading stations, a continuation of the Viking tradition under the flag of Christ. Church approval of wars of conquest supplied ideological gloss for existing habits. In the twelfth century, the Danes fought the Wends and other pagans in the southern Baltic, while their fleets penetrated eastwards in pursuit of increasing regional trade. Swedes started to harry the shores of the Gulf of Finland and the Gulf of Riga. Such aggression against non-Christians traditionally gained ecclesiastical support. When an attack on non-Christian pirates led by the Danish Archbishop Absalon of Lund (1178–1201), a vigorous pagan-basher, was described as 'making an offering to God not of prayers but of arms', this was not an account of a crusade, but a reflection of a far older tradition of war against the pagans *deo auctore*; as was a promise of heaven to those who died fighting pagans in defence of the Norwegian *patria* made during a royal synod held at Trondheim (1164).[22] Nonetheless, by presenting such wars as extending or defending Christianity, papal approval could be sought, enhancing regal image.[23] Alexander III's 1171 offer to Valdemar I of Denmark of a year's Holy Land plenary indulgence to participants on an expedition against pagans in the eastern Baltic, probably the Estonians, and a full remission for those who died on campaign, while lacking the full crusade apparatus of vow, cross, preaching and temporal privileges, confirmed available justifications and incentives.[24]

Yet, however much Valdemar I was a devotee of holy war against pagans, no Danish crusade to the eastern Baltic occurred until 1206 when, according to the not always reliable chronicler Henry of Livonia, the troops accompanying Valdemar II's raid on the island of Osel were given the cross by the archbishop of Lund.[25] The Danish invasion of northern Estonia in 1219–20, in coalition with the Swordbrothers and King John I of Sweden (1216–22), was backed by a papal crusade bull. The Swedes briefly occupied Leal on Estonia's west coast while the Danes built a fort overlooking Reval's large natural harbour. Thereafter, the Danes acted as absentee landlords, taking profits from trade and land as the new town at Reval was settled chiefly by Germans. Danish overlordship was recognised by the Teutonic Knights (1238). Further Danish conquests eastwards provoked confrontation with the Russians of Novgorod, branded hostile schismatics by successive popes who provided crusading support for campaigns against them in the hope of further converts in the pagan lands of the eastern Gulf of Finland. The results were meagre. Valdemar II joined the Teutonic Knights and Swedes from Finland in the disastrous anti-Russian crusade of 1240–2 that saw defeats for the Swedes on the River Neva in 1240 and for the Teutonic Knights at Lake Chud-Peipus on 5 April 1242; Alexander Nevsky of Novgorod's victory received vividly iconic if fanciful reworking in Sergei Eisenstein's famous patriotic 1938 film. Eric IV of Denmark's (1241–50) taking the cross in 1244 led nowhere. A fresh crusade in 1256 to the lower Narva failed to achieve converts. Danish interest in the eastern Baltic waned; in 1346, Danish Estonia was sold to the Teutonic Knights.

106. The Battle on the Ice, 5 April 1242.

Increasingly only the Swedes, already established on the Gulf of Finland, seemed attracted to further military action in the bleak unproductive area further east where material returns were exiguous and conversion hardly a priority. Swedish incursions into Finland began in the twelfth century, later accompanied by missionary attempts. After some success in south-west Finland, resistance became stiffer further east in Tavastria where the Swedes confronted the neighbouring Karelians and Novgorod Russians in wars that lasted into the fourteenth century. Crusades were attached to Swedish expansion into eastern Finland, in 1237, 1249, 1257 and 1292. Appropriate histories of Swedish martyrs and a saintly royal holy warrior, Eric IX (1156–60), were invented retrospectively. Holy war was urged on Magnus II (1319–63) by his cousin, St Bridget, conveniently as a legitimate excuse for royal taxation.[26] Magnus, supported by another crusade enthusiast, Pope Clement VI (1342–52), responded with two crusades (1348 and 1350) against the Russians that achieved little. A subsequent papally backed scheme in 1351 produced rich tax pickings from a church tithe which, in the absence of any military action, the papacy demanded be paid back. Later efforts to drum up support for an anti-Russian crusade by King Albert (1364–89) failed. Ideas for crusades still circulated into the late fifteenth century as Karelian raiding continued, but the last Swedish crusade bull in 1496 never even arrived, confiscated in transit by King John of Denmark (1481–1513). Although Swedish rule of Finland lasted until 1809, the role of the crusade in its beginnings was insignificant.

Prussia

By contrast, crusading created German Prussia. Through conquest and rule from the 1220s, the Teutonic Knights built an unprecedented *Ordenstaat*, a state run by a Military Order, a polity to which the Livonian Swordbrothers had aspired but failed to realise. Polish rulers, eager for greater access to the Baltic, had campaigned against the Prussians throughout the twelfth century in wars that, at least in retrospect, were afforded a gloss of quasi-crusading holiness; one early thirteenth-century Polish chronicler even described the Prussians as '*Saladinistas*'.[27] However, it was only in 1217 that a crusade bull was issued on behalf of a mission to the lower Vistula valley by Bishop Christian (1215–45), supported by German and Polish lords. The failure of their efforts, confronted by local resistance, led in 1225 to an invitation from the Polish Duke Conrad of Mazovia to the Teutonic Knights to intervene. Since 1211, the Knights had been serving King Andrew of Hungary in Transylvania against the Cumans. In 1226 their Master, Hermann of Salza (1209–39), a sharp political operator and close associate of Emperor Frederick II, secured an imperial bull authorising the Order's invasion of Prussia. Any conquests in Kulmerland and Prussia were to be held by Hermann as a *Reichsfürst*, an independent imperial prince. Conrad of Mazovia abandoned his role as patron of the enterprise. In 1234, Hermann secured the additional protected status of papal fief for the Order's Prussian lands. The removal into Prussian captivity of Bishop Christian (1233–9) left the Order without rivals, a position consolidated by Innocent IV's delegation to it in 1245 of the power to call and recruit crusades without prior papal consent.[28] The Order thus became the arbiter of its own fate, sole political authority in Christian Prussia, and manager of any future crusades there.

The conquest of Prussia began in 1229 with the Teutonic Knights' deployment of a small garrison in the upper Vistula. This allowed the invaders to interrupt Prussian trade in the interior, enabling easy access to home bases and recruits via Poland and Pomerania. Proximity made Prussian crusades more popular than those to distant Livonia and among German nobles even usurped the Holy Land as the crusade destination of choice.[29] Once again, campaigns focused on rivers, with forts and trading posts used to control and exploit conquered territory. The invaders' technological superiority and land frontier further secured their advantages during the advance down the Vistula towards the Baltic and the Frisches Haff which, with aid from regular crusading armies recruited mainly from across eastern Europe, was reached by 1237. As well as estates granted to German lords, the conquest rested on a network of forts built by the slave labour of the conquered: Thorn (1231); Marienwerder (1233); Reden (1234); the tellingly named Christburg (1237); Elbing (1237). The Knights soon attracted Dominican preachers and German settlers, drawn by special civil privileges: Silesians in Kulmerland; citizens of Lübeck in Elbing. Further advances in the late 1230s towards Samland and the Order's recently acquired Livonia threatened to deny indigenous Prussians access to the sea, thereby completing Latin Christian control of the Baltic seaboard.

The Military Order's early successes provoked a decade-long revolt from the Prussians aided by a fearful and jealous Duke Swantopelk of Danzig. Beginning in 1242, the rebels, using guerrilla tactics to neutralise the Germans' heavy cavalry and crossbows, soon swept aside the Order's conquests except in Pomerania and a few isolated outposts such as Elbing. The Order's response combined renewed commitment to war and local reprisals. The so-called treaty of Christburg (1249) offered Prussian converts, chiefly aristocrats, civil rights under the jurisdiction of church courts, in other words obedience to the Order. The consequent emergence of an elite of Christianised Prussians provided a new buttress to the German regime. Pagans were cast beyond the rules and protections of civil society. Such limited accommodation extended to diplomacy. In 1253, to forestall Polish intervention along the Vistula, a deal was struck with Duke Swantopelk. King Ottokar II of Bohemia assisted the annexation of Samland (1254–6) to blunt the ambitions of Lübeck and of Hakon IV of Norway, who had been promised it by the pope. Even King Mindaugas of Lithuania (1236–61) was induced to convert and ally with the Order as protection from the Russians, allowing the incorporation of Samland and the construction of Memel (1252) and Georgenburg (1259).

These successes were immediately thrown into hazard by a well-organised general Prussian rising in 1260 supported by Swantopelk's son Mestwin of Danzig. Limited acculturation had lent the Prussians German military technology: crossbows, siege engines and field tactics. Between 1260 and 1264 two of the Military Order's Prussian Masters were killed; a crusade was destroyed at Pokarvis near Königsberg; forts were overrun; settlers massacred. Savagery in the name of faith was mutual; devastation and displacement of people extensive. The Order survived through regular assistance from large, well-funded crusade armies. By 1283, with the surrender of the Yatwingians, the Prussian tribes had been subdued or annihilated. The Coronians, Letts and Semigallians were conquered by 1290. Revolts in 1286 and 1295 failed to loosen the Order's grip. Opponents were left with the choice of slavery or exile. The Prussian *Ordenstaat* emerged as a regime in its own right: enclosed, brutal, exploitative, defined by God and the sword.

Recruitment for the crusades that saved Prussia for the Teutonic Knights far outstripped that for the Livonia wars. The 1230s saw Polish nobles, German princes; townspeople from Silesia, Breslau, Magdeburg and Lübeck; minor lords from Saxony and Hanover. Leading German princes soon followed: Rudolph of Habsburg (1254), Otto III of Brandenberg (1254 and 1266); Albert I of Brunswick and Albert of Thuringia (1264–5); and Dietrich of Landsberg (1272). Ottokar II of Bohemia (1254–5 and 1267) gave his title to the new castle of Königsberg. Some recruits may have used these crusades to escape the political dilemmas thrown up by extended German civil wars from the late 1230s. The Military Order's skilful diplomacy maintained relations with both warring parties of pope and emperor, securing its own independence and soothing papal doubts over the Order's increasingly notorious activities. As well as defeating the Prussians, the Order contained or repelled other challenges to its monopoly of power. Besides incorporating the Livonian Swordbrothers in 1237, the Order absorbed Bishop Christian's Militia of Dobryzn in 1235 while their patron was in Prussian captivity. In 1243 the new Prussian episcopacy was reduced in size, jurisdiction and share of new possessions.[30] After a failed coup in Livonia in 1267–8, the legate Albert Subeer (archbishop of Prussia 1246–53 and of Riga 1253–73) even spent a short time imprisoned by the Order. Innocent IV's devolution to the Order of the authority to call crusades in 1245, while not eliminating papal appeals and preaching campaigns, provided the Knights with the means to pursue their wars as crusade at will, a privilege extended in 1260 by Alexander IV's mandate for the cross to be preached by the Order's own priests.[31] These arrangements gave the Order free rein, the crusade forming an integral element in military policy and the rhetorical projection of the Knights as champions of the faith.

The Later Middle Ages

Frontier wars and military aggression, frequently in the guise of crusades, did not cease with the consolidation of the Military Order's control within Prussia, Livonia and southern Estonia. Encouragement of trade and German – 'New Prussian' – immigration prompted attempts to expand control over the whole southern and eastern Baltic. Besides the purchase of north Estonia in 1346, Danzig and eastern Pomerania were annexed in 1308–10. In 1337, Emperor Louis IV of Germany invited the Order to conquer pagan Lithuania and its Christian Polish allies, the crossed-wires of Baltic politics finding Poles both as allies of pagan Lithuania and, in papal eyes, potential crusaders against them. Additional incentive for continued crusading militarism came from the Order's precarious international status following the fall of the last mainland outpost of Outremer in 1291. Despite ruling Prussia, the Order initially maintained its Mediterranean base, moving its headquarters to Venice, an indication of the continuing importance of its Mediterranean origins. Events subsequently forced a change. The violent suppression of a rebellion against the Order by the archbishop, clergy and citizens of Riga in 1297–9 led victims to appeal to the pope, feeding growing disquiet in some quarters at the Order's general behaviour in the Baltic. Although retaining vociferous supporters, such as Bishop Bruno of Olmutz who wrote in laudatory terms for Pope Gregory X in 1272, persistent complaints led Clement V (1305–14) to instigate an inquiry in 1310 into the Order's methods and performance. The Livonian brothers were briefly excommunicated in 1312. Fortuitously or not, this coincided with new attacks on Livonia and Prussia by the pagan Lithuanian Grand Prince Vytenis. Even more immediately, the whole function and legitimacy of Military Orders, the subject of academic debate for a generation, were cast into jeopardy by the arrest and trials of the Templars, beginning in 1307–8, culminating in their suppression in 1312. To avoid scandal and escape from harm's way while simultaneously polishing their credentials as holy warriors, just as the Hospitallers responded by supervising the occupation of Rhodes (1306–10) and moving their central Convent there in 1309, so in the same year the Teutonic Knights established their headquarters at Marienburg.

The fourteenth-century crusades against Lithuania provided ideological cover for the Military Order's power, justifying its privileged international status and attracting military recruits. At its largest, alone the Order's knights only numbered about 1,000 to 1,200 divided between Prussia and Livonia. Regular winter and summer *Reisen* (raids) against Lithuania, until 1386 a pagan power, sustained the tradition of meritorious religious war for a European aristocracy increasingly embroiled in unequivocally secular conflicts such as the Hundred Years War. Although conditions across the wilderness between Prussia/Livonia and Lithuania were consistently grim – frozen in winter and waterlogged in summer – foreign nobles could take the opportunity (and risk) to show off in difficult and often dangerous combat. Conversion of the enemy was not an issue. With stalemate with Lithuania prevailing, *Reisen* assumed features of chivalrous grand tours, decked with feasts, heraldry, souvenirs and

107. Marienburg Castle.

prizes. These attracted clients from western Europe, beyond Germany or central Europe. While part of a dour violent struggle for power and profit, *Reisen* ostentatiously incorporated recruits' cultural aspirations, as in 1375 under Grand Master Winrich of Kniprode (1352–82), when selected nobles received badges with the motto 'Honour conquers all', despite its stark crusading incongruity. Baltic *Reisen* proved particularly attractive during truces in the Hundred Years War in the 1360s and 1390s.

Between 1304 and 1423 the bulk of recruits came from Germany, although many came from other regions. Some campaigned many times: John of Luxembourg, king of Bohemia, William IV count of Holland and the Frenchman Marshal Boucicaut three times each; William I of Gelderland on seven occasions between 1383 and 1400. Summer campaigns could be substantial: in 1377, Duke Albert III of Austria brought 2,000 knights with him. At least 450 French and English nobles made the journey over the century, so Chaucer's Knight became a familiar type:

> Ful ofte time he hadde the bord bigonne
> Aboven alle nacions in Pruce;
> In Lettow hadde he reysed, and in Ruce,
> No Cristen man so ofte of his degree.[32]

English evidence confirms the extended social networks involved.[33] Anglo-French peace in 1360 prompted relatively large-scale plans and expeditions, notably one led by the earl of Warwick. However flamboyant, such commitment was not necessarily light-hearted. The reality of combat, injury and death elevated the enterprise beyond the merely self-serving or ludic. The Marienkirche in Königsberg acted as a mausoleum. The experiences of recruits linked the Baltic crusades with other theatres of war against the infidel: Marshal Boucicaut, Humphrey Bohun earl of Hereford and Richard Waldegrave, a future Speaker of the English House of Commons (1381), each fought in the Mediterranean as well as against the Lithuanians. In 1365, Pope Urban V saw Thomas Beauchamp, earl of Warwick's vow as applying equally to Prussia or Palestine.[34] Although it is difficult to determine whether those who fought with the Military Order had ceremonially taken the cross, the trappings, language and perhaps the emotions of religious war remained as the knights continued to proclaim their *Reisen* as crusades. Recruits such as Henry Bolingbroke, the future Henry IV of England, visited Prussian shrines offering indulgences. Despite the growing gap between military strategy and religious purpose, the popularity of the Baltic campaigns emphasised the tenacity of crusading tradition while the Order restricted foreigners to military assistance alone. In alliance with the Hanseatic League, the Order resisted external penetration of its markets, negotiated tight trading concessions, fought over control of fish stocks, and exacted heavy fines for trading irregularities.[35]

The Military Order's success in Prussia and Livonia contrasted awkwardly with the failure of the Lithuanian crusades. Generations of war produced no resolution; Prussia remained German and Lithuania independent. In 1386 the

108. The reconstructed Königsberg/Kaliningrad Cathedral.

political and religious context radically altered when Jogaila of Lithuania (1377–81; 1382–1434) became king of Poland (1386–1434) and converted to Christianity, calling into doubt in some minds the very legitimacy of Baltic crusading, the Order's purpose and its rule in Prussia/Livonia. Still employing traditional crusading rhetoric, the Order, with some success, sought foreign allies to unpick the Lithuania and Poland alliance. With larger contingents even than in the 1360s and 1370s, the Order made ground: Dobryzn in the 1390s and Samogitia between 1398 and 1406. This aggressive policy came to a disastrous end with the Lithuanian-Polish victory at Tannenberg/Grunwald (15 July 1410) at which Grand Master Ulrich von Jungingen, most of the Order's high command and 400 knights were killed. Although territorial losses were modest, a brief revival of international aid after Tannenberg soon waned, perhaps because the Hundred Years War restarted in 1415. It seems that non-Germans ceased to campaign in the Baltic after 1413, concluding a trend apparent before Tannenberg. After 1423, even the Germans stayed away.

109. The battle of Tannenberg, 1410.

Tannenberg exemplified the problem: a Christian army defeated by another Christian army. The Council of Constance (1414–18) that healed the Great Schism (1378–1417) debated the Order's future. Although rejecting radical criticisms and refusing to censure the Order, in 1418 the Council declined to approve the Order's request for a new crusade against its enemies. Tellingly, the new pope, Martin V (1417–31), made the rulers of Poland and Lithuania his vicars-general for a planned war against the schismatic Russians. The whole basis for continuing crusading against Lithuania-Poland collapsed, along with the Order's reputation and credentials. With the last foreign crusade to Prussia ending in 1423, the Order's power declined, undermined internally by competing landed and civic interests and externally by a resurgent Poland. A Thirteen Years War (1454–66) unpicked the Order's dominance. At the Treaty of Thorn in 1466, west Prussia, including the Order's seat at Marienberg and most of the earliest conquests dating back to the mid-thirteenth century were lost, leaving only an eastern rump. The Grand Masters in their new capital at Königsberg were now little more than Polish clients.

Holy war was not wholly abandoned. In 1429 a detachment of Teutonic Knights fought the Ottoman Turks for Sigismund, Holy Roman Emperor and king of Hungary. In Livonia the interminable struggle with the Russians continued. However, popes, not averse to allowing crusades elsewhere, refused to assign crusades to the Order's wars. Between 1495 and 1502, Alexander VI consistently rejected Livonian appeals for a crusade against the Russians. Although technically able to authorise crusades themselves, the Order unavailingly sought international support. The Baltic crusades had helped turn the Baltic region Christian. Regional demography, economy, even flora and fauna, had been fundamentally changed in one of the most radical, harsh and extensive colonial transformations in Europe since the barbarian invasions.[36] Once the process had achieved maturity, the justification for further crusades became harder to sustain. Now they ended. In 1525 the Prussian Order secularised itself. In 1562 the Livonian convent followed suit.

CHAPTER NINE

CRUSADES AGAINST CHRISTIANS

ars between Christians had been presented as earning spiritual merit long before Urban II's Jerusalem campaign of 1095. Once Christianity became identified with political authority, dissent could be treated as a challenge to the religious as well as secular establishment. To defend the state was to defend its Church and vice versa. Early medieval Christian armies sought divine approval before fighting other Christians, carrying religious images and relics into battle and enjoying church blessings of troops, banners and weapons. Individual warriors welcomed the comforts of religion before the deadly hazard of battle through prayer, confession or the sacrament. While religious war against non-Christians remained easier to justify, claiming divine sanction in battles against co-religionists became commonplace. By the tenth century, popular liturgies were including prayers likening victory in temporal battle to Christ's victory on the cross.[1] From the eighth century, the image of active Christian warriors received increasing clerical respect, as protectors of the faith and even models of conduct. Martial saints became more prominent in church dedications and iconography. Popes explicitly promoted military champions of the Church. In 1053, Leo IX granted remission of penance and absolution of sins to his followers fighting the Normans of southern Italy. Gregory VII further moralised war in consecrating the violence of his supporters in Milan in the 1070s as a war of God (*bellum Dei*), offering 'absolution of all your sins and blessing and grace in this world and the next' to adherents fighting against Henry IV, and recruiting what he and his partisans called *milites Sancti Petri*.[2] Secular wars against supposed religious disobedience or schism attracted papal blessing as they had enjoyed local episcopal approval for generations. In 1066, William of Normandy fought Harold II of England, stigmatised as a perjured protector of a schismatic archbishop (Stigand of Canterbury), under a papal banner. Gregory's framing of political conflict in spiritual terms received academic gloss from sympathetic scholars who approved of the penitential service of an 'ordo pugnatorum' fighting just wars to defend the Church and the weak against tyrants, excommunicates, schismatics and heretics.

While these precedents formed a significant context for Urban II's Jerusalem war, the new institutions of the crusade – preaching, vow, cross, privileges – did not automatically transfer to these older forms of ecclesiastically justified inter-Christian conflict. Conservatism prevailed in practice and legal theory. Policing operations by Louis VI of France (1108–37) were supported by parish priests bearing banners to join royal armies along with their parishioners in operations described by sympathetic memorialists in terms of war directly approved by God and the clergy ('the pious slaughtered the impious'), including, one observer suggested, absolution of sins and salvation for those who died.[3] One account of the Anglo-Scottish battle of the Standard in 1138 suggested that the English who died would receive remission of penalties of sin. Offers of remission for those killed in battle, for example against mercenary war-bands in Languedoc in 1139, appeared more frequently. This may reflect the generally greater precision in describing the Church's penitential and legal systems, as witnessed by Gratian's canon law compendium, the *Decretum* (1139), in which wars against Christians occupy much space (the crusade against the infidel none).

Elsewhere, direct links to the crusade were made. Paschal II, in the afterglow of the First Crusade, offered plenary remission or absolution for conflicts against his political opponents and, under the masquerade of a new crusade to Palestine, to Bohemund's campaign against Byzantium in 1107–8. The influence of the First Crusade provisions was apparent in spiritual rewards offered to papalists in the war against the anti-pope Anacletus in the 1130s, an association explicit in the indulgence proposed at the Council of Pisa in 1135. However, the First Lateran Council of 1123 reserved the Jerusalem war institutions to conflicts in the Holy Land and Spain, a restriction tangentially extended to Wendish pagans by Eugenius III in 1147. During campaigns *crucesignati* did fight Christians: Greeks during the First, Second and Third Crusades and the Venetian crusade in 1122–5; and Sicilians in 1190; but none was the stated object of crusade vows. In

1197 an exasperated Celestine III exceptionally authorised Holy Land privileges to those who sought to bring Alfonso IX of León to heal after he had campaigned with Moors against fellow Christians. However, the material advantages of crusading as they had matured by the 1190s – legal protection, debt relief, access to special taxation and church funds – coupled with the militant evangelising and political agenda of the papacy, made the association of crusading with wars against Christians likely. In 1199, Innocent III granted Holy Land plenary indulgences to those who campaigned against the German Markward of Anweiler (d. 1202), 'another Saladin', who was challenging papally supported regents in the kingdom of Sicily. Innocent argued that Markward threatened the Papal States and the new Jerusalem crusade.[4] As other crusade features such as vow, cross and temporal privileges were absent, this hardly constituted radical departure, more logical opportunism.

Crusades against Christians

Innocent's logic went further. In 1208 the full Holy Land paraphernalia of preaching, cross, indulgence and temporal privileges were deployed to deal with the heretics of Languedoc, an initiative confirmed and reinforced by the Fourth Lateran Council in 1215.[5] As the practice developed, three different categories of Christian opponent attracted crusades: heretics, classed as religious deviants, who consciously refused to accept the orthodox teachings and authority of the Church, notably but far from exclusively the Cathars in Languedoc; the religiously ignorant, such as sections of the German peasantry or Bosnian faithful in the 1220s and 1230s, whose failings were deemed to require forcible discipline; and those whose political actions endangered the integrity of the Roman Church, its territory or its client states, and who therefore could be accused of fomenting schism, which readily equated with heresy. Chief antagonists in this last category were the Hohenstaufen rulers of Germany and Sicily until 1266 and, thereafter, anti-papal powers in Italy and the western Mediterranean. As obedience to social and political hierarchies mirrored God's ordered world, disruption or disturbance invited scriptural condemnation (e.g. 'Kingdom/House divided against itself cannot stand', Mark 3:24–5; 'foxes in the vineyard', Song of Solomon 2:15). Heresy, in reality rejecting existing ecclesiastical establishments, was branded as treason to God, offering falsehood instead

110. A contemporary depiction of Markward of Anweiler.

of truth, corrupting the Church, weakening its ability to save souls or, in a crusading context, restore the Holy Land. Heresy was thus deemed to pose an existential danger to every faithful Christian. Like a cancer, it needed excision. Political opponents who attacked the pope's lands in Italy threatened the pope's security and, thus, given the Roman Church's claim to embody the universal Church, constituted an assault on the whole Church. To counter possible disquiet, crusades against Christians were repeatedly equated with less controversial targets, with opponents branded as obstructions to the cause of the Holy Land, collaborators with infidels, similar to or worse than 'Saracens' or pagans. The Hohenstaufen excited particularly fevered papal excoriation as enemies of the Church, 'treacherous and impious', Frederick II a 'limb of the devil, minister of Satan and calamitous harbinger of the Anti-Christ', likened to the Biblical Pharaoh and Herod and the Roman Nero, his son a closet Muslim.[6] Not everyone was convinced.

Developing academic canon law on categories of just war made war against fellow Christians easier to justify on general grounds of legitimate violence, defence, retribution, the recovery of land and rights denied or wrongfully invaded, and the restoration of peace. The clergy attached to the Fourth Crusade persuaded crusaders to fight the Greek Christians in 1204, arguing that the Greeks were regicides, or tacitly complicit in regicide and 'above and beyond all this' schismatics, so 'this battle is right and just (*droite et juste*)'; those killed in the fighting qualified for the crusaders' indulgence provided they had fought with the 'right intention' of returning Byzantium to obedience to Rome and had confessed their sins.[7] As crusade preaching and propaganda became increasingly the preserve of theologians and canonists trained, like Innocent III himself, at the universities of Paris and Bologna, crusade rhetoric adopted just-war arguments. In the mid-thirteenth century the canonist and crusade preacher Henry of Segusio (Hostiensis, *c.* 1200–71) identified seven different types of just war, arguing for the priority of crusading within Christendom (the *crux cismarina*) over the overseas crusade (*crux transmarina*). As well as condoning papal crusades against the Hohenstaufen, this drew on the older legal criteria for just war against heretics, seen as a greater threat to Christian souls than infidel possession of the Holy Land.[8] Not all wars fought against Christians on behalf of Church or pope after Innocent III's reign attracted the trappings of crusading. Nonetheless, the crusade within Christendom became the most exploited use of the war of the cross in the later thirteenth and fourteenth centuries.

Four long-term trends contributed to this. Two were financial: the extension of the uniquely generous crusade indulgence to non-combatants who, from 1213, could redeem their vows for material contributions; and the introduction of church crusade taxes (proposed in 1199; implemented in 1215). These provided obvious incentives for rulers to get their wars proclaimed crusades. The third development arose from the consolidation of a papal state in central Italy from Innocent III's pontificate onwards that required policing and defending. Finally, the thirteenth century saw the general promotion of the crusade as a model of Christian life within a belea-guered *societas Christiana* threatened by sin, temporal enemies and religious dissidents. Initiative for crusades against fellow Christians came from the pope but also from regional secular and ecclesiastical authorities pursuing local interests. This denied many internal crusades the universal appeal of wars with infidels and attracted more critical scrutiny than their Holy Land exemplars.

The Albigensian Crusades, 1209–29

The suppression of heresy, broadly defined as false beliefs and disobedience to the authority of the Church, provided an established justification for the use of physical force. Gratian of Bologna's mid-twelfth-century *Decretum* conveniently collated patristic and later texts defining heresy and the measures that legitimately could be employed against them. Events pushed the issue into prominence as religious diversity and dissent proliferated during the eleventh and twelfth centuries across western Christendom. The reasons for this are contested and complex: the quickening of the transmission of ideas following the expansion of regional and international commerce; a simultaneous growth of literacy, the technology of writing and access to learning; the encouragement of criticism of ecclesiastical structures and traditions by church reformers, including some eleventh-century popes; the erosion of customary hierarchical alliances between lay and church authorities in the wake of the Investiture dispute; the emergence of greater urban political autonomy; the popularity of ideals of puritanical austerity in reaction to the increased materialism of a wealthier society; the emergence of a self-conscious clerical elite jealous of its authority and privileges; the encounter with different Christian and infidel belief systems. The move towards greater definition in theology and canon law inevitably placed uniformity at a premium, threatening eccentricity or deviation with exclusion and condemnation and making anomalies in law, doctrine or ritual more obvious and more dangerous. Heresy was defined by shifting orthodoxy. Nevertheless, in the sense of adherents to different belief systems or lived patterns of expression, heretics existed, more visible to the vigilant gaze of fresh-minted guardians of religious truth.

Heresies fell into different categories. Refined academic disputes; evanescent charismatic personality cults exploiting popular anxiety over death, divine judgement and the end of the world; and organised social revolts that embraced aggressive anti-clericalism. Most proved fleeting, arcane or ephemeral. More challenging were groups of believers with resilient corporate identity possessing distinctive shared literature, doctrine and ritual. Notable among these were the followers of Peter Valdes (*c.* 1140–*c.* 1205), the Poor Men of Lyons or Waldensians, whose puritanical scriptural fundamentalism contradicted the official Church's development of an elaborate sacramental penitential system. After papal investigation condemned them as heretics from the 1170s and 1180s, Waldensian communities established themselves, chiefly in the French and Italian Alps, suffering a crusade as late as in 1488, before being subsumed into the sixteenth-century Protestant Reformation.

More threatening than cells of radical Christian dissenters appeared to be the adherents to a wholly alternative Christian theology to trinitarian Christianity, now known as Cathars (from the Greek *katharos*, 'clean' or 'pure', a term used by some of their opponents). Cathars regarded creation as controlled by two principles, Good and Evil, expressed through the different spheres of the spiritual and material. Some thought that Evil/the material came from a rebellion against the Good God, a view not that far removed from orthodox Christian teaching. Others, more radically, believed the two forces were co-eternal, the material world being the creation of Lucifer, the Evil force, not the Good God. This dualist doctrine contradicted the most fundamental tenets of traditional Christianity as it denied the Good God could in any material sense become part of the Evil temporal world and so rejected the Incarnation. The more absolutist position became prevalent across Cathar communities from the 1160s. As with orthodox Catholic believers, precise details of doctrinal theory were filtered by Cathar faithful, the *credentes*, into simpler articles of belief: the reality of sin; the evil inherent in creation and the material world; the primacy of asceticism; the rejection of the carnal, including marriage, sex and procreation. The central ritual to which the faithful aspired, often on their deathbeds, was the *consolamentum* (derived from the Latin for 'strengthening' or 'comforting'), a sacramental rite in which the believer received the Holy Spirit and absolution of sin, becoming a *perfectus* (or *perfecta*: unlike the Catholic Church the Cathars lacked formal institutional misogyny). *Perfecti*, sometimes known as *Boni Homines*, or Good Men, acted as preachers, delivering the *consolamentum*, and leading exemplary lives avoiding meat and sexual intercourse.

Cathar communities apparently produced written theological and doctrinal texts, in Latin and the vernacular. The circulation of these texts was mirrored by international contacts between dualist groups in northern and southern France, west Germany, northern Italy, the Balkans (another name for Cathars was 'Bulgarian heretics') and Constantinople. Some of these communities appear, by the second half of the twelfth century, to have been organised into recognised bishoprics that shadowed Catholic provinces. Cathars were Christian, just not Catholic or Trinitarian, rejecting the Catholic sacramental system and the humanity of Christ. Large parts of the New Testament and a few passages from the Old Testament were incorporated and reinterpreted by Cathar preachers and theologians, their discussions, as recorded, littered with scriptural references. Theirs was a wholly different version of the Christian message, which nonetheless confronted many of the same issues as Catholic teaching: the problem of sin and evil; anxiety over materialism; the dangers of moral and venal corruption of the Church and churchmen; the desire to return to some pristine austerity. In many ways, the similarities and points of contact with mainstream Catholicism made Cathars in the eyes of church authorities appear more insidious, especially where organised in regional social networks supported by believers with property, money and status.[9]

The origins of western Christian dualism – the belief in two competing cosmic forces – probably lay in evangelism from the Bogomil dualist Church, established in the Balkans in the tenth century. As part of the increasing flow of commerce and people between Byzantium and western Europe in the eleventh and early twelfth centuries, Bogomil dualist doctrines were possibly mediated by western, Latin converts in Constantinople. Probably from at least the 1140s, dualist communities existed in the Rhineland, Champagne, western Languedoc and Lombardy. By the 1170s, dualist bishops had been established in Lombardy, northern France and across Languedoc – Agen, Albi, Carcassonne and Toulouse – and were likely in contact with a bishop from Constantinople. The number of Cathar believers is hard to assess through lack of statistical evidence and because the nature of the faith blurred confessional boundaries. Dualism existed socially in tandem with Catholicism, one strand in a diverse popular religious culture, the plurality of which added to the disquiet of church authorities. A Catholic knight justified his refusal to pursue heretics from his lands: 'we cannot; we were brought up with them, there are many of our relatives amongst them, and we can see that their way of life is a virtuous one'.[10] Where lay and ecclesiastical authorities worked in harmony, as in parts of the Rhineland, northern France, or England, heretics were vigorously policed and contained by orchestrated repression and swift joint legal action.

Where no such alliance existed and where the Church's increasingly prescriptive intrusions into social behaviour were matched by popular dislike of clerical wealth and hierarchical solipsism, alternative doctrines could flourish.

Languedoc between the Garonne and Rhône rivers proved especially fertile ground, a region of distinctive cultures, commerce, political rivalries, loose centralised lordship, and ineffective pastoral leadership, with intractable geography, distant from the centres of reformist Catholicism. The Cathar heresy attracted members of social elites, not just the excluded or marginal. The papacy began to take notice, from the 1170s planning counter-measures that within a generation led to the unleashing of a crusade to eradicate heresy in the region. Heresy was not new to Languedoc in the 1170s. Bernard of Clairvaux had preached against heretics there in 1145. However, the rise of organised Catharism prompted Count Raymond V of Toulouse (count 1148–94) to seek outside assistance. A mission to Toulouse led by a papal legate, Peter of Pavia, and Henry of Marcy, abbot of Cîteaux, in 1178 excommunicated a number of prominent local heretics. They probably observed how heretics were accepted members of Languedoc society, freely engaged in

111. Fragment of a Cathar text.

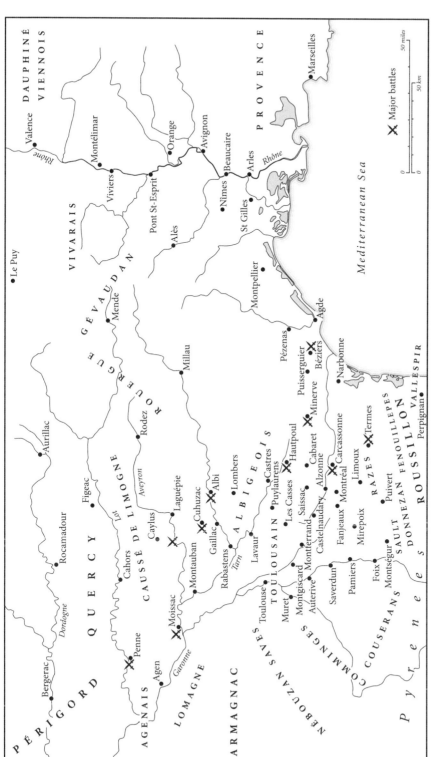

15. *Languedoc and the Albigensian Crusade.*

trade, employment, landholding, and mundane communication with their Catholic neighbours and relatives. A more strident policy was proposed by Canon XXVII of the Third Lateran Council of 1179, which offered the threat of physical coercion as well as excommunication. Those who fought heretics in southern France were to receive papal protection of person and property, 'as we do those who visit the Lord's Sepulchre', and a limited, two-year remission of penance; those who were killed would be rewarded with a full indulgence and salvation. The politicisation of the campaign against heresy was reinforced by the canon's inclusion of similar provisions for those who enlisted against rapacious mercenary companies terrorising Christian communities 'like pagans'.[11]

The response was modest. A small military campaign in 1181 under Henry of Marcy, now Cardinal Bishop of Albano (and future preacher of the Third Crusade), briefly besieged Lavaur, a major Cathar centre between Albi and Toulouse, securing the conversion of two prominent Cathars who were then installed in canonries in Toulouse – an ironic demonstration of the fluidity of allegiances that made eradicating heretics so problematic. In 1184, Lucius III's bull *Ad Abolendam* decreed condemned heretics should be delivered to the secular powers for unspecified punishment. However, only with the failure of Innocent III's legatine missions (1198, 1200–1, 1203–4) did a new policy of direct action emerge that bypassed the inertia of Count Raymond VI of Toulouse (1194–1222), increasingly seen by the pope as an obstacle if not an outright enemy, and a supporter of heretics. In 1204, when appointing a new legate in Languedoc, Innocent offered Holy Land crusade indulgences to those who joined the struggle against the heretics, at the same time trying to persuade Philip II of France to support the 'material sword' against them.[12] Efforts to engage Philip failed, despite a further offer of Holy Land indulgences in 1207. The direction of Innocent's policy was clear: 'wounds that do not respond to the healing of poultices must be lanced with a blade'. In January 1208 the assassination of the papal legate Peter of Castelnau near St Gilles on the Rhône by an employee of Raymond VI provided Innocent with the opportunity to launch a full crusade in the cause of 'faith and peace', urging 'knights of Christ' against 'the perverters of our souls', worse than Saracens: 'we must not be afraid of those who kill the body but of him who can send the body and soul to hell'.[13] Command, preaching and recruitment for the crusade army were entrusted to the papal legate Arnaud Aimery, abbot of Cîteaux. Recruits were clear that they were *crucesignati* 'against the heretic

Albigensians' (*hereticos Albigenses*), and, like those in the Jerusalem wars, their mission was penitential, their status akin to pilgrims.[14]

In practice, the Albigensian crusades differed from other theatres of crusading. With recruits from across much of France, the proximity of the battlefields – not more than a very few weeks' march – encouraged short-term commitment. In 1210 the legates insisted that at least forty days of service were required before crusaders could receive the full indulgence, a term that soon became standard. Rhetoric was tailored to elevate the war against heretics and their supposed protectors to equivalence with the Holy Land crusade. From the start the Albigensian crusades involved regime change across western and southern Languedoc. This held serious implications alike for the invading crusaders and the local counts and lords threatened with dispossession, but also for other interests: the kings of Aragon, France and England (in his role as duke of Aquitaine), each of whom had claims to overlordship in the region; the compromised southern French ecclesiastical establishment; urban communities in cities such as Toulouse, eager to assert autonomy; and the papacy, whose policy never lost sight of wider international implications. The objective of extirpating heresy provided a raw, at times vicious religiosity, inciting, if chroniclers can be believed, often fanatically barbarous ferocity in treating opponents and captives. Until subsumed into French royal policy in the 1220s, the Albigensian crusades lacked consistent or adequate external funding beyond the resources of participants and the lands they invaded. Socially, the crusades exposed a cultural gulf: the crusaders' genuine or confected horror at the existential threat of heresy collided with the daily experience of Languedoc where fellow Catholics and heretics had lived together without violent confessional conflict.

For the first campaign in 1209, Abbot Aimery recruited widely in northern France, despite Philip II remaining aloof. The leading nobles included Duke Odo III of Burgundy (1193–1218) and the counts of Nevers, St Pol and Boulogne. They were self-funded; their followers were paid. Duke Odo recruited Count Simon V of Montfort (d. 1218), the future leader of the crusade, with 'substantial gifts'.[15] This did not suggest a lack of emotional or ideological commitment: Simon proved a stern, tenacious uncompromising zealot against heretics. Given the temporary seasonal nature of most crusaders' commitment, material incentives of conquest alone cannot explain recruitment. Rather, motives conformed to similar church-approved expeditions: peer-group enthusiasm; reputation; spiritual reward; payment; and putting military habits to recognised good use.

Although the crusaders identified their enemies as 'Albigensians', after Albi, a major centre for heretical support, the initial target in 1209 was Toulouse and its excommunicate count. This quickly changed when Raymond VI prudently submitted, taking the cross in June 1209 as the crusading army neared. This deflected the invasion to Béziers and Carcassonne, lands held by Viscount Raymond Roger Trencavel (also lord of Albi) who, though personally orthodox, refused to comply with the crusaders' demands to persecute heretical subjects. The tone for the crusade was set on 22 July with the sack of Béziers and the massacre of its inhabitants, regardless, the legates with the army reported, 'of rank, sex or age'.[16] Even if the notorious story of Aimery Arnaud dismissing qualms over killing fellow Catholics ('Kill them. The Lord knows who are his own', II Timothy 2:19)[17] is apocryphal, making an example of Béziers showed the religiously inspired invasion as determinedly political in execution. Previous failures of direct evangelism had persuaded crusade planners that eradication of heresy depended on the removal of complaisant or complicit local rulers and their substitution by energetic promoters of Catholic orthodoxy. The first step came after the surrender of Carcassonne on 14 August 1209 with the election of Simon V of Montfort as commander of the crusade and ruler of the Trencavel lands. Over the following twenty years, to the accompaniment of calculated self-justifying sanctimonious atrocities, the Albigensian crusades redrew the political map of Languedoc, redesigning its social and tenurial contours through dispossession and the redistribution of loyalties, lordships and estates. The consequent disruption, devastation and lawlessness scarred the region for decades. Yet, with cruel irony, while heresy was driven underground, it was far from obliterated.

The Albigensian crusades fell into four rough periods: the conquest of the Trencavel lands, 1209–11; the Montfortian annexation of the county of Toulouse and the Pyrenean counties to the south, 1211–16; a messy revival of concerted local resistance, 1216–25; and the final decisive campaigns of Capetian armies, 1226–9. Until 1226 regular crusading reinforcements, while militarily significant, merely added temporary makeweights to existing and shifting political balances of power; even the interventions of Philip II's son Louis (1215, 1219) made little lasting impact. Until his defeat and death at the battle of Muret against the Montfortians

112. Stone relief showing the siege of Carcassonne, 1209.

(2 September 1213), Peter II of Aragon, a crusader against the Moors at Las Navas de Tolosa only the year before, presented the most serious challenge to the reordering of Languedoc. Historic Aragonese claims of overlordship were incompatible with the creation of a separate Montfortian principality, pushing Peter towards support for the dispossessed Raymond VI. However, even Muret's apparent resolution of the fate of Languedoc proved temporary.

Apart from the resistance of local baronage, concerned less with religious orthodoxy than their freedoms, traditions and property, and sharp rivalries between Montfort and the new church hierarchy, geography posed the chief obstacle to conquest. The hill country of the Pyrenees foothills and between the valleys of the Aude, Tarn and Lot, speckled with castles and fortified villages, often remote and protected by forbidding terrain, made political control from distant centres on the Garonne or Mediterranean coastal plain difficult. The landscape forced an unceasing round of arduous policing sorties long after nominal control had initially been seized from local lords. Tenacity proved Montfort's most necessary quality.[18] Closely linked to reformist academics and orthodox evangelical groups, such as the early Dominicans, Montfort on the Fourth Crusade had baulked at fighting fellow Catholics at Zara in 1202, reportedly announcing before he left the expedition that 'I have not come here to destroy Christians'.[19] His orthodox horror at heresy appears sincere; it also proved convenient in his attempt to carve out a Montfort principality.

The military campaigns revolved around sieges and piecemeal investment of castles, villages and towns. Precariously funded by church taxes, booty, and income and tributes from conquered territory, the core of Montfort's armies was modest, although repeatedly swelled by brief attendance by recruits from the north. The conquest of Trencavel lands was complete by May 1211. Attention then turned to the lands of the re-excommunicated Raymond VI and his Pyrenean allies, the counts of Comminges and Foix. After victory at Castelnaudary in September 1211, one of the few pitched battles of the wars (Muret 1213, Baziège 1218 the others), in 1212 Montfort conquered large swathes of territory from Agen on the Garonne towards the Pyrenees, although Toulouse itself eluded him. Signalling his dominance in

113. *Languedoc castles: Tour Cabaret and Tour Regine, near Lastours.*

the creation of a new polity, in December 1212 he issued the so-called Statute of Pamiers, establishing judicial, tenurial and ecclesiastical rights in his new lordship, privileging northern French incomers, who would enjoy the 'usages and customs observed in France around Paris'.[20] However, in January 1213, Innocent III, now focused on a new crusade to the Holy Land, cancelled further crusade indulgences for Languedoc in response to slick diplomacy by Peter of Aragon, whose attempt to broker Raymond VI's rehabilitation was rejected by the militantly hostile papal legates. Montfort was instructed to return his conquests of 1212. However, pressure from his legates forced a papal volte face. The bull *Quia Maior* (April 1213) launching the Fifth Crusade allowed inhabitants of Languedoc to take the cross against the Albigensians once more, and Montfort's position was restored in May, provoking Peter II's invasion and Montfort's crushing victory over Aragonese and Toulousan forces at Muret.

In 1214–15, Montfort tightened his hold over the county of Toulouse, extending his control northwards towards the Dordogne and the frontier with Angevin-held Guyenne. His title to the county of Toulouse was recognised by the Church and Philip II's only son, Louis, who toured Languedoc in the spring of 1215, fulfilling a crusade vow taken in 1213. The Fourth Lateran Council (November 1215), while restoring the count of Foix to his lands, confirmed Montfort in possession of the county of Toulouse and the Trencavel possessions, titles with which Montfort was invested by Philip II in April 1216. By the end of that year even the city of Toulouse was in Montfort's hands. However, the completeness of his victory provoked reaction, facilitated by the French court's distraction over Prince Louis' invasion of England in 1216–17. Raymond VI began to regain support and territory. In September 1217, Toulouse opened its gates to him leading to another siege at which, on 25 June 1218, Montfort was killed, struck on the head by a stone hurled by a mangonel in the city, operated, some claimed, by women. With the tables now turned, a new crusade was announced by Honorius III in August 1218, led in 1219 by Prince Louis. Some initial success was followed by failure to take Toulouse. Louis withdrew in August 1219, leaving Montfort's less talented son, Amaury, to preside over a gradual deterioration of the Montfortian position. By 1223, a truce between Amaury and Raymond VII (1222–49) found much of Languedoc, including the Trencavel lands, regained by the families of its pre-1209 rulers. By 1225, Amaury had effectively given up, ceding his rights in the south to the new French king, Louis VIII (1223–6), the crusade apparently a military, political and, given the survival of heresy, religious failure.

This verdict was rejected by Louis VIII. The crusade posed unfinished business for a twice-sworn Languedoc crusader eager to promote his new kingship in sacral terms and anxious to further dominate the south following his conquest of Poitou from the Angevins in 1224. With the pope still implacably hostile to reconciliation, Raymond VII was excommunicated in late 1225 and a clerical crusade tithe ordered. Louis took the cross for the third time in January 1226, leading a large army south in June. A three-month siege of Avignon led to its negotiated surrender in September and the submission of Provence and most of Languedoc. Although Louis died on his return journey north (in November 1226), remaining Toulousan resistance was broken by vicious ravaging campaigns in 1227 and 1228 led by Humbert of Beaujeu, the Capetian agent in Languedoc. The Albigensian crusades ended when Raymond VII submitted to Capetian terms at the treaty of Paris in 1229. Besides accepting reduced lands and the prospect of their absorption after his death into Capetian lordship, Raymond agreed to assist in the suppression of heresy, a tacit admission that the crusade had failed in its primary aim. Over the following decades heresy was rooted out, occasionally by military force, as with the siege and capture of the Cathar stronghold of Montségur in 1244, but more conclusively by the alliance of the new political and ecclesiastical establishments championing direct evangelism, especially by friars, and new processes of clerical inquisition, legal intimidation and punishment. While pivotal in the political reordering of southern France, the crusades had proved ineffective in creating an obedient Catholic community cleansed of error. Yet the former proved vital in the subsequent achievement of the latter, once more confirming the ineradicable fusion of the secular and spiritual, the cultural rationale of crusading in the first place.

The Extension of Crusading

The Albigensian crusades let the genie out of the bottle. Accusations of heresy and schism against a protean array of opponents flowed freely. The association of crusading and the defence of rights suited political contests, such as the civil wars in England in 1215–17 and 1263–5: at the battle of Evesham in 1265 both royalists and rebels wore crusade crosses (respec-

114. *From the* Customs of Toulouse, *1296: torture.*

115. *Heretics thrown to the fire.*

tively red and white). On one occasion, in Germany in 1240, a pseudo- or anti-crusade, complete with preaching, giving the cross and granting of indulgences, was directed against a papal legate promoting a crusade against King Frederick II.[21] Crusades were directed against the Colonna family in Italy (1297–8), enemies of Pope Boniface VIII (1294–1303), and to crush the disruptive northern Italian charismatic cult of Fra Dolcino (1306–7). As a tool of social and political discipline, crusading became a weapon of choice for rulers who energetically (and not always successfully) petitioned popes for access to crusade indulgences and money.

Papal enthusiasm could be impressive. Gregory IX (1227–41), a canon lawyer and veteran crusade preacher, demonstrated particular versatility in authorising, with careful legal justification, full-blown crusades or the reward of plenary indulgences. Targets included the supposedly heretical Stedinger peasants in the Lower Weser valley (1232–5) and German heretics more generally (1228–32, 1233–4); Bosnians suspected of heresy and inadequate orthodoxy (1233–8); Italian heretics and their alleged protectors (1231, 1235); Greek Orthodox rulers (1231, 1235–8); the Bulgarian King John Asen (1238), who threatened the Latin empire of Constantinople established in 1204; and Russian Orthodox enemies of the Teutonic Knights (1240). Gregory's eagerness provided precedents for his successor, the even more distinguished canon lawyer Innocent IV (1243–54), whose crusade attention fell on Bosnians, Italian heretics, Greeks and Sardinians. For both Gregory and Innocent, the main enemies were the Hohenstaufen: Frederick II, his descendants and their supporters.

The Hohenstaufen

The wars against the Hohenstaufen provided the most dramatic example of the crusade used to redress a political problem, in this case the prevention of territorial encirclement of papal lands in Italy by Emperor Frederick II (1197–1250). Indelible distrust between successive popes and what Urban IV (1261–4) called a 'viper race' prevented a settlement, the feud becoming increasingly venomous under a succession of popes: Gregory IX, Innocent IV, Alexander IV (1254–61), Urban IV and Clement IV (1265–8). Frederick had first been excommunicated in 1227; a campaign against him led by the former king-regent of Jerusalem John of Brienne in 1228–30 had attracted clerical taxes. However, only after Frederick had again been excommunicated in March 1239 did Gregory IX declare a crusade against him in the winter of 1239–40, hoping to reassure local allies and extend support in northern Italy and Germany where, renewed in 1240 and 1243, the crusade was preached. The full vial of papal vitriol was liberally poured on the Hohenstaufen as schismatics, heretics, harbingers of the Anti-Christ, fomenters of disorder and covert Muslims. After Innocent IV had deposed Frederick at the First Council of Lyons (1245), anti-kings were set up in Germany (Henry Raspe of Thuringia, 1246–7; William of Holland, 1247–56), perhaps encouraged by funds generated by the crusade. Thereafter, the crusade provided a focus and respectable cover for local rivalries in Italy and Germany as well as papal hostility that persisted after Frederick's death. Crusades continued in Germany against his son Conrad IV (1250–4) and his illegitimate son, Manfred (regent, then, after 1258 king of Sicily; d. 1266), in Italy where, after 1254, the military action took place. In 1255, Henry III of England accepted from Alexander IV the crown of Sicily on behalf of his second son, Edmund, the pope wishing to harness the resources of a secular kingdom to the cause. English involvement failed to materialise, as Henry's optimistic financial guarantees almost cost him his throne when leading English magnates rebelled at what they saw as the cost and caprice of the 'Sicilian Business'. In place of the English, Urban IV and Clement IV enlisted Louis IX of France's youngest brother, Charles of Anjou (d. 1285), to tackle Manfred. Following a swift, daring campaign in the winter of 1265–6, Charles defeated and killed Manfred at the battle of Benevento (February 1266). In 1268, Charles repulsed an attempted Hohenstaufen restoration, defeating Conrad IV's son Conradin at Tagliacozzo (in August) and executing him in Naples (October), the last Hohenstaufen in the male line.

The anti-Hohenstaufen wars further embedded crusading in western European politics. Crusades were directed against Ezzelino and Alberigo of Romano (1256) (see 'A Day in Venice', p. 356); Sardinia (1263); and English rebels (1263, 1265). After a Sicilian revolt against Charles of Anjou in 1282 (the so-called Sicilian Vespers) and the occupation of the island by Frederick II's son-in-law, Peter III of Aragon, a fresh crusade was promulgated (January 1283), which led to a disastrous invasion of Aragon by Philip III of France (1270–85) in 1285. Fresh crusading was instituted when Frederick of Sicily (1296–1337), younger son of Peter III, refused to surrender the island to the Angevins. Only the treaty of Caltabellota in 1302, which left Sicily in Aragonese hands, ended the Sicilian crusades.

116. Charles of Anjou and Manfred.

The Later Middle Ages

In the fourteenth century, Italy remained the chief arena for crusades against Christians. They were employed when Louis IV attempted to revive German imperial claims in the peninsula (1328–30); to prevent Venetian control of Ferrara (1309–10); and against anti-papal (so-called Ghibelline) city rulers, or *signori*, prominently the Visconti of Milan. (Florence and Naples tended towards the papal – Guelph – side.) However, alliances were necessarily fluid: in 1334, Guelph Florence joined Milan to prevent a papal scheme to erect a Lombard puppet state. Defence of the Papal States, orchestrated by cardinal-legates, such as Bertrand du Poujet after 1319 and Gil Albornoz after 1353, regularly employed crusades. This was chiefly in order to allow the papacy, now settled in Avignon (1309–76), to raise huge sums of money to pay for the wars against Milan (1321, 1324, 1360, 1363, 1368); Ferrara (1321); Mantua and Ancona (1324); Cesena and Faenza (1354). In 1357, 1361 and 1369–70 crusades were directed against freelance mercenary companies (*routiers*) in the peninsula. Despite conventional rhetoric and privileges, these

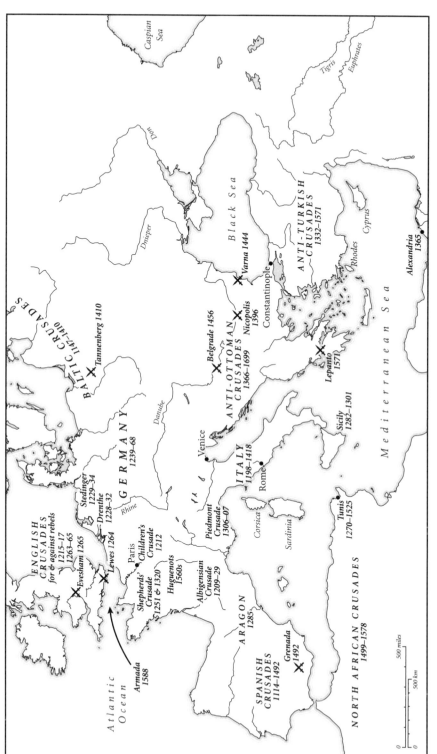

16. Crusades against Christians in Europe, fourteenth–sixteenth centuries.

Caspian Sea

Tigris

Euphrates

Don

Black Sea

Dnieper

ANTI-TURKISH
CRUSADES
1332–1571

Varna 1444

Constantinople

Cyprus

Rhodes

Alexandria
1365

BALTIC CRUSADES 1147–1410

Tannenberg 1410

Belgrade 1456

Nicopolis
1396

ANTI-OTTOMAN
CRUSADES
1366–1699

Lepanto
1571

Mediterranean Sea

GERMANY 1239–68

Stedinger
1229–34

Drenthe
1228–32

Lewes 1264

Paris

Children's
Crusade
1212

Shepherds'
Crusade
1251 & 1320

Huguenots
1560s

Albigensian
Crusade
1209–29

Danube

Venice

Rome

Rhine

Piedmont
Crusade
1306–07

ITALY
1198–1418

Sicily
1282–1301

Corsica

Sardinia

Tunis
1270–1525

ENGLISH
CRUSADES
for & against rebels
1215–17
1263–65

Evesham 1265

Armada
1588

Atlantic
Ocean

ARAGON
1285

Grenada
1492

SPANISH
CRUSADES
1114–1492

NORTH AFRICAN CRUSADES
1499–1578

500 miles

500 km

A DAY IN VENICE, 1258

By the thirteenth century, crusade preachers were well used to employing props and histrionic devices in support of oral rhetoric. However, few could have outdone the scene that unfolded in Venice's Piazza San Marco sometime in 1258,[22] as recorded by the gossipy judgemental Franciscan, Salimbene de Adam (1221–c. 1289). A crusade had been authorised by Pope Alexander IV against the supposedly tyrannical and – in hostile accounts – sadistic ruler of Treviso, Alberigo of Romano, at the time a supporter of the anti-papal Hohenstaufen. One of Alberigo's alleged atrocities had been the abuse of thirty Treviso noble-women who had been stripped of their clothes below their breasts and forced to watch their husbands, sons, brothers and fathers being hanged before expulsion from the city. Apparently they made their way to Venice where the papal legate (identified by Salimbene as Cardinal Ottaviano degli Ubaldini), feeding off public outrage, theatrically exploited their predicament to excite the crowd: 'in order to anger the people more against Alberigo . . . the cardinal . . . had the women come forth in the same shameful and nude condition that the wicked Alberigo had reduced them to'.[23] To reinforce his message that the demonised Alberigo needed to be combated by force, the legate rehearsed a string of the more bellicose revenge texts from the Bible before, amid cries of 'So be it! So be it!', and by popular demand, he preached and dispensed the cross to the hysteri-cally enthusiastic audience. Salimbene attributed such mass fervour to a combi-nation of deference to the legate, the attraction of indulgences and the witness to Alberigo's crimes. The friar's account is lurid, probably more than a little embroidered: if the show did occur, the cardinal may have used actors, as the idea that he, let alone the women themselves, would have agreed to any such a public naked parade defies credulity. Yet, however formal or imaginative, the essential outline features of Salimbene's story are consistent with many other descriptions of crusade sermons: the emphasis on the lure of spiritual reward; the explicit scriptural support for the justice of authorised violence; the power of atrocity narratives; the validation of reciprocal popular consent; and the skilled mechanics of crowd manipulation, from rhetoric to theatricals and crowd

117. The Venice piazza in Bellini's Procession of the True Cross.

chanting. Effective preaching of the cross, whether outside St Mark's or else-where, involved entertainment as much as conviction.

Italian crusades were restricted to regional politics and local recruitment. Outside Italy, successive popes declined to gild other temporal conflicts with the cross, whether French ambitions on Flanders or the Hundred Years War.

The rivalries of the Great Schism (1378–1417) provided new crusading opportunities: the Roman Pope Urban VI against his Avignon rival Clement VII (1378); both Roman and Avignon popes authorised crusades during succession wars in Naples (1382, Clement VII; 1411 and 1414, John XXIII). Urban VI associated the crusade with Bishop Despenser of Norwich's campaign in Flanders in 1383. This was no casual association. Bishop Despenser milked the traditional symbolism in a dramatic performance when he assumed the cross at a ceremony in December 1382 at St Paul's Cathedral in London, the bishop lifting then carrying a large, heavy cross onto his shoulders in a physically theatrical display of observing the central crusading command of Christ to 'take up his cross'.[24] The crusade still provided incentives, not least financial. Despenser's crusade, for instance, offered the English government a cheap, if in the event drearily unsuccessful, French campaign, while crusade bulls elevated the status of John of Gaunt's bid to become king of Castile in 1386. However, the nature of the schism meant that neither side's crusades had access to adequate church taxes to underwrite substantial campaigns. At the same time papal universalist claims underpinning crusade theory were degraded even if crusading against overt heretics, pagans, Mamluks and Ottomans retained cultural lustre. Following the end of the schism in 1417, popes refrained from using the crusade to defend the Papal States until Julius II (1503–13) briefly revived the habit in Italy. Julius also afforded crusade status to Henry VIII of England's French campaign of 1512–13. Crusade detritus still littered the political landscape. Occasionally, as in Hungary in 1514, it became enmeshed in civil revolt, although in this case the crusaders' violence was provoked by the Hungarian nobility's reluctance to fight Ottomans.

The exception to the decline in crusades against Christians came with six crusades fought against the Hussites of Bohemia (1420, 1421, 1422, 1427, 1431, 1465–71) and another planned (1428–9) and with a rhetorically grand but, in execution, petty and squalid assault on Waldensian communities in Savoy (1488). The Hussites combined organised religious radicalism – vernacular texts, distinct liturgies, Bible-based theology, and a rejection of traditional ecclesiastical authority – with the political cause of anti-German Czech nationalism. This gained it important allies among the Bohemian nobility. A policy of a crusade to crush Hussite heresy attempted to demonstrate the new unity of the western Church after the end of the papal schism (1417) and successfully drew international attention and support across western Europe. However, the continuing Hundred Years War sapped Franco-English support. The leadership of the German Emperor Sigismund (king of Hungary, 1387–1437; of Germany, 1411–37), also king of Bohemia (1419–37), emphasised how far the crusades were enmeshed in discrete regional politics, with religion forming only a part of the cause of conflict. The crusaders' successive military failures between 1420 and 1431, coupled with their indiscriminate violence, served to reinforce Czech identity and independence while hardly adding lustre to the crusade as a weapon against Christian European powers. The 1465–71 crusade concerned politics and diplomacy rather than faith; Bohemia had long since been recognised by fellow rulers less as a rogue state and more as a potential partner. Inevitably, the following century, the Reformation stimulated revived crusade talk, but talk it chiefly remained (see Chapter 12).[25]

Criticism and Opposition

Given the pre-1095 tradition of holy war and the kudos of the Jerusalem war, the use of crusading against Christians was inescapable. Its rapid extension in the thirteenth century rested on clearer categories of holy and just war, the arrival of a settled theology of plenary indulgences and the new availability of funds. Inevitably, crusades against Christians aroused controversy. Victims and opponents naturally objected: Languedoc poets loudly lamented the rape of their land and culture.[26] Such crusades could easily be characterised as tawdry political and financial rackets, sometimes with justice. The popes' arguments that their enemies were distracting efforts to help the Holy Land could be turned back on them. In the thirteenth century, otherwise crusade sympathisers condemned papal wars against the Hohenstaufen in Italy and Germany. Clergy, such as the rectors of Berkshire in 1240, resented taxation for them. English and French nobles objected to attempts to force them to commute their Holy Land vows to fight the Greeks in the 1230s and 1240s. Opponents were found from citizens of Lille in 1284 to Florentines who refused to permit crusade legacies to be diverted. The papalist preacher and canon lawyer Hostiensis ran into trouble on an anti-Hohenstaufen preaching tour of Germany where he was heckled by crowds who preferred the Holy Land crusade. The diversion of

118. Hussite wars.

church taxes granted in 1274 and 1312 from the Holy Land to Italy appeared
fraudulent. Wars in the Holy Land and against pagans and heretics retained
primacy of respect; those against fellow Christians attracted limited international approval and inconsistent papal enthusiasm. While Gregory IX,

Innocent IV, Clement IV, Boniface VIII or John XXII (1316–34) eagerly promoted such wars, Gregory X (1271–6) or Nicholas IV (1288–91) worked for internal peace in pursuit of a new eastern expedition. The curia was not deaf to critics: in 1246, Innocent IV wished his order to stop preaching the Holy Land crusade in favour of the Hohenstaufen crusade to remain secret.[27] As the disgruntled responses of *crucesignati* in the 1230s and 1240s showed, the coincidence of different crusade objectives caused unease. To some in the later thirteenth century, the erosion of Outremer while crusades in Italy intensified appeared deplorable.

However, the German and Italian crusades elicited support, chiefly from those with immediate political interests in play. Crusades against Christians failed to tarnish other wars of the cross and played only a subordinate part in attacks on papal authority. The English radical theologian John Wyclif's coruscating attack on Despenser's Crusade of 1383 fitted wider anxieties exposed by the crisis of the Great Schism. Papal crusades against Christians produced some dramatic political successes: the conquest of Languedoc; Charles of Anjou's success in Sicily; the destruction of the Hohenstaufen. Yet papal territory remained insecure and the aura of sanctity wore very thin during the interminable Ghibelline–Guelph wars. As with crusade grants in Iberia and elsewhere, the later Middle Ages saw crusades against Christians become financial expedients. By the early fifteenth century, even that failed to compensate.

CHAPTER TEN

THE END OF THE JERUSALEM
WARS, 1250–1370

The failure of the Egyptian crusade of 1248–50 could not be reversed. The succession of aggressive Mamluk sultans in Egypt bent on proving their Islamic credentials made conquest of enfeebled Frankish Outremer a clear objective once the immediate threat of Mongol lordship in Syria had receded after the Mamluk victory at the battle of Ain Jalut in 1260. Thereafter, Outremer survived through piecemeal treaties and increasingly desperate and ineffectual military and diplomatic expedients. Louis IX could do little more than follow the pattern during his stay at Acre between 1250 and 1254: shoring up the defences of Outremer's remaining cities and castles; futile diplomacy, such as the abortive treaty with Egypt in 1252 against Damascus or pursuing contacts with an indifferent Mongol Great Khan; and funding modest garrisons at Acre after his departure. In the west, since the 1230s, competing threats, such as the Mongols, or distracting alternative opportunities, such as crusades with the Teutonic Knights in the Baltic, against supposed religious dissidents or even papal crusades against the Hohenstaufen, may have blunted active engagement with the Holy Land and provoked criticism.[1] However, especially in Italy and France, generalised enthusiasm for the original cause continued to resist strategic reality, the concept of divine retribution for sin providing cover for logistical contradictions that three generations of planners, theorists and lobbyists sought and failed to unravel. Ideas for Eurasian alliances, maritime blockades, economic embargos, fiscal innovations and professional armies regularly reached the council chambers of rulers whose lip service to the Holy Land failed to override domestic political obligation, a dilemma appreciated by the veteran crusader John of Joinville when he condemned

Louis IX's crusade to Tunis in 1270 as damaging to the peace and security of France.[2]

The Shepherds' Crusade, 1251

A striking illustration of Joinville's dilemma came with the so-called Shepherds' Crusade in France during 1251, which exposed the impotence of popular enthusiasm and the perils of absentee rulers. News of Louis IX's defeat and capture reached western Europe in the summer and autumn of 1250, provoking disturbances in Italian cities and outpourings of communal grief in France. By the spring of 1251 people in rural Brabant, Flanders, Hainault and Picardy, described slightingly as 'shepherds and simple people', mobilised with the stated intention of travelling to join Louis in the Holy Land.[3] Echoing the 1212 Children's Crusade in criticising the crusade failings of the nobility, disparate groups of *pastoureaux* (shepherds) across northern France parodied the crusade processions familiar since the early thirteenth century. Some marched on Paris carrying banners with symbols of the Passion (including the paschal lamb that may have provided their nickname) and the Virgin Mary, while handing out crosses and absolution of sins. Far from an inarticulate formless rabble, they were initially supported by the Regent, Blanche of Castile (d. 1252). Some may have actually reached the Holy Land, indicating means beyond those of shepherds.[4] Demonstrations, expressing social frustrations as well as crusade enthusiasm, spread from Normandy to the Loire and south into Berry and beyond. Degenerating into armed gangs, they provoked violence in Rouen, Orléans and Bordeaux, particularly directed at clerics. At Bourges, one band, led by an educated man called 'the Master of Hungary', allegedly trilingual in French, German and Latin, attacked Jews before being dispersed and their leader killed.

While, for the mass of followers, the uprisings led nowhere, they demonstrated significant popular acquaintance with official policy and high politics: the use of crusading symbols, such as images of the Passion, favoured by King Louis himself; indulgences; cross-giving; the desire for government approval; criticism of the nobility and clergy; predatory hostility towards Jews, another royal habit; and the call for political action in the service of God. Clerical accusations of disorder, criminality and sexual excess concealed the movement's coherence and the popular resonance of targets such as venal clergy, feather-bedded scholars and Jews. Of varied economic status, the '*pastoureaux*', proclaiming loyalty to the king, expressed the frustrations of the marginalised not the ignorant. They revealed wide social diffusion of crusading practices and mentalities achieved through preaching, communal ceremonies, taxation and gossip. Like their social superiors in the Nile Delta, they also showed how devotion alone was not enough, a fact confirmed by Louis IX's crusade to Tunis in 1270.

The 1270–2 Crusade

Louis IX did not abandon Outremer after 1254. He provided for a French garrison at Acre and annual subsidies. At home, he fashioned an image of royal asceticism and Christian devotion, for which his sufferings in Egypt provided unimpeachable witness, the commitment to the Holy Land supporting a programme of moral authority crafted in art, architecture, anti-Semitism, religious observance and politics.[5] Charles of Anjou's victory in southern Italy and Sicily (1266–8) and the triumph of the royalists in the English Civil War (1263–7) freed Louis to try reversing the verdict of 1250. By September 1266, partly in response to worsening news from the Holy Land, he was planning to take the cross once more.

The survival of Outremer was in increasing jeopardy. The arrival of the Mongols had transformed the regional balance of powers. After capturing Baghdad and killing the last Abbasid caliph in 1258, the Mongols conquered Syria in early 1260, briefly occupying Sidon and raiding as far as Gaza.[6] Bohemund VI of Antioch-Tripoli (1252–75) submitted to Mongol overlordship, accepting a Mongol garrison in Antioch that remained until 1268 when the city fell to the Mamluks. Armenian Cilicia also accepted Mongol overlordship. By contrast, the Franks of Acre refused to ally with the Mongols but equally declined to assist the new Mamluk sultan of Egypt, Qutuz, against them. Given Mamluk hostility and the Mongols' uncompromising unilateral approach to alliances, this may have appeared prudent. However, both Acre and Tripoli-Antioch were left vulnerable after the Egyptian victory at Ain Jalut in southern Galilee (3 September 1260) over a modest Mongol force left behind when the main army had withdrawn eastwards. With Mongol attention subsequently focused on Iraq, Iran and the Caucasus, the Mamluks rapidly proceeded to annex Muslim Syria, ejecting or overawing the surviving Ayyubid princes. By the end of October 1260 when the Bahriyya Mamluk commander Baibars (1260–77) assassinated Qutuz and

119. Hulagu captures Baghdad, 1258.

assumed the sultanate, the unification of Egypt and Syria was more complete than at any time since 1193.

Baibars, who had played a central role in the Egyptian military campaigns and internal violence of 1249–50, now used the conquest of Outremer to cement his political and ideological authority, in the process denying the Mongols a potential ally. From 1265 he proceeded to dismantle the remains of Outremer through asymmetrical diplomacy and irresistible siege warfare: Caesarea, Arsuf, Toron and Haifa fell in 1265; Safed, Galilee, Ramlah and Lydda in 1266; Jaffa, Beaufort and, with a punitive massacre, Antioch in 1268. Baibars' aggression provoked Pope Clement IV to revive crusade plans begun in 1263 under his predecessor Urban IV. On 25 March 1267, the Feast of the Annunciation, before the relics of the Passion in the Sainte Chapelle in Paris, Louis IX took the cross with his immediate family and the leading magnates in France.[7]

The 1270 crusade was expertly organised. Repeating techniques familiar from the 1240s, finance came from a French clerical tithe, legacies, redemptions, taxes on towns and tenants, expropriation of Jewish funds and sales of private assets. Ships were commissioned from Genoa, Marseilles and ports in

120. Baibars and his court.

Catalonia. As in 1248–9, the king underwrote the expenses of leading companions, including the duke of Burgundy and the counts of Poitiers, Champagne, Brittany and Flanders. English and Gascon involvement was attracted by loans of 70,000 *livres tournois* to Louis' English nephew, Edward, the future Edward I. As well as the usual recruiting devices of kinship, lordship, friendship and geographic association, formal contracts were issued on both sides of the English Channel specifying pay and other rewards for a stated number of knights: Louis paid for a contracted core of 325 knights; Edward paid for one of 225. In total, a combined force of between 10,000 and 15,000 could have been assembled. Beyond France, recruits came from Frisia, the Netherlands, Aragon, Scotland, England and the kingdom of Sicily, now ruled by Louis' brother, Charles of Anjou. Louis secured the adherence of James I of Aragon. In England, Edward and his brother Edmund took the cross in 1268; in 1270 they managed to extract a parliamentary tax on moveables of a twentieth, perhaps worth £30,000, the first lay subsidy granted to the English crown since 1237.[8]

Yet, despite central contracts and royal funding, the new crusade was a disjointed affair. Louis planned to depart in May 1270 and did so in July; James of Aragon had embarked in June 1269; Charles of Anjou only took the cross in February 1270, starting to equip his fleet in July when his brother was already at sea en route for Tunis; Edward only set out from England in August 1270, arriving at Tunis in November just as the crusaders were packing up to leave; and his brother Edmund did not set out until the winter of 1270–1. Storms wrecked the Aragonese fleet, only a few ships reaching Acre. Recruitment in France fell short of initial estimates. The long papal interregnum from the death of Clement IV in November 1268 to the election of Gregory X in September 1271 exactly coincided with final preparations and the campaign itself. In 1268 or 1269 the original French plan for direct aid for the Holy Land and another assault on Egypt was replaced by a scheme to attack Tunis, confusingly an ally of the king of Aragon. Despite the declared muster ports in Sardinia and western Sicily, the fiction of an eastern objective was maintained, the public announcement of Tunis as the destination only coming after Louis had embarked in July 1270.

As a staging post for an invasion of Egypt, Tunis may have appeared more convenient than Cyprus. Commercial and diplomatic relations between western Mediterranean Christian powers and the emirs of Tunis were of long standing, alternately of alliance, competition and conflict. A Tunisian embassy was in negotiation with Louis in 1269, while Louis' Dominican contacts may have argued that Tunis and north Africa were ripe for evangelism, a common optimistic mendicant trope in this period. Although possibly suiting the Sicilian ambitions of Charles of Anjou, Louis' decision may have owed more to a combination of a mendicant-inspired commitment to convert non-Christians, a vague strategic hope of denying Egypt an ally, and securing the north African route to attack the Nile that had been suggested since the early twelfth century. The Tunis crusade reflected lasting networks of contact, commerce, competition and exchange between the powers around the western Mediterranean that belied any two-dimensional model of religious conflict.

Louis' departure followed the precedents of 1147, 1190 and 1248, with the king receiving the oriflamme and pilgrim's scrip and staff at St Denis (14 March 1270), and that of 1248 with him setting out from Paris as a barefoot penitent. Immediately things went wrong. At Aigues Mortes, commissioned ships arrived late and illness broke out in the army. After a stormy passage from Aigues Mortes to Sardinia (2–4 July), Louis, unsure of where he was, is said to have been shown a map of Cagliari and its situation, probably a Genese *portolano*, or navigational map, the first recorded instance of a crusader consulting a map or chart on campaign.[9] After Tunis was revealed as the destination on 13 July, the French fleet made landfall on 17 July, the troops disembarking the next day before moving camp to Carthage a few miles away on 24 July to be nearer adequate water. Apart from some perfunctory skirmishing, operations stalled while the army waited for Charles of Anjou. Heat, poor food and dire sanitation soon sparked disease, typhus or dysentery, which ravaged the high command as well as the mass of the army. Louis (25 August 1270) and his son John Tristan (born at Damietta in the dark days of 1250) died; the king's eldest son and successor Philip III fell seriously ill. When Charles of Anjou arrived in late August and assumed command, he had little option but to negotiate a withdrawal. With the Hafsid emir Mohammed eager to pay the crusaders to go away, terms were agreed (1 November) including an exchange of prisoners, agreement to allow Christian worship and evangelising in Tunis, and payment of 210,000 gold ounces (*c.* 500,000 *livres tournois*) of which Charles claimed a third. The crusaders, now reinforced by Edward of England, sailed for Sicily where a storm (15/16 November) destroyed dozens of ships and claimed over 1,000 lives. Thereafter, only Edward wished to continue to Acre. The convalescent Philip III returned to France with the remains of his father, brother, brother-in-law, wife and stillborn son. In Tunis, trading relations were soon restored with Sicily, Aragon and the Genoese.

The Tunis campaign, in a traditional crusading perspective a disaster, tested but failed to break the resilience of the ideal. Louis' death in August 1270 provided the crusade with a popular martyr, even if, when canonised in 1297 it was as a confessor, to his friend Joinville's annoyance. In 1271 the cardinals elected the well-connected archdeacon of Liège, Tedaldo Visconti, as pope (Gregory X, 1271–6), while he was in Acre on crusade with Edward of England. His attempts to recruit western rulers to a new eastern expedition culminated in the Second Council of Lyons (1274).[10] Meanwhile Edward, ignoring appeals to return home where his aged father Henry III was nearing death, sailed to Acre in the spring of 1271 with a small force, possibly only 1,000 strong, carried in thirteen ships, arriving on 9 May 1271. He remained for a year, being joined in September by his brother Edmund. Edward's stay was little more than a morale-boosting promenade. He largely avoided the traps of local Frankish infighting but, apart from helping see off a Mamluk attack on Acre in December 1271 and a couple of raids into Acre's hinterland, contributed nothing to alleviate Outremer's predicament. His diplomatic links with the Mongol Il-Khan of Persia proved typically nugatory. Baibars had captured Crac des Chevaliers in April 1271 and was hardly deflected from his grand design: his emollient May 1272 truce with the Franks ignored Edward's presence. Edward's followers, including his brother Edmund (May 1272), began leaving. The famous attempt on Edward's life by a Mamluk assassin in June provided the most memorable incident of his Holy Land crusade, which ended when Edward sailed from Acre in October 1272 leaving behind a small English garrison and a mountain of debts. Although Edward's quixotic crusade had cost a vast sum (perhaps more than £100,000) for no concrete achievement, in terms of fame and honour the investment paid handsomely: for the rest of his life as King Edward I (1272–1307), with the Holy Land's fate an inescapable feature of western diplomacy and public discussion, he remained the only western monarch who had actually been there to fight for the cross, a status he reinforced by taking the cross again in 1287.

The Loss of the Holy Land

Despite statements of intent, Edward I never returned east. By pleading, not entirely disingenuously, pressing business at home, he exposed a central contradiction in attempts to rescue or restore Outremer. The application of the resources of kingdoms to crusading had shown, in 1248–50 and 1270 as in 1188–90, how costs and administration could be covered. However, the more powerful monarchs became, the more extensive their domestic obligations. Expanding bureaucracies ensured that the huge expenses of Holy Land crusades were now dauntingly measurable: the financial accounts of Louis IX's crusades were still being examined in the 1330s.[11] Extensive discussion of practical problems provoked by repeated failure inspired ideas such as the amalgamation of the Military Orders to achieve economies of scale, but inevitably tempered political enthusiasm. Before the Second Council of Lyons (1274), Gregory X collected advice and information. This revealed the scale of the challenge and, equally inconvenient, the largely negative impact exerted by the diverse theatres of crusading on the Holy Land enterprise.

Gregory X was committed to the relief of the Holy Land. On his election he preached to the text 'If I forget thee, O Jerusalem, let my right hand forget her cunning' (Psalm 137:5). The council he summoned to consider church reform and a new crusade, to be led by the pope himself, met at Lyons in May 1274. Armed with written and oral advice from a wide range of interested parties, the council produced the most complete programme for planning a new crusade yet achieved. The decree *Constitutiones pro ⟨eli fidei* (18 May 1274) authorised indulgences, a trade embargo, a sexennial ecclesiastical tithe, and a voluntary lay poll tax. The collection of the church tax was organised into twenty-six collectories. Diplomatic provision included the council's reception of Mongol ambassadors and a proposed union between the Roman and Greek Orthodox Churches negotiated with the Greek emperor Michael VIII Palaeologus (1261–85), part of his efforts to parry the Balkan ambitions of Charles of Anjou. Only in 1261 had Michael expelled the westerners from Constantinople, but he now needed allies against this new Mediterranean power. Yet only one western monarch attended, the veteran James I of Aragon, and even his offer of 500 knights and 2,000 infantry came to nothing. Following the council, preaching was authorised in September 1274 and Philip III of France, Charles of Anjou and the new king of Germany, Rudolf of Habsburg, took the cross in 1275. Large sums were raised, a departure date was fixed (April 1277), a papal fleet planned. Yet concerted political will was absent, as speakers at Lyons had warned.[12] Impressive papal administrative reach failed to translate into action. The indifference of the Military Orders at Lyons spoke loudly. Gregory X's crusade died with him in January 1276. The crusade tithes were redirected to papal crusades in Italy. Despite continued diplomacy, the Mongol alliance remained illusory. Church union foundered on rejection by the Greek Orthodox faithful. A pattern was set, copied in varying detail after the Council of Vienne (1311–12), in the 1330s and in the 1360s: papal or royal initiatives; public endorsement; diplomacy, fund-raising, administrative preparations; then delay, distraction and cancellation. As the Italian Franciscan commentator Salimbene of Adam remarked: 'it does not seem to be the Divine Will that the Holy Sepulchre should be recovered'.[13]

By 1272, mainland Outremer had been reduced to a few castles and ports. Despite Christian bases in Cyprus and Cilician Armenia and maritime superiority, recovery was stymied by western inertia and Baibars' systematic destruction of the harbours and coastal cities he had captured. The pause in attacks after Baibars' 1272 treaty with the Franks followed by his death in 1277 combined with continuing Mongol ambitions in Syria to distract the Mamluks and delay Outremer's final collapse. With the defeat of the

121. The fall of Tripoli, 1289.

SIEGES

The military history of the crusades is punctuated by decisive sieges, the commonest form of set-piece large-sale armed encounter in the Middle Ages. In the west they occurred in a landscape of castles; in the eastern Mediterranean in a world of cities. The course of crusades rested on sieges: Nicaea, Antioch, al-Bara, Ma'arrat al-Numan, Arqah, Jerusalem on the First Crusade; Lisbon and Damascus on the Second; Acre on the Third; Zara and Constantinople on the Fourth; Damietta on the Fifth and in 1249; Tunis in 1270. The fate of Outremer was similarly mapped by sieges, both in its establishment and demise: Jerusalem (1099) and the coastal ports from Jaffa (1099) to Tyre (1124) and Ascalon (1153); Jerusalem and Tyre (1187); Acre (1189–91); Beirut (1197); and the systematic Mamluk capture of cities and castles from 1265, including Antioch (1268) and Tripoli (1289), until the conclusive siege of Acre in 1291. Power in the region depended on urban centres and strategic strong-points, possession of which did not rest on rare pitched battles, Hattin excepted. The nature and conduct of sieges differed depending on whether the target was a walled city or a castle, as well as local topographical or architectural circumstances. Cities could rarely be completely sealed by blockade, while castles could more easily be deprived of provisions.

However, three consistent factors determined the outcome of sieges: morale; numbers, especially of besiegers; and the availability or prospect of relief. The Franks' successes on the First Crusade and in the twelfth century rested on their ability to resist land and sea relieving forces, as did their final victories at Acre in 1191 and Damietta in 1219. Throughout the twelfth century, Frankish sea-power, provided severally by Genoa, Pisa and Venice, played a vital role in effective investment of cities. Even the timbers of derelict ships could supply necessary materials for siege engines, from Jerusalem in 1099 onwards. The collapse of Outremer in 1187–8 and after 1265 was hastened as garrisons of even the strongest castles saw no prospect of relief. Such considerations obviously played directly to the morale of either side. Numerically, garrisons could be modest – a few score or hundreds at most in castles or a few thousand in cities – while besiegers tended to prevail if possessed of enough manpower to with-

122. *Artillery, archery and assault in the thirteenth century.*

stand inevitably heavy casualties, as with the constant western reinforcements at Acre in 1189–91 or during the later thirteenth century when Mamluk attackers massively outnumbered the besieged Franks: at Acre in 1291, it has been calculated, by 11 to 1.[14] Numbers also dictated tactics. The Franks, usually needing to preserve troops even during large crusades, tended to opt for the slower technique of surrounding, harrying and starving opponents into submission, while the Turks and Mamluks, with greater access to additional local forces, adopted more aggressive direct assaults, more able to sustain the ensuing casualties. Successful Frankish sieges tended to last months (Antioch, 1097–8; Tyre, 1124; Damietta, 1217–19) and even years (Acre: 653 days, 1189–91); Turkish and especially Mamluk operations, days and weeks (six weeks at Acre, 1291).

This was not due to very different siege weapons or tactics. All sides employed ladders; wooden siege towers on wheels or rollers; battering rams; and a range of artillery. Traction- or torsion-propelled throwing machines (mangonels and petraries) and, from the mid-twelfth century, counterweight trebuchet catapults capable of throwing horses or weights over 100kg were used by besiegers and defenders alike.[15] They were considered so important that crusaders brought models with them by sea in 1191 and 1202. During their final push to eradicate Outremer in 1265–91, the Mamluks perfected their own massive versions, some, like a number of Frankish ones, prefabricated in transportable sections. Franks, Turks and Mamluks all used sappers, resistance to whom drove many aspects of castle defensive systems, such as elaborate talus (or glacis) structures that also kept siege engines at a distance. All siege warfare was conducted under a mutual hail of arrows and crossbow bolts. However, it appears that only the Franks' enemies used varying forms of Greek Fire (a preparation of crude oil or naphtha; Byzantine Greek Fire comprised distilled crude oil). However generated, fire proved a very effective weapon in its own right, as gates and many defensive superstructures were wooden as were vulnerable, slow-moving or stationary siege engines. Various mixtures of vinegar were employed to combat flames, with uneven rates of success. However, for all the sophisticated technology, the outcome of sieges depended on the human element on both sides: adequate provisioning for both sides; starvation; disease; hope or prospect of relief; morale; weight of numbers; leadership. Most sieges included efforts to negotiate, not all successful or honest. Depending on the intent of the successful besiegers, defenders were massacred (Antioch in 1098; Jerusalem in 1099; the early Frankish conquests of coastal ports; Antioch in 1268; Acre in 1291); taken into captivity; allowed to leave; or even the civilian elements permitted to remain or return (Tyre in 1124). Castle garrisons most commonly agreed terms. As with any static military confrontation, opponents engaged in various forms of contact, not all violent or hostile.[16]

Mongols at Homs in 1281 and the death of Abaqa, the expansionist Mongol Il-Khan of Persia, in 1282, Sultan Kalavun (1279–90) was given a free hand. Marqab fell in 1285; Latakia in 1287; and Tripoli in 1289, after 180 years of continuous Frankish rule, accompanied by a massacre and the demolition of the city's defences. Although Acre still received aid, men and money, visiting crusaders, with their modest military entourages, and western-funded garrison troops could only observe, not counter the approaching end. Attempts by Charles of Anjou (1277–85) to absorb the kingdom of Jerusalem into a trans-Mediterranean empire exacerbated factional contests within Acre, while the War of the Sicilian Vespers from 1282 destroyed prospects of a united western crusade. Philip III of France died on crusade in 1285, but against Aragon not Egypt. Edward I was occupied with conquering Wales (to 1284) and the Scottish succession (from 1290). German involvement was compromised by the divisions left by the imperial interregnum (1250–73). After Charles of Anjou's death in 1285, the restoration of unified rule in Acre under Henry II of Cyprus and I of Jerusalem did nothing to stem the crisis. No meaningful help came from the west.

The remaining Frankish lordships succumbed piecemeal, some, like Beirut, to temporary Mamluk clientage or shared lordship, others, as at Tripoli, to destruction. The final siege of Acre, prepared by Kalavun in 1290 and completed by his successor al-Ashraf Khalil, lasted from 6 April to 18 May 1291, before the city, pummelled by huge mangonels and overwhelmed by vastly superior numbers, fell amidst incandescent scenes of bravery, mayhem, butchery and despair. The fortified Templar quarter held out for a further ten days before being overrun. Frankish survivors were killed. On the sultan's orders, the city was 'razed to the ground'.[17] By August, the last Frankish holdings on the mainland – Tyre, Sidon, Beirut, Tortosa and Athlit – had surrendered or been abandoned.

The Failure of Recovery

There was no return. Despite loud ululations, the loss of Outremer reinforced perceptions of the immense task of reconquest, now discussed in terms of budgets, manpower, training, logistics, intelligence and diplomacy as much as faith and devotion. Pope Nicholas IV (1288–92) authorised another ecclesiastical tenth and, like Gregory X, appealed for advice, some of which proved very detailed, accompanied with illustrative, if not particularly useful maps.[18] Any attempt to coordinate a new crusade was wrecked by the fractious politics of the 1290s: the War of the Sicilian Vespers spluttered on; Philip IV of France (1285–1314) fought Edward I of England over Gascony, challenged papal authority over the French Church and failed to resolve tensions with Flanders; Edward I became embroiled in trying to dominate then annex Scotland; Pope Boniface VIII (1294–1303) used a crusade against his Italian rivals, the Colonna. News of the victory of the Mongol Il-Khan Ghazan (1295–1304) over the Mamluks, and his brief re-occupation of Syria (1299–1300) in alliance with Christian Cilician Armenia, provoked illusory optimism.[19] Diplomacy continued. The Templars briefly occupied the island of Ruad off Tortosa (1300–3). Prospects for an anti-Mamluk coalition with the Persian Mongols proved a mirage.

Nonetheless, planning, advice and research into the recovery of the Holy Land continued to flourish. A strong literary tide of 'recovery literature' only ebbed with the outbreak of the Hundred Years War between France and England in the late 1330s, leaving an increasingly attenuated tradition that persisted for generations. While the possibility of re-occupying the Holy Land had long ceased to be practical, instead it was partly refashioned into a metaphor or allegory for the reform of Christendom.[20] The fourteenth century saw only three major attempts to organise a new international crusade to reverse the decision of 1291 – under Clement V (1305–14); by Philip VI of France (1328–50) in the 1330s; and by Peter I of Cyprus (1359–69) during a lull in the Anglo-French wars in the 1360s. Only the last produced military action, an attack on Alexandria in 1365. Sporadic raids on the Levant littoral continued into the early fifteenth century, and Mamluk resources remained a subject of concern for the defenders of Frankish Cyprus and for western merchants. Nevertheless the expansion of Turkish emirates in the Aegean and the subsequent rapid emergence of the Ottoman Turkish Empire in Asia Minor and the Balkans in the second half of the fourteenth century rendered the recovery of the Holy Land a second-order objective even before the Cypriot-Mamluk treaty of 1370 effectively brought the Palestine crusades to an end.

Clement V and Philip IV

Clement V attempted to use the Holy Land crusade as a means to restore the papacy's position after damaging conflicts during Boniface VIII's reign had seen a dramatic collapse in Franco-papal relations, which ended with the pope being manhandled by agents of the French king at Anagni in 1303. France, with its substantial resources, direct access to Mediterranean ports and public devotion to the legacy of St Louis (canonised 1297), remained central to any scheme for a major new eastern campaign. With Philip IV of France asserting an increasingly strident quasi-imperial form of royal sovereignty in the Church as well as the State, Clement found he had little room to manoeuvre, especially once Philip demanded papal support as he began to persecute the Templars in 1307. The Templar affair, which dominated Franco-papal relations between 1307 and 1312 (see 'The End of the Templars', p. 380), and prompted fresh proposals for the recovery of the Holy Land. French courtiers and hangers-on developed ideas for a French-led crusade that conveniently served extravagant claims of royal supremacy. Shows of papal independence were greeted with threats and bullying. While consistently and possibly sincerely proclaiming his devotion to the cause of the Holy Land, Philip failed to contribute to the independent Hospitaller crusade of 1309. Ostensibly designed to relieve Cilician Armenia and blockade Egypt, in line with current strategic orthodoxy, this planned crusade attracted considerable popular enthusiasm across north-west Europe but, lacking sufficient logistical resources, failed to employ the masses who had taken the cross. The small professional expedition that did embark in 1310 delivered nothing more than completion of the Hospitaller conquest of the Greek island of Rhodes, the Order's front-line bolt hole to escape the fate of the Templars.

Clement resorted to the familiar precedent of calling a general council of the Church that linked the crusade with wider church reform as well as the immediate crisis of the Templars. Although having to accept the suppression rather than condemnation of the Templars, Philip IV effectively, if temporarily, secured their funds and stood as the main beneficiary of a new crusade sexennial church tithe agreed by the council. The king assumed leadership of the proposed enterprise, in 1313 taking the cross with his three sons, son-in-law, Edward II of England, and large numbers of French nobles and members of the Parisian urban elite. The promise of 1313 soon vanished. In 1314, Philip IV died as did Clement V (leading to a two-year papal interregnum), and Edward II was defeated by the Scots at Bannockburn. The following year saw the start of a catastrophic northern European famine (1315–22). Yet the French court remained committed beyond rhetorical clichés and appropriation of church funds, despite a disruptively rapid

123. Cilician Armenia, a continental crossroads: Archbishop John of Cilicia in 1287 wearing a robe decorated with a Chinese dragon.

succession of monarchs (Louis X, 1314–16; Philip V, 1316–22; Charles IV, 1322–8). Philip V consulted crusade veterans and experts and floated the idea of a lay crusade tax; plans for a relief force to beleaguered Cilician Armenia were briefly entertained by Charles IV in 1323.[21] Such activity stimulated a wealth of written commentary, plans, studies and advice on the recovery of the Holy Land, as well as the production and collection of literary and historical crusade-related manuscripts in and around the French court, an interest that sustained fresh plans for a general crusade in the 1330s.[22]

Planning the Recovery of the Holy Land

Advice on recovering the Holy Land fell into several categories, from visions of transforming the world to details of ships' biscuits, occasionally in the same work. Usually framed by religious, missionary, political or commercial interests, most considered some or all of the means to conduct long-distance military campaigns: geography, routes, strategy, diplomacy, recruitment, training, fund-raising, taxation, wages, weaponry, shipping, logistics, implications for trade, intelligence on the enemy, arrangements for the rule of a reconquered Outremer. While much advice between 1270 and 1340 comprised special-interest lobbying, some was commissioned by popes, such as Gregory X, Nicholas IV or Clement V, or by putative crusade commanders, such as Count Louis of Clermont (*c.* 1280–1342), a grandson of Louis IX, who asked Marseilles for detailed information on shipping in 1318. Writers included kings (James I of Aragon, Charles II of Sicily, Henry II of Cyprus); Hospitallers (Master Fulk of Villaret and a former prisoner of war in Egypt, the Englishman Roger of Stanegrave); the last Master of the Templars (James of Molay); mendicants with experience of the east (the Franciscans Fidenzio of Padua and Galvano of Levanto; the Dominican William Adam); associates of the French court (Philip IV's minister William of Nogaret, the Norman lawyer Pierre Dubois, Bishop William de Maire of Angers and the southern French Bishop Durand of Mende); maritime corporations (Marseilles and Venice); merchants (most notably an indefatigable Venetian lobbyist Marino Sanudo Torsello); visionaries (such as Ramon Lull); and an Armenian prince, Hethoum (or Hayton) of Gorigos.[23]

Beneath the gloss of piety and sectional *parti pris* certain general features were agreed: Christian peace; united leadership; the destruction of Mamluk power in Egypt; the massive costs, many times royal and papal annual revenues; effective sea power. The need for disciplined professional troops was emphasised, at least for any preliminary campaign (known as a *passagium particulare*) that most advocated to secure bridgeheads for the mass crusade of conquest (*passagium generale*). Knowledge of Egyptian and western Asian politics, geography and resources was considered a desideratum. It was to be supported by reference to or – in the case of a Franciscan friar, Fidenzio of Padua, and a Genoese doctor, Galvano of Levanto, in the late thirteenth century, and the Venetian merchant Marino Sanudo in the early fourteenth – the inclusion of maps or detailed navigational charts known as

THE END OF THE TEMPLARS

The destruction of the Order of the Temple of Solomon, the Templars, between 1307 and 1314 provides one of the most dramatic, notorious and sordid episodes in the civil history of the western European Middle Ages. Despite contemporary slanders and later fantasies, the only sinister aspects in the process against the Templars came from the malignancy of their persecutors and the craven subservience of church authorities. As the fortunes of Outremer careered from dire to hopeless, the reputation of the Military Orders inevitably came under scrutiny. Given their history of rivalry, some argued that the Orders should amalgamate the better to provide moral as well as military leadership against the infidel. The loss of their final bases on the Levant mainland caused the Templars to move headquarters to Cyprus. From there, they continued to harass the Mamluks. With extensive estates and banking interests across Christendom, the Order remained prominent in political establishments throughout Europe, not least in France. The sudden coordinated arrest of all Templars in France by royal officers and confiscation of their property on Friday 13 October 1307 therefore came as a surprise and shock.

The French king, Philip IV (1285–1314), claimed he was acting on behalf of the Church to eradicate gross misconduct and heretical beliefs within the secretive order. Charges levelled by Philip's aggressive, sanctimonious and mendacious legal team included denial of Christ, spitting on the cross, idol worship, and a range of sanctioned homosexual activities and indecent kissing. In a technique later familiar from twentieth-century show trials, to achieve well-publicised confessions torture was freely applied, including on the Templar leadership. Although accepting the fait accompli of the arrests and ordering the detention of Templars across Christendom, Pope Clement V (1305–14) remained sceptical, suspending the inquiry (February 1308) after the Master of the Temple, James of Molay, revoked his earlier confession in front of cardinals sent to investigate. This provoked a sustained French campaign of political bullying, including more Templar forced confessions, until the pope renewed inquiries (summer 1308), one conducted by papal commissioners and another by local bishops. More confessions were extracted by French bishops in 1309, but where torture was not threatened or used, as mostly in England, Scotland and Ireland, Templars refused to admit to the charges. In 1310, Templar resistance to French persecution grew into organised denial of the accusations and the earlier confessions made under duress. The French government reacted savagely. On 12 May 1310 fifty-four Templars were burnt to death outside Paris after being condemned as relapsed heretics by the archbishop of Sens, a royal stooge; Templar resistance leaders were imprisoned or vanished. Increasingly, the issue became less about Templar guilt than about church authority versus royal power; defence of the former demanded accommodation with the latter, with the Templars paying the price.

At a general council of the Church at Vienne (1311–12), despite widespread opposition, Clement, constrained by the attendance of Philip IV and his army, imposed a pusillanimous compromise. On the grounds that their reputation had been irretrievably damaged, the Templars were not condemned but suppressed (March 1312). Their property was granted to the Order of St John, the Hospitallers (May 1312), from whom, over the next few years the French crown extracted over 300,000 *livres tournois* in supposed compensation for costs

124. *The burning of James of Molay.*

incurred by the arrest and pursuit of the fallen Order. Some Templars were or remained imprisoned; others were despatched to retirement in religious houses; some returned to their families and the minor aristocratic obscurity from which many had come. Finally, in Paris, on 18 March 1314, the four leading Templars still in custody were sentenced by papal judges to perpetual imprisonment. Two, James of Molay and Geoffrey of Charny, protested their innocence and that of

125. *The destruction of the Templar Order.*

their Order. King Philip immediately rushed them to be burnt at the stake on the Ile des Javiaux (now the Quai Henri IV) in the Seine as relapsed heretics.

Two questions hang over the trial and suppression of the Templars: the truth of the charges and the motives of Philip IV and his ministers. The only sustained evidence of guilt came from confessions extracted under torture or the threat of torture. Despite some modern Roman Catholic apologists and literary hucksters, few give them much credence. The Templars, like other closed institutions, may well have developed idiosyncratic rituals hard to explain to outsiders, but reflecting a homosocial not homosexual environment. As with other religious orders, wealth was no necessary bar to the sincere performance of vocation. Without torture, inquiries failed to uncover coherent evidence of doctrinal unorthodoxy beyond the levels of eccentricity and ignorance common throughout Christian society. Why then the persecution? And why just the Temple? Part of the answer lay in French politics and finance. Since the twelfth century, the Templars had played a central role in the administration of royal finance, providing a tempting target for Philip IV's cash-strapped but hugely ambitious centralising regime. Whether Philip himself was a useful idiot or evil genius remains contested, but if, as is likely, he played the lead in activating the anti-Templar policy, it is just possible that he sincerely believed in their demonic quality. The attack also played directly into his government's wider assertion of the French monarchy as a rival if not superior to the papacy as guardian and leader of Christendom, a policy that had led to the attempted abduction of Pope Boniface VIII in 1303, sustained bullying of Clement V, and insistence, at the council of Vienne, on a new crusade with associated taxes under French command.

For the crusades, the consequences of the Templar affair involved the other international Military Orders' rapid reassertion of their primary military role and relocation of their headquarters: the Hospitallers to Rhodes (1306–10) and the Teutonic Knights to Marienburg in the Baltic (1309). Inevitably there were loose ends. In 1340 a German pilgrim in the Holy Land encountered two ex-Templars, former prisoners of the Mamluks after 1291, living near the Dead Sea. They knew nothing of the grim fate of their colleagues. Persuaded to return to the west, they found themselves welcomed at the papal court.[24]

portolans.[25] Some writers went into minute detail. Sanudo advised on everything from the prime season for felling timber for ships, to detailed estimated annual naval and military budgets, to precise calculations of crusaders' daily consumption of biscuits, wine, meat, cheese and beans. While such information had been available from earlier arrangements with troops and shippers, its collation provided an unprecedented resource of information, some of which, notably the level of expense, was distinctly off-putting. The range of advice was impressive, as in Guy of Vigevano's tract of 1335, *Texaurus Regis Franciae*, which combined fanciful illustrated war machines with practical advice on maintaining healthy ears, eyes, teeth and diet, and how to avoid poisoning. Guy, physician to Queen Joan of France, dedicated his work to his employer's husband, Philip VI, then engaged in trying to put some of these plans into action.

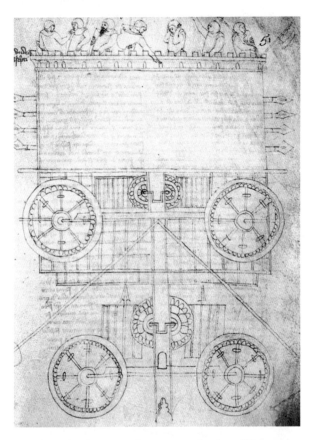

126. A plan for a crusade siege tower by Guy of Vigevano.

Philip VI's Crusade

The crusading legacy of St Louis continued to frame projections of French regality, creating tension between political necessity, public expectation and operational possibility. As the first French king of a new cadet dynasty, Philip VI of Valois (1328–50) embraced the crusade between 1331 and 1336 to bolster his legitimist credentials at home and international standing abroad. He may also have believed it was the right thing to do. Preparations included diplomacy that stretched to the eastern Mediterranean; consulting current and past expert advice; scrutiny of the financial records of Louis IX's crusades; negotiations with Pope John XXII (1316–34) over money from the Church; and cultivating domestic support through a series of public assemblies at which the crusade was preached. Even knightly salaries were determined. Courtiers and nobles commissioned luxury copies and translations of crusade histories equally as icons of commitment as for scholarly enlightenment.[26] In July 1333, Philip was created 'Rector and Captain-General' of the crusade by the pope and took the cross the following October. Crucial to Philip's commitment was the pope's grant of a new sexennial tithe, the last such general ecclesiastical crusade tax. Much diplomatic wrangling concerned Philip's access to these funds. While assisting a joint Hospitaller, Byzantine and Venetian naval league against the Turks in the Aegean (1332–4) and considering help to Armenia, Philip appears to have decided on a traditional unitary mass campaign, a so-called *passagium generale*, without a coordinated preliminary expedition favoured by contemporary strategic orthodoxy. Departure was fixed for 1336.

However, the whole scheme rested on the impractical premise of international peace. Papal hostilities against Italian enemies and suspicions of the German emperor Louis IV after his invasion of Italy in 1328–30 and Spanish indifference were compounded by the deteriorating relations between England, France and Scotland. Edward III of England (1327–77), involved in the French crusade plans from 1332, proved to be the first English monarch since Stephen (1135–54) not to take the cross. Another monarch with something to prove, his bellicose attempts to impose his own candidate as king of Scotland (1332–5) in place of Philip's ally David Bruce reignited Anglo-French hostility, provoking Philip to link the crusade with agreement over Scotland. This reassertion of traditional rivalries quickly pushed the crusade to the margins of practical politics. The accession of the austere and meticulous Pope Benedict XII (1334–42) further complicated Philip's

MAPS

The traditional image of crusaders heading off into the unknown directed only by hope and prayers is wholly untrue. From the beginning, their leaders knew where they were going and how to get there. They knew the world was a sphere and understood a tripartite continental division – Europe, Asia and Africa. The learned knew of the third-century BC Greek Eratosthenes' nearly accurate calculation of the earth's circumference of *c.* 25,000 miles. A thirteenth-century English monk was well aware of the equator where the sun stood exactly overhead twice a year. However, a sense of geography or knowledge of possible routes was not necessarily or primarily derived from or enshrined on maps. Crusaders' information rested on memory (e.g. of pilgrims or crusade veterans), experience (e.g. of merchants or sailors), and oral testimony and written literary descriptions rather than visual cartography. From the First Crusade onwards, many chroniclers who had travelled on crusade, or recorded the witness of those who did, produced detailed itineraries of land and sea routes and times taken between cities or landfalls. By the time of the Third Crusade there existed a mass of detailed geographical, nautical and topographical information for planners to use. Nautical handbooks, such as the late twelfth-century Pisan *On the existence of the coasts and form of our Mediterranean sea* or the English *De viis maris* (*Sea Journeys*), exploited Arabic and Sicilian geographic texts. It is likely that some of this information was transcribed onto maps and charts, although none survives until a century later.

However, pictorially visualising the world was not conditioned solely by practical utility. Rather, it operated at two levels, representation of the actual physical world initially being overshadowed by virtual, schematic *mappae mundi*, world maps. These depicted an idealised globe and portrayed images derived from the Bible or popular neo-classical fables, commonly placing Jerusalem at the centre of the world, illustrating religious or imaginative not geographical trigonometry. *Mappae mundi* were diagrammatic and indicative of an orderly imagined world, not intended as accurate guides to the physical world but rather as illustrations of scripture or history. However, their Jerusalem-centred vision of the world matched the idealism of the crusade. Mirroring

127. The Hereford Mappa Mundi.

chroniclers' and preachers' depictions of the cosmic centrality of the Holy City, they suggested the scale of the crusaders' task and may have been employed in crusade promotion: by the mid-thirteenth century, crusade preachers were being encouraged to acquaint themselves with *mappae mundi*. By this time, however, written travelogues were being illustrated and supplemented by maps. The English chronicler Matthew Paris produced detailed linear maps of pilgrim routes from England to southern Italy as well as maps of the Holy Land and the city of Acre festooned with text. Increasingly, stylised illustrative maps accompanied pilgrim narratives and crusade advice that proliferated in the later thirteenth century and beyond. In particular, the map accompanying the Dominican Burchard of Mount Sion's detailed description of the Holy Land (1274–85) inspired a whole cartographical tradition.[27]

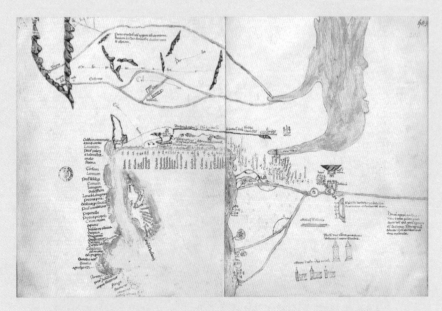

128. *Pietro Vesconte's portolan for Marino Sanudo's crusade advice, 1320s: a chart of the Near East.*

These maps were aids, more or less practical, for pilgrimages and religious devotion. More directly functional were the nautical charts that began to be produced in the later thirteenth century in the ports of Italy and the western Mediterranean. Known as portolan charts (from the Italian adjective *portolani*, 'to do with ports'), they showed with some precision coastlines, ports, harbours and the distances between, connected with directional gridlines from a number of fixed points. Such charts supplemented the greater knowledge of winds and currents and the use from the twelfth century of compasses, chiefly employed when sun, moon or stars were not visible. Both navigation and forward planning became more informed if not more certain. The habit of creating and consulting maps reflected both practical needs and cultural developments that increased the role of writing and record-keeping, in this case visual, as evinced by the survival of larger numbers of *mappae mundi* and geographical handbooks from the time of the Third Crusade. However, the earliest explicit evidence for a crusade commander consulting a map, probably a portolan chart, dates from 1270 when Genoese sea captains were reported as showing Louis IX a chart of the port of Cagliari in Sardinia during the king's stormy passage from Aigues Mortes en route to Tunisia.[28]

In the specialist advice generated by the decline and fall of Outremer between 1270 and 1330, considerations of the geography of the Levant became central to discussions of military options and logistics. The irruption of the Mongols into Europe and western Asia in the thirteenth century opened new geographical as well as diplomatic horizons, underlining Europe's inferior size relative to Asia and Africa. By the early fourteenth century, any potential leader of an eastern crusade could be expected to have consulted maps. Some of the earliest portolans were produced between *c.* 1310 and 1330 by a Genoese cartographer, Pietro Vesconte, working in Venice, many of whose maps were used by the Venetian crusade lobbyist Marino Sanudo Torsello (*c.* 1270–1343). When he presented his voluminous crusade tract the *Liber Secretorum Fidelium Crucis* (*Book of the Secrets of the Faithful of the Cross*) to Pope John XXII (1316–34) in 1321, Sanudo included a portfolio of maps of the world, the eastern Mediterranean and Asia and Palestine, plans of Acre and Jerusalem and five portolans of the Mediterranean and the Black Sea. Maps became an essential tool in Sanudo's continuing campaign of persuasion into the 1330s, integral to, occasionally cross-referencing, his written texts, as with his grid-plan map of the Holy Land.[29] These charts and maps demonstrated the twin pragmatic and prophetic cartographical traditions so appropriate for the promotion of the crusade. While Vesconte's portolans represented the most up-to-date nautical charts, the map of Acre harked back to before 1291, and that of Jerusalem mixed modern topography with Biblical site-spotting. The plan of Palestine followed Burchard of Mount Sion's combination of the Biblical past and physical present, deliberate or not, a metaphor for the crusade phenomenon as a whole.[30]

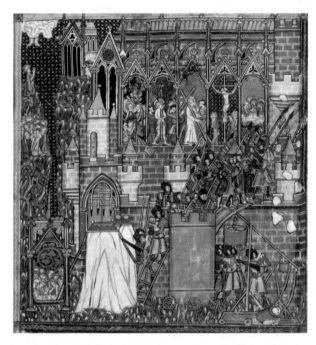

129. *The siege of Jerusalem, 1099, in a luxury copy of William of Tyre's* Historia *commissioned by a member of Philip VI's court.*

schemes, as the new pope was vigilant lest church taxes were diverted away from the crusade. With prospects for an eastern expedition receding and suspicion of French motives and misappropriation of resources growing, Benedict cancelled the crusade in 1336, paradoxically hastening the outbreak of the Anglo-French war he had tried to avoid. The French crusade fleet was diverted to the Channel, and crusade funds misappropriated to pay for French armies, giving the English the excuse to brand Philip's crusade intentions disingenuous and bogus. Although Philip had encountered delay and difficulty in providing men, materiel and money, his emotional, ideological, political and diplomatic investment in the crusade appears serious. However, the collapse of relations with England destroyed the necessary conditions for such a huge and risky enterprise, a situation rendered near permanent by the subsequent Hundred Years War.[31]

Alexandria, 1365, and the End of a Tradition

Realpolitik determined the final stages of the Holy Land wars. By 1343–4, Pope Clement VI (1342–52), who had led Philip VI's crusade propaganda

130. Armed galleys, like those of the anti-Turkish naval leagues and the planned passagium particulare.

campaign in the 1330s, was issuing licences to trade with Mamluk Egypt while simultaneously encouraging a campaign against Turkish predators in the Aegean. While lip service was still paid to the needs of the Holy Land in attempts to end the Anglo-French war, only with the long truce following the treaty of Brétigny (1360–9) did prospects for a new eastern expedition revive. The driving force was Peter I of Cyprus. As well as asserting a brand of energetic chivalric kingship, confronting Mamluk Egypt furthered Peter's attempts to sustain Cypriot commercial interests in the Levant for which the dilapidated Palestinian ports and cities were peripheral. Economics not religion propelled Peter's occupation of Armenian Gorhigos and Turkish Adalia on the southern coast of Asia Minor in 1360–1. Not a realistic strategic target, recovering the Holy Land nonetheless acted as a recruiting agent during a tour that Peter conducted between 1362 and 1365 across Italy, France, England, Flanders, Poland and Bohemia. At Avignon in March–April 1363, at a conference organised by Pope Urban V (1362–70), King Peter, John II of France (1350–64), Count Amadeus of Savoy, the Master of the Hospitallers and nobles from across western Europe (including an English crusade enthusiast Thomas Beauchamp, earl of Warwick) took the cross, preaching was instituted, indulgences offered, taxes proposed, and a legate appointed – the experienced diplomat Elias of Perigord, Cardinal Talleyrand.

The momentum of Avignon soon dissipated. John II and Cardinal Talleyrand died in 1364. John's successor, the cautious, pragmatic Charles V (1364–80), did not share his father's crusading commitment. However, by June 1365, Peter and the new legate, Pierre de Thomas (d. 1366), supported by papal subsidies, had assembled a polyglot force of perhaps 10,000 at Venice, including hired troops and recruits from France, England, Scotland and Geneva. Although the papal crusade bull had not distinguished between Mamluks and Turks, the Cypriot leadership took the bold decision to attack Alexandria, Egypt's main and massively defended port. In one of the most spectacular military coups of the age, the city fell by storm to the crusaders on 10 October 1365 after just one day's fighting. The following week was spent in massacre and pillage. However, the victorious crusaders immediately faced a familiar strategic conundrum of what to do next. Their army lacked the numbers, materiel or cohesion for a serious invasion of the Nile Delta or even, many thought, to defend their conquest. It was later claimed that the Cypriots wished to retain Alexandria as a bargaining tool, ostensibly for the restoration of Jerusalem. More likely, beyond securing enormous booty, they hoped to persuade the Mamluks to accommodate Cypriot trading interests, enhance the position of Famagusta as a Levantine entrepôt while also attracting friendly western European engagement in the region unseen for decades. Whatever the intention, the crusaders evacuated Alexandria on 16 October. Thereafter, the army soon dispersed. The next western European invasion of Egypt was led by Napoleon Bonaparte in 1798.

Beyond a glorious and memorialised triumph of western chivalry, and, one distant English observer noted, pushing up the price of spices,[32] the sack of Alexandria failed to benefit Cyprus. Cypriot raids on the Levantine coast continued and Peter toured western Europe once more to drum up support in 1367–8, without much effect. More western concern was directed at the growing Ottoman threat, with a new crusading venture led by Amadeus of Savoy to the Dardanelles and the Black Sea in 1366–7. Yet in parallel, from 1366, Peter had begun negotiations with Egypt for a peace treaty. These continued despite his assassination in 1369. Pressure for a deal with Egypt came from Genoa and Venice as well as the Cypriot merchant community, all suffering from the commercial dislocation caused by the 1365 campaign and subsequent Cypriot raids on Levantine ports. Agreement was finally reached with the Mamluk sultanate by Cyprus, Genoa and the Hospitallers of Rhodes and Venice in October 1370. This marked the end of prospects, although not dreams, of the recovery of the Holy Land, three centuries after Gregory VII's scheme to lead an army to Jerusalem and Urban II's realisation of it. Regional conflict did not vanish. The remains of the Cilician Armenian kingdom were conquered by the Mamluks in 1374–5; the efforts of the exiled King Leo V (d. 1393) notwithstanding, no retaliation was forthcoming. The Great Schism (1378–1417) intervened. Despite the assertiveness of the 1360s, Cypriot trade, already in decline since the 1340s, was fatally compromised as the Genoese captured Famagusta in 1373 and Italian merchants increasingly traded directly with Syrian and Egyptian ports. A raid on the Syrian coast in 1403 by Jean le Maingre, Marshal Boucicaut, was under the Genoese colours, linked to their continued occupation of Famagusta rather than any lingering hopes for Jerusalem, now accessible to western Christians through organised and regulated pilgrim package tours.[33]

The recovery of the Holy Land continued to haunt western Christian imagination, attract literary attention and colour diplomatic rhetoric into the sixteenth century.[34] Glamorisation of the Holy Land crusades slid as easily into allegory as planning did into wishful thinking. The career and literary trajectory of Peter I of Cyprus's chancellor Philippe de Mézières (1327–1405) bore striking witness to the process. After joining a crusade led by Humbert Dauphin of Vienne in the Aegean (1345–7), Mézières, a Picard by birth and knight by profession, conceived the idea of a new crusading order, the Order of the Passion, the rules and recruitment for which he refined over thirty years from the 1360s to 1390s. A natural courtier, he played a central role in the organisation of Peter I's Alexandrian crusade of 1365 and was later associated with the French royal court. However, by the time he composed his chief literary works calling for a new crusade, such as *The Dream of the Old Pilgrim* (1387) or the *Letter to Richard II* (1395), he used the crusade more as an emblem and metaphor of Christian morality, faith and unity than a call to arms. Even his later regulations for the Order of the Passion lost touch with reality in their prohibition on initiates fighting anywhere but the Holy Land, despite the advance of the Turks into the Balkans; while his reaction to the Turkish victory at Nicopolis on the Danube in 1396, when a coalition Franco-Hungarian army was crushed by forces under the Ottoman Sultan Bayezid I, relied on arcane allegory, not serious recipes for counter-attack.[35] The Jerusalem wars were over.

A MEAL IN PARIS, 6 JANUARY 1378

On Wednesday, 6 January 1378, during a state visit to Paris, after visiting Louis IX's Sainte Chapelle with its relics of the Passion, the Emperor Charles IV of Germany was entertained to dinner by his nephew King Charles IV of France in the great hall of the neighbouring royal palace on the Ile de la Cité. The feast was sumptuous: three courses, each of ten dishes, followed by spiced wine, served to a gathering of five tables of nobles plus a further 800 'below the salt'. The emperor, his son and future successor, Wenceslas, and King Charles sat at the high table facing the hall. The diners were presented with a fancifully elaborate theatrical presentation of the siege of Jerusalem in 1099, complete with armed crusaders in a moving ship and a large tiered stage-set of the Holy City defended by soldiers dressed as Turks. Above the defenders perched a figure who 'in Arabic cried the law'. Led by Godfrey de Bouillon, the crusaders, identified by heraldic flags and surcoats, attacked up ladders, with some falling off, until the city was won. Watching the proceedings from the stern of the pantomime ship was the figure of Peter the Hermit, whose costume, according to the detailed official account of the event, was modelled as closely as possible on chronicle descriptions of him. The lavish production values of this remarkable performance were confirmed by a stunning fine-detailed illumination of the event that accompanied the description in the manuscript text (Bibliothèque Nationale Fr 2813, fol. 473 verso). While unusual in showing a secular, if sanctified, historical scene, the 1378 Jerusalem show was not unique. On 20 June 1389, to celebrate the entry into the city of Charles VI's queen, Isabelle of Bavaria, Paris staged an outdoor production of a Third Crusade romance, the *Pas Saladin*.[36]

The crusades evidently still made good theatre if not good politics. Charles V (1364–80) was the first king of France since Philip I (1060–1108) not to take the cross. However, the idea of and plans for a renewed attempt to retake the Holy Land persisted, if only, by the 1370s, as an idealised cause that might encourage political and ecclesiastical reform in the west and a cessation of the Hundred Years War. Such a policy had been advocated over many years by one of Charles V's associates, Philippe de Mézières (*c.* 1327–1405), crusader, former

131. *The play of the siege of Jerusalem, Paris 1378: the figure in the bottom left portraying Peter the Hermit may depict Philippe de Mézières who possibly helped design and direct the performance.*

chancellor to the crusading Peter I of Cyprus, and writer of tracts urging moral renewal and a new eastern crusade. He also may have had some experience directing staged performances. The Jerusalem dinner play may have been his idea or staged under his direction. He may even have played the part of Peter the Hermit, strikingly depicted in the manuscript illumination, a role that well suited his later self-image of a poor pilgrim. If so, he subsequently appeared to repent his involvement, writing a decade afterwards criticising the wasteful expense of the lavish feast and lamenting that it had not even served its diplomatic purpose as one of the guests, Wenceslas, had shortly after married off his sister to France's enemy, Richard II of England.[37] Yet, for all that, the Jerusalem show offers tangible evidence of the continued cultural traction of the crusade if only in its dramatic historical resonance, still able to generate recognition, interest and excitement.

CHAPTER ELEVEN

THE OTTOMANS

fter 1291, crusading became increasingly regionalised, fragmented, its institutions more bureaucratic, devotion channelled into administrative form and fiscal expediency. Continuing to inform a state of mind, crusading was sustained by habit, liturgy, appeals for alms, taxation, buying indulgences and occasional active service. In a late medieval paradox, there were more crusades, more varied preaching campaigns yet fewer *crucesignati*. Imaginative association with the Holy Land became formalised. Western Christians' physical engagement settled on visits by pilgrims, spies, merchants and visiting clergy. Package tours of Jerusalem from the 1330s were officially delegated by the Mamluk authorities to Franciscan friars, who devised suitably moving ceremonies and itineraries, even rerouting the Via Dolorosa for convenience. By contrast with such chaperoned site-seeing, new Islamic powers further west provided fresh, urgent settings for holy war. By the middle of the fourteenth century, the Ottoman sultanate of north-west Asia Minor presented the most serious challenge to Christendom's integrity since the Mongols in the 1240s. By the sixteenth century, with the Turks battering at the gates of Austria, the survival of Christendom itself appeared at stake, seemingly reduced, in the words of Pope Pius II in 1463, 'to an angle of the world'.[1]

The Ottoman Turks

The origins of the Ottoman Empire lay in the fragmentation of political power in the Balkans and Asia Minor during the thirteenth century. From the Danube and Adriatic to the Taurus Mountains, new or attenuated older lordships jostled for survival and expansion. After 1204, the Byzantine Empire had dissolved into successor principalities at Nicaea (then after 1261 Constantinople as capital of an enfeebled restored empire), Epirus and Trebizond; Frankish statelets in Attica, Boeotia and the Peleponnese; Venetian possessions around the coasts and on the islands of the Aegean and Ionian Seas; independent Bulgarian and Serbian kingdoms; and Hungarian penetration south of the Danube into Bosnia and Wallachia. The collapse of the Seljuk sultanate of Rum in the later thirteenth century similarly opened Asia Minor to competitive Turkish emirates sustained by banditry, privateering and service as mercenaries: Aydin, Menteshe and Tekke in western Asia Minor; Karaman in the south-east; and the Ottomans in the north-west, well placed to take particular advantage of political disruption in the neighbouring Byzantine Empire. As well as control of territory and tax revenues, at stake was regional trade, which directly involved Italian powers.

Western attention initially focused on the emirate of Aydin's piracy operating from the Aegean port of Smyrna (Izmir). The threat to Venetian, Hospitaller and Byzantine interests provoked papally sponsored naval leagues in 1332–4 and 1343–5: Smyrna was occupied (1344–1405) and a crusade mounted by Humbert, Dauphin of Vienne (1345–7), which proved a damp squib. In contrast, by the 1330s, the land-based Ottomans under Osman and his son Orkhan (1326–62) had extended their territory from the region around Bursa to the Sea of Marmora, the Bosporus and Dardanelles. By the 1340s, Orkhan was employed by the Byzantine emperor John VI Cantacuzene (1345–54) against his rivals for the Byzantine imperial throne, giving the Ottomans the opportunity to occupy the Gallipoli peninsula, capturing Gallipoli itself in 1354, the beginning of a European land empire that lasted until the early twentieth century. Subsequent Ottoman progress in Thrace produced contradictory Byzantine responses of alternating alliance and confrontation. Western reactions were complicated by the competing ambitions of Venice and Genoa. While a limited campaign by Count Amadeus VI of Savoy in 1366–7 recaptured Gallipoli and a few Black Sea ports, the Ottoman conquest of the Balkan interior continued from Thrace (Adrianople/Erdine, taken c. 1369, becoming their capital) northwards into Serbia and south into Greece. By the end of the century, the Ottomans had redrawn the political map of the whole region. After overawing the Serbians at the battle of Kossovo in 1389, through conquest, alliance, direct lordship and client rulers, the Ottomans controlled the

132. *Turks defeating Christians, from Sercambi's* Luccan Chronicle, *late fourteenth century.*

Balkans from the Danube to the Gulf of Corinth, threatening both Hungary and Constantinople. The Ottoman victory over French crusaders and Hungarians at Nicopolis in 1396 confirmed a new hegemony.

The Ottoman threat to western Christendom dawned only slowly. Most of the early victims were Orthodox not Catholic Christians. The confused politics of Byzantium, Latin Greece and the Orthodox Christian Balkans presented few clear strategies, Urban V's elision of Mamluks and Turks in promulgating the crusade in 1363 revealing characteristically limited understanding.[2] The naval expeditions and costal raids of 1332–67 in Greece and Asia Minor failed to confront the Ottomans' land-based power or their access to the sea, where they were regularly assisted by the Genoese, eager to seize advantage from the Venetians whose post-1204 maritime empire the Ottomans were dismantling. The idea of a mass land crusade in coalition with local Christians was never fully realised.

No longer dependent on a steppe nomadic economy and culture, the Ottoman polity was settled, confident and accommodating, centred on loyalty to the ruling dynasty and its religion, not on origins, ethnicity or past associations ('Ottoman' means follower of the dynasty's semi-legendary Osman/Uthman). Thus anyone – Turk, Slav or Greek – could become an Ottoman, even, after the fall of Constantinople in 1453, members of the Byzantine imperial family. Although flaunting the *ghazi* (holy warrior) rhetoric of *jihad*, Ottoman policy revolved around secular dynastic power not

Islamic mission. While Islam provided cohesion for the ruling elite, alliances were rooted in convenience not faith; subjects' loyalty counted for more than their religion. The parallels between Ottoman and traditional Byzantine policies of accommodation and incorporation of neighbours, rivals and conquered peoples are striking. Communal boundaries were porous. The fifteenth-century Christian Albanian resistance leader George Castrioti (d. 1468) was a Catholic convert who had previously served Sultan Murad II (1421–51) as a Muslim and received a Turkish name, Scanderbeg (Alexander Bey). A future crusader at Nicopolis, the Frenchman Marshal Boucicaut offered to serve Bayezid I (1389–1403).[3] The Ottomans began their European conquest as vassals and allies of the Byzantine emperor: rival Greek imperial families married into the Ottoman dynasty (Islamic polygamy proving of great diplomatic use). Christian Serbs fought for the Turks against crusaders at Nicopolis in 1396 and against the Turco-Mongol Timur at Ankara in 1402; Genoese fought with Murad II against crusaders in 1444; Christian allies stormed Constantinople alongside the Turks in 1453. Some Greeks preferred the tax rates of Ottoman rather than Byzantine rulers and even the monks at Mount Athos could argue in favour of the Muslim Turks against the heretical emperor John V Palaeologus (1341–76, 1379–90, 1390–1).[4] The view peddled by crusade enthusiasts, despite the evidence of travellers, spies, merchants and diplomats, of uncompromising Muslim enslavement of embittered subject Christian people, ignored reality. Flexible self-interest contradicted rigid idealism as the Ottomans based their new empire in the Orthodox Christian Balkans not Muslim Anatolia.

Regional support for western involvement was patchy at best. The Italian cities were guided by shifting competitive commercial advantage. Defence of the Frankish territories scattered across central Greece and the Peloponnese had never proved popular with western crusaders. The Slav princes, intent on autonomy, were suspicious of foreign interference from Roman Catholic powers, an obstacle magnified in dealings with the Byzantine Empire. Since 1274, the papal price for a crusade to help Byzantium was church union, a euphemism for Greek obedience to Rome, which consistently proved unacceptable to leaders of the Orthodox Church and their lay followers. Increasingly after 1204, the Greek Orthodox Church rather than the emperor provided the focus of Byzantine cultural identity, reinforced by the fourteenth-century Orthodox mystical Hesychast movement. The first reunion agreed at the Second Lyons Council (1274) to suit

133. *Recruiting local Christians for Ottoman service.*

the diplomacy of Michael VIII Palaeologus (1261–82) against Charles of Anjou was rejected in 1282 by Andronicus II (1282–1328). Facing Ottoman overlordship and later conquest, John V offered reunion in 1355 and travelled to the west in 1369 to secure it, a journey copied by Manuel II (1391–1425) in 1400–1 and John VIII (1425–48) in 1423. Revived Ottoman power after 1420 persuaded elements of the Greek elite to accept church union at the Council of Florence in 1439, a deal that found little support from Greek Orthodox believers. The Union of Florence only served to alienate the Orthodox hierarchy from the last two emperors John VIII and Constantine XI (1448–53) and complicate crusade diplomacy with front-line Orthodox rulers. It was left to Mehmed II the Conqueror (1451–81) to restore the Orthodox patriarchate to Constantinople.

In any case, church union did not work; no grand crusade was forthcoming. Steady erosion of territory and revenue, accelerated by civil wars and the consequent presence of expensive foreign mercenaries such as the Ottomans, reduced Byzantium to military, economic and political dependency, hardly more than a client city state under Turkish sufferance or protection. Commercial prosperity, largely sustained by Italians such as the Ottoman-allied Genoese, shielded Byzantine elites while imperial government withered and the emperors faced bankruptcy. For much of the Greek Orthodox and Greek-speaking Mediterranean, the imperial writ was no longer valid. By the 1380s, emperors had become tributaries and vassals of the sultan. In 1346, Sultan Orkhan had married a daughter of John VI; in 1358 one of his sons married a daughter of John VI's nemesis John V. Manuel II, who cut a bedraggled figure as he traipsed around western Europe in search of aid in 1400–1, had served in the Ottoman army in the 1390s. The complexity and contradictions of Byzantium's predicament were matched by the inability of western powers to respond. John V's plan for a crusade in 1355 clashed with major campaigns in the Hundred Years War and papal crusades in Italy. A decade later, the Alexandria crusade diverted energies to the Levant, Amadeus of Savoy's small crusade in 1366–7 excepted. The resumption of the Hundred Years War (1369) and papal schism (1378) further undermined military resistance to the Ottoman conquests; the western crusade of 1396 only temporarily distracted Bayezid I's eight-year blockade of Constantinople begun in 1394. The walls of Constantinople proved more effective, at least until the Ottomans employed gunpowder in their siege armoury in the fifteenth century.

The Tunis Crusade, 1390

Regular papal offers of crusade privileges from the 1360s onwards failed to ignite concerted action in the Mediterranean. Coastal raids and occupation of ports such as Gallipoli and Smyrna provided temporary help for local Frankish rulers, Italian merchants and the Hospitallers of Rhodes, but hardly challenged Ottoman land power. After an Anglo-French truce of 1389, the first revival of active anti-Muslim crusading was directed at furthering Genoese commercial interests. In 1389–90 the French government of Charles VI (1380–1422) agreed to a Genoese plan to seize the Tunisian port of al-Mahdiya following their capture of the island of Jerba off the Tunisian coast in 1388. Supported by indulgences from both Roman and Avignon popes and commanded by Charles VI's uncle, Louis II, duke of Bourbon (1337–1410), the campaign assumed the character of a chivalric promenade rather than a serious attempt at conquest. Recruits included several English nobles, but numbers remained modest, perhaps 2,000 to 3,000 knights, infantry and archers, carried in forty Genoese galleys and transport ships.[5] Lacking the support of church funds or government subsidies, the expedition was necessarily the preserve of wealthy aristocrats, eager to gild martial and social credentials. Although justified with indulgences and eulogised in the language of holy war, there appears to be no firm evidence of anyone taking the cross. Embarking from Genoa in July 1390, the Franco-English army besieged al-Mahdiya for nine disease-afflicted weeks before agreeing to withdraw. The chief consequence was a general re-establishment of long-standing commercial links between Genoa and the Hafsids of Tunis in 1391 followed by similar agreements with Venice (1392) and Pisa (1397). In image a noble crusading endeavour, in practice the Tunis expedition played a minor role in the shifting business relations that had united western Mediterranean trade across religious divisions for centuries. It sat outside the expansionist interventions into north Africa by Castilians and Portuguese backed by papal grants of crusade indulgences and money. Nonetheless, the Tunis expedition provided members of the Franco-English nobility with a chance to flex their sinews as holy warriors. Numerous al-Mahdiya veterans later fought in Prussia or joined the Nicopolis crusade six years later.

134. The Tunis crusade under sail.

The Nicopolis Crusade, 1396

The Anglo-French truce of 1389 encouraged more elaborate crusading schemes, stimulated by the Ottoman threat to Hungary following their annexation of Serbia and by a transient mood of sentimental optimism at the English and French courts. Grandiose revivalist ideas incorporating the end of the papal schism, final peace between France and England, and the recovery of the Holy Land were circulated on both sides of the Channel by Philippe de Mézières, now living in Parisian retirement. French and English knights were recruited to Mézières' New Order of the Passion (*Nova religio passionis*), which between 1390 and 1395 received the patronage of Charles VI (who went mad in 1392) and Richard II (1377–99).[6] The influence of enthusiasts should not be exaggerated. In response to appeals from King Sigismund of Hungary (1387–1437), a plan was prepared in 1392–4 to relieve the Balkans, to be led by Charles VI's brother, Louis, duke of Orléans, his uncle Philip the

Bold, duke of Burgundy, and Richard II's uncle, John of Gaunt, duke of Lancaster. Money was raised, troops commissioned and negotiations opened with Venice for a campaign expected in 1395. Indulgences were granted by Boniface IX (Rome, 1389–1404) and Benedict XIII (Avignon, 1394–1423), although, as in 1390, no one may have actually taken the cross.[7]

The scheme soon shrank in scope amid rivalries around the mad king of France, Richard II's progressive alienation of much of his higher nobility, a Gascon revolt against the English, Anglo-French diplomatic tensions, and difficulties coordinating with the Hungarians. Leadership devolved onto the

135. Bayezid I routs the infidels at Nicopolis.

Burgundians under the duke's eldest son, John of Nevers: Louis of Orléans opted out and English participation, if any, was meagre. The whole army probably numbered only a few thousand, including a few hundred men-at-arms. Little could be expected from such a modest force. Leaving Burgundy in April 1396, the French travelled overland, reaching Buda, the Hungarian capital, late in July where they combined with Sigismund's forces. Advancing down the Danube into Bulgaria, taking the frontier fortresses of Vidin and Rahova and massacring the defenders, the army reached Nicopolis (8–10 September) where Bayezid I (1389–1402) confronted them. True to his nickname, 'Thunderbolt', Bayezid had rapidly assembled a significant force of Ottoman levies and Serbian allies. His hurried arrival unnerved the French and Hungarians, who were forced into battle on 25 September. As so often in this period, poorly considered battlefield aggression ensured the destruction of French cavalry, while the Hungarians, deserted by their Wallachian and Transylvanian allies, fared no better. The Christian army was destroyed. French casualties were heavy, the captured, including John of Nevers, later ransomed for huge sums.

The Defence of Christendom

The disaster at Nicopolis confirmed Ottoman power in the central Balkans while exposing the inadequacy of traditional crusade strategies and the problems of coordinating the defence of eastern Europe. Resistance to Ottoman advance now lay firmly with the frontier kingdoms of central and eastern Europe and Venice, supported by papal grants of indulgences and money with occasional recruitment of western troops. Urgency was deferred as Bayezid failed to capitalise on Nicopolis with further conquests along the Danube or by capturing Constantinople. After 1400, his priority to control Turkish emirates in Anatolia drew him into conflict with Timur the Lame (1336–1405) when the Turco-Mongol steppe ruler, whose Asiatic empire stretched from Mongolia to northern India and Persia, turned his attention to western Asia. In 1402, Timur defeated and captured Bayezid at the battle of Ankara, provoking two decades of Ottoman civil war and disintegration of their control over territories both in Europe and Asia Minor. Domestic political crises prevented western powers taking advantage: instability in Germany following the deposition of Sigismund's brother Emperor Wenceslas in 1400; civil wars in France, over control of the mad king Charles VI, and in England in the aftermath of the deposition of Richard II (1399); continued efforts to end the papal schism, only finally achieved by the Council of Constance (1414–18) in 1417; the renewal of the Hundred Years War by Henry V of England in 1415; and the revolt of the Czech Hussites in Sigismund's kingdom of Bohemia and the subsequent launch of crusades in 1420. The Anglo-French peace treaty of Troyes (1420) was accompanied by predictable talk of uniting to confront the infidel. A Flemish traveller, knight and diplomat, Ghillebert of Lannoy was sent east as a spy. However, Henry V's death (1422), the long minority of Henry VI, the continuation of the French wars, and the concentration by Sigismund, now emperor, on the Hussites diverted attention away from eastern Europe where, under Mehmed I (1413–21) and Murad II (1421–51), Turkish rule was restored over much of the central Balkans. By the late 1430s, most of Serbia was again annexed, the Danube provinces of Hungary and Wallachia threatened, and a new siege of Constantinople begun (1442). While fourteenth-century Ottoman rule had relied on delegated authority to Turkish governors, regional allies or clients, after the re-imposition of authority the empire became more highly centralised. Reassertion of control over the sub-Danubean Balkans took just a generation as the Ottomans began to employ cannon and naval power, with local responses conditioned by self-interest not holy war. The subsequent increase in Ottoman raids across the Danube and the prospect of Constantinople's fall invited a new international effort.

The Crusade of Varna, 1444

Pope Eugenius IV (1431–7) took a serious interest in the eastern question. He secured advice from veterans, merchants and self-styled experts, some of whom identified the Ottomans as the chief threat. The nominal union with the Orthodox Church at the Council of Florence (1439) was followed by making two Greek clerics with knowledge of the Turks cardinals. In 1442–3 indulgences were issued, a fleet planned and a legate, Julian Caesarini (previously a legate on the anti-Hussite crusade of 1431), appointed to eastern Europe. Eugenius hoped to capitalise on the effective resistance to the Ottoman advance by John Hunyadi, voivode of Transylvania (1441–56; regent of Hungary, 1445–56). Although the new king of Hungary, Wladislav III of Poland (king of Poland, 1434–44; Hungary, 1440–4), had recent diplomatic accords with the sultan, he agreed the scheme. A coalition was assembled. The Venetians were to blockade the Dardanelles to prevent Ottoman rein-forcements by sea, while Hunyadi led a Hungarian and Serbian army into Bulgaria. Initial coordination failed. Neither the Venetians nor a western fleet were on station when the first land attack began in the autumn of 1443. The operation was hampered by conflicting allied objectives. The Hungarians sought security of their frontiers; the Serbs the recovery of their indepen-dence. Neither supported Caesarini's ambition to relieve Constantinople as they saw there was no Byzantine Empire left to revive, with much of the immediate European hinterland of Constantinople already substantially Turcified. Murad II had played on the allies' divided expectations by offering peace terms, which George Brancovic of Serbia (1427–56) accepted while Wladislav of Hungary declined. These negotiations delayed the muster of the Christian army, allowing the Ottomans time to assemble their defence.

Hunyadi's initial campaign in 1443–4 with a large Serbo-Hungarian army, with recruits from Bohemia, Moldavia and a few from the west, had been a success. Attacking through Bulgaria, Nish and Sofia were captured and Erdine (Adrianople), the Ottoman capital, menaced, before Hunyadi withdrew to Belgrade. Plans for 1444 called for the land army to link up with an allied fleet on the Black Sea coast of Bulgaria. However, when the Venetian flotilla of twenty-two or twenty-four galleys, paid for by the papacy, Burgundy and Venice, finally appeared in the Dardanelles in July 1444, it did not move into the Bosporus and Black Sea as planned, failing to intercept a large Ottoman army crossing to Europe north of Constantinople in October 1444. Fear of losses and provoking the Turks induced paralysis in the Venetian naval commander. The allied army under Hunyadi and King Wladislav was abandoned to face the much superior Ottoman force at the Bulgarian port of Varna. The battle on 10 November lasted all day. Casualties on both sides were enormous. King Wladislav and Cardinal Caesarini were killed, sapping morale and persuading Hunyadi's Hungarians to withdraw.

The Ottoman victory further consolidated their rule over Rumelia (their Balkan provinces) while highlighting their enemies' divisions. Varna's slaughter confirmed the scepticism of many Serbs, Hungarians, Moldavians, Poles and Venetians at the wisdom of aggressive policies towards Ottoman power favoured by western strategists. There were exceptions. Hunyadi, now regent of Hungary (for Ladislas V, 1444–56), persisted in challenging the Turks across the Danube frontier, in 1448 obtaining crusade indulgences from Nicholas V (1447–55) for a campaign into Serbia where he was defeated by Murad II at Kossovo, the site of the battle of 1389. The 1448 bull fitted a familiar fifteenth-century papal stand-by, issuing crusade credentials as a means of focusing diplomacy, asserting papal authority and, through the sale of indulgences and church taxation, supporting front-line commanders with financial assistance. Only in the 1450s and early 1460s did this pattern stretch to attempts to organise substantial crusading in western Europe in response to the fall of Constantinople (1453) and the defence of Belgrade (1456).

The Fall of Constantinople 1453: Another Crusade that Never Was

Constantinople fell to the Turkish armies of Mehmed II (1451–81) on 29 May 1453 after a fifty-three-day siege. The last Byzantine emperor, Constantine XI, was killed during the final assault. Bankrupt, diplomatically isolated, heavily outnumbered, reliant on Italian mercenaries, the defenders of Constantinople, reduced to a beleaguered city state, had been left to face the Turkish heavy artillery and massed infantry without allies. News of the city's fall and subsequent sack and massacre provoked the most concerted international efforts by the major western powers to gather a grand crusade of the fifteenth century. Horror stories of the slaughter, enslavement and ransoming of Greek civilians excited polemic narratives of barbarism overthrowing civilisation ('a second death of Homer and Plato' in the words of the humanist Aeneas Sylvius Piccolomini, the future Pope Pius II)[8] to complement familiar ritualised hysteria and the traditional trope of Christendom in danger. The crisis deepened as the Ottomans consolidated their hold over Serbia (1454–5), threatening Hungary and the middle Danube, and conquered the remaining Frankish and Greek territories on mainland Greece: Athens fell in 1456; the Peloponnese between 1458 and 1460; Venetian Euboea (Negroponte) in 1470. Central Europe, the remaining Venetian holdings in the Aegean and Ionian Seas and the Hospitallers on Rhodes all appeared vulnerable.

Once again, western reaction hardly addressed reality. Byzantium had long been a failed state, its demise the consequence of regional forces not western hostility or indifference. Ottoman rule did not plunge the region into barbaric tyranny, many in the Balkans finding satisfactory degrees of accommodation with the new rulers. The Ottomans avoided systemic religious persecution while providing harsh security and reviving the regional economy, with Constantinople once more the centre of an eastern Mediterranean commercial as well as political empire. European neighbours, trading partners and regional clients adopted pragmatic strategies at odds with the crusade revivalism generated at the papal curia and among sympathetic rulers such as the dukes of Burgundy.[9]

Nevertheless, from Germany to Spain, a new crusade was aired. Pope Nicholas V (1447–55) issued a crusade bull, *Etsi ecclesia Christi* (30 September 1453). War with the Turks was considered by the German imperial *Reichstag* in 1454–5, with Duke Philip of Burgundy (1419–67) present at Regensburg in April 1454. New techniques of publicity and propaganda were employed. Pamphlets circulated widely, exploiting the very recent invention of printing. Nicholas V's successor, Calixtus III (1455–8), authorised preaching, church taxes and the sale of indulgences, built galleys in a short-lived arsenal on the Tiber, and sent a fleet to the Aegean in 1456–7. This recovered Lemnos, Samothrace and Thasos and defeated a Turkish fleet at Mytilene before

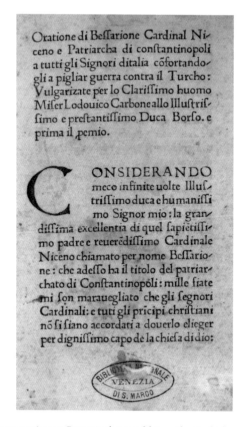

136. *Epistolae et orationes: Bessarion's pamphlet on the Turkish war, printed 1471.*

raiding the Levant towards Egypt. Calixtus established a separate curial department for proceeds of indulgence sales and clerical taxes, the *camera sanctae cruciatae*. While clergy complained about taxation, the indulgence campaign went well. Printed forms of sale were introduced. To give a lead, Calixtus sold papal assets including plate and valuable bindings from the Vatican Library founded by Nicholas V. Calixtus's former employer King Alfonso V of Aragon (1416–58; also king of Naples, 1442–58) took the cross as did the German emperor Frederick III (1440–93), whose Habsburg family lands bordered Hungary. Although Philip of Burgundy did not take the cross, Burgundian commitment was glamorously displayed at Lille in February 1454 during the lavish and gaudy Feast of the Pheasant at which 200 nobles swore to fight the infidel.

Fantasy was not confined to festive theatricals. Duke Philip's proposal for a campaign in 1455 ignored modest German enthusiasm, the opposition of Charles VII of France (1422–61) and, crucially, Venice's treaty with the Ottomans in 1454. The death of Nicholas V (April 1455) further postponed action. Apart from taxing his subjects, Duke Philip hardly moved to organise military or naval operations, perhaps surprisingly given his previous sustained patronage of crusading projects and his contributions to fleets to help Rhodes (1429, 1441, 1444) and Constantinople (1444–5). International diplomacy failed to coordinate western policy or investment despite Cardinal John Carvajal's crusade legation to Hungary (1455–61) during which he oversaw preaching and cross-giving. Alfonso V's proposal for a massive amphibious attack in 1457 seemed to owe more to a desire to burnish moral credentials than serious policy. Much rhetoric still harked back to historic Holy Land wars of the cross. Deep-seated conflicts of interest and divisions between the western powers prevented any muster of a large international army. Despite significant numbers taking the cross and many more buying indulgences, the limits of practical crusading were further exposed. Thereafter, crusading institutions primarily supplied moral status, public support, finance for modest naval expeditions, and occasional aid for local front-line resistance to the Turks.

Belgrade 1456

The urgency of the Ottoman threat contrasted with the costive responses of western rulers. The ubiquitous use of crusade bulls and preaching chiefly to raise taxes or sell indulgences undermined public confidence, not in the cause or the efficacy of the spiritual rewards so much as in prospects for action. Pope Pius II wryly observed of crusade preaching a few years later: 'People think our sole object is to amass gold. No one believes what we say. Like insolvent tradesmen we are without credit.'[10] Yet preaching and marketing indulgences sustained popular awareness, even alarm, which could translate into active engagement, as shown in events surrounding the defence of Belgrade. In the summer of 1456, Mehmed II advanced up the Danube. The siege began in early July, Mehmed assuming an easy victory as the small garrison was prepared to agree terms. However, the city was unexpectedly reinforced by a substantial army assembled and led by John of Capistrano, a septuagenarian Observant Franciscan enthusiast for crusading and moral renewal.

A prominent figure in an Order that held a tradition of preaching against Jews and other perceived enemies of the Church, John's mission had begun in 1454 as he made a round of visits to Burgundy and to the imperial diet. Whilst trying to interest Regent Hunyadi of Hungary in a fanciful scheme for an army of 100,000 crusaders, John toured Hungary between May 1455 and June 1456, a figure of conspicuous sanctity, austerity and honesty which he combined with shrewd organisational skills. His carefully orchestrated progress was unhurried – 375 miles in fourteen months, less than a mile a day – culminating in a grand ceremony at Buda in February 1456 where he received the cross from the papal legate, John of Carvajal. While Hunyadi enlisted the nobility, John, his team of preachers and local bishops recruited non-nobles, exploiting the Hungarian system of military levies known as the *militia portalis* that provided a ready supply of armed peasants.[11] From beyond Hungary, John signed up followers from Austria and Germany including Viennese students, many attracted by his appeal for people not just money. While John's carefully crafted aura of sanctity later encouraged an exaggerated retrospective hagiography, alongside mundane secular organisation his preaching and charismatic leadership clearly helped inspire a crusader army of many thousands whose numbers and morale played a significant part in relieving Belgrade. Mehmed's calculation on the modest size of the Belgrade garrison and the repeated preference of Hungarian nobles for accommodation was upset by the appearance of John's crusaders after 2 July. They altered the military balance, helping Hunyadi break the Turkish naval blockade (14 July) and the defenders repel the main Turkish

137. *Moravian fresco of 1468 showing the siege of Belgrade.*

attack on the night of 21–22 July. On 23 July they led the destructive counter-attack on the Turkish positions as Mehmed prepared to withdraw, his expectations of a quick victory decisively dashed.

The image of simple peasant faith triumphing where noble professionalism had failed proved irresistible. Not only conforming to well-worn polemic tradition, it also reflected the potency of peasant armies in late medieval and early modern Europe mobilised for political or ideological causes and grievances, as seen from the Shepherds' Crusades of 1251 and 1320 to the Hungarian peasant crusaders' anti-noble insurrection of 1514 and the German Peasants' War of 1524–5. The element of social challenge was displayed at Belgrade when John's crusaders and Hunyadi's nobles and professionals briefly fell out over the division of booty and chain of command. The crusaders at Belgrade appeared to embody a rhetorical model of practical virtue: temporal success through the highest spiritual standards, with John's personal charisma and revivalist message providing a dynamic unifying force. Yet, as with other populist movements, John of Capistrano's crusade proved evanescent, no more than a summer's dramatic promenade. He disbanded his army immediately its objective had been achieved in late July 1456 and died of the plague in October. While the crusaders had saved Belgrade and the central Danube, it was left to local garrisons, truces and practical accommodations to maintain the integrity of the Hungarian frontier against the Ottomans until the 1520s. Despite constant diplomatic talk, there were no further significant Danubian crusades; the Ottomans continued to consolidate their power from the Black Sea and Serbia to Cilicia. The Belgrade victory receded into poetic and pious commemoration: in 1457, Calixtus III instituted general observance of the Feast of the Transfiguration to be held on 6 August in honour of the day the previous year that news of the Belgrade victory had reached Rome. In England a poetic romance, *Capystranus*, found its way into print half a century later.

The Crusade of Pius II

When Aeneas Sylvius Piccolomini (1405–64), prominent humanist scholar, diplomat and late convert to the priesthood, was elected Pope Pius II in 1458, he immediately revived calls for a crusade, a cause he had been advocating for two decades. Closely involved in crusade diplomacy since 1453, he summoned a council at Mantua (summer 1459–January 1460) to discuss it. Pius pressed ahead despite lukewarm international response and deteriorating international prospects: civil war in England; French opposition to what they regarded as Burgundian crusade posturing; and papal involvement in a protracted succession contest in Naples that pitted the French against the Aragonese. Pius's old-fashioned rhetoric suggested a traditional mass crusade not just to defeat the Ottoman Turks but also recover Jerusalem. This struck some as impractical but also thin cover for an attempt to assert papal authority. Little came from Mantua. Trapped by his cosmic rhetoric and lurid demonisation of the Turks, early in 1462, Pius decided to lead the crusade himself, perhaps the only way to convince a sceptical international community. The preaching campaign relied on conservative rituals of encouragement, the liturgy of taking the cross minutely choreographed down to the placing (on the breast), colour (red), and material (silk or cloth) of the crosses to be sewn onto the clothes of *crucesignati*.[12] Yet, prematurely aged, already an invalid, Pius hardly generated confidence, his gesture appearing more sacrificial than practical, an act of martyrdom not leadership. However, when he renewed the crusade appeal in October 1463, support seemed available from Burgundy and Venice. A fresh plan advocated a smaller, more realistic expedition against the Turks in the western Balkans. Preaching, cross-giving, Holy Land indulgences, privileges and financial arrangements were announced. While trying to attract other Italian states to his scheme, Pius forged a new coalition between Burgundy, Hungary and Venice. Ancona was set for the campaign's muster. A Venetian fleet would convey the crusaders across the Adriatic to combine with the Hungarians or the Albanian resistance leader Scanderbeg.

On 22 October 1463, Pius formally declared war on Mehmed II. The response was mixed. Despite another lavish crusade *fête* at Christmas 1463, Philip of Burgundy only despatched 3,000 men under his bastard Anthony in May 1464. While a few other small bands from north of the Alps and Italy moved towards Ancona, only one cardinal provided a galley, Rodrigo Borgia, nephew and protégé of the crusade enthusiast Calixtus III, later notorious as Pope Alexander VI.[13] Pius also provided galleys and, in St Peter's on 18 June 1464, took the cross, possibly the only pope in office to do so to fight the infidel rather than political enemies in Italy. However, when he set out for Ancona in late June, he was already seriously ill. The Venetian fleet commanded by Doge Cristoforo Moro was delayed. Soldiers in the papal army at Ancona began to desert: the curtains of Pius's litter were said to have been drawn shut to stop the now dying pope see them go. He died on 14 August. His crusade died with him. Pius's heroic, pathetic pursuit of a grand crusade definitively underlined the difficulty if not futility of such designs, a lesson not lost on his successors. His most tangible contribution to the crusade lay elsewhere, in initiating the process of reserving to the papal crusade treasury the monopoly profits from alum (used to fix dyes in textiles) discovered at Tolfa in the Papal States in 1461.[14]

From Crusade to Realpolitik

Pius II's crusade scheme had recognised one element of the new political reality. The immediate frontier with the Turks lay along the Danube and down the Adriatic. Regions such as Croatia became war zones. By 1478, a

138. Crusade economics: alum mines at Tolfa.

decade after Scanderbeg's death, Albania had been absorbed into the Ottoman Empire. In 1480–1 the Turks briefly occupied Otranto on the south-east tip of Italy, a shocking incursion into the heart of western Christendom that provoked another round of hand-wringing, crusade bulls and fund-raising. In the Aegean, the Hospitallers only narrowly survived a long Turkish siege of Rhodes in 1480. The death of Mehmed II in 1481 and an Ottoman succession dispute under Bayezid II (1481–1512) lessened the immediate pressure in the Adriatic: Bayezid even struck a deal in 1495 with western powers to keep his rival claimant, Djem, captive. However, Venice lost its remaining mainland holdings in Greece between 1499 and 1502, including the Adriatic port of Durazzo, while the Ottomans continued to harden their control over Rumelia and completed their annexation of the Black Sea and lower Danube.

Pius's successors reverted to pragmatism: selling indulgences to fund front-line rulers, and building anti-Ottoman alliances, which in the 1470s included Uzun Hassan, a Turcoman warlord in Azerbaijan, and approaches

139. *Turks preparing to attack Rhodes, 1480, from William of Caoursin's account, 1483.*

to the Tartars of the Golden Horde north of the Black Sea, as well as front-line rulers such as Stephen III of Moldavia (1457–1504). Awkwardly, the heretical Hussite ruler of Bohemia, George Podiebrad (1458–71), promoted his own scheme for a new international crusade in 1463 but instead faced a crusade against him in 1466–7. Crusade credentials helped secure a royal title for Hunyadi's son Matthew Corvinus as king of Hungary (1458–90). The Poles and Hungarians sought rival patriotic solidarity and international advantage by promoting their kingdoms as bastions (*antemurales*) of Christendom against the infidel. However, political disunity in the west and

17. The Ottoman advance in Asia Minor and the Balkans.

on the Balkan frontier undermined attempts to gather effective coalitions to combat the Turks. For those on the front line, such as the Moldavians, advantage and survival not ideology determined policy. Innocent VIII's crusade council of Rome in 1490 proved abortive and Alexander VI's crusade proclamation of 1500 was largely ignored.

The draining Italian wars (1494–1559) pitted Italian states and the major powers of continental Europe against each other, further compromising crusade diplomatic solidarity and political will. Combatants, such as Genoa, Florence, Milan and Naples, felt no compunction in allying against Venice or with the Ottomans. In 1500 the Polish king Jan Olbracht (1491–1501) voiced widely shared suspicions that Venice itself habitually sought to shirk its responsibility by 'searching for ways to transfer the war from their lands to ours, if they can'.[15] The Venetian-Turkish treaty of 1503 effectively acknowledged the Ottomans as legitimate political partners and rivals. The efforts of Leo X at the Fifth Lateran Council (1512–17), the issue of a crusade bull (1513), church taxation and indulgences (1517) generated some short-lived diplomatic momentum, expressed in the general European pacification agreed at the treaty of London (1518), and the despatch of two French flotillas to the east in 1518 and 1520. However, the Lutheran schism, the renewal of the Italian wars, and the persistent armed rivalry of Francis I of France (1515–47) and Charles V (1500–58) of Spain (1516–56), Naples (1516–54) and Germany (1519–58) prohibited any concerted response to the new surge in Ottoman aggression under Selim the Grim (1512–20) and Suleiman the Magnificent (1520–66).

140. Suleiman the Magnificent at the battle of Mohacs, 1526.

Sultan Selim's conquest of Syria, Palestine and Egypt (1516–17) created an eastern Mediterranean territorial empire not seen since seventh-century Byzantium, stretching from the Danube to the Sahara, although the rise of the Shi'ite Safavid Empire based in Iran and Iraq prevented the reunification of the Fertile Crescent while offering western powers a potential new ally. Selim's conquests made the whole Mediterranean basin a war zone between Ottomans, their allied privateers and pirates, and the Venetians, Hospitallers and Habsburgs under Charles V. Over the next two centuries, the Habsburg–Ottoman contest played out from Tunisia to Austria, punctuated by wars and truces. In central Europe, Belgrade fell to the newly emboldened and resourced Ottomans in 1521, most of Hungary after the crushing Turkish victory at Mohacs in 1526. Vienna was unsuccessfully besieged by the Turks in 1529 and Austria attacked again in 1532, with the seat of action settling across the middle Danube. At sea, the main theatres of confrontation included the Aegean, Adriatic and the narrows between Sicily and Tunisia. Rhodes fell in 1522, the Hospitallers being relocated further west on Malta in 1530. The Ottoman victory over a papal-Habsburg-Venetian fleet off Prevesa in Epirus in 1538 gave supremacy in the eastern Mediterranean until their heavy defeat at Lepanto in 1571, a setback balanced by their conquest of Cyprus the same year. Charles V did succeed in capturing Tunis in 1535, which was held until 1574, and Malta successfully resisted a sustained Ottoman siege in 1565.

141. The battle of Lepanto.

Such shifting intercontinental engagement encouraged dialogue, exchange, even alliance, as well as hostility. With both sides grappling with the problems of managing large fissiparous empires, Ottoman-Habsburg truces were agreed in 1533 and 1545. Iberian crusading energy was increasingly focused on the western Mediterranean, north Africa and the east Atlantic. A defining moment came in 1536 when Francis I allied with Suleiman I against Charles V, the first of a series of such treaties. In 1542–4, naval cooperation saw a Turkish fleet joining the French in besieging Habsburg-held Nice and being allowed to use Toulon as a base. In such circumstances, Pope Paul III's hope in 1544 that the Council of Trent he was summoning would initiate a new anti-infidel crusade showed the tenacity of the ideal allied to a level of wishful thinking that lacked credibility even in Catholic circles.[16] Growing economic stability and prosperity in the Ottoman Empire stimulated local, regional and international commerce regardless of faith, politics or persistent formal papal trade embargos. Venice secured an Ottoman truce in 1573 that stuck for seventy years; Spain, since 1556 separate from the empire, followed suit in 1580. In central Europe a recrudescence of war between 1593 and 1606 ignited embers of crusade enthusiasm

142. A new dispensation: the siege of Nice by a Franco-Turkish alliance, 1543.

in the west, for example in France, as did the Ottoman conquest of Crete (1669) and the central European Holy League from 1683 to 1699. However, in Habsburg lands the crusade remained chiefly a device to raise money.

Elsewhere, by the mid-seventeenth century the Ottomans, while still demonised as decadent violent tyrants, were regarded in terms chiefly of power, territory and trade, formalised in the English and French Levant companies. The Turkish policy of Louis XIV of France (1643–1715) in the 1660s briefly encouraged ideas of holy war before subsequently emphasising commercial cooperation and political advantage.[17] Bulls continued to be issued. The cross could still be taken by individuals for personal penance and salvation. Association with the naval power of the Hospitallers on Malta always possessed a religious dimension, seen by some in terms of wider Roman Catholic revivalism. War in defence of the faith still appealed across the new confessional divides. Despite generations of alliance, French troops helped defeat the Ottomans at Saint Gotthard in 1664. Traditional rhetoric could strike chords across Europe's nobilities, attracting recruits to defend Crete in the 1660s. However, as the seventeenth century drew to a close and attitudes towards the Turks slid from fear to contempt as the Ottoman military threat diminished, crusade institutions and idealism as tools in anti-Ottoman politics ceased to be relevant and slipped into complete disuse.

CHAPTER TWELVE

NEW CHALLENGES AND THE END
OF CRUSADING

The Italian Wars (1494–1559), conquests in the New World (after 1492), the opening of a sea route to the Indian Ocean and southern Asia (from 1487) and the Protestant upheaval (from 1517) reshaped European culture, attitudes and politics. In an increasingly diverse religious universe, the crusade retained a place, for some still addressing urgent issues of conviction, salvation and identity. The Old and New Worlds could meet. Charles V paid for his capture of Tunis in 1535 with conventional church taxes and sale of indulgences (authorised by a papal *bula de crozada*) but also with loot from South America. For many Roman Catholics, the Protestant schism of the sixteenth century presented as serious a challenge to their concept of the right order of the world as did the Ottoman advance. Reformists rejected the crusade's ideological basis in papal authority and the late medieval penitential system epitomised by the sale of indulgences, seen as materially corrupt and theologically wrong. Yet a sense of Christian solidarity in the need to combat the infidel Turk was shared. Protestant London celebrated the crusading victory at Lepanto in 1571; Luther condoned war to repulse the Ottoman. Yet, while its rhetoric thrived, not least at the papal curia, active crusading faded. The emotions and policies once the crusade's preserve found expression elsewhere.

This slow transformation was hardly predestined. In 1400 crusades featured prominently in the armoury of western Christendom across a wide range of conflicts. Crusading raised money and framed diplomacy, in tune with popular enthusiasm and elite chivalric self-image. The reign of Pope Eugenius IV (1431–47) indicated crusading's vibrancy. The Council of Florence in 1439 secured the nominal union of the Latin and Greek Churches. The pope received treatises and pamphlets on the Ottomans and the recovery of the Holy Land. He welcomed representatives from the Coptic Churches of Palestine, Egypt and Ethiopia, and made approaches to minority Christian communities in Armenia, Iraq and Cyprus. Two Greeks with knowledge of the Turks were created cardinals, Isidore of Kiev and John Bessarion. Eugenius took an active role in the anti-Turkish crusade in 1439 and 1444, and issued crusade bulls for Castilian attacks on Granada and Portuguese attacks on Tangiers in 1437 and 1443.[1] Dealing separately with Portuguese aggression along the coast of west Africa and in the islands of the western Atlantic, in 1436 he reversed an initial ban on force to coerce pagan natives (1434) after pressure from King Duarte of Portugal (1433–8), a volte face allowing for the subjugation of pagan natives before conversion, a precedent later employed to devastating effect in the Americas. While invasions of north Africa were treated as extensions of the Iberian *Reconquista*, Atlantic pagans lived in regions that had never been part of Christendom and so did not easily fit canon law categories as legitimate targets for religious violence.[2] Although in the Maghreb and the Atlantic the crusade and papal licences were subordinate to royal policy, they still demonstrated a role for the pope's leadership after the challenges of the Great Schism, the rival claims to ecclesiastical authority by the representative church Council of Basel (1431–47), and the failed Hussite crusades of the 1420s. Tradition also acted as a cloak: Holy Land formulae covered the use of the term *cruciata*, which actually meant standardised sales of indulgences.[3]

The Dukes of Burgundy

Secular support for crusading rested on popular devotional practices, aristocratic cultural identification and memories of past heroics, sustained in visual and material culture, history and imaginative literature. Political dividends were pursued in western Europe most strenuously by the dukes of Burgundy, Philip the Good (1419–67) and Charles the Rash (1467–77), son and grandson of the commander of the Nicopolis crusade, John the Fearless (duke 1404–19), both eager to break the shackles of their non-royal titles to assert an independent authority commensurate with their wide territories and immense wealth. As dukes of Burgundy, counts of Flanders and descendants of Louis IX, they stood as legatees of the grandest crusade inheritances, which they exploited loudly even if their material aid failed to match their belligerent rhetoric and ritual investment.[4]

Philip the Good sponsored intelligence-gathering trips to the eastern Mediterranean, such as Guillebert de Lannoy's in 1421. He employed crusade experts such as Bertrandon de la Broquière (d. 1459), who scrutinised the Greek diplomat John Torcello's crusade advice to Eugenius IV in 1439 and in 1457 published his own memoirs of his travels around the Near East in 1432–3, during which he had met Sultan Murad II.[5] Another Burgundian courtier, Geoffrey of Thoisy, campaigned in the eastern Mediterranean and the Black Sea between the 1440s and 1460s. He wrote a memorandum on anti-Turkish war in the early 1460s as did another Burgundian veteran of the Ottoman conflict, Waleran of Wavrin. Jean Germain, bishop of Chalon-sur-Saône (1436–61), acted as the Burgundian court's resident commentator on crusade involvement from the 1430s to 1450s. He served as chancellor of the Order of the Golden Fleece, founded n 1431, which laid on the Feast and anti-Turkish Vow of the Pheasant at Lille in 1454. Another chancellor of the Order, William Filastre, bishop of Tournai, led crusade discussions with Pius II in the 1460s. For half a century, the Burgundian court entertained crusade planners, such as John of Capistrano, and voiced enthusiasm for proposals. Duke Philip played a prominent part in crusade diplomacy after the fall of Constantinople and in the 1460s. Church taxes were regularly levied and indulgences sold. Philip supported both Iberian and anti-Hussite crusading. Small squadrons of galleys were sent to Rhodes (1429, 1441, 1444) and Constantinople (1444–5), and a regiment despatched to Ancona to aid Pius II's crusade in 1464. Duke Charles maintained the dynastic commitment that was continued by his grandson, the emperor Charles V, who combined the Burgundian crusade tradition with his Spanish *reconquista* inheritance.

However, Burgundy's failure to convert showy enthusiasm into effective policy suggested a changing role for crusading that now competed with parallel forms of civic devotion, with kingdoms proclaiming their status as new Israels, holy lands in their own right, their defence a moral priority. The Burgundian court's engagement followed a ritualised pattern of diplomatic expectations. The dukes raised crusade money and promoted nostalgic fancies of recovering the Holy Land, yet declined major unilateral investments in conflicts in eastern Europe, the Adriatic or Aegean. France, England and western Germany always posed more immediate problems than the Turks. Burgundian rhetoric and emotion appeared driven by history not future conquests; John of Capistrano discussed the recovery of Jerusalem on his visit in 1454. The extent of popular engagement is hard to assess, although local recruitment initiatives bore some fruit in the 1450s and 1460s: for example, in March 1464, eighty men from Ghent took the cross.[6] Even at court, commitment could appear divorced from mundane serious war planning. The Vow of the Pheasant (1454) represented displacement: theatrical ducal glorification not a policy to recapture Constantinople. This was not, as it could have been, a ceremony of taking the cross. Only a very few volumes among Duke Philip's considerable collection of crusade texts even dealt with the Turks.[7] The supposedly practical information contained in Broquière's memoir of his Near Eastern travels was twenty-five years out of date. Escapist theatricals were not necessarily cynical or mendacious, but reflected only a general conceptual frame not a political revival.

Popular Responses

Evidence for social engagement with crusading came from the popularity of buying indulgences, now a bureaucratised international system of purchasing spiritual privileges of absolution, either immediate or on the point of death. Prices were not insignificant. In Germany around 1500 an indulgence cost about a week's household expenditure. In 1501 in England, rates varied: on property, a sliding scale charged the richest 0.16 per cent of estimated income to 0.33 per cent for the least wealthy; on non-property income rates were more consistent at about 0.2 per cent, i.e. a few shillings to a few pounds. Money from other indulgence sales, such as those for the increasingly regular papal Jubilees (1450, 1475, 1500, etc.) could be diverted to the crusade or, more generally, to defence against the Turks. In England between 1444 and 1502 twelve such indulgence drives were conducted. Although receipts could be modest – hundreds rather than thousands of pounds a time in England – perceptions that large sums were being drained out of the nation became standard, especially in Germany.[8] Indulgence campaigns quickly exploited the new technology of printing. Previously written on durable vellum, indulgence forms now appeared as printed pro forma sheets, with blank spaces kept for the names of the beneficiaries to be filled in by hand. The earliest surviving examples date from Mainz in 1454/55. Printers began producing them in batches of hundreds a day. In England from the 1470s, the top pioneer printers, William Caxton, John Lettou, Wynkyn de Worde and Richard Pynson, all took advantage of this lucrative staple of their business.

143. *Money being assembled to pay for indulgences.*

144. *A Gutenberg indulgence from 27 February 1455.*

Printing accelerated the speed and widened the reach of the circulation of news, ideas and crusade texts: sermons, treatises, poems, popular songs, pamphlets, public correspondence, newsletters and devotional works. The new technology allowed for the inclusion of woodcut illustrations to add vivid immediacy and mould public perceptions. Whereas Cardinal Bessarion's Latin *Orationes* (1471, see p. 409), prompted by the loss of Venetian Negroponte in 1470, attracted a print run of fewer than one hundred copies, William of Caoursin's lively account of the siege of Rhodes (1480), also originally in Latin, with its array of striking woodcut images, became a best-seller, with editions published between 1481 and 1489 in Venice, Ulm, Salamanca, Paris and Bruges. An English translation appeared in London by 1484.[9] Printing stimulated translation generally. In 1481, Caxton produced an English version (from the French) of William of Tyre's account of the First Crusade (the first nine books) under the title *Godfrey de Bouillon*. Pynson published a translation of the early fourteenth-century encyclopaedic crusade treatise and Asian gazetteer, the *Flowers of the History of the East*, by the Armenian Hetoum of Gorigos in 1520. The Middle English romance, *Capystranus*, commemorating the 1456 defence of Belgrade, appeared in numerous editions, fragments surviving from 1515, 1527 and 1520.[10] The first century of European printing massively increased the volume, availability and social reach of material on the crusade and the Turkish threat, reflecting what was believed to be popular. The literary confections of fifteenth-century Italian humanists appealed to a narrower audience than the more demotic, often garishly illustrated, front-line German pamphlets, the *Turkenbüchlein* and *Flugschriften* of the 1510s to 1540s.[11] However, in their respective spheres, both offered debates on necessity, urgency, legitimacy, efficacy and conduct of crusading to social groups beyond traditional political, ecclesiastical and academic hierarchies.

Despite the absence of regular mass cross-taking, the ceremony remained available in various different versions across Christendom. Innocent VIII (1484–92) included a revised formula in his Roman Pontifical that reflected current practice by describing the cross being taken 'to assist and defend the Christian faith or the recovery of the Holy Land'.[12] Cross-giving still featured prominently in high-profile fifteenth-century crusade initiatives, including Cardinal Carvajal's legation to Hungary in 1455–61 involving John of Capistrano, and Pius II's crusade.[13] *Crucesignati* fought with the Hungarians against the Turks in 1458 and with Matthias Corvinus in Bosnia

145. Woodcut of the siege of Rhodes, 1480.

in 1464. Recruitment centred on towns, even if quite modest ones, such as Axel in the Netherlands. Individual examples of cross-takers continued. Some, such as two Norwich worsted weavers in 1499, were hardly grand.[14] However, recruitment of non-professional troops scarcely met the needs of generals or politicians, a familiar gap between expectations and practice. The infrastructure to generate enthusiasm and stimulate anxiety remained available in liturgies, Masses and processions while crusading was still promoted as a metaphor for Christian behaviour.[15] In Hungary in 1514 the tension between popular expectations and the reality of crusade politics even helped ignite social revolt. Recruited by anti-Turkish preaching, an army of *cruce-signati* from poorer marginal sections of the community, eager to believe the militant revivalist rhetoric, confronted the prudent caution of nobles more interested in diplomatic accommodation and crusade money and reluctant to divert their workforce from their lands.[16] The ensuing atrocities and extremes of violence from both sides pointed to how the crusade could excite unrelated social tensions.

Cross-taking rituals became increasingly obsolete as preaching was divorced from raising men. The last time the cross was generally preached in France may have been in 1517–18. In Germany, between 1486 and 1504, an energetic crusade proponent, Cardinal Raymond Perault (1435–1505), emphasised the infidel menace to Christendom and Christian souls: but he was there to sell indulgences.[17] As a fiscal mechanism, the system inevitably invited abuse and attracted criticism, courting rulers' hostility except, as in Spain, where they secured a monopoly over proceeds. Imagery of the cross of redemptive violence still resonated, not least with the cultural aspirations of Roman Catholic nobilities. Preachers and pamphleteers continued to thunder against Ottoman threats to Christendom and Christianity. Yet by the end of the fifteenth century, for most of the faithful, the crusade bypassed religious passion, reduced in practice to a bureaucratic process by which money or goods were handed to Church or State to be used more or less at will. The inherent dangers of corruption, incompetence, and the distance between oratory and action invited indulgence fatigue, a problem identified as early as the 1270s.[18] The fifteenth century witnessed a paradox: indulgences continued to be bought extensively while official perception of disenchantment mounted, provoking Pius II's remark that crusade preachers had become 'like insolvent tradesmen . . . without credit'.[19] Between 1458 and 1523 the German *Reichstag* regularly questioned the use of crusade money.

Suspicion undermined Perault's preaching in Germany around 1500. Leo X's attempts to fund a new crusade were dismissed by Francis I of France in 1517 as 'clever tricks to extract money', adding that 'the people's devotion is so small that almost nothing will be raised'.[20] Such disenchantment charted the distance between traditional popular enthusiasm for holy war, as it became generally known in the sixteenth century, and its more complex political and military reality.

New Worlds

The expansion of Iberian kingdoms into and across the Atlantic exposed different features of religious violence, some not specifically crusading. Traditional crusade ideology and institutions remained integral to Iberian national identities, notably in Castile where the culture of *reconquista* suffused popular romances, matching an economy of plunder. Continuing inter-faith conflict on the peninsula and in north Africa attracted standard crusade incentives and finance.[21] To improve their appeal, indulgences were offered at decreasing flat rates and, after 1456, open to souls in purgatory. Although often placed in the context of the international conflict with Muslim powers, with Sixtus IV in 1482 explicitly equating the Granada campaign with wars in the Holy Land,[22] Iberian crusading remained distinct. The *reconquista* tradition persisted in Spanish and Portuguese wars to annex Morocco and Tunisia into the later sixteenth century with the Spanish conquest of Tunis and the disastrous Portuguese invasion of Morocco in 1578. Even if driven primarily by incentives of martial glory, commerce and African gold, these north African wars could be presented in traditional terms of Christian defence and recovery. They could also be promoted as opportunities for conversion. Despite the canon law prohibition on forced conversion, since the twelfth century some had seen crusading as enabling the extension of the faith, *dilatatio fidei*. Sixtus IV's 1482 Granada bull linked defence with the spread of Christian faith and conversion.

Castilian and Portuguese expansion in west Africa and the Atlantic islands could not be justified in terms of recovery or defence of Christian land, but canon law going back to Innocent IV in the thirteenth century allowed for the conquest of pagans who resisted missionary work. More contestably, some defenders of Iberian Atlantic conquests deployed concepts of racial inferiority and innate barbarism to deny indigenous populations political agency or even independent human rights.[23] This racist argument was not the monopoly of Iberian apologists, mirroring humanist depictions of Ottomans as barbarians beyond the pale of civilisation, in Pius II's word, *immanis*, inhuman.[24] Denying autonomous rights to indigenous Atlantic and American pagans pointed to fundamental differences between conquest in the New World and crusading in the Old. Despite arousing conventional crusading emotions and rhetoric, wars in the Canaries or later the Americas could only be related to the *reconquista* or the Holy Land by distant analogy. Christopher Columbus imagined his voyages in the context of the recovery of Jerusalem.[25] In Mexico, Hernán Cortés compared Tlaxcala with Granada. This generic crusading identification helped incorporate the New World into familiar cultural patterns of the Old, but there were no crusades in America, a point reinforced by Alexander VI's bull *Inter cetera* in 1493 that gave the Spanish monarchs the right to conquer and rule native Americans. Alexander, a veteran of Pius II's Turkish crusade schemes of the 1460s, based his grant on the pope's duty to protect all mankind. He insisted that Spanish conquest be aimed at conversion not material exploitation. Alexander's concern to base the right to dominion on the promotion of conversion followed Eugenius IV's precedent in 1436 over the Portuguese annexation of the Canaries rather than Nicholas V's grant in 1455 allowing the Portuguese to conquer and enslave the infidels of Africa. Although citing the recent end of the Granada war, *Inter cetera* did not proclaim a crusade in the New World. It was in any case immediately rendered redundant by the treaty of Tordesillas in 1494 that carved up the globe between Spain and Portugal without papal approval.[26] European colonisation was pursued under Christian banners and furthered by Christian missionaries and ecclesiastical settlement, but, unlike conquests of pagans in the Baltic, independent of direct papal authority and without the use of the crusade. The crusade only reached the Americas as a region of the Spanish Empire subject to *cruzada* taxation. It has been argued that only the speed of Spanish conquests prevented grants of crusade privileges.[27] This is contradicted by the early date of *Inter ceteros* and subsequent rejection of crusade precedents for the Americas despite crusade bulls for the Spanish in the Mediterranean and the Portuguese in the western Atlantic. The Spanish do not seem to have requested crusade privileges, despite trading on equivalent religious emotions or psychology. As contemporaries noticed, the conquistadors' chief driver lay in unabashed material gain, conversion acting as a weapon of conquest.

146. *Cross and conquest: a late sixteenth-century depiction of Columbus in Hispaniola.*

In the absence of crusade certainties, doubts concerning the conduct and legitimacy of New World conquests revived late medieval debates over just war and infidel rights. The Dominican theologians and canonists Bartolomé de Las Casas (1484–1566) and Francis Vitoria (1492–1546) asserted Amerindian human rights with arguments derived in part from thirteenth-century canon law on the crusade and just war even if Vitoria, for instance, rejected the appropriateness of traditional crusade categories. Others, more wedded to reassuring self-serving conservatism, sought to brand Amerindians as fair game for subjugation, analogous to Turks and Muslims or as uncivilised natural slaves.[28] Despite legal arguments familiar to late medieval crusading, and although American conquests indulged ambitions previously associated with holy warriors, conquistadors were not *crucesignati*. The absence of the crusade in America signalled its irrelevance to the most important and transformative new area of Christian war, conquest, mission and expansion since late antiquity, marking a break with the past and a lessening of crusading's role in Christian society.

The Protestant Challenge

The diminishing of the crusade was further accelerated by the combat against the religious reformers of the sixteenth century. The reformist Christian opponents of the Roman Catholic Church presented a fundamental critique of the crusade's ideology and devotional practices. As such, like the fifteenth-century Hussites, they offered obvious targets for traditional crusading. However, these opportunities were only equivocally pursued, perhaps as a result of the previous century's experience. The use of crusades against dissident Christians and political opponents by opposing sides during the papal schism had undermined the credibility of crusading as a tool of secular statecraft. Nicholas V's offer of crusade indulgences to Charles VII of France for an invasion of Savoy, the county of anti-pope Felix V (1439–49), led nowhere.[29] Julius II's (1503–13) renewal of Italian crusades and his grant of crusade status to Henry VIII of England's invasion of France in 1512 proved eccentric not prescient.[30] Nonetheless, after 1417, the restored papacy had continued to approve crusades against heretics: the Hussites in Bohemia or the nasty little crusade in 1487–8 against Alpine communities of Waldensians.[31] Inevitably, new schemes for crusades against the reformers were floated: against Henry VIII of England in the 1530s and Elizabeth I after her excommunication in 1570; German Protestants in the 1540s; or in favour of Irish Catholic resistance to Protestant English rule between 1577 and 1600. In 1536, Lord Darcy, a leader of the English Catholic traditionalist uprising the Pilgrimage of Grace, supplied the rebels with badges of the Five Wounds of Christ originally manufactured for a planned campaign to Morocco in 1511. Indulgences to fight 'foes of our holy faith', as those granted to the English privateer and veteran of Lepanto, Thomas Stuckeley, in 1575 by Gregory XIII (1572–85), could as easily be applied to Ireland as to north Africa: in the event Stuckeley died at the battle of Alcazar (1578).[32] Sixtus V (1585–90) based his indulgences for the Spanish Armada against Elizabeth I of England

147. The badge of Five Wounds of Christ worn during the Pilgrimage of Grace in 1536.

(1588) on those issued for fighting the Turks by Gregory XIII in 1585, complete with Holy Land remissions, an association included in Gregory XIII's earlier 1580 indulgences to Irish opponents of Elizabeth I. Protestants were frequently demonised as agents of Anti-Christ, similar or worse than Turks, impediments in the struggle with the Ottomans.

Yet no general anti-Protestant crusade was launched. Politics trumped religion. Competition between the Habsburgs and the kings of France, the divergent interests of Spain, religious divisions within France and the German Empire, and Catholic princes' suspicion of papal authority, prevented a united front against English or German reformers. Holy war was by no means dead. Inspired by Old Testament precedent, Protestants could argue from scripture for direct divine approval of war for the faith, shorn of Roman Catholic theology and penitential accretions. Roman Catholic devotees maintained the crusade tradition, its mentality, language and forms apparent

148. *Spanish Armada of 1588, with a ship flying the flags of Spain, the papacy and the crusaders' cross.*

149. *An English Knave of Hearts playing card showing the pope paying for the Spanish Armada.*

during the French Wars of Religion (1562–98). Defenders of Toulouse against Huguenots in 1567–8 wore white crosses and were given plenary indulgences by Pius V to create a militia or association (*sodalitium*) of *cruce-signati*.[33] Yet these local instances merely emphasised the crusade's absence on a grander scale, conforming to counter-Reformation Roman Catholicism's increased concentration on individual as well as communal devotional practice. As with the conquests in America, anti-Protestant wars provided alternative non-crusading expressions for fighting for the faith. There were no crusades in the great confessional confrontation of the Thirty Years War (1618–48).

Crusade and Nation

Throughout the later Middle Ages, as kingdoms developed greater political and administrative articulation, the nation increasingly provided a focus for a sense of divinely ordained and protected community parallel to that of Christendom, a process stimulated by cults of monarchy and national exceptionalism. During the Hundred Years War, both English and French propagandists projected images of national providence, one English bishop in 1377 claiming in Parliament that English victories in the French wars proved that God 'as he did Israel' had chosen England 'as his heritage'. The red cross of royalist crusaders in the 1260s became the badge of later medieval English soldiery.[34] Assertion of a crusading reputation, a feature of royal propaganda since the twelfth century, continued in the fifteenth and sixteenth centuries: Emperor Frederick III of Germany (1440–93) taking the cross and holding crusade Diets after 1453; Matthew Corvinus of Hungary using his own and his father John Hunyadi's crusading credentials to bolster his parvenu dynasty; Emperor Charles V fighting Turks, Protestants and conquering Tunis; the claims of Hungary and other eastern European, Balkan and Italian principalities for special treatment as Christendom's bastions, *antemurales*. National pride attached to crusade heroes: Richard I in England; Louis IX in France; Baldwin IX of Flanders in Flanders/Burgundy; the champions of the Iberian *Reconquista*. Philip II of Spain's messianic insistence that Spain's wars were God's wars witnessed perhaps the most strident transfer of crusading ethos into national holy war.

The nationalisation of crusading found reflection in literary commentary. While fifteenth-century Italian humanists tended to use the crusades to

150. El Greco's Adoration of the Name of Jesus, *c. 1578, an allegory of the union of Spain, Venice and the papacy against the Turks; Philip II of Spain is the kneeling figure in black at the front.*

discuss the idea of a threat to western post-classical Christian civilisation as a whole, by contrast, Christine de Pisan's *Ditié de Jehanne d'Arc* (1429), in language saturated with familiar crusade tropes ('He who fights for justice gains Paradise'; 'God wills it'), elevated the French monarchy to God's providential favour ('He finds more faith in the royal house than anywhere else'), confirmed by the deeds of Joan of Arc: a restored Charles VII (1422–61) would recover the Holy Land. For Christine, heaven was the reward for those who fought just wars for the *patria*.[35] Each side in the Hundred Years War was claimed as the new Israelites. The *Gesta Henrici Quinti* (1417), by one of Henry V's chaplains, describes English soldiers the night before Agincourt (1415), as 'God's people', like the Maccabees, donning 'the armour of penitence'. A *Te Deum* is ordered by the king 'to the praise and glory of God Who had so marvellously deigned to receive His England and her people as His very own'. Henry, 'God's knight', rules 'his people Israel'.[36] This sanctification of the secular world was not confined to Catholic orthodoxy. The Czech Hussites created a new holy landscape in Bohemia, including a Mount Tabor and a Mount Horeb, to express their national religion, the association with Old Testament Israel demonstrating a clear rejection of the crusades launched against them. Such sanctified patriotism mirrored crusading. Armies took the sacrament, spoke the general confession and received absolution before battle. The cross became an increasingly common military uniform for national armies (red for the English and troops of the Habsburg emperors) and popular insurgents, such as the German peasant rebels in 1524–5 and, according to one observer, the English Pilgrimage of Grace in England in 1536. Precise crusade association may have faded, yet the cross's religious significance in symbolising particular communal solidarity remained. Soldiers of the Swiss Confederacy wore white crosses against Burgundy and the Habsburgs. So did the defenders of the Florentine Republic, a city with long crusade credentials, described in the 1490s as a New Jerusalem. As a banner of armed struggle, the iconography of the cross was unmistakable.[37]

With crusade images recruited to wars for the *patria*, academic study adopted a nationalist tinge, not least in regions of religious contest, Germany and France. The French Huguenot Jacques Bongars (1554–1612) produced a massive edition of crusade chronicles and texts, *Gesta Dei Per Francos* (1611), the most significant single tool for crusade research until the nineteenth century. Explicitly in the preface and implicitly in choice of texts, Bongars was praising the crusading tradition of France and its Roman Catholic monarchy (as a diplomat he was employed by the convert Henry IV), annexing the crusade to a supra-confessional national myth. A French translation of William of Tyre in 1574 was titled *Histoire de la Guerre Sainte, dire proprement, La Franciade orientale*, while the encyclopaedist Etienne Pasquier in the 1590s, like Bongars, associated the Holy Land wars with 'la grandeur de nostre France'.[38] This French literary enthusiasm was maintained during the seventeenth century, not least under Louis XIV with such royalist Francophile works as Louis Maimborg's *History of the Crusades* (1675), by which time crusading had become for all but a very few simply a matter of antiquarian curiosity and historiographical interest.

The Image of the Crusade

The fading of the crusade as a dynamic element in Christian society was slow and uneven. Its image retained force, through preaching, literature, communal memory and visible iconography long after calls to arms and offers of indulgences had become nugatory, remote, insincere or controversial. Vocabulary traced the transformation. In the fifteenth century, the word *cruciata* and related vernacular versions increasingly referred to fundraising while war against the Turks assumed the general language of war such as *bellum* or *expeditio*.[39] After Belgrade in 1456, few actual *crucesignati* fought the Turks. Yet the crusade continued to provide an ideal against which to assess political action and morality in the tradition of Philippe de Mézières' response to the Nicopolis defeat of 1396, urging general spiritual regeneration as a precondition for Christian success.[40] Blaming defeat on the pious deficiencies of crusaders or Christendom more generally retained currency, from works of advice to those of encouragement.[41] The debate on collective moral deficiency was maintained both by Italian humanist crusade advocates and critics of military crusading such as, in the mid-fifteenth century, the Spanish John of Segovia and the German Nicholas of Cusa, or, two generations later, Erasmus of Rotterdam. The familiar uneasy literary relationship between historical commentary and political exhortation persisted.[42] William of Tyre became the standard narrative, with numerous printed versions, including editions of the whole Latin text in 1549, 1564 and 1611, the Basel printer Johannes Herold's *De bello sacro* (1549) (holy war being the near-ubiquitous name for the crusades in the early modern period; Herold was not a Roman Catholic) extending William of Tyre to the accession of Suleiman the Magnificent in 1520.

Herold's hardly penetrating observation that religious divisions were obstructing resistance to the Turks became a common motif across confessional boundaries, as in the massive but popular *Generall Historie of the Turks*

(1603) by the English Protestant schoolmaster Richard Knolles.[43] Such common ground identified an aspect of Christian universalism that survived changing patterns of devotion. Although the crusades no longer dominated Ottoman wars or infra-religious Christian conflict, the fight against the Turks retained a generalised religious dimension in popular perceptions of Islam as more alien than other Christian confessions. Recognition of the moral as well as political benefits of war against the Turks was shared by Protestant and Roman Catholics alike, but shorn of the formal trappings of the crusade. Thus the great Roman Catholic victory at Lepanto in 1571, with all its hallmarks of crusading, could be welcomed by the young Calvinist James VI of Scotland in a long Virgilian epic (1585) as a 'wondrous worke of God', and was celebrated at the time by Protestant commentators and Londoners as a victory 'against the common enemy of our faith . . . of so great importance unto the whole state of Christian commonwealth'.[44]

The often laudatory concern with the crusades shown by non-Catholic scholars indicates a final irony. Detoxified by its irrelevance to fighting the Turks or Protestants, study of the crusades was used to suggest cultural continuity across the confessional caesura of the Reformation either, by Bongars, in weaving the crusades into the national epic or, by Knolles, in projecting a view of Christian Europe as a 'commonweale' of princes defined not by religious disagreements but by collective opposition to Muslims. Even the English reformist polemicist John Foxe's excoriating anti-Roman Catholic account of the crusades, *History of the Turks* (1566), noted the courage and religious devotion of ordinary Catholic believers in the wars against common enemies of Christ and Christendom, even if he insisted that 'the Turks . . . were never so repulsed and foiled as at the present time in encountering with the protestants and defenders of sincere religion'.[45] The Protestant challenge had destroyed universal acceptance of the religious systems behind traditional crusading but not the emotional attraction. Confessionally neutral concepts of holy war were fashioned that avoided arguments over crusading.

This did not mean universal agreement that holy war was any more justified than crusading, a point underlined in the English lawyer, scholar and politician Francis Bacon's fragmentary *Advertisement Touching an Holy Warre* (1622–3; published 1629) on the legitimacy of 'the propagation of the Faith by arms'.[46] Bacon's discussion, presented as a debate between contending intellectuals, rested on history and the new perspectives provided by the conquests of natives in the Americas. While famously having one of his protagonists describe the crusade as 'a *rendez-vous* of cracked brains that wore their feather in their head instead of their hat', Bacon's treatment – what there is of it – is notably balanced.[47] Rejecting wars for profit and crusading's religious dogma, and suspicious of arguments based on necessity, prudence and law, Bacon's presentation of the idea of a just war against the Turks nonetheless displayed familiarity with the legacy of the crusade. Religious wars continued to excite massive bloodshed far into the seventeenth century, in Germany, Britain and on frontiers with the Turk, but, despite an equivalence of emotional and psychological dynamics, it was not conditioned by the apparatus of the crusade. While individual crusaders still fought in the Mediterranean and eastern Europe for another century, and the Hospitallers maintained an increasingly lordly hold on Malta until expelled by Napoleon Bonaparte in 1798, crusading as a vital element of public policy and private ambition dimmed into the margins of European experience, a gilded or reviled memory.

CHAPTER THIRTEEEN

CRUSADING: OUR CONTEMPORARY?

No medieval events have possessed a more contested afterlife than the crusades. Few are more recognisable to modern audiences, in rhetoric and visual imagery. Later debates have become part of crusade history, classic examples of past events being shaped in retrospect. In western Europe and North America, the crusades have been perceived variously through the filters of Roman Catholic apologia, Protestant condemnation, nationalist appropriation, humanist materialism, Enlightenment disgust, Romantic empathy, imperial enthusiasm, modernist condescension and post-colonial disquiet. They have been seen as barbaric invasions, conduits of economic development and cultural exchange, transmitters of European supremacy, witnesses to spiritual devotion, expressions of religious bigotry, acts in a cosmic clash of civilisations or squalid self-interested land-grabs. The heirs of victims and opponents share some of these opinions, but add particular elements of inherited outrage, anger, bitterness, disgust and sadness. The crusades have transcended historiography to find a place in popular culture, in operas, novels, elite art and public monuments, but also in children's books and folklore, Arabic as well as western. From literature and art to entertainment and politics, the crusades have long possessed power to inspire or appal.

The crusades attracted, in David Hume's phrase, 'the curiosity of mankind' both for their role in international mayhem and for the startling emotional paradox of religious violence presented as an act of charitable love.[1] The duopoly of materialism and idealism has provoked judgemental assessments: were the crusades aberrant, malign, eccentric or, in some ways, central to the European experience, of 'limitless effect'?[2] Interpretations since 1600 have mixed admiration, revulsion and astonishment. Words for the crusades became lodged in modern vernaculars. By the eighteenth century, descriptive terms *Kreuzzug* or *croisade* replaced the generically neutral 'holy war' in Germany and France, while in Spain, the *bula de cruzada* remained a living part of the fiscal system. Samuel Johnson's *Dictionary* (1755) included four words for the phenomenon – crusade (of early eighteenth-century coinage, later popularised by Hume and Gibbon), crusado, croisade and croisado. By the mid-eighteenth century, 'crusade' also began to be applied analogically to campaigns for good causes or issues of principle (e.g. J. G. Hamann's *Die Kreuzzüge des Philologen* [*Crusades of the Philologian*], 1762; Voltaire's *croisade* against smallpox, 1767–8; Thomas Jefferson's 'crusade against ignorance', 1786). Such awareness owed more to imaginative literature than to academic disputes or scholarly accuracy, as does much modern appreciation.[3]

Accounts of the crusades had always straddled the fine line between history and fiction. Probably the most influential early modern work was Torquato Tasso's *Gerusalemme Liberata* (1580–1), which translated the story of the First Crusade and Godfrey of Bouillon into an epic of chivalric romance and magic, creating an exotic never-never land of amorous crusaders and Muslim warrior maidens ripe for love, death and conversion. Although hardly liable to be confused with the sober historical accounts being written at the time, Tasso's work, regularly republished and translated, distanced the image of crusading from its involvement in urgent contemporary concerns with papal authority or the Ottoman threat. Placed in a fantastical space available to imaginations free from historical, confessional or political constraints, owing as much to Renaissance classicism as to medieval religious war, Tasso's romance, by taking the crusades out of the council chamber, scholar's library and pedant's schoolroom, offered a sentimental perception that reduced the crusades to exotic (and often erotic) adventure stories seen through a soft-focus western lens. The impact was immediate and far reaching. By 1639, the Englishman Thomas Fuller's influential, critical *Historie of the Holy Warre* was seen by one enthusiast as robbing Tasso's poem 'of its long-liv'ed glory . . . Thou canst not feigne so well as he relate.'[4] This proved optimistic. Tasso's legacy penetrated far into the mortar of European high culture, inspiring music by Monteverdi, Lully, Handel, Vivaldi, Gluck, Haydn, Rossini, Brahms and Dvořák, and paintings by Tintoretto, Poussin, van Dyck, Tiepolo and Delacroix. In literature and,

151. The crusades through Tasso's lens: Poussin's Rinaldo and Arminda.

later, film, Tasso's influence was profound, part of a lasting unequal exchange between the popular and the learned.

Crusades and Progress

Given such dramatic raw material, it is unsurprising that historians have incorporated the crusades into wider patterns of European experience. For Thomas Fuller and savants of the earlier seventeenth century, the crusades addressed issues of immediate significance: the expression or corruption of faith; the materialism behind the crusade's emphasis on possession of physical space; the advance of the Turks. Waste formed a common theme, the crusades being blamed for a dissipation of resources that led to the decline in traditional aristocratic power and the rise of national monarchies. Perspectives shifted with the decline of the Ottomans as a political threat after the repulse of the siege of Vienna in 1683 and confirmation of Ottoman retreat at the end of the Turkish war in 1699. The eradication of religion as a stated cause of European war after the end of the Thirty Years War; the expansion of European trading and colonial empires from the Americas to the East Indies; and increased

European commercial penetration of the Mediterranean and Levant – led to a reformulation of the crusades into a story of contact and exchange. This materialist turn was signalled in the influential *Discourse on Ecclesiastical History* (1691) by the French lawyer, priest, theologian and church historian Claude Fleury. Avoiding confessional point scoring or patronising the past, Fleury identified, beneath the wars and conquests, the growth of navigation and commerce. This afforded Italian merchants in the Mediterranean 'freedom of trade' (*liberté du commerce*), starting a commercial revolution that led to an urban renaissance in arts, manufacture and industry.[5] This positive if accidental material consequence allowed the crusades a place in the construction of progressive modernity and European global hegemony.

Subsequent intellectual debates pursued Fleury's themes in contrasting ways. The new European global reach and the retreat of Ottoman power inspired greater interest in Arabic and non-European sources in confident accounts of the rise of Christian Europe and their opponents; accounts of the crusades using Arabic texts were integrated into a much wider materialist narrative of Eurasian invasions and cultural exchange devoid of nationalist or moralising charge. Within a general materialist consensus, no united 'Enlightenment' view of the crusades existed. The French *philosophes*, Denis Diderot and Voltaire, decried the crusades' superstition and irrationality, using them as oblique criticism of the manners, culture and pretensions of the *ancien régime*. Implicitly, crusaders' superstition, hypocrisy, greed and imposition of social inequality were analogous to the conduct of their modern aristocratic heirs. This negative assessment was far from unchallenged. Although few were more acidly hostile to the whole crusade phenomenon than David Hume, his Scottish associates, William Robertson, Adam Smith and Adam Ferguson, integrated the crusades into a persuasive account of the rise of western Europe. In the introductory chapter to his *History of the Reign of Charles V* (1769), 'The Progress of Society in Europe', Robertson, like Fleury, argued that the crusades, despite their superstition and folly, inadvertently produced increased international commerce, cultural exchange with the sophisticated east and the growth of western cities, which fostered civic values fundamental to the improvement of civilisation. Thus to the crusades 'we owe the first gleams of light which tended to dispel barbarity and ignorance'.[6] Robertson apparently derived this idea of economically determined progress directly from Adam Smith's lectures, just as his observations on beneficial cultural borrowing were taken from Ferguson's *Essay on the History of Civil Society* (1767). The contrast with the French *philosophes* lay in the different contemporary targets. In France, Voltaire and Diderot were confronting an illiberal, reactionary hierarchy under a divine-right monarchy whereas in Scotland Robertson and Smith were analysing a society that had seen rapid and, they would have argued, positive developments in the economy and legal, religious and political freedom, seen by them as the fruits of the Act of Union with England (1707).

However, this Smithian concept of progress was not universally accepted even by anglophone writers. Gilbert Stuart's *View of Society in Europe* (1778) turned Robertson's economic argument on its head by insisting that the material and human waste in Europe caused by the crusades actually discouraged trade and the development of the civilising arts while simultaneously promoting superstition. The Robertsonian scheme of progress was similarly rejected by Edward Gibbon in his *Decline and Fall of the Roman Empire* (the chapters on the crusades were published in 1788). In a pointed phrase, Gibbon insisted that the crusades marked 'the final progress of idolatry', the material advances that came in their wake insignificant and peripheral.[7] Yet Gibbon accepted the orthodoxy that the crusades in some measure contributed to the rise of independent cities and hence to a growth of liberty. The idea that the crusades contributed positively to the development of European civilisation and its global dominance became an academic orthodoxy across western Europe by the end of the eighteenth century, helped by the absence of any serious attempt to analyse, still less empathise or understand the religious motivations. Academic prizes were offered for theses supporting positive materialist interpretations, which were lent apparent credence by the consolidation of European world empires, and the American, French and early industrial revolutions. Each appeared to demonstrate a progressive tendency in the historical process from which the crusades could not be excluded. Moral judgements were relegated to a series of Enlightenment or neo-Protestant clichés of bewilderment or disapproval only balanced by recognition of the crusaders' commitment and bravery, however misguided.

French Romance and Empire

Such academic discussions, aimed at using history instrumentally to explain the modern world, operated in parallel to a very different approach. Even before the French Revolution exposed for many the aridity and cost of the cult of Reason and its Enlightenment apologists, a very different literary response to the Middle Ages had flourished. Beyond the intellectual salon, customary religion still played a central role in popular attitudes to history. Interest in the social aspects of the medieval past, such as chivalry, remained lively in aristocratic circles on many levels from the literary and antiquarian to the nostalgic and snobbish. Study of medieval literature produced fanciful pictures of chivalric hierarchy, codes of honour, valour and public service, with bold and selfless knights errant defending the weak or embarking on crusade. Chivalry could be depicted as tempering the barbarism of a violent militarist society, an agent of progress towards post-medieval civility, a secular code of moral behaviour contrasted with the supposedly ignoble materialism of modern society. Such sentimental evocations of medievalism were more closely attuned to public impressions than rarefied academic debates. The imagined Middle Ages offered an escape, an antithesis to modernity. At the same time, the crusades touched current concerns: empire; the relative cultural power of Europe; religion in secular society; mass support for popular political causes. The branding of the crusades as central to the development of European society could thus ally with conservative empathy for a lost world of social and religious certainties.

This combination of materialist and empathetic assessments of the crusades directed the revival of interest in the nineteenth century. One of the most influential champions of the crusades, François-René de Chateaubriand (1768–1848) had read Robertson's *Charles V* essay on progress (translated into French in 1771). The context was propitious for a revival of crusade enthusiasm as Napoleon's extravagant campaign in the Levant in 1798–9 led to renewed interest in the crusading past. A Roman Catholic re-convert and royalist, Chateaubriand's romantic evocation of the crusades in his account of his Near Eastern travels in 1806 (*Itinéraire de Paris à Jérusalem*, 1811) combined religious empathy with pride in 'French' crusader achievements. In his *Génie de christianisme* (1802), Chateaubriand had insisted that Christianity itself, *pace* Enlightenment thinkers, played a central role in furthering the progress of arts and learning. Chateaubriand expressed a visceral, patronising dislike of Islam, offering a clear message that the crusade presented an admirable precedent for new western conquests in a decadent and impoverished Levant. The crusade soon became a central event for conservatives as well as progressives, widely accepted as 'one of the greatest revolutions that has ever taken place in the history of the human race'.[8]

This view was shared by another French conservative, the former publisher Joseph-François Michaud (1767–1839), whose monumental epic narrative *Histoire des croisades* (1811–22, revised until a final posthumous edition in 1841), supplemented by his collection of translated sources *Bibliothèque des croisades* (1829), recast the crusades as moral exemplars of devotion and heroism, of Christian values and European cultural dynamism. A populariser with an ear for historical romance (he was not above using Tasso as a primary source) and eye for political uses of history, Michaud, like Chateaubriand, wrapped his francophile analysis in a sheen of cultural supremacism. Islam was cast as the eternal enemy, the Near East as ripe for new French colonisation and the crusades as part of an age-old conflict between civilisation (Christian Europe) and barbarism (the Muslim east). Armed with the appeal of an exciting story, extensive if uncritical and sometimes distorting employment of primary sources, a novelist's power of credible invention, a clear moral tone and an attractive conservative political agenda, Michaud's influence spread beyond Imperial and Restoration France. His *Histoire* ran into nineteen editions in the nineteenth century as well as translations into English,

152. King Louis Philippe and family visiting the Salle des Croisades *at Versailles in 1844, with Merry-Joseph Blondel's* Surrender of Acre to Philip Augustus and Richard I *in the background.*

153. Blondel's Surrender of Ptolemais [Acre] to King Philip II Augustus of France
and Richard Lionheart on 13th July 1191.

German, Italian and Russian. His vivid prose, along with Gustave Doré's wonderfully powerful illustrations to the 1877 edition and the crusade paintings – essentially illustrations of Michaud – commissioned from 1837 by Louis Philippe for his *Salle des croisades* at Versailles, could be said to have provided the modern image of the crusades and crusaders, recognisable two centuries after Michaud began to mine the crusades for publishing profits.

Partly thanks to Michaud, the marshalling of the crusades to create patriotic myth was especially prevalent in France. The irony of using a quintessentially supranational cause to promote national identity was largely lost. One less meretricious consequence of the nationalist turn was the encouragement given to academic study of crusade texts, notably the monumental collection of western and eastern sources published as the *Recueil des historiens des croisades* (1841–1906). The purpose was explicitly nationalist: 'France has played such a glorious part in the wars of the crusades that the historical documents that contain the accounts of these memorable expeditions seem to enter her domain.'[9] The focus on the 'colonies chrétiens en

Palestine' was equally deliberate: Spain, the Baltic or the Albigensian crusades were absent. The crusades were harnessed to the chariot of French cultural and political imperialism, Outremer – 'La France du Levant' – studied by French scholars for the next century and more as a precursor to modern colonisation. The tradition of imagining the crusaders as prototype French colonists reached a zenith under the Third Republic (1870–1940),

154. *Gustave Doré's extraordinary 1888 image of angelic support for Louis IX embarking on crusade in 1248.*

155. *The headline of* L'Epoque, *10 June 1945, reads 'France will not renounce its thousand-year influence in the states of the Levant'.*

eager to assert an imperial destiny to distract and unite a fractious, divided political nation. French historians identified supposedly typical 'French' elements in the buildings and social systems of Outremer. The post-First World War French mandates in Syria and Lebanon invited further parallels. Academic arguments for the existence of a Franco-Syrian society in Outremer reflected concurrent French settlement in Algeria as much as anything medieval. Into the twentieth century in France, as elsewhere, the crusades attracted writers of nationalist, conservative, Roman Catholic or right-wing persuasion. It took a Marxist, Claude Cahen, to debunk the westernised approach to Outremer history in his monograph using Arabic as well as western sources, *La Syrie du Nord à l'époque des croisades* (1940).

German Variations

A distinct German tradition in many ways paralleled the French. A definitive German crusades narrative had been provided by Friedrich Wilken (1777–1840), *Geschichte des Kreuzzüge nach morgenländische und abendländische Berichten* (*A History of the Crusade from Eastern and Western Sources*, 7 volumes, 1807–32). Wilken's history, as its title indicated, rested on Arabic as well as western sources, lending his account a neutral air, far removed from Michaud's triumphalist clash of civilisations. However, Wilken's survey implicitly subscribed to the positive materialist interpretation, sustained by the inclusion of the Baltic crusades to which his employer, the kingdom of Prussia, owed its existence. This allowed his history to be mined for a positive German legacy which, in extreme form, became almost as anachronistically nationalist as its French equivalent, the crusading feats of Frederick Barbarossa being harnessed in the creation of a mythic national hero. The crusades were respectably integrated into a German narrative of development, 'an agitation favourable to liberty and progress'. This fitted a wider project of identifying a unifying German spirit in medieval sources, demonstrated in the editing of specifically German texts under the auspices of the *Monumenta Germaniae Historica* (founded in 1818–19).

In parallel, the German academic tradition transformed study of the crusades through forensic critical study of sources (*Quellenkritik*) pioneered by Leopold von Ranke. Building on one of Ranke's insights, his pupil Heinrich von Sybel (1817–95) in his *Geschichte des ersten Kreuzzüges* (*History of the First Crusade*, 1841) placed crusade scholarship on a wholly new footing in using textual analysis to challenge the primacy of the account of the First Crusade by William of Tyre that had largely held sway since the thirteenth century. Von Sybel saw that no text could be taken at face value without interrogating its sources, origins and context. In the process he demolished the intellectual credentials of almost all previous supposed experts on the crusades, being notably harsh on Michaud. Yet while ostensibly setting the crusades free from uncritical histories 'of a purely national or patriotic tendency', von Sybel's work did not release the subject from nationalist appropriation.[10] The identification of a distinctive German dimension within a scheme that saw the crusades as furthering cultural progress towards a destined national unification was not politically neutral. While von Sybel's work led to the forensic scrutiny of texts, it also cast a

156. The ruins of Königsberg Castle, 1944.

legitimising penumbra around wilder nationalist fancies, such as state-sponsored attempts to unearth Barbarossa's remains in Tyre or the excesses of Wilhelm II's much publicised visit to Palestine and Syria in 1898 during which he essayed the remarkable trick of posing both as a neo-crusader and as an admirer of Saladin. Study of the Baltic crusades and the Teutonic Knights sharpened awareness of the roots of German cultural and political imperialism. This fed a strand of aggressive German nationalism that found its most grotesque manifestation in Heinrich Himmler's promotion of SS admiration for the Teutonic Knights. A more positive consequence saw the lengthy nineteenth-century restoration of the former Teutonic Knights' castle at Marienburg/Marlbork. The fate of the other great Teutonic Knights' castle, at Königsberg/Kaliningrad, capital of the Teutonic Order and later of East Prussia, confirmed the powerful symbolism of crusade history. In 1968 the castle ruins, which had survived bombardment by the RAF and the Russians in the Second World War and were now in the centre of Russian Kaliningrad, were blown up on the orders of the Russian leader Leonid Brezhnev.

Popular Fictions

Of greater public impact than scholarship were the recreations of crusades and crusaders provided by a former pupil of William Robertson, the Scottish novelist Walter Scott (1771–1832). In the early nineteenth century, anglophone responses to the world of the crusades were couched in terms of the Protestant scepticism of Fuller, the Enlightenment disdain of Gibbon, and the insular view popular since the beginning of the seventeenth century that the crusades, in the guise of Richard I, represented a diversion from the national mission of reconciling Normans and Saxons to create the united world power of Scott's day. In Scott's novels *Ivanhoe* (1819) and *The Betrothed* (1825) the crusades provide a distant backdrop for the action while *The Talisman* (1825) is set in Palestine during the Third Crusade and *Count Robert of Paris* (1831) at the Byzantine court during the passage of the First Crusade. Scott's crusaders were pre-Michaud and Wilken, more Tasso than Fuller. While the focus of each is on adventure, character, plot and, in the last two, extravagant romantic fantasy, Scott's verdict on the crusades is clearly expressed in his essay on chivalry in the *Encyclopaedia Britannica* (1818 edition). The enterprise was flawed, an expensive, futile, if individually heroic, distraction. While encouraging noble deeds, the worth of Scott's crusades may be assessed in the stiff-necked and morally compromised villains of *Ivanhoe* and *The Talisman*, the Templars. Unlike Michaud, Scott avoids demonising Muslims (or Jews); Saladin is the moral exemplar in *The Talisman*. Scott's historical fiction became wildly popular across Europe, the vivid evocation of setting and character, despite the unreal plots, providing a sort of alternative history, one that inspired artists and musicians even more than Michaud did.

Scott's view that the crusades were not admirable, while crusaders often were, influenced a whole non-Roman Catholic tradition. The emphasis on crusaders' devotion, tenacity and self-sacrifice allowed the crusades to be seen as totems for both neo-colonialists and political reactionaries, nervous about the social and economic forces unleashed by early industrialisation. The crusades occupied a conspicuous place in the nineteenth-century cult of medievalism that emphasised religion, social hierarchy and moral discipline, cherishing an essentially aristocratic and rural lost world in contrast to the commercial, increasingly urban and socially mobile, disruptive realities of the early nineteenth century. Medievalism's glamorous escapism provided a

157. J.A. Atkinson's 1775–1831 depiction of the death of the Templar Brian de Bois-Gilbert in Ivanhoe.

canvas on which reactionaries and reformers alike could sketch their critiques of the moral and social ills of the new industrial world: the political reactionary's selfless idealist knight errant, the social reformer's honest artisan or worker in touch with the process and fruits of production. Escapism it remained. Despite being presented as precursors of colonial expansion, such as the French conquest of Algeria after 1830, there were no serious attempts to revive actual crusades, a few eccentric dreams apart. Even the Hospitallers, exiled from Malta in 1798, abandoned any military role once they were established in Rome after 1834. The crusade's appeal as a symbol of nostalgia in the face of the perceived mercenary tawdriness of material progress attracted romantic reactionaries and social critics, like the young Benjamin Disraeli in *Tancred: The New Crusader* (1847), who affected to be both.[11] For the actual or parvenu aristocrat, the crusades also paid snobbish dividends: to boast a crusading ancestor – real or invented – conferred an aura of distinction both in fiction and in certain social circles into the modern era.[12] For most, the crusades became entertainment, the vogue for medievalism securing their recognition in theatrical re-enactments, operas, paintings and popular novels. Impressionist images, not details, of the crusades remained embedded in popular culture across Europe. Even John Wisden reached for a list of the eight main eastern crusades to pad out his first edition of the *Cricketers' Almanack* of 1864. Such cultural penetration was underpinned by continued analogous use of crusading language in religious settings, such as Christian youth associations or Sabine Baring-Gould's hymn *Onward Christian Soldiers* of 1865 (music by Arthur Sullivan, 1871; Sullivan also composed music for an opera based on *Ivanhoe* in 1891), and in secular application to vigorous campaigning, military or not.

Religion and War

The two elements that most characterised the crusades supplied the trickiest legacies: religion and war. While certain Roman Catholic devotees in Europe and the colonies sought and found inspiration in the crusades,[13] for liberal, Protestant or secular nationalists, colonialists and imperialists the attraction lay in what they imagined the crusade taught of human endeavour, economic development and social progress. Although obviously seen as anti-Islamic, the crusades tended to be placed by nineteenth- and twentieth-century observers in a cultural not religious context. Specifically

158. Statue of Godfrey of Bouillon, Brussels.

religious aspects could be rendered secular – the desire to conquer the Holy Places becoming a form of early colonialism, or merely eccentrically archaic and baffling – such as pilgrimages and relics. Religion cut across nineteenth-century nationalism and vice versa. In the new, religiously divided nation of Belgium, created in 1830, Godfrey de Bouillon could only act as a national symbol, and his statue placed in the Grand Place in Brussels in 1851, by ignoring the religious specifics of his crusading. The emphasis fell on crusaders' 'spirit', not their spirituality. Crusading also provided rhetorical cover for racist imperialism: the Belgian conquest and exploitation of central Africa was described as a crusade by its instigators.

The violence of crusader warfare was discreetly transmuted into adventure stories of heroism and suffering, with little empathy for the victims, similar to how colonial wars were reported in home countries. When war came to western Europe, crusade analogies were paraded but soon exposed as threadbare. During the Crimean War (1854–6), fought in part over control of the Holy Places, crusader parallels fell foul of the inconvenience that the

western 'crusading' powers were in alliance with the Ottomans against
Christian Russians. Both the First and Second World Wars drew excited
comparisons with crusades, as sacred national causes, or contests with
barbarians, generalised right versus specific, secular evil (as in Dwight D.
Eisenhower's war memoirs, *Crusade in Europe*), not as specifically religious
conflicts even if God was an early recruit. The chivalric overtones in sentimental enthusiasm for the First World War choked in the blood and mud of
Flanders and Gallipoli. The only modern war that adopted the crusade as a
clear religious parallel was General Franco's revolt and successful civil war
in Spain (1936–9), which to the Fascists was a *cruzada española*. By comparison, the use of the crusade as a motif by Franco's republican and commu-
nists opponents, 'crusaders for freedom', while ideological, was wholly
secular, a crusade by literary analogy not emotional emulation. In the 1960s,
faced with the neo-crusading ideology of South American Liberation

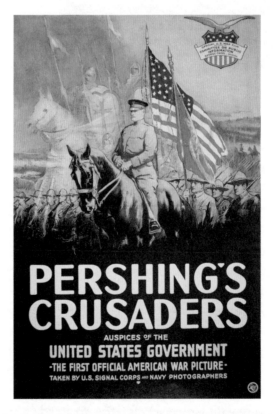

*159. Continuing parallels: 'Pershings Crusaders', a poster for an official US First
World War film.*

theology that urged the faithful to fight social and political oppression as a religious duty, the Roman Catholic church hierarchy declined to endorse it, and not just because it was often in cahoots with the repressive regimes that Liberation Theology was designed to challenge. To those historically alert, the notion of holy war no longer appeared attractive.

New Lamps for Old

With the withdrawal from empire after 1945, French politicised academic interest in the crusades slackened, and the French model of an integrated Outremer society was systematically dismantled, contradicted by the primary evidence of a social structure harshly stratified on religious, racial and cultural grounds, and by closer scrutiny of other theatres of crusading and the crusaders' own inspirations. Yet critics of the French model were no less politically engaged. The Israeli historian Joshua Prawer (1917–90), the leading post-1945 scholar of Outremer, in pointedly describing society in the kingdom of Jerusalem as characterised by a system of 'apartheid', was keen to establish how the Zionist settlement in Israel differed fundamentally from that of the crusaders in depth and permanence of occupation, while also asserting the impossibility of social and cultural merging of settler and indigenous communities. Prawer's crusaders became part of continuing debates over the nature of modern Zionism.[14] More broadly, the mid-twentieth-century intellectual as well as political retreat from western imperialism changed how historians examined the nature of the crusaders' conquests and their cultural and economic impact, in the Levant and in the Baltic, eroding the idea of the crusades as instrumental in a 'rise of Europe'.

If changing geopolitics refocused views on the material consequences of the crusades, they also stimulated a renewed interest in their ideology. In 1935, Carl Erdmann (1989–1945), a German scholar of medieval political ideas and an expert on eleventh-century papal correspondence, published *Die Entstehung des Kreuzzugsgedankens* (*The Origins of the Idea of Crusading*), the single most original monograph on the crusades in the twentieth century. This tackled the central issue of the alliance of religion with war and the background to its application by Urban II. The crusades are placed in the long perspective of Christian acceptance of the military values of the ruling elites. Erdmann's exploration of the parallel impulses of official church policy and popular knightly mores set the crusades firmly within the general orbit of European culture. By exploring the pathology of early medieval Church-sanctioned public violence, Erdmann, while far from offering a direct critique of the militarism of German National Socialism, addressed a subject of obvious contemporary and not just German relevance: the communal mobilisation of violence in support of ideologies, religious or secular. His unsentimental approach to church history and ecclesiastical leaders was matched by coolness towards the whole concept of holy war and crusading, more informed by the experience of the popular militarism of the Second Reich before the First World War than the immediate challenge of the Nazis. Erdmann took the intellectual and psychological forces behind crusade ideology seriously on their own terms not as a disguise for something else – fanaticism, adventurism, greed, hysteria or escapism. In rejecting the crude material and economic reductionism of the previous Franco-German model, Erdmann restored the crusades as an aspect of internal European culture and as a religious enterprise.

Erdmann was not alone in rebalancing of crusader studies in sympathy with the twentieth-century experience of ideological conflict and popular political movements. However, some historians still clung to the old idea that religion was a cover, one prominent American crusade expert suggesting that to argue for the religious cause of the crusade was 'like accepting the statements of *Pravda* that the USSR is only altruistically interested in establishing "truly democratic peoples' governments"'.[15] This was written in 1948, in the early years of the Cold War. However, other scholars in the 1930s and 1940s, especially in France, followed the same path as Erdmann, studying crusading mentalities, rhetoric, liturgy, art, canon law, popular religion, mass psychology and the means of transmitting church doctrine to the laity.[16] This tradition of treating the religious motivations of lay crusaders seriously and framing the crusade within medieval developments in doctrine and canon law underpinned much of the anglophone recrudescence of crusade scholarship in the later twentieth century. This religious turn coincided with similar approaches adopted by scholars of Arabic and Hebrew sources, shadowed by the rise of new militant Islamism in the Near East and the Christian religious Right in the United States, Europe and Russia.

Twentieth-century academic reassessment of the crusades may have suited the times, but it exerted limited public impact. The popular image of the crusade, in the west as across Islamic Asia and Africa, remained stubbornly traditional: undefined fanaticism, avaricious motives, brutal and mercenary conquests. The whole enterprise was assigned to an inferior past world of irrationality, almost in disregard of the brutality of the twentieth century. The crusaders still stood, as they did for Walter Scott, as energetic barbarians blundering with varying degrees of sincerity into the sophisticated Orient (itself a crude unhistorical Orientalist construct), a brute example of culture wars. This view received apparently scholarly affirmation in Steven Runciman's *History of the Crusades* (1951–4), by far the most read and socially cited work on the crusades of the twentieth century, the most popular study since Michaud's *Histoire* with which it shares not a few characteristics: moral certainty, literary imagination and historical invention.

Runciman, a Byzantinist and scholar of the medieval Balkans, relied heavily for his epic narrative on secondary sources for his factual structure, ideas and details, especially French scholarship of the 1920s and 1930s, to which he added an inimitable stylish gloss. He expanded the traditionally hostile view of the crusaders as barbaric disrupters of the sophisticated Muslim Levant to include Byzantium, promoting the crusades as a central feature of Byzantine history. By undermining the eastern Christian empire, the crusaders' misplaced zeal betrayed the allies they had initially come to assist and so – in terms familiar to previous writers as far back as Knolles and Fuller – allowed the Ottoman conquest of eastern Europe, a circumstance Runciman instinctively assumed to be deplorable. However, Runciman reached beyond the crusades in a threnody for a lost world of reason, twentieth century no less than medieval. The crusades bore witness to the eternal dangers of unbridled ideological passion pitted against civility. This was not an attack on religion but on cultural philistines, demagogues and self-righteous, intolerant followers of totalitarian systems of belief, religious or secular – by implication nationalism, communism, fascism or capitalism. Like Gibbon, he lamented the damage caused by untempered enthusiasm. Like Walter Scott, whose novelist's skill he shared in creating believable scenes of action, Runciman saw little admirable in the crusades except individual courage and endeavour. From a vertiginous pose of confident intellectual eminence, Runciman passed timeless adamantine judgements, none more so than his famous condemnation of the crusaders' sack of Constantinople in 1204: 'there never was a greater crime against humanity than the Fourth Crusade', a verdict delivered in 1954, just years after the principle of crimes against humanity had first been defined and internationally accepted in the aftermath of the atrocities of the Third Reich, Japanese imperialism, the

Holocaust and the Second World War. The immediate contemporary resonance was deliberate: in Runciman's memoirs of 1991, 'crime' had changed to
'tragedy'.[17]

Modern Politics

Runciman's *History of the Crusades* sustained a familiar attitude to the
crusades (and the Middle Ages in general) as irrational and materialist,
destroyers of the superior and peaceful worlds of Byantium and Islam,
impressive but essentially shameful. While this opinion may be of only
cocktail-party interest in western countries, it becomes more significant
when exported to the political arena. Modern responses to the crusades can
retain a presentist political tinge, implied or deliberate. In First World discussion, while the neo-colonial view still persists, the rise of Christian fundamentalism of various hues has encouraged a rejection of the materialist
interpretation of crusader aggression and Muslim victimhood in favour of
an insistence that the crusades were a legitimate defence against Islamic invasions, even part of a supposed age-old clash of civilisations. Such a Manichean

160. Saladin as modern Arab hero: President Hafez al-Assad's statue of him in Damascus.

view is mirrored in parts of the Islamic world. General cultural responses to the crusades which, over the centuries, have proved as local, varied, complicated and shifting as those in the west, have been lent a sharp modern edge through propagandist exploitation by two distinct Near Eastern groups: secularist regimes eager to wrap themselves in the legitimising robe of pan-Arab champions (Saladin was a public hero alike for Presidents Gamal Abdel Nasser of Egypt, Saddam Hussein of Iraq and Hafez al-Assad of Syria); and their domestic, especially Islamist opponents (such as the Muslim Brotherhood or al-Qaeda), who use the continued western incursions into the region as standing condemnation of the existing status quo.

This use of the memory of the crusades to assert Muslim unity and identity, while offering a critique of existing rulers, echoes some of the oldest traditions of Near Eastern reactions to the historical crusades. Each generation writes its own version of the crusades to suit contemporary interests. As in the west, there has never been a uniform 'Muslim' view of the crusades. Historically, Near Eastern Muslim responses have displayed flexibility on a spectrum including twelfth-century Palestinian, Syrian and Lebanese refugees; time-serving *jihad*-promoting apologists of Zengid, Ayyubid or Mamluk rulers; critics of supposedly supine Islamic governments; promoters of ideal Koranic rule; and writers who regarded the Franks as little different to other invaders of the *dar al-Islam* and who expressed little concern, especially after the final expulsion of the Franks from the Levant mainland in 1291. These diverse views were held concurrently as well as sequentially, with perspectives inevitably differing in Iraq, Syria or Egypt. Whilst heroes such as Nur al-Din, Saladin and Baibars entered street folklore across the eastern Mediterranean into the early modern period and beyond, the ultimate victory over the crusaders, the long rule of the Mamluks and Ottomans, and the absence of aggressive western intervention in the region until Napoleon in 1798–9, consigned the crusades to popular memory and antiquarian footnote. Until the late nineteenth century, there was not even a specific Arabic word for the crusades. Even then, the need for one (e.g. *al-hurūb al-Ṣalibiyya*, the cross wars, or *harb al-Ṣalib*, the war of the cross) was generated by Ottoman and Egyptian writers drawing parallels between current western European colonialism and the crusades. Ironically, the idea of the crusades as a colonial adventure was encouraged by a direct import from the west, for example the translation of Michaud's *Histoire des croisades* into Turkish (1866–7). Thus the west's own vulgar politicisation of the

161. Saladin enters Jerusalem in 1187: a modern Egyptian image.

crusades spawned a toxic legacy made more virulent with the shameless French assertion of historic claims to mandates in Syria and Lebanon at the Versailles Peace Conference in 1919.

As a strand in modern polemic, the crusades possess obvious attractions for those in the Near East wishing to portray themselves as victims of western aggression. Hence the dismay in Europe (although not so obviously in the United States) at George W. Bush's ill-judged use of the term in describing his 'war on terror' as 'this crusade' (17 September 2001), shortly after 9/11. The crusades and hostility to the State of Israel, with its apparent geographic and demographic parallels with the European settlement of the medieval kingdom of Jerusalem, have been harnessed by groups such as al-Qaeda, the Muslim Brotherhood and ISIS in the shorthand of 'crusaders and Zionists', a historical oxymoron. Yet studies of how the crusades are portrayed in school textbooks suggest subtler distinctions, with a range of attitudes from balanced historicism (e.g. in Lebanon) to Manichean confrontation and Muslim supremacism (e.g. in Egypt and Saudi Arabia). With Israelis also reassessing attitudes to the crusading Franks in the context of inherited space and shared antagonists, across the region images of the crusades continue to resonate and divide, even as Arabic scholarship establishes distinctive academic credentials.[18] Western historians' focus on the crusades' origins, ideals, motives and organisation scarcely helps to obscure the perception of the political and territorial reality of the original invasion of the eastern Mediterranean.

The Near East is not the only crusade frontier of contested memories. The Spanish crusades had been folded into the *reconquista* mythology of national identity and power, a vibrant symbol of the union of Church and State that long excluded the past dispossessed (Jews and Moriscos) and modern dissidents (socialists and democrats), especially under the Franco regime. In the Baltic the legacy was harder to accommodate. The Teutonic Knights had created Prussia, until its abolition in 1945 a major cultural as well as political constituent of German nationalism. In 1701, Frederick I, the first king of Prussia, was crowned at the Teutonic Knights' Königsberg Castle. Further east, in the less Germanised former Teutonic Knights' state of Livonia (Latvia and Estonia), shifting political regimes – German, Swedish, Russian – determined how the crusaders were perceived: civilising Christian liberators or confiscating tyrannical invaders who destroyed the primary freedoms and culture of the indigenous people. The interpretation of the crusades played out between alternate sympathy for the Germans as modernisers, Russians as allies against the German yoke, or a nascent local nationalism. Since the end of the Cold War, Scandinavian and Baltic medievalists have sought to escape these stereotypes, looking towards links with Europe beyond the awkward Russo-German duopoly.[19] The crusades have provided a means to achieve this, by associating the far north with developments and policies derived from and pursued by interests at the heart of medieval European Christendom, in its way a mirror to the region's increasing ties with the rest of Europe through NATO and the European Union. However, this approach in turn runs the risk of concentrating on the dynamic of invasion (which is where the written sources come from) in a teleology of conquest and integration. Recent archaeology has raised questions of the nature, wealth and complexity of the silent conquered communities, research that accidentally or not accords with the post-Cold War and newly independent eastern Baltic. Thus in Estonia as in Egypt and across the globe, the crusades, as for centuries past, remain contemporary.

DO THE CRUSADES MATTER?

The crusades offer features to fascinate and disturb modern audiences. Surviving evidence – literary, archival, archaeological, visual and material – allows access in some detail to individual experiences as well as large movements, to perpetrators but also to opponents and victims. Much of the western historical record of the Levant crusades presents a rare instance of history written by losers. The physical legacy is extensive. The drama of events involving armed conflict across vast geographic distances and sharp cultural, communal and faith boundaries, together with the claims made at the time and later about their significance, have made study of the crusades highly sensitive to intellectual, cultural or political fashion. Each generation writes its own crusades, so current western scholarship now pays attention to memory, memorialisation, inter-faith and cross-cultural community relations, race, popular religious belief, identity and gender, as previous observers concentrated on politics, war, cultural supremacy, colonialism or religious value judgement. For many modern audiences the essential strangeness of the phenomenon still intrigues.

The crusades disturbed patterns of life in startling and bewildering ways, for those who experienced them as much as for later observers. The earnest violence and disruption of long-distance campaigns mirrored the emotional and ideological force of the driving ideals. While crusading shared psychologies with other wars for perceived good causes, it depended on an especially stark legitimacy. 'God wills it!' is not only unprovable; it is also unanswerable, free from customary social or legal considerations and constraints, or even the discipline of failure. Behind its theological, liturgical and canonical trappings, crusading displayed a bleak binary model of human belief and behaviour. Its strenuous self-righteousness enshrined a formal intolerance and rejection of empathy, a devotional observance that shackled crusaders to performing a series of expiatory acts with no final resolution except in the unknowable fate of individual souls or the collective providence of the Apocalypse and Last Judgement. That many crusaders saw themselves as acting out of charity for their faith and fellow Christians in a willing sacrifice of self-interest for a higher transcendent purpose adds to the fascination. To attempt empathy with crusaders is not to approve or disapprove but to accept an imaginative challenge, to recognise the existence of very different, possibly rebarbative systems of social values. To these, the material witness bears direct witness.

How important were the crusades to medieval contemporaries? Active participation in crusading was always a minority activity, appealing to different sections of society in different ways in different places and at different times, or even differently to the same groups in the same places and at the same time. There were always voices in the crowds decrying the crusade as there were devotees profoundly moved by it. Established as a normative feature of Catholic Christian teaching and observance by the early thirteenth century, taxation, almsgiving, liturgical performances and vow redemptions lent crusading wide social and imaginative presence. Increasingly, dissemination of crusading stories and images across artistic genres and social borders created its own atmosphere, inseparable from the air men breathed.[1] Among certain royal and noble families and in certain cities, traditions of involvement became entrenched, producing generations of recruits and particular habits of ecclesiastical patronage. For centuries, western European diplomacy rang with calls and commitments to aid the Holy Land, fight the Moors, combat heresy or resist the Ottomans. For the ruling elites, and for those aspiring to join them, the Jerusalem war of 1096–9 provided a new, precise and lasting model of respectable violence, religious obedience and chivalric glamour. However, the crusades were far from all-consuming. They reflected as much as formed concurrent mentalities. The traction of crusading among the majority, serving populations can chiefly be surmised only through the testimony of their social masters. Only occasionally, as during the Third Crusade, did crusading exert more than a temporary or marginal effect on major diplomacy or domestic politics. Success on crusade could enhance fame and reputation, but these could be, and were, won in many other settings. For much of the time, even for enthusiasts, the crusade, lit by a glorious past, always remained for the future, the next thing to be done, or the one after that. Away from the campaigns themselves, crusading added a tone and a flavour to Christian culture, politics and society in western Europe, not a determining causal principle.

Nonetheless, the wars and conquests in the guise of the crusades helped shape the political map of Europe, from the Iberian Peninsula to north-eastern Germany and the eastern Baltic. They remain flecked across cultural memories in Scandinavia (as in the myth of the Dannebrog, the flag of Denmark), regions of eastern Europe and the Balkans. They provide national heroes (and villains) in France, Germany, Italy (notably in Venice) and England. For certain zealots, the crusades present a relevant model of religious conflict. For others, the crusades prove the alien quality of the past: impenetrable, irrational, inferior and conveniently distant. The Roman Catholic Church has even taken steps towards apologising for the effects of the crusades. Ironically, outside polemics, in the Levant, imposing ruins apart, only the Maronite Christian Church of Lebanon, officially united with the papacy since 1181, survives as a significant living heir of the crusading era. Besides physical remains and a few place-name elements (e.g. Qala 'at Sanjil in Tripoli – castle of St Gilles', i.e. Raymond of St Gilles who built a fort on the site in 1103), in Syria and Palestine the crusades have only left shadows and contested memories.

Yet the crusades still claim attention, not as precursors to modern political or religious conflict nor yet as David Hume's 'most signal and most durable monument of human folly that has yet appeared in any age or nation'.[2] They deserve consideration for their own sake, as prominent features of half a millennium of European and Mediterranean history, as witnesses to the present's complex and conflicted relationship with the past, and as testimony to the challenges and contradictions of the human experience. Some of the material evidence illustrated here invites direct historical contemplation and contact with a past on its own terms, not ours. The crusades occupied a real world that it is too easy to claim we have lost. Much remains; much still to be examined and disputed. This is as it should be. It is called history.

CHRONOLOGY

c. 400	Augustine of Hippo outlines a Christian theory of just war
638	Jerusalem is captured by the Arabs under Caliph Umar
800	Charlemagne the Frank is crowned Roman Emperor of the West
9th century	Holy wars proclaimed against Muslim invaders of Italy
11th century	Peace and Truce of God movements in parts of France mobilise arms bearers to protect the Church
1053	Leo IX offers remission of sins to his troops fighting the Normans of southern Italy
1050s–1070s	Seljuk Turks invade Near East; occupy Syria and Palestine; become sultans in control of caliph of Baghdad
1071	Seljuk Turks defeat Byzantines at Manzikert; they overrun Asia Minor and establish a capital at Nicaea
1074	Pope Gregory VII proposes a campaign from the west to help Byzantium against the Turks and to liberate the Holy Sepulchre
1095	Byzantine appeal to Pope Urban II for military aid against the Turks; Urban II's preaching tour of France (ends 1096); Council of Clermont proclaims crusade
1096–9	First Crusade; Rhineland massacres of Jews (1096); Peasants' Crusade (1096); capture of Nicaea (1097); Edessa and Antioch (1098); Jerusalem (15 July 1099)
1101 onwards	Smaller crusades to Holy Land
1104	Acre captured
1108–9	Crusade of Bohemund of Taranto against Byzantium; defeated in the Balkans
1109	Tripoli captured
c. 1113	Order of the Hospital of St John in Jerusalem recognised; beginning to be militarised by *c.* 1130
1114 onwards	Crusades in Spain
1119	Defeat of Antioch at battle of Field of Blood
1120	Order of the Temple founded in Jerusalem to protect pilgrims
1123	First Lateran Council extends Jerusalem privileges to Spanish crusades
1122–5	Venetian Crusade; Tyre captured (1124)
1129	Crusade to Damascus
1135	Jerusalem privileges extended to war against papal enemies in Italy
1144	Edessa captured by Zengi of Aleppo
1145–9	Second Crusade; preaching of St Bernard (1146–7); Rhineland massacres of Jews (1146–7); Louis VII and France and Conrad III of Germany go on crusade (1147–8); Saxon crusaders campaign in southern Baltic (1147); crusaders help capture Lisbon en route to Holy Land (1147); failure of siege of Damascus (1148)

1149	Battle of Inab; Antioch defeat; Nur al-Din of Aleppo, Zengi's son, begins unification of Syria
1154	Nur al-Din of Aleppo captures Damascus in process of unifying Syria
1163–9	Franks of Jerusalem contest control of Egypt with Nur al-Din's mercenary commander Shirkuh; Shirkuh wins
1169	Saladin succeeds Shirkuh as ruler of Egypt
1171	Saladin abolishes the Fatimid caliphate of Egypt, which returns to nominal allegiance of Abbasid caliph of Baghdad
1174	Death of Nur al-Din; Saladin begins to unify Syria with Egypt (Damascus 1174; Aleppo 1183; Mosul 1186)
1177	Saladin defeated at Montgisard
1179	Saladin captures Jacob's Ford
1187	Battle of Hattin; Saladin destroys army of kingdom of Jerusalem; Jerusalem falls to Saladin
1188–92	Third Crusade: Saladin Tithe (1188); siege of Acre (1189–91); Frederick I of Germany leads land army (1189); defeats Turks in Asia Minor but drowns in River Saleph (1190); crusade of Richard I of England (1190–2) and Philip II of France (1190–1); capture of Cyprus (1191); fall of Acre (1191); Saladin defeated at Arsuf (1191) and Jaffa (1192); Richard withdraws from Jerusalem twice (1192); treaty of Jaffa partitions Palestine (September 1192); Jerusalem stays in Muslim hands
1193	Saladin dies
1196–7	German Crusade of Henry VI
1198–1230	Crusades to Livonia in Baltic
1198	Foundation of Teutonic Knights in Acre (the militarisation of German hospital, founded at Acre 1190–1)
1198	Pope Innocent III proclaims Fourth Crusade
1199	Church taxation suggested by Innocent III for the crusade; crusade against Markward of Anweiler in Sicily
1201–4	Fourth Crusade; treaty with Venetians (1201); sack of Zara (1202); diversion to Constantinople (1203); sack of Constantinople (1204)
13th century	Crusades in the Baltic by Teutonic Knights (Prussia), Sword Brothers (Livonia); Danes (Prussia, Livonia, Estonia)and Swedes (Estonia and Finland); crusades against German peasants, Bosnians etc.
1208–29	Albigensian Crusade; sack of Beziers (1209); battle of Muret (1213); death of Simon de Montfort at siege of Toulouse (1218); crusade of Louis VIII of France (1226); treaty of Paris (1229)
1212	Children's Crusade
1212	Almohads defeated by Spanish Christian coalition at Las Navas de Tolosa
1213	Innocent III proclaims Fifth Crusade and extends crusade privileges to those who contribute but do not go on crusade
1215	Fourth Lateran Council authorises regular crusade taxation
1217–21	Fifth Crusade; siege of Damietta (1218–19); Damietta occupied (1219–21)
1228–9	Frederick II of Germany in Holy Land; treaty with Sultan of Egypt restores Jerusalem (1229–44)
1231 onwards	Crusades against the Byzantines to defend western conquests in Greece
1239–41	Crusades to Holy Land of Theobald, count of Champagne and Richard, earl of Cornwall; crusaders defeated at Gaza (1239)
1239–68	Crusades against Hohenstaufen rulers of Germany and Sicily
1242	Teutonic Knights defeated by Alexander Nevsky at Lake Chud
1244	Jerusalem lost to Muslims; Louis IX of France takes the cross
1248–54	First Crusade of Louis IX of France; Damietta occupied (1249–50); battle of Mansourah (1250); Louis in Holy Land (1250–4)
1250	Mamluks take rule in Egypt (to 1517)
1251	First Shepherds' Crusade
1260	Mamluks repulse Mongols at Ain Jalut; Baibars sultan of Egypt (to 1277)

1261	Greeks recover Constantinople
1267	Louis IX takes cross again
1268	Fall of Antioch to Baibars of Egypt
1269	Aragonese crusade to Holy Land
1270	Louis IX's crusade ends at Tunis where he dies
1271–2	Crusade to Holy Land of Lord Edward, later Edward I of England
1272–91	Small expeditions to Holy Land
1282–1302	Wars of the Sicilian Vespers; French crusade to Aragon (1285)
1289	Fall of Tripoli
1291	Fall of Acre to al-Ashraf Khalil of Egypt and evacuation of mainland Outremer
1306–1522	Hospitallers rule island of Rhodes
1307–14	Trial and suppression of Templars
14th century	Papal crusades in Italy; crusading continues against heretics in Italy; Moors in Spain; Lithuanian pagans in Baltic (to 1410)
1309	Popular crusade; Teutonic Knights move headquarters from Venice to Prussia
1320	Second Shepherds' Crusade
1330s onwards	Naval leagues against Turks in Aegean; Smyrna occupied (1344–1402)
1345–7	Crusade of Humbert of Vienne
1350s onwards	Ottoman Turks established in Balkans; soon establish overlordship over Byzantine emperors
1365–6	Crusade of Peter of Cyprus; Alexandria sacked (1365)
1365	Crusade of Count Amadeus of Savoy to Dardanelles
1383	Crusade of Bishop Despenser of Norwich against supporters of Pope Clement VII in Flanders
1390	Christian expedition to Tunisia
1396	Christian expedition under John of Nevers against the Ottomans defeated at Nicopolis on the Danube (September)
15th century	Numerous small crusading forays against the Ottomans in eastern Mediterranean and east/central Europe
1420–71	Crusades against the Hussite heretics in Bohemia
1444	Crusaders defeated at Varna in Bulgaria (November)
1453	Fall of Constantinople to Ottoman Turks under Mehmed II
1456	Belgrade successfully defended from Ottoman Turks with help of crusaders under John of Capistrano
1460–4	Abortive crusade of Pope Pius II
1480	Turks besiege Rhodes; Otranto occupied by Turks (1480–1)
1492	Granada falls to Spanish Monarchs
1499–1503	Venetian-Ottoman war
1513–17	Fifth Lateran Council; crusade still promoted
16th century	More crusade schemes against Turks in Mediterranean and central Europe; Hungary conquered by Suleiman the Magnificent after battle of Mohacs (1526); from 1530s crusades threatened against heretics (i.e. Protestants)
1522	Rhodes falls to Turks
1525	Secularisation of Teutonic Order in Prussia
1529	Turks besiege Vienna
1530–1798	Hospitallers rule Malta
1535	Charles V captures Tunis
1536	Francis I of France allies with Ottomans
1560s–1590s	French Wars of Religion; some Catholics receive crusade privileges
1561–2	Secularisation of Teutonic Order in Livonia
1565	Turks fail to conquer Malta
1571	Holy League wins a naval battle against the Turks at Lepanto; Cyprus falls to Turks
1578	King Sebastian of Portugal defeated and killed at Alcazar on crusade in Morocco
1588	Spanish Armada attracts crusade privileges for the Spanish

1618–48	Thirty Years War; religious war without formal crusading
1669	Crete falls to Turks
1683	Turks besiege Vienna
1684–97	Holy League begins to reconquer Balkans from Turks
1798	Hospitallers surrender Malta to Napoleon Bonaparte
1830	French invasion of Algeria
1854–56	Crimean War; Britain and France ally with Ottomans against Russia
1898	Kaiser Wilhelm II of Germany visits Jerusalem and Damascus
1914–18	First World War; Ottoman Turkey allies with Germany, which encourages proclamation of *jihad* against the Turks' enemies
1917	British under General Allenby take Jerusalem
1919	Versailles Peace Treaty negotiations confirm Mandates for Britain and France in Syria, Palestine, Iraq and the Lebanon
1922	End of the Ottoman Empire
1948	Creation of the State of Israel (defended in wars 1948, 1967, 1973)
1982	Israeli invasion of Lebanon
1990	First Gulf War
2001	al-Qaeda attack on US; President George W. Bush likens conflict with al-Qaeda to crusade
2003	Iraq War
2004 and 2011	Papal apologies for crusade violence
2014	Isis declares new caliphate in Syria and Iraq

RULERS

Papacy

Gregory VII 1173–85
(Anti-pope Clement 1080–1100)
Victor III 1086–7
Urban II 1088–99
Paschal II 1099–1118
Gelasius II 1118–19
Calixtus II 1119–24
Honorius II 1124–30
Innocent II 1130–43
(Anti-pope Anacletus 1130–38)
Celestine II 1143–4
Lucius II 1144–5
Eugenius III 1145–53
Anastasius IV 1153–4
Hadrian IV 1154–9
Alexander III 1159–81
Lucius III 1181–5
Urban III 1185–7
Gregory VIII 1187
Clement III 1187–91
Celestine III 1191–8
Innocent III 1198–1216
Honorius III 1216–27
Gregory IX 1227–41
Celestine IV 1241
Innocent IV 1243–54
Alexander IV 1254–61
Urban IV 1261–4
Clement IV 1265–8
Gregory X 1271–6
Innocent V 1276
Hadrian V 1276
John XXI 1276–7
Nicholas III 1277–80
Martin IV 1281–5

Honorius IV 1285–7
Nicholas IV 1288–92
Celestine V 1294
Boniface VIII 1294–1303
Benedict XI 1303–4
Clement V 1305–14
John XXII 1316–34
Benedict XII 1334–42
Clement VI 1342–52
Innocent VI 1352–62
Urban V 1362–70
Gregory XI 1370–78
Urban VI 1378–89
(Avignon Clement VII 1378–94)
Boniface IX 1389–1404
(Avignon Benedict XIII 1394–1423)
Innocent VII 1404–6
Gregory XII 1406–15
Alexander V 1409–10
John XXIII 1410–15
Martin V 1417–31
Eugenius IV 1431–47
(Anti-pope Felix V 1439–49)
Nicholas V 1447–55
Calixtus III 1455–8
Pius II 1458–64
Paul II 1464–71
Sixtus IV 1471–84
Innocent VIII 1484–92
Alexander VI 1492–1503
Pius III 1503
Julius II 1503–13
Leo X 1513–21
Hadrian VI 1522–3
Clement VII 1523–34

Paul III 1534–49
Julius III 1550–55

Marcellus II 1555
Paul IV 1555–9

Germany
(*denotes also Holy Roman Emperor)

Henry IV* 1056–1106
Henry V* 1106–25
Lothar VII* 1125–37
Conrad III 1138–52
Frederick I* 1152–90
Henry VI* 1190–97
Philip of Swabia 1198–1208
Otto IV* 1198–1214
Frederick II* 1212–50
Conrad IV 1250–54
(Contested rule 1247–73)
Rudolf I 1273–91

Adolf of Nassau 1292–98
Albert I 1298–1308
Henry VII* 1308–13
Louis IV* 1314–47
Charles IV* 1346–78
Wenzel 1378–1400
Rupert 1400–10
Sigismund* 1410–37
Albert II (I of Hungary) 1438–9
Frederick III* 1440–93
Maximilian* 1493–1519
Charles V* 1519–55

Byzantine Empire

Alexius I 1081–1118
John II 1118–43
Manuel I 1143–80
Alexius II 1180–83
Andronicus I 1183–5
Isaac II 1185–95; 1203–4
Alexius III 1195–1203
Alexius IV 1203–4
Nicholas 1204
Alexius V 1204
Latin Empire of Constantinople:
    Baldwin I 1204–5
    Henry 1205–16
    Peter of Courtenay 1217–18

Robert of Courtenay 1221–8
Baldwin II 1228–61
John of Brienne (co-emperor)
    1231–7
Michael VIII 1261–82
Andronicus II 1282–1328
Andronicus III 1328–41
John V 1341–7, 1354–77, 1379–90, 1390–91
John VI 1347–54
Andronicus IV 1376–9
John VII 1390
Manuel II 1391–1425
John Vlll 1425–48
Constantine XI 1448–53

France

Philip I 1060–1108
Louis VI 1108–37
Louis VII 1137–80
Philip II 1180–1223
Louis VIII 1223–6
Louis IX 1226–70
Philip III 1270–85
Philip IV 1285–1314
Louis X 1314–16
John I 1316
Philip V 1316–22

Charles IV 1322–8
Philip VI 1328–50
John II 1350–64
Charles V 1364–80
Charles VI 1380–1422
Charles VII 1422–61
Louis XI 1461–83
Charles VIII 1483–98
Louis XII 1498–1515
Francis I 1515–47

England

William I 1066–87
William II 1087–1100
Henry I 1100–1135
Stephen 1135–54
Henry II 1154–89
Richard I 1189–99
John 1199–1216
Henry III 1216–72
Edward I 1272–1307
Edward II 1307–27
Edward III 1327–77
Richard II 1377–99

Henry IV 1399–1413
Henry V 1413–22
Henry VI 1422–61
Edward IV 1461–70, 1471–83
Henry VI 1470–71
Edward V 1483
Richard III 1483–85
Henry VII 1485–1509
Henry VIII 1509–47
Edward VI 1547–53
Mary I 1553–8
Elizabeth I 1558–1603

Sicily

Roger I 1062–1101
Simon 1101–5
Roger II 1105–54
William I 1154–66
William II 1166–89
Tancred 1189–94
William III 1194
Henry I (VI of Germany) 1194–7
Frederick I (II of Germany) 1197–1250
Conrad I (IV of Germany) 1250–54
Conrad II (Conradin) 1254–8

Manfred 1258–66
Charles I 1266–85 (Naples only 1282–5)
Naples:
Charles II 1285–1309
Robert I 1309–43
Sicily:
Peter I (III of Aragon) 1282–5
James I (II of Aragon) 1285–96
Frederick II 1296–1337
    (these kingdoms continued independ-
    ent until the sixteenth century)

Castile

Ferdinand I 1036–65
Sancho II 1065–72
Alfonso VI 1072–1109
Urraca 1109–26
Alfonso VII 1126–57
Sancho III 1157–8
Alfonso VIII 1158–1214
Henry I 1214–17
Ferdinand III 1217–52
Alfonso X 1252–84
Sancho IV 1284–95
Ferdinand IV 1295–1312

Alfonso XI 1312–50
Peter I 1350–69
Henry II 1369–79
John I 1379–90
Henry III 1390–1406
John II 1406–54
Henry IV 1454–74
Isabella 1474–1504
Ferdinand V (II of Aragon) 1475–1516
as Spain:
Charles I (V of Germany) 1516–56
Philip II 1556–98

León

Ferdinand I 1037–65
Alfonso VI 1065–1109
    (1109–57 as Castile)
Ferdinand II 1157–88

Alfonso IX 1188–1230
Ferdinand III 1230–52
    (from 1252 as Castile)

Aragon

Sancho I 1063–94
Peter I 1094–1104
Alfonso I 1104–34
Ramiro II 1134–7
Petronilla and Ramon Berenguer 1137–62
Alfonso II 1162–96
Peter II 1196–1213
James I 1213–76
Peter III 1276–85
Alfonso III 1285–91

James II 1291–1327
Alfonso IV 1327–36
Peter III 1336–87
John I 1387–96
Martin I 1396–1410
Ferdinand I 1412–16
Alfonso V 1416–58
John II 1458–79
Ferdinand II 1479–1516
    (from 1516 as Castile/Spain)

Hungary

Ladislas I 1077–95
Coloman 1095–1116
Stephen II 1116–31
Bela II 1131–41
Geza II 1141–62
Stephen III 1162, 1163–72
Stephen IV 1162–3
Bela III 1172–96
Emeric 1196–1204
Ladislas II 1204–5
Andrew II 1205–35
Bela IV 1235–70
Stephen V 1270–72
Ladislas III 1272–90

Andrew III 1290–1301
Wenceslas III 1301–4
Otto of Bavaria 1304–8
Charles Robert 1308–42
Louis I 1342–82
Mary, 1382–6, 1386–7
Charles II 1385–6
Sigismund 1387–1437
Albert I 1438–9
Ladislas IV 1439–44
Ladislas V 1444–57
Matthias Corvinus 1458–90
Ladislas VI 1490–1516
Louis II 1516–26

Ottoman Empire

Osman d. 1326
Orkhan 1326–62
Murad I 1362–89
Bayezid I 1389–1402
(Interregnum civil wars 1403–13)
Mehmed I 1413–21

Murad II 1421–51
Mehmed II 1451–81
Bayezid II 1481–1512
Selim I 1512–20
Suleiman I 1520–66
Selim II 1566–74

Jerusalem

Godfrey of Bouillon 1099–1100
Baldwin I 1100–1118
Baldwin II 1118–31
Fulk 1131–43 and Melisende 1131–52
Baldwin III 1143–63
Amalric 1163–74
Baldwin IV 1174–85
Baldwin V 1185–6
Guy of Lusignan 1186–92; with his
    wife Sybil 1186–90, daughter of
    Amalric

Isabel I 1192–1205; with Conrad I 1192;
    Henry 1192–7; Aimery 1197–1205
Maria 1205–12
John of Brienne 1210–25
Isabel II 1212–28; with Frederick
    (II of Germany) 1225–8
Conrad II (IV of Germany) 1228–54
Conrad III (Conradin) 1254–68
Hugh I (III of Cyprus) 1268–84
John 1284–5
Henry I (II of Cyprus) 1285–1324

RULERS

Antioch

Bohemund 1098–1105
Tancred regent 1101–3, 1105–8; prince
    1108–12
Roger of Salerno 1113–19
Baldwin II of Jerusalem 1119–26, 1130–1
Bohemund II 1126–30
Fulk of Jerusalem 1130–36
Raymond of Poitiers 1136–49

Constance 1149–53, 1161–3
Raynald of Châtillon 1153–61
Bohemund III 1163–1201
Bohemund IV 1201–16, 1219–33
Raymond Roupen 1216–19
Bohemund V 1233–52
Bohemund VI 1252–68

Tripoli

Raymond IV of Toulouse, I of Tripoli 1102–5
William-Jordan 1105–9
Bertrand 1109–12
Pons 1112–37
Raymond II 1137–52

Raymond III 1152–87
Bohemund IV of Antioch 1187–1233
Bohemund V 1233–52
Bohemund VI 1252–75
Bohemund VII 1275–87

Edessa

Baldwin I of Boulogne 1098–1100
Baldwin II of Le Bourcq 1100–18
Joscelin I of Courtenay 1119–31

Joscelin II 1131–50
(Joscelin III titular count 1150–88)

Valois dukes of Burgundy

Philip the Bold 1363–1404
John the Fearless 1404–19

Philip the Good 1419–67
Charles the Rash 1467–77

GLOSSARY

Abbasids	Caliphs of orthodox Sunnis, 750–1258, based in Baghdad
al-Andalus	Muslim Spain
Almohads	Fundamentalist Muslim dynasty and movement originating in early twelfth-century Morocco; created an empire in north Africa and al-Andalus that lasted until the mid-thirteenth century
Almoravids	Fundamentalist Muslim dynasty and movement from Morocco that established an empire in north Africa and al-Andalus between the 1050s and the mid-twelfth century
askars	Groups of professional soldiers in the service of Arab and Turkish rulers
assise	Literally a sitting, its meaning transferring from a meeting of a court to legal processes and then to the actual laws themselves
atabeg	Regent or guardian of Turkish or Mamluk princes
Ayyubids	Family of the Kurdish commander Ayyub, Saladin's father; a dynasty that ruled parts of the Near East from the 1160s
Byzantium	Modern name given to the surviving eastern Roman Empire based in Constantinople; finally extinguished by the Ottoman Turks in the mid-fifteenth century
caliph	Successor to the Prophet Muhammed (d. 632), religious and political leader of Islam, a role contested between different Islamic traditions
canon law	The rules, laws, principles and ordinances governing the Church and the conduct of the faithful, increasingly codified in the twelfth and thirteenth centuries although quiet on the legal theory of crusading
Cathars	A name given by their persecutors to twelfth- and thirteenth-century dualist believers (from the Greek *katharos*, clean or pure); those in Languedoc also called Albigensians
Chalcedonian Christians	Those denominations, including Catholics and Eastern Orthodox, that subscribe to the definition of the Trinity of Father, Son and Holy Ghost agreed at the Council of Chalcedon; other substantial Christian groups in the Near East, such as the Nestorian, Maronite and Jacobite communities, held different views on the nature of the Trinity and the relationship of the human and divine in Jesus
cogs	Round, clinker-built, single square-rigged sailing transport ships, central to Baltic trade and warfare, and increasingly used on crusades to the Levant from the later twelfth century
commune	Formal sworn civil association pooling command, jurisdiction and funds; crusade examples created before and during campaigns
crucesignatus/a	A man or woman who, in recognition of swearing a vow to pursue holy war, has received, been 'signed with', a cross; a crusader

dar al-Islam	The house of Islam; Muslim lands, as opposed to the *dar al-harb*, the house of war, or the *dar al-ahd*, the house of truce
Fatimids	Caliphs of Shia Muslims, 909–1171, based in north Africa, then Egypt
frangopouloi	Western Europeans settled in Byzantium
Franks	A generic term for western settlers in Outremer, *ifranj* in Arabic, sometimes derisively known in western Europe as *poulains*; also the name applied to the early medieval populations of modern France and western Germany
Great Schism	1378–1417 when two then, from 1409, three rival popes were recognised by different groups across western Christendom; crusades were occasionally used in the conflict
Hohenstaufen	German imperial dynasty producing four crusaders, Conrad III, Frederick I Barbarossa, Henry VI and Frederick II; also rulers of Sicily from 1194; target of papal hostility and crusades, 1239–68
Hussites	Followers of the religious ideas of Jan Hus (d. 1415) in Bohemia, a combination of ideological dissent and Czech nationalism; they survived repeated crusades to suppress them
Il-Khans of Persia	Mongol rulers of Iraq and Iran, 1261–1353; until 1323 putative but not actual allies of crusaders against Mamluk Egypt
indulgence	The remission of God's punishment for sin, available to the sinner after confession to a priest and authorised by the pope acting as the successor to St Peter as Christ's vicegerent with the power according to Christ's command in Matthew 16:19 to bind and loose on earth and heaven
jihad	Literally 'struggle' or 'striving' in Arabic; in Islamic tradition denotes either inner spiritual struggle or the external struggle or holy war against infidels and heretics
Khwarazmians	Turkish nomadic freelance mercenaries displaced from the steppes by the Mongols; invaded Outremer in the pay of the sultan of Egypt in 1244, capturing Jerusalem
madrasa	Islamic religious school or college
Mamluks	Slave soldiers, usually steppe Turks; organised into regiments attached to Arab and Turkish rulers, played an increasingly prominent and independent military and hence political role until they usurped rule in Egypt, creating a Mamluk sultanate, 1250–1517
mendicants	Literally beggars; applied to members of the religious Orders founded by Francis of Assisi and Dominic of Osma, the Franciscan and Dominican friars, who were prominent in promoting crusading from the 1220s
Mongols	Asiatic steppe people of Altaic stock, united under Genghis Khan (d. 1227) before forging the largest land empire in history from China to Iraq and southern Russia; renowned for ruthlessness but adept at incorporating conquered people into their armies; in the 1240s their campaigning reached eastern and central Europe but, as non-Muslims, they were sometimes seen as potential allies for crusaders in the Levant against the mutual enemy, Egypt
Moors	Non-Muslim designation of Muslim inhabitants of the western Mediterranean
Mozarabs	Christians living in al-Andalus
mudejars	Muslims living under Christian rule in Spain
Ottomans	Turkish rulers of a small thirteenth-century principality in north-west Asia Minor who from the fourteenth to sixteenth centuries created an empire that stretched from the Danube to the Sahara; based from 1453 at Constantinople/ Istanbul, the Ottoman Empire lasted until 1922
Outremer	The land beyond the sea, the principalities in Syria and Palestine settled by western Europeans after the First Crusade
papal bull	Public letter of the pope (a decree, order, grant of rights or privileges, etc.) authenticated by a lead seal (*bulla*); *bula de cruzada* authorising the sale of indulgences became a regular fiscal feature of Spanish rule into the twentieth century

GLOSSARY

passage	Term used to describe naval activity – civilian, commercial and military – during the twice-yearly windows when the winds and currents allowed for easier sea communication between the western Mediterranean and the Levant; also became used as synonym for sea-borne crusades, either of mass (*passagium generale*) or smaller, professional nature (*passagium particulare*)
penance	In Christian terms, a punishment performed in expiation of sin and demonstration of repentance, customarily imposed by priests after the sinner has confessed to the sin
pilgrimage	Journeys to holy sites; regarded as spiritually beneficial or imposed as a penance; also a metaphor for internal spiritual journeying
portolan	Navigational charts and maps based on compass points and observed distances between ports; in use by the late thirteenth century and probably earlier
reconquista	The name given somewhat tendentiously to the conquest of al-Andalus by Iberian Christian rulers from the late eleventh century
redemption of vows	A system developed from the late twelfth century and perfected between 1213 and 1234 that allowed the faithful to take the cross and fulfil their obligation and enjoy the privileges by redeeming their oath not by participation but through paying money or other material contributions; this developed into the direct sale of remissions and indulgences
Reisen	Raids; short winter and summer Baltic campaigns by the Teutonic Knights against the Lithuanians in the fourteenth century attracting western European recruits
Rumelia	The European territories of the Ottoman Empire, chiefly the Balkans
Seljuks	Nomadic Turks from the Eurasian steppes who invaded and conquered much of the Near East in the eleventh century
Shi'ites	Muslims who believe authority in Islam rightfully descends through the immediate family of Muhammed via his son-in-law Ali (caliph assassinated 661) and his descendants, spiritual leaders called imams, opposed to the authority of Sunni caliphs
sultan	Islamic ruler, beneath the notional authority of the caliph
Sunnis	The majority of Muslims who followed the *sunna* or custom, the accepted sayings and practices of Muhammed, which developed and clarified doctrine and law beyond the Koran
tithes	Taxes on laity and/or clergy for the crusade calculated on a tenth of annual surplus income; most famously used in 1188 in England and France, the so-called Saladin Tithe; from 1215 it became an irregular tax on the Church for the crusade
trebuchet	Effective large-scale throwing machine or catapult in use at sieges by 1200
ulema	Body of specialist Muslim religious and legal scholars
Umayyads	Muslim dynasty of caliphs, 661–750, who later established themselves as rulers of al-Andalus based at Cordoba, 756–1031, proclaiming themselves caliphs in 919
umma	The community of all Muslim people
Zengids	Turkish dynasty related to Imad al-Din Zengi (d. 1146), ruler of Mosul and Aleppo

NOTES

PREFACE

1. Ralph Glaber, *Opera*, ed. J. France (Oxford 1989), pp. 36–7; 61.
2. C. Morris, *The Sepulchre of Christ and the Medieval West* (Oxford 2005); M. Biddle, *The Tomb of Christ* (Stroud 1999).

INTRODUCTION

1. From the only surviving version of the decree of Urban II's Council of Clermont, November 1095, J. and L. Riley-Smith, *The Crusades: Idea and Reality 1095–1274* (London 1981), p. 37; trans. from R. Somerville, *The Councils of Urban II: 1. Decreta Claromontensia* (Amsterdam 1972), p. 74; cf. pp. 108, 124.
2. P. Jackson, 'The Crusade against the Mongols (1241)', *Journal of Ecclesiastical History*, 42 (1991), 1–18, esp. 6–7, 17–18; E. T. Kennan, 'Innocent III, Gregory IX and Political Crusades', *Reform and Authority in the Medieval and Reformation Church*, ed. G. F. Lytle (Washington, DC 1981), pp. 26–9; C. Tyerman, *God's War: A New History of the Crusades* (London 2006), pp. 705 (Baltic) and 904 and nn. 63–5 (anti-crusade crusades).
3. C. Tyerman, *How to Plan a Crusade* (London 2015), pp. 45–50, 204–7; A. Bysted, *The Crusade Indulgence: Spiritual Rewards and the Theology of the Crusades c. 1095–1216* (Leiden 2015); J. Brundage, *Medieval Canon Law and the Crusader* (Madison 1969).
4. M. C. Gaposchkin, *Invisible Weapons: Liturgy and the Making of Crusade Ideology* (Ithaca, NY 2017).
5. J. B. Pitra, *Analecta Novissima* (Paris 1885–8), ii, Sermon XI, pp. 328–31; cf. F. H. Russell, *The Just War in the Midde Ages* (Cambridge 1975), p. 205; in general, G. Constable, 'The Cross of the Crusaders', *Crusaders and Crusading in the Twelfth Century* (Farnham 2008), pp. 45–91.
6. C. Tyerman, *The Invention of the Crusade* (Basingstoke 1998), p. 79 and n. 210 p. 147; idem, *How to Plan a Crusade*, p. 84.
7. Trans. J. and L. Riley-Smith, *The Crusades*, p. 139.
8. *Curia Regis Rolls* (London 1922–), viii, 324; in general Brundage, *Medieval Canon Law*, pp. 159–90.
9. T. Van Cleve, *The Emperor Frederick II of Hohenstaufen* (Oxford 1972), p. 528 and n. 1.
10. C. Tyerman, *England and the Crusades 1095–1588* (Chicago 1988), pp. 111, 185, 414 n. 132; Constable, 'Cross of the Crusaders', p. 90.
11. Tyerman, *The Invention of the Crusade*, pp. 76–83, esp. 82–3; idem, *How to Plan a Crusade*, p. 87.
12. The son of Merot the Jew in 1239, *Recueil des historiens des Gaules et de la France*, ed. M. Bouquet et al. (Paris 1738–1876), xxii, 600.
13. Tyerman, *How to Plan a Crusade*, pp. 150–77.
14. *Chanson de Roland*, ed. J. Dufornet (Paris 1973), v. 1015.

15. N. Morton, *The Field of Blood: The Battle for Aleppo and the Remaking of the Medieval Middle East* (New York 2018)

16. J. Powell, *Anatomy of a Crusade 1213–1221* (Philadelphia 1986), p. 167; John of Tubia, *De Iohanne Rege Ierusalem*, ed. R. Röhricht, *Quinti Belli Sacri Scriptores Minores* (Geneva 1879), p. 139; Tyerman, *How to Plan a Crusade*, pp. 165–7; in general C. Maier, 'The Roles of Women in the Crusade Movement: A Survey', *Journal of Medieval History*, 30 (2004), 61–82.

17. J. Migne, *Patrologia Latina* (Paris 1844–64), 216, col. 1262; cf. Brundage, *Medieval Canon Law*, p. 77.

18. For text, P. G. Schmidt, 'Peregrinatio periculosa: Thomas von Froidmont über die Jerusalem-Fahrten seiner Schwester Margareta', *Kontinuität und Wandel. Lateinische Poesie von Naevius bis Baudelaire. Franco Munari zum 65. Geburtstag*, ed. U. J. Stache et al. (Hildesheim 1986), pp. 461–85; cf. Maier, 'Roles of women', pp. 64–7.

19. Albert of Aachen, *Historia Ierosolimitana*, ed. S. Edgington (Oxford 2007), pp. 126–9; Matthew 10:37–8; Vincent of Prague, *Annales, Monumenta Germaniae Historica. Sciptores*, ed. G. Pertz et al. (Hanover etc. 1826–1934), 17, 663.

20. Brundage, *Medieval Canon Law*, p. 77 and n. 38.

21. Augustine of Hippo, *City of God*, Bk XIX, c. 7; cf. Bk I, c. 21; trans. H. Bettenson (London 1984), pp. 32, 862.

22. E.g. Exodus 32:26; Joshua 6:21; I Samuel 15:3; Psalm 137; II Maccabees 15:27–8.

23. P. Buc, 'Some Thoughts on the Christian Theology of Violence, Medieval and Modern', *Rivista di Storia del Christianismo*, 5 (2008), 9–28; in general C. Tyerman, 'Violence and Holy War in Western Christendom', *The Routledge History of Medieval Christianity 1050–1500*, ed. R. N. Swanson (London 2015), pp. 185–96; Tyerman, *God's War*, pp. 28–57; Russell, *Just War*, pp. 1–39 and *passim*; C. Erdmann, *The Origins of the Idea of the Crusade*, trans. M. W. Baldwin and W. Goffart (Princeton 1977).

24. Bede, *Ecclesiastical History of the English People*, ed. B. Colgrave and R. A. B. Mynors (Oxford 1969), pp. 214–15, 240–3, 251 for the example of Oswald of Northumbria, a new Constantine.

25. R. Bartlett, *Why Can the Dead Do Such Great Things?* (Princeton 2013), pp. 321–4, 378–83.

26. D. Boutet, 'Le sens de mort de Roland dans la literature des XIIe et XIIIe siècles', *Chevalerie et christianisme au XIIe et XIIIe siècles*, ed. M. Aurell (Rennes 2011), pp. 257–69, esp. 264–6.

27. MGH *Epistolarum*, v (Berlin 1898), p. 601, s.a. 853; vii (Berlin 1912), pp. 126–7, no. 150.

28. Trans. J. F. O'Callaghan, *Reconquest and Crusade in Medieval Spain* (Philadelphia 2003), p. 30.

29. *The Register of Pope Gregory VII 1073–1085*, trans. H. E. J. Cowdrey (Oxford 2002), p. 123.

30. *Register of Gregory VII*, p. 380.

31. Guibert of Nogent, *Gesta Dei Per Francos*, RHC Occ., iv, 124.

32. See recent studies by M. C. Gaposchkin, 'Origins and Development of the Pilgrimage and Cross Blessings', *Medieval Studies*, 73 (2011), 261–86; 'The Place of Jerusalem in Western Crusading Rites of Departure', *Catholic Historical Review*, 99 (2013), 1–28; 'From Pilgrimage to Crusade: The Liturgy of Departure 1095–1300', *Speculum*, 88 (2013), 44–91, and her book, *Invisible Weapon: Liturgy and the Making of Crusade Ideology* (Ithaca, NY 2017).

33. Bysted, *The Crusade Indulgence*, esp. chap. 4.

34. *Joinville and Villehardouin. Chronicles of the Crusades*, trans. C. Smith (London 2008), p. 176.

35. *On Cutting his Hair before Going on Crusade, The Penguin Book of Irish Poetry*, ed. P. Crotty (London 2010), pp. 125–6.

36. *Yorkshire Charters*, viii, ed. C. T. Clay (London 1949), pp. 84–5; cf. M. Clanchy, *From Memory to Written Record* (London 1979), pp. 24–5.

37. Tyerman, *The Invention of the Crusades*, pp. 49–55 ('Language').

38. C. Tyerman, 'Paid Crusaders: Money and Incentives on Crusade', idem, *The Practices of Crusading* (Farnham 2013), no. XIV, pp. 1–40.

39. *Recueil des actes de Philippe Auguste*, i, ed. H. F. Delaborde et al. (Paris 1916), no. 286.

40. For examples from a large literature, P. Deschamps, 'Combats de cavalerie et episodes des croisades dans les peintures murales de xiie et du xiiie siècle', *Orientalia Christiana Periodica*, xiiii (1947), 454–74; C. Morris, 'Picturing the Crusades', *The Crusades and their Sources*, ed. J. France et al. (Aldershot 1998), esp. pp. 201–6; J. Munns, 'The Vision of the Cross and the Crusade in England before 1189', *The Crusades and Visual Culture*, ed. E. Lapina et al. (Farnham 2015), pp. 57–73.

41. Ed. H. R. Luard (London 1872–84); for criticism, M. Aurell, *Des chrétiens contres les croisades* (Paris 2013); E. Siberry *Criticism of Crusading 1095–1274* (Oxford 1985); P. Throop, *Criticism of the Crusades* (Amsterdam 1940).

42. Rutebeuf, '*La desputizons dou croisié et dou descroisié, Onze poems concernant la croisade*', ed. J. Bastin and E. Faral (Paris 1946), pp. 84–94.

43. C. Douais, ed., *Documents pour servir à l'histoire de l'Inquisition dans le Languedoc* (Paris 1900), ii, 94.

44. S. Lambert, 'Translation, Citation and Ridicule: Renart the Fox and Crusading in the Vernacular', *Languages of Love and Hate*, ed. S. Lambert and H. Nicholson (Turnhout 2012), pp. 65–84.

45. S. Lambert, 'Playing at Crusading: Cultural Memory and its (Re)creation in Jean Bodel's *Jeu de St Nicholas*', *Journal of Medieval History*, 40 (2014), 361–80.

46. See now L. Paterson, *Singing the Crusades* (Woodbridge 2018).

47. Gerald of Wales, *De principis instructione*, *Opera*, ed. J. S. Brewer et al. (London 1861–91), viii, 207.

I THE MEDITERRANEAN CRISIS AND THE BACKGROUND TO THE FIRST CRUSADE

1. *The Annals of the Saljuk Turks: Selections from al-Kamil fi'l Ta'rikh of Izz al-Din Ibn al-Athir*, trans. D. S. Richards (London 2002), p. 192; *Gesta Francorum*, trans. R. Hill (London 1962), pp. 91–2.

2. In general on structures in the Islamic empire, see J. Berkey, *The Formation of Islam: Religion and Society in the Near East 600–1800* (Cambridge 2003), esp. chaps 18–23.

3. *Nāser-e Khusraw's Book of Travels*, trans. W. M. Thackston (New York 1986), esp. pp. 2–4, 9–10, 13, 21, 35, 37–45, 52 *passim*. On the Near East, very generally, *New Cambridge Medieval History*, 4 vols, ed. D. Luscombe and J. Riley-Smith (Cambridge 2004), vol. II, chaps 22 and 23.

4. See esp. D. Wasserstein, *The Rise and Fall of the Party Kings: Politics and Society in Islamic Spain 1003–1086* (Princeton 1985).

5. For a political overview, M. Angold, *The Byzantine Empire 1025–1204* (London 1984).

6. E.g. *The Damascus Chronicle of the Crusades Extracted and Translated from the Chronicle of Ibn al-Qalānisī*, trans. H. A. R. Gibb (London 1932), pp. 41–4.

7. On climate, R. Ellenblum, *The Collapse of the Eastern Mediterranean: Climate Change and the Decline of the East 950–1072* (Cambridge 2012); on Seljuks, A. C. S. Peacock, *Early Seljuk History: A New Interpretation* (London 2010), and idem, *The Great Seljuk Empire* (Edinburgh 2015), and, briefly, P. M. Cobb, *The Race for Paradise: An Islamic History of the Crusades* (Oxford 2014), pp. 81–4.

8. *Annals of the Saljuk Turks*, p. 139.

9. N. Morton, 'The Saljuq Turks' Conversion to Islam: The Crusading Sources', *Al-Masdaq*, 27 (2015), 109–18; and idem, *The Field of Blood* (New York 2018), pp. 74–7.

10. *Annals of the Saljuk Turks*, p. 23.

11. Usama ibn Munqidh, *Book of Contemplation: Islam and the Crusades*, trans. P. M. Cobb (London 2008), pp. 162–3.

12. On Syria's status, Cobb, *Race for Paradise*, pp. 33–5, and pp. 78–88 for the Seljuk intervention.

13. J. Shepard. 'When Greek Meets Greek', *Byzantine and Modern Greek Studies*, 12 (1988), 185–278.

14. J. Harris, *Byzantium and the Crusades* (London 2003); *Cambridge History of Byzantium*, ed. J. Shepard (Cambridge 2009); P. Lock, *The Franks in the Aegean 1204–1500* (London 1995).

15. For an accessible account, D. Crouch, *The Birth of Nobility* (Harlow 2005).

16. Guibert of Nogent, *Gesta Dei Per Francos*, RHC Occ., iv, 141, trans. R. Levine, *The Deeds of God through the Franks* (Woodbridge 1997), p. 47. In general on planning, C. Tyerman, *How to Plan a Crusade: Reason and Religious War in the High Middle Ages* (London 2015), refs to First Crusade.

17. Guibert of Nogent, *Gesta Dei Per Francos*, RHC Occ., iv, 184; trans. p. 89; on the Byzantine connection, P. Frankopan, *The First Crusade: The Call from the East* (London 2012).

18. Orderic Vitalis, *Ecclesiastical History*, ed. M. Chibnall (Oxford 1969–80), III, pp. 134–6, vol. V, pp. 156–9; in general, C. Tyerman, *God's War: A New History of the Crusades* (London 2006), pp. 81–3, 112–14 and refs.

19. Albert of Aachen, *Historia Ierosolimitana*, ed. S. Edgington (Oxford 2007), pp. 154–5, 160–1, 190–1, 230–3, 476–9.

20. For a summary and refs, J. France, *Victory in the East: A Military History of the First Crusade* (Cambridge 1994), pp. 165–6, 211, 252–4, 302, 304, 317, 325–6, 334, 358, 368.

21. E.g. Anselm of Ribemont to the archbishop of Rheims, Antioch, July 1098, in E. Peters, ed., *The First Crusade* (2nd edn, Philadelphia 1998), pp. 289–91; *Gesta Francorum*, ed. and trans. Hill, pp. 20–1, 66–7.

22. Albert of Aachen, *Historia*, pp. 146–7, 164–5; Raymond of Aguilers, *Historia Francorum qui ceperunt Iherusalem*, *RHC Occ.*, iii, 278; trans. J. H. and L. L. Hill, *The History of the Frankish Conquerors of Jerusalem* (Philadelphia 1968), p. 91.

23. Anna Komnene, *The Alexiad*, trans E. R. A. Sewter and P. Frankopan (London 2003), pp. 115, 183–5, 410.

24. Above, notes 15 and 16; K. Ciggaar, 'Byzantine Marginalia to the Norman Conquest', *Anglo-Norman Studies*, ix (1986), 43–63; J. Shepard, 'The Use of Franks in Eleventh-Century Byzantium', *Anglo-Norman Studies*, xv (1993), 275–305.

25. W. J Aerts, 'The Latin-Greek Wordlist in MS 236 of the Municipal Library of Avranches, fol. 97v', *Anglo-Norman Studies*, ix (1986), 64–9.

26. Ibn Khaldun, *The Muqaddimah: An Introduction to History*, trans. F. Rosenthal (Princeton 1958), vol. II, p. 42.

27. See now R. D. Smith, 'Calamity and Transition: Re-imagining Italian Trade in the Eleventh-Century Mediterranean', *Past and Present*, 228 (2015), 15–56.

28. C. Tyerman, *How to Plan a Crusade: Reason and Religious War in the High Middle Ages* (London 2015), pp. 104–7 and refs; in general, S. Menache, *The Vox Dei: Communication in the Middle Ages* (London 1990); cf. C. Maier, *Preaching the Crusades* (Cambridge 1994), chap. 5.

29. *De expugnatione Lyxbonensi*, trans. C. W. David (New York 1976), pp. 70–1.

30. Aerts, 'The Latin-Greek Wordlist in MS 236', 64–9

31. *Gesta Francorum*, ed. and trans. Hill, pp. 66–7.

32. *The Chronicle of Henry of Livonia*, trans. J. Brundage (New York 2003), p. 53.

33. D. Abulafia, 'Trade and Crusade 1050–1250', *Cultural Convergences in the Crusader Period*, ed. M. Goodich et al. (New York 1995), p. 15, and generally pp. 1–20; on Pisan *bacini*, idem, 'The Pisan *bacini* and the medieval Mediterranean: A historian's viewpoint', *Italy, Sicily and the Mediterranean* (London 1987), no. XIII; K. R. Mathews, 'Other Peoples' Dishes: Islamic *Bacini* on Eleventh-Century Churches in Pisa', *Gesta*, 53 (2014), 5–23; in general, A. Metcalfe and M. Rosser-Owen, 'Forgotten Connections? Medieval Material Culture and Exchange in the Central and Western Mediterranean', *Al-Masdaq*, 25 (2013), esp. 1–8.

34. *The Register of Pope Gregory VII 1073–1085*, trans. H. E. J. Cowdrey (Oxford 2002), pp. 204–5.

2 THE FIRST CRUSADE

1. Trans. J. and L. Riley-Smith, *The Crusades: Idea and Reality, 1095–1274* (London 1981), p. 39.

2. D. Richards, trans., *The Chronicle of Ibn al-Athir for the Crusading Period from* al Kamil fi'l-Ta'rikh (Aldershot 2006), vol. 1, 13.

3. Anna Comnena, *The Alexiad*, trans. E. R. A. Sewter, intro. P. Frankopan (London 2009), pp. 101–3.

4. A. Jotischky, 'The Christians of Jerusalem, the Holy Sepulchre and the Origins of the First Crusade', *Crusades*, 7 (2008), 35–57.

5. A. Becker, *Papst Urban II* (Stuttgart 1964–2012); cf. H. E. J. Cowdrey, 'Pope Urban II's Preaching of the First Crusade', *History*, 55 (1970), and for the general context, C. Morris, *The Papal Monarchy: The Western Church from 1050 to 1250* (Oxford 1989).

6. William of Malmesbury, *Gesta Regum Anglorum*, ed. W. Stubbs, Rolls Series (London 1887–9), vol. II, p. 390.

7. J. P. Migne, *Patrologia Latina* (Paris 1844–64), vol. cli, col. 504.

8. Migne, *Patrologia Latina*, vol. cli, col. 303; generally A. Becker, 'Urbain II, pape de la croisade', in Y. Bellenger and D. Quéruel, eds, *Les champenois et la croisade* (Paris 1989), pp. 9–17.

9. R. Somerville, *The Councils of Urban II, Decreta Claromontensia* (Amsterdam 1972), p. 74 and *passim*.

10. *The Register of Pope Gregory VII 1073–1085*, trans. H. E. J. Cowdrey, p. 128 and generally pp. 122–4, 127–8; cf. Urban II's letters, in J. and L. Riley-Smith, *The Crusades*, pp. 38–40.

11. J. and L. Riley-Smith, *The Crusades*, p. 39.

12. C. Tyerman, *God's War: A New History of the Crusades* (London 2006), pp. 72–3 and refs; for crusaders' letters, see trans. E. Peters, *The First Crusade* (2nd edn, Philadelphia 1998), pp. 284–96.

13. Albert of Aachen, *Historia Ierosolimitana*, ed. and trans. S. Edgington (Oxford 2007), p. 4 and generally pp. 2–45.

14. Jotischky, 'The Christians of Jerusalem', 35–57.

15. Albert of Aachen, *Historia Ierosolimitana*, ed. and trans. Edgington, p. 4 and generally pp. 2–45; for an apparent eyewitness physical description, Guibert of Nogent, *The Deeds of God through the Franks*, trans. R. Levine (Woodbridge 1997), pp. 47–8.

16. E. Blake and C. Morris, 'A Hermit Goes to War', *Studies in Church History*, 22 (1985), 79–107; J. Flori, *Pierre l'ermite et la première croisade* (Paris 1999).

17. Jotischky, 'The Christians of Jerusalem,' 35–57.

18. See now D. Park, *Papal Protection and the Crusader* (Woodbridge 2018).

19. C. Tyerman, *How to Plan a Crusade: Reason and Religious War in the High Middle Ages* (London 2015), pp. 170–7.

20. J. and L. Riley-Smith, *The Crusades*, pp. 44, 52.

21. *Gesta Francorum*, ed. and trans. R. Hill (London 1962), pp. 19–20.

22. Caffaro, *De liberatione civitatum Orientis*, RHC Occ., vol. v, 49.

23. For the example of Rotrou III of Perche, see J. Riley-Smith, *The First Crusaders 1095–1131* (Cambridge 1997), pp. 104–5; K. Thompson, *Power and Border Lordship in Medieval France: The County of Perche 1000–1226* (Woodbridge 2002), pp. 54–85.

24. J. France, *Victory in the East: A Military History of the First Crusade* (Cambridge 1994), p. 142 and generally on numbers, pp. 122–42.

25. Baldric of Bourgueil, *Historia Jerosolimitana*, RHC Occ., iv, 17; C. Tyerman, 'Paid Crusaders', *The Practices of Crusading* (Farnham 2013), no. XIV, pp. 1–40.

26. *Recueil des chartes de l'abbaye de Cluny*, ed. A. Bruel (Paris 1894), vol. V, 51–3, no. 3703; A. V. Murray, 'Money and Logistics in the First Crusade', *Logistics of Warfare in the Age of the Crusades*, ed. J. H. Pryor (Aldershot 2006), pp. 239–41.

27. For the formula *pro anima mea* – for my soul – C. Bouchard, *Sword, Mitre and Cloister* (Ithaca, NY 1987), pp. 241–3.

28. *Chartes originals antérieurs à 1121 conservées en France*, ed. C. Giraud et al. (Nancy and Orléans 2010), no. 3133; Tyerman, *How to Plan a Crusade*, p. 206.

29. P. Frankopan, *The First Crusade: The Call from the East* (London 2012), p. 116.

30. Descriptions in Albert of Aachen, *Historia*, pp. 50–1; R. Chazan, *European Jewry and the First Crusade* (Berkeley and Los Angeles 1987), pp. 223–97, for the earliest Hebrew accounts.

31. H. Hagenmeyer, *Die Kreuzzugsbriefe aus den Jahre 1088–1100* (Innsbruck 1901), pp. 138, 140; Albert of Aachen, *Historia*, pp. 86–7; cf. pp. 72–3; Fulcher of Chartres, *A History of the Expedition to Jerusalem*, trans. F. R. Ryan (Knoxville 1969), pp. 80, 83; Ralph of Caen, *Gesta Tancredi*, trans. B. S. and D. S. Bachrach (Aldershot 2005), pp. 42–3.

32. Chazan, *European Jewry and the First Crusade*; idem, *The Jews of Medieval Western Christendom* (Cambridge 2006); R. Rist, *Popes and Jews 1095–1291* (Oxford 2016).

33. Fulcher of Chartres, *History*, p. 80.

34. Peters, *The First Crusade*, pp. 283–4, for the Patriarch's and crusaders' joint letter to the west, January 1098.

35. Hagenmeyer, *Kreuzzugsbriefe*, p. 149.

36. Matthew of Edessa, *Chronique*, RHC Docs Arméniens, vol. II, p. 41; cf. Albert of Aachen, *Historia*, pp. 316–21.

37. Raymond of Aguilers, *Historia Francorum Qui Ceperunt Iherusalem*, trans. J. H. and L. J. Hill (Philadelphia 1968), p. 80; Albert of Aachen, *Historia*, pp. 384–5.

38. C. Tyerman, '"Principes et Populus": Civil Society and the First Crusade', *Practices of Crusading*, no. XII, pp.1–23.

39. B. Z. Kedar, 'The Jerusalem Massacre of July 1099', *Crusades*, 3 (2004), 15–75.

40. Letter of the crusade leadership to Pope Paschal II, September 1099, trans. Peters, *The First Crusade*, p. 295; *Gesta Francorum*, ed. and trans. Hill, p. 70.
41. Baldric of Bourgueil, *Historia Ierosolimitana*, ed. S. Biddlecombe (Woodbridge 2014), p. 9.
42. Caffaro, *Annali Genovesi*, trans. M. Hall and J. Phillips, *Caffaro, Genoa and the Twelfth Century Crusades* (Farnham 2013), p. 56.
43. C. Tyerman, *How to Plan a Crusade* (London 2015), pp. 140–50 and refs.
44. Ralph of Caen, *Gesta Tancredi*, trans. B. S. and D. S. Bachrach (Aldershot 2005), pp. 145, 152.
45. *Gesta Francorum*, ed. and trans. Hill, pp. 19–20; A. Andrea, 'Deeds of the Bishops of Halberstadt', *Contemporary Sources for the Fourth Crusade* (Leiden 2000), p. 253 and n. 57.
46. D. Queller and T. Madden, *The Fourth Crusade* (Philadelphia 1997), pp. 294–5.
47. B. and G. Delluc, 'Le suaire de Cadouin et son frère: le voile de sainte Anne d'Apt', *Bulletin de la Société Historique et Archéologique de Périgord*, 128 (2001), 607–28.
48. H. Nickel, 'A Crusader's Sword: Concerning the Effigy of Jean d'Alluye', *Metropolitan Museum Journal*, 26 (1991), 123–8.
49. In general, Tyerman, *How to Plan a Crusade*, pp. 140–50, 166, 186, 196, 209, 234, 247–8, 251 and refs; N. Paul, *To Follow in Their Footsteps* (Ithaca, NY 2012), pp. 90–134.
50. In general, Paul, *To Follow in Their Footsteps*; J. Riley-Smith, *The First Crusade and the Idea of Crusading* (London 1986), 'Theological refinement', pp. 135–52.
51. *Chronicon S. Andreae Castro Cameracensii*, ed. L. C.Bethmann, MGH SS, vii (Hanover 1846), pp. 544–5.
52. Tyerman, *God's War*, pp. 156–7.
53. *Historia Peregrinorum*, RHC Occ, vol. III, p. 206.
54. Riley-Smith, *The First Crusaders*, p. 155; Paul, *To Follow in their Footsteps*, pp. 85–6, 106–7; F. Arbellot, 'Les chevaliers limousins à la première croisade', *Bulletin de la Société archéologique et historique de Limousin*, 29 (1881), 37.
55. B and G. Delluc, 'Le suaire de Cadouin et son frère', 607–28.
56. The phrase is that of the English baron Brian FitzCount, *c*. 1143, R. H. C. Davis, 'Henry of Blois and Brian FitzCount', *English Historical Review*, XXV (1910), 301.
57. M. Cecilia Gaposchkin, *Invisible Weapon: Liturgy and the Making of Crusade Ideology* (Ithaca, NY 2017), esp. chaps 4 and 5. Cf. memorial sermons, P. Cole et al., 'Application of Theology to Current Affairs. Memorial Sermons and the dead of Mansourah and on Innocent IV', *Historical Research*, 63 (1990), 227–47.
58. In general, the pioneering N. Paul, *To Follow in Their Footsteps*, and pp. 91–3 for Pompadour.
59. *Chronicles of the Crusades*, ed. C. Smith (London 2008), pp. 346–8.
60. H. Nickel, 'A Crusader's Sword', *Metropolitan Museum Journal*, 26 (1991), 123–8; in general, M. Cassidy-Welch, *Remembering the Crusades and Crusading* (London 2017).

3 'THE LAND BEYOND THE SEA'

1. D. Richards, trans., *The Chronicle of Ibn al-Athir for the Crusading Period from* al Kamil fi'l-Ta'rikh (Aldershot 2006), Part I, pp. 78, 278–9.
2. William of Tyre, *A History of Deeds Done Beyond the Sea*, trans. E. A. Babcock and A. C. Krey (New York 1941; 1976 reprint), vol. I, p. 55.
3. *Willelmi Tyrensis Archiepiscopi Chronicon*, ed. R. B. C. Huygens (Turnhout 1986); cf. P. W. Edbury and J. G. Rowe, *William of Tyre: Historian of the Latin East* (Cambridge 1988).
4. *Libellus de expugnatione Terrae Sanctae per Saladinum*, ed. J. Stevenson (London 1875), p. 218; cf. M. Barber, *The Crusader States* (New Haven and London 2012), p. 299. On settlement, see R. Ellenblum, *Frankish Rural Settlement in the Latin Kingdom of Jerusalem* (Cambridge 1998); cf. J. Prawer, *The Latin Kingdom of Jerusalem* (London 1972); idem, *Crusader Institutions* (Oxford 1980).
5. W. D. Phillips Jr, 'Sugar Production and Trade in the Mediterranean at the Time of the Crusades', *The Meeting of Two Worlds*, ed. V. P. Goss et al. (Kalamazoo 1986), pp. 393–406.
6. William of Tyre, *History*, trans. Babcock and Krey, vol. II, pp. 374–5; Ellenblum, *Frankish Rural Settlement*, pp. 73–94.
7. For a summary and references to sources, C. Tyerman, *God's War: A New History of the Crusades* (London 2006), pp. 219–25; cf. P. Mitchell and A. Millard, 'Approaches to the Study of Migration during the Crusades', *Crusades*, 12 (2013), 1–12.

8. Fulcher of Chartres, *A History of the Expedition to Jerusalem*, trans. F. R. Ryan (Knoxville 1969), p. 271.
9. John of Würzburg in *Jerusalem Pilgrimage*, ed. J. Wilkinson (London 1988), p. 259.
10. Tyerman, *God's War*, pp. 222 and 936, n. 22.
11. On this see now Barber, *Crusader States*, pp. 56–62.
12. William devoted the first eight books of his *History*, out of twenty-two completed taking the narrative up to the early 1180s, to the First Crusade; see Edbury and Rowe, *William of Tyre*.
13. H. E. Mayer, 'Abū 'Alis am Berliner Tiergarten', *Archiv für Diplomatik* (1992), 113–33; *The Travels of Ibn Jubayr*, trans. R. Broadhurst (London 1952), p. 300 and cf. pp. 316–23.
14. Ellenblum, *Frankish Rural Settlement*, p. xviii for map.
15. D. M. Metcalf, *Coinage of the Crusades and the Latin East in the Ashmolean Museum, Oxford* (London 1995), esp. pp. 23, 52–3.
16. E.g. in the conflict between Tancred of Antioch (allied with Aleppo) and Baldwin of Edessa (allied with Mosul) in 1108, according to Ibn al-Athir, *Chronicle*, trans., vol. I, p. 141; cf. N. Morton, *The Field of Blood: The Battle for Aleppo and the Remaking of the Medieval Middle East* (New York 2018).
17. For the 1183 tax, William of Tyre, *History*, trans. Babcock and Krey, vol. ii, pp. 486–9.
18. Metcalf, *Coinage*.
19. *Cartulaire general de l'Ordre des Hospitaliers de Saint-Jean de Jérusalem*, ed. J. Delaville le Roulx (Paris 1894–1905), vol. I, pp. 222–3, no. 309.
20. William of Tyre, *History*, trans. Babcock and Krey, vol. II, pp. 486–9.
21. In general on the circumstances and politics of Outremer, Barber, *Crusader States*; Tyerman, *God's War*, chaps 5–7 and 11; B. Hamilton, *The Leper King and his Heirs* (Cambridge 2000).
22. B. Z. Kedar, 'The Battle of Hattin Revisited', *The Horns of Hattin*, ed. B. Z. Kedar (London 1992), pp. 190–207; J. France, *Hattin* (Oxford 2015); N. Morton, *The Field of Blood* (New York 2018).
23. T. Asbridge, *The Creation of the Principality of Antioch 1098–1130* (Woodbridge 2000), pp. 189–94.
24. J. Riley-Smith, 'Some Lesser Officials in Latin Syria', *English Historical Review*, lxxxvii (1972), 1–26.
25. *Livres des Assises de la Cour des Bourgeois*, chap. 241, RHC Lois (Paris 1843), vol. II, p. 172.
26. A. Boas, *Crusader Archaeology* (London 1999), pp. 77, 84, 87, 102, 113, 118–19, 163–5, 168–70, 174, 178–9, 188, 217, 219, 237; P. Mitchell, *Medicine in the Crusades* (Cambridge 2004), pp. 856, 118–19, 148; R. Kool, 'Coins at Vadum Jacob', *Crusades*, 2 (2002), 73–88; R. Ellenblum, 'Frontier Activities: The Transformation of a Muslim Sacred Site into the Frankish Castle of Vadum Iacob', *Crusades*, I (2003), 83–97.
27. K. J. Lewis, 'Medieval Diglossia: The Diversity of the Latin Christian Encounter with Written and Spoken Arabic in the "Crusader" County of Tripoli', *Al-Masāq*, 27 (2015), 119–52; idem, *The Counts of Tripoli and Lebanon in the Twelfth Century* (Abingdon 2017), pp. 16–17, 150, 214–19.
28. C. Cahen, *La Syrie du Nord* (Paris 1940), pp. 41–2, 343–4, 405, 540; Usama ibn Munqidh, *The Book of Contemplation*, trans. P. M. Cobb (London 2008), p. 110; Tyerman, *God's War*, pp. 224, 229–30; B. Z. Kedar, 'Subjected Muslims of the Frankish Levant', *Muslims under Latin Rule*, ed. J. M. Powell (Princeton 1990), pp. 135–74.
29. Usama, *Book of Contemplation*, p. 147.
30. B. Z. Kedar, 'The Samaritans in the Frankish Period', in idem, *The Franks in the Levant* (Aldershot 1993), chap. XIX, pp. 86–7.
31. William of Tyre, *History*, trans. Babcock and Krey, vol. II, pp. 323–5.
32. C. MacEvitt, *The Crusades and the Christian World of the East: Rough Tolerance* (Philadelphia 2008); cf. in general, B. Hamilton, *The Latin Church in the Crusader States: The Secular Church* (London 1980).
33. R. Röhricht, ed., *Regesta regni Hierosolymitani* (Innsbruck 1893–1904), no. 502.
34. Tyerman, *God's War*, pp. 231–2.
35. A. E. Doustourian, *Armenia and the Crusades: The Chronicle of Matthew of Edessa* (New York and London 1993), pp. 245–57.

36. For a general survey, D. Pringle, 'Architecture in the Latin East', *Oxford Illustrated History of the Crusades*, ed. J. Riley-Smith (Oxford 1995), pp. 160–83; and idem, *Secular Buildings in the Crusader Kingdom of Jerusalem* (Cambridge 2009); A. Boas, *Crusader Archaeology* (London 1999).

37. William of Oldenburg saw it in 1211/12, *Peregrinatores medii aevi quatuor*, ed. J. C. M. Laurent (Leipzig 1864), p. 166 *et seq. passim*, trans. D. Pringle, *Crusades*, 11 (2012); cf. J. Folda, *Crusader Art in the Holy Land* (Cambridge 2005), p. 136.

38. Above notes 12 and 29; Usama, *Book of Contemplation*, p. 43.

39. Metcalf, *Coinage*, esp. pp. 14, 22–3, 40–65; see now A. M. Stahl, 'The Denier Outremer', *The French of Outremer*, ed. L. Morreale and N. Paul (New York 2018), pp. 30–43.

40. Barber, *Crusader States*, p. 204.

41. For wall inscriptions, al-Harawi's memories in *A Lonely Wayfarer's Guide to Pilgrimage*, trans. J. W. Meri (Princeton 2004), pp. 70, 72.

42. William of Tyre, *History*, trans. Babcock and Krey vol. II, pp. 292–3; F. Michaeu, 'Les médecins orientaux au service des princes latins', *Occident et Proche Orient: Contacts scientifiques au temps des croisades*, ed. I. Draelants et al. (Louvain 2000), pp. 95–115; cf. Tyerman, *God's War*, pp. 212–13.

43. B. Kühnel, *Crusader Art of the Twelfth Century* (Berlin 1994), pp. 67–125; J. Folda, *The Art of the Crusaders in the Holy Land 1098–1187* (Cambridge 1995), pp. 137–63; J. Backhouse, 'The Case of Queen Melisende's Psalter', *The Making and Meaning of Illuminated Medieval and Renaissance Manuscripts, Art and Architecture*, ed. S. L'Engle and G. Guest (London 2006), pp. 457–70.

44. C. Burnett, 'Antioch as a Link between Arabic and Latin Culture in the Twelfth and Thirteenth Centuries', *Occident et Proche Orient*, ed. Draelants et al., pp. 1–78 (perhaps slightly over-egged).

45. Lewis, 'Medieval Diglossia', p. 136; Fulcher of Chartres, *Historia*, trans. Ryan, p. 222; William of Tyre, *History*, trans Babcock and Krey, vol. II, p. 294.

46. *Itinerarium Ricardi Regis*, trans. H. Nicholson (Aldershot 1997), pp. 167, 171, 204.

47. *De constructione castri Saphet*, trans. H. Kennedy, *Crusader Castles* (Cambridge 1994), pp. 190–8.

48. Kennedy, *Crusader Castles*; R. Ellenblum, *Crusader Castles and Modern Histories* (Cambridge 2006); D. Pringle, *Secular Buildings in the Crusader Kingdom of Jerusalem* (Cambridge 1997); Boas, *Crusader Archaeology*, pp. 91–120.

49. J. France, 'Warfare in the Mediterranean Region in the Age of the Crusades 1095–1291: A Clash of Contrasts', *The Crusades in the Near East: Cultural Histories*, ed. C. Kostick (London 2011), pp. 9–26.

50. Ralph Niger, *De Re Militari et Triplici Via Peregrinationis Ierosolimitanae*, ed. L. Schmugge (Berlin 1977), pp. 186–7, 193–9.

4 CRUSADES AND THE DEFENCE OF OUTREMER, 1100–1187

1. Fulcher of Chartres, *A History of the Expedition to Jerusalem*, trans. F. R. Ryan (Knoxville 1969), pp. 149–50.

2. Quoted in L. Melve, ' "Even the very laymen are chattering about it": The Politicisation of Public Opinion 800–1200', *Viator*, 44 (2013), 42–3.

3. M. Cecilia Gaposchkin, 'The Echoes of Victory: Liturgical and Para-Liturgical Commemoration of the Capture of Jerusalem in the West', *Journal of Medieval History*, 40 (2014), 237–59, esp. 251–2.

4. C. Tyerman, *God's War: A New History of the Crusades* (London 2006), pp. 170–5.

5. H. E. Mayer, 'Henry II of England and the Holy Land', *English Historical Review*, xcvii (1982), 721–39; C. Tyerman, *England and the Crusades 1095–1588* (Chicago 1988), pp. 46–7, 54–6.

6. Orderic Vitalis, *Ecclesiastical History*, ed. M. Chibnall (London 1969–80), vol. VI, pp. 68–73, 100–4.

7. C. Tyerman, *The Invention of the Crusades* (Basingstoke 1998), pp. 22 and 27; for disparate cross-giving rites, M. C. Gaposchkin, 'The Place of Jerusalem in Western Crusading Rites of Departure (1095–1300)', *Catholic Historical Review*, xcix (2013), 1–28.

8. M. Barber, *The New Knighthood: A History of the Order of the Temple* (Cambridge 1994).

9. Roger of Howden, *Chronica*, ed. W. Stubbs (London 1868–71), vol. II, p. 346; in general, J. Riley-Smith, *The Knights Hospitaller in the Levant*, c. *1070–1309* (Basingstoke 2012).

10. H. Kennedy, *Crusader Castles* (Cambridge 1994), esp. pp. 54–61; for transfer of castles, S. Tibble, *Monarchy and Lordships in the Latin Kingdom of Jerusalem 1099–1291* (Oxford 1989).

11. A. Forey, *The Military Orders from the Twelfth to Fourteenth Centuries* (Basingstoke 1992), for a concise survey.

12. Fulcher of Chartres, *History*, trans. Ryan, pp. 237–45, 255–8, 264–6; cf. William of Tyre, *A History of Deeds Done Beyond the Sea*, trans. E. A. Babcock and A. C. Krey (New York 1941; 1976 reprint), vol. I, pp. 548–56; vol. II, pp. 1–21.

13. Fulcher of Chartres, *History*, trans. Ryan, pp. 238–9, 243–5; cf. William of Tyre, *History*, trans. Babcock and Krey, vol. I, pp. 548–50, and for the siege of Tyre, vol. I, pp. 550–6 and vol. II, pp. 1–21; Tyerman, *God's War*, pp. 265–6 and refs.; Barber, *Crusader States*, pp. 139–41.

14. Cf. J. Riley-Smith, 'The Venetian Crusade of 1122–4', *I Communi Italiani nel Regno Crociato Gerusalemme*, ed. G. Airaldi and B. Kedar (Genoa 1986), pp. 337–50.

15. *Anglo-Saxon Chronicle*, trans. S. I. Tucker, *English Historical Documents*, gen. ed. D. Douglas (London 1955–75), vol. II, p. 195.

16. Michael the Syrian, cited in Barber, *Crusader States*, p. 148.

17. *Chronicle of Ibn al-Qalanisi* in *The Damascus Chronicle of the Crusade*, trans. H. A. R. Gibb (London 1932), p. 196.

18. Trans. Niall Christie, *Muslims and Crusaders: Christianity's Wars in the Middle East 1095–1382, from the Islamic Sources* (London 2014), pp. 133–5, quotation at p. 134; P. Cobb, *The Race for Paradise: An Islamic History of the Crusades* (Oxford 2014), pp. 38–41.

19. *Damascus Chronicle*, trans. Gibb, pp. 200–2.

20. D. Richards, trans., *The Chronicle of Ibn al-Athir for the Crusading Period from* al Kamil fi'l-Ta'rikh (Aldershot 2006), vol. II, p. 320.

21. M. Lyons and D. Jackson, *Saladin: The Politics of Holy War* (Cambridge 1982), pp. 56–7.

22. *Chronicle of Ibn al-Athir*, trans. Richards, vol. I, p. 337.

23. J. Berkey, *The Formation of Islam: Religion and Society in the Near East 600–1800* (Cambridge 2003), pp. 197–8.

24. C. Hillenbrand, *The Crusades: Islamic Perspectives* (Edinburgh 1999), pp. 110–11; cf. idem, '"Abominable Acts": The Career of Zengi', *The Second Crusade*, ed. J. Phillips and M. Hoch (Manchester 2002), pp. 111–32; in general, N. Morton, *Encountering Islam on the First Crusade* (Cambridge 2016).

25. Y. Lev, 'The *jihad* of Nur al-Din', *Jerusalem Studies in Arabic and Islam*, 35 (2008), 275.

26. *Chronicle of Ibn al-Athir*, trans. Richards, vol. II, p. 334; Hillenbrand, *Crusades*, pp. 151–61.

27. Ibn Shaddad's biography is translated by D. S. Richards, *The Rare and Excellent History of Saladin* (Aldershot 2002); S. Mourad and J. Lindsay, *The Intensification and Reorientation of Sunni Jihad Ideology in the Crusader Period* (Leiden 2012), for Ibn Asakir.

28. Berkey, *Formation of Islam*, p. 189.

29. Trans. J. and L. Riley-Smith, *The Crusades: Idea and Reality, 1095–1274* (London 1981), pp. 57–9.

30. Trans. G. Loud, 'Texts and Documents-2 A', *The Crusades: An Encylcopedia*, ed. A. V. Murray (Santa Barbara 2006), p. 1,298 and note 1.

31. Vincent of Prague, *Annales*, MGH, vol. XVII, 663; G. Constable, 'A Further Note on the Conquest of Lisbon in 1147', *The Experience of Crusading*, vol. I, ed. M. Bull et al. (Cambridge 2003), p. 43 and n. 16 for refs.

32. Bernard of Clairvaux, *Letters*, trans. B. S. James (Stroud 1998), nos 391–5.

33. C. Tyerman, *How to Plan a Crusade: Reason and Religious War in the High Middle Ages* (London 2015), p. 112.

34. Otto of Freising, *The Deeds of Fredrick Barbarossa*, trans. C. Mierow (New York 1966), p. 74.

35. Bernard of Clairvaux, *Letters*.

36. Bernard of Clairvaux, *Letters*, no. 394, p. 467.

37. Odo of Deuil, *De profectione Ludovici VII in orientem*, ed. V. Berry (New York 1948), p. 125.

38. Tyerman, *How to Plan a Crusade*, pp. 247–51.

39. *De expugnatione Lyxbonesni*, ed. C. W. David (New York 1976), p. 57 *et passim*.

40. C. Marshall, *Warfare in the Latin East* (Cambridge 1992), pp. 76–7 and n. 134.

41. Tyerman, *How to Plan a Crusade*, pp. 167–70 and refs.

42. William of Tyre, *History*, trans. Babcock and Krey, vol. II, pp. 192–4

43. R.C. Smail, 'Latin Syria and the West, 1146–1187', *Transactions of the Royal Historical Society*, 5th ser. 19 (1969), 1–20; cf. the more positive J. Phillips, *Defenders of the Holy Land: Relations between the Latin East and the West 1119–1187* (Oxford 1996); for a less rosy view, Tyerman, *England and the Crusades*, pp. 36–56.

44. B. Hamilton, *The Leper King and his Heirs* (Cambridge 2000).

45. J. Rubenstein, 'Putting History to Use: Three Crusade Chronicles', *Viator*, 35 (2004), 131–68; *The* Historia Iherosolimitana *of Robert the Monk*, ed. D. Kempf and M. Bull (Woodbridge 2013), pp. xliv–xlvii.

46. *De expugnatione Lyxbonensi*, ed. and trans. David, pp. 26–46 for MS; (new edn and forward by J. Phillips, 2000).

47. H. Livermore, 'The "Conquest of Lisbon" and its Author', *Portuguese Studies*, 6 (1990–1), 1–16; but see the doubts of C. West, 'All in the Same Boat', *East Anglia and the North Sea World*, ed. D. Bates et al. (Woodbridge 2013), pp. 287–300, esp. nn. 16 and 19.

48. *De expugnatione Lyxbonensi*, ed. and trans. David, p. 104 note 'b'.

49. S. Edgington, 'The Lisbon Letter of the Second Crusade', *Historical Research*, 69 (1996), 328–39.

50. *De profectione Ludovici VII in orientem*, ed. and trans. V. Berry (New York 1948), pp. xxxii–xl for MS.

51. B. Schuster, 'The Strange Pilgrimage of Odo of Deuil', *Medieval Concepts of the Past*, ed. G. Althoff et al. (Cambridge 2002), pp. 253–78; J. Phillips, 'Odo of Deuil's *De profectione Ludovici VII in Orientem* as a Source for the Second Crusade', *The Experience of Crusading*, vol. 1, ed. M. Bull et al. (Cambridge 2003), pp. 80–95.

5 THE THIRD CRUSADE AND THE REINVENTION OF CRUSADING, 1187–1198

1. M. Lyons and D. Jackson, *Saladin: The Politics of Holy War* (Cambridge 1982), pp. 280–1.

2. J. Folda, *The Nazareth Capitals and the Crusader Shrine of the Annunciation* (Philadelphia 1986).

3. *Audita Tremendi*, trans. J. and L. Riley-Smith, *The Crusades: Idea and Reality, 1095–1274* (London 1981), p. 64.

4. D. Richards, trans., *The Chronicle of Ibn al-Athir for the Crusading Period from* al Kamil fi'l-Ta'rikh (Aldershot 2006–8), vol. II, p. 323; cf. J. France, *Hattin* (Oxford 2015).

5. Roger of Howden, *Gesta Regis Henrici Secundi*, ed. W. Stubbs (London 1867), vol. I, pp. 341–2; cf. J. Richard, 'The Adventure of John Gale, Knight of Tyre', *The Experience of Crusading*, vol. II, ed. P. Edbury and J. Phillips (Cambridge 2003), pp. 189–95.

6. Y. Harari, 'The Military Role of the Frankish Turcopoles: A Reassessment', *Mediterranean Historical Review*, 12 (1997), 75–116.

7. Ibn al-Athir, *Chronicle*, trans. Richards, vol. II, pp. 337, 351–2, 364; for the Alexandria refugees, 'The Old French Continuation of William of Tyre', trans. P. Edbury, *The Conquest of Jerusalem and the Third Crusade* (Aldershot 1998, pp. 65–6.

8. *Pilgrimages to Jerusalem and the Holy Land, 1187–1291*, ed. and trans. D. Pringle (Farnham 2012), pp. 120–1.

9. *Itinerarium Ricardi Regis*, trans. H. Nicholson (Aldershot, 1997), p. 48 (repeated by a later compiler, p. 142).

10. *Itinerarium*, trans. Nicholson, p. 143.

11. Baha al-Din ibn Shaddad, *The Rare and Excellent History of Saladin*, trans. D. S. Richards (Aldershot 2002), p. 125; Ibn al-Athir, *Chronicle*, trans. Richards, vol. II, p. 363; Henry of Albano, *De peregrinante civitate Dei*, J. P. Migne, *Patrologia Latina* (Paris 1844–64), vol. CCIV, col. 355.

12. J. and L. Riley-Smith, *Crusades*, pp. 64–7.

13. Alan of Lille, quoted by G. Constable, 'The Cross of the Crusaders', *Crusaders and Crusading in the Twelfth Century* (Farnham 2008), pp. 45–91 at p. 90; cf. Roger of Howden, *Gesta Henrici*, ed. Stubbs, vol. II, pp. 26–8, for Bertier of Orléans' poem; C. Tyerman, *God's War: A New History of the Crusades* (London 2006), esp. pp. 379–80, 388–9; J. and L. Riley-Smith, *Crusades*, p. 66. For the liturgy of the cross, see now C. Gaposchkin, *Invisible Weapons: Liturgy and the Making of Crusade Ideology* (Ithaca , NY 2017).

14. Produced in the Bavarian abbey of Schäftlarn, now in the Vatican Library (Bibliotheca Apostolica Vat Lat 2001).
15. Roger of Howden, *Gesta Henrici*, ed. Stubbs, vol. II, p. 32.
16. N. Barrat, 'The English Revenues of Richard I', *English Historical Review*, 116 (2001), 639–41; cf. C. Tyerman, *England and the Crusades* (Chicago 1988), pp. 75–80.
17. C. Tyerman, *How to Plan a Crusade: Reason and Religious War in the High Middle Ages* (London 2015), 'Finance', pp. 181–227.
18. Ambroise, *The Crusade of Richard Lion-Heart*, trans. M. J. Hubert (New York 1976), ll. 67–8, p. 33.
19. R. Chazan, 'Emperor Frederick I, the Third Crusade, and the Jews', *Viator*, 8 (1977), 83–93.
20. Tyerman, *How to Plan a Crusade*, esp. pp. 278–81 and, generally, pp. 231–92.
21. C. Tyerman, 'Paid Crusaders', *The Practices of Crusading* (Farnham 2013), no. XIV; idem, *How to Plan a Crusade*, pp. 182–91.
22. *Itinerarium*, trans. Nicholson, p. 83, cf. p. 22; for a blow-by-blow account of the siege, J. D. Hosler, *The Siege of Acre 1189–91* (London 2018).
23. Richard of Devizes, *Chronicle*, ed. and trans. J. T. Appleby (London 1963), p. 15.
24. Ibn Shaddad, *Saladin*, trans. Richards, p. 145.
25. In general, Tyerman, *How to Plan a Crusade*, pp. 258–64 and refs.
26. John of Joinville, *Life of St Louis*, trans. C. Smith, *Chronicles of the Crusades* (London 2008), p. 187.
27. P. Mitchell, *Medicine in the Crusades* (Cambridge 2004), pp. 1, 66.
28. For archaeological evidence, A. Boas, *Crusader Archaeology* (London 1999), pp. 170–80; D. Nicolle, *Arms and Armour of the Crusading Era 1950–1300* (London 1999); J. France, *Victory in the East* (Cambridge 1994), pp. 26–51, 144–9.
29. *Itinerarium*, trans. Nicholson, p. 74; William of Newburgh, *Historia Rerum Anglicarum*, ed. R. Howlett (London 1889), p. 374; Ibn Shaddad, *Saladin*, trans. Richards, p. 26.
30. Ibn al-Athir, *Chronicle*, trans. Richards, vol. II, pp. 346–7.
31. Ibn Shaddad, *Saladin*, p. 212.
32. Ibn al-Athir, *Chronicle*, trans. Richards, vol. II, p. 392; Al-Harawi, *A Lonely Wayfarer's Guide to Pilgrimage*, trans. J. W. Meri (Princeton 2004), p. 78.
33. Ibn al-Athir, *Chronicle*, trans. Richards, vol. II, p. 397.
34. Trans. W. Lunt, *Papal Revenues in the Middle Ages* (New York 1965), vol. II, pp. 485–7.
35. On the evidence for Celestine's Baltic policy, I. Fonnesberg-Schmidt, *The Popes and the Baltic Crusades 1147–1254* (Leiden 2007), pp. 67–75.
36. See now G. Loud, 'The German Crusade of 1197–1198', *Crusades*, 13 (2014), 143–71.
37. Odo of Deuil, *De profectione Ludovici VII in orientem*, ed. V. Berry (New York 1948), pp. 122–3.
38. Bernard of Clairvaux, *Letters*, trans. B. S. James (London 1998), no. 391.
39. John of Joinville, *Life of St Louis*, trans. C. Smith, *Chronicles of the Crusades* (London 2008), p. 187.
40. Tyerman, *How to Plan a Crusade*, pp. 150–77; idem, 'Who Went on Crusades to the Holy Land?', *Practices of Crusading* (Farnham 2013), chap. XIII.
41. *Itinerarium*, trans. D. Pringle, *Pilgrimage to Jerusalem and the Holy Land 1187–1291* (Farnham 2012), pp. 61–94. The account of the Beirut palace is at pp. 65–6.
42. J. Folda, *Crusader Art in the Holy Land from the Third Crusade to the Fall of Acre* (Cambridge 2005), p. 136.

6 RESHAPING THE EASTERN MEDITERRANEAN

1. Quoted in P. Throop, *Criticism of the Crusades* (Amsterdam 1940), p. 232.
2. For background, A. V. Murray, 'The Place of Egypt in the Military Strategy of the Crusades 1099–1221', *The Fifth Crusade in Context*, ed. E. J. Mylod et al. (London 2017), pp. 117–34; J. H. Pryor, 'The Venetian Fleet for the Fourth Crusade', *The Experience of Crusading*, vol. I, ed. M. Bull and N. Housley (Cambridge 2003), esp. pp. 114–23.
3. D. Richards, trans., *The Chronicle of Ibn al-Athir for the Crusading Period from* al Kamil fi'l-Ta'rikh (Aldershot 2006), vol. I, 13–14.
4. Raymond of Aguilers, *Historia Francorum Qui Ceperunt Iherusalem*, trans. J. H. and L. L. Hill (Philadelphia 1968), p. 115.

5. Innocent III to Archbishop Hubert Walter of Canterbury, *Crusade and Christendom*, ed. and trans. J. Bird et al. (Philadelphia 2013), p. 49.

6. See William of Tyre, *A History of Deeds Done Beyond the Sea*, trans. E. A. Babcock and A. C. Krey (New York 1941; 1976 reprint), vol. II, p. 408.

7. Geoffrey of Villehardouin, *The Conquest of Constantinople*, in *Chronicles of the Crusade*, trans. C. Smith (London 2008), p. 11.

8. For examples, *Crusade and Christendom*, ed. and trans. Bird et al., pp. 37, 40, 149.

9. P. Edbury, *The Conquest of Jerusalem and the Third Crusade: Sources in Translation* (Aldershot 1998), pp. 181–2.

10. On the 1204 raid on Egypt, B. Z. Kedar, 'The Fourth Crusade's Second Front', *Urbs Capta*, ed. A. Laiou (Paris 2005), pp. 89–110.

11. Robert of Clari, *The Conquest of Constantinople*, trans. E. H. McNeal (New York 1976), p. 40.

12. Geoffrey of Villehardouin, *Conquest of Constantinople*, in *Chronicles of the Crusades*, trans. Smith, pp. 16–17.

13. For Fulk of Neuilly, James of Vitry, *Historia Occidentalis*, ed. J. F. Hinnebusch (Freiburg 1972), p. 101.

14. E.g. *Contemporary Sources for the Fourth Crusade*, trans. A. Andrea (Leiden 2000), p. 84, a letter from the crusaders to Otto IV of Germany, August 1203.

15. *Contemporary Sources*, trans. Andrea, pp. 188–9.

16. For a translation of Gunther of Pairis, *Historia Constantinopolitana*, which provides the account of Abbot Martin's preaching, crusade and theft, *The Capture of Constantinople*, ed. and trans, A. J. Andrea (Philadelphia 1997); Gunther's other works include a versification of the First Crusade chronicle by Robert of Rheims, a clear influence along with the works of Bernard of Clairvaux.

17. Peter of Les Vaux-de-Cerney, *The History of the Albigensian Crusade*, trans. W. A. and M. S. Sibly (Woodbridge 1998), p. 58.

18. *Contemporary Sources*, trans. Andrea, p. 48.

19. Niketas Choniates, *Annals*, trans. H. J. Margoulias, *O City of Byzantium* (Detroit 1984), p. 296.

20. The Anonymous of Soissons, *Contemporary Sources*, trans. Andrea, p. 234.

21. Villehardouin, *Conquest*, in *Chronicles of the Crusade*, trans. Smith, pp. 59–60.

22. D. Queller and T. Madden, *The Fourth Crusade* (Philadelphia 1997), pp. 294–5.

23. Gunther of Pairis, *The Capture of Constantinople*, ed. and trans. Andrea, p. 111.

24. Ibn al-Athir, *Chronicle*, trans. Richards, vol. III, 76; Innocent III letter to legate Peter of Capuano, 12 July 1205, *Contemporary Sources*, trans. Andrea, p. 166.

25. B. Z. Kedar, 'The Fourth Crusade's Second Front', *Urbs Capta*, ed. A. Laiou (Paris 2005), pp. 89–110.

26. *Crusade and Christendom*, ed. and trans. Bird et al., pp. 107–12 at p. 110.

27. C. Kohler, 'Documents inédits concernant l'Orient Latin et les croisades', *Revue de l'Orient Latin* (Paris 1893–1911), vol. VII, 1–9.

28. *Narratio quomodo reliquiae martyris Georgii ad nos aquicinensis pervenerunt*, *RHC Occ.*, vol. V, 251.

29. For the Sacro Catino, William of Tyre, *History*, trans. Babcock and Krey, vol. I, 437; in general N. Paul, *To Follow in Their Footsteps* (Ithaca 2012), pp. 79, 99–104, 122–3.

30. The phrase is that of Gunther of Pairis, *Capture of Constantinople*, trans. Andrea, p. 111.

31. Gunther of Pairis, *Capture of Constantinople*, p. 124; 'The Anonymous of Soissons' and 'Deeds of the Bishops of Halbetrstadt', *Contemporary Sources*, trans. Andrea, pp. 235–8, 260–3.

32. P. Riant, *Exuviae sacrae constantinopolitanae* (Geneva 1876–7), vol. I, XCV, XCVII, pp. 127–40.

33. M. Barber, 'The Impact of the Fourth Crusade in the West: The Distribution of Relics after 1204', *Urbs Capta*, ed. A. Laiou (Paris 2005), pp. 325–34; Riant, *Exuviae*, vol. II, pp. 290–304.

34. *Decrees of the Ecumenical Councils*, trans. N. P. Tanner (London and Washington, DC 1990), Lateran IV, canon 62, pp. 263–4.

35. M. Cecilia Gaposchkin, *The Making of St Louis: Kingship, Sanctity and Crusade in the Late Middle Ages* (Ithaca, NY 2010).

36. *The Chronicle of Henry of Livonia*, trans. J. A. Brundage (New York 2003), p. 152; *Song of the Cathar Wars*, trans. J. Shirley (Aldershot 1996), pp. 74–5.

37. G. Dickson, *The Children's Crusade: Medieval History, Modern Mythistory* (Basingstoke 2008).

38. In general, J. M. Powell, *Anatomy of a Crusade 1213–1221* (Philadelphia 1986).

39. Oliver of Paderborn, *Capture of Damietta*, in *Crusade and Christendom*, ed. and trans. Bird et al., pp. 166–7.

40. Dickson, *Children's Crusade*.

41. Trans. in Powell, *Anatomy of a Crusade*, pp. 100–1.

42. C. Tyerman, *England and the Crusades 1095–1588* (Chicago 1988), p. 98 and n. 49.

43. The poet Freidank quoted by T. Van Cleve, *The Emperor Frederick II of Hohenstaufen* (Oxford 1972), p. 217, n. 5.

44. Matthew Paris, *Itinerary from London to Jerusalem*, trans. D. Pringle, *Pilgrimage to Jerusalem and the Holy Land 1187–1291* (Farnham 2012), p. 206.

45. In general, see D. Jacoby, *Studies in the Crusader States and on Venetian Expansion* (Northampton 1989); idem, *Commercial Exchange across the Mediterranean* (Aldershot 2005); idem, 'Silk Economies and Cross-Cultural Artistic Interaction', *Dumbarton Oaks Papers*, 58 (2004), 197–240.

46. T. Vorderstrasse, 'Trade and Textiles from Medieval Antioch', *Al-Masdaq*, 22 (2011), 151–71.

47. D. Pringle, *The Churches of the Crusader Kingdom of Jerusalem*, 3 vols (Cambridge 2009–10).

48. Z. Jacoby, 'Crusader Sculpture in Cairo', *Crusader Art in the Twelfth Century*, ed. J. Folda (Oxford 1982), pp. 121–38; K. R. Mathews, 'Mamluks and Crusaders: Architectural Appropriation and Cultural Encounter in Mamluk Monuments', *Languages of Love and Hate*, ed. S. Lambert et al. (Turnhout 2012), pp. 177–200.

49. D. Pringle, 'Architecture in the Latin East', *Oxford Illustrated History of the Crusades*, ed. J. Riley-Smith (Oxford 1995), pp. 160–83.

50. E. Lapina, ed., *The Crusaders and Visual Culture* (Farnham 2015), p. 63.

51. D. H. Weiss and L. Mahoney, *France and the Holy Land: Frankish Culture and the End of the Crusades* (Baltimore 2004); J. Lowden review of D. Weiss, *Art and Crusade in the Age of Saint Louis* (Cambridge 1998) http://www.history.ac.uk/reviews/review/92; accessed 28 June 2018; R. Abels, 'Cultural Representation of Warfare in the High Middle Ages', *Crusading and Warfare in the Middle Ages*, ed. S. John et al. (Farnham 2014); C. Maier, 'The *bible moralisée* and the Crusades', *The Experience of Crusading*, vol. I, ed. M. Bull et al. (Cambridge 2003), pp. 209–24.

52. J. Folda, *Crusader Art: The Art of the Crusaders in the Holy Land 1099–1291* (Aldershot 2008), and refs there to his earlier works and comments; idem, 'Figurative Arts in Crusader Syria and Palestine 1187–1291, *Dumbarton Oaks Papers*, 58 (2004), 315–31.

53. *Crusade and Christendom*, ed. and trans. Bird et al., pp. 266–98; M. Lower, *The Barons' Crusade* (Philadelphia 2005).

54. Guibert of Nogent, *Gesta Dei Per Francos*, trans. R. Levine, *The Deeds of God through the Franks* (Woodbridge 1997), p. 47.

55. Matthew Paris, *Historia Anglorum*, ed. F. Madden (London 1866–9), vol. III, p. 55.

56. Ralph of Caen, *Gesta Tancredi*, trans. B. S. and D. S. Bachrach (Aldershot 2005), pp. 42–3; for Barzella's will, J. and L. Riley-Smith, *The Crusades: Idea and Reality, 1095–1274* (London 1981), pp. 174–5.

57. M. S. Giuseppi, 'On the Testament of Sir Hugh de Nevill', *Archaeologia*, 56 (1899), 352–4; A.-M. Chazaud, 'Inventaires et comptes de la succession d'Eudes, comte de Nevers', *Mémoires de la Société Nationale des Antiquaires de France* 32, 4th ser., ii (1871), 164–206; cf. J. Folda, *Crusader Art in the Holy Land 1187–1291* (Cambridge 2005), pp. 356–8; J. Gillingham, *Richard I* (New Haven and London 1999), pp. 4, 141.

58. W. C. Jordan, *Louis IX and the Challenge of the Crusade* (Princeton 1979).

59. John of Joinville, *Life of Saint Louis*, in *Chronicles of the Crusades*, trans. Smith, esp. pp. 199–207.

60. John of Joinville, *Life of St Louis*, p. 190.

61. Matthew Paris, *Chronica Majora*, ed. H. R. Luard (London 1872–84), vol. V, p. 107; vol. VI, p. 163.

62. A. Leopold, *How to Recover the Holy Land* (Aldershot 2000).

63. S. Stanchev, *Spiritual Rationality: Papal Embargo as Cultural Practice* (Oxford 2014).

64. Albert of Aachen, *Historia Ierosolimitana*, ed. S. Edgington (Oxford 2007), pp. 142–5.

65. *Itinerarium Ricardi Regis*, trans. H. Nicholson (Aldershot 1997), p. 55.

66. *Itinerarium*, trans. Nicholson, pp. 237, 255.
67. In general, the pioneering study by P. Mitchell, *Medicine in the Crusades* (Cambridge 2004); see also S. Edgington, 'Medical Knowledge of the Crusading Armies', *The Military Orders*, ed. M. Barber (Aldershot 1994), vol. I, pp. 320–6.
68. Hayton (or Hetoum), *La Flor des estoires de la Terre Sainte, Recueil des historiens des croisades, Documents Arméniens* (Paris 1869–1906), vol. II.
69. C. Tyerman, *How to Plan a Crusade: Reason and Religious War in the High Middle Ages* (London 2015), pp. 275–82 and figs 1, 2, 23, 24, 25, 26, 29.
70. Pierre Dubois, *De recuperatione Terrae Sanctae*, trans. W. I. Brandt, *The Recovery of the Holy Land* (New York 1956); in general P. Biller, *The Measure of Multitude* (Oxford 2000).
71. John of Joinville, *Life of St Louis*, pp. 222, 242–3; Tyerman, *How to Plan a Crusade*, pp. 167, 252.

7 CRUSADES IN SPAIN

1. P. M. Holt, *The Age of the Crusades: The Near East from the Eleventh Century to 1517* (London 1986), p. 27.
2. Trans. J. and L. Riley-Smith, *The Crusades: Idea and Reality, 1095–1274* (London 1981), p. 40.
3. D. Wasserstein, *The Rise and Fall of the Party Kings* (Princeton 1985).
4. R. Fletcher, *Moorish Spain* (London 1992), p. 99.
5. R. Fletcher, *The Quest for El Cid* (London 1990).
6. Trans. J. F. O'Callaghan, *Reconquest and Crusade in Medieval Spain* (Philadelphia 2003), pp. 8, 30.
7. *The Register of Pope Gregory VII 1073–1085*, trans. H. E. J. Cowdrey (Oxford 2002), p. 7; cf. pp. 66–9; O'Callaghan, *Reconquest*, p. 29.
8. Bishop Pelayo of Oviedo, *Chronicon regum Legionensium*, trans. S. Barton and R. Fletcher, *The World of El Cid* (Manchester 2000), pp. 87–8 and n. 95.
9. For example, *Historia Compostellana*, ed. E. Falque Rey (Turnhoult 1987); *Chronica Adefonsi Imperatoris*, trans. Barton and Fletcher, *World of El Cid*, pp. 162–263; cf. S. Barton, 'Islam and the West: A View from Twelfth-Century León', *Cross, Crescent, and Conversion*, ed. S. Barton and P. Linehan (Leiden 2008), pp. 153–74, esp. p. 162. Pope Paschal II also called the Almoravids 'Moabites', trans. O'Callaghan, *Reconquest*, p. 34.
10. Trans. O'Callaghan, *Reconquest*, pp. 31–2.
11. A. Ubieto Arteta, *Colección diplomática de Pedro I de Aragón y Navarra* (Zaragoza 1951), p. 113 and n. 6 and p. 115 n. 9.
12. *Historia Silense*, trans. Barton and Fletcher, *World of El Cid*, pp. 50–2.
13. *Historia Roderici*, trans. Barton and Fletcher, *World of El Cid*, pp. 90–147; *The Poem of the Cid*, ed. and trans. R. Hamilton et al. (London 1984).
14. R. Bartlett, *The Making of Europe* (London 1994), pp. 240–2; N. Housley, *Religious Warfare in Europe 1400–1536* (Oxford 2002), pp. 75–82, 201–4.
15. *Historia Compostellana*, ed. Falque Rey, pp. 25–6, 77–8.
16. J. D. Mansi, *Sacrorum Conciliorum nova amplissima*, vol. XXI (Venice 1776), col. 284; trans. O'Callaghan, *Reconquest*, p. 38; J. and L. Riley-Smith, *Crusades*, p. 74.
17. R. Fletcher, *St James's Catapult* (Oxford 1984), pp. 298–9.
18. E. Lourie, 'The Will of Alfonso I', *Speculum*, 50 (1975), 635–51; A. Forey, 'The Will of Alfonso I', *Durham University Journal*, 73 (1980), 59–65.
19. C. Tyerman, *God's War: A New History of the Crusades* (London 2006), p. 665 and nn. 31 and 32, p. 967; trans. O'Callaghan, *Reconquest*, pp. 44–6.
20. *Poem of Almeria*, trans. Barton and Fletcher, *World of El Cid*, pp. 250–63.
21. A distinction usefully advanced by R. Rist, *The Papacy and Crusading in Europe 1198–1245* (Bloomsbury 2009), p. 225.
22. J. Bird et al., *Crusade and Christendom* (Philadelphia 2013), p. 110; for the 1188 bull, trans. O'Callaghan, *Reconquest*, pp. 57–8.
23. N. Housley, *Religious Warfare in Europe 1400–1536* (Oxford 2002), pp. 75–82, 201–4.
24. *Documents on the Later Crusades 1274–1588*, trans. N. Housley (Basingstoke 1996), pp. 156–62, at p. 158.

25. J. Muldoon, *Popes, Lawyers and Infidels* (Liverpool 1979).
26. A. Hamdani, 'Columbus and the Recovery of Jerusalem', *Journal of the American Oriental Society*, 99 (1979), 39–48.

8 BALTIC CRUSADES

1. Bernard of Clairvaux, *Letters*, trans B. S. James (London 1953, 1998), no. 394, p. 467; Innocent III to Valdemar II, trans. J. and L. Riley-Smith, *The Crusades: Idea and Reality, 1095–1274* (London 1981), p. 77.
2. Trans. J. and L. Riley-Smith, *Crusades*, p. 40.
3. Trans. J. and L. Riley-Smith, *Crusades*, pp. 75–7.
4. H. Richter, '*Militia Christi*', *Journeys Towards God*, ed. B. N. Sargent-Baur (Michigan 1992).
5. Helmold of Bosau, *Chronicle of the Slavs*, trans. F. Tschan (New York 1966), pp. 169, 176–7.
6. Otto of Freising, *The Deeds of Frederick Barbarossa*, trans. C. C. Mierow (New York 1966), p. 76.
7. Helmold of Bosau, *Chronicle*, p. 180.
8. J. P. Migne, *Patrologia Latina* (Paris 1844–64), 200, cols 860–1.
9. Helmold of Bosau, *Chronicle*, p. 188.
10. Helmold of Bosau, *Chronicle*, p. 221.
11. E. Christiansen, *The Northern Crusades* (2nd edn London 1997), pp. 61–2, 69–70, 72; R. Bartlett, *The Making of Europe* (London 1993), pp. 268, 274–8.
12. In general, I. Fonnesberg-Schmidt, *The Popes and the Baltic Crusades 1147–1254* (Leiden 2007).
13. Arnold of Lübeck, *Chronica Slavorum*, ed. J. M. Lappenberg (Hanover 1868), p. 215.
14. A. Pluskowski, *The Ecology of Crusading, Colonisation and Religious Conversion in the Medieval Eastern Baltic* (Turnholt 2017).
15. Henry of Livonia, *Chronicle*, trans J. Brundage (Madison 1961), *passim*; C. Tyerman, 'Henry of Livonia and the Ideology of Crusading', in idem, *The Practices of Crusading* (Farnham 2013), no. VII; Innocent III to Valdemar II of Denmark, in J. and L. Riley-Smith, *Crusades*, p. 78.
16. Henry of Livonia, *Chronicle*, p. 152.
17. Christiansen, *Northern Crusades*, p. 128.
18. Tyerman, 'Henry of Livonia', p. 30; Fonnesberg-Schmidt, *Popes and the Baltic Crusades*, pp. 99–104, 111.
19. *The Chronicle of Henry of Livonia*, trans. J. Brundage (New York 2003); *Crusading and Chronicle Writing on the Medieval Baltic Frontier*, ed. L. Kaljundi et al. (Farnham 2011).
20. Arnold of Lübeck, 'De conversione Livonie', *Chronica Slavorum*, pp. 212–31; Henry of Livonia, *Chronicle*, pp. 6–12.
21. For Livonia after 1300, W. Urban, *The Livonian Crusade* (Washington DC 1981).
22. Saxo Grammaticus, *Danorum Regum Historia*, Books X–XVI, trans. E. Christiansen (Oxford 1980–1), vol. II, p. 611; R. Rist, *The Papacy and Crusading in Europe 1198–1245* (London 2009), p. 25 and n. 112.
23. T. Lindkvist, 'Crusades and Crusading Ideology in the Political History of Sweden', *Crusade and Conversion on the Baltic Frontier 1150–1500*, ed. A. Murray (Aldershot 2001), pp. 119–30; K. Villads Jensen, 'Denmark and the Second Crusade: The Formation of a Crusading State?', *The Second Crusade*, ed. J. Phillips and M. Hoch (Manchester 2001), pp. 164–79.
24. Migne, *Patrologia Latina*, 200, cols 860–1.
25. Henry of Livonia, *Chronicle*, p. 64.
26. Christiansen, *Northern Crusades*, pp. 190–2, 276 n. 135.
27. D. von Güttner-Sporzynski, 'Constructing Memory: Holy War in the *Chronicle of the Poles* by Bishop Vincentius of Cracow', *Journal of Medieval History*, 40 (2014), 289 and n. 63.
28. *Codex Diplomaticus Prussicus*, ed. J. Voigt (Königsberg 1836–61), vol. I, pp. 59–60.
29. N. Morton, '*In subsidium*: The Declining Contribution of Germany and Eastern Europe to the Crusades to the Holy Land 1187–1291', *German Historical Institute Bulletin*, 33 (2011), 38–66.
30. *Epistolae saeculi XIII e regestis pontificum romanorum*, ed. G. Pertz and C. Rodenberg, vol. II (Berlin 1887), no. 5.
31. Alexander IV, *Registres*, ed. C. Bourel de la Roncière et al. (Paris 1895–1953), no. 3068.
32. Geoffrey Chaucer, *General Prologue*, *Canterbury Tales*, ll. 52–4.

33. T. Guard, *Chivalry, Kingship and Crusade: The English Experience in the Fourteenth Century* (Woodbridge 2013).

34. *Calendar of Papal Registers*, ed. W. T. Bliss et al. (London 1893–1960), vol. IV, p. 19.

35. Tyerman, *England and the Crusades*, pp. 272–4.

36. A. Brown and A. Pluskowski, 'Detecting the Environmental Impact of the Baltic Crusades', *Journal of Archaeological Science*, 38 (2011), 1,957–66; *Science*, 338 (2012), 1,144–5.

9 CRUSADES AGAINST CHRISTIANS

1. C. Erdmann, *The Origin of the Idea of Crusade*, trans. M. Baldwin and W. Goffart (Princeton 1977).

2. Gregory VII, *Epistolae Vagantes*, ed. and trans. H. E. J. Cowdrey (Oxford 1972), p. 135. In general, idem, 'Pope Gregory VII and the Bearing of Arms', *Montjoie*, ed. B. Z. Kedar et al. (Aldershot 1997), pp. 21–35, and esp. Erdmann, *The Origins of the Idea of Crusade*, trans. Baldwin and Goffart; and above, Introduction, pp. 19.

3. Guibert of Nogent, *Autobiographie*, ed. E.-R. Labande (Paris 1971), pp. 410, 412–14; Orderic Vitalis, *Historia Ecclesiatica*, ed. and trans. M. Chibnall (Oxford 1969–80), vol. VI, pp. 156–7; Suger, *The Deeds of Louis the Fat*, trans. R. Cusimo and J. Moorhead (Washington DC 1992), pp. 80, 84–9, 106–9.

4. J. P. Migne, *Patrologia Latina* (Paris 1844–64), 214, cols. 780–2.

5. Migne, *Patrologia Latina*, 215, cols 1,469–71; J. and L. Riley-Smith, *Crusades: Idea and Reality, 1095–1274* (London 1981), pp. 79–85.

6. For a summary, C. Tyerman, *How to Plan a Crusade: Reason and Religious War in the High Middle Ages* (London 2015), pp. 56–7.

7. Geoffrey of Villehardouin, *The Conquest of Constantinople*, in *Chronicles of the Crusade*, trans. C. Smith (London 2008), p. 60, cc. 224–5.

8. See discussion in F. H. Russell, *The Just War in the Middle Ages* (Cambridge 1975), esp. p. 205 and refs.

9. On Cathars, M. Barber, *The Cathars* (London 2000; 2nd edn 2013); on recent debates, *Cathars in Question*, ed. A. Sennis (Woodbridge 2016). On reconstructing Cathar texts, J. Arnold and P. Biller, *Heresy and Inquisition* (Manchester 2016); on circulation, B. Hamilton, 'Wisdom from the East', *Heresy and Literacy*, ed. P. Biller and A. Hudson (Cambridge 1994), pp. 38–61.

10. William of Puylaurens, *Chronicle*, trans. W. A. and M. D. Sibley (Woodbridge 2003), p. 25.

11. N. Tanner, *Decrees of the Ecumenical Councils* (London and Washington DC 1990), vol. I, p. 224.

12. Migne, *Patrologia Latina*, 215, cols 360, 361–2.

13. J. and L. Riley-Smith, *Crusades*, pp. 79, 80–5.

14. D. Power, 'Who Went on the Albigensian Crusade?', *English Historical Review*, cxxviii (2013), 1,047–85.

15. Peter of les Vaux-de-Cernay, *The History of the Albigensian Crusade*, trans. W. A. and M. D. Sibley (Woodbridge 1998), p. 56.

16. William of Puylaurens, *Chronicle*, p. 128.

17. Caesarius of Heisterbach, *Dialogus Miraculorum*, ed. J. Strange (Cologne 1851), vol. I, p. 302.

18. See now G. Lippiatt, *Simon V of Montfort and Baronial Government 1195–1218* (Oxford 2017).

19. Peter of Les Vaux-de-Cernay, *History of the Albigensian Crusade*, p. 58, perhaps a *post hoc* gilding of Simon's pious credentials.

20. Peter of Les Vaux-de-Cernay, *History of the Albigensian Crusade*, pp. 320–9.

21. C. Tyerman, *England and the Crusades* (Chicago 1988), pp. 133–51; *Albert von Behan und Regesten Pabst Innocenz IV*, ed. C. Höfler (Stuttgart 1847), pp. 16–17.

22. Or possibly 1259, N. Housley, *The Italian Crusades* (Oxford 1982), p. 167, n. 101.

23. For a translation of Salimbene's account, see J. Bird et al., *Crusade and Christendom* (Philadelphia 2013), pp. 414–17.

24. T. Guard, 'Pulpit and Cross: Preaching the Crusade in Fourteenth-Century England', *English Historical Review*, cxxix (2014), 1,319.

25. Tyerman, *England and the Crusades*, pp. 343–70; N. Housley, *Religious Warfare in Europe 1400–1536* (Oxford 2002), pp. 195–7 and below esp. pp. 433–6.

26. See now, L. Patterson, *Singing the Crusades* (Woodbridge 2018), esp. chaps 6 and 8.

27. *Epistolae selectae saeculi XIII*, ed. C. Rodenberg (Berlin 1883–94), no. 214, pp. 161–2.

10 THE END OF THE JERUSALEM WARS, 1250–1370

1. For the decline in noble German involvement in Holy Land crusading, N. Morton, '*In subsidium:* The Declining Contribution of Germany and Eastern Europe to the Crusade to the Holy Land 1221–91', *German Historical Institute Bulletin*, 33 (2011), 38–66. For critical German attitudes, M. Fischer, 'Criticism of Church and Crusade in Ottokar's *Österreichische Reimchronik*', *Forum for Modern Language Studies*, 22 (1986), 157–70; generally, for criticism, see Throop and Aurell in the bibliography for Chapter 9.

2. John of Joinville, *Life of St Louis*, in *Chronicles of the Crusades*, trans. C. Smith (London 2008), p. 329.

3. C. Tyerman, *God's War: A New History of the Crusades* (London 2006), p. 803 and nn. 92–3, p. 977.

4. Matthew Paris, *Chronica Majora*, ed. H. R. Luard (London 1872–84), vol. V, p. 253.

5. W. C. Jordan, *Louis IX and the Challenge of the Crusade* (Princeton 1979); J. Le Goff, *St Louis* (Paris 1996); M. C. Gaposchkin, *The Making of St Louis* (Ithaca, NY 2008).

6. In general, P. Jackson, *The Mongols and the Islamic World* (London 2017).

7. J. Richard, *St Louis: Crusader King of France*, trans. J. Birrell (Cambridge 1992), pp. 293–332.

8. For the English preparations, S. Lloyd, *English Society and the Crusade 1216–1307* (Oxford 1988), esp. pp. 113–53; J. R. Maddicott, *The Origins of the English Parliament 924–1327* (Oxford 2010), pp. 266–72.

9. C. Tyerman, *How to Plan a Crusade: Reason and Religious War in the High Middle Ages* (London 2015), p. 281 and n. 23.

10. P. B. Baldwin, *Gregory X and the Crusades* (Woodbridge 2014).

11. Tyerman, *How to Plan a Crusade*, pp. 194–5.

12. P. Throop, *Criticism of the Crusade* (Amsterdam 1940), pp. 229–30, for James I's account.

13. Salimbene of Adam, *Chronicle*, ed. and trans. J. L. Baird (Binghampton 1986), pp. 504, 505.

14. C. Marshall, *Warfare in the Latin East 1192–1291* (Cambridge 1992), p. 223, and generally pp. 210–56; cf. R. C. Smail, *Crusading Warfare 1097–1193* (Cambridge 1956); R. Rogers, *Latin Siege Warfare in the Twelfth Century* (Oxford 1992).

15. Tyerman, *How to Plan a Crusade*, pp. 272–3 and refs.

16. For a detailed study of an exceptional siege, J. Hosler, *The Siege of Acre 1189–91* (London 2018).

17. Quoted P. Holt, *The Age of the Crusades* (London 1986), p. 104.

18. See below, n. 21.

19. S. Schein, '*Gesta Dei Per Mongolos*: The Genesis of a Non-Event', *English Historical Review*, xciv (1979), 805–19.

20. C. Tyerman, 'New Wine in Old Skins? Crusade Literature and Crusading in the Eastern Mediterranean in the Later Middle Ages', *Byzantines, Latins and Turks in the Eastern Mediterranean World after 1150*, ed. J. Harris et al. (Oxford 2012), pp. 265–89.

21. W. C. Jordan, *The Great Famine* (Princeton 1996); C. Tyerman, *The Practices of Crusading* (Farnham 2013), articles II, III, IV.

22. A. Leopold, *How to Recover the Holy Land* (Aldershot 2000).

23. Leopold, *How to Recover the Holy Land*, for a summary.

24. M. Barber, *The Trial of the Templars* (Cambridge 1978); idem, *The New Knighthood* (Cambridge 1994), esp. pp. 1 and 280–313; for another dimension, *The Proceedings against the Templars in the British Isles*, ed. and trans. H. Nicholson (Farnham 2011).

25. Tyerman, *How to Plan a Crusade*, esp. pp. 274–92. For Sanudo's book, see the translation by P. Lock, *The Book of the Secrets of the Faithful of the Cross* (Farnham 2011).

26. S. Throop, 'Mirrored Images: The Passion and the First Crusade in a Fourteenth-Century Parisian Illuminated Manuscript', *Journal of Medieval History*, 41 (2015), 184–207.

27. P. D. A. Harvey, *Medieval Maps of the Holy Land* (London 2012), esp. chaps 9–12.

28. Guillaume de Nangis, *Gesta Sancti Ludovici, Recueil des historiens des Gaules et de la France*, ed. M. Bouquet et al. (Paris 1738–1876), vol. XX, pp. 444–5.

29. Marino Sanudo Torsello, *The Book of the Secrets of the Faithful of the Cross*, trans. Lock, esp. pp. 20, 25, 392–8 for the use of the map grid in the text; Harvey, *Medieval Maps of the Holy Land*, p. 107 n. 1 and pp. 107–27.

30. In general, Tyerman, *How to Plan a Crusade*, pp. 91, 276–82 and plates 1, 2, 23–7, 29.

31. C. Tyerman, 'Philip VI and the Recovery of the Holy Land', *English Historical Review* (1985), 25–52.
32. Thomas Walsingham, *Historia Anglicana*, ed. H. T. Riley (London 1863–4), vol. I, pp. 301–2.
33. P. W. Edbury, 'The Crusading Policy of King Peter I of Cyprus 1359–69', *The Eastern Mediterranean Lands in the Period of the Crusades*, ed. P. M. Holt (Warminster 1977), pp. 90–105; idem, *The Kingdom of Cyprus and the Crusades 1191–1374* (Cambridge 1991), pp. 141–79.
34. C. Tyerman, *The Debate on the Crusades* (Manchester 2011), esp. chap. 2.
35. Tyerman, 'New Wine in Old Skins?', pp. 274–80.
36. L. H. Loomis, 'Secular Dramatics in the Royal Palace, Paris, 1378, 1389, and Chaucer's "Tregetours"', *Speculum*, 33 (1958), 242–55; cf. D. A. Bullough, 'Games People Played: Drama and Ritual as Propaganda in Medieval Europe', *Transactions of the Royal Historical Society*, 5th ser., xxiv (1974), 97–122.
37. *Le Songe du Vieil Pèlerin*, ed. G. W. Coopland (Cambridge 1969), vol. II, p. 318.

11 THE OTTOMANS

1. Quoted in C. Tyerman, *God's War: A New History of the Crusades* (London 2006), p. 837 and n. 24 for refs.
2. K. Setton, *The Papacy and the Levant* (Philadelphia 1976), vol. I, p. 245.
3. Tyerman, *God's War*, p. 846.
4. N. Oikonomides, 'Byzantium between East and West', *Byzantium and the West*, ed. J. Howard-Johnstone (Amsterdam 1988), pp. 326–7 and n. 17.
5. Setton, *Papacy and the Levant*, vol. I, pp. 329–41 and refs.
6. J. J. N. Palmer, *England, France and Christendom* (London 1972), esp. pp. 180–210.
7. Setton, *Papacy and the Levant*, vol. I, pp. 341–69; A. S. Atiya,. *The Crusade of Nicopolis* (London 1934); N. Housley, *The Later Crusades* (Oxford 1992), pp. 76–81.
8. Quoted in N. Bishaha, 'Pope Pius II and the Crusade', *Crusading in the Fifteenth Century*, ed. N. Housley (Basingstoke 2004), p. 40.
9. J. Paviot, *Les Ducs de Bourgogne, la croisade et l'Orient* (Paris 2003); B. Weber, *Lutter contre les Turcs: Les formes nouvelles de la croisade pontificale au xve siècle* (Rome 2013).
10. Setton, *Papacy and the Levant*, vol. II, p. 235.
11. N. Housley, 'Giovanni da Capistrano and the Crusade of 1456', and J. M. Bak, 'Hungary and Crusading in the Fifteenth Century', *Crusading in the Fifteenth Century*, ed. Housley, pp. 94–127.
12. Cardinal Bessarion's instructions to preachers in Venice in August 1463, *Documents of the Later Crusades 1274–1580* (Basingstoke 1996), pp. 147–54.
13. M. Mallet, *The Borgias* (London 1969), p. 92.
14. S. K. Stantchev, *Spiritual Rationality: Papal Embargo as Cultural Practice* (Oxford 2014), p. 171 and n. 40.
15. N. Nowakowska, 'Poland and the Crusade', *Crusading in the Fifteeenth Century*, ed. Housley, p. 139.
16. Setton, *Papacy and the Levant*, vol. III, p. 486.
17. P. McCluskey, '"Les ennemis du nom Chrestien": Echoes of the Crusade in Louis XIV's France', *French History*, 29 (2015), 46–61; G. Poumarède, *Pouir finir avec la croisade* (Paris 2004).

12 NEW CHALLENGES AND THE END OF CRUSADING

1. C.-M. de Witte, 'Les bulles pontificales et l'expansion Portugaise', *Revue d'histoire ecclésiastique*, xlviii (1953), 699–718; xlix (1954), 438–61.
2. J. Muldoon, *Popes, Lawyers and Infidels* (Liverpool 1979), esp. pp. 119–31; in general, C. R. Boxer, *The Portuguese Seaborne Empire 1415–1825* (London 1969). F. Fernández-Armesto, *Before Columbus: Exploration and Colonisation from the Mediterranean to the Atlantic 1229–1492* (London 1987); P. E. Russell, *Henry the Navigator* (Oxford 1984).
3. B. Weber, 'Nouveau mot ou nouvelle réalité? Le terme *cruciata* et son utilisation dans les textes pontificaux', *La papauté et les croisades, Crusades: Subsidia*, vol. 3, ed. M. Balard (Farnham 2011), pp. 11–25. On indulgences, N. Housley, 'Indulgences for Crusading 1417–1517', *Promissory Notes*

on the Treasury of Merits: Indulgences in Later Medieval Europe, ed. R. Swanson (Leiden 2006), pp. 277–307.

4. J. Paviot, *Les ducs de Bourgogne, la croisade et l'Orient* (Paris 2003); idem, 'Burgundy and the Crusade', *Crusading in the Fifteenth Century*, ed. N. Housley (Basingstoke 2004), pp. 70–80; R. J. Walsh, 'Charles the Bold and the Crusade', *Journal of Medieval History*, iii (1977), 53–87.

5. *Voyage d'outremer de Bertrandon de la Broquière*, ed. C. Schefer (Paris 1892), pp. 1–262.

6. Paviot, 'Burgundy and the Crusade', p. 79.

7. Paviot, *Ducs de Bourgogne*, p. 238.

8. N. Housley, *Crusading and the Ottoman Threat: 1453–1505* (Oxford 2012), pp. 174–210; C. J. Tyerman, *England and the Crusades* (Chicago 1988), pp. 315–17.

9. J. Ing, 'The Mainz Indulgences of 1454/5', *British Library Journal* (1983), 14–31; F. Heal, 'The Bishops and the Printers', *The Prelate in England and Europe 1300–1560*, ed. M. Heale (Woodbridge 2014), p. 142; Tyerman, *England and the Crusades*, pp. 304–7; J. Hankins, 'Renaissance Crusaders', *Dumbarton Oaks Papers*, 49 (1995), pp. 117–18.

10. Tyerman, *England and the Crusades*, p. 305; *Capystranus*, ed. S. H. A. Shepherd, *Middle English Romances*(New York and London 1985), pp. 391–408.

11. J. W. Bohnstedt, *Infidel Scourge of God* (Philadelphia 1968), *passim*.

12. M. Andrieu, *Le pontificale romain au môyen âge* (Vatican 1940), vol. III, 30, 228, 243, 330.

13. Trans. *Documents on the Later Crusades: 1274–1588*, ed. N. Housley (Basingstoke 1996), pp. 147–54; idem, *Crusading and the Ottoman Threat*, p. 84, for Carvajal's crosses; Paviot, 'Burgundy and the Crusade', p. 79, for Ghent *crucesignati*.

14. Tyerman, *England and the Crusades*, p. 308; for Axel, Paviot, 'Burgundy and the Crusade', p. 79.

15. A. Linder, *Raising Arms: Liturgy in the Struggle to Liberate Jerusalem in the Late Middle Ages* (Turnhout 2003).

16. N. Housley, 'Crusading as Social Revolt: The Hungarian Peasant Uprising of 1514', *Journal of Ecclesiastical History*, 49 (1998), 1–28.

17. See the commentary on Perault's work throughout Housley, *Crusading and the Ottoman Threat*.

18. P. Throop, *Criticism of the Crusade* (Amsterdam 1940), pp. 82–95.

19. *Memoirs of a Renaissance Pope: The Commentaries of Pius II*, trans. F. A. Gragg, ed. L. C. Gabel (London 1960), p. 237; for Gilbert of Tournai's comments, *Crusade and Christendom*, trans. J. Bird et al. (Philadelphia 2013), p. 455.

20. E. Charrière, ed., *Négotiations de la France dans le Levant*, vol. I (Paris 1848), p. 47.

21. For a descriptive summary, N. Housley, *The Later Crusades, 1274–1580: from Lyons to Alcaẓar* (Oxford 1992), pp. 291–321; for Portuguese bulls, C.-M. de Witte, 'Les bulles pontificales et l'expansion portugaise au XVe siècle', *Revue d'histoire ecclésiastique*, xlviii (1953), 683–718; xlix (1954), 438–61; li (1956), 413–53, 809–36; liii (1958), 1–46, 443–71; idem, *Les lettres papales concernant l'expansion portugaise au XVIe siècle* (Uznach 1986); J. Goñi Gaztambide, *Historia de la bula de la cruẓada en España* (Vitoria 1958); and above, pp. 300–5.

22. Trans. *Documents on the Later Middle Ages*, ed. Housley, pp. 156–62 at p. 158.

23. Muldoon, *Popes, Lawyers and Infidels*, pp. 119–52.

24. Hankins, 'Renaissance Crusaders', pp. 121–2.

25. A. Milhou, *Colón y su mentalidad mesiánica en el ambiente franciscanista español* (Valladolid 1983); A. Hamdani, 'Columbus and the Recovery of Jerusalem', *Journal of the American Oriental Society*, 99 (1979), 39–48.

26. J. Muldoon, 'Papal Responsibility for the Infidel: Another Look at Alexander VI's *Inter Cetera*', *Catholic Historical Review*, 64 (1978), 168–84; trans. of *Inter Cetera* and the Tordesillas treaty, F. G. Davenport, ed., *European Treaties bearing on the History of the United States and its Dependencies to 1648* (Washington, DC 1917), pp. 61–3, 86–100.

27. Housley, *Later Crusades*, pp. 311–12. For a wider view, J. J. Lopez-Portillo, *'Another Jerusalem'* (Leiden 2018).

28. Muldoon, *Popes, Lawyers and Infidels*, pp. 139–52; A. Grafton, *New Worlds: Ancient Texts* (Cambridge, MA 1992), pp. 136–7; A. Pagden, *The Fall of Natural Man: The American Indian and the Origins of Comparative Ethnology* (Cambridge 1982), esp. pp. 15–16, 29, 30–8, 50–3, 65–118.

29. Housley, *Later Crusades*, p. 249; for a general survey, pp. 234–66.
30. C. Tyerman, *The Invention of the Crusades* (London 1998), p. 103; idem, *England and the Crusades*, p. 359 and n. 74.
31. S. Morland, *The History of the Evangelical Churches of the Valleys of Piedmont* (London 1658), pp. 196–214, for the papal bull; E. Cameron, *The Reformation of the Heretics* (Oxford 1984), pp. 38, 46.
32. Tyerman, *England and the Crusades*, pp. 343–5, 351–4, 360–7.
33. N. Housley, *Religious Warfare in Europe 1400–1536* (Oxford 2002), pp. 194–8; B. B. Diefendorf, *Beneath the Cross: Catholics and Huguenots in Sixteenth-Century Paris* (Oxford 1991).
34. Housley, *Religious Warfare*, pp. 190–3, 199–204; Tyerman, *England and the Crusades*, pp. 324–42, quotation at p. 326; idem, *God's War: A New History of the Crusades* (London 2006), pp. 906–12.
35. Trans. *Documents on the Later Crusades*, ed. Housley, pp. 132–3 and note 2.
36. *Gesta Henrici Quinti*, ed. F. Taylor and J. S. Roskell (Oxford 1975), pp. 78–9, 88–9, 146–7, 150–1.
37. Housley, *Religious Warfare*, pp. 120–3; Tyerman, *England and the Crusades*, pp. 149, 360, 363; idem, *God's War*, p. 908 and refs.
38. C. Tyerman, *The Debate on the Crusades* (Manchester 2011), pp. 41–50.
39. E.g. Pius II, *Commentaria*, vol. I, ed. M. Meserve and M. Simonetta (Cambridge, MA 2003), pp. 134, 136, 160, 209, 264.
40. Philippe de Mézières, *Epistre lamentable et consolatoire*, ed. K. de Lettenhove, *Oeuvres de Froissart*, vol. xvi (Brussels 1872), pp. 444–523; C. J. Tyerman, 'New Wine in Old Skins? Crusade Literature and Crusading in the Eastern Mediterranean in the Later Middle Ages', *Byzantines, Latins, and Turks in the Eastern Mediterranean World after 1150*, ed. J. Harris, C. Holmes and E. Russell (Oxford 2012), pp. 265–89.
41. On this see Housley, *Crusading and the Ottoman Threat*, p. 126.
42. R. Black, *Benedetto Accolti and the Florentine Renaissance* (Cambridge 1985), pp. 299–315.
43. Tyerman, *Debate on the Crusades*, pp. 39–40, 59–60; J. Herold, *De bello sacro* (Basel 1560); R. Knolles, *The Generall Historie of the Turks* (London 1603).
44. Quoted Tyerman, *England and the Crusades*, pp. 349 and 350, and generally, pp. 346–54.
45. Foxe, 'The History of the Turks', *Acts and Monuments*, vol. IV, 62; generally, pp. 18–122, esp. p. 41 (Belgrade 1456), 55–62 (Vienna 1529), and prayer, pp. 121–2. See now L. Mannion, *Narrating the Crusades* (Cambridge 2014), esp. pp. 151, 203–11; Tyerman, *England and the Crusades*, p. 348.
46. F. Bacon, *Advertisement Touching an Holy Warre*, *Works*, ed. J. Spedding et al. (London 1859), vol. VII, p. 18 and generally, pp. 17–36.
47. Bacon, *Advertisement*, p. 24.

13 CRUSADING: OUR CONTEMPORARY?

1. D. Hume, *History of Great Britain* (London 1761), vol. I, 209.
2. C. Tyerman, *The Debate on the Crusades* (Manchester 2011), p. 222 and n. 12, p. 242, and for what follows, chaps 2–4.
3. See *Seven Myths of the Crusades*, ed. A. J. Andrea and A. Holt (Indianapolis 2015), although this inadvertently demonstrates the *de haut en bas* solipsism of professional academics as much as the ignorance of popular opinion.
4. T. Fuller, *The Historie of the Holy Warre* (Cambridge 1639), commendatory verse in Preface.
5. C. Fleury, *Discours au l'histoire ecclésiastique* (Paris 1691, 1763 edn), p. 267.
6. Quoted, with refs, Tyerman, *Debate on the Crusades*, p. 84 and generally, pp. 77–91.
7. Quoted, with refs, Tyerman, *Debate on the Crusades*, p. 90.
8. Heinrich von Sybel, *The History and Literature of the Crusades*, trans. Lady Duff Gordon (London 1861), p. 1.
9. Trans. Tyerman, *Debate on the Crusades*, p. 142 and generally, pp. 141–50.
10. *History and Literature of the Crusades*, trans. Lady Duff Gordon, p. 312.
11. E. Siberry, 'Images of the Crusades in the Nineteenth and Twentieth Centuries', *Oxford History of the Crusades*, ed. J. Riley-Smith (Oxford 1999), pp. 366–7.
12. Eg N. L. Paul, *To Follow in Their Footsteps* (Ithaca, NY 2012), pp. 6–8.

13. J. Riley-Smith, *The Crusades, Christianity and Islam* (New York 2008).

14. B. Z. Kedar, 'Joshua Prawer (1917–90)', *Mediterranean Historical Review*, 5 (1990), pp. 107–16; Tyerman, *Debate on the Crusades*, pp. 170–6, 180, n. 30.

15. J. L. La Monte review of P. Rousset, *Les origines et les caractères de la première croisade*, *Speculum*, 23 (1948), 329–30.

16. Tyerman, *Debate on the Crusades*, pp. 182–92.

17. Tyerman, *Debate on the Crusades*, pp. 192–9; cf. M. Dinshaw, *Outlandish Knight: The Byzantine Life of Steven Runciman* (London 2016).

18. C. Hillenbrand, *The Crusades: Islamic Perspectives* (Edinburgh 1999), pp. 589–616; E. Sivan, 'Modern Arabic Historiography of the Crusades', *Asian and African Studies*, 8 (1972), 109–49; A. Mallett, 'Muslim Memories of the Crusades', *Remembering the Crusades and Crusading*, ed. M. Cassidy-Welch (London 2017), p. 230; M. Determann, 'The Crusades in Arab School Textbooks', *Islam and Christian-Muslim Relations*, 19 (2008), pp. 199–214; Tyerman, *Debate on the Crusades*, pp. 235–42; P. Cobb, *The Race for Paradise* (Oxford 2014); *The Crusades: An Arab perspective*, TV documentary, Al-Jazeera English, December 2016 (available on YouTube). On Israelis and the crusade, R. Ellenblum, *Crusader Castles and Modern Histories* (Cambridge 2007), pp. 57–61; M. Benvenisti, *Scared Landscape: The Buried History of the Holy Land since 1948* (London 2000), esp. pp. 192–3, 299–303, 309–10; Tyerman, *Debate on the Crusades*, pp. 170–6 and refs nn. 26, 30, 36, 37, pp. 180–1.

19. C. S. Jensen, 'Appropriating History: Remembering the Crusades in Latvia and Estonia', *Remembering the Crusades and Crusading*, ed. M. Cassidy-Welch (London 2017), pp. 231–46.

POSTSCRIPT

1. F. M. Powicke, *The Thirteenth Century* (Oxford 1962), p. 80.

2. D. Hume, *History of Great Britain* (London 1761), vol. I, p. 209.

BIBLIOGRAPHY

Introduction

On definition, J. Riley-Smith, *What Were the Crusades?* (London; many edns since 1977); G. Constable, 'The Historiography of the Crusades', *Crusaders and Crusading in the Twelfth Century* (Farnham 2008); C. Tyerman, *The Invention of the Crusades* (London 1998); idem, *The Debate on the Crusades* (Manchester 2011); on narratives, structures and analysis of the movement, C. Tyerman, *God's War: A New History of the Crusades* (London 2006); idem, *How to Plan a Crusade: Reason and Religious War in the High Middle Ages* (London 2015); H. E. Mayer, *The Crusades* (Oxford 1988); N. Housley, *Fighting for the Cross* (London 2008); A. Jotischky, *Crusading and the Crusader States* (Harlow 2004); J. Riley-Smith, *The Crusades: A Short History* (London 1987 and edns to 2014); in addition on ideology, F. H. Russell, *The Just War in the Middle Ages* (Cambridge 1975); C. Erdmann, *The Origin of the Idea of the Crusade*, trans. from 1935 German original M. W. Baldwin and W. Goffart (Princeton 1977); on the legend of Charlemagne, M. Gabriele, *An Empire of Memory* (Oxford 2011); on crusade institutions, J. Brundage, *Medieval Canon Law and the Crusader* (Madison 1969); A. Bysted, *The Crusade Indulgence: Spiritual Rewards and the Theology of the Crusades c. 1095–1216* (Leiden 2015); on Jews and the crusades, R. Chazan, *European Jewry and the First Crusade* (Berkeley 1987); idem, *God, Humanity and History: The Hebrew First Crusade Narratives* (Berkeley 2000); on women, S. Edgington and S. Lambert, *Gendering the Crusades* (New York 2002); N. Hodgson, *Women, Crusading and the Holy Land in Historical Narrative* (Woodbridge 2007); on criticism, M. Aurell, *Des chrétiens contre les croisades* (Paros 2013); E. Siberry, *Criticism of Crusading 1095–1274* (Oxford 1985); P. Throop, *Criticism of the Crusades* (Amsterdam 1940).

Chapter One

In general, see *New Cambridge Medieval History*, vol. IV, ed. D. Luscombe and J. Riley-Smith (Cambridge 2004). On Islam and the Near East, *New Cambridge History of Islam*, ed. M. Cook (Cambridge 2010); J. P. Berkey, *The Formation of Islam: Religion and Society in the Near East 600–1800* (Cambridge 2003); *The Cambridge History of Egypt*, vol. I: *Islamic Egypt 640–1517*, ed. C. F. Petry (Cambridge 1998); P. M. Cobb, *The Race for Paradise: An Islamic History of the Crusades* (Oxford 2014); C. Hillenbrand, *The Crusades: Islamic Perspectives* (Edinburgh 1999); A. C. S. Peacock, *Early Seljuk History: A New Interpretation* (London 2010), and idem, *The Great Seljuk Empire* (Edinburgh 2015); on environment, R. Ellenblum, *The Collapse of the Eastern Mediterranean: Climate Change and the Decline of the East 950–1072* (Cambridge 2012); on trade, R. S Lopez and I. W. Raymond, *Medieval Trade in the Mediterranean World* (New York 1955); E. Ashtor, *Economic and Social History of the Near East in the Middle Ages* (London 1976); S. Goitein, *A Mediterranean Society: The Jewish Communities of the Arab World as Portrayed in the Documents of the Cairo Geniza* (Berkeley 1967–88); P. Frankopan, *The Silk Roads. A New History of the World* (London 2015), chaps 7 and 8; R. D. Smith, 'Calamity and Transition: Re-imagining Italian Trade in the Eleventh-Century Mediterranean', *Past and Present*, 228 (2015),

14–56; on Spain, H. Kennedy, *Muslim Spain and Portugal* (London 1996); D. Wasserstein, *The Caliphate on the West* (Oxford 1993); idem, *The Rise and Fall of the Party Kings: Politics and Society in Islamic Spain 1002–1086* (Princeton 1985); on Byzantium, *Oxford History of Byzantium*, ed. C. Mango (Oxford 2002); *Cambridge History of the Byzantine Empire* c. *500–1492*, ed. J. Shepard (Cambridge 2008); M. Angold, *The Byzantine Empire 1025–1204* (London 1984); K. Cigaar, *Western Travellers to Constantinople: The West and Byzantium 962–1204* (Leiden 1996); P. Frankopan, *The First Crusade: The Call from the East* (London 2012); on the Normans in southern Italy, G. Loud, *The Age of Robert Guiscard: Southern Italy and the Norman Conquest* (London 2000); on Fatimid influence on Norman Sicily, J. Johns, *Arabic Administration in Norman Sicily* (Cambridge 2002).

Chapter Two

The First Crusade was then and is now one of the most heavily studied episodes of European medieval history. The scholarly literature is commensurately vast. What follows is anglophone, general, and inevitably highly selective. On context and narrative, C. Tyerman, *God's War: A New History of the Crusades* (London 2006). On the Muslim background and response, C. Hillenbrand, *The Crusades: Islamic Perspectives* (Edinburgh 1999), and P. M. Cobb, *The Race for Paradise* (Oxford 2014). On the western European contribution, with the stress on piety, J. Riley-Smith, *The First Crusade and the Idea of Crusading* (London 1986) and *The First Crusaders 1095–1131* (Cambridge 1997). J. France's essay 'Patronage and the Appeal of the First Crusade' on recruitment, Colin Morris's on 'Peter the Hermit and the Chroniclers' and Jonathan Shepard's 'Cross-Purposes: Alexius Comnenus and the First Crusade' in J. Phillips, ed., *The First Crusade: Origins and Impact* (Manchester 1997), provide important interrogations of the evidence. A distinctive take, emphasising the apocalyptic dimension, is J. Rubinstein, *Armies of Heaven: The First Crusade and the Quest for the Apocalypse* (New York 2011). A gallant attempt at material sociological analysis is C. Kostick, *The Social Structure of the First Crusade* (Leiden 2008). The best military account is J. France, *Victory in the East: A Military History of the First Crusade* (Cambridge 1994). Planning is discussed in C. Tyerman, *How to Plan a Crusade: Reason and Religious War in the High Middle Ages* (London 2015). Some important insights into logistics are contained in the contributions in J. H. Pryor, ed., *Logistics of Warfare in the Age of the Crusades* (Aldershot 2006), and on contemporary attitudes and historiography in M. Bull and D. Kempf, *Writing the Early Crusades: Text, Transmission and Memory* (Woodbridge 2014). The Byzantine perspective is explored in P. Frankopan, *The First Crusade: The Call from the East* (London 2012), and using a wider lens, J. Harris, *Byzantium and the Crusades* (London 2003). For the 1096 anti-Jewish attacks, R. Chazan, *European Jewry and the First Crusade* (Berkeley and Los Angeles 1987). For the memorialisation of the First Crusade, N. L. Paul, *To Follow in Their Footsteps* (Ithaca, NY 2012).

Chapter Three

For overviews, apart from the general histories already cited, M. Barber, *The Crusader States* (London 2012); A. Jotischky, *Crusading and the Crusader States* (Harlow 2004). On the Jerusalem nobility, J. Riley-Smith, *The Feudal Nobility and the Kingdom of Jerusalem 1174–1277* (London 1973); S. Tibble, *Monarchy and Lordships in the Latin Kingdom of Jerusalem 1099–1291* (Oxford 1989); H. E. Mayer, *The Crusades* (2nd edn Oxford 1988), and his many articles, e.g. 'Studies in the History of Queen Melisende', *Dumbarton Oaks Papers*, 26 (1972), 95–182. For Antioch, T. Asbridge, *The Creation of the Principality of Antioch 1098–1130* (Woodbridge 2000); A. D. Buck, *The Principality of Antioch and its Frontiers in the Twelfth Century* (Woodbridge 2017); for Edessa, obliquely, C. MacEvitt, *The Crusades and the Christian World of the East: Rough Tolerance* (Philadelphia 2008); for Tripoli, K. J. Lewis, *The Counts of Tripoli and Lebanon in the Twelfth Century* (London 2017); see also N. Morton, *The Field of Blood: The Battle for Aleppo and the Remaking of the Medieval Middle East* (New York 2018). For the settlement debate, J. Prawer, *Crusader Institutions* (Oxford 1980) and *The Latin Kingdom of Jerusalem* (London 1972), and the major revision by R. Ellenblum, *Frankish Rural Settlement in the Latin Kingdom of Jerusalem* (Cambridge 1998). B. Hamilton, *The Latin Church in the Crusader States: The Secular Church* (London 1980), can be supplemented by Jotischky and MacEvitt above. For Muslim reactions, as well as C. Hillenbrand, *The Crusades: Islamic Perspectives* (Edinburgh 1999), A. Mallett, *Popular Muslim Reactions to the Franks in the Levant 1097–1291* (Farnham 2014). The cultural mix has been a theme of B. Z. Kedar, for example his collected papers *The Franks in the Levant* (Aldershot 1993). An indicative selection of papers may be found in *East and West in the Crusader States*, ed. K. Cigaar et al. (Louvain 1996); *Occident et Proche Orient*, ed. I. Draelants et al. (Louvain 2000); and *The Crusades and the Near East: Cultural Histories*, ed. C. Kostick (London 2011). For the most obvious symbol of Frankish power, H. Kennedy, *Crusader Castles* (Cambridge 1994), and R. Ellenblum, *Crusader Castles and Modern Histories* (Cambridge 2007). For art, J. Folda, *The Art of the Crusaders in the Holy Land 1098–1187* (Cambridge 1997). A usefully full bibliography can be found in Barber, *Crusader States*.

Chapter Four

As in Chapter Three, see M. Barber, *The Crusader States* (London 2012); A. Jotischky, *Crusading and the Crusader States* (Harlow 2004); C. Tyerman, *God's War: A New History of the Crusades* (London 2006); P. M. Cobb, *The Race for Paradise: An Islamic History of the Crusades* (Oxford 2014). On the Military Orders, M. Barber, *The New Knighthood: A History of the Order of the Temple* (Cambridge 1994); J. Riley-Smith, *The Knights Hospitaller in the Levant* c. *1070–1309* (Basingstoke 2012); A. Forey, *The Military Orders from the Twelfth to the Fourteenth Centuries* (Basingstoke 1992). On the Second Crusade, J. Phillips, *Second Crusade: Extending the Frontiers of Christendom* (New Haven and London 2007), but cf. A. Forey, 'The Second Crusade: Scope and Objectives', *Durham University Journal*, lxxxvi (1994), 165–75, and G. Loud, 'Some Reflections on the Failure of the Second Crusade', *Crusades*, 4 (2005), 1–14. On the Muslim 'revival' and unification, C. Hillenbrand, *The Crusades: Islamic Perspectives* (Edinburgh 1999); P. M. Holt, *The Age of the Crusades: The Near East from the Eleventh Century to 1517* (London 1986); N. Elisséef, 'The Reaction of Syrian Muslims after the Foundation of the First Latin Kingdom', *Crusaders and Muslims in Twelfth-Century Syria*, ed. M. Shatzmiller (Leiden 1993), pp. 162–72, and *Nur al-Din: Un grand prince musulman de Syrie au temps des croisades* (Damascus 1967); and S. Humphreys, 'Zengids, Ayyubids and Seljuks', *New Cambridge Medieval History*, IV, ii, ed. D. Luscombe and J. Riley-Smith (Cambridge 2004), pp. 721–52; on Saladin, A.-M. Eddé, *Saladin*, trans. J. M. Todd (Cambridge, MA 2011); M. Lyons and D. Jackson, *Saladin: The Politics of the Holy War* (Cambridge 1982); on Islamic thought, J. Berkey, *The Formation of Islam: Religion and Society in the Near East, 600–1800* (Cambridge 2003). On Outremer's defence, H. Kennedy, *Crusader Castles* (Cambridge 1994); S. Tibble, *Monarchy and Lordships in the Latin Kingdom of Jerusalem 1099–1291*, and the classic R. C. Smail, *Crusading Warfare 1097–1193* (Cambridge 1956). For Outremer and the west, J. Phillips, *Defenders of the Holy Land: Relations between the Latin East and the West 1119–1187*, for a study in commitment; for memorialisation, N. Paul, *To Follow in Their Footsteps* (Ithaca, NY 2012), and C. Tyerman, *The Invention of the Crusade* (London 1998).

Chapter Five

Besides general works already cited, for Outremer politics pre-1187, B. Hamilton, *The Leper King and His Heirs* (Cambridge 2000); on Hattin, J. France, *Hattin* (Oxford 2015); for the chief players during the Third Crusade, M. Lyons and P. Jackson, *Saladin: The Politics of the Holy War* (Cambridge 1982); A.-M. Eddé, *Saladin* (Cambridge, MA 2011); J. Gillingham, *Richard I* (London 1999); there is no modern scholarly work dedicated to the Third Crusade, but it is dealt with in previously cited general studies and now in part by J. D. Hosler, *The Siege of Acre 1189–91* (London 2018); on planning, recruitment and logistics, C. Tyerman, *How to Plan a Crusade: Reason and Religious War in the High Middle Ages* (London 2015). On the development of the ideology and liturgy of the crusaders' cross, see now M. C. Gaposchkin, *Invisible Weapons: Liturgy and the Making of Crusade Ideology* (Ithaca, NY 2017). On the remaking of the crusade, C. Tyerman, 'Ehud's Sharpened Sword', *God's War* (London 2006), pp. 477–500; on the German Crusade, G. Loud, 'The German Crusade of 1197–98', *Crusades*, 13 (2014), 143–71.

Chapter Six

On the Near East in the thirteenth century, P. M. Holt, *The Age of the Crusades: The Near East from the Eleventh Century until 1517* (London 1986); C. Hillenbrand, *The Crusades: Islamic Perspectives* (Edinburgh 1999), esp. chap. 4; R. S. Humphreys, *From Saladin to the Mongols: The Ayyubids of*

Damascus 1193–1260 (Albany 1977); M. Chamberlain, 'The Crusader Era and the Ayyubid Dynasty', *Cambridge History of Egypt*, ed. C. F. Petry, vol. I (Cambridge 1998), R. S. Humphreys, 'Ayyubids, Mamluks and the Latin East in the Thirteenth Century', *Mamluk Studies Review*, 2 (1998); R. Irwin, *The Middle East in the Middle Ages: The Early Mamluk Sultanate 1250–1382* (Carbondale 1986); N. Christie, *Muslims and Crusaders* (London 2014), chap. 7. On thirteenth-century eastern crusades, M. Angold, *The Fourth Crusade* (Harlow 2003); D. Queller and T. Madden, *The Fourth Crusade* (Philadelphia 1997); J. M. Powell, *Anatomy of a Crusade 1213–1221* (Philadelphia 1986); M. Lower, *The Barons' Crusade* (Philadelphia 2005); W. C. Jordan, *Louis IX and the Challenge of the Crusade* (Princeton 1979); P. Jackson, *The Seventh Crusade* (Aldershot 2007); C. Tyerman, *God's War: A New History of the Crusades* (London 2006), chaps 15–17, 18, 19, 22–4. On the development of planning and logistics, C. Tyerman, *How to Plan a Crusade: Reason and Religious War in the High Middle Ages* (London 2015).

Chapter Seven

For accessible accounts of medieval Spain, A. MacKay, *Spain in the Middle Ages: From Frontier to Empire 1000–1500* (London 1977); H. Kennedy, *Muslim Spain and Portugal: A Political History of Al-Andalus* (London 1996); R. Fletcher, *Moorish Spain* (London 1992); B. Reilly, *The Medieval Spains* (Cambridge 1993); P. Linehan, *Spain 1157–1300: A Partible Inheritance* (Oxford 2008); and, for the later Middle Ages, J. N. Hillgarth, *The Spanish Kingdoms 1250–1516* (Oxford 1976–8), and generally, N. Housley, *The Later Crusades: From Lyons to Alcázar 1274–1580* (Oxford 1992), chaps 9 and 10. On the *taifa* period, D. Wasserstein, *The Rise and Fall of the Party Kings* (Princeton 1985); R. Fletcher, *The Quest for El Cid* (London 1990). On the Reconquest, B. Reilly, *The Contest of Christian and Muslim Spain 1031–1157* (Cambridge 1992); J. F. O'Callaghan, *Reconquest and Crusade in Medieval Spain* (Philadelphia 2003); and a classic teleological account by R. Menéndez Pidal, *The Cid and His Spain* (trans. London 1934, 1971 of *España del Cid*, Madrid 1929); but now cf. A. J. Kosto, 'Reconquest, Renaissance and the Histories of Iberia *c.* 1000–1200', *European Transformations*, ed. T. F. X. Noble and J. Van Eugen (Notre Dame 2012), pp. 93–116. On sources, P. Linehan, *History and the Historians of Medieval Spain* (Oxford 1993), and the useful collection of early Reconquest texts, *The World of El Cid*, ed. S. Barton and R. Fletcher (Manchester 2000). On papal bulls and ideology, J. Goñi Gaztambide, *Historia de la bula de la cruzada en España* (Vitoria 1958); J. Muldoon, *Popes, Lawyers and Infidels* (Liverpool 1979). A starting point for the Military Orders is A. Forey, *The Military Orders* (London 1992), pp. 23–32, and bibliography, pp. 253, 257, 258, 260; his article 'The Military Orders and the Spanish Reconquest', *Traditio*, 40 (1984). On wider perspectives, B. Kedar, *Crusade and Mission: European Approaches Toward the Muslims* (Princeton 1984); B. Catlos, *The Victors and Vanquished: Christians and Muslims of Catalonia and Aragon* (Cambridge 2004); F. Fernández-Armesto, *Before Columbus: Exploration and Colonisation from the Mediterranean to the Atlantic 1229–1492* (London 1987).

Chapter Eight

The best introduction in English remains E. Christiansen, *The Northern Crusades* (2nd edn London 1997); for background, B. and P. Sawyer, *Medieval Scandinavia* (Minneapolis 1993); for the wider context, R. Bartlett, *The Making of Europe* (London 1993). Narratives can be found in W. Urban's quartet, *The Livonian Crusade* (Washington DC 1981); *The Prussian Crusade* (Lanham 1980); *The Samogitian Crusade* (Chicago 1989); *The Baltic Crusade* (2nd edn Chicago 1994). There has been a recent revival of interest in the Baltic crusades, not least from Scandinavian scholars, in numerous collections of essays, for example, *Crusade and Conversion on the Baltic Frontier 1150*–1500, ed. A. V. Murray (Aldershot 2001); *Crusading and Chronicle Writing on the Medieval Baltic Frontier*, ed. M. Tamm et al. (Farnham 2011). On conversion, N. Blomkvist, *The Discovery of the Baltic* (Leiden 2005). On papal policy, I. Fonnesberg-Schmidt, *The Popes and the Baltic Crusades 1147–1254* (Leiden 2007). The ideological background is sketched by F. Lotter, 'The Crusading Idea and the Conquest of the Region East of the Elbe', *Medieval Frontier Societies*, ed. R. Bartlett and A. MacKay (Oxford 1989), pp. 267–306. For Denmark as a 'crusading state', the work of K. V. Jensen, esp. 'Denmark and the Second Crusade: The Formation of a Crusader State?', *The Second Crusade*, ed. J. Phillips and M.

Hoch (Manchester 2001), pp. 164–79. On the Teutonic Knights, another W. Urban narrative, *The Teutonic Knights* (London 2003); more recent and scholarly, *The Teutonic Order in Prussia and Livonia*, ed. R. Czaja et al. (Cologne 2015); for their decadence, M. Burleigh, *Prussian Society and the German Order* (Cambridge 1984), and, generally, idem, 'The Military Orders in the Baltic', *New Cambridge Medieval History*, vol. V, ed. D. Abulafia (Cambridge 1999). S. Turnbull, *The Crusader Castles of the Teutonic Knights* (London 2003–4), has not entirely speculative illustrated reconstructions. The environmental context and consequences are being reassessed by field research currently being conducted under Professor Aleks Pluskowski of Reading University; see A. Pluskowski, *The Archaeology of the Prussian Crusade: Holy War and Colonisation* (Abingdon 2013). For Baltic crusaders, W. Paravicini, *Die Preussenreissen des europäischen Adels* (Sigmaringen 1989–95); for English involvement, see T. Guard, *Chivalry, Kingship and Crusade* (Woodbridge 2013).

Chapter Nine

In general the work of N. Housley, *The Italian Crusades* (Oxford 1982); 'Crusades against Christians', *Crusade and Settlement*, ed. P. Edbury (Cardiff 1985); *The Avignon Papacy and the Crusades* (Oxford 1986); *The Later Crusades* (Oxford 1992), chap. 8; *Religious Warfare in Europe 1400–1536* (Oxford 2002). On the papacy, R. Rist, *The Papacy and Crusading in Europe 1198–1245* (London 2009). For political crusades, E. T. Kennan, 'Innocent III and the First Political Crusade', *Traditio*, XXVII (1971), and 'Innocent III, Gregory IX and Political Crusades', *Reform and Authority in the Medieval and Reformation Church*, ed. G. F. Lytle (Washington, DC 1981). For papal ideology, J. Riley-Smith, *What Were the Crusades?* (London 1992); J. R. Strayer, 'The Political Crusades of the Thirteenth Century', *History of the Crusades*, gen. ed. K. Setton, vol. II (Madison 1969). For different nuances, C. J. Tyerman, 'The Holy Land and the Crusades of the Thirteenth and Fourteenth Centuries', *Crusade and Settlement*, ed. P. Edbury (Cardiff 1985); *The Invention of the Crusades* (London 1998); *God's War: A New History of the Crusades* (London 2006). On the Cathars and Albigensian crusades, M. Barber, *The Cathars* (London 2000), and, for a decent narrative, J. Sumption, *The Albigensian Crusade* (London 1978); for the vigorous arguments over Catharism, *Cathars in Question*, ed. A. Sennis (Woodbridge 2016). On criticism, see the contrasting P. Throop, *Criticism of the Crusade* (Amsterdam 1940), and the more apologist E. Siberry, *Criticism of Crusading 1095–1274* (Oxford 1985), but now the robust M. Aurell, *Des Chrétiens contre les croisades* (Paris 2013), and H. E. Mayer, *The Crusades*, trans. J. Gillingham (Oxford 1988), pp. 320–1.

Chapter Ten

On Louis IX, J. Richard, *St Louis: Crusader King of France*, trans. J. Birrell (Cambridge 1992); J. Le Goff, *St Louis* (Paris 1996); M. C. Gaposchkin, *The Making of St Louis* (Ithaca, NY 2008); M. Lower, 'Conversion and St Louis' Last Crusade', *Journal of Ecclesiastical History*, 58 (2007), 211–31, and *The Tunis Crusade of 1270* (Oxford 2018); W. C. Jordan, *Louis IX and the Challenge of the Crusade* (Princeton 1979). On the crusades post-1274, S. Schein, *Fideles Crucis: The Papacy, the West, and the Recovery of the Holy Land 1274–1314* (Oxford 1991); A. Leopold, *How to Recover the Holy Land* (Aldershot 2000); C. Tyerman, *The Practices of Crusading* (Farnham 2013), articles I–V and IX; N. Housley, *The Later Crusades* (Oxford 1992), esp. chap. 1. Still useful, A. S. Atiya, *The Crusade in the Later Middle Ages* (London 1938); on Cyprus, P. W. Edbury, *The Kingdom of Cyprus and the Crusades 1191–1374* (Cambridge 1991); on trade embargos, S. Stantchev, *Spiritual Rationality: Papal Embargo as Cultural Practice* (Oxford 2014); in general, K. Setton, *The Papacy and the Levant* (Philadelphia 1976), vol. I. On the Mongol context, P. Jackson, *The Mongol and the West 1221–1410* (London 2005), and *The Mongols and the Islamic World* (London 2017).

Chapter Eleven

For the western crusade perspective, N. Housley's *The Later Crusades* (Oxford 1992), *Religious Warfare in Europe 1400–1536* (Oxford 2002) and *Crusading and the Ottoman Threat* (Oxford 2012) are crucial. Also useful are the collected essays he has edited, *Crusading in the Fifteenth Century* (Basingstoke 2004), *Reconfiguring the Fifteenth-Century Crusade* (Basingstoke 2017), and his edited *Documents on the*

Later Crusades 1274–1588 (Basingstoke 1996). For a recent Pontic and Danubian perspective, A. Pilat and O. Cristea, *The Ottoman Threat and Crusading on the Eastern Border of Christendom during the 15th Century* (Leiden 2018). On papal policy, B. Weber, *Lutter contre les Turcs: Les formes nouvelles de la croisade pontificale au xve siècle* (Rome 2013), and on embargos, S. K. Stantchev, *Spiritual Rationality: Papal Embargo as Cultural Practice* (Oxford 2014); on Burgundy and the crusade, J. Paviot's article in *Crusading in the Fifteenth Century* and his *Les Ducs de Bourgogne, la croisade et l'Orient (fin de XIVe siècle–XVe siècle)* (Paris 2003); on crusade liturgy, A. Linder, *Raising Arms: Liturgy in the Struggle to Liberate Jerusalem in the Later Middle Ages* (Turnhout 2003); on the end of the crusade, G. Poumarède, *Pour finir avec la croisade* (Paris 2004); on ideas and polemics, N. Bisaha, *Creating East and West: Renaissance Humanists and the Ottoman Turks* (Philadelphia 2004); J. Hankins, 'Renaissance Crusaders', *Dumbarton Oaks Papers*, 49 (1995), 111–207; C. Tyerman, *The Debate on the Crusades* (Manchester 2011), and *God's War: A New History of the Crusades* (London 2006), chaps 25 and 26; now on Mézières, *Philippe de Mézières and his Age*, ed. R. Blumenfield-Kosinski and K. Petkov (Leiden 2011), and, as an example of his work, C. W. Coopland's translation *Letter to King Richard II* (Liverpool 1975); on Burgundy, J. Paviot, *Les ducs de Bourgogne, la croisade et l'Orient* (Paris 2003); on the Ottomans, C. Kafadar, *Between Two Worlds: The Construction of the Ottoman State* (Berkeley 1995); C. Imber, *The Ottoman Empire 1300–1650* (Basingstoke 2009), and his edited volume of documents, *The Crusade of Varna 1443–45* (Aldershot 2006); for Byzantium, D. Nicol, *The Last Centuries of Byzantium 1261–1453* (Cambridge 1983), J. Harris, *The End of Byzantium* (London 2010); in general, the pioneering A. S. Atiya, *The Crusade in the Later Middle Ages* (London 1938), is more than an antiquarian curio; on the Hospitallers of Rhodes, A. Luttrell, *The Hospitallers of Rhodes and their Mediterranean World* (Aldershot 1992).

Chapter Twelve

For details and some relevant discussion, N. Housley, *The Later Crusades* (Oxford 1992); *Crusading and the Ottoman Threat 1453–1505* (Oxford 2012); essays in his edited volume *Crusading in the Fifteenth Century* (Basingstoke 2004); especially *Religious Warfare in Europe 1400–1536* (Oxford 2002); and 'Indulgences for Crusading 1417–1517', in *Promissory Notes on the Treasury of Merits*, ed. R. Swanson (Leiden 2006); J. Goñi Gaztambide, *Historia de la bula de la cruzada en España* (Vitoria 1958); for factual details, K. Setton, *The Papacy and the Levant 1204–1571* (Philadelphia 1976), which ranges beyond the eastern Mediterranean; J. Paviot, ed., *Les projets de croisade. Géostrategie et diplomatie européen du XIVe au XVIIe siècle* (Toulouse 2014); G. Poumarède, *Pour finir avec la croisade. Mythes et réalités de la lutte contre les Turcs au XVIe et XVIIe siècles* (Paris 2004); J. W. Bohnstedt, *The Infidel Scourge of God: The Turkish Menace as Seen by German Pamphleteers of the Reformation Era* (Philadelphia 1968); M. J. Heath, *Crusading Commonplaces: La Noue, Lucinge and Rhetoric* (Geneva 1986); for some early modern ideas, C. Tyerman, *The Debate on the Crusades* (Manchester 2011), chap. 2.

Chapter Thirteen

For crusades historiography, C. Tyerman, *The Debate on the Crusades* (Manchester 2011); G. Constable, 'The Historiography of the Crusades', in his *Crusaders and Crusading in the Twelfth Century* (Aldershot 2008); J. Richard, 'National Feeling and the Legacy of the Crusades', *Palgrave Advances in the Crusades*, ed. H. Nicholson (Basingstoke 2005); N. Housley, *Contesting the Crusades* (Oxford 2006); R. Ellenblum, *Crusader Castles and Modern Histories* (Cambridge 2007); for modern impact, E. Siberry, *The New Crusaders* (Aldershot 2000), and 'Images of the Crusades in the Nineteenth and Twentieth Centuries', *Oxford Illustrated History of the Crusades*, ed. J. Riley-Smith (Oxford 1995); on Jewish memory, R. Chazan, *European Jewry and the First Crusade* (London 1987); on Islam and the crusades, C. Hillenbrand, *The Crusades: Islamic Perspectives* (Edinburgh 1999); E. Sivan 'Modern Arab Historiography of the Crusades', *Asian and African Studies*, 8 (1972); P. Cobb, *The Race for Paradise* (Oxford 2014); and now articles in Part IV, 'Cultural Memory', in *Remembering the Crusades and Crusading*, ed. M. Cassidy-Welch (London 2017).

INDEX